S0-CFO-944

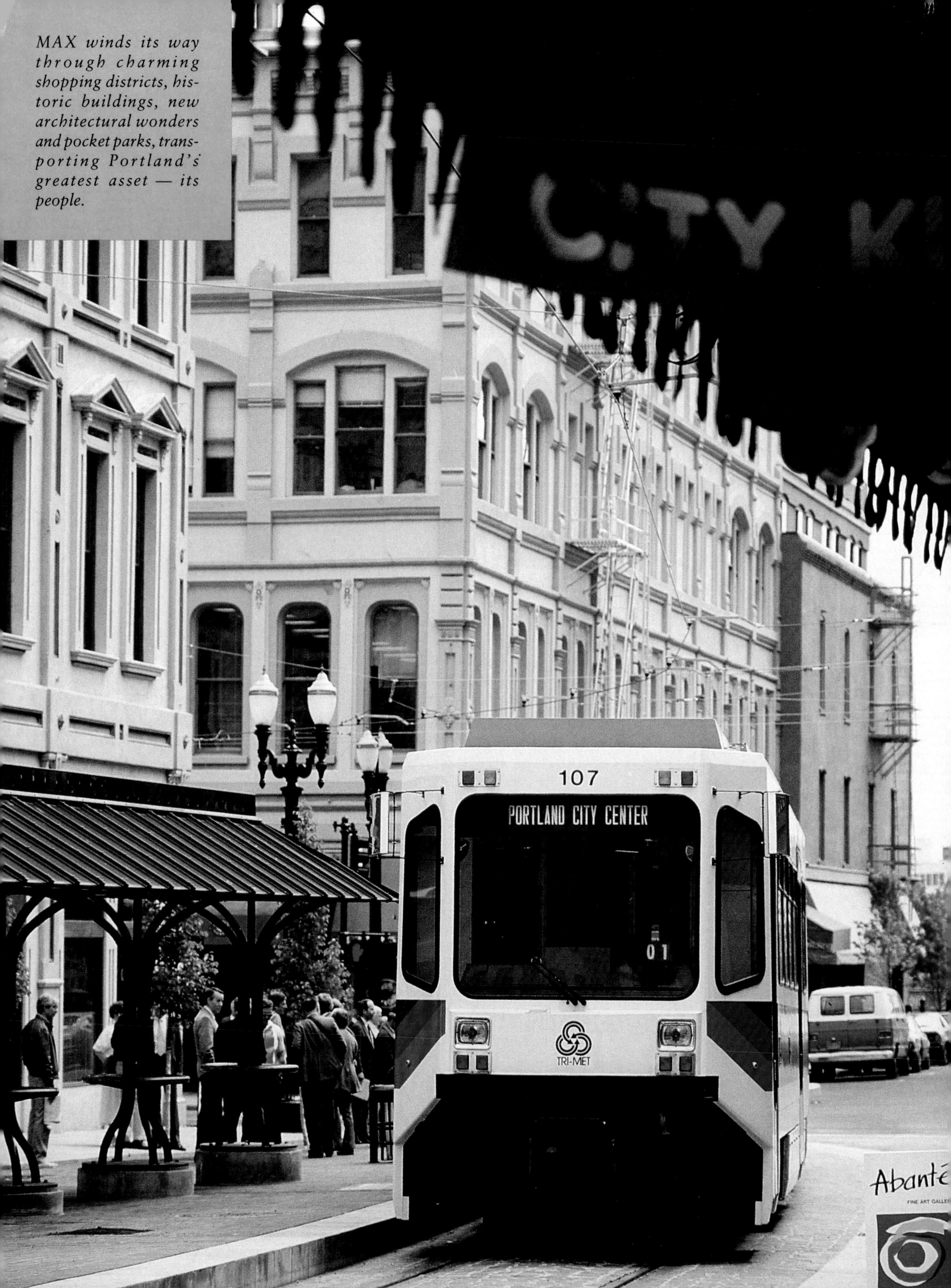

MAX winds its way through charming shopping districts, historic buildings, new architectural wonders and pocket parks, transporting Portland's greatest asset — its people.

THE FIRST PORTLAND CATALOGUE™

FOURTH EDITION

EARTHLIGHT PRESS LTD.
ENSEMBLE PUBLICATIONS INC.

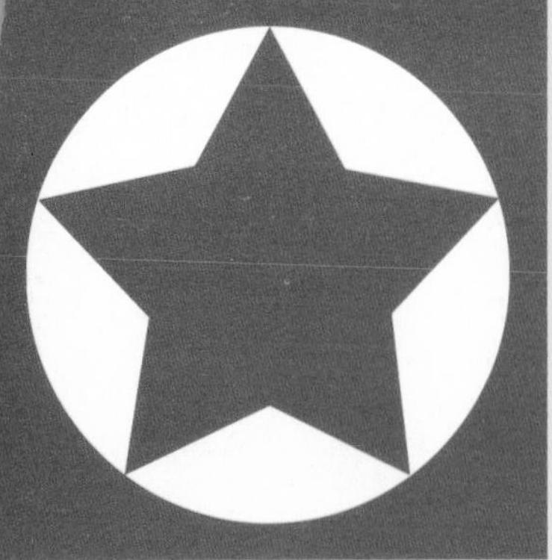

Publisher: Ann Marra

Project Coordinator: Ronald Kirk

Editorial Director: Catherine Windus

Editors: Sheilah Jones, International Wordsmiths Ltd.; Diana Masarie Leach; Malcolm Dean

Production Coordinators: Diana Masarie Leach, Nicole Sung

Production Assistant & Research: Deanne Wong

Marketing Staff: Ronald Kirk, Sharon Kolb, Joanne Forman, Tracy Farnsworth

Copywriters: Thomas H. Ryll, Renardo Barden

Photographers: Steven Bloch, Edward Gowans, Cathy Cheney, Wayne Aldridge

Graphic Design: Marra & Associates Graphic Design

Seating Plans: Steve Wilson, Becky Gyes

Paste-up: Becky Gyes

Word Processing: Susan Singer, Joanne Johnson

Maps: Liz Kingslien, Becky Gyes

Typography: Type-a-graphic, Paul O. Giesey/ Adcrafters, Studio Source

Camera and Prep: Camart Studio Ltd.

Printing: Graphic Arts Center

Cover Photo: Steven Bloch

Earthlight Press also wishes to acknowledge the advice and support extended by many individuals, and to thank in particular Jacqueline Babicky, Rita Capponi, Malcolm Dean, Sharon Yoes, Jane Willard, Robin Lawton, Colin Dobson, William Atkinson, Barbara Krane, Margaret Baricivec, Meredyth Schaffer, Cromwell Formal Wear, ProLab N.W., Joanne Barker, Janet Hume, Joanne Johnson, Gail Hauschka and Kerry Rigby.

The locations listed in this book were researched and handpicked by the staff. Every effort has been made to ensure that the information is current and correct. However, conditions beyond our control may change the accuracy over time.

ISBN 0-944328-00-8
Printed in the United States of America

The First City Catalogue™ concept originally published by Ensemble Publications Inc. in Portland, Seattle, Vancouver B.C., Denver, Phoenix, Atlanta, San Antonio, Edmonton and Victoria. Since 1987, *The First City Catalogues*™ have been published in the United States by Earthlight Press Ltd.

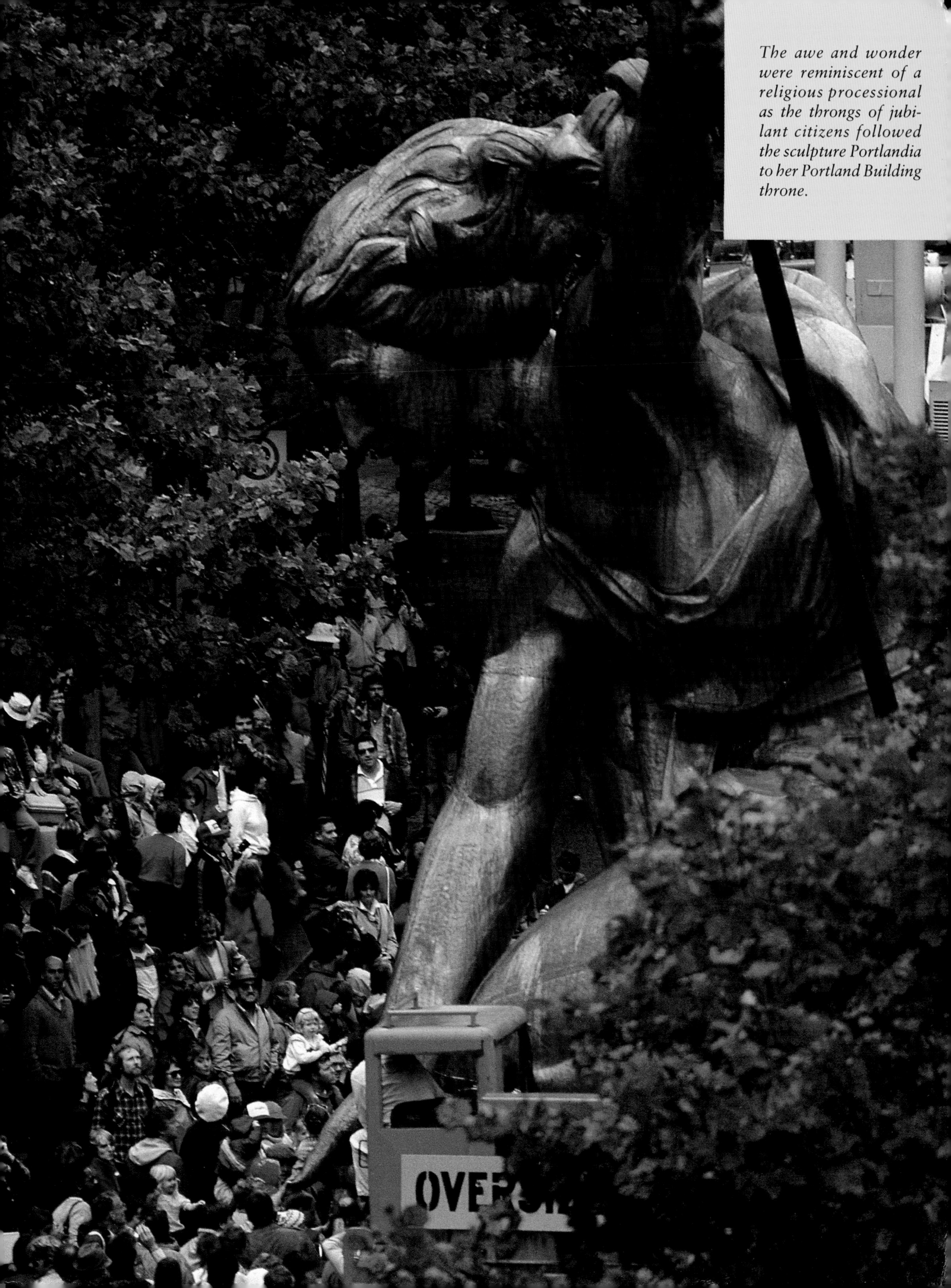

The awe and wonder were reminiscent of a religious processional as the throngs of jubilant citizens followed the sculpture Portlandia to her Portland Building throne.

CONTENTS

10

INTRODUCTION

11

HOW TO USE THIS BOOK

Not just how, but when and where. This is a book for people who live here, people who visit. Flip its pages to find a fabulous dinner. Study it to plan a shopping trip or a Sunday drive. The Catalogue is information for the imagination, a book full of fun.

12

PORTLAND: A PERFECT FIT

Architect Bob Frasca muses from a personal point of view about the Portland experience. Discover all the diversity you would expect to see in Manhattan in one quick half-hour stroll through Portland's neighborhoods.

16

DESTINATIONS

From food to furniture, from knick knacks to nights on the town, our selected stores and restaurants are grouped by neighborhood to guide you into a new look at the city. Take your book and sally forth!

19

MAPS

A whole gatefold of visual information. Our three new maps take you in progression from a broad view, to a detail of the downtown streets. Keyed from inside, they are also your guide to selectivity in shopping, dining out, having fun. As well, we've assembled check lists of the town's landmark hotels, charming bed and breakfast inns, and postcard favorite locations.

SIGHTS

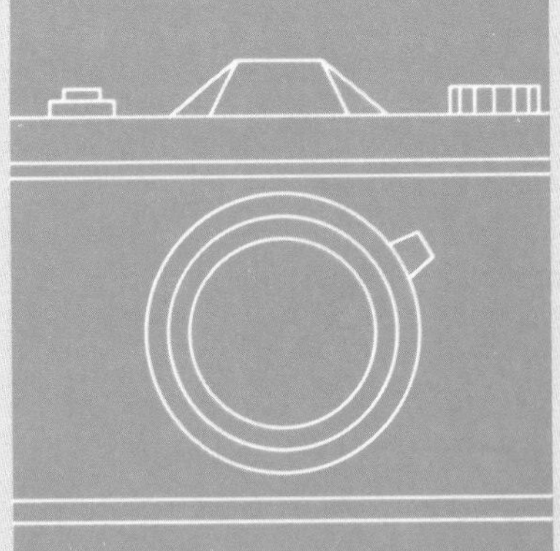

25

Gardens, parks, museums, architecture...from one end of town to the other, all the wonderful sights. The Catalogue introduces 16 new pages, many bursting with color, that take a look at both the natural beauty of Portland and the delightful additions created by our citizenry to complement the natural surroundings. From a kick on the bricks to a frolic in the grass, it's all here!

FOOD

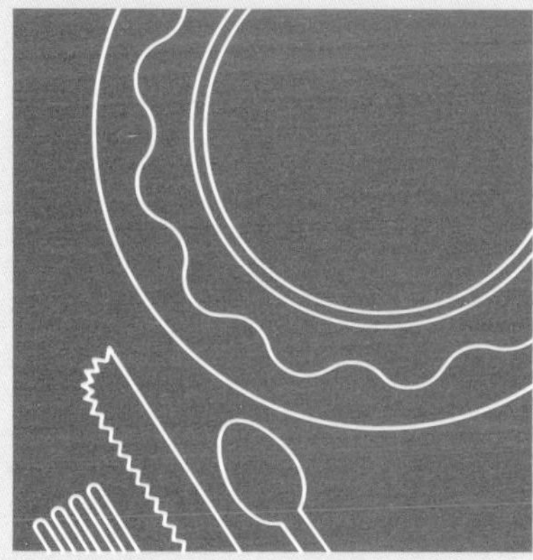

41

Introduction by Emily Crumpacker

43

DINING

From formal to casual, from seats over the water to seats in high places, we pass by the grills and sample the stock pots and the sushi bars of cosmopolitan Portland.

68

CAFÉS AND CASUAL RESTAURANTS

Congenial gathering places for breakfasts, lunches, supper and twenty-four hour cravings; hot spots for cold beer, pasta and salsas, low-cal and healthy, fattening and fabulous.

88

CATERING AND GOURMET FOODS

Personalized catering and classy take-out; wine tastings and cooking classes. The best sources for specialty foods from frozen yogurt to shiitake mushrooms to sushi makings. Fresh is the word.

ENTERTAINMENT

107

Introduction by Mike Lindberg

109

MUSIC

Somber cellos, synthesizers, baroque on brass, early music, new music — sounds you will hear for the first time tonight. Portland offers two seats on a variety of musical aisles for the traditional and inventive.

112

THEATER

Theater as sport, theater as mime, theater at its traditional best. Reflections in a variety of fascinating venues to show us another side of ourselves.

115

DANCE

We've shown our best to the world—ballet, jazz, the boldest of experimental. Companies and individuals who are recognized nationally and internationally. We list the best.

117

NIGHTBEAT

Going for a joke, blowin' the hurtin' blues, catching the buzz as opening night ends, or a jug of suds to set you up for the weekend, our club scene is more than rock or R & B. It's chasin' down the action!

120

SEATING PLANS

The new Portland Center for the Performing Arts has opened up a whole new world of options for those in search of front row and center. Are you in the mood for intimate theater in the round, a crashing wave of Wagner, a heart-stopping leap into the poised arms of the lead dancer? The seating plans for Portland's favorite theaters help you choose.

125

ANNUAL EVENTS CALENDAR

Dull days in Portland? Not in our book. This is a city of celebrations. Find out what special treats await you day by day and month by month.

FASHION

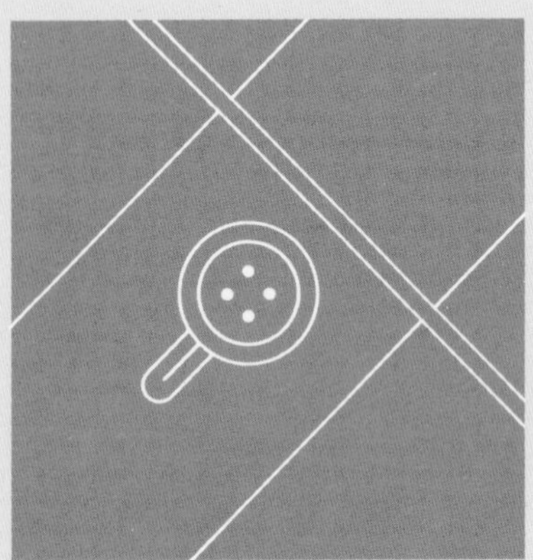

133

Introduction by Tim Leigh

135

FOR WOMEN

Clothing and accessories for every taste and occasion. European and American designers, maternity and petite sizes, plus wardrobe and image consultation.

152

MEN AND WOMEN

A distinguished selection of clothiers for men and those catering to both sexes. The finest in classic and contemporary, casual and formal, plus accessories and grooming sources.

169

JEWELRY

Designers of gold and silver jewelry, dealers in precious and semi-precious stones. Zsa Zsa, eat your heart out! Special services include gem appraisals, repair and restoration.

KIDS AND TEENS

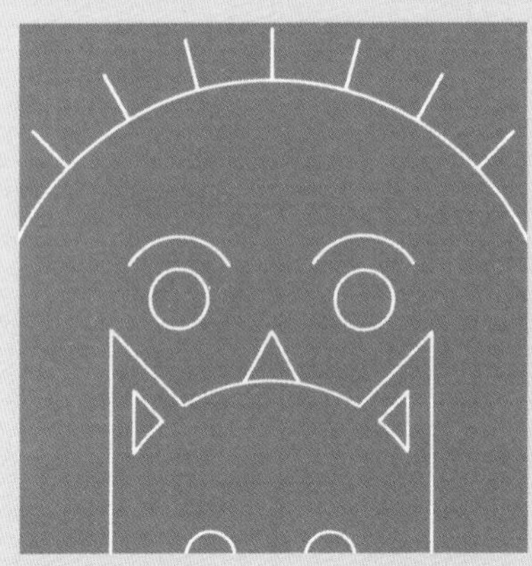

175

Introduction by Catherine Windus

European, Japanese and American designer clothing, special edition dolls, furniture that grows with you, toys, games and a very special hair dresser. Plus a gym and a museum especially for children.

SPORTS AND RECREATION

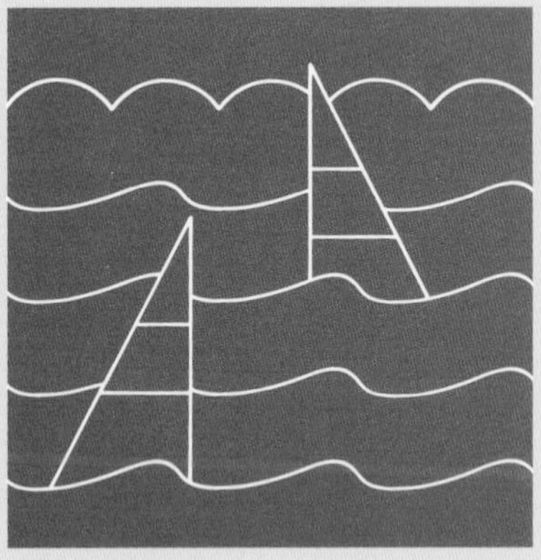

193

Introduction by Chris Boehme

Where else but Portland can you attend a regatta, baseball game, golf match and major league basketball all in the same day? Whether you're an avid fan or a participant, you'll find an overwhelming variety of games and sports, from windsurfing to croquet.

HOME

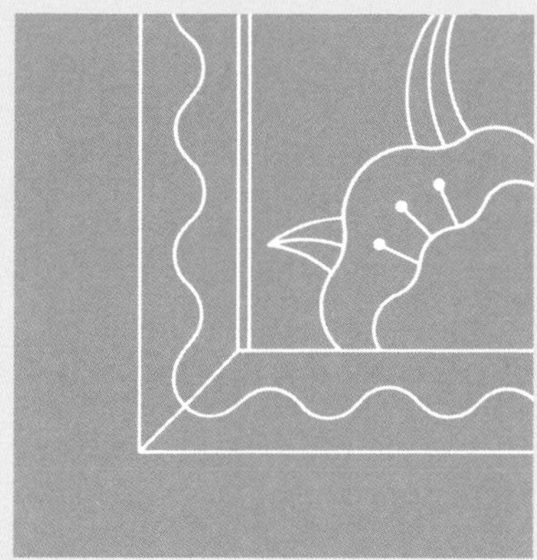

211

Introduction by Megan McMorran

213

INTERIORS

Contemporary, traditional, and unfinished furniture, along with art and antiques from around the world, silver and porcelain. And, a host of things to create your very own look at home.

229

FINAL TOUCHES

For indoors and out, the ultimate accoutrements for your home. Decorative objects, grandfather clocks, lighting and kitchen supplies, storage advice. Plants and flowers from floral designers or nurseries.

243

ART AND CRAFT GALLERIES

Regional artists share the billing with established masters in art and fine crafts, contemporary and classic, national and international. Also find consultants, framers and sources of supplies.

SPECIALTIES

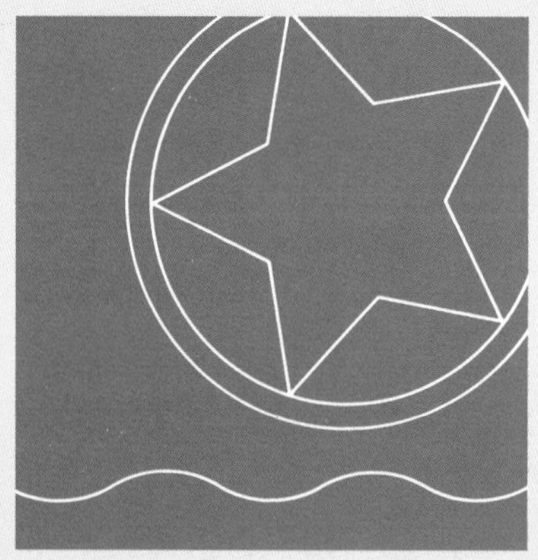

261

Introduction by Susan Stanley

263

BOOKS AND MUSIC

Literary specialists for fiction classics, travel, foods, feminist concerns, holistic health, international magazines and periodicals; audio systems, video libraries and pianos new and restored.

285

INCREDIBLES

One-of-a-kind shops and services so varied that no other category quite applies. Boutiques devoted to paper and cards, horse farms and Teddy bears, textiles and games and rentals for all occasions.

ENVIRONS

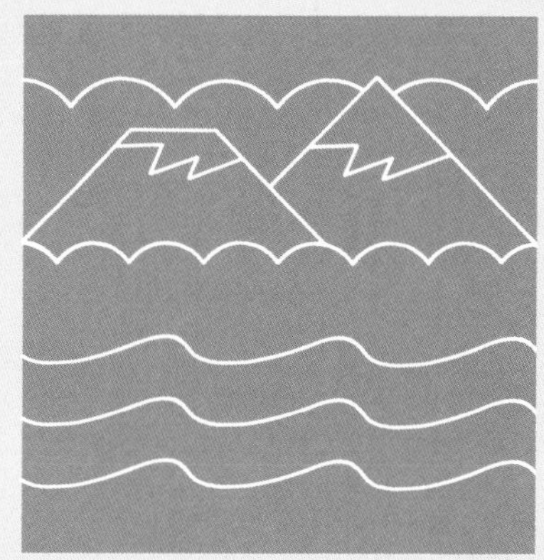

303

The grapes glistening on the vines near Newburg, the sunrise sparkling pink on a snowfield on Mount Hood, the salt air, seagulls and seafoam, the enveloping warmth of natural mineral springs, all within an hour of Portland? The stunning photographs in this section prove it's possible! Just look at where you can be in no time!

313

INDEX

The book's first, last and best source for everything that starts with a letter of the alphabet. Start with A in our Product Index for an American primitive antique and work through the town's selected best. Plug into A in our Places Index for A Children's Place and you're on your way to more discoveries.

Captured within these pages are the vitality and celebration that is Portland. Obviously not your average, everyday guidebook. It's an insightful commentary on a very special city. It's a color explosion of graphics and big, friendly photos, and an exhilarating compilation of the best things to do, see and explore.

We create a picture of Portland, leading you through a festival of options, from the essential to the unusual. The First Portland Catalogue™ addresses the big city, yet features more of its small and often overlooked elements. It's a book that meets the needs of people who like living in cities and want a more personal involvement with their surroundings.

Following on the heels of the overwhelmingly popular Third Edition, the new Fourth Edition is livelier than ever. Now, all of the fascinating details, the personality and the color are wrapped in a graphic presentation that matches today's highly visual world.

It's also paced for today, designed for frequent and fast use. Information is yours at a glance, or settle in for a good browse when you desire a great source of fresh ideas. Locations are highlighted, maps have been added and we offer more information about our selected restaurants, stores and services—who they are, what they do and what makes them special.

We had a wonderful time getting to the inside of Portland. This is your invitation to see what we found and discover it for yourself!

The answer book.

When it's late in the afternoon and no-one's had a moment to think about dinner, it will steer you swiftly to a sizzling night out—or gourmet home-delivery. It's an answer when you've been given the job of picking up something for someone very special. It lets you know what's new, and what's old and worth collecting, what events to attend and what day-trips to take.

It's a book to present to your house guests or send to a relative in faraway anywhere.

Use it when you want to pick the best seat at the Schnitzer. Call in for a fifth of Beethoven! Call out for Sunday brunch, in bed! Use the product index on page 313 for more ideas. From American primitive antiques to non-violent toys you'll find it there.

Keep it by the phone, on top of the fridge, in the reading room or the back seat of your car. It's ready when you are. And the more you use it, the better it gets.

We could go on, but you get the idea. It's a book to entertain, to give you new insights into your city. But, most of all, it's information — up front and easy to find.

The First Portland Catalogue!

Here's one of our pages.

We've packed each page full of quick reference details to help you get the picture at a glance. The legend below will show you how to get around the book.

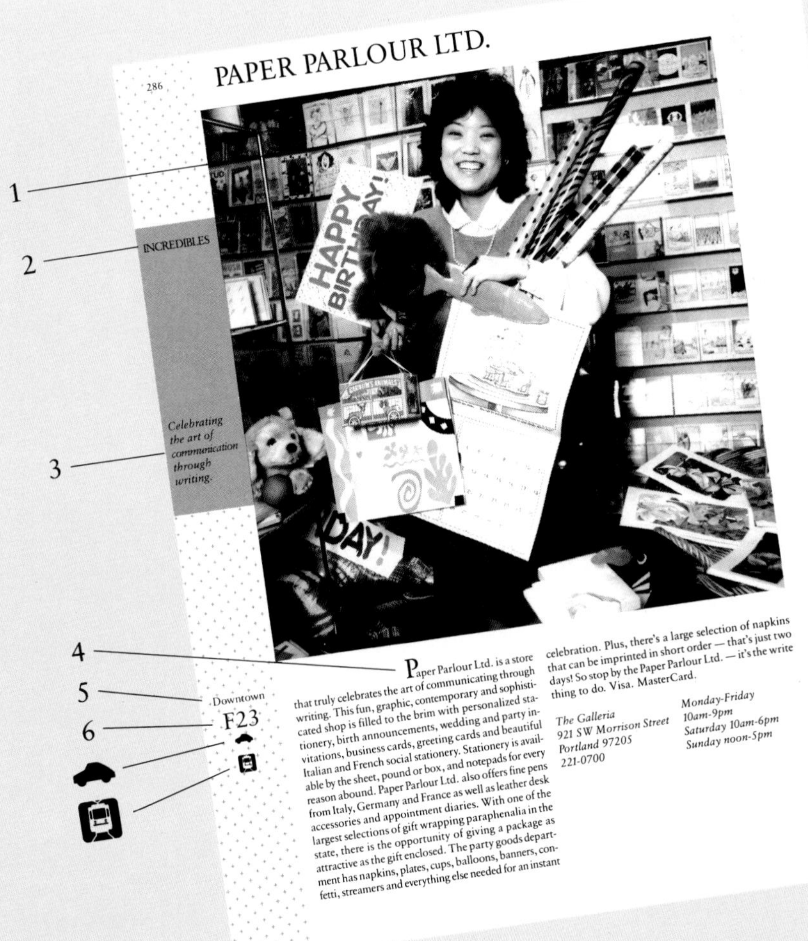

286

PAPER PARLOUR LTD.

INCREDIBLES

Celebrating the art of communication through writing.

Downtown

F23

Paper Parlour Ltd. is a store that truly celebrates the art of communicating through writing. This fun, graphic, contemporary and sophisticated shop is filled to the brim with personalized stationery, birth announcements, wedding and party invitations, business cards, greeting cards and beautiful Italian and French social stationery. Stationery is available by the sheet, pound or box, and notepads for every reason abound. Paper Parlour Ltd. also offers fine pens from Italy, Germany and France as well as leather desk accessories and appointment diaries. With one of the largest selections of gift wrapping paraphenalia in the state, there is the opportunity of giving a package as attractive as the gift enclosed. The party goods department has napkins, plates, cups, balloons, banners, confetti, streamers and everything else needed for an instant celebration. Plus, there's a large selection of napkins that can be imprinted in short order — that's just two days! So stop by the Paper Parlour Ltd. — it's the write thing to do. Visa. MasterCard.

The Galleria
921 SW Morrison Street
Portland 97205
221-0700

Monday-Friday
10am-9pm
Saturday 10am-6pm
Sunday noon-5pm

1 The picture *Big and friendly, this is photo journalism at its best. Each on-location photograph was specially taken for the catalogue. Our photographers where directed to show products, atmosphere and people—to bring them together, to make each an invitation. It's a great place to start browsing.*

2 The category *This lets you know where you are within one of our eight major sections. It further defines the nature of the business and how you can best use it.*

3 The tag *A sentence, a phrase, that brings the activity into focus and makes each business distinctive.*

4 The story *More warmth, more detail than in any other medium. Behind-the-scenes information to make it easier for you to make decisions. History, anecdotes, people, features, menu information; each has been written to capture the flavor.*

5 The destination *You will find this as well on our fold-out map. A quick study of Portland's neighborhoods and what's in them will entice you to a shopping adventure in another part of town—perhaps a foray into late-afternoon fashion, topped off with a fine dinner at night.*

6 Map co-ordinates *The location is pinpointed by these vertical and horizontal co-ordinates on the maps on page 19. Easy? You're on your way!*

Parking *This symbol means that parking (sometimes limited) is provided in the immediate vicinity of the store or restaurant (other than on the street) or parking-lot tickets will be validated.*

MAX *When you see this symbol you know the store is located right on the line of Portland's hot, new, fun-to-ride light rail system. Have a blast zipping from store to park to river, to more stores.*

PORTL

Immigrants are like converts; they become shameless boosters of their newfound truth. In my case it's a place: Portland, Oregon.

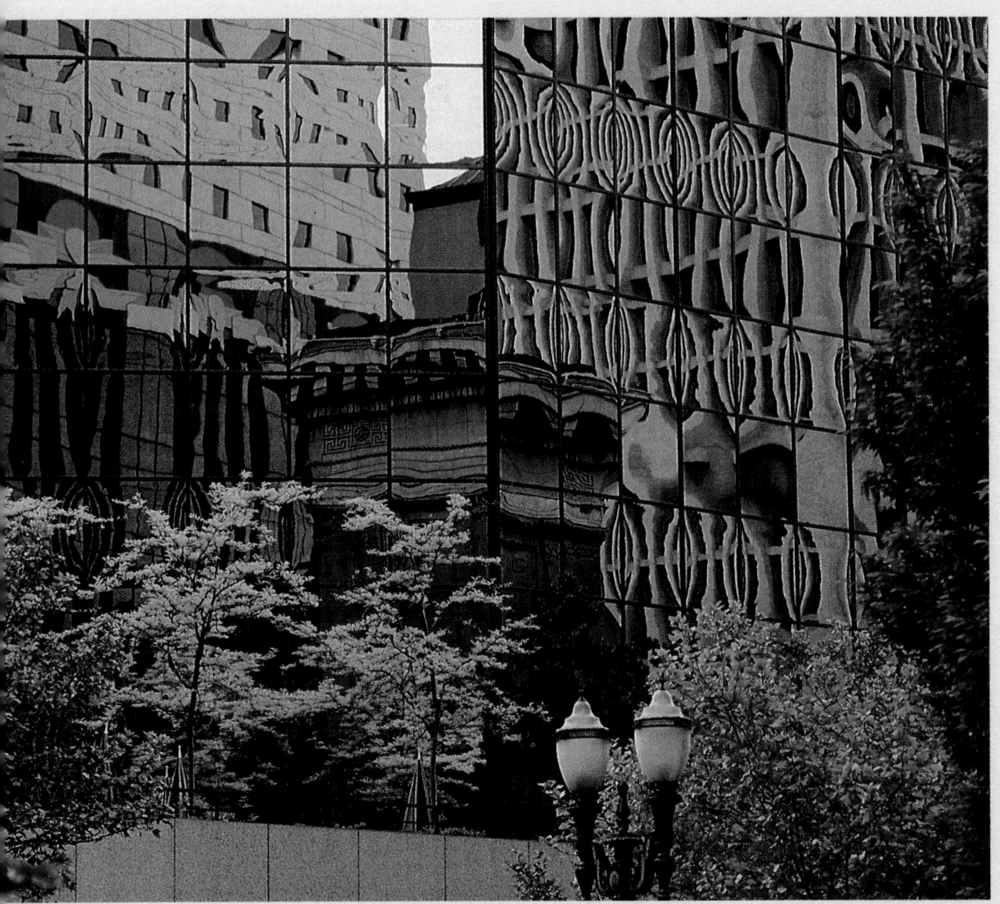

As a refugee from the blizzards and humidity of western New York State, by way of Ann Arbor, Michigan and Cambridge, Massachusetts some 25 years ago, I may no longer qualify as an immigrant in the purest sense. But memories of life on the other side of the continent die hard, and inevitably invite comparison.

Some of my enthusiasm for Portland may come from the fact that I ended up here by luck. Someone I knew in Boston had two cars to transport across the country, and I volunteered to drive one, deciding to look for a job upon my arrival. The other source of my enthusiasm stems from what I like to call the "Oregon experience." For some people, myself included, Portland simply offers a perfect fit.

On one hand, the "experience" is made up of the landscape and climate. On the other, the ethic. Both manifest themselves in how Oregonians build their cities, in that the overwhelming quality of the natural environment has fostered a similar respect for the built environment. Like places in New England, Oregon is a very civilized place, carefully conceived by the forebearers who

LAND

A Perfect Fit

Bob Frasca

settled here. The major difference is that, unlike the East coast, there still remains a frontier quality to the mindset here. In Boston and New York, people were always talking about how they were going to knock them dead if they ever "made it on Broadway." Portland, on the other hand, is definitely "off Broadway." People here spend most of their time exploring the advantages of it.

Portland is a Lilliputian City, in that it has most of the qualities and diversity of a large metropolis, only at a more human, diminutive scale. It serves as the financial and cultural capital of a large region, yet the central city has a forced density, due to its confinement by hills on one side and the river on the other. Even our blocks are less than one-half the size found in most cities.

For example, a walk from Portland State University to the Skidmore Fountain in Old Town offers all of the diversity you'd find in a journey from one tip of Manhattan to the other. The major difference is that, in Portland, you're talking about a half-hour stroll. In New York it would take the better part of a weekend. Portland may have similarities or

A collector of cities will find a permanent corner for Portland.

pretenses to New York, such as our in-town housing area on Southwest Park Avenue, our soon-to-open Saks on Southwest 5th Avenue, our Southwest Broadway theater district — but that's where it ends.

Portland by contrast is a very "readable" place, in that it's easy to go exploring with a slight tingly feeling of adventure, but without the fear of ever getting lost. In addition to the hills and the river which set the overall context, Portland's numerous parks, squares, unique districts and streets, and its distinct buildings and monuments, break the city down into bite-size images that permanently burrow their way into one's consciousness. It's a feeling that extends everywhere, from the Ira Keller Fountain, a notion transplanted from Big Sur, to Pioneer Square, the physical and spiritual hearth of the city.

Good cities are more than a collection of buildings or monuments, but you can't have a memorable city without them. The Portland Building is this city's newest and brashest — a 13-story jukebox, upon which is perched a 27-foot high (and that's kneeling) "Portlandia," contemplating the traffic below. Like it or not, it serves as testament to a civic courage that says ideas can be built in Portland, not just discussed. A collector of cities will find a permanent corner for this place, in that mental scrapbook that we all carry around, as one of the minor class acts on this planet.

Cities and places are like stages where we act out our lines. We consciously choose them because, after awhile, we find the right fit. Portland is that way for me. I wait impatiently for the rains after an especially dry, distracting summer, so that I can finally go back to work. If I had driven that car to San Diego instead of Portland 25 years ago, I'm sure the salt from the margaritas would have killed me by now!

Bob Frasca *was quoted as saying "I want to leave my thumbprint on the environment" in an interview with* Willamette Week *in 1982. By 1984 the firm Zimmer Gunsel Frasca was the 23rd largest architectural firm in the United States. Notable recent additions to the cityscape include The Portland Justice Center, Willamette Center and the Koin Center. So much of the southern end of downtown Portland is Zimmer Gunsel Frasca's work that it is sometimes known as "Frascaland."*

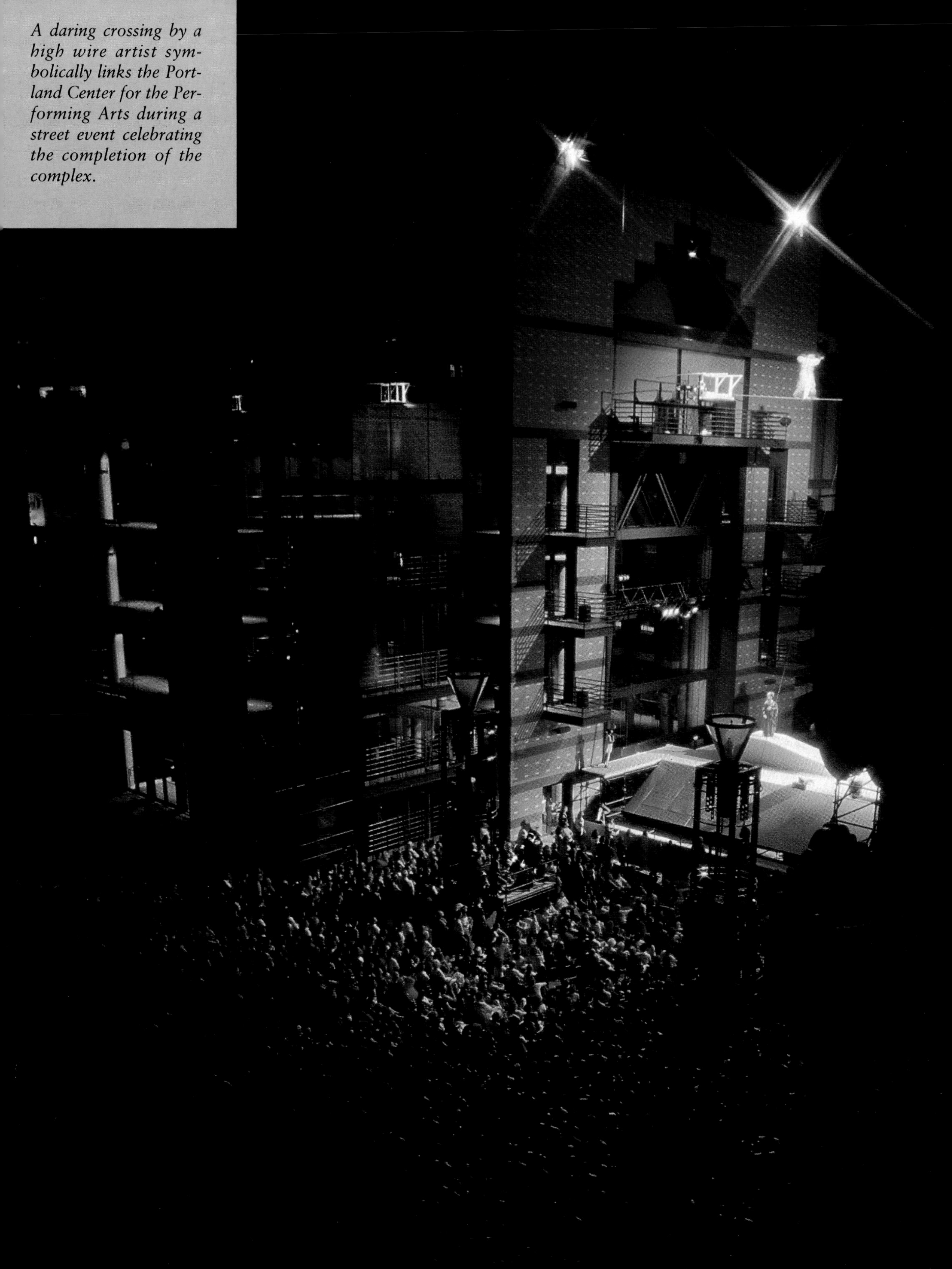

A daring crossing by a high wire artist symbolically links the Portland Center for the Performing Arts during a street event celebrating the completion of the complex.

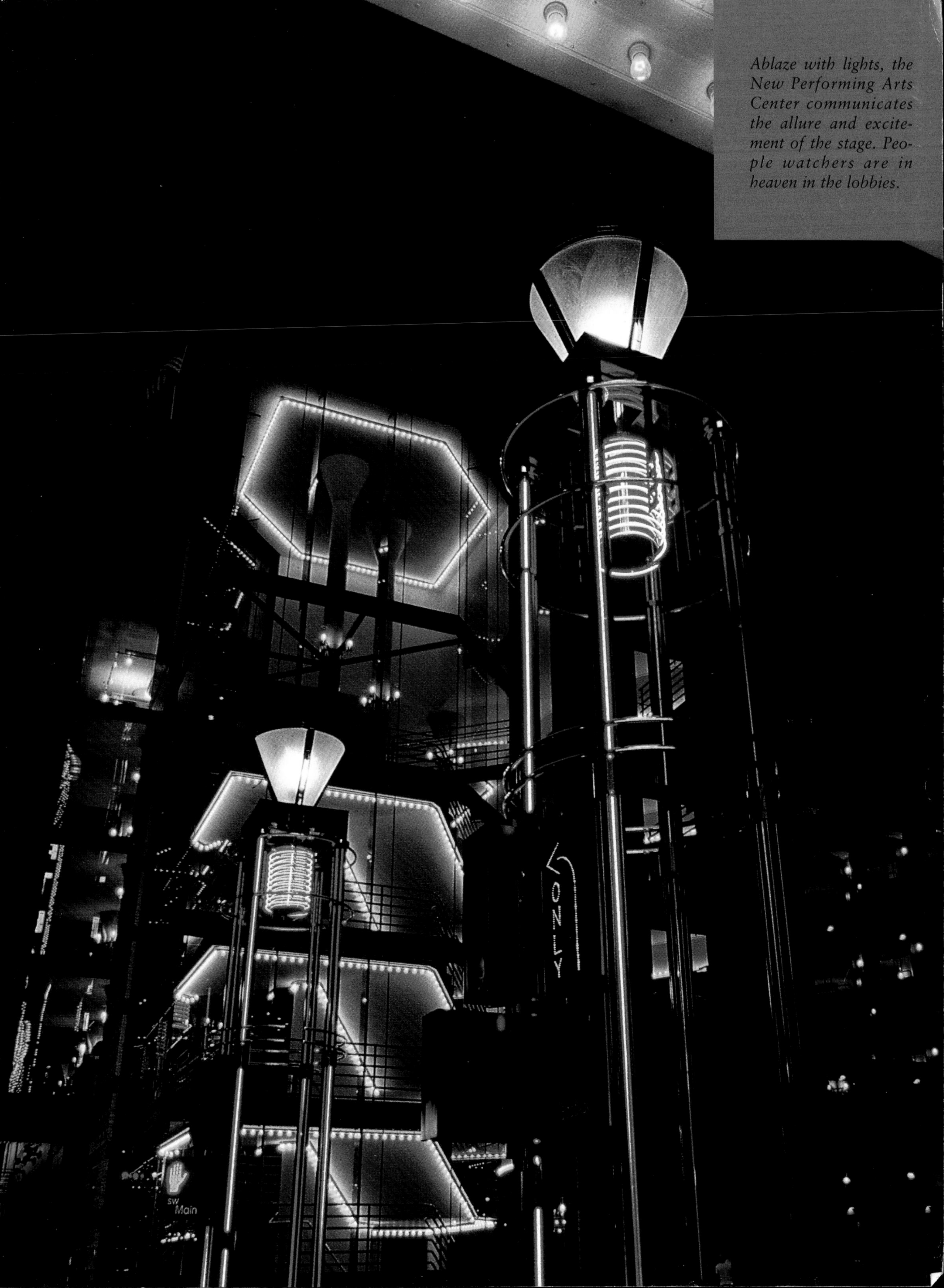

Ablaze with lights, the New Performing Arts Center communicates the allure and excitement of the stage. People watchers are in heaven in the lobbies.

DESTINATIONS

Every Portland neighborhood, with its undefined yet definite borders, has a distinct character and evergrowing pride. Imagination, muscle and dedication is the glue that bonds our neighborhoods. On nearly every corner a Victorian has closed its doors on a dingy past and emerged as a bright retail shop or a cozy family dwelling. Poking about a Portland neighborhood can easily occupy a day. A casual stroll down a row of fanciful shops leads us (how lucky we are) to our favorite pastry retreat. Satisfactorily snacked, we (what next?) gallery hop. Later, armed with a formidable picnic, we sally forth to claim our place in the park for the free concert. A day in the life of a neighborhood—ain't it grand?

DOWNTOWN

Downtown Portland celebrates the pedestrian. Here is the heart of the city—colorful, bustling, alive—served by a transit mall and MAX, the recently completed light rail. The elegance and grandeur of historic buildings have been preserved and restored, mirrored images of the bustle and activity. People places abound—parks, squares, fountains and plazas. Stroll the waterfront, peruse the shops, dally in the parks, or dine in any of a delectable array of eateries. Downtown Portland has grown up, so join the crowd and check it out.

► SIGHTS

Chapman and Lownsdale Squares
Ira Keller Fountain
KOIN Tower
Oregon Art Institute
Oregon Historical Society
PacWest Center
Park Blocks
Pioneer Courthouse Square
Portland Building
Portland Center for the Performing Arts
Portlandia
Terry Schrunk Plaza
Tom McCall Waterfront Park
U.S. Bank Tower

► FOOD

13 Coins *71*
Atwater's Restaurant & Lounge *48*
Bogart's Joint *85*
Brasserie Montmartre *56*
Café Vivo *53*
Chen's Dynasty *65*
Coffee Ritz *77*
Cool Temptations *93*
Edelweiss Sausage & Delicatessen *99*
Executive Sweets, Desserts Etc. *106*
The Heathman Hotel & Restaurant *50*
Hot Lips Pizza *82*
Huber's *60*
Hunan Restaurant *57*
Jake's Famous Crawfish *61*
Macheesmo Mouse *83*
Metro on Broadway *79*
The Veritable Quandary *87*

► FASHION

Alan Costley *161*
Alder West *165*
Cromwell Formal Wear *155*
Element 79 *171*
Equinox Fine Jewelry *173*
Expecting the Best *138*
Faces Unlimited *141*
Goldmark Jewelers *170*
Harrington's Executive Clothiers *166*
Hickox & Friends *167*
Hot Cities *158*
M. Willock *146*
Mario's *154*
Mario's For Women *142*
Mercantile *136*
Nofziger *163*
Richard Ltd. *153*
Robert Eaton Jeweler-Designer *172*

► KIDS AND TEENS

Finnegan's *183*

► SPORTS AND RECREATION

Nike Downtown *207*

► HOME

Art Media *259*

Kitchen Kaboodle *232*
The Kobos Company *235*
Portland Cutlery Company *234*
The Real Mother Goose *256*
Shannon & Co. *260*
Shogun's Gallery *219*
Storables *238*

► SPECIALTIES
Byrne's Luggage *288*
The Catbird Seat Bookstore *271*
Chelsea AudioVideo *267*
Endgames *291*
Josephine's Dry Goods *293*
Looking Glass Bookstore *277*
Oregon Historical Society *274*
Paper Parlour Ltd *286*
Portland Music Co. *282*
Portland State Bookstore *275*
Powell's Travel Store *279*
Powell's Books *264*
Rich's Cigar Store *290*
Shannon & Co. Reprographics *297*

RIVERPLACE

RiverPlace's addition to downtown Portland's waterfront is significant. Consisting of specialty shops, several restaurants, the RiverPlace Alexis Hotel, an athletic club, condominiums and an esplanade extending along the water's edge, connecting RiverPlace to Tom McCall Waterfront Park, RiverPlace has added life and vitality to the south waterfront. RiverPlace's 200 slip marina offers many public and private uses such as rowing, windsurfing and sailing.

► FOOD
Harbor Side Restaurant Shanghai Lounge *62*

► FASHION
Suite 360 *148*

► SPECIALTIES
Book Port *269*

YAMHILL HISTORIC DISTRICT

The sense of history is everywhere in the Yamhill Historic District where many of the buildings date from the mid-1800's and are now on the National Historic Register. It's a great area to gawk at gargoyles and cast-iron facades, and shop for everything from fresh food to art. In the Antique Carousel Museum, the only one in the country, you can see the only antique carousel still working. In the midst of all the history is the Yamhill Marketplace, a new, light, bright atrium building designed to take up where the old Yamhill Public market left off. It provides a wealth of fresh food choices from produce to pasta plus a spectrum of international quick food restaurants and interesting retail shops. A fun place for friendly people-watching and mingling.

► FOOD
Crane & Company *90*
Great Harvest Bread Co. *102*
Kashmir Restaurant *66*
Le Panier Very French Bakery *98*
Pasta Cucina *101*

► FASHION
Trade Secrets *168*

► KIDS AND TEENS
City Kids *185*

► HOME
Abanté Fine Art Gallery *250*
Augen Gallery *245*
The Country Willow *230*
Lawrence Gallery *249*
Northwest Futon Company *218*
O'Connell Gallery *251*
Scandia Down Shops *239*
Sunbow Gallery *252*

► SPECIALTIES
Bookmerchants Bookshop Cafe Espresso Bar *268*
Present Perfect *300*

SKIDMORE HISTORIC DISTRICT

The Skidmore area is part of Portland's oldest development. The Skidmore Fountain; the new Market Village, the many small shops, galleries and restaurants housed in historic buildings, all contribute to a contemporary bustle in the charm of a historical setting. It is also home of the new Portland Maritime Museum. The greenway of the riverside Tom McCall Waterfront Park gives a feeling of quiet and spaciousness. On weekends the entire Skidmore area is even busier with the Saturday Market activities under the Burnside Bridge.

► SIGHTS
Oregon Maritime Center and Museum
Saturday Market

► FOOD
Abou Karim *80*
Bijou Cafe *73*
Crêpe Faire Restaurant & Bistro *64*
Le Panier Very French Bakery *98*
McCormick & Schmick's Seafood Restaurant *54*

► FASHION
Gazelle Natural Fibre Clothing *162*

► HOME
Attic Gallery *248*
Elizabeth Leach Gallery *244*
Gango Gallery *255*
Jamison/Thomas Gallery *246*
Oriental Rug Gallery *223*
The Poster Gallery Etc. *254*
Studio Artists *258*

► SPECIALTIES
The Nor'wester Bookshop *270*
Salutations *299*

OLD TOWN

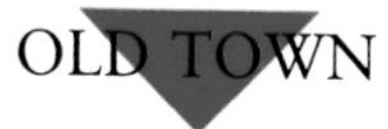

The original Portland was built in this riverfront area north of Burnside. Much of the old architecture has been restored and refurbished for an exciting array of shops, galleries and ethnic food restaurants. Portland's Chinatown has a sparkling new structure, China Gate, commemorating 135 years of Chinese contributions to the city. Also new, is the American Advertising Museum which is the first museum of its kind in the world. The museum is the culmination of three years of research, acquisitions and design of an extensive collection of business and advertising Americana. To explore Portland's history, visit the Historic Preservation League of Oregon which has films, books, and an array of tours for everyone.

► SIGHTS
American Advertising Museum
China Gate
Historic Preservation League of Oregon
Portland Police Historical Museum

► FOOD
Alexis Restaurant *76*
Couch Street Fish House *45*
Juleps *63*
Opus Too/Jazz de Opus *52*

► SPORTS AND RECREATION
Ciclo Sport Shop *204*
Oregon Mountain Community *198*

► SPECIALTIES
Old Town Car Tunes *278*
Portland Music Co. *282*

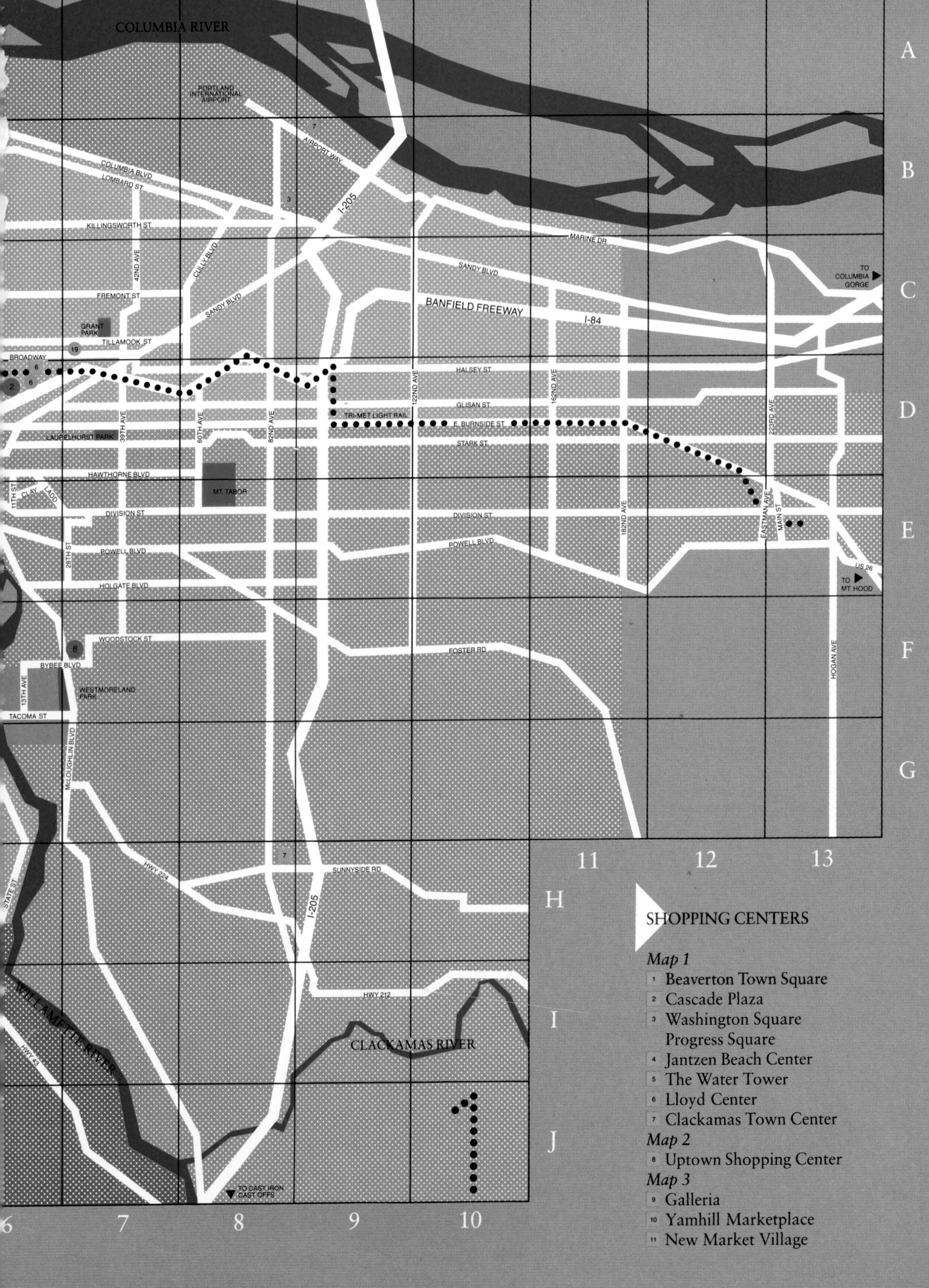

SHOPPING CENTERS

Map 1

1 Beaverton Town Square
2 Cascade Plaza
3 Washington Square
Progress Square
4 Jantzen Beach Center
5 The Water Tower
6 Lloyd Center
7 Clackamas Town Center

Map 2

8 Uptown Shopping Center

Map 3

9 Galleria
10 Yamhill Marketplace
11 New Market Village

Three maps and a wash of color paint the town for your adventure. Filled with information, from right to left, Map 1 is the big picture showing parks and neighborhoods in the greater Portland area; Map 2 is a Northwest neighborhood detail; Map 3 is Downtown. The map coordinate numbers you will also find in the margin of each page inside. Welcome to the Portland experience.

DESTINATIONS

Map 1

- North Portland
- Northeast Portland
- Northwest Portland
- Old Town
- Downtown
- Southwest Portland
- Corbett-John's Landing
- Multnomah/Hillsdale
- Raleigh Hills
- Beaverton
- Progress
- Lake Oswego
- Southeast Portland
- Sellwood
- Gresham

Map 3

- Old Town Historic District
- Skidmore Historic District
- Yamhill Historic District
- RiverPlace

BRIDGES

North to South:

St John's
Fremont
Broadway
Steel
Burnside
Morrison
Hawthorne
Marquam
Ross Island
Sellwood

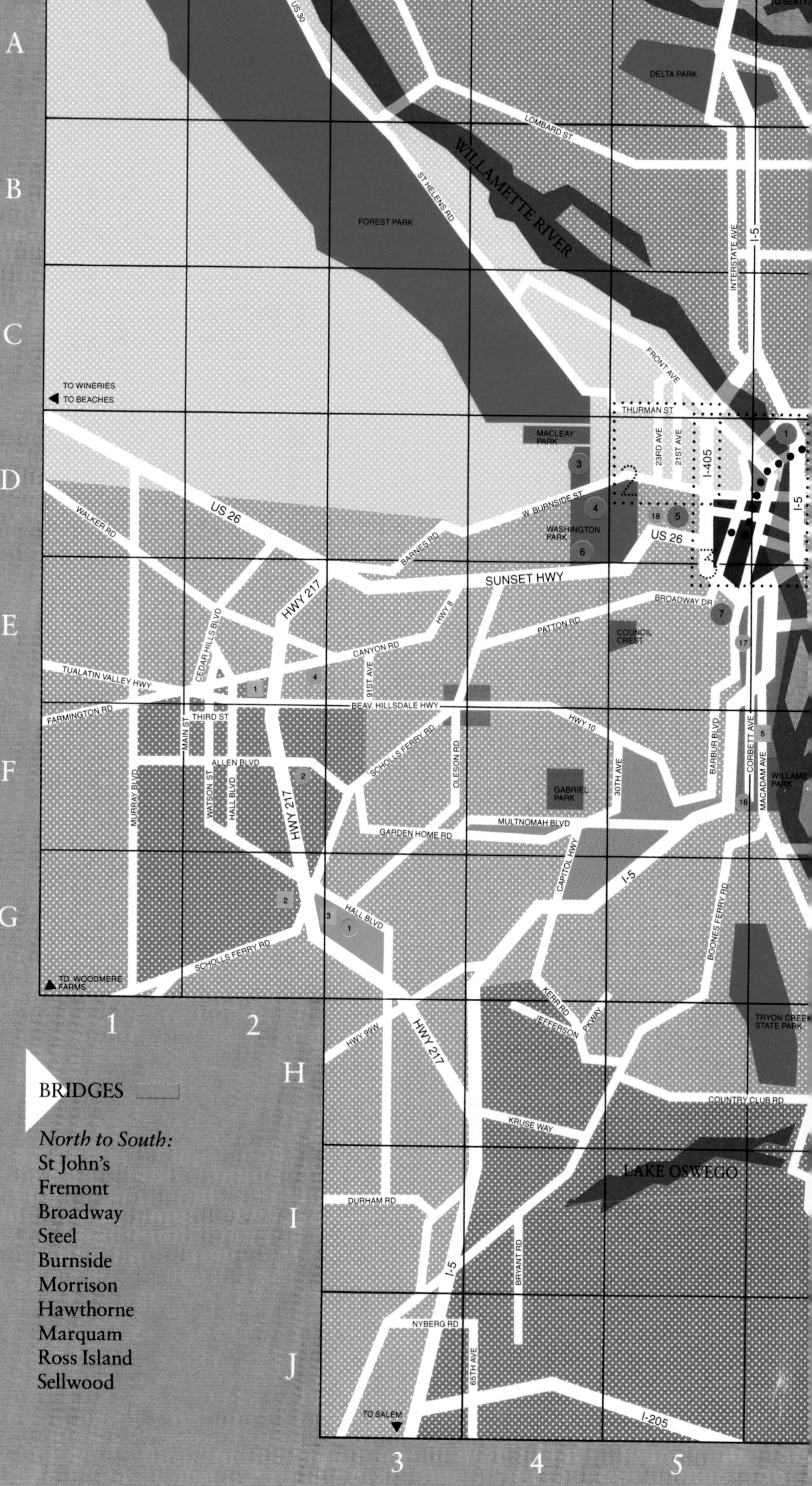

NORTHWEST PORTLAND

Urbane, sophisticated, rowdy, and colorful, Northwest Portland is many different things to many different people. In age — from preschoolers to pensioners — and in lifestyles — from artists to financiers, Yuppies to hippies, and communal singles to nuclear families, a wide variety of people make this neighborhood their home and workplace. The built environment, no less eclectic, ranges from snappy contemporary condos to street upon street of historic houses, with warehouses and commercial buildings thrown in for good measure. Forest Park begins here with 5,000 acres of wilderness and 58 miles of hiking trails. It's the largest urban wilderness park in America. Back in civilization, stop for a tour of the French Renaissance Pittock Mansion. It offers a spectacular view of the city and four snow-capped mountain peaks.

► SIGHTS
Forest Park
Macleay Park
Pittock Mansion
Wallace Park
► FOOD
Bogart's Joint *85*
Casa-U-Betcha *81*
The Coffee People *97*
Cool Temptations *93*
Delphina's *58*
Elephants Delicatessen *96*
Foothill Broiler *84*
L'Auberge *46*
Macheesmo Mouse *83*
Papa Haydn *70*
Paul*Bergen Catering and Charcuterie *92*
Pettygrove House and Gardens *55*
Pharmacy Fountain *84*
The Ringside *47*
Rose's Restaurant *75*
Rose's Viennese Bakery *105*
ThirtyOne Northwest *51*
► FASHION
Elizabeth Street *137*
Jean-Marie Fine Lingerie *144*
Norm Thompson *157*
Sylvie, An Image Perfected For You *150*
The Towne Shop *139*
23rd Avenue Sweaters *140*
Victoria's *149*
West End Ltd. *145*
► KIDS AND TEENS
Child's Play *186*
Dimples *184*
Early Childhood Bookhouse *182*
Hanna Andersson *179*
Mako *181*
Portland Family Calendar *190*
► SPORTS AND RECREATION
Howell's Uptown Sports Center *203*
► HOME
Ann Sacks' Tileworks *225*
Beyond Reason *257*
Kitchen Kaboodle *232*
Portland Antique Company *220*
Recollections *221*
Shogun's Gallery *219*
Uptown Hardware *241*
► SPECIALTIES
Annie Bloom's Books *276*
Daisy Kingdom *296*
Dazzle *287*
Plâte du Jour *298*
Westover Wools *292*

NORTH PORTLAND

The confluence of the Willamette and Columbia Rivers provides a scenic setting for Kelley Point Park, a wonderful place for swimming, picnicking and watching oceangoing vessels wind their way back to the Pacific. South of the park the small community of St. Johns has charming historic buildings as well as a large indoor tennis center, open to the public. Along the Columbia River, public boat landings can be found at Hayden Island and Jantzen Beach, which also features a large shopping mall complete with carousel. Along the Willamette River are the busy Port of Portland facilities which features five marine terminals and four dry docks.

► SIGHTS
Cathedral Park
Delta Park
Kelley Point Park
► FASHION
Norm Thompson *157*
► HOME
Paul Schatz Fine Furniture *217*
► SPECIALTIES
HK Limited *289*
Teddy Bears Picnic *301*

NORTHEAST PORTLAND

Tree-lined avenues and quiet parks provide the setting for one of the city's most popular residential areas. An eclectic mix of architectural styles, ranging from the ubiquitous Bungalow to elegant Colonial Revival are found throughout the area. Broadway Avenue, with its clusters of small commercial buildings and shops, is a reminder of the days of the streetcars which once plied the street between downtown and the newly developing residential areas. You'll also find the Memorial Coliseum, where large exhibitions and conventions are held and which is also home of the NBA Trail Blazers. Only a few blocks away is Lloyd Center, one of the world's first shopping malls, complete with a large indoor ice rink.

► SIGHTS
Grant Park
The Grotto
Laurelhurst Park
► FOOD
Anzen Oriental Foods and Imports *100*
Macheesmo Mouse *83*
Nature's Fresh Northwest *103*
Rose's Restaurant *75*
The Ringside *47*
► KIDS AND TEENS
A Children's Place *187*
The Children's Gym *192*
► SPORTS AND RECREATION
Nike Factory Outlet *207*
► HOME
The Arrangement *231*
Kasch's Garden Centers *240*
The Kobos Company *235*
Lloyd's Interiors *214*
Parker Furniture Design Center *215*
Stanton's Unfinished Furniture *224*
► SPECIALTIES
A Woman's Place Bookstore *280*
HK Limited *289*
Sign Wizards *302*
Stiles For Relaxation *284*
Teddy Bears Picnic *301*

SOUTHEAST PORTLAND

If you are in the market for antiques, collectibles, old books, or wares, you've come to the right spot. The Hawthorne Boulevard area — blossoming with new shops as well as old — or Sellwood, where Thirteenth Avenue is known as Antique Row, offer a wide variety of selec-

tions. A number of delectable restaurants as well as old neighborhood movie theaters are found throughout both areas. Or if you are yearning for more wide open spaces, Southeast has plenty of those as well. Consider the parks: Mt. Tabor Park—the only park in the city on the site of an extinct volcano—and Laurelhurst Park where duck ponds abound, are only two of the many which beckon the outdoor enthusiast. In the midst of it all are the beautiful grounds and hallowed halls of Reed College, one of the most prestigious private liberal arts colleges in the nation.

► SIGHTS

Crystal Springs
Rhododendron Gardens
Leach Botanical Gardens
Mt. Tabor Park
Oaks Pioneer Park
Westmoreland Park

► FOOD

Edelweiss Sausage & Delicatessen *99*
Genoa *44*
Le Panier Very French Bakery *98*
Macheesmo Mouse *83*
Papa Haydn *70*
Parchman Farm Restaurant and Bar *86*
Pastaworks *89*

► HOME

Fathertime Clocks *236*
Kasch's Garden Centers *240*
Kitchen Kaboodle *232*
Northwest Futon Company *218*
Stanton's Unfinished Furniture *224*

► SPECIALTIES

Day Music Company *266*
Endgames *291*
HK Limited *289*
Moe's Pianos *273*

GRESHAM

Gresham has grown-up from its former status as a simple outpost on the way to Mt. Hood. With its proximity to the mountain and wilderness areas, Gresham attracts skiers, hunters and fishermen who need only drive a short distance for the sport of their choice. This major suburban area is growing rapidly. Starting for some—ending for others—Portland's new Light Rail is the "new" ticket to Gresham. Mt. Hood Community College plays an important part in the area's growth. It sponsors the annual Mt. Hood Festival of Jazz in August, a nationally acclaimed get-together of some of the world's finest jazz musicians and their fans. For the sporting type, the Multnomah Kennel Club offers Greyhound racing. For family outings, there's picnicking nearby at Blue Lake park. The fresh produce stands that circle Gresham offer irresistible spring, summer and fall pickings right out of nearby gardens.

► FOOD

Cloudtree & Sun and Main Street Grocery *94*

► FASHION

Pacific Crest Clothing Co. *156*

► SPECIALTIES

Portland Music Company 282

SOUTHWEST PORTLAND

Looking to the west from downtown you see Portland Heights, the home of some of Portland's grandest manors and oldest families. Drive up Southwest Vista to see the hillside homes and breath-taking views of the city. Washington Park on the edge of the area can be reached by turning west off Vista onto Park Avenue. From Washington Park, roads wind through the hills to the Rose Test Gardens, the Shakespearean Garden, the Japanese Gardens, the Washington Park tennis courts, the Hoyt Arboretum and the Washington Park Zoo. The Zoo is famous for having the largest herd of breeding elephants, its penguinarium and a well-developed primate center. Across from the Zoo, the Oregon Museum of Science and Industry offers extensive displays and interesting programs at the Planetarium. The World Forestry Center nearby shows the story of the wood products industry through an audio-visual presentation, and is host to a variety of wood related activities year round.

► SIGHTS

Council Crest Park
Hoyt Arboretum
International Rose Test Gardens (Washington Park Rose Gardens)
Japanese Gardens
Oregon Museum of Science and Industry (OMSI)
Oregon School of Arts and Crafts
Washington Park
Washington Park Zoo
World Forestry Center

► FOOD

Crane & Company *90*
Hot Lips Pizza *82*
Strohecker's *95*

► FASHION

Chris H. Foleen Goldsmith *174*
Gary McKinstry Hair Design *159*

► HOME

Olde Favorites *227*
Paul Schatz Fine Furniture *217*
Virginia Jacobs *233*

► SPECIALTIES

The Audio Alternative *272*
Westside Rentals & Gifts *295*

CORBETT-JOHNS LANDING

Delightful Victorian houses, many of which have been lovingly restored by young professionals who like their style and close proximity to downtown, are the hallmark of this neighborhood. On Corbett Avenue you will find The Contemporary Crafts Gallery, the nation's oldest craft gallery which consistently presents compelling work of both local and national artists. You will find the Water Tower at Johns Landing, a shopping complex — crammed with gifts, fashion, food shops and restaurants. Across Macadam Avenue the developed riverside includes restaurants, condominiums, and offices. Nearby Willamette Park provides a wealth of picnic areas and tennis courts as well as a boat launch for power boaters and sailors.

► FOOD

Buffalo Gap Saloon and Eatery *78*
Caro Amico *74*
Koji Osakaya Fish House *59*
Nature's Fresh Northwest *103*
Piccolo Mondo *53*

► FASHION

Eye of Ra *151*
Francesca's Fragrances *164*
The Petite Woman's Shoppe *147*

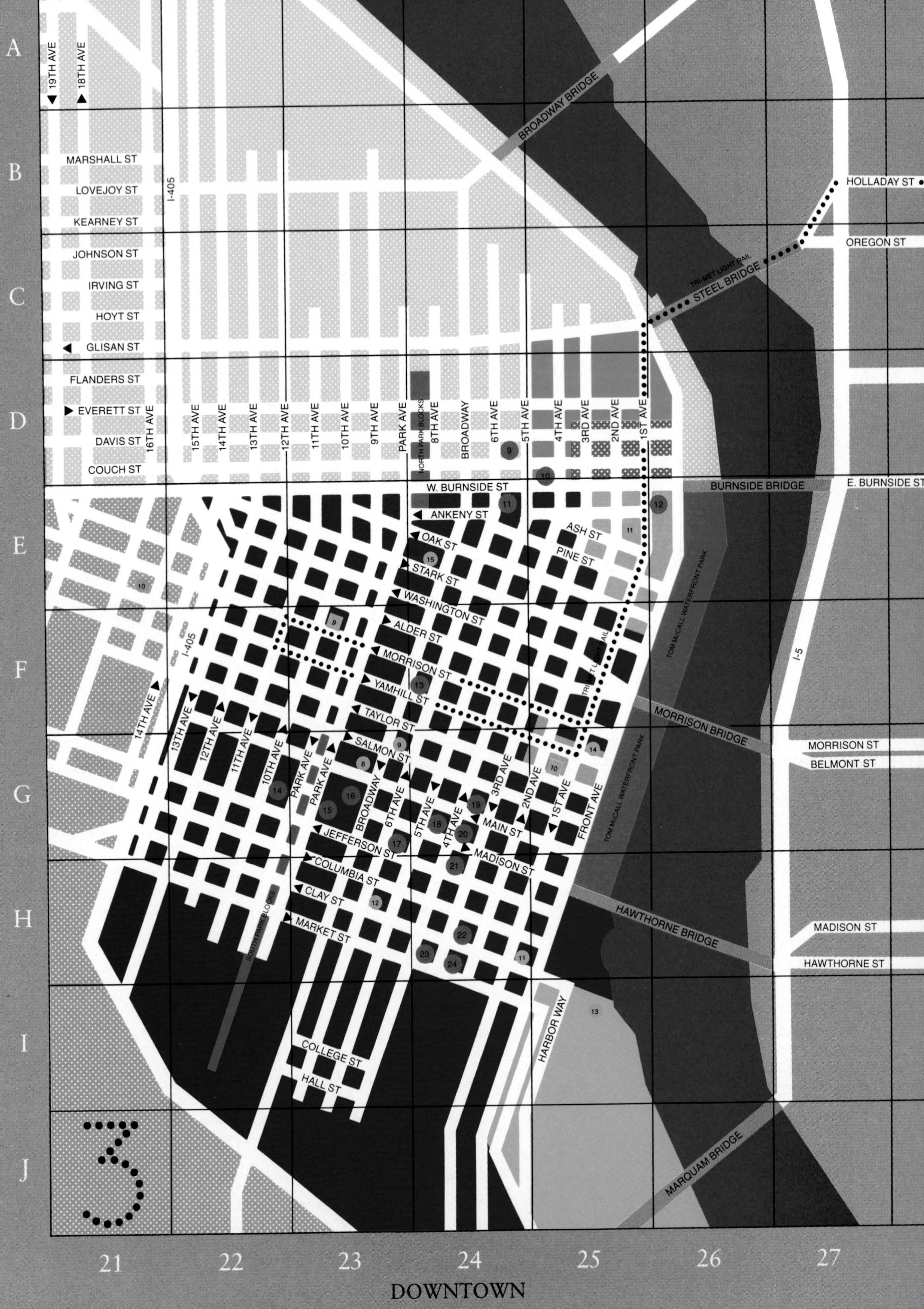

A
B
C
D
E
F
G
H
I
J
21
22
23
24
25
26
27
19TH AVE
18TH AVE
MARSHALL ST
LOVEJOY ST
KEARNEY ST
JOHNSON ST
IRVING ST
HOYT ST
GLISAN ST
FLANDERS ST
EVERETT ST
DAVIS ST
COUCH ST
I-405
16TH AVE
15TH AVE
14TH AVE
13TH AVE
12TH AVE
11TH AVE
10TH AVE
9TH AVE
PARK AVE
NORTH PARK BLOCKS
8TH AVE
BROADWAY
6TH AVE
5TH AVE
4TH AVE
3RD AVE
2ND AVE
1ST AVE
BROADWAY BRIDGE
HOLLADAY ST
OREGON ST
TRI-MET LIGHT RAIL
STEEL BRIDGE
W. BURNSIDE ST
BURNSIDE BRIDGE
E. BURNSIDE ST
ANKENY ST
ASH ST
OAK ST
PINE ST
STARK ST
WASHINGTON ST
ALDER ST
MORRISON ST
YAMHILL ST
TAYLOR ST
SALMON ST
MAIN ST
JEFFERSON ST
MADISON ST
COLUMBIA ST
CLAY ST
MARKET ST
COLLEGE ST
HALL ST
SOUTH PARK BLOCKS
14TH AVE
13TH AVE
12TH AVE
11TH AVE
10TH AVE
PARK AVE
PARK AVE
BROADWAY
6TH AVE
5TH AVE
4TH AVE
3RD AVE
2ND AVE
1ST AVE
FRONT AVE
TOM McCALL WATERFRONT PARK
TOM McCALL WATERFRONT PARK
TOM McCALL WATERFRONT PARK
TRI-MET LIGHT RAIL
I-5
MORRISON BRIDGE
MORRISON ST
BELMONT ST
HAWTHORNE BRIDGE
MADISON ST
HAWTHORNE ST
HARBOR WAY
MARQUAM BRIDGE
3

DOWNTOWN

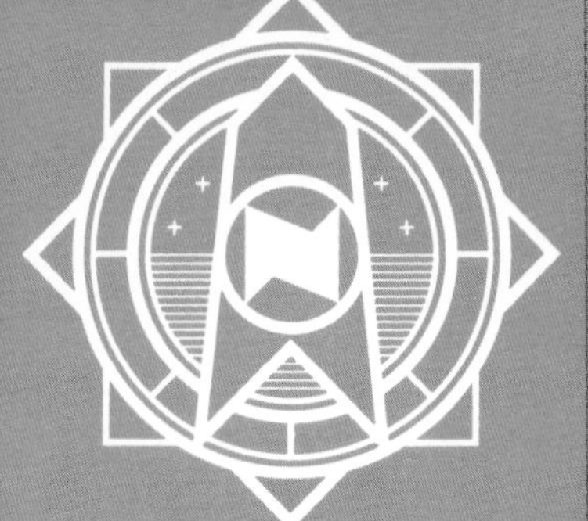

HOTELS

Map 1

1. Embassy Suites
2. Greenwood Inn
3. Holiday Inn — Columbia
4. Nendel's Inn
5. Red Lion — Jantzen Beach
6. Red Lion — Lloyd Center
7. Sheraton Inn

Map 3

8. Heathman
9. Hilton
10. Mallory Motor Hotel
11. Marriot
12. Portland Inn
13. RiverPlace Alexis
14. Riverside Inn
15. Westin Benson

BED & BREAKFAST

Map 1

16. Corbett House
17. General Hooker's House
18. McMaster House
19. Portland's White House

Map 2

20. Allenhouse

SIGHTS

Map 1

1. Memorial Coliseum
2. Proposed Convention Center Site
3. Pittock Mansion
4. Washington Park Rose Gardens
5. Civic Stadium
6. Washington Park Zoo World Forestry Center OMSI
7. Duniway Park
8. Rhododendron Test Garden

Map 3

9. Portland Center for the Visual Arts (PCVA)
10. China Gate
11. U.S. Bank Plaza
12. Portland Saturday Market
13. Pioneer Courthouse Square
14. Oregon Art Institute
15. Oregon Historical Center
16. Performing Arts Center Arlene Schnitzer Concert Hall
17. PacWest Building
18. Portland Building Portlandia
19. Lownsdale Square
20. Chapman Square
21. Schrunk Plaza
22. KOIN Tower
23. Ira Keller Fountain
24. Civic Auditorium

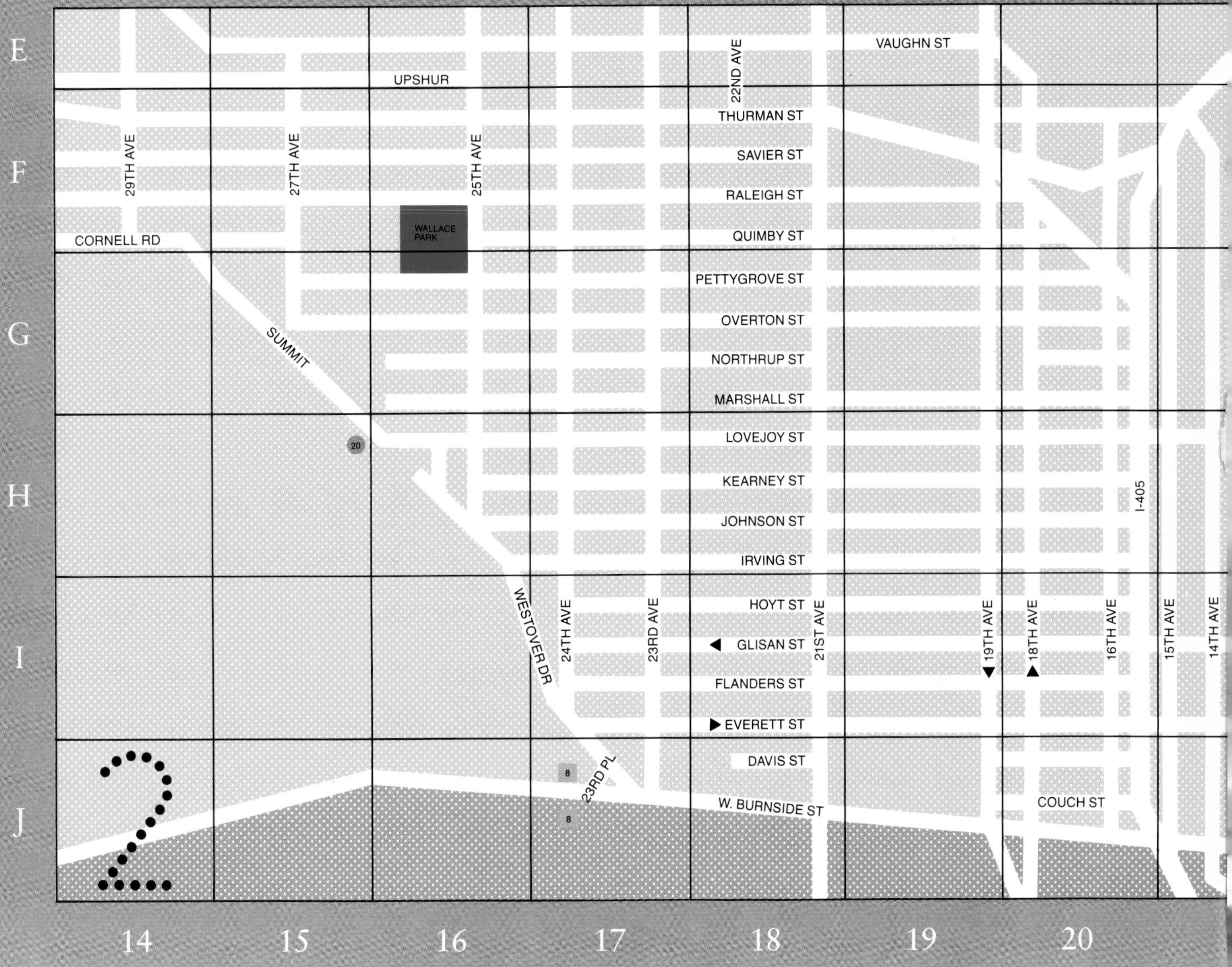

NORTHWEST PORTLAND

► KIDS AND TEENS
Children's Museum *191*
► SPORTS AND RECREATION
Ebb and Flow Kayak Center *202*
Mastercraft of Oregon *208*
► HOME
Contemporary Crafts Gallery *247*
The Kobos Company *235*
Recollections *221*
Storables *238*
► SPECIALTIES
House of Titles *265*

MULTNOMAH/ HILLSDALE

Multnomah is named for the Indians who inhabited Sauvie Island. Today it is a neighborhood known for its collection of unique specialty shops — especially those touting books and antiques. The charming grid of the streets and the diagonal parking give it a quaint, small-town feeling. Hillsdale is nestled within the southwest hills just northeast of Multnomah. At one time it served as a stopping place for travelers on their way from Portland to a ferry crossing on the Tualatin River.

► SIGHTS
Gabriel Park
► FOOD
Comella & Son & Daughter *91*
► FASHION
La Paloma *143*
► HOME
More or Less Collectibles *222*
► SPECIALTIES
Annie Bloom's Books *276*
Lasky's Video Library *283*

BEAVERTON

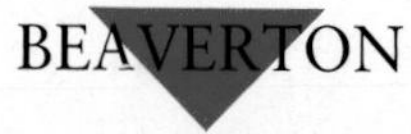

Beaverton is booming. It's alive with new businesses — a whole corridor of high-tech firms and the corporate headquarters of some of Oregon's largest and most famous companies, such as Tektronics, Nike, Floating Point Systems, and Intel. New housing developments are keeping apace. Restaurants throughout the area offer a wide range of options for family dining. A car is a must to get around this large and rapidly growing suburban community. It's a place where life is good and the shopping is easy; especially at Beaverton Town Square — an open, well-designed shopping mall full of specialty shops and restaurants.

► FOOD
Anzen Oriental Foods and Imports *100*
Coffee Bean *104*
Echo Restaurant *49*
Hall Street Bar & Grill *69*
Nature's Fresh Northwest *103*
Rose's Restaurant *75*
► FASHION
Cromwell Formal Wear *155*
Expecting the Best *138*
Northwest Passage Boots & Clothing Company *160*
► KIDS AND TEENS
Children's Country Store *180*
Book Barn for Children *182*
Kid's Hair Parlour *189*
► SPORTS AND RECREATION
Tailwind Outfitters *199*
Woodmere Farm *210*
► HOME
Fathertime Clocks *236*
Floral Trends Ltd. *242*
Kasch's Garden Centers *240*
The Kobos Company *235*
Ludeman's Fireplace & Patio Shop *228*
Parker Furniture Design Center *215*
Stanton's Unfinished Furniture *224*
Storables *238*
► SPECIALTIES
Beaverton Book Company *281*
Chelsea AudioVideo *267*
Portland Music Co. *282*
Teddy Bears Picnic *301*

PROGRESS-WASHINGTON SQUARE

With Cascade Plaza on one side of Highway 217 and Washington Square on the other, there's a full spectrum of shops for grown-ups and entertainment for the kids. Besides many specialty shops, six major department stores at Washington Square are a big draw at the covered mall. You'll enjoy special exhibits of prize roses, antiques, old cars and many other interesting features throughout the year. For golfers, two courses are nearby. For kids, a multiscreen movie theater is just a short walk from Washington Square as well as the Malibu Grand Prix, a racetrack where you can drive miniature race cars.

► KIDS AND TEENS
City Kids *185*
Le Papillon *178*
► HOME
Claytrade *253*
Gango Gallery *255*
Kitchen Kaboodle *232*
Malacca Rattan *216*
The Poster Gallery Etc. *254*
The Real Mother Goose *256*
Scandia Down Shops *239*
► SPECIALTIES
HK Limited *289*
The Paper Station *294*
Powell's Books *264*

LAKE OSWEGO/ LAKE GROVE

Lake Oswego — getting there is half the fun because the route along the Willamette River is so scenic. For bicyclists a special route on the Terwilliger Path makes riding to Lake Oswego safe, easy and scenic. Call the City Bike Program for specific information. Lake Oswego proper, resting between the river and the lake for which it was named, is a toney town with some extravagant lakeshore homes and shopping amenities for a quality-minded community. Public areas are available on the lake and at Tryon Creek State Park north of Lake Oswego where you can hike, jog, bicycle, picnic or ride your own horse on the many trails within this large, natural preserve. Lake Grove has become an extension of Lake Oswego and is a sprawling area of beautiful farmland, suburban residences and specialty shops and services.

► SIGHTS
Mary S. Young State Park
Tryon Creek State Park
► FOOD
Cool Temptations *93*
The Gazebo *72*
► KIDS AND TEENS
Bambini's Children's Boutique *188*
► SPORTS AND RECREATION
Ciclo Sport Shop *204*
Mt. Park Pro Shop *206*
Phidippides Fitness Center *201*
► HOME
Naomi's *237*
► SPECIALTIES
The Paper Station *294*

25

SIGHTS

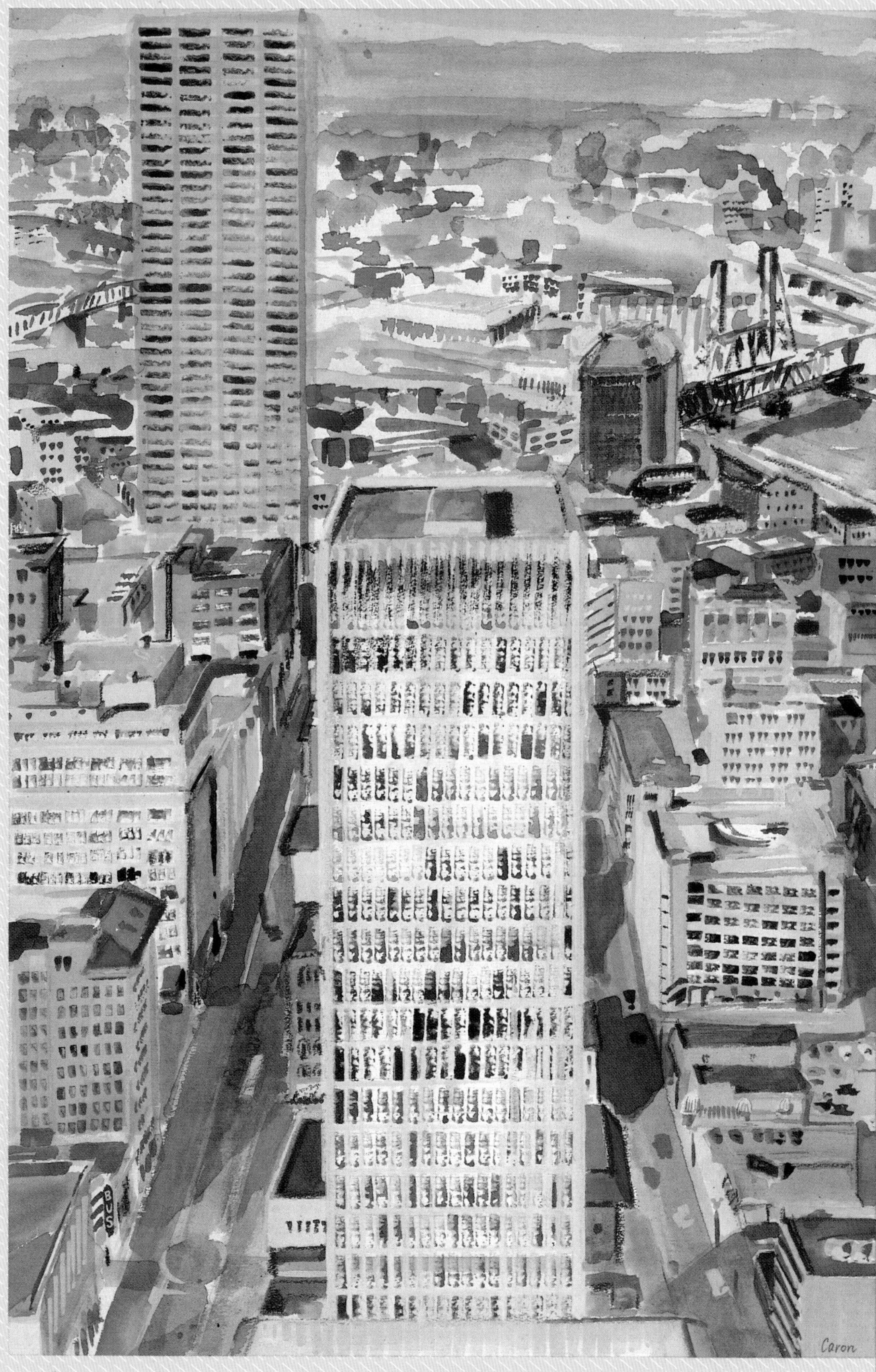

Sidonie Caron *North From First Interstate Tower* ATTIC GALLERY

No matter how long you've lived here, kicking around town is still a process of discovery. For many of us it's one of life's chief delights. And, on any given day we find ourselves mingling with the camera-laden and foot-weary visitors, always ready to proffer a warm smile and directions to the closest museum, park, garden or gallery. We take great pride in following the latest developments — any erstwhile MAX rider could tell you that Chant Dee is the proud mother of Me Tu. Or that OMSI's recent extravaganza includes a volcano you can walk right through. Join us for a new look at Portland's most interesting venues.

PARKS AND GARDENS

You want parks? We got parks!

The countrys largest city park, and the world's smallest. Waterfront parks, neighborhood parks, parks atop dormant volcanoes. One of the highest park area per capita ratios in the United States.

The smallest park is Mill Ends Park located in the crosswalk at S.W. Front and Taylor. Measuring a mere 24″ in diameter,the park contains a bronze plaque which reads: "From his office on the second floor of the old Oregon Journal, journalist Dick Fagan periodically gazed down the busy Front Avenue thoroughfare. It was his keen imagination that turned a utility pole hole in the avenue median strip at Taylor Street into Mill Ends Park." Where else but Stumptown?

A few miles to the northwest, you'll find Forest Park, the largest inner-city park in the U.S. Here, within minutes of downtown, is the solitude and peace of remote wilderness areas. Miles of trails beckon hikers, birdwatchers, and nature lovers of every creed. Touch a tree, meditate in the quiet of a summer evening, follow the tracks of a black-tailed deer.

Neighborhood parks abound. In fact, we enjoy a park system which includes everything from community centers, swimming pools, and city art centers, to tennis courts and golf courses. Throughout the year, we can participate in everything from team sports to dance, art, theatre and music classes. So if Frisbee and hackeysack are getting a little old, dig out your tutu and point shoes and leap into something new.

Our passion for parks may be outdone only by our infatuation with gardens! And although roses get a great deal of press, there's no shortage of evidence suggesting that they share equal time with a multitude of other wonderful varieties. What better place to garden than Portland? With the temperate climate and perfect year-round mix of sunshine and rain, there are few times of the year when we can't be active — growing everything from rutabagas to rhubarb, and turnips to tulips.

Sidonie Caron, *represented by the Attic Gallery, has lived in and utilized Portland for over twenty years as an inexhaustible source of visual stimulation. Eclectic best describes Sidonie's range of work: landscape, cityscape, pattern painting using oriental rug motifs or computer hardware and nude drawings.*

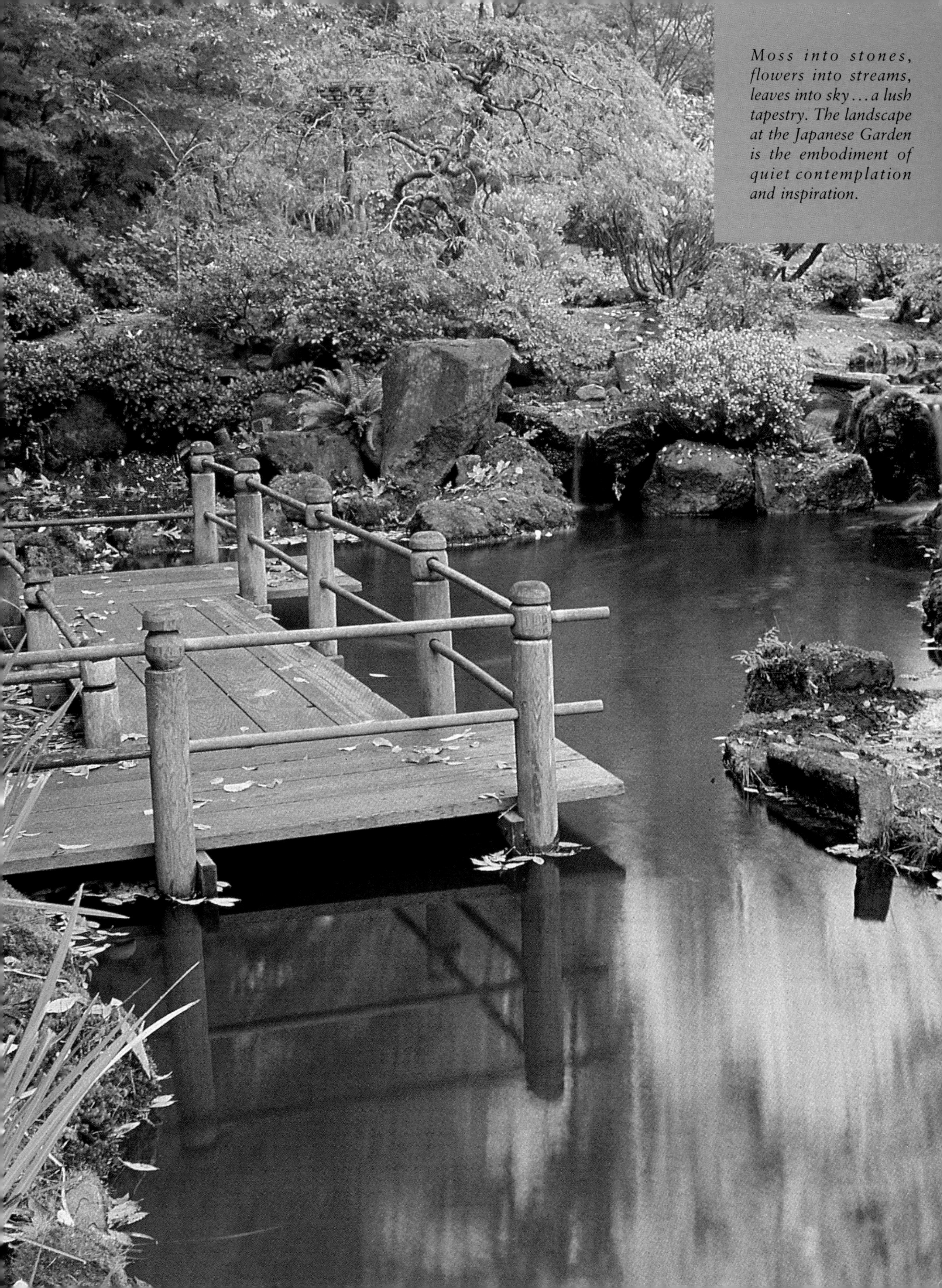

Moss into stones, flowers into streams, leaves into sky…a lush tapestry. The landscape at the Japanese Garden is the embodiment of quiet contemplation and inspiration.

MAIN ATTRACTIONS

Washington Park, west terminus of SW Park Place. One hundred acres of beautiful green hillside—much in a semi-natural state. Includes plantings of heather, lilacs, azaleas, camellias, and rhododendrons. Picnic areas abound. For the sports enthusiast there are tennis courts, an archery range, and miles of walking and jogging paths. In the summer an outdoor amphitheater provides a variety of musical extravaganzas, and for the railroad buff a narrow gauge line winds through the park linking the lower park with the Zoo above. Two of the most popular attractions in the park are the International Rose Test Garden and the Japanese Gardens. Map D4

Washington Park Zoo and **Elephant Museum,** 4001 SW Canyon Road. 226-1561. Feathered and fierce, slothful and sleek, over five hundred creatures of every size and shape inhabit Portland's exciting zoo. Over the last few years there have been some big changes! Take a look at the award-winning Cascades Exhibit, for example — it's nestled in a lush ravine and filled with critters and plant life native to the beautiful Cascade Mountains. Then there is the Penguinarium — so like the warm, rocky coast of Peru, you'll think you've left Portland. And the elephants. Have you met Chant Dee or Me Tu yet? Map D4

NEIGHBORHOOD PARKS

Alberta Park, NE 19th Avenue at Killingsworth. A 20-acre urban oasis complete with tennis courts, wading pool, handball and horseshoe courts, baseball and football fields, play equipment for the little guys and six covered basketball hoops! Map B6

Cathedral Park, beneath St. Johns Bridge on the east side of the river. Fishing piers and a boat ramp, a small amphitheater and a picnic shelter offer a variety of options for recreation. The soaring arches of the bridge overhead are reminiscent of the great cathedrals of medieval Europe. Map A3

Cedar Hills Park, Cedar Hills Boulevard, north of Walker Road in Beaverton. A great place for summer afternoon picnics. If tennis isn't your game you'll also find volleyball nets and a softball field. Map E2

Council Crest, head of SW Council Crest Drive. With an elevation of slightly over 1000 feet, Council Crest is the city's highest point. The vehicle turnaround at the top offers a stunning view of the city and five snowcapped mountain peaks. Map E5

Delta Park, N Denver. Acres of green for kite flying, frisbee toss, and football, not to mention four softball fields, ten soccer fields, as well as archery and model airplane fields! Map A5

Duniway Park, SW Barbur Boulevard & Terwilliger. This park, famous for its lilac gardens, is also one of Portland's most visible havens for runners. An all weather track, soccer field, par course and close proximity to the Metro Y make this a big hit. Map E5

Gabriel Park, between SW 37th and 45th Avenues, south of Vermont Street. In the midst of the Multnomah/Hillsdale residential area this large park includes eight lighted tennis courts, ballfields, playground apparatus, extensive picnic facilities and several wood bridges spanning small streams. Map F4

Grant Park, NE 33rd adjacent to Grant High School. This is a great park for the kids complete with lots of play equipment and a large wading pool. It also has an outdoor track, swimming pool and lighted tennis courts. Map C7

Laurelhurst Park, SE 39th Avenue at Oak Street. Famous for its beautiful picnic areas, this park also has an open air theater, lake with waterfowl, wading pool and sandbox, as well as lighted horseshoe, basketball and tennis courts. Map D7

Mt. Tabor Park, 60th Street between Yamhill and Division. Spectacular views greet visitors at this park atop an extinct volcano. Two hundred acres of attractively terraced grounds, gardens, tennis courts and picnic areas make it an enjoyable retreat. It also has a theater with stage and lights. Map E8

Wallace Park, NW 25th Avenue at Pettygrove. Towering shade trees, two playgrounds, one standard and one scaled down for toddlers, along with a sheltered recreation area are popular features. Basketball hoops, tennis courts and softball fields are also available. Map F16

Westmoreland Park, SE 22nd Avenue at McLoughlin Boulevard. This 47 acre tract has four ballfields, one which is a stadium field, lighted tennis courts, casting pool and model yacht basin, twin bowling greens and throngs of migratory waterfowl! What more does anyone need? Map F7

DOWNTOWN

Chapman and Lownsdale Squares, SW 4th between Main and Madison. Originally dedicated in 1852, these two city blocks have witnessed many celebrations, political debates and rallies. Today they are a popular spot for "brown baggers". Map G24

Governor Tom McCall Waterfront Park, SW Front between Clay and Glisan. A verdant mile-long park bordering the ever changing Willamette River. A promenade for all to enjoy. Great for jogging, fishing, picnicking or simply a respite from the bustle of the adjacent downtown. The park comes alive when ships from around the world dock here for Portland's famous Rose Festival. Throughout the spring, summer and fall the park hosts a wide variety of other festivals and concerts. Map F25

Ira Keller Fountain, SW 3rd between Market and Clay Streets. Also known as the Forecourt Fountain, this beautiful piece of landscape architecture was described by Ada Louise Huxtable in The New York Times as "perhaps the greatest open space since the Renaissance." Quiet pools and billowing cascades of water are interspersed with islands, terraces and open spaces for people to relax and enjoy. Map H24

Lair Hill Park, SW 2nd at Woods. The Children's Museum is located in this park, along with a tennis court and picnic facilities. Map E5

O'Bryant Square, SW Park Avenue between Washington & Stark. Outdoor concerts are scheduled throughout the summer months at the square which includes a fountain, wonderful shade trees and lots of sittin' space for "brown baggers." Map E23

Park Blocks: North, Park and SW Ankeny to NW Glisan; **South,** Park and S W Salmon to Jackson. Pre-schoolers and professors, joggers and shoppers — people from all walks of life find the Park Blocks a beautiful, peaceful and convenient place to play, paint, rest or simply pass through. The park, created in 1852 and nicknamed "The Boulevard", originally consisted of 25 full city blocks, although portions have since been developed. Map H22 and D24

Pettygrove Park, SW 4th and Harrison. Sculpture in a pool. Hollows, hidden nooks, an acre of park in the heart of the city. Great for sunning, lunching and people-watching. Map I23

Pioneer Courthouse Square, SW Broadway between Morrison and Yamhill. The heart of Portland, and a great people-watching place, where the past, present and future of the city blend into a wonderfully fanciful square. A refreshing waterfall cascades over brightly colored tiles and purposely collapsed columns add a touch of antiquity. A glass-enclosed restaurant proffers delectable treats. Also located in the Square are the Tri-Met Information Center and the well-stocked Powell's Travel Bookstore. Completed in 1984, the Square is a joyous merging of classicism and modern urbanism, and has been hailed as one of the most innovative urban plazas any American city has constructed in years. Map F24

Proof that Portland is the City of Roses resides in the Rose Test Gardens.

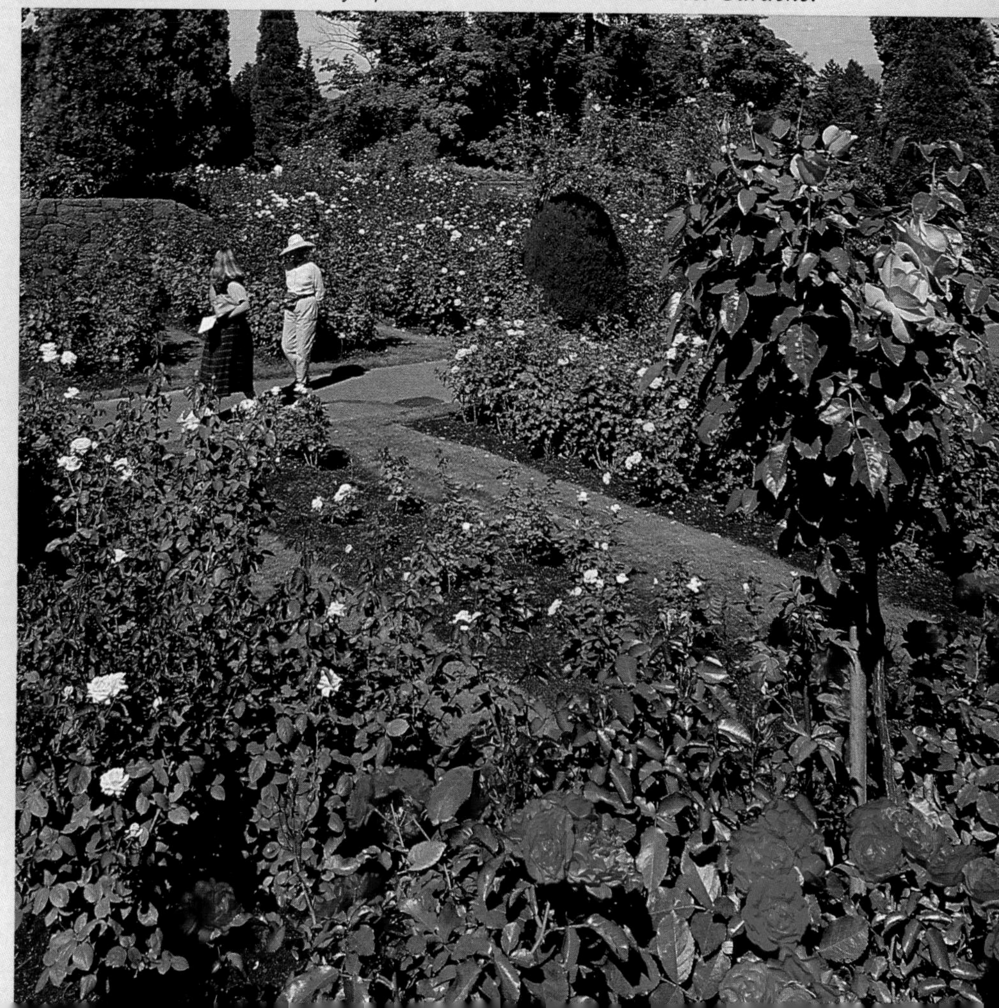

GARDENS

Crystal Springs Rhododendron Garden, SE 28th & Woodstock. Admission fee for Mother's Day show. The Rhododendron Garden is nestled along the quiet waters of Crystal Springs. Stunning varieties of both native and hybrid rhododendron species have been interwoven to create a garden rich in color and texture. The garden includes an island setting for observing waterfowl. This is a favorite site for feeding ducks, strolling, or just enjoying the peaceful beauty of this unique garden. Map F7

Hoyt Arboretum, 400 SW Fairview Boulevard. Over 700 species of woody plants and a myriad of different bird species are found in this beautiful forested preserve. It is renowned for having one of the country's most notable collections of gymnosperms (needle-bearing trees). Lovely picnic areas and 10 miles of trails among the trees, including a paved handicapped access trail. Trails in the Arboretum connect with the 50 mile trail system in Forest Park. Map D4

International Rose Test Gardens, 400 SW Kingston. High above Portland in Washington Park, the Rose Test Gardens allow visitors to experience roses on a grand scale. Established in 1917 by the Portland Rose Society, these are the oldest and one of the largest continuously operating test gardens in the country. There are 10,000 bushes representing more than 400 varieties covering over four and one-half acres! The view of the city and Mt. Hood from this point is spectacular. The gardens bloom from June through November and include the Shakespeare Garden which features seasonal displays of annuals. A kiosk provides information on the history and care of roses as well as directions to the miniature and traditional gardens. Map D4

Japanese Gardens, west of SW Kingston and Washington Park Drive. Tucked into the hillside on a terrace above the Rose Gardens lie the Japanese Gardens. The complex consists of five traditional gardens — each with its own theme — and a pavilion. The gardens were designed by P. Takuma Tono of the University of Tokyo and are considered by even the most discriminating gardeners to meet the Shibui standards. The gardens are a quiet place for meditation, for reflection on the intricacies of Japanese architecture and landscape design, or for exploration of the enchanting distinctions among the gardens. Map D4

Leach Botanical Gardens, 6704 SE 122nd. 761-9503. Lilla and John Leach were a unique couple. They explored Northwest wilderness in the '20s and '30s in search of rare and previously unknown plants and created a garden; a stunning expression of their devotion to each other and the world around them. Today it is a rich and colorful botanical garden for everyone to enjoy. Map F10

HIKING

Dodge Park, East of Gresham on I-84, Dodge Park exit. This park hugs the banks of the Sandy River, with miles of trails all along the water. Bring your fishing pole, inner tube, raft, or, if you're feeling more like relaxing, a book and perhaps some suntan lotion will do just fine.

Forest Park, From NW 29th and Upshur to Newberry Road between NW Skyline and St. Helens Road. Forest Park is a wilderness within a city — the largest of its kind in the United States. Twenty-five miles of trails lead the visitor through four thousand acres of lush, forested parkland. Stretching for seven miles along the eastern flank of the Tualatin Mountains, the area teems with wildlife — deer, quail, even an occasional bear and bobcat — and a rich variety of native plants. A map of trails is available from the Park Bureau. Map B3

Macleay Park, NW Cornell Road. Adjacent to Forest Park on the south, Macleay Park is an extension of the larger park providing additional trails for hiking. Map D4

Marquam Nature Trail, from Council Crest to Marquam Hill. Part of a 40 mile loop, this trail is great for everything from birdwatching to jogging. The views are great too. Map D5

Mary S. Young State Park, 3 miles south of Lake Oswego on Highway 43. Trails through the woods lead to the Willamette River and lots of open meadows provide opportunities for everything from volleyball to kite flying. There's also a cooking shelter, so pack a picnic and join the fun. Map I6

Tryon Creek Park, Terwilliger extension between Lewis and Clark Law School and Macadam Avenue. Eleven miles of trails for horseback riding, hiking or jogging in a lush preserve of native plants and wildlife. An excellent Nature Center provides information on the flora and fauna. The birdwatching is great. Map H6

MUSEUMS AND GALLERIES

Look through windows on the past, present, future.

Buildings and monuments, statues and fountains, cedar bark canoes and root baskets, calligraphy scrolls and raku-fired bowls ... precious artifacts of our culture collected together in a city-sized shoebox. The richness of Portland's historical, artistic and architectural tradition is evident everywhere. Museums and galleries are proliferating here at a rapid pace, with a wide variety to choose from, whether it's art museums, crafts galleries, historical museums, museums for children, maritime museums, even the first museum for advertising.

On any given day you can be entertained by 200 years of classic advertising (how many do you remember?), look into the Renaissance or our own Northwest Coast Indian culture, research the history of your block or view a nationally traveling Amish quilt exhibit, live the romance of our early maritime history, see a beehive or anthill from the inside, ride an antique carousel horse, hug a tree or watch the construction of musical instruments, chuckle at lucite-and-computer-chip jewelry or admire an iridescent glaze on a ceramic plate (how did they do that!).

Gallery-hopping has become a favorite avocation here, whether you choose to take in the exhibits or take in those who are taking in the exhibits. The variety of offerings brings out a variety of viewers, as much a part of our culture as that which is enshrined behind glass.

Return visits can be habit-forming, as regularly changing shows maintain a high level of curiosity and permanent collections always offer something you didn't see before. Plan an entire day!

PUBLIC ART GALLERIES

Oregon Art Institute, 1219 SW Park Avenue. 226-2811. Tuesday-Thursday 11-7, Friday 11-9:30, Saturday and Sunday Noon-5. Free admission Tuesdays 4-7. Long, low and elegant, the Oregon Art Institute building was designed by prominent architect Pietro Belluschi. Inside, visitors will find an impressive collection of Northwest Coast Native American Art, Asian Art, Art of the Cameroons, the Roberts Collection of Contemporary Art and the Kress Collections of Renaissance Painting and Sculpture, as well as exhibitions of contemporary art and special events throughout the year. Be sure to visit the Memorial Sculpture Mall adjacent to the building — a fascinating example of what can be done with a vacated street! Map G22

Advertising history is gathered at the American Advertising Museum.

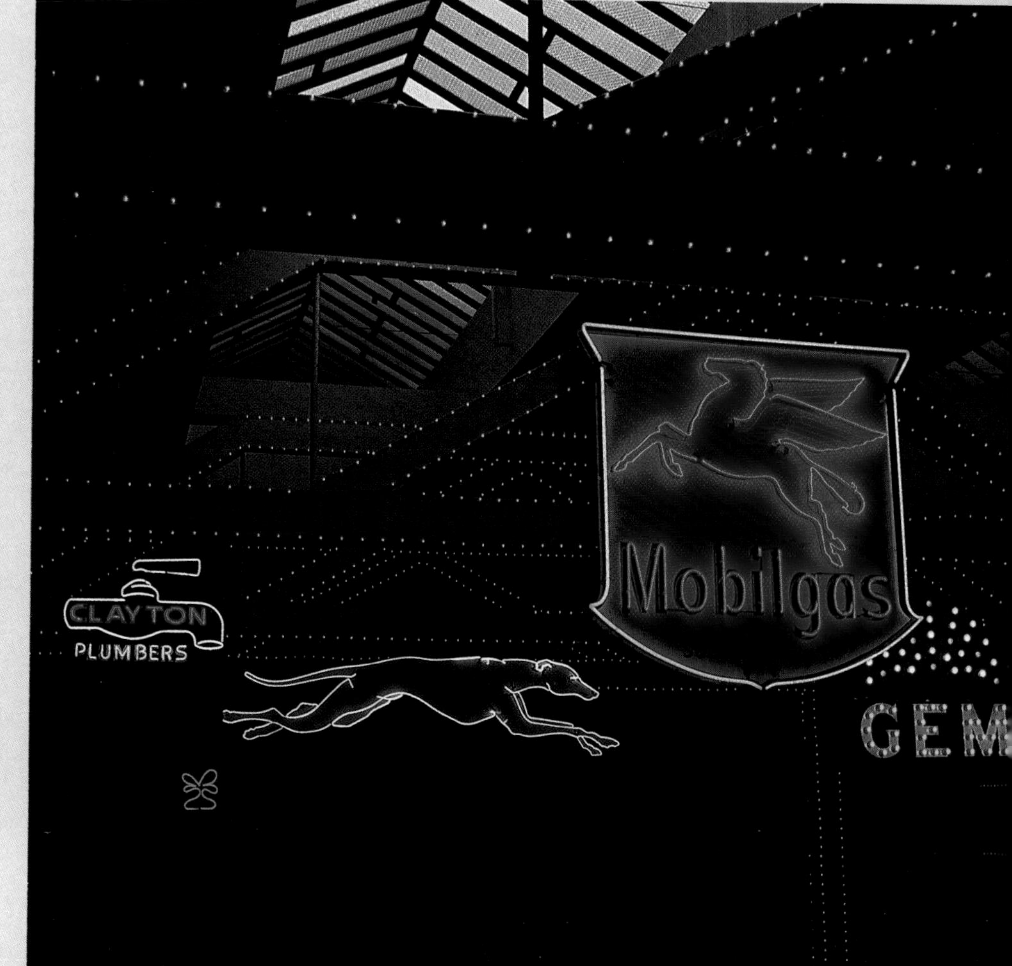

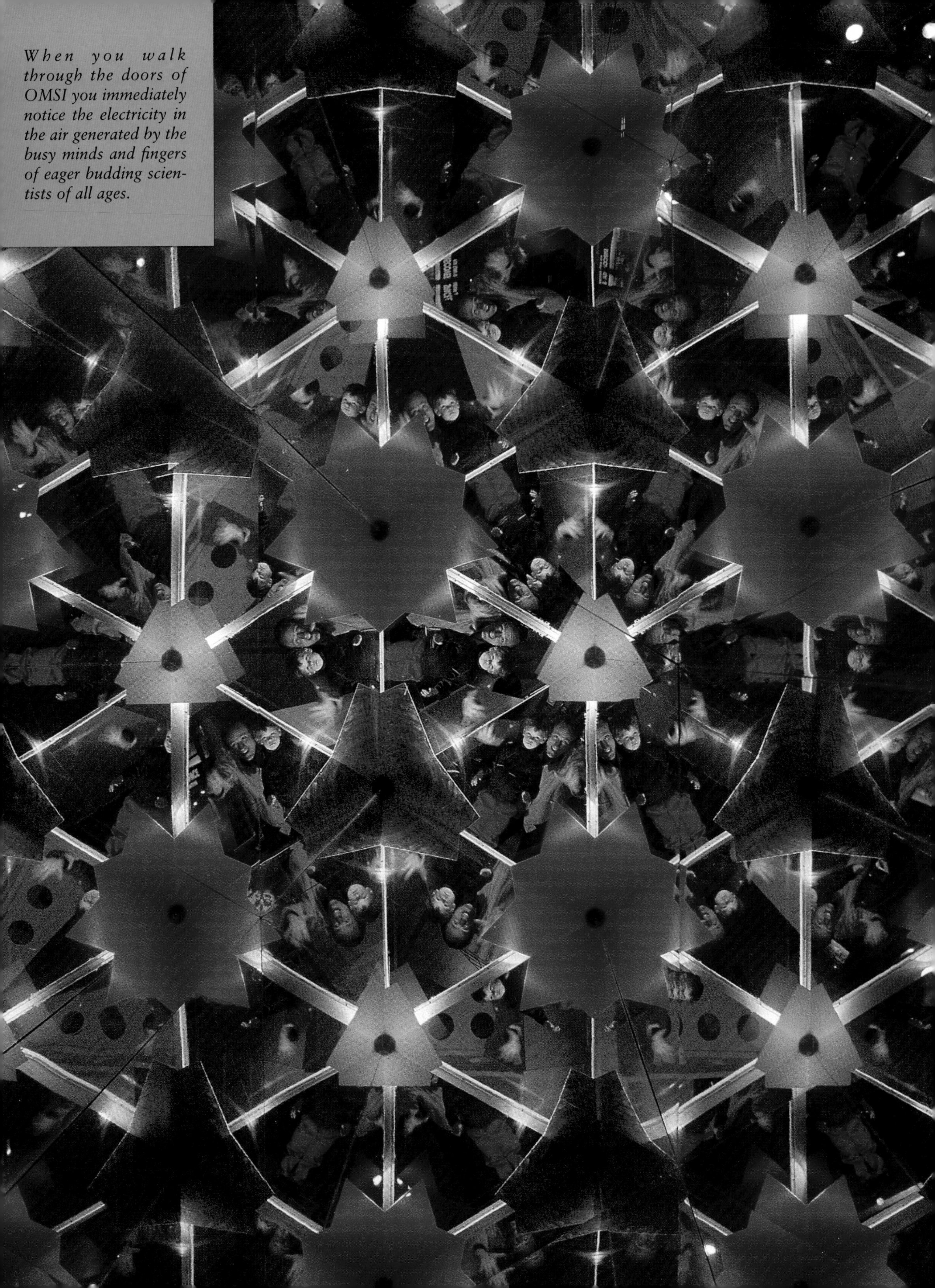

When you walk through the doors of OMSI you immediately notice the electricity in the air generated by the busy minds and fingers of eager budding scientists of all ages.

Contemporary Crafts Gallery, 3934 SW Corbett. 223-2654. Tuesday-Friday 11-5, Saturday 12-5, Sunday 1-5. Established in 1937, the Contemporary Crafts Gallery just recently celebrated its 50th anniversary. During its tenure as one of the city's oldest arts and crafts galleries, it has received a number of prestigious awards including the American Craft Council Gold Medal — the first ever awarded to a gallery. Dedicated to encouraging artists and craftspeople, the large gallery space displays works from throughout the Northwest and the nation. Map E6

Oregon School of Arts and Crafts, 8245 SW Barnes Road. 297-5544. Gallery hours: Monday-Friday 10-5, Saturday-Sunday 10-4. Beautifully sited on 7 acres of wooded hillside, the rustic buildings of the Oregon School of Arts and Crafts were designed by noted local architect John Storrs. Architectural finishes and details throughout the buildings were created by local craftspeople. In addition to the Hoffman Gallery, which carries artists' work on consignment, you'll find an extensive library as well as a wonderful cafe for lunch and light suppers. Map D3

PUBLIC MUSEUMS

Children's Museum, 3037 SW Second Avenue. 248-4587. Tuesday-Thursday, Saturday 9-5, Friday 9-8, Sunday 11-5. Admission fee. Kids will find a world of fun to explore at the Children's Museum. It offers a wide range of activities aimed at assisting children to develop crucial age-appropriate skills that help them grow into productive, creative adults. Map E5

Oregon Historical Center, 1230 SW Park Avenue. 222-1741. Monday-Saturday 10-4:45. Free admission. The Oregon Historical Center is headquarters for the Oregon Historical Society including its museum, regional research library, press and bookstore. Adults and children alike will marvel at the colorful exhibits and dioramas depicting the richness of Oregon history. The research library on the third floor contains one of the country's most extensive collections of maps, books and other documents related to the history of the West. Map G23

Oregon Museum of Science and Industry (OMSI), 4015 SW Canyon Road. 222-2828. Winter hours daily 9-5. Summer hours daily 9-6. The fascinating world of science is depicted through ever-changing exhibits, live demonstrations, hands-on activities and permanent installations geared for all ages and all interests. Map D4

THEME MUSEUMS

American Advertising Museum, 9 NW Second Avenue. 226-0000. Saturday-Sunday 12-4, Wednesday-Friday 11-5. Admission fee. An absolutely engrossing, first-of-a-kind museum featuring an eclectic array of commercial memorabilia and advertising history in both exhibition and theater format. Map D25

Historic Preservation League of Oregon, 26 NW Second Avenue. 243-1923. Monday-Friday 9-5. The League is a statewide organization dedicated to promoting, preserving and protecting the buildings and sites which are a part of our rich cultural heritage. Visit its office, gallery and library, and find out what historic preservation is all about. Great collection of videotapes, slideshows and tour brochures! Map D25

Jeff Morris Fire Department Museum, 55 SW Ash. Viewable at all hours. A fascinating window display depicting the history of fire fighting at the Fire Department Headquarters. Map E25

Oregon Maritime Center and Museum, 113 SW Front. 224-7724. Winter hours Friday, Saturday 11-4, Sunday 12-5. Summer hours Tuesday, Thursday, Friday, Saturday 11-4, Sunday 12-5. The romance and hardship of maritime history are reflected in the Museum's collection of model ships, navigation instruments, photographs, and shipboard hardware. Special focus on Portland's own maritime history. Map E25

Portland Carousel Museum, SW First and Taylor. 241-2560. Open daily May through August 11-4. Off-season hours subject to change. Portland residents spearheaded the preservation of this charming part of Americana. You can't resist a ride on an animal of your choice when it is sculpture in motion — a camel, a giraffe, a bear or even a sea monster. A nostalgic treat for all. Map G25

World Forestry Center, 4033 SW Canyon Road. 228-1367. Winter hours daily 10-5. Summer hours daily 9-6. Nestled in the hillside adjacent to Hoyt Arboretum, the Western Forestry Center is a monument to Oregon's primary resource: wood. Here visitors can enjoy exhibits and demonstrations about forest products and their uses—wooden toys, musical instruments, wood sculptures, furniture making, recreational equipment and much more. Interested in learning how to identify one mushroom from another? Or perhaps how to catch the wily steelhead? Call the Center! It has a wide range of classes and tours ranging from day hikes in the Cascades to tropical forests of Kenya. Map D4

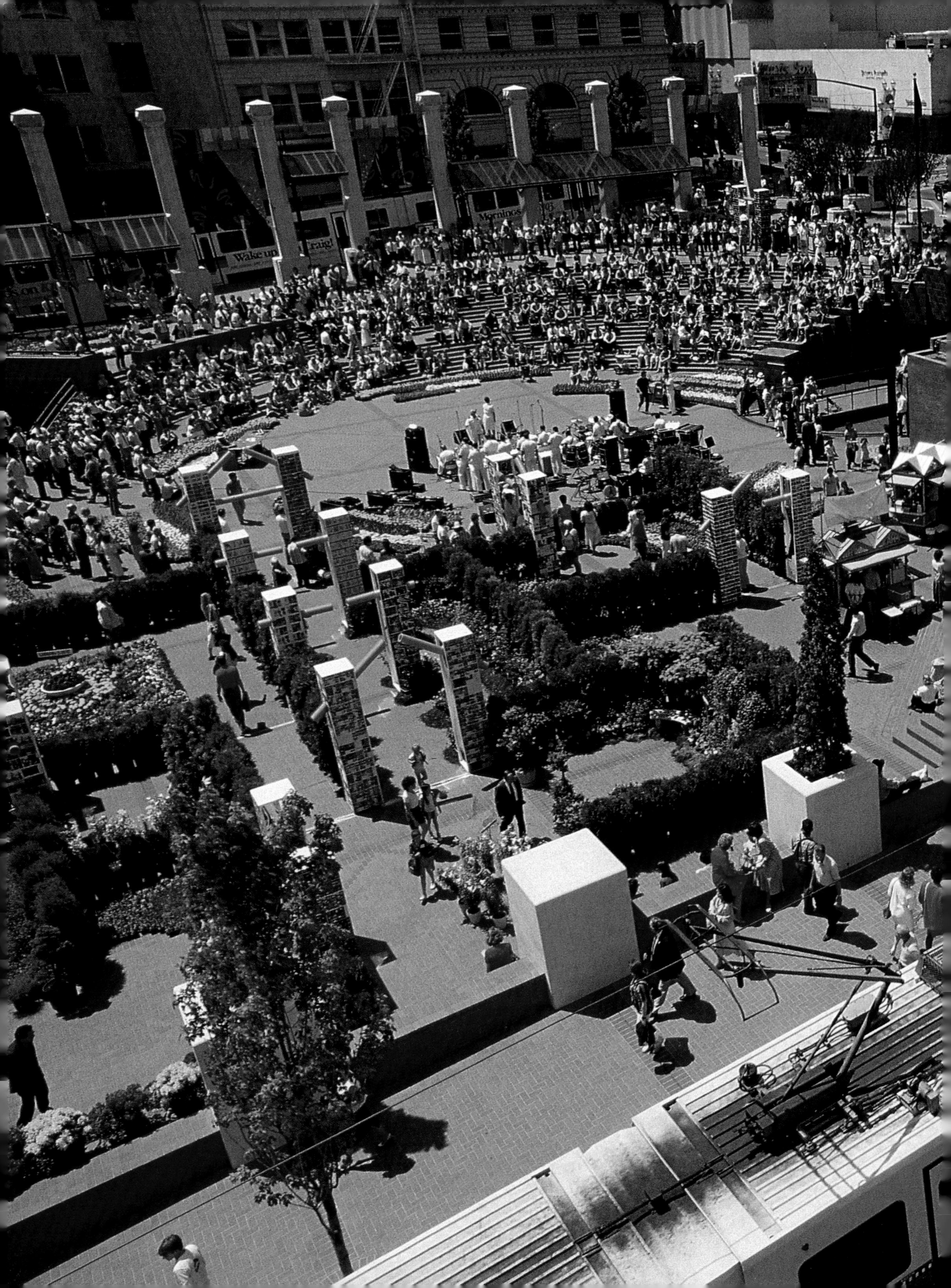
Wake up
Craig!
Mornings

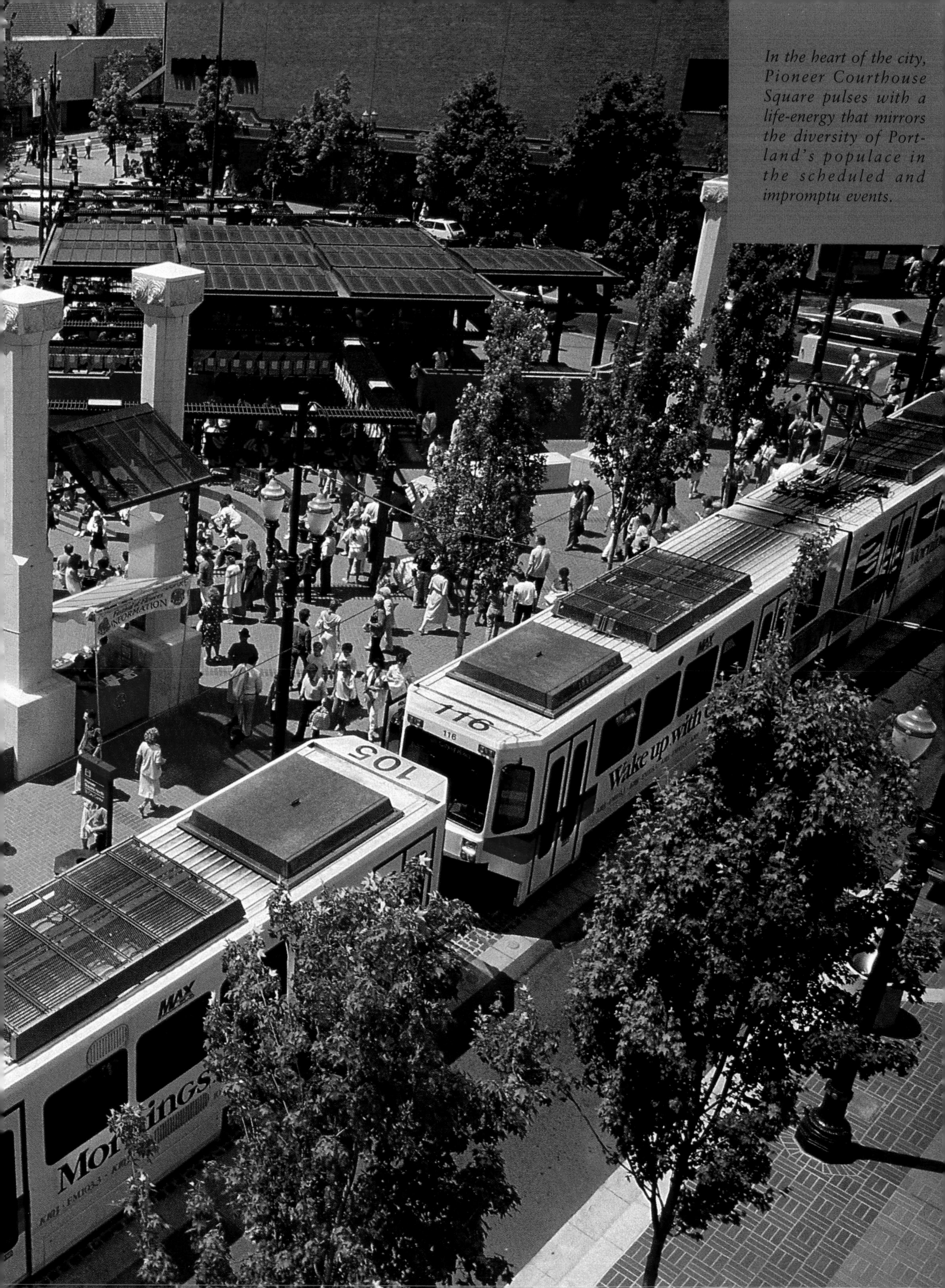

In the heart of the city, Pioneer Courthouse Square pulses with a life-energy that mirrors the diversity of Portland's populace in the scheduled and impromptu events.

ARCHITECTURE

Stretch your neck to take in the details.

Working in a stunning natural setting, our architects and urban designers have fostered an exciting tradition of innovative design. They've created an exotic urban environment where buildings and monuments are as bold and beautiful as nature's bounties. A museum in itself, our city is a microcosm of architectural history. In fact, our rich and eclectic heritage, combined with an exciting sense of risk and adventure, has catapulted Portland into the international architectural limelight.

In recent years we've all marveled at the dramatic changes in the downtown skyline. Striking contemporary buildings have been incorporated into the fabric of the existing architectural fiber, creating a colorfully woven cloth: classical columns mirrored in the gleaming expanse of aluminum-clad skyscrapers; the rhythm and grace of cast-iron colonnades; and elegant facades of terra cotta juxtaposed with the sleek, minimalist forms of the International Style.

If you were here in the 70's you may recall it was an unusually exuberant time, during which the City created two major historic districts —Skidmore/Old Town and Yamhill. Since then the districts have experienced tremendous growth as a result of restoration and revitalization efforts. Each is an incredible showplace for period architecture dating to the 19th Century — magnificent settings for shopping, dining, strolling, or simply stretching your neck to take in the fanciful details of yesterday's architectural indulgences!

U.S. Bancorp Tower, 111 SW Fifth. At 43 stories, "Big Pink", as it is affectionately called by many, is our tallest skyscraper. Voted Portland's best-liked building in 1983, the subtle pink marble facade and tawny bronzed windows reflect a rosy Portland, which, oddly enough, gets rosier as the day gets grayer. Skidmore, Owings, and Merrill.

The Equitable (Commonwealth) Building, 421 SW Sixth Avenue. The Equitable Building was a technological triumph upon completion in 1948. The first building in the country to be completely sealed, the first to use double-glazed windows, the first to be air-conditioned, the first to be sheathed in aluminum, and the first to employ traveling cranes for window washing! Pietro Belluschi.

Charles F. Berg Building, SW Broadway and Morrison. Constructed in 1926, the Berg Building is one of Portland's most outstanding examples of the Art Deco Style, with its polychrome-glazed terra cotta in black, cream, aquamarine and 18-karat gold.

The Justice Center, 1120 SW Third Avenue. Our Justice Center is undoubtedly one of the most sophisticated jails in the country! Drawing on the architectural vocabulary of historic buildings, the architects created a giant, luminous salute to the Postmodern era while expressing a highly refined image of civic dignity. Zimmer Gunsul Frasca, 1983.

Multnomah County Public Library, 801 SW Tenth Avenue. Undeniably one of the city's most elegant examples of Georgian-inspired architecture. A. E. Doyle, 1913.

Pioneer Courthouse, 620 SW Morrison Street. One of Portland's earliest and most acclaimed preservation projects, the restoration of Pioneer Courthouse saved one of our most-loved landmarks. The severely dilapidated 118-year-old building was restored in 1970. Today the glistening sandstone pilasters and the exquisite octagonal cupola stand in glorious tribute to a colorful past. Allen, McMath and Hawkins.

The Benson Hotel, SW Broadway and Oak. Liveried doormen greet you as you swish through the revolving doors into a magnificent lobby of rich, dark wood that truly says Old World and Old Wealth. The Circassian walnut came from the Old World of Czarist Russia and the Old Wealth, at least in Northwest terms, came from timber baron Simon Benson who constructed the building for the pricey 1912 sum of one million dollars. A. E. Doyle.

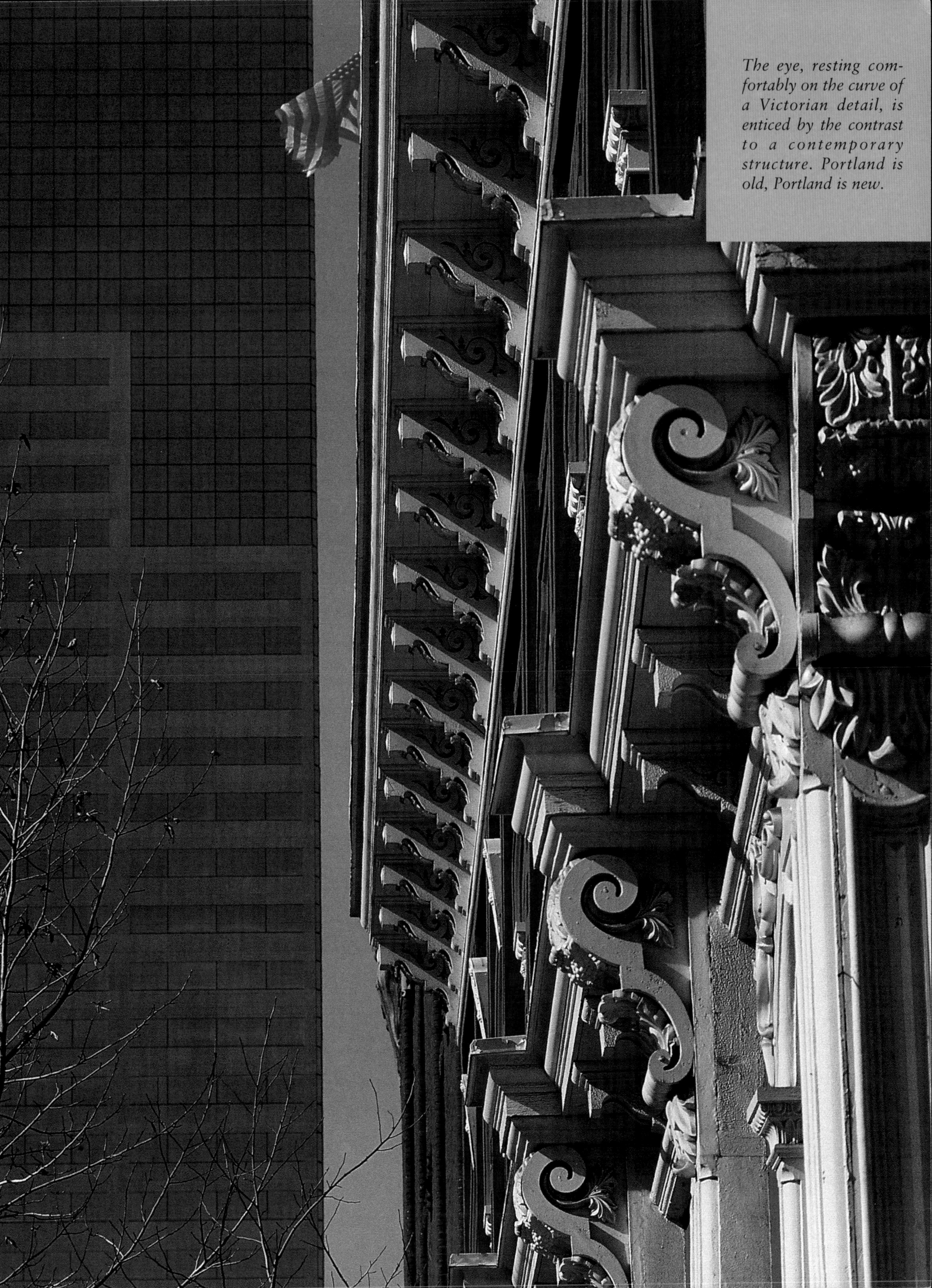

The eye, resting comfortably on the curve of a Victorian detail, is enticed by the contrast to a contemporary structure. Portland is old, Portland is new.

U.S. National Bank Building, 321 SW Sixth Avenue. The 54-foot Corinthian columns and the huge bas-relief bronze doors, complete with Oregon historical scenes, all contribute to the towering message of this beautifully scaled building—"your money is safe here." A. E. Doyle, 1917.

New Market Theatre, 50 SW Second Avenue. In 1872 this building opened with the plushest theater north of San Francisco upstairs — "The High-Class Theater" — and a bustling produce market downstairs. The bustle is back with renovated space for offices and lots of eateries, boutiques, galleries and flower and confectionery shops.

Temple Beth Israel, 1931 NW Flanders. Perhaps one of Portland's most passionate buildings, Temple Beth is a true architectural triumph. The building is one of our most distinctive examples of the Byzantine style. Whitehouse, Herzog and Brookman, 1927.

The Portland Building, 1120 SW Fifth Avenue. The Portland Building may well by one of the most hotly-debated structures of all time — at least here in River City. Built in 1983 to house City Government, it has drawn worldwide attention to our fair city. Regardless of one's sentiments, most everyone agrees it is a colorful postmodern addition to the skyline. Michael Graves.

The PacWest Center, 1211 SW Fifth Avenue. In sheer defiance of the trendy "historic" buildings so popular in the '80s, the PacWest Center is a marvel of computer aesthetics — clean lines, grid-like design, geometric efficiency. Sleek and sexy, it nevertheless harkens to the "streamlined" decade of the '30s when sculptural forms came to symbolize the promise of a brighter future. Skidmore, Owings and Merrill, 1984.

Exotic treats await the explorer who travels through the China Gate.

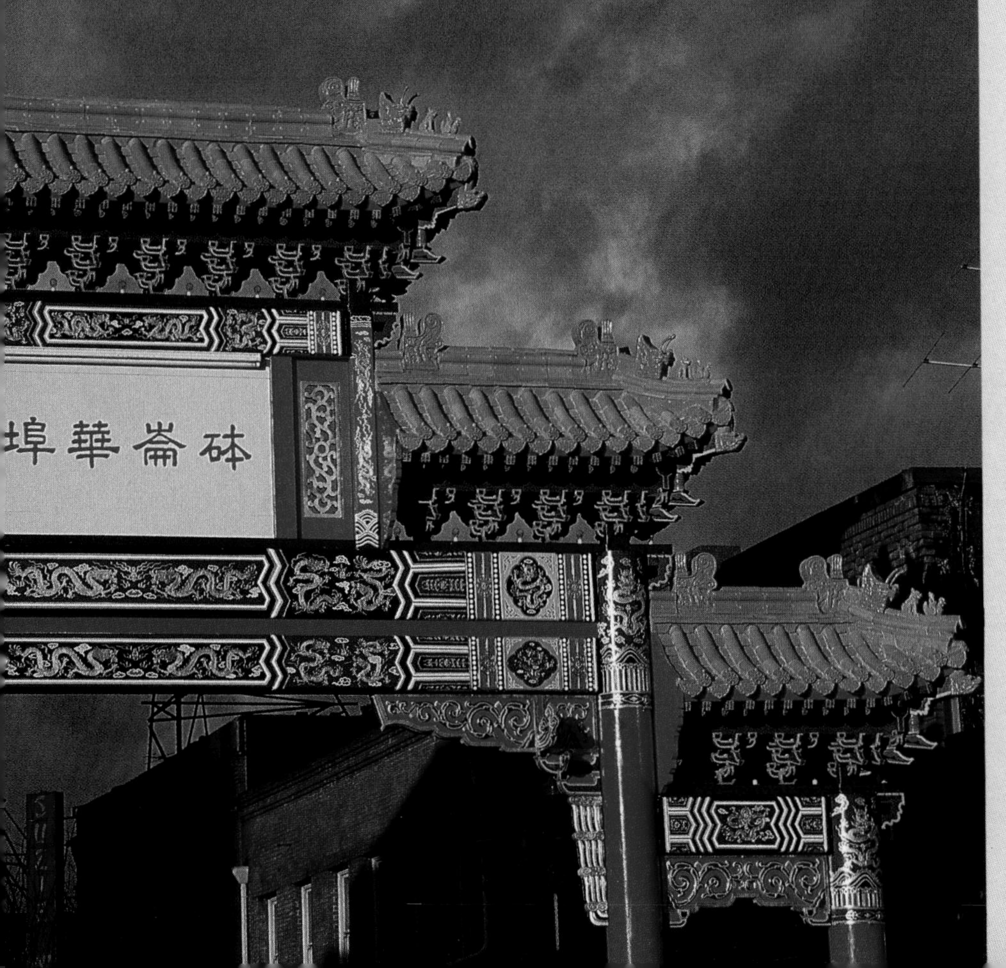

The Blagen Block, 30-34 NW First Avenue. High Victorian Italianate at its best! The Blagen Block was designed in 1888 by one of Oregon's most fashionable architects. A master creator of pastiches, Warren Williams infused the building with a rich variety of cast-iron ornamental elements — stars, stripes, arrows, laurel leaves, and much more.

Jackson Tower, 806 SW Broadway. Ablaze with thousands of sparkling lights each night, Jackson Tower is one of the most elegant buildings on the skyline. Sheathed in gleaming white brick, the building is adorned with a prominent square tower sporting a giant timepiece, as well as stunning terra cotta decorative elements seen in the rusticated base, Doric columns, and roof balustrade. Reid and Reid, 1912.

Smith Block, 111-117 SW Front. Colonnades of rhythmic beauty grace the Italianate facade of the Smith Block, a rare and elegant reminder of the early days when Portland's commercial area was lined with row upon row of exquisite cast-iron fronted buildings. W. W. Pipero, 1872.

The Old Church, 1422 SW Eleventh. Constructed in 1883 in the "Carpenter Gothic" style, The Old Church has been sensitively restored and is one of the City's finest examples of this popular late-19th Century style.

Pittock Mansion, 3229 NW Pittock Drive. 248-4469. Open daily 1-5. The Pittock Mansion is a landmark restoration of a 1912 French Renaissance mansion. The 22-room house is furnished with antiques and objets d'art from the period. Perched nearly 1,000 feet above sea level, the house commands a breathtaking view of two states, the Columbia and Willamette Rivers, and five majestic peaks in the Cascade Range.

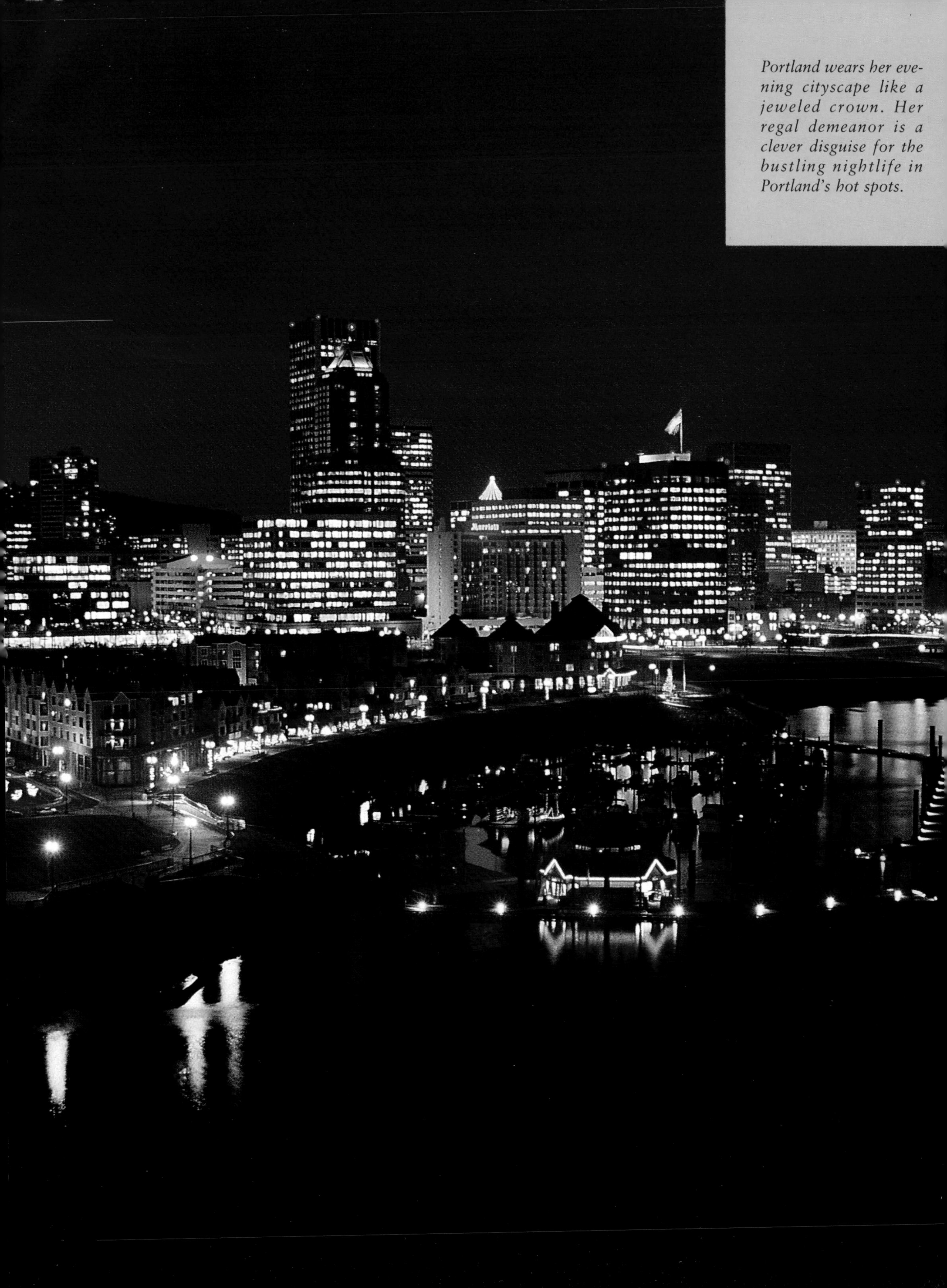

Portland wears her evening cityscape like a jeweled crown. Her regal demeanor is a clever disguise for the bustling nightlife in Portland's hot spots.

TOURS

Be a tourist in your own town.

No need to wait for out-of-town house guests to be the usual excuse for a tour. The following excursions are unique enough to budge the most smug among us. Grab the camera and don your walking shoes and discover what visitors have known for a long time: Portland is a visual smorgasborg.

Tour companies have mushroomed in our town over the last few years offering a wide range of tour packages — city tours, wine country tours, gorge tours, tours of art galleries—you name it you're likely to find it! Pilots point out the geological fireworks of active volcanoes as you fly over molten lava, and colorful octogenarians expound on the marvels of Portland history and architecture in any number of walking or driving tours through the city's historic neighborhoods. *Julie Koler, Peter Donahue*

BY AIR

Eagle Flight Center, Inc., 648-7151. Variety of custom flights available including Mount St. Helens, Columbia Gorge, Oregon Coast, Portland Metro Area and more.

Hillsboro Helicopters Inc., 648-2831. Scenic tours of Portland and environs. Custom tailored flights statewide.

Northwest Aviation, 228-0089. Oregon's oldest balloon excursion company offers trips throughout the state. Scenic Champagne Flight from Wilsonville to Woodburn is a favorite.

Oregon Balloon Adventures, 244-5676. Hot air balloon and blimp tours of the greater metropolitan area????

BY BOAT

Sternwheeler River Cruises, 223-3928. Columbia Gorge and Portland waterfront tours. Lunch, dinner and Sunday brunch cruises. Private charters available.

Yachts-O-Fun Cruises, Inc., 289-6665. Willamette River and Columbia Gorge cruises. Charter boats and regular sightseeing excursions. Dinner cruises, Sunday brunches and harbor tours.

BY BUS

AES Transportation Inc., 285-4040. Daily winter schedule from Portland to Mt. Hood. Discount ski packages and sightseeing tours.

Discovery Tours, 241-2520. Group motor coach tours. Specialists offering out of city historic, forestry and shopping tours with a professional escort.

Gray Line Scenic Tours, 226-6755. Itinerary planning and package city and statewide tours.

WALKING TOURS

Portland On Foot, 235-4742. Two and one-half hour narrated tours of Portland's Skidmore/Old Town and Yamhill Historic District. Saturdays, April through September. Private tours available.

Walk Portland, 274-9769. One hour narrated tours of downtown Portland.

Urban Tour Group, 227-5780. Downtown city tours for school children.

Greater Portland Convention and Visitors Association, 222-2223. Variety of self-guided tour brochures available.

Historic Preservation League of Oregon, 243-1923. Self-guided tour brochures available focusing on historic districts and neighborhoods throughout Oregon.

MISCELLANEOUS

Arlene Schnitzer Concert Hall — Portland Center for the Performing Arts, 248-4496. Tours of the historic 1920's "Palace of Splendor".

Western Culinary Institute: Taste and Tour, 223-2245. Behind the scenes look at what it takes to become an international culinarian.

Port of Portland, 231-5000. Bus tours of Port facilities including airport and ship repair yards during summer months. Special arrangements for large groups during off season.

Oregon Vineyard Tours, 232-3232. Tours of Oregon's vineyards led by the witty, knowledgeable Howard MacAllister.

Kitty Wheeler Tours, 223-0527. Tailor-made tours for individuals and groups includes Portland and environs. Step-on guide service available as well as walking and driving tours.

FOOD

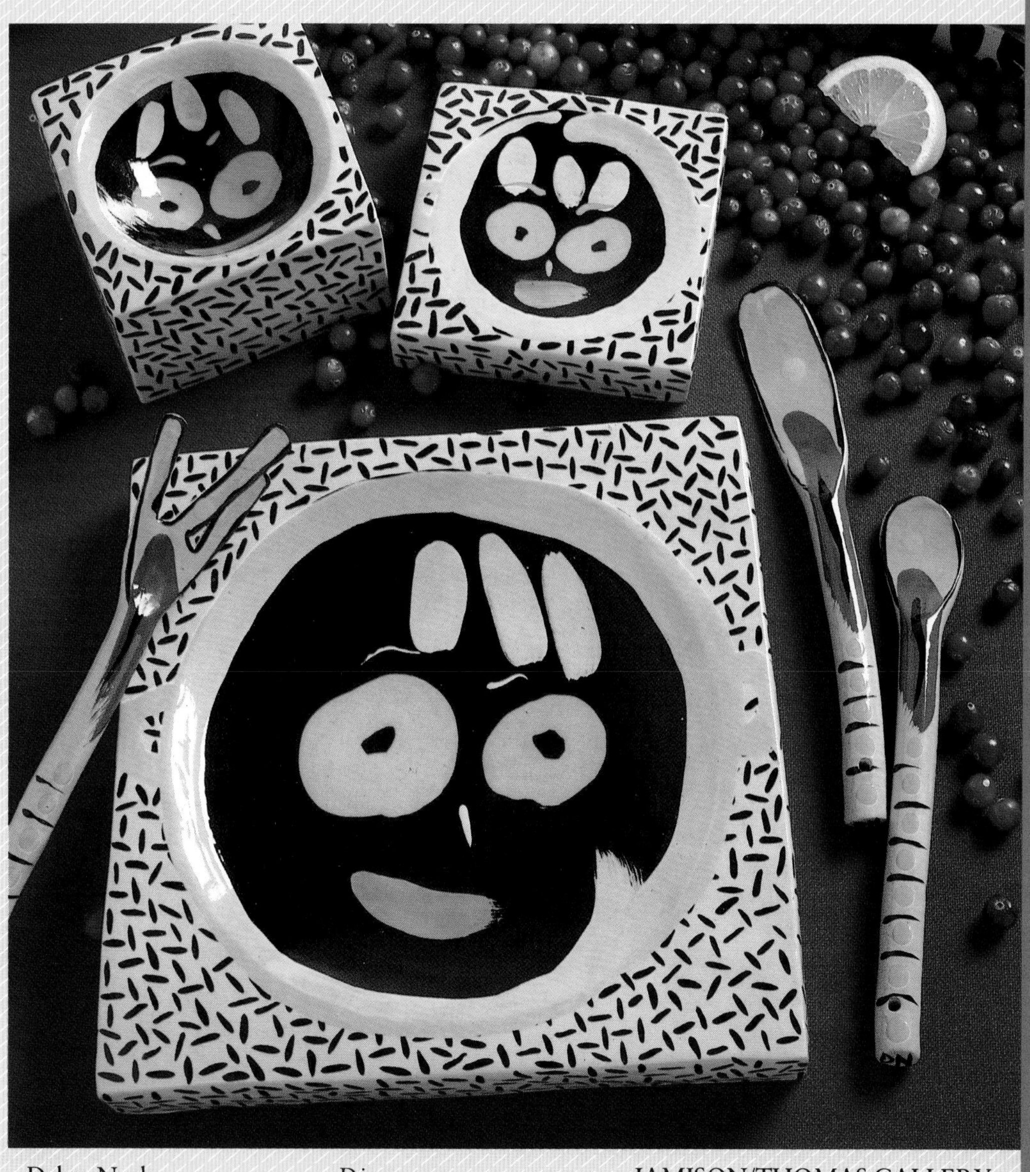

Debra Norby *Dinnerware* JAMISON/THOMAS GALLERY

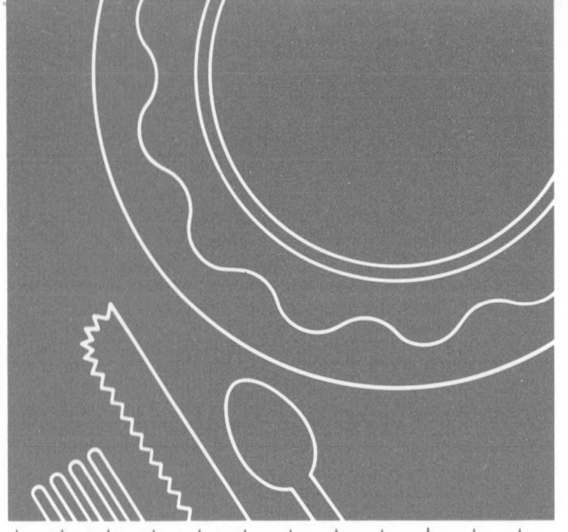

Portland has a wonderfully relaxed food style.

During the past several decades certainly more than the skyline of Portland has changed. We zip in our autos or in MAX quickly about town amid renovated old buildings, head-turning new architecture, cozy city parks and the tree-lined transit mall. Exploring Portland, and, no less, exploring eating in Portland has become an adventure.

The food adventures here are inspired by the rich supply of seasonal delicacies nature has seen fit to heap upon us. The abundance of edible natural resources made possible a glorious cooking history in Portland that began long before Captain Cook sailed along our shores. And, the exploration of cooking continues!

Seasonal produce abounds, from the fragrant carpets of wild strawberries that appear in July, the onset of autumn grapes ready to be pressed into wine, the wild mushrooms that pop up overnight, the produce stands creaking under the weight of varieties of apples, to the pears, prunes and figs. The changing seasons offer us an abundance of Dungeness crab, salmon, crawfish, trout, scallops and oysters.

It is interesting to note that the very foods the early settlers harvested and hunted are still relished by Portland cooks. Portland restaurants use the seasonal offerings to full advantage with the "special of the day." Ethnic restaurants and specialty seafood houses both are enticed by the same fresh, crimson salmon, but the former will add pinches of their traditional seasoning, while the latter may simply broil or alder smoke the glorious fish.

It is true that our proximity to the sea is often reflected in our cooking, yet the Willamette Valley and the fields of Eastern Oregon are well represented on our tables by chicken, duck and wild fowl. One doesn't need to drive far to see the farms from whence the hazelnuts, wheat or livestock came.

Portland has a wonderfully relaxed food style. Describing it is nothing as simple as portraying Tex-Mex as "spicy" or Midwestern as "beefy." Here it is "do-whatever-you-wish-with-our-fine-available-ingredients."

This style interests many, and often visitors "into" food find it so appealing that they stay and set up business. Hence, the many new specialty food shops offering everything from homemade pasta to pastries straight from the oven. How lucky we are in Portland to have experts making sausages, divine pizzas and bakeries grinding and using their own flour on the premises. New delis and meat markets, coffee houses and take-out spots dot the city, giving us a wide variety of choices.

This variety is reflected in our restaurants. Portlanders now have the opportunity to sample truly authentic Mexican cuisine. Our Vietnamese food rivals that of any city in the U.S. We have more than a handful of restaurants that create irresistible ethnic and regional specialties. And the old favorites, where tradition runs as deep as the variety is broad, still offer great classic fare.

Portland's food market tradition is also a strong one, providing a cornucopia of specialty foods from our region. The cottage industry that creates these specialties has virtually exploded. Delicacies now available include freeze-dried chanterelle mushrooms grown around Corvallis and the coast, and plum barbecue sauce made from the sumptuous fruit of Oregon's Plum Hills. The local version of the Italian twice-cooked bread, filbert biscotti, is wonderful with tea. The list continues with fruit syrups, berry jams, salsas made from the peppers that grow here so well, pear preserves from the Comice pear, (available only from southern France and southern Oregon) and, last but not least, those Walla Walla sweet onions!

Ecclectism, be it represented by chocolate truffles, Indonesian spices or the quintessential all-American hamburger, is alive in Portland. The discoveries in Portland's food world make a happy adventure indeed.
Emily Crumpacker

Emily Crumpacker *is the Food Merchandising Coordinator for Norm Thompson Outfitters and Northwest Cooking Expert on KATU-TV.*

Debra Norby, *represented by the Jamison/Thomas Gallery, has a growing national reputation for her work in clay and found objects. Her "Egomaniac" dinnerware and flatware shown overleaf are lead-free and can be hung on the wall. She also creates whimsical animal teapots and hanging fish, and is currently working on sculptures based on the human figure.*

DINING

From formal to casual, from seats over the water to seats in high places, we pass by the grills and sample the stock pots and the sushi bars of cosmopolitan Portland.

Atwater's
Restaurant & Lounge *48*
Brasserie Montmartre *56*
Chen's Dynasty *65*
Couch Street Fish House *45*
Crêpe Faire
Restaurant & Bistro *64*
Delphina's *58*
The Echo Restaurant *49*
Genoa Restaurant *44*
Hall Street Bar & Grill *69*
Harbor Side Restaurant *62*
The Heathman
Hotel & Restaurant *50*
Huber's *60*
Hunan Restaurant *57*
Jake's Famous Crawfish *61*
Juleps *63*
Kashmir *66*
Koji Osakaya Fish House *59*
L'Auberge *46*
McCormick & Schmick's
Seafood Restaurant *54*
Opus Too *52*
Pettygrove House
and Gardens *55*
Piccolo Mondo *53*
The Ringside *47*
ThirtyOne Northwest *51*

GENOA

Exquisite northern Italian dinners.

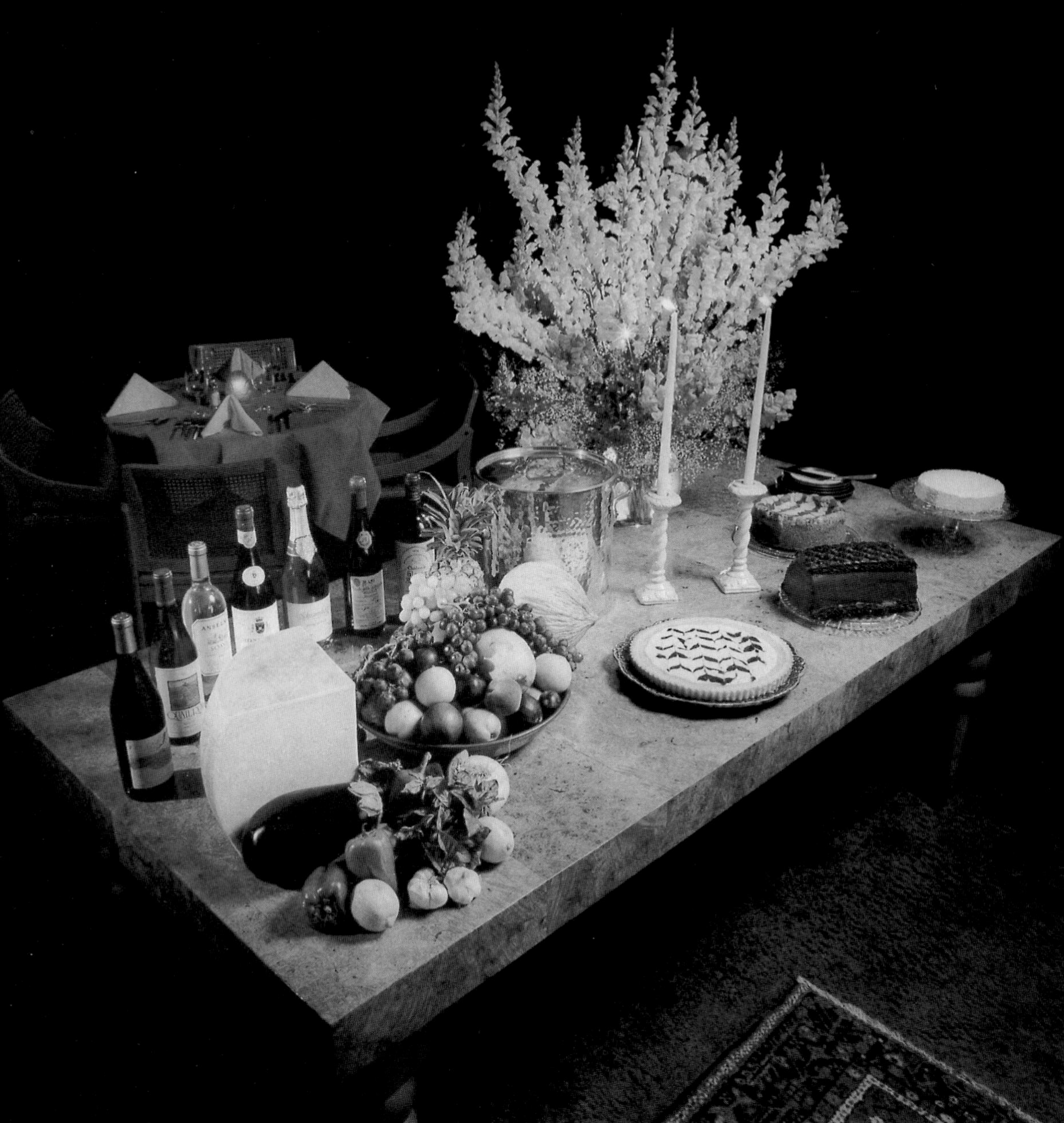

Southeast Portland

D7

Northern Italians consider fine dining to be the ultimate entertainment. A special occasion in Genoa, Milan or Venice is spent enjoying leisurely conversation while sampling antipasto, hearty entrées, fine wines, and luscious desserts. Here in Portland, the Genoa successfully recreates this tradition with its unique seven-course dinner served in an informal, romantic atmosphere. Conversation flows easily while diners enjoy the skillfully prepared pasta, fish and meat dishes made with the freshest local and imported ingredients. For a rare treat, fresh white truffles are flown in from Italy in season. The Genoa's fine wine list is fairly priced and features appropriate wines for every course — and the service is attentive yet unobtrusive. Don't miss the tempting array of sensational desserts. A delighted Andre Gregory, star of "My Dinner with Andre," said: "There are no restaurants in New York to match the Genoa." *The Best Places* guidebook awarded Genoa its highest four-star rating — only two other restaurants in Oregon share this distinction. Do you enjoy the theatre? Four course dinners are available before or after the performance, with reservations of course. But devoted patrons will tell you: the Genoa is a special occasion all by itself. Visa. MasterCard. American Express. Diners Card. Carte Blanche.

2832 SE Belmont Street
Portland 97214
238-1464

Monday-Saturday
7 course dinners:
6pm-9:30pm
4 course dinner seating only at: 5:30pm, 6pm, 10pm, & 10:30pm

COUCH STREET FISH HOUSE

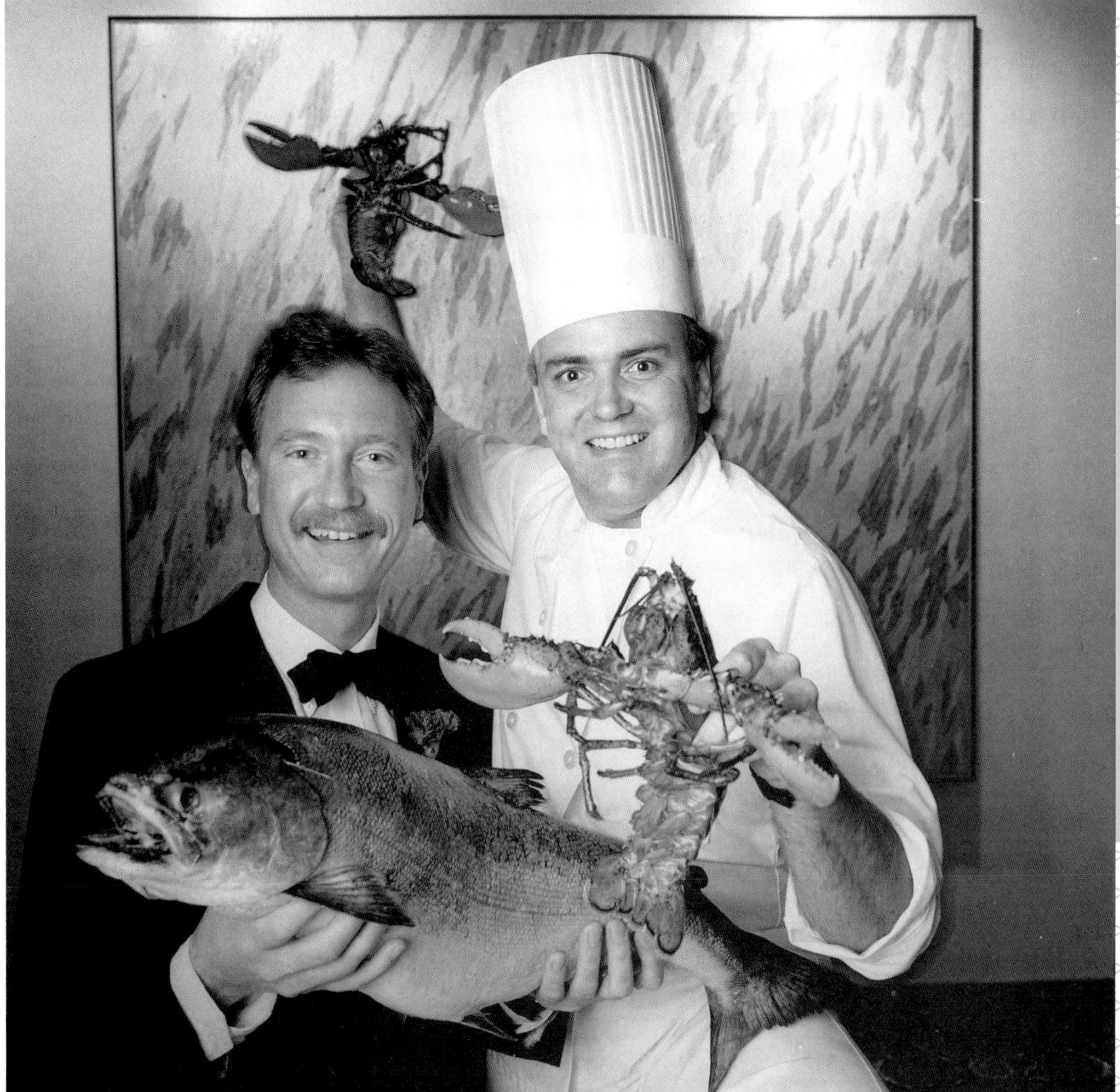

Extraordinary dining and fresh seafood at its finest.

From the moment you enter the Couch Street Fish House's arched facade and are absorbed by the elegant interior ambience, it is apparent that an uncommon dining experience awaits. Every waiter wears a tuxedo; every place setting holds a carnation that is yours to keep. By the time dinner arrives, your highest expectations will be met. This will not surprise maitre 'd Stanley Hoff and executive chef Ronald Glanville: they are accustomed to the customer satisfaction that has given the Couch Street Fish House its sterling reputation. Here, a triumphant meal begins with carefully chosen local and exotic foods and reaches a grand finale with artistic, appealing presentations. The choice is yours: crab legs Toscana; salmon, sturgeon, trout and mussels smoked on the premises; mesquite-broiled salmon; lobster bisque with brandy and cream; live Maine lobster, poached or Thermidor style; and the unforgettable Grand Marnier strawberries, injected and double-dipped with white and dark chocolate. All of this is served in warm, rich surroundings of red brick, high-backed chairs, semi-circle booths and antiques that blend flawlessly with this turn-of-the-century storefront building. The restaurant's long list of accolades, among them the Travel Holiday dining award for the past seven years, will merely reinforce what every customer soon learns: Couch Street Fish House is the standard by which fine dining is measured. Visa. MasterCard. American Express.

NW Third and Couch
Portland 97209
223-6173

Dinner
Sunday-Thursday
5pm-10pm
Friday-Saturday
5pm-11pm

Old Town
D25

L'AUBERGE

DINING

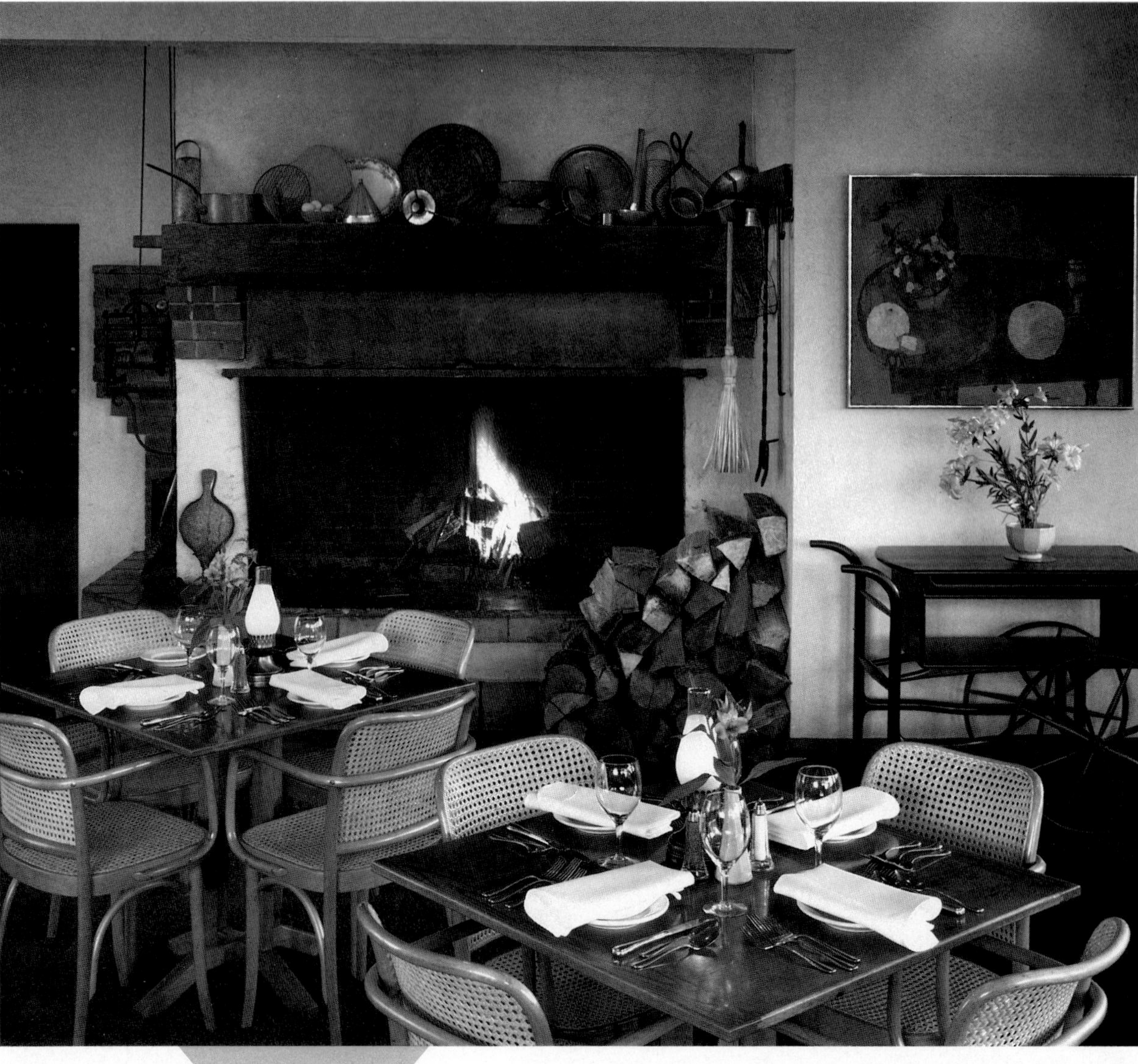

Intimate French dining in understated elegance.

Northwest Portland

E16

"L' Auberge" is the French word for inn, and a fitting name for Bill McLaughlin's intimate French restaurant, where the fine food, wine, and good company carry the evening in an atmosphere of understated elegance. When Playboy recently published its list of the top restaurants in the country, L' Auberge was included. The menu in the dining room has French origins, but has been adapted to showcase Oregon's delectable local resources, including lamb, veal, quail, pheasant, salmon, sturgeon, and scallops. L' Auberge makes a commitment to serious dining, promising consistent, original presentations every evening, from a menu that changes daily. All courses are set except the entrée — which you select from four alternatives — and the dessert, when six or seven heavenly creations are presented. Local and French wines are highlighted, with several local wines poured by the glass. At L' Auberge, pace is an integral part of the dining experience, so you can relax and enjoy each course fully before the next one is served. You can also dine in the bar, where the menu is lighter and more international. As in the dining room, the menu changes daily and is served until late in the evening. L' Auberge has developed a citywide following for its Sunday night movies, shown in the casual atmosphere of its bar. Many patrons order the now famous burgers filled with gruyere cheese and served on L' Auberge's own onion buns. Enjoy dining alfresco on the bistro deck when weather permits. Visa. MasterCard. American Express. Diners Club. Carte Blanche. Discover.

2601 NW Vaughn Street
Portland 97210
223-3302

Dining: Six-course meals
Monday-Saturday
6pm-10pm

Bistro/Bar Menu: Daily
5:30pm-midnight

Bar: Monday-Thursday
5pm-midnight
Friday-Saturday
5pm-1am
Sunday
5:30pm-midnight

THE RINGSIDE

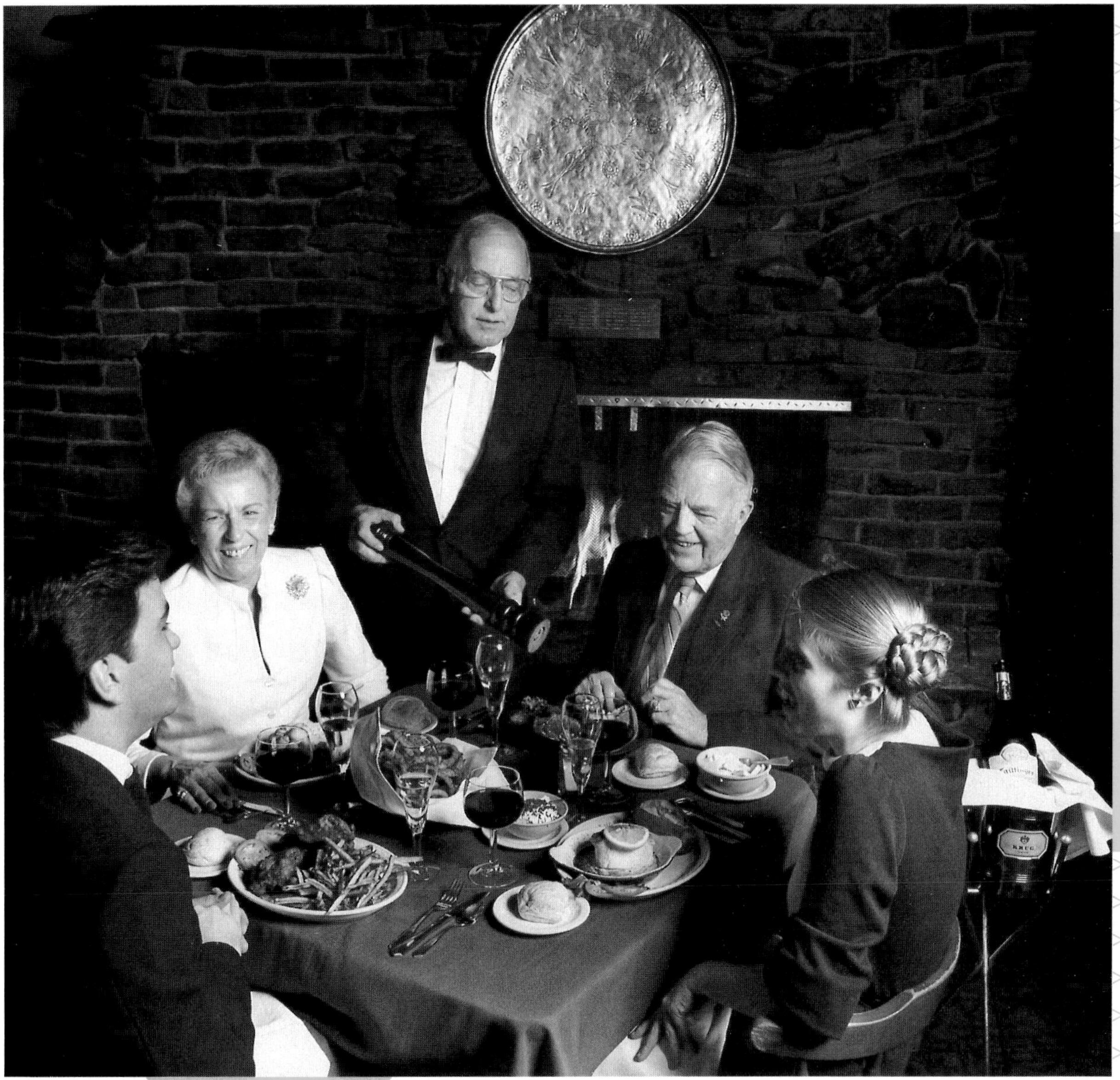

DINING

A Portland institution for over 40 years.

No one can argue that Portland does not have its share of fine restaurants of all shapes and sizes. But there is perhaps just one that can be called legendary: The Ringside. For forty-two years, impeccably dressed servers have presented The Ringside menu to customers who have come to expect the finest. Perhaps it's because The Ringside chefs always take that extra step: the halibut is steamed and then baked; the chicken baked and then fried. And then there are those famous onion rings — James Beard, the late culinary expert extraordinaire, once pronounced them the best in the world! The batter is a secret, no short cuts are taken in preparation and the result is worth bicycling in for — from anywhere. Equally remarkable is The Ringside hallmark: beef, generous cuts of it — eight to twenty-two ounces — with no flavor-enhancing chemicals or tenderizers. There's no need to doctor this meat, it's the prime or choice grade corn-fed variety from the Midwest. More? Try the Australian rock lobster tail, peruse the extensive wine list and, if you are at The Ringside East, indulge in ice cream cocktails for dessert. Reservations are gladly accepted, but certainly not required. The secret is out — and has been for years. Visa. MasterCard. American Express.

2165 West Burnside
Portland 97210
223-1513

The Ringside East
14021 NE Glisan Street
Portland 97230
255-0750

Monday-Saturday
5pm-midnight
Sunday 4pm-11:30pm

Lunch
Monday-Friday
11:30am-2:30pm

Dinner
Monday-Thursday
4pm-11pm
Friday-Saturday
4pm-midnight
Sunday 3pm-10:30pm

Northwest Portland

J18

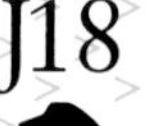

Northeast Portland

D10

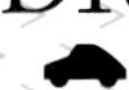

ATWATER'S RESTAURANT & LOUNGE

DINING

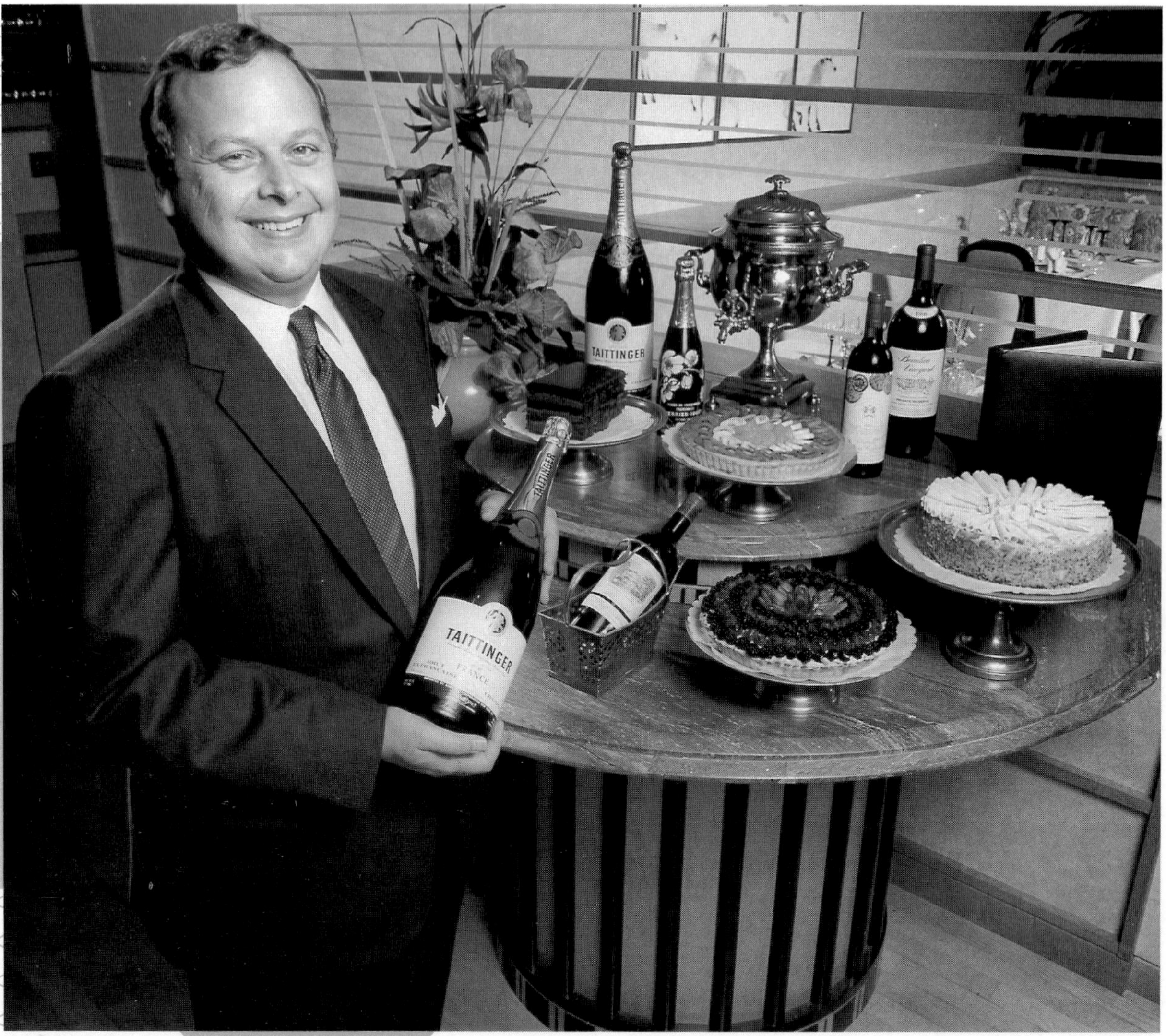

Elegant dining with a view.

Downtown

E25

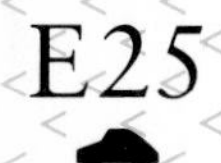

Rising thirty floors above the city lights, Atwater's Restaurant and Lounge brings out the best of Portland. At Atwater's, you'll find an unparalleled view of the city, rivers and mountains combined with beautiful decor, delicious food and impeccable service. The menu highlights fine American cuisine, featuring fresh items from the Pacific Northwest and select ingredients from around the country. Diners may order à la carte or choose the six-course Fixed Price menu which includes an appetizer, fish course, sorbet, entrée, salad and dessert. Either way, guests at Atwater's are assured of the finest and freshest in preparation and presentation. Dessert selections are prepared daily by Atwater's own pastry chef. Dining is an experience for all the senses at Atwater's. The elegant yet comfortable decor designed by a local architecture firm was awarded a certificate for excellence from the American Institute of Architects. Furniture and fine art from around the world has been collected to create an atmosphere of warmth and graciousness. Private dining rooms may accommodate a small, intimate dinner for a few friends or a party for 200. The same spectacular view is always available. From 11am 'til 3pm, Monday through Friday, the facility operates as The Founders Club, a private luncheon club catering to business executives. It provides an unmatched setting to entertain clients or conduct an impressive business meeting. From the fresh orchids gracing every table to the award-winning decor, attentive service and outstanding cuisine, Atwater's offers its guests an unforgettable experience. Reservations recommended. Visa. Mastercard. American Express. Diners Club. Carte Blanche. Discover.

111 SW Fifth Avenue,
30th Floor
Portland 97204
220-3600

Lounge
Monday-Saturday
3pm-midnight

Dinner
Monday-Saturday
5:30pm-10:30pm

Sunday Brunch
10am-3pm

THE ECHO RESTAURANT

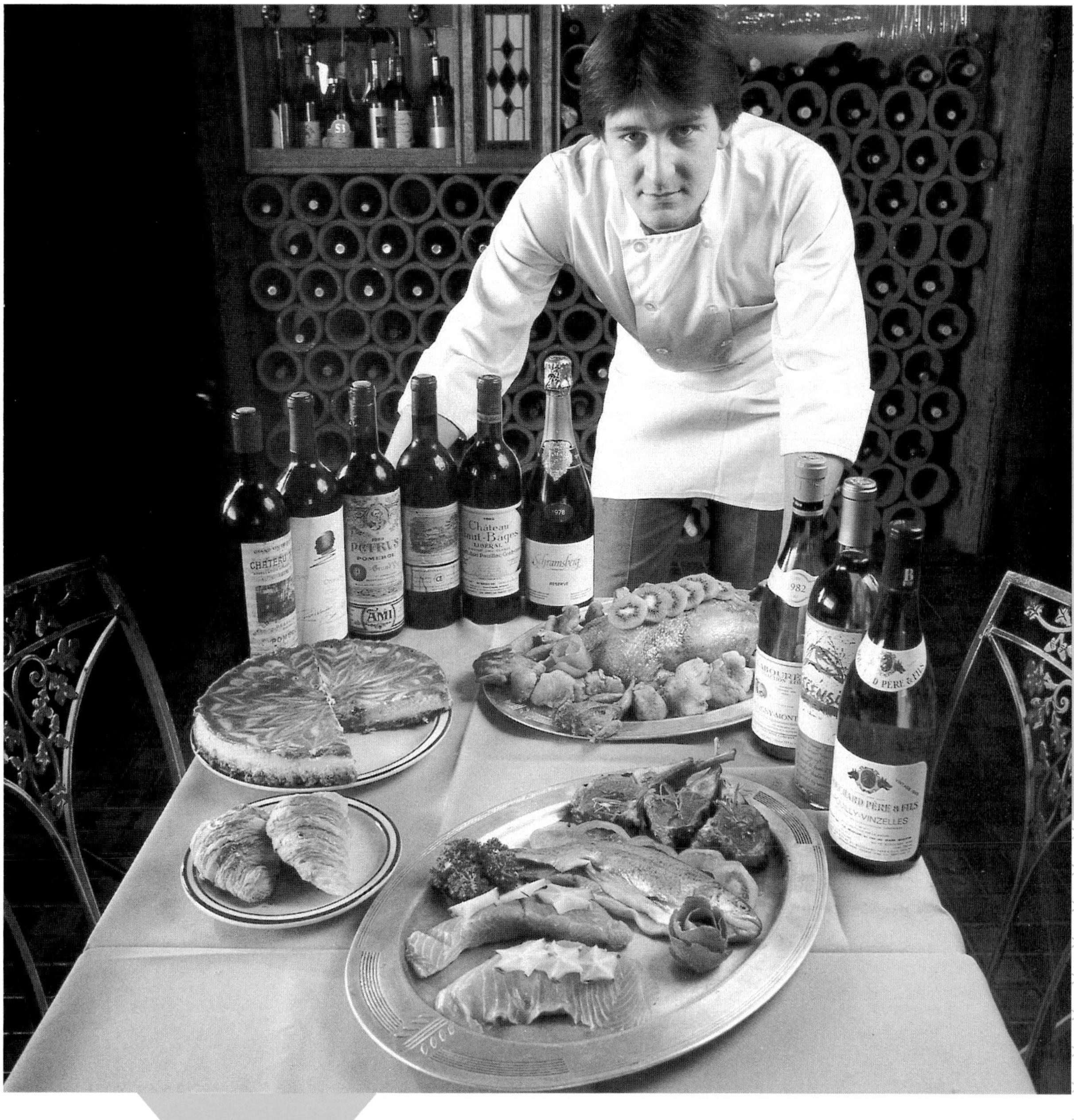

DINING

Informal, affordable, gourmet dining.

James R. Van Buren, chef and owner of The Echo Restaurant brings a varied background to the table. A 1980 graduate of the Culinary Institute of Hyde Park, he has worked as pastry chef in the Caribbean, as executive chef in Santa Cruz and he's traveled and tasted throughout Asia and Europe. This combination of culinary experience and worldwide travel brings Portlanders some exceptional cuisine. Van Buren transforms the freshest fruits, vegetables, seafoods, lamb, veal, duck, quail and pheasant into a sumptuous repast from appetizers to dessert. Start with rabbit pâté or a strudel composed of halibut, salmon, dill, sherry and Pernod. Then move on to an imaginative entrée — quail stuffed with homemade chutney; two small lamb chops with cream and green peppercorns, or fettucine al dente tossed with bits of red snapper, garlic, herbs and cream. Finish with an equally delectable dessert, such as cheesecake topped with chestnut purée, fresh cream and Grand Marnier; rum raisin ice cream and brandy, or the ultimate chocolate mousse made with Belgian chocolate, brandy and cream. For exquisite and imaginative tastes, dinner at The Echo may become a frequent affair. Visa. MasterCard. American Express. Diners Club. Carte Blanche.

6175 SW Lombard
Beaverton 97005
643-5252

Lunch
Tuesday-Friday
11:30am-2pm

Dinner
Tuesday-Saturday
5:30pm-9:30pm

Beaverton

F2

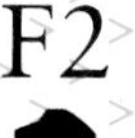

THE HEATHMAN HOTEL & RESTAURANT

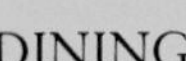

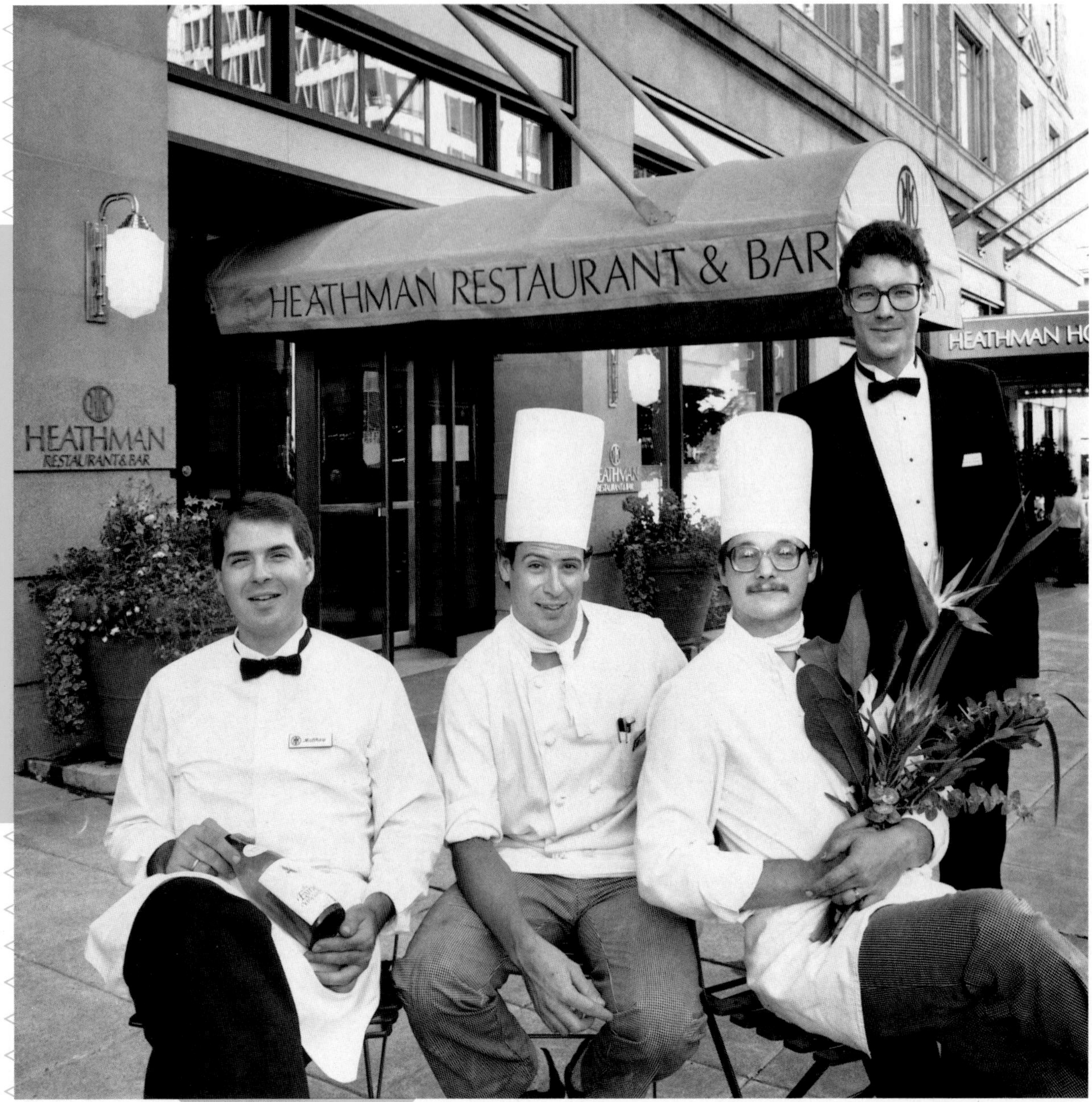

DINING

Service extraordinaire, fresh Northwest cuisine, Tapas Bar.

Downtown

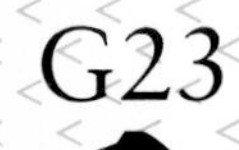

G23

Hotels and wines have something in common. Both have the potential to improve with age. With wines it takes a robust grape and enormous care. With hotels it takes a burning dedication to service, quality and ambience, as well as a relentless enthusiasm for tradition. When The Heathman Hotel opened its doors in 1927, it was praised as the "most modern of appointments" and singled out for its "unexcelled cuisine". These days it's equally admired for the care that has been taken in its luxurious restoration: the gumwood paneling, graceful stairway and ornate, wrought iron railings, black granite and teak, and the understated elegance of its 152 Regency, Empire, Ming, and Biedermeier style guest rooms. But let's not overlook the food. From a menu that changes quarterly, Heathman diners sample such succulent delicacies as Northwest rabbit, Oregon lamb, Spring Chinook salmon, often preceded by an array of imaginative appetizers such as Northwest game pâté! For added variety there's the Tapas Bar, serving an ever-changing selection of delectables for the lighter appetite, along with fine wines and beers from all over the world. Afternoon tea served seven days a week can be accompanied by baked scones, delicate mouth-watering snacks or pâté, and come evening there is live piano music. Heathman's hallmark, service extraordinaire, proves its vintage greatness, like the best of wines. Complimentary valet parking is available for dinner guests. Visa. MasterCard. American Express. Diners Club. Carte Blanche.

SW Broadway at Salmon
Portland 97205
241-4100

Daily
6:30am-11pm

THIRTYONE NORTHWEST

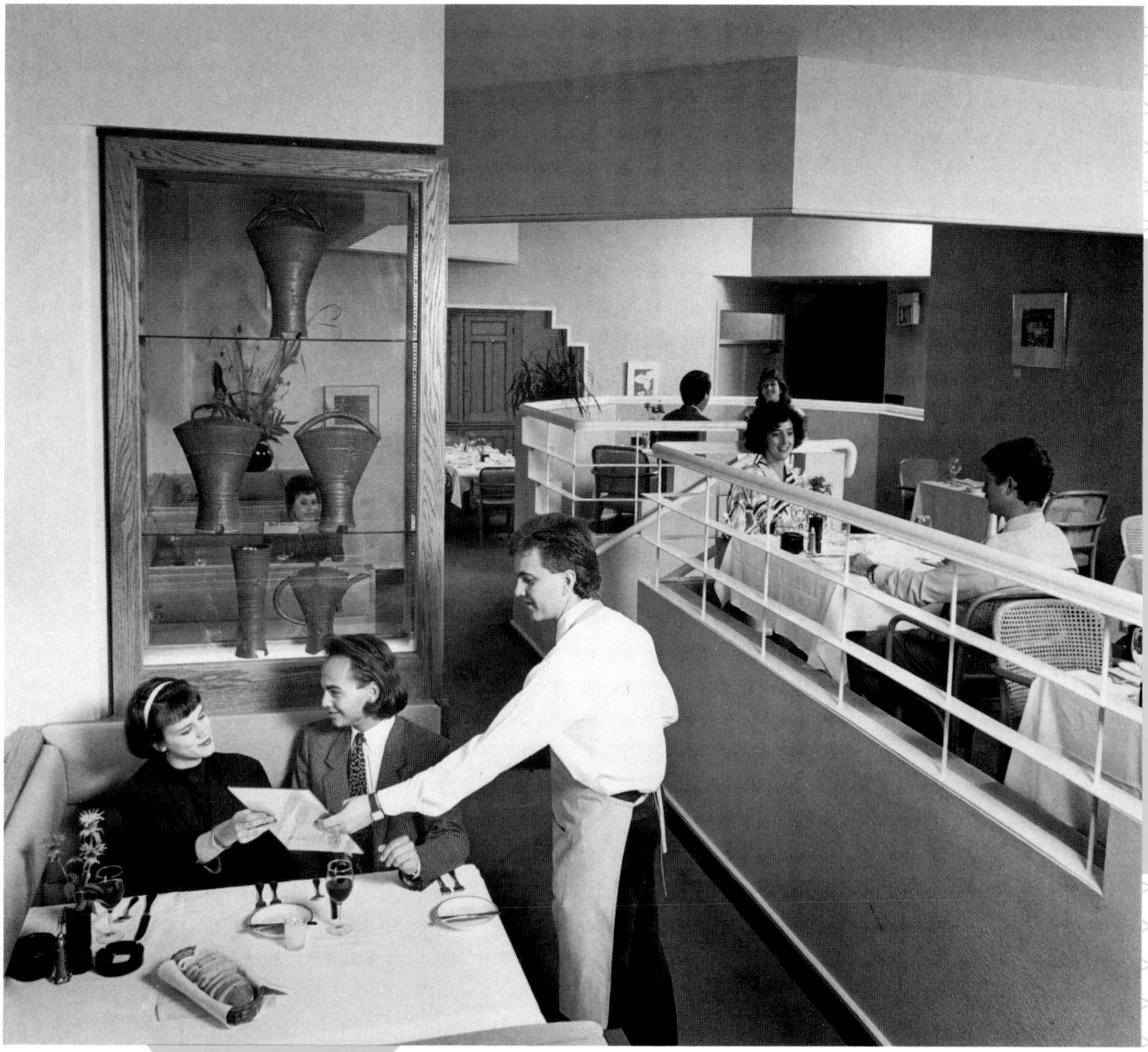

DINING

Delicious food beautifully presented.

Like a colorful kaleidoscope, ThirtyOne Northwest thrives on changes — with never a loss of interest. Enlivened by fresh flowers, crisp linens and a constantly changing display of paintings, the restaurant evolves from a sunny, Venetian pink by day to a candlelit peach after dark. Freshness of ingredients is paramount, of course, particularly in a restaurant as partial to seafood as ThirtyOne Northwest. Yet not by entrées alone do Portlanders thrive. Knowing this, ThirtyOne Northwest provides splendid appetizers, artistically presented salads, fresh breads baked on the premises, scrumptious desserts, and a new light menu for the smaller appetite. The light menu features Tapas, the various and delicious Spanish canapé which takes its name from its traditional position, served on a plate atop the wineglass. Available daily in the bar, Tapas include a variety of delectables such as lamb brochette, garlic chicken with capers, and seafood mousseline with saffron sauce. These can be enjoyed with a glass of fine wine or sherry, a cocktail, or perhaps a micro brewery Widmer beer, served with a hint of lemon. For groups of up to 32 there's private dining to be had for lunch, dinner or special occasions. Spare and tasteful decor along with delicious food in a kaleidoscope of pleasing presentations: That's what you'll find at ThirtyOne Northwest. Visa. MasterCard. American Express. Discover.

31 NW 23rd Place
Portland 97210
223-0106

Lunch
Monday-Friday
11:30am-2:30pm

Dinner
Monday-Saturday
5:30pm-10pm

Tapas
Monday-Friday
2:30pm-10pm
Saturday
5:30pm-10pm

Northwest
Portland

J17

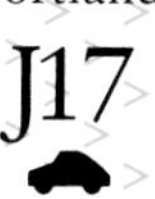

OPUS TOO RESTAURANT AND BAR

DINING

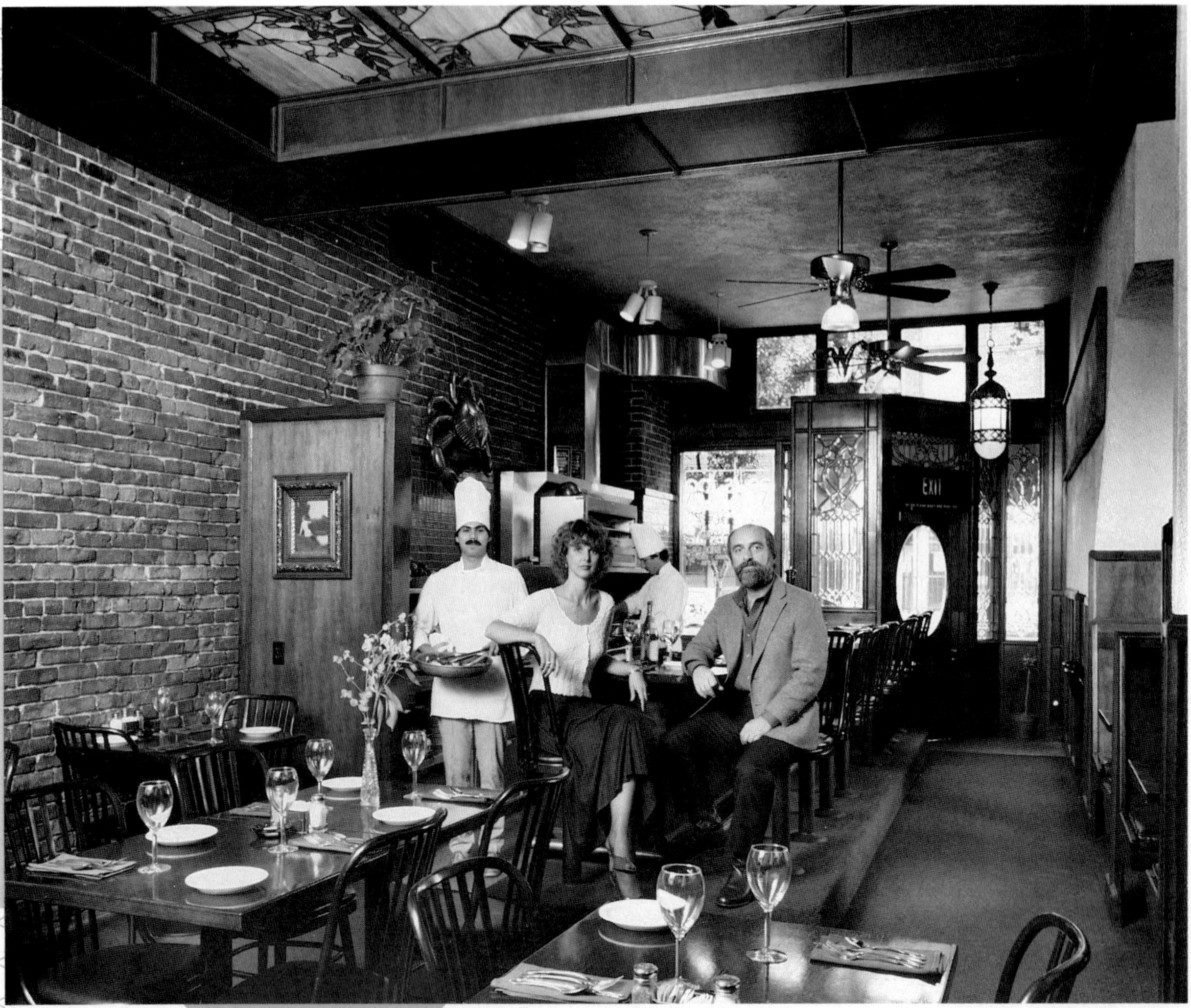

Life's great pleasures... romantic setting, exquisite food and soft jazz.

At Opus Too, the rich aroma of the mesquite grill tempts hungry folk to enter and enjoy. The stained glass ceiling and rich, mahogany booths are reminiscent of New York style dining, as is the sophisticated menu. Exotic seafood like baby blue marlin, tiger prawns, shark and ono are offered at their freshest — and choices change daily. The mixed grill plate — lamb chop, pork chop, beef tenderloin, Greek, German, or Italian sausages; Carne Azada — mesquite-broiled tenderloin in salsa — and mesquite-broiled rack of lamb are specialties of the house. Home-made pasta, great appetizers, and delicious desserts — such as the chocolate decadent cake or the cheese cake du jour — along with an extensive wine list complete the menu. Private party and banquet facilities are available too. After dinner, the finest in jazz listening awaits — over 3,000 selections — just through the archway at Jazz de Opus. Since 1972 jazz greats like Cal Tjader, Milt Jackson, and Charlie Bird have frequented Jazz de Opus and delighted Portland enthusiasts. Visa. MasterCard. American Express. Carte Blanche. Diners Club.

Old Town
D25

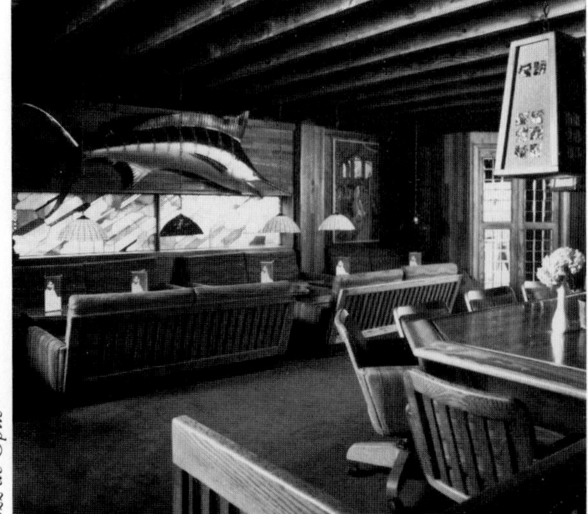

Jazz de Opus

33 NW Second Avenue
Portland 97209
222-6077

Lunch
Monday-Saturday
11am-3pm

Bar
Monday-Saturday
11am-2am
Sunday noon-2am

Dinner
Monday-Saturday
5pm-midnight
Sunday 5pm-11pm

PICCOLO MONDO RISTORANTE

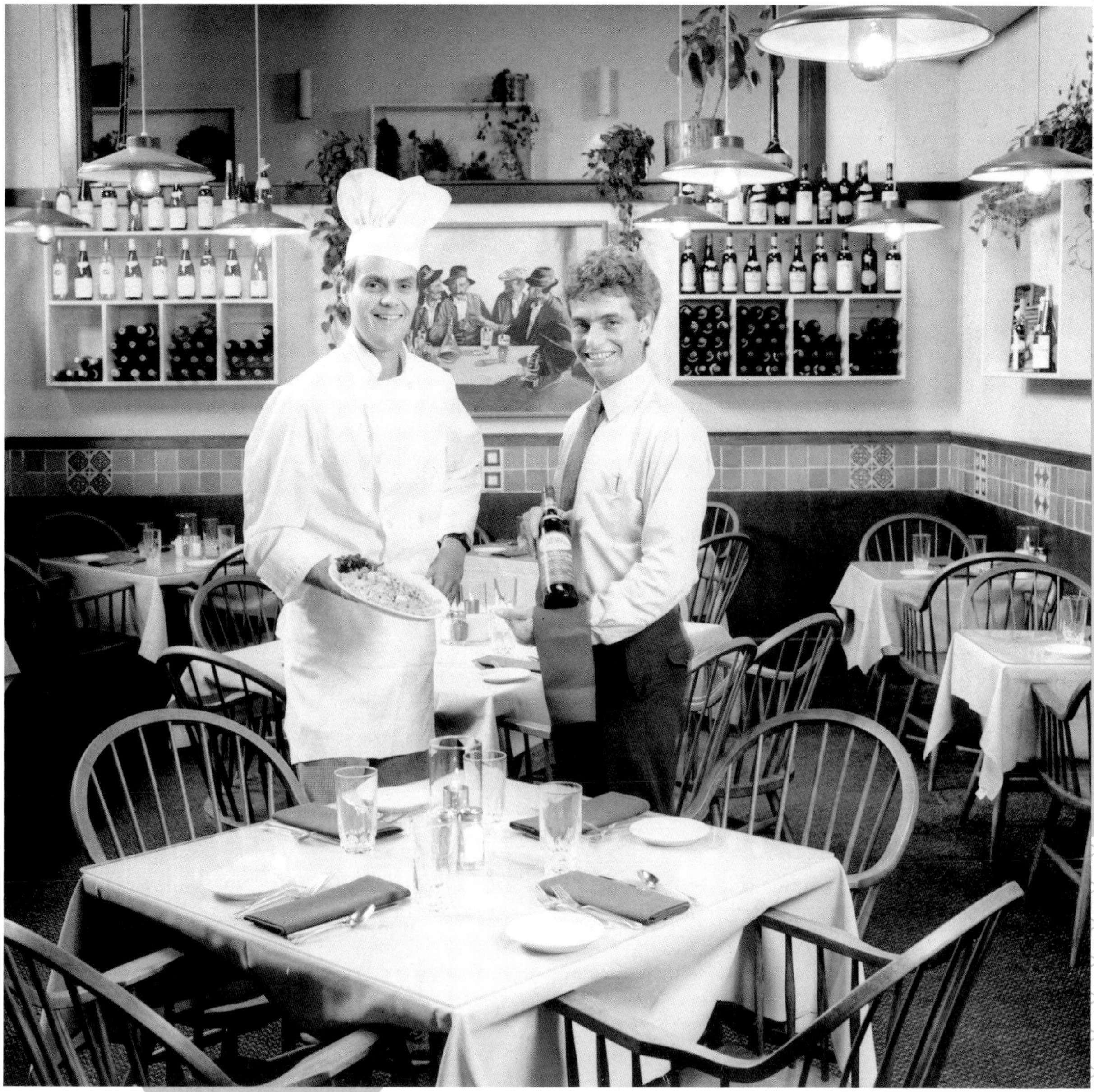

Northern Italian cuisine in a casually elegant atmosphere.

The critics are unanimous. Piccolo Mondo is a dining experience not to be missed. Every major publication has reviewed and raved about this quaint, casually elegant Northern Italian restaurant, situated in a corner of a renovated turn-of-the-century factory. "Intelligent recipes and skillful hands," the Oregonian reported. "One of Portland's finest-quality and best-value restaurants," wrote Willamette Week's critic. But the menu and milieu speak fluently for themselves at Piccolo Mondo, where the pasta is fresh and consistent, the nightly seafood specials tempting. The prime veal is milk-fed Provimi and a full-service bar offers generous premium brand drinks. Piccolo Mondo means small world, and the restaurant's surroundings of Italian tile, wraparound armchairs, skylights, relaxing colors, candlelight and large displays of wine leave no doubt: this little world is a restaurant that picks up where most leave off. And for your special occasions, Piccolo Mondo will bring its culinary expertise to you, via a catering service that extends the promise, "any time, anywhere, any number, any menu." Or while you're downtown, come and indulge in some eclectic Italian cuisine and treat yourself to some great entertainment at Café Vivo. Visa. MasterCard. American Express.

The Water Tower
5331 SW Macadam Avenue
Portland 97201
248-9300

Café Vivo
U.S. Bank Tower
555 SW Oak
Portland 97204
228-8486

Lunch
Monday-Saturday
11:30am-4:30pm

Dinner
Monday-Thursday
5pm-9:30pm
Friday-Saturday
5pm-10pm
Sunday 4:30pm-9pm

Corbett-Johns Landing
F6
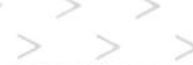

Downtown
E24

McCORMICK & SCHMICK'S SEAFOOD RESTAURANT

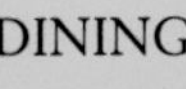

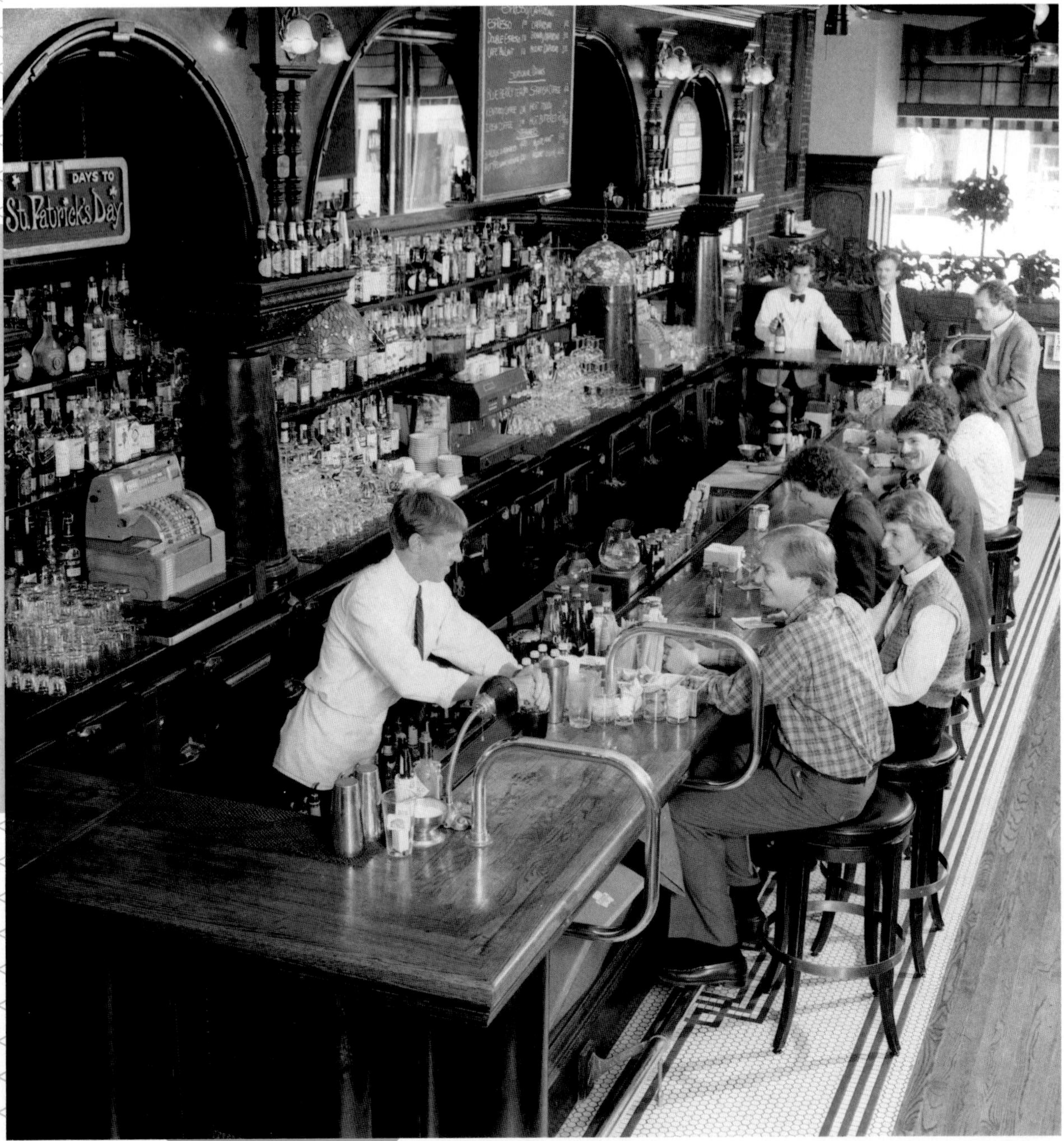

DINING

Lively bistro atmosphere where impeccably fresh seafood reigns.

Skidmore Historic District

F25

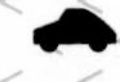

Seafood — fresh seafood — is the specialty here. Standard fare includes Alder smoked chinook salmon, live Maine lobster, and broiled Columbia River sturgeon, to name a few. The daily menu reflects the immediate availability of seafoods — grilled razor clams, swordfish, crab legs and sauce bernaise, yellow fin tuna and pan fried oysters. There is also a wealth of enticing non-seafood offerings including prime rib, peppered duck, New York steak medallions sautéed with artichoke hearts and one of the city's best hamburgers: the seven ounce New York cheeseburger. McCormick & Schmick's full service bar offers such specialties as espresso, Irish coffee, steamer drinks, more than twenty single malt and blended scotches and, delightfully, from the piano loft, there's contemporary piano music Wednesday through Saturday. Housed in the 19th century Italianate style Henry Failing Building, this establishment's rich interior reflects its dedication to comfortable dining, excellent food and professional service. Visa. MasterCard. American Express. Diners Club. Carte Blanche. Discover.

235 SW First Avenue
Portland 97204
224-7522

Lunch
Monday-Friday
11:30am-2pm

Dinner
Monday-Saturday
5pm-11pm
Sunday 5pm-10pm

PETTYGROVE HOUSE AND GARDENS

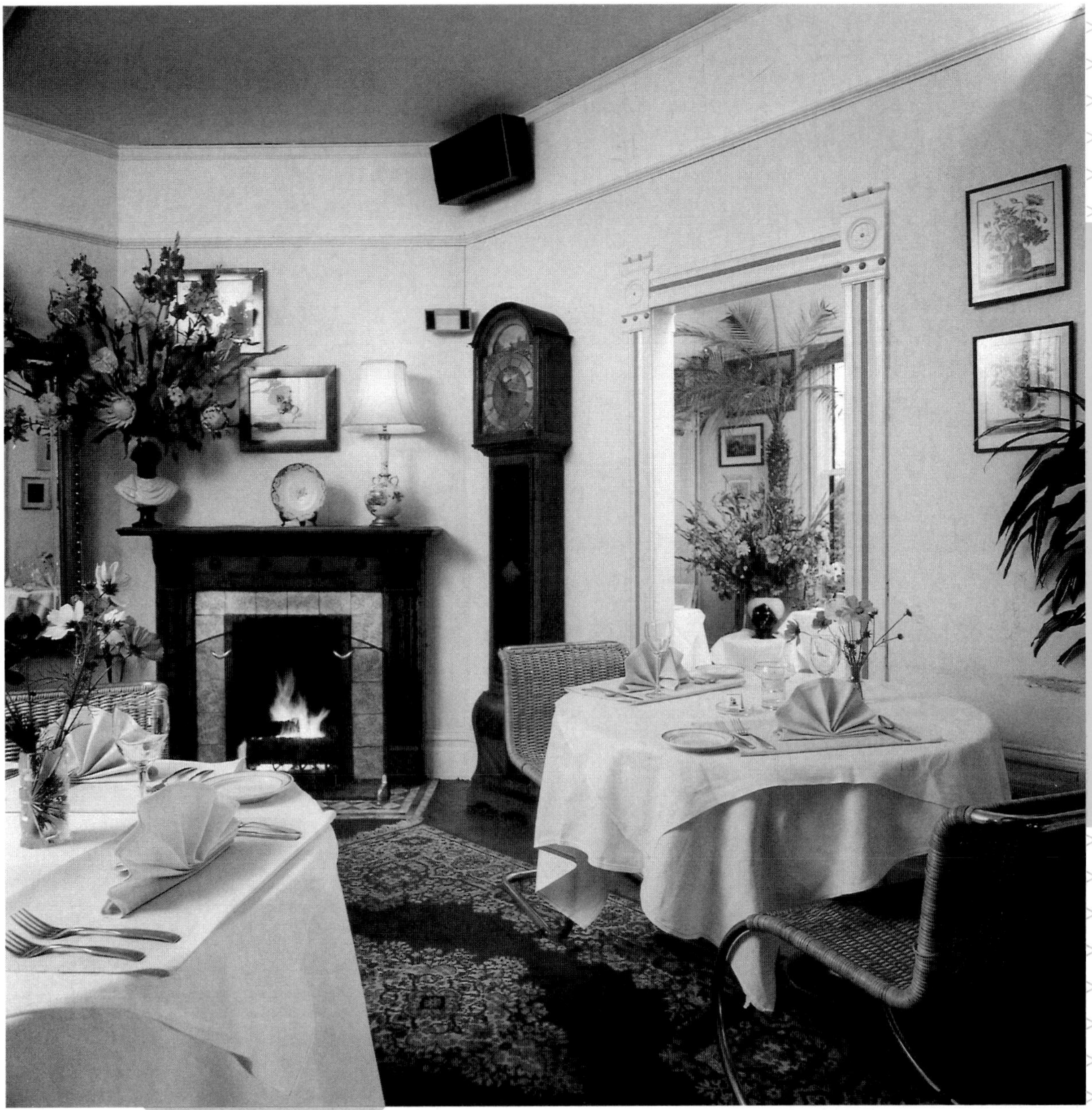

DINING

Satisfying the wild and more tame palate.

Northwest Portland

G17

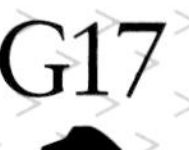

An 1883-vintage Victorian home, decorated with original art and European antiques, is the setting for a culinary diversion referred to as "Avant Garde Nouvelle Cuisine" that proves Portland's finest restaurants are not all cast from the same mold. The century-old building, converted to a restaurant without loss to its original charm, is home to the Pettygrove House. From filet mignon Portlandia to Australian wild boar flamande or fresh fish du jour to bahmi goreng, the breadth of selections caters to every taste, wild or tame. "Lest you think, though, that Jenaer is a culinary snob, unwilling to use anything common or inexpensive in his preparations," wrote one reviewer, "let me assure you his menu is reflective of a desire to be different and open to experimentation, not a desire to be snooty." For the diner in search of more typical fare, the Pettygrove House offers the fresh seafood, filet mignon and chicken dishes, all executed with the same care as the most exotic items, in addition, Paul Jenaer has incorporated into the Pettygrove menu Paillard entrées — entrées without sauces and creams. Weather permitting, enjoy Pettygrove's patio dining amidst seventy rose bushes. Visa. MasterCard. American Express. Diner's Club. Carte Blanche.

2287 NW Pettygrove
at 23rd
Portland 97210
221-4254

Lunch
Tuesday-Saturday
11:30am-3pm

Dinner
Tuesday-Thursday
5pm-10pm
Friday-Saturday
5pm-11pm

BRASSERIE MONTMARTRE

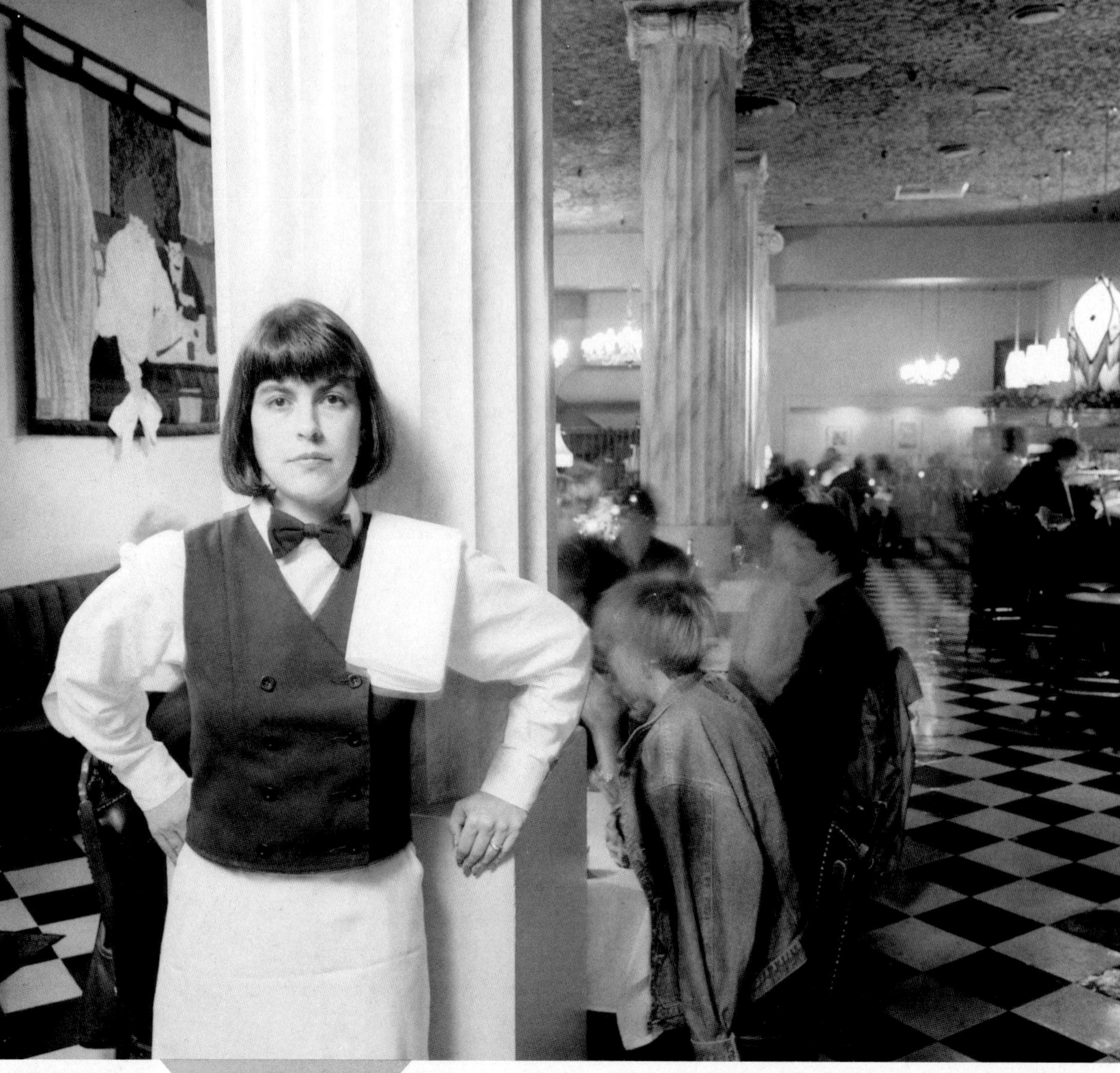

DINING

Unique Parisian flavor and live jazz.

Downtown
F23

Portland may be half a world and fifty years from Paris of the 1930's, but the Brasserie Montmartre rekindles the excitement and mystique with unmistakable élan. This nightclub and dinner house creates an atmosphere unique in Oregon. But the massive white pillars, black-and-white checkerboard floor and newly remodeled stage tell only a part of the story. The unique Parisian flavor comes from live jazz, seven nights a week. The rest comes in savory installments as you choose among succulent lamb, rabbit, Chicken Roquefort, smoked salmon or the finest New York steak. Here the light meal is not ignored; there are more than 40 choices, from basic salads, croissant sandwiches — or even a grilled hamburger — to Beluga Caviar. Don't overlook the homemade pastries and the bar's famous fresh steamed milk drinks. The relaxing, romantic surroundings are elegant yet casual; the chandeliers European, and the lighting soft. Two whimsical touches are certain to bring a smile: on weekends, a magician travels table-to-table to practice his sleight of hand; the unusual tables are covered with butcher paper — and crayons are provided. You supply the art, Brasserie supplies the sounds of jazz and the tastes of Paris. It's a pleasure! Visa. MasterCard. American Express. Diners Club. Carte Blanche.

626 SW Park Avenue
Portland 97205
224-5552

Light meals in Lounge
Sunday-Thursday
till 2am
Friday-Saturday
till 3am

Live jazz 7 nights a week
till 2:30am

Breakfast
Sunday-Thursday
10pm-2am
Friday-Saturday
11pm-3am

Lunch
Monday-Friday
11:30am-2:30pm

Dinner
Monday-Saturday
5:30pm-10pm
Sunday 5:00pm-9:30pm

HUNAN RESTAURANT

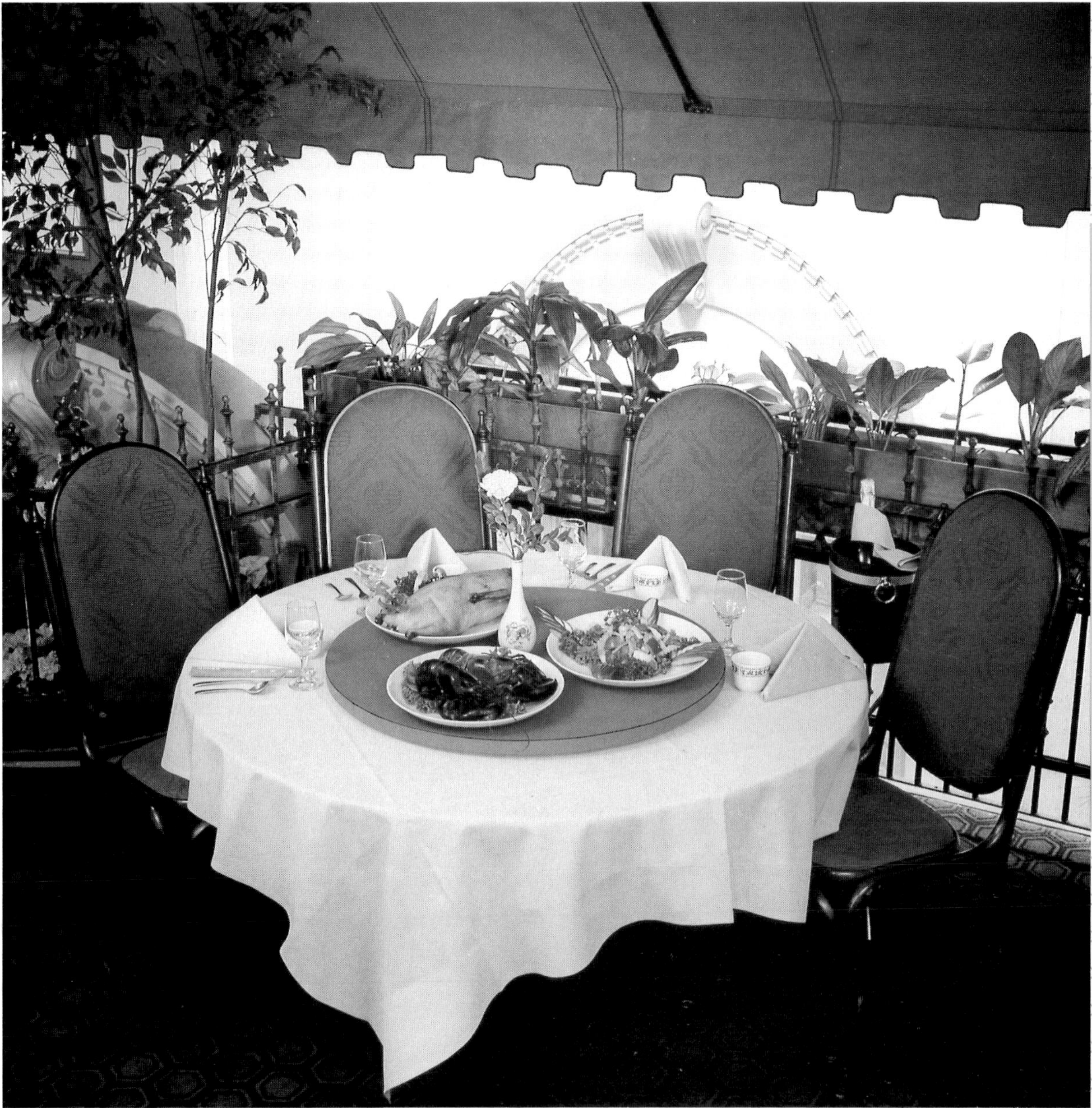

DINING

Exotic Hunan and Szechuan Chinese cuisine.

Downtown
F24

You're craving Chinese food. Something out of the ordinary. How about General Tso's Chicken with the chef's special sauce? Or tender slices of spicy sweet and sour Sesame Beef? Perhaps a Double Ocean Delight of prawns and scallops sautéed with hot peppers? The Hunan Restaurant beckons with unique and exotic dishes from the Hunan and Szechuan provinces of Mainland China. But red pepper reigns supreme in Hunan cuisine, so prepare your palate for a spectrum of tastes from delicate to fiery. A bottle of cool, delicious Chinese wine is a must. Your fellow patrons will likely be members of a delegation from mainland China, a business group from Taiwan, or the Japanese consulate staff — all frequent visitors to Hunan. Located in Morgan's Alley, one block from Pioneer Courthouse Square in the heart of downtown, Hunan provides convenient lunch, dinner and banquet facilities. Once introduced to the restaurant which brought Hunan cuisine to Portland, you'll want to return again and again for your favorites from Hunan's enticing menu — and to master the chopsticks! Visa. MasterCard.

Morgan's Alley
515 SW Broadway
Portland 97205
224-8063

Monday-Thursday
11am-9:30pm
Friday 11am-10:30pm
Saturday noon-10:30pm
Sunday 5pm-9:30pm

11814 NE Eighth Street
Bellevue, WA 98005
(206) 451-3595

DELPHINA'S

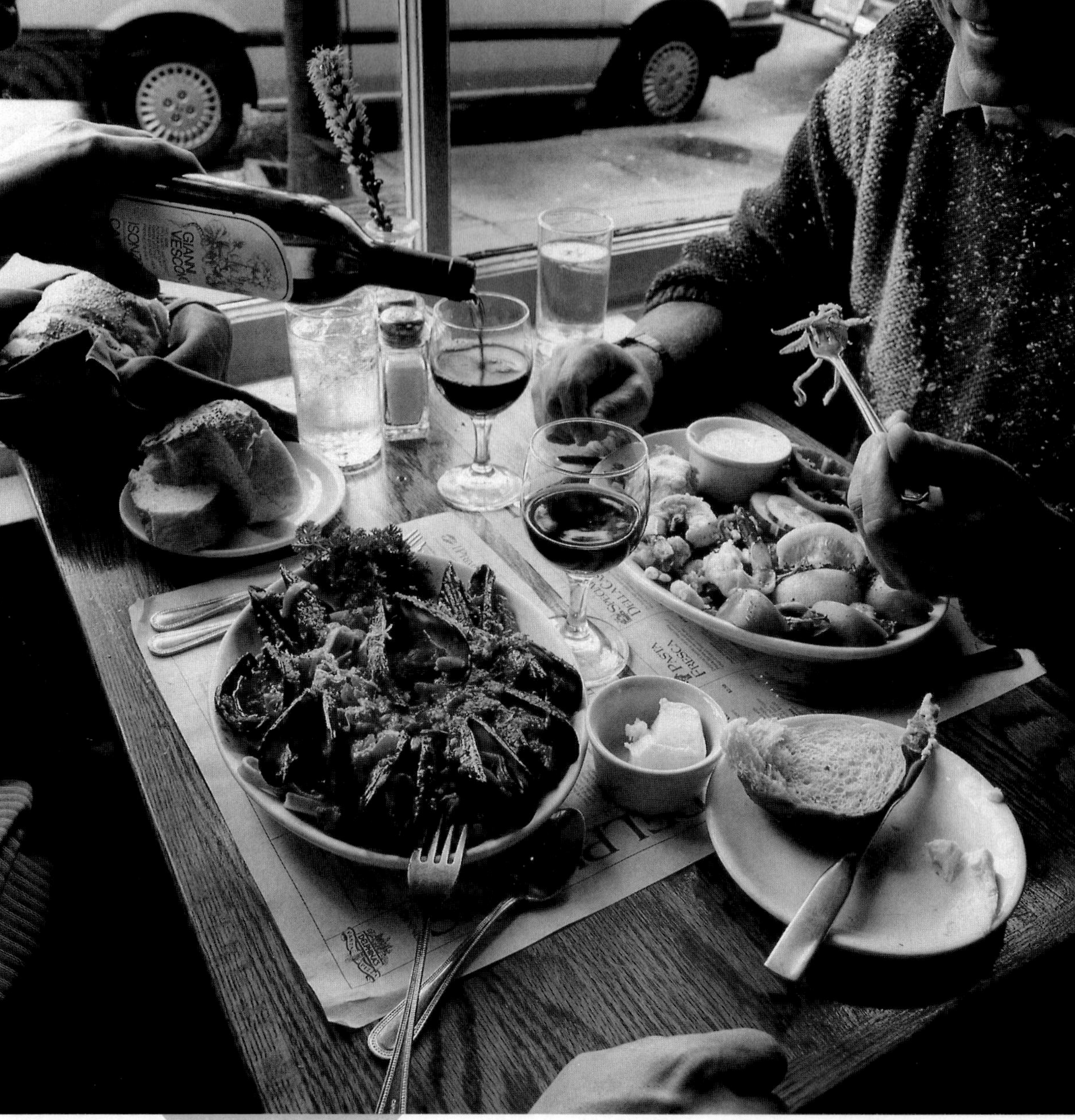

DINING

Mastering the pastabilities.

Northwest Portland
H18

There are Italian restaurants and there is Delphina's. Dining here is comfortable, engaging, entertaining and exquisite; it also can be festive or intimate, depending on where you sit in a restaurant that has captured Portland's imagination and appetite for more than seven years. Dinner is served every night until eleven; fresh lamb, flavorful tenderloin of pork, enchanting ravioli al pesto and zesty calamari Dijon are but a few of the choices. An undeniable ingredient in Delphina's appeal is the atmosphere, warmed by exposed brick, and enlivened with multiple levels. In any case, atmosphere and cuisine set Delphina's apart. In the summer you can sip a drink on the patio or eat lunch and dinner outside. If you're hungry at mid-afternoon, there's never a problem: Delphina's lunch fare is at your fingertips Monday through Friday, all afternoon until five. Night owls will find pizza by the slice, desserts, drinks and cappuccino in the bar. The service is courteous and attentive, and you'll feel at home whether you're in blue jeans or all dressed up. Sample a fine Italian wine, pair it with an elegant entrée or a simple dish and you'll be set for a sensational meal. Visa. MasterCard. American Express.

2112 NW Kearney Street
Portland 97210
221-1195

Monday-Friday
11:30am-2am
Saturday-Sunday
5pm-2am

KOJI OSAKAYA FISH HOUSE

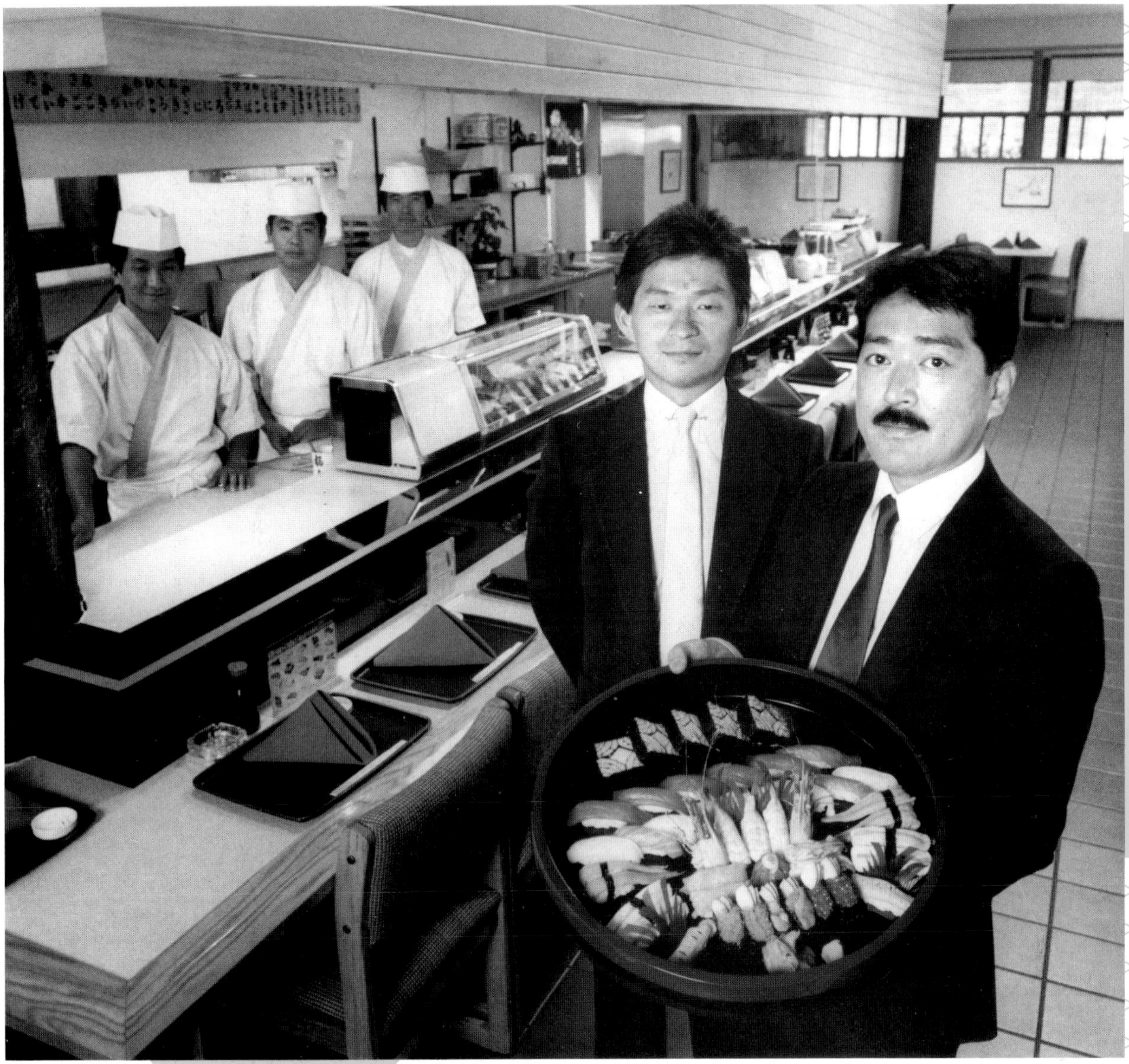

DINING

One of the largest sushi bars in the Northwest.

Sushi fanatics, oblivious to all but their own gustatory pleasures, are slow to realize that Koji Osakaya consists of more than its elegant sushi bar where chefs sculpt, entertain, slice and serve those oh-so-aesthetic delights. Nevertheless, a cursory glance proves that surrounding these hedonists is a full service restaurant happily serving somewhat less exotic, but equally tasty Japanese cuisine — including popular lip-licking teriyaki, teppan and tempura. Sister restaurant to its namesake in Osaka, Japan, the Koji atmosphere pleases the eye with vaulted ceilings, skylights, beautiful wood and private dining areas. Whether in the full service bar or the dining area, customers are easily distracted by two giant-screen TVs showing — of all things — Sumo wrestling from Japan. If, at first, you can't follow this decidedly Japanese sport, don't fret. Order a tangy Japanese beer, or better, sample from the most extensive sake list around. A few nips of this heated beverage will warm you from the toes up and you'll begin to understand the sport's attraction. Don't cheer too loudly, though. You're in one of the finest Japanese restaurants hereabouts and likely to disturb the folks at the sushi bar in sushi heaven. Special party catering and takeout is available. Visa. MasterCard. American Express. Diners Club. Carte Blanche.

7007 SW Macadam Avenue
Portland 97219
293-1066

Dinner
Tuesday-Sunday
5pm-11pm

Sushi Bar
Tuesday-Sunday
5pm-11pm

Corbett-John's Landing

F6

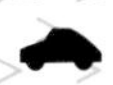

HUBER'S

DINING

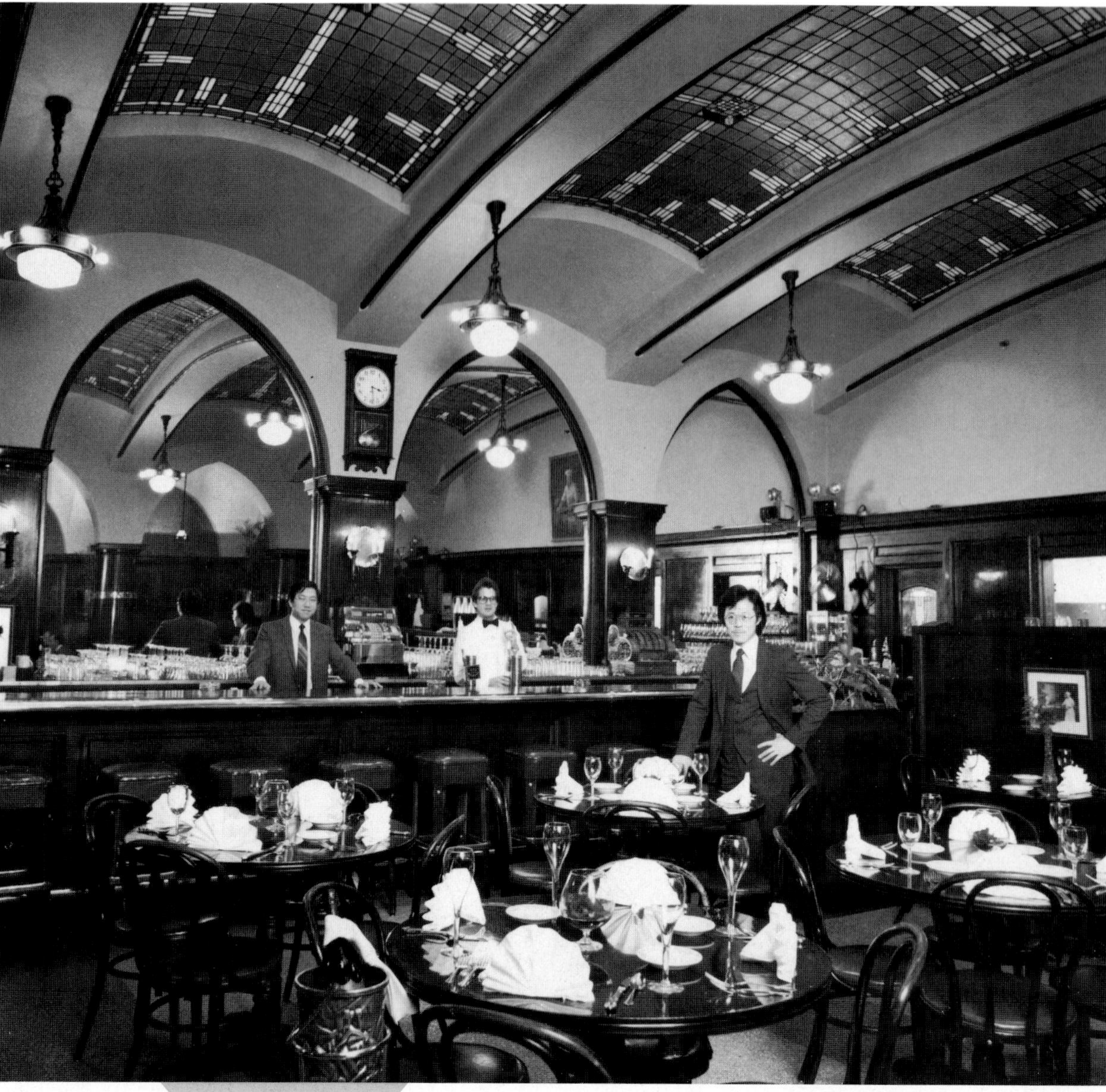

Turn of the century deluxe restaurant and bar.

Downtown

F25

Mixing efficiency with old world elegance, Huber's is the place where business meets pleasure. Now in the third generation of family ownership, this establishment maintains the crisp, traditional air of a pinstripe suit. The stained-glass skylight, mahogany paneling and terrazo floor are part of the original fixtures from 1911, as are the brass cash register, the brass ship's clock, pewter wine bucket and its silver wine stand. Huber's recently celebrated 105 years of continuous operation by securing a place on the National Registry of Historic Places. The menu, as well as the decor, has historic significance. Turkey sandwiches and coleslaw were once components of a complimentary lunch served with drinks at the original saloon. During Prohibition, the emphasis at Huber's changed to eating. Today, Huber's specializes in fine food at reasonable prices. Turkey, ham and duck dinners can be accompanied by fine wines from around the world. A specialty is Spanish coffee, flamed tableside with understated flair. Whether it be a turkey dinner, a special seafood entrée, a light meal after the concert, or a fifth of Dom Perignon, Huber's offers it at a reasonable price. Huber's is still the place in Portland where business people meet to talk turkey. Visa. MasterCard. American Express. Diners Club.

411 SW Third Avenue
Portland 97204
228-5686

Lunch
Monday-Friday
11am-4pm

Dinner
Monday-Saturday
5pm-10pm

Cocktails
Monday-Thursday
till Midnight
Friday & Saturday
till 1am

JAKE'S FAMOUS CRAWFISH

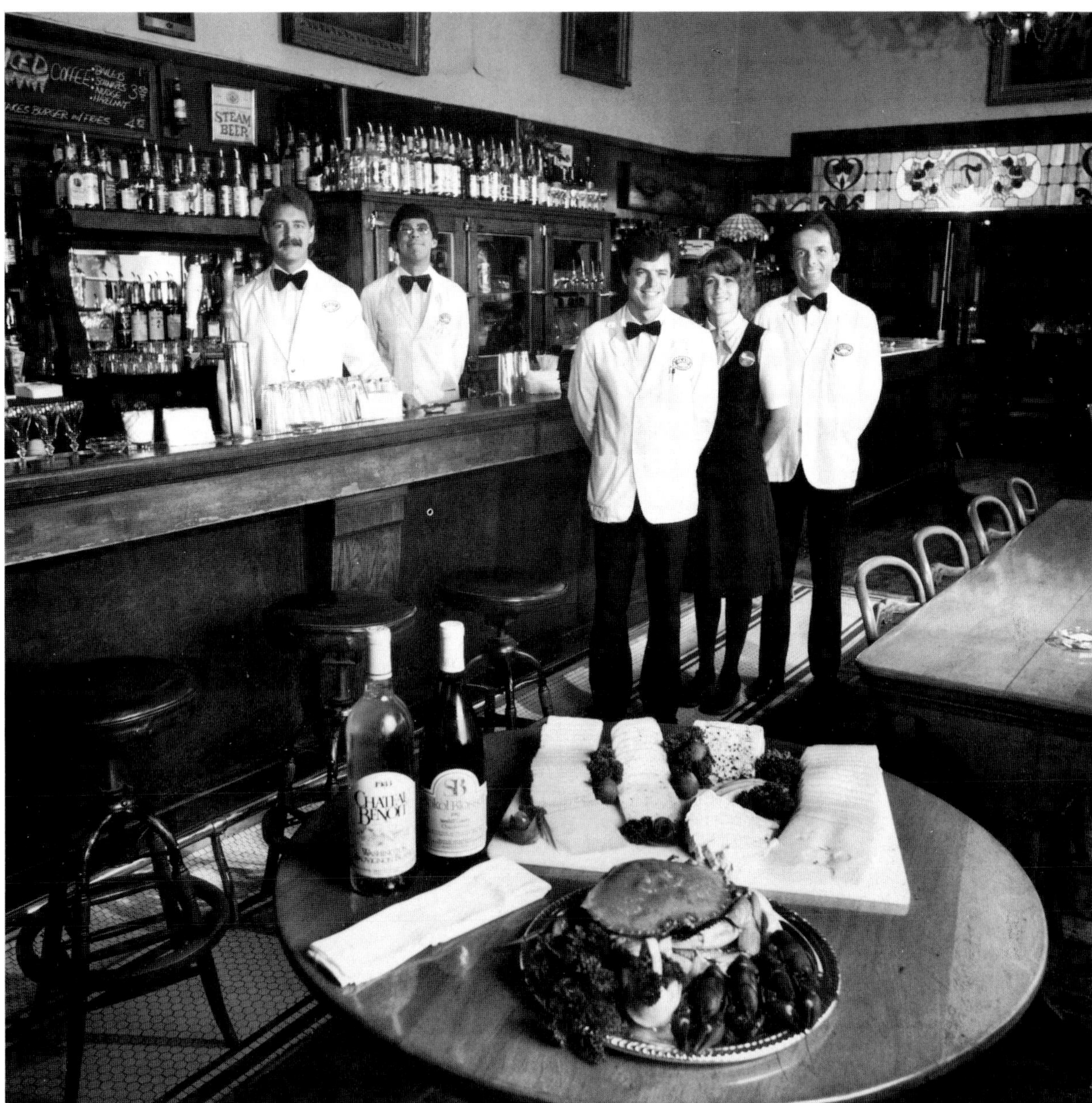

DINING

A Portland tradition specializing in fresh seafood.

Among Pacific Northwest seafood restaurants, Jake's Famous Crawfish is undeniably in the Ivy League; prestigious, nationally recognized, and a tradition for many. Occupying the same corner of the historic Whitney Gray Building for nearly eighty years, Jake's has been familiar to literally generations of customers. As you enter this warm establishment you are immediately emmersed in a Manhattan-style bar, known for its Irish coffee, lively atmosphere and animated conversation. As you proceed through to the second and third dining rooms you will find them more formal and serene. If you continue on you will discover the Back Bar, an intimate retreat serving hors d'oeuvres and after-theater coctails. Both lunch and dinner at Jake's provide a vast array of tempting seafoods which are brought in daily from around the world. A sampling of their award-winning cuisine includes signature presentations of bouillabaisse, salmon, sturgeon, swordfish and — of course there's crawfish in season. The restaurant's truffle cake, worshipped by chocolate-lovers nationwide, is always available and the list of Oregon wines is the longest in the city. Visa. MasterCard. American Express. Diners Club. Discover.

401 SW 12th Avenue
Portland 97205
226-1419

Lunch
Monday-Friday
11am-3pm

Dinner
Monday-Thursday
5pm-11pm
Friday-Saturday
5pm-midnight
Sunday 5pm-10pm

Downtown
E23

HARBOR SIDE RESTAURANT SHANGHAI LOUNGE

DINING

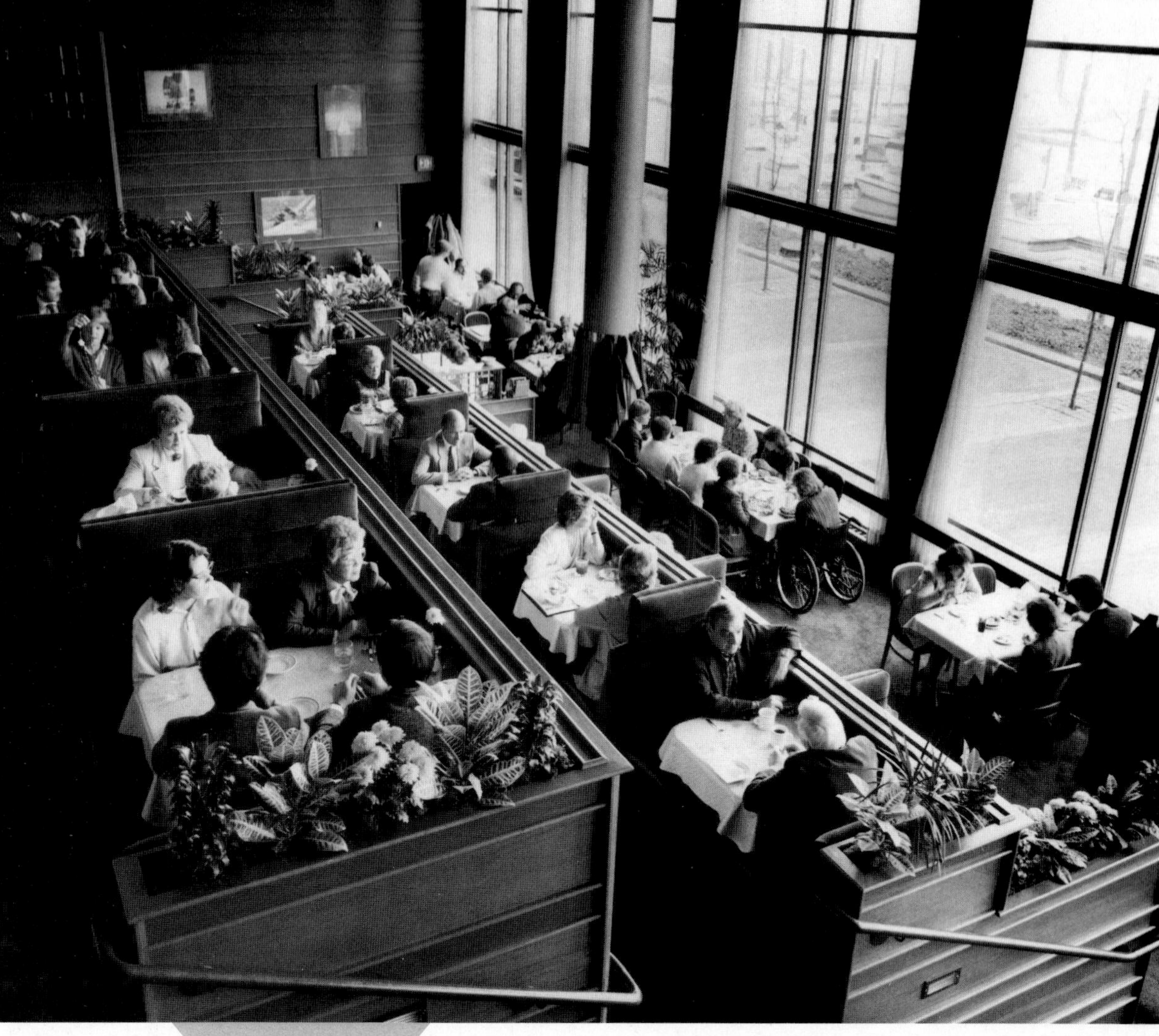

Spectacular waterfront dining and dancing.

RiverPlace
125

It wasn't long after the opening of Harbor Side Restaurant and Shanghai Lounge that critics and customers alike began delivering praise by the boatload. *Oregon Magazine* named Harbor Side's astounding menu selection the best in the state in 1985. The 1986 Downtowner Awards, a readers' poll, added the title of best Saturday night restaurant, and best waiter; the *Oregonian* reported that the Harbor Side has "the most determinedly fashionable menu around" and that it "creates a substantial new resource for Portland diners." All of this should come as no surprise, in that the Harbor Side's proprietors are Bill McCormick and Doug Schmick of McCormick and Schmick's and Jake's Famous Crawfish fame. Their newest undertaking blends a four-tier restaurant with a lounge featuring state-of-the-art sound and light systems. The tiers offer all diners a view of the Willamette River from the Harbor Side's splendid RiverPlace location, and the Shanghai, winner of *Oregon Magazine's* "Best Singles Bar" title in 1985, features live music seven nights a week. Seafood, Cajun recipes, pasta and gourmet pizza are but a tiny fraction of the Harbor Side's 110 luncheon and dinner entrees — not to mention the Sunday brunch which offers an additional 75 items, setting the standard for sumptuous feasts. For lunch or dinner you'll find pan-fried oysters and stir-fry chicken, steamed clams and New York Steak, hamburgers and seafood sauté, linguini and calzone, Joe's Special, Hangtown Fry, Caeser salad and escargot, crab cocktail and spinach salad, and much, much more. If the perfect meal can't be found on this menu, then you simply aren't hungry. Visa. MasterCard. American Express. Diners Club. Discover.

0309 SW Montgomery
Portland 97201
220-1865

Daily 11am-11pm
Buffet Brunch
Sunday at 10:30am

Shanghai Lounge
Monday-Saturday
11am-2:30am
Sunday 10:30am-1:30am
Live music nightly

JULEPS

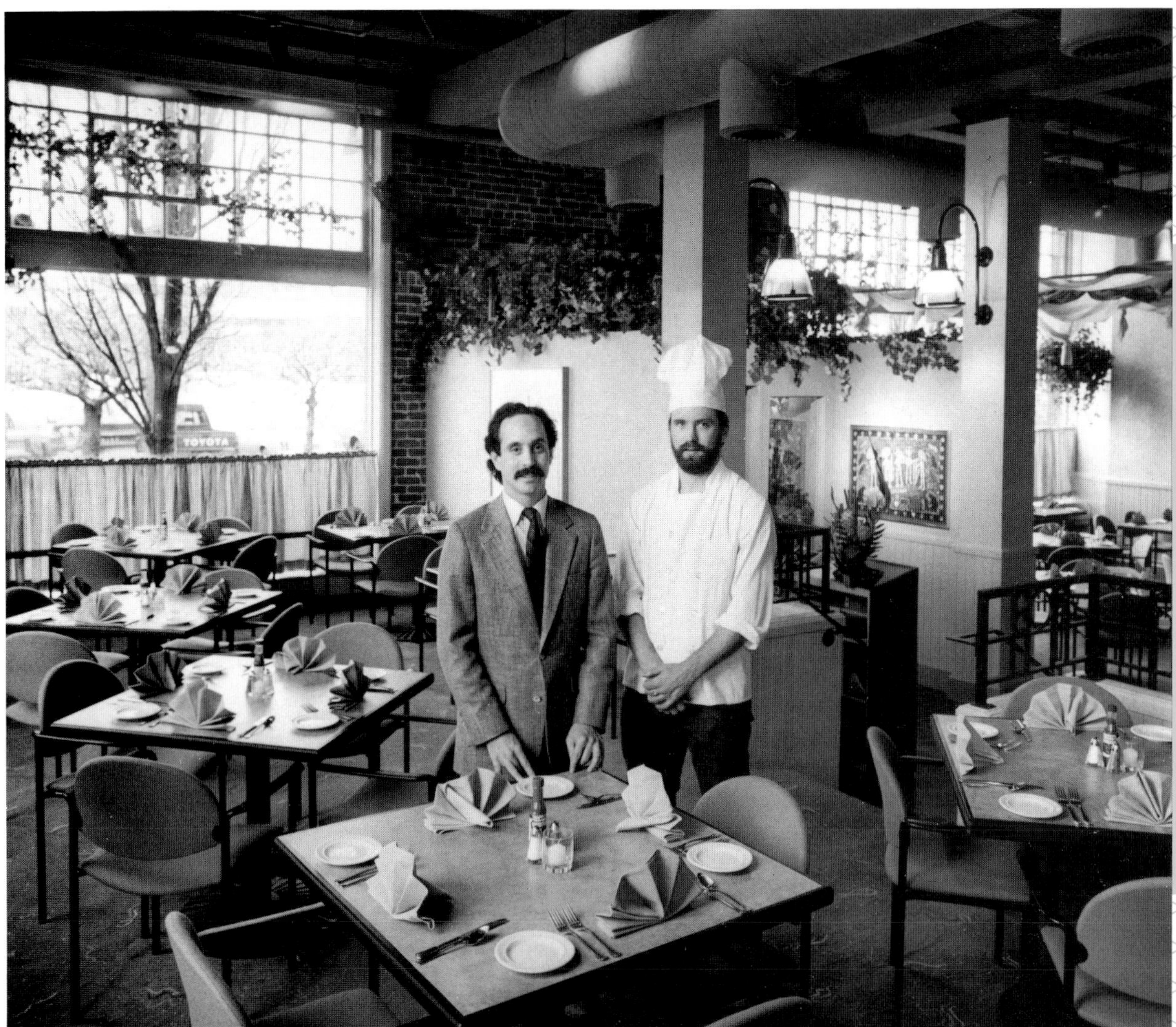

DINING

Southern comfort . . . simply Juleps.

In its native state of Kentucky, the mint julep is as sacred as Derby Day or the memory of Henry Clay. As a symbol of Dixie's friendly leisure, its blend of mint, mellow bourbon and sugar is without equal. So too is Juleps, a young Portland restaurant that does justice to classic and contemporary cuisine of the South. Featuring regional southern food from Chesapeake Bay, down the Atlantic coast to New Orleans these unerringly authentic recipes have now reached the Northwest. Restaurateur Randy Stern turned to professional food consultants Nathalie Dupree and Elise Griffin from Atlanta. Dupree is a well-known southern gourmet chef and instructor; Griffin is food development director for Atlanta's top restaurant group. Their efforts have brought a menu, reflecting both old and new southern cuisine that includes Maryland style crab cakes, fried catfish and hush puppies, southern fried chicken, sweet potato fries in a tasty French-fry cut, Brunswick stew, Creole shrimp salad, oysters pan roast (spicy New Orleans mixture of oysters and andouille sausage served with house grits), and soft shell crab, lightly fried and served with two dipping sauces. Dessert brings such delicacies as Georgia peach cheesecake, pecan roll, homemade cobbler along with the house specialty, mint julep pie. To make the effect complete, a festive atmosphere pervades the dining spaces, with brick walls, colorful carpet, street lamps and stylized wrought-iron railing separating the intimate seating areas. Visit Juleps and have an affordable sampling of the South. Visa. MasterCard. American Express.

135 NW Fifth Avenue
Portland 97209
274-9819

Lunch
Tuesday-Friday
11:30am-4pm

Dinner
Tuesday-Thursday
5:30pm-10pm
Friday-Saturday
5:30pm-11pm
Sunday 5:30pm-10pm

Old Town
D25

CRÊPE FAIRE RESTAURANT & BISTRO

DINING

Simple elegance, creative French and regional dishes, outdoor dining.

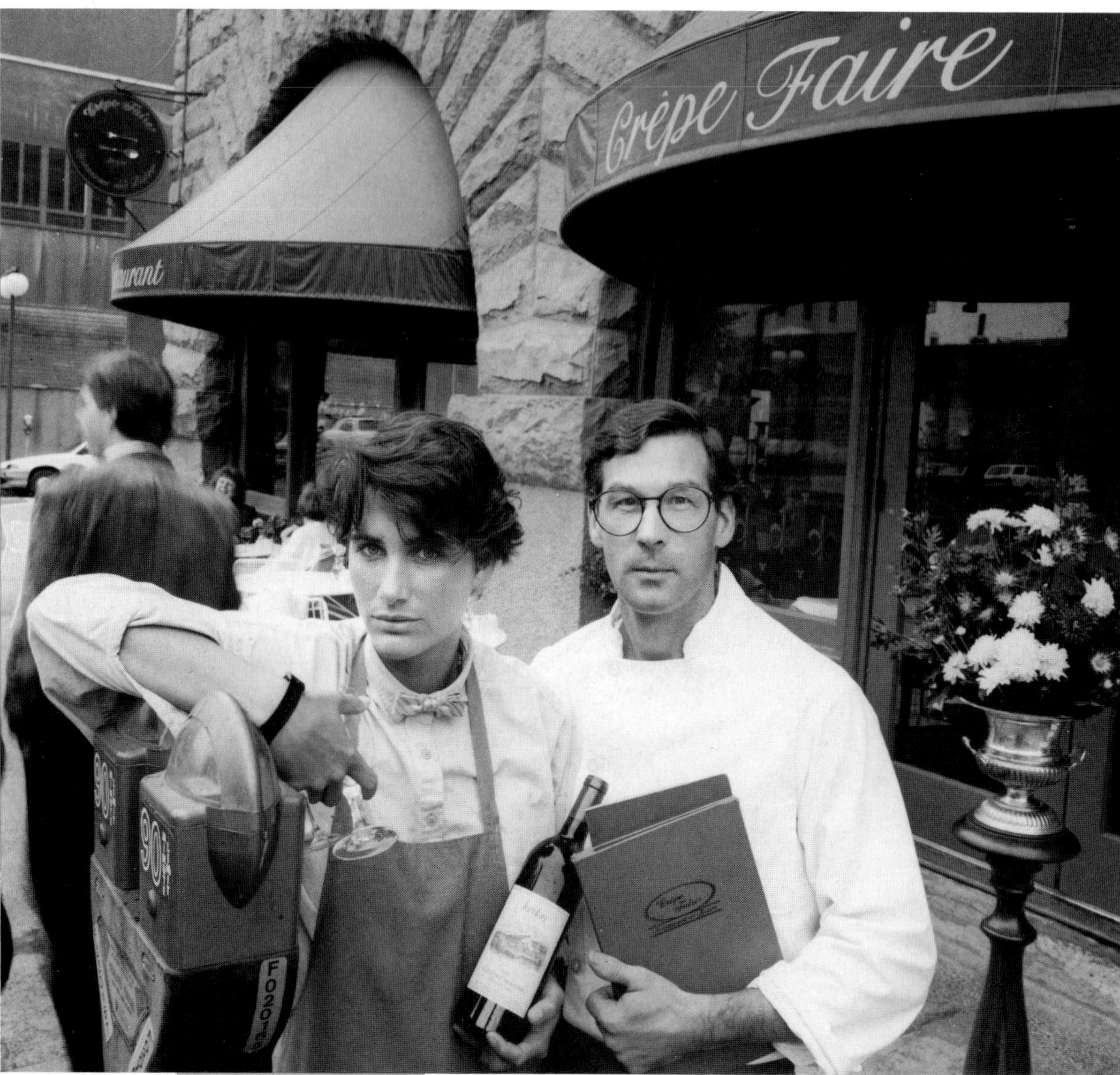

Skidmore Historic District

E25

Tired of standard restaurant fare? Next time, sample the intriguing selections at the Crêpe Faire Restaurant and Bistro established in 1974. There's no mass-production of this timeless treat at Crêpe Faire, where crêpes are all made by hand in the traditional pans. The restaurant is located in the Hazeltine Building, a recent recipient of the Historic Preservation Award as the finest example of commercial building restoration in the city. Although the Brandied Apple Gateau, Shrimp Curry Crêpe, and many other crêpe dishes are still prominent, Crêpe Faire has become a well rounded dining establishment featuring such international dishes as Scallops Moutarde, Seviché, Green Peppercorn Chicken and Croute au Fromage. Indeed, from an early morning breakfast to an after theatre light dinner, Crêpe Faire has a perfect selection for any appetite. Complementing their meals is freshly baked bread, a house blend Stash Tea and a wine list featuring a fine selection of imported and domestic wines highlighted by a sampling of many Oregon wines available by the glass. Oh, on that perfect day this summer, remember Crêpe Faires' sidewalk cafe. Visa. MasterCard. American Express. Carte Blanche. Diners Club.

133 SW Second & Pine
Portland 97204
227-3365

Bistro: Seasonal light fare menu after 2pm

Breakfast
Monday-Friday
7am-10:30am
Saturday 8am-11:30am

Lunch
Monday-Friday
11:30am-2:30pm
Saturday til 3:30pm

Dinner
Monday-Thursday
5:30pm-10pm
Friday-Saturday
6pm-11pm

CHEN'S DYNASTY

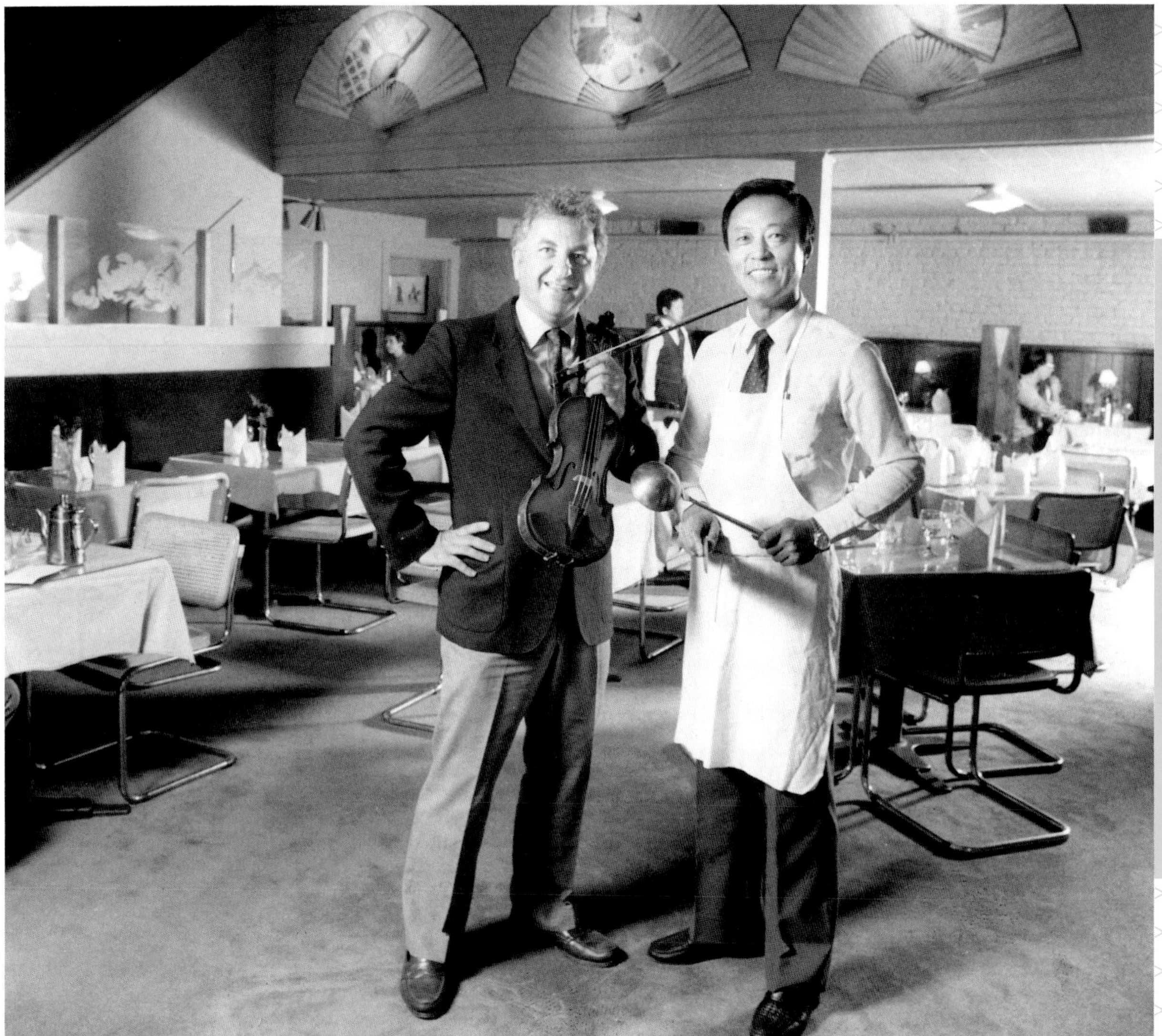

DINING

Impeccably prepared cuisine representing the four main Chinese provinces.

Downtown
F24

A shared passion for impeccably prepared, authentic Chinese cuisine brought Chi-Siung Chen, Master Chef, and Sergiu Luca, internationally renowned violinist, together in a partnership that promises to redefine Portland's expectations about Chinese food forever. Chen's Dynasty is a collaborative effort between two acknowledged masters — "Uncle" Chen, whose culinary pedigree traces directly back to Chiang Kai-shek's personal chef, and Luca, who plays his violin in the major concert halls of the world. The result is Chinese haute cuisine, elegantly prepared and served in a sophisticated environment, combining oriental and contemporary themes. The extraordinary seventeen page menu encompasses a great variety of dishes, and is uniquely divided into four separate sections, representing the major regional cooking styles in China. A number of the dishes prepared at Chen's Dynasty are Portland firsts and are seldom found outside of the People's Republic of China, Taiwan, New York or San Francisco; and full course "imperial banquets" can be arranged with advance notice. Try the "Dragon and Phoenix," a dynamic combination of two dishes — sautéed lobster meat and fiery General Tso's chicken, or "Minced Squab in Nest," an elegant and savory dish, wrapped in lettuce leaves... obviously, the stuff of which dynasties are made. Visa. MasterCard. American Express. Diners Club.

622 SW Washington Street
Portland 97205
248-9491

Sunday-Thursday
11am-10pm
Friday-Saturday
11am-11pm

805 Broadway
Vancouver, WA 98668
(206) 695-1553

China North
12319 Roosevelt Way NE
Seattle, WA 98125
(206) 362-3422

Uncle Chen's
2010 Iowa Street
Bellingham, WA 98225
(206) 733-5255

KASHMIR RESTAURANT

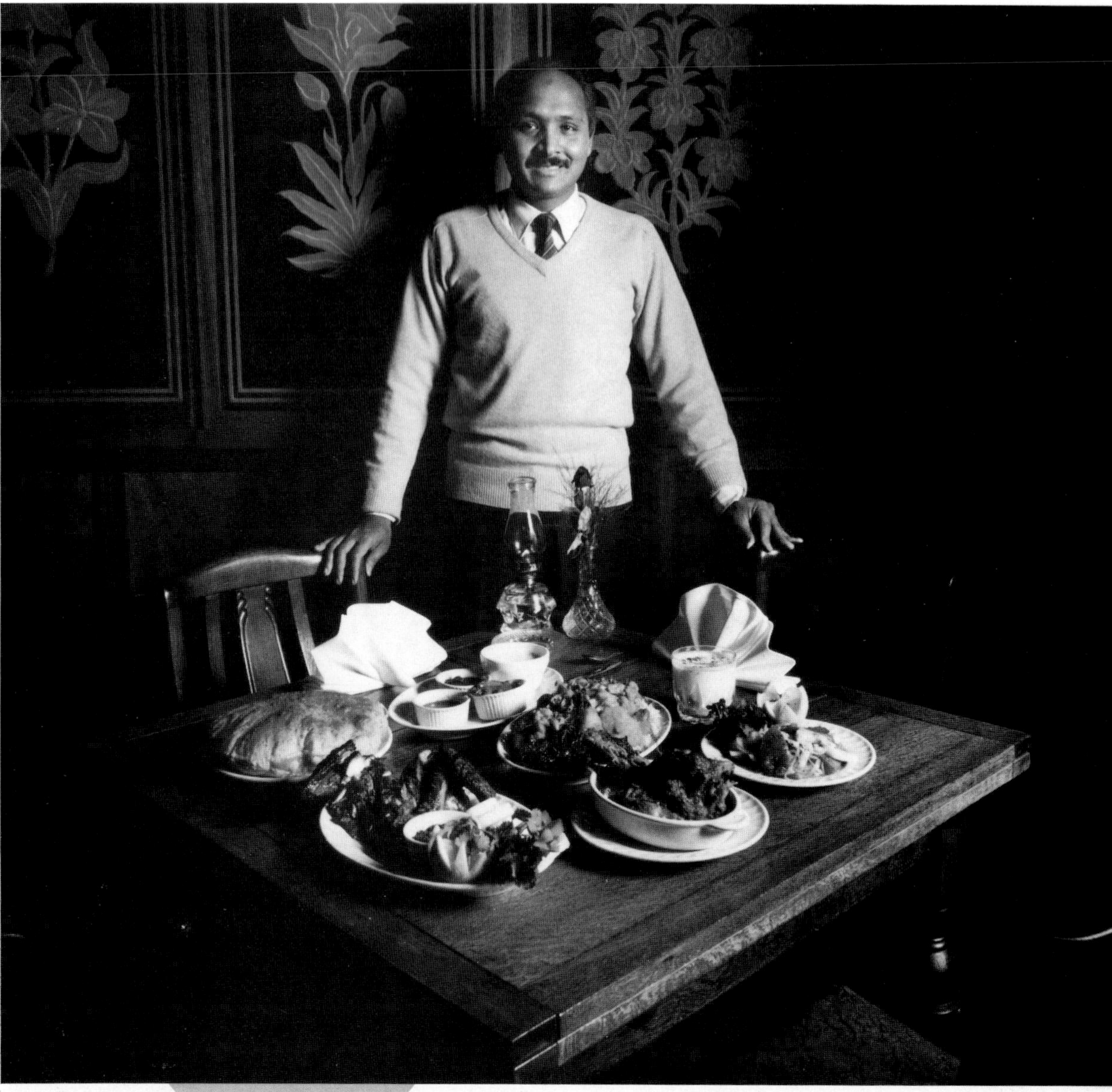

DINING

Offering the great tastes of East India and Pakistan.

Yamhill Historic District

F25

Readers of Oregon Magazine will recognize Kashmir Restaurant, the subject of a cover story in February 1984. As one of the only restaurants in the state devoted to East Indian and Pakistani food, Kashmir has earned critics acclaim: "If any restaurant in Portland has gone from adequate to superlative in the past year, it is Kashmir." Here is the chance to try an exotic dish in an atmosphere that is as colorful as the countries themselves. Select the Lamb Korma, tender morsels of lamb sauteed in special seasonings, saffron and almonds. Or the Tandori Murgh, a whole breast of chicken marinated overnight in spices and yogurt and baked in the oven. Then there is the Kashmiri Biryani, blending the delicacy of lamb with basamati rice and the Alu Ghobi, a tempting dish of cauliflower and potatoes flavored with Kashmir's special seasonings. But the selection does not end with chicken and lamb dishes; Samosa is ground beef wrapped in a dough shell, deep fried and served with chutney; Jhinga Curry is a prawn dish. At Kashmir, even the chapati — a whole wheat leavened bread — is authentic. The Kashmir Restaurant offers a taste of East India and Pakistan at their best. Visa. MasterCard. American Express. Diners Club.

223 SW Stark Street
Portland 97204
222-5247

Lunch
Monday-Friday
11am-2pm

Dinner
Monday-Thursday
5:30pm-9:30pm
Friday-Saturday
5:30pm-10pm

Espresso Bar
Monday-Friday
11am-3pm

When we were very young we had a grandmother who would challenge us to say two dozen double damask dinner napkins very quickly. It was always a struggle to maintain any degree of precision. We think of her at restaurants, where damask and not so damask comes in all shapes and sizes. Napkins serve many useful purposes. In candlelight they add warmth to any table. They are also most effective for hiding inopportune yawns, giggles, smirks and even spills. Restaurants call them linen, even if they're cotton. The washing, ironing and folding of linen is an endless and costly business. Unless you're folding for fun. Then you can be Robin Hood, Napoleon, or even Mr. Gumby.

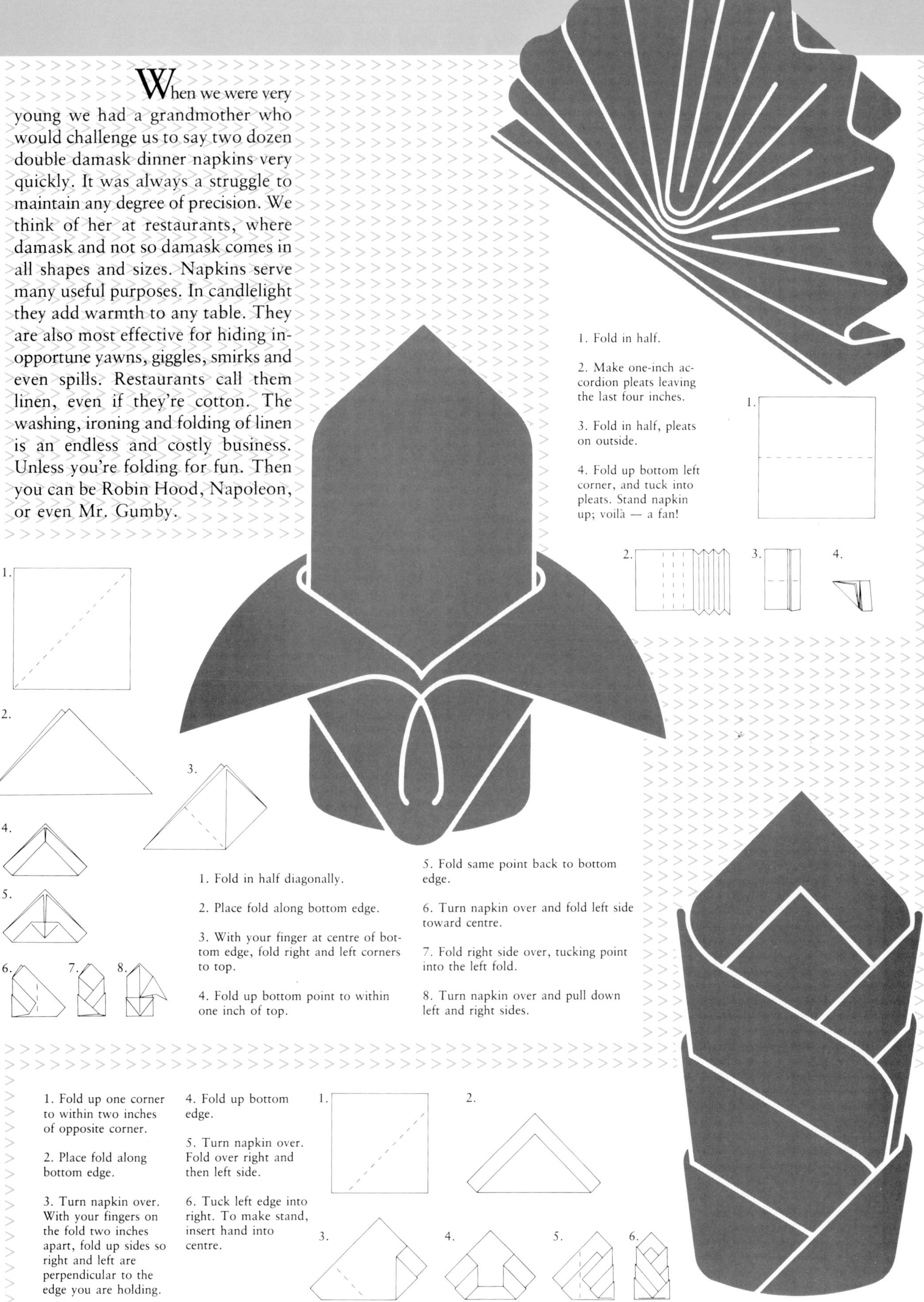

1. Fold in half.

2. Make one-inch accordion pleats leaving the last four inches.

3. Fold in half, pleats on outside.

4. Fold up bottom left corner, and tuck into pleats. Stand napkin up; voilà — a fan!

1. Fold in half diagonally.

2. Place fold along bottom edge.

3. With your finger at centre of bottom edge, fold right and left corners to top.

4. Fold up bottom point to within one inch of top.

5. Fold same point back to bottom edge.

6. Turn napkin over and fold left side toward centre.

7. Fold right side over, tucking point into the left fold.

8. Turn napkin over and pull down left and right sides.

1. Fold up one corner to within two inches of opposite corner.

2. Place fold along bottom edge.

3. Turn napkin over. With your fingers on the fold two inches apart, fold up sides so right and left are perpendicular to the edge you are holding.

4. Fold up bottom edge.

5. Turn napkin over. Fold over right and then left side.

6. Tuck left edge into right. To make stand, insert hand into centre.

CAFÉS AND CASUAL RESTAURANTS

Congenial gathering places for breakfasts, lunches, supper and twenty-four hour cravings; hot spots for cold beer, pasta and salsas, low-cal and healthy, fattening and fabulous.

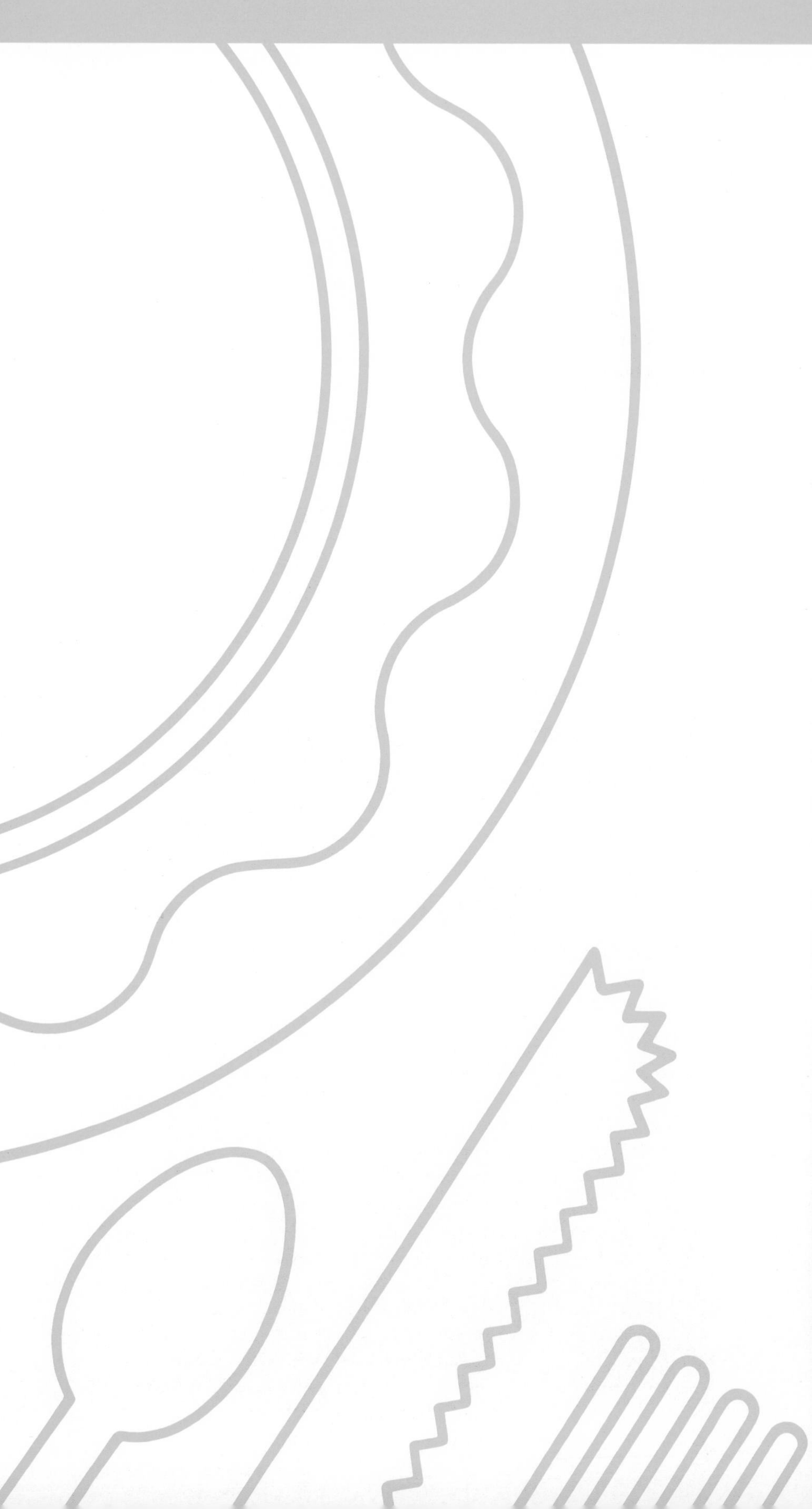

Abou Karim *80*
Alexis Restaurant *76*
Bijou Cafe *73*
Bogart's Joint *85*
Buffalo Gap Saloon and Eatery *78*
Café Vivo *53*
Caro Amico *74*
Casa-U-Betcha *81*
Coffee Ritz *77*
Crêpe Faire Restaurant & Bistro *64*
Edelweiss Sausage & Delicatessen *99*
Executive Sweets, Desserts Etc. *106*
Foothill Broiler *84*
The Gazebo Gallery-Restaurant *72*
Hall Street Bar & Grill *69*
Hot Lips Pizza *82*
Huber's *60*
Jazz de Opus *52*
Macheesmo Mouse *83*
Main Street Grocery *94*
Metro on Broadway *79*
Papa Haydn *70*
Parchman Farm Restaurant and Bar *86*
Paul*Bergen Catering and Charcuterie *92*
Pharmacy Fountain *84*
Rose's Restaurant *75*
13 Coins *71*
The Veritable Quandary *87*

HALL STREET BAR & GRILL

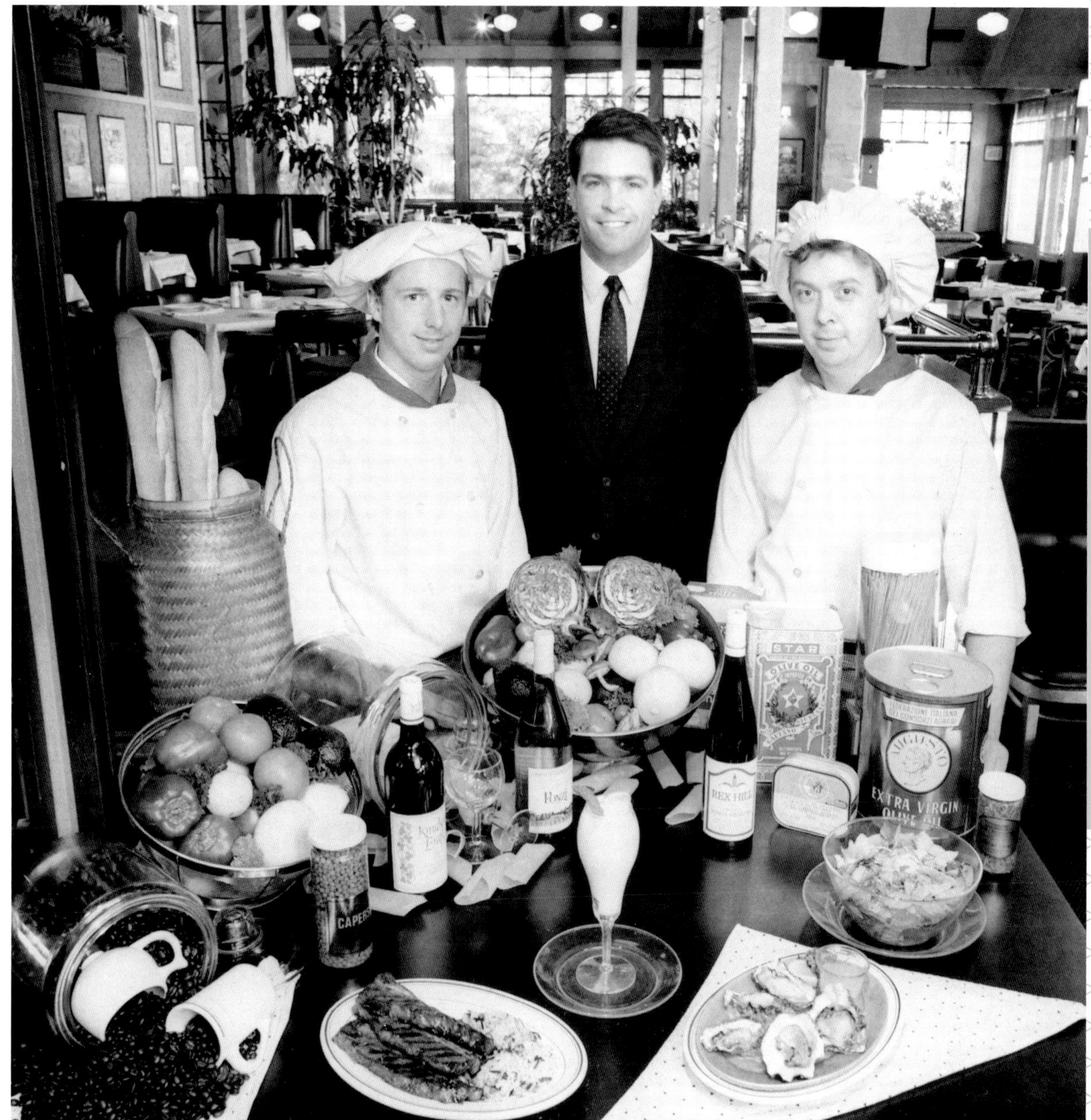

Foods for all moods.

With a promise of "foods for all moods", the Hall Street Bar & Grill earns praise as a rewarding dining experience. Hall Street is sophisticated yet informal. And although dining at Hall Street is an easy-going experience, the kitchen staff is serious about providing memorable foods for every occasion. Oak floors lead to the Hall Street's dining room, decorated with natural-finish wainscoting and a wonderful collection of historic photographs of the Pacific Northwest. By day, large windows amplify the airy feeling of high ceilings supported by rough-hewn timbers; by night, lamps shed their warmth on your menu. The emphasis here is on the bounty of the sea: fresh fish is always part of a daily sheet featuring just-caught selections and other unique specials. A recent touch — the addition of lighter cuts at reduced prices — allows the not-so-hungry diner to save room for Hall Street's spread of unforgettable desserts. The faithful turn to burnt creme, a creamy custard dish with a burnt sugar topping that gives calories a good name. A covered patio and lounge offer full dining and cocktails, and the bar features an extensive beer selection and more than 20 varieties of scotch. Over the years, several personalities from the world of food including Victor and Marcella Hazan and beer expert Michael Jackson, have visited the establishment. Isn't it time to add your name to the list? Reservations available. Visa. MasterCard. American Express.

3775 SW Hall Boulevard
Beaverton 97005
641-6161

Monday-Saturday
11:30am-closing
Sunday 4pm-closing

Beaverton
E3

PAPA HAYDN

CAFES AND CASUAL DINING

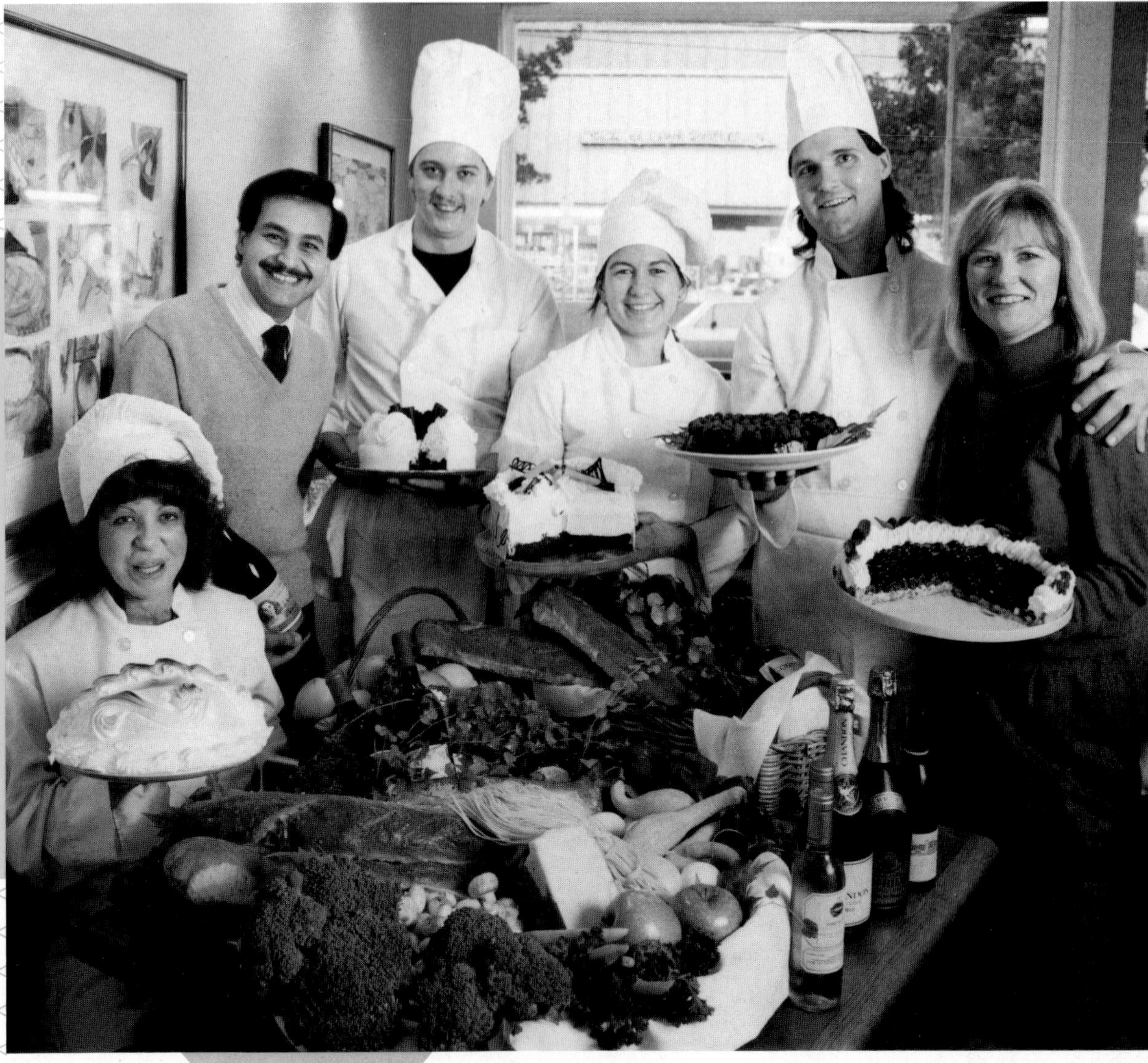

Fresh Northwest cuisine.

Northwest Portland
H17

Southeast Portland
F6

Inspired Northwest cuisine and some of the very best desserts in all the land are to be found at Papa Haydn. Whether it is fresh Columbia salmon or sturgeon, hand-picked chanterelles, Pacific Coast oysters and mussels, or Oregon lamb, all are prepared by creative chefs and served by a courteous staff. Sample the Oregon breast of chicken, petite sirloin and Italian sausage, all grilled over an open fire, or the local salmon en papillote, the ravioli of the week or Papa Haydn's own club sandwich. Then there's dessert. In Portland, dessert and Papa Haydn are synonymous. Consistently rated the city's best by local newspapers, they range from the simple but elegant Almond Torte to the visually stunning Autumn Meringue — three tiers of Swiss Meringue and chocolate mousse wrapped in wide ribbons of dark chocolate. In season there are always fresh local berries for cobblers and fruit tarts, and no less than 25 varieties of delicious pastries are always on display. To complement the food or dessert, both locations have a carefully chosen wine list featuring many premium selections by the glass, including a delightful sampling of dessert wines, fine sherries and ports. On the Westside there is a full-service bar featuring a wide array of specialty drinks, from French aperitifs and margaritas to cognac and coffee drinks. To bring all this goodness to you, Papa Haydn now caters banquets and parties. Visa. MasterCard. American Express.

701 NW 23rd Avenue
Portland 97210
228-7317

Tuesday-Thursday
11:30am-11pm
Friday-Saturday
11:30am-midnight
Sunday Brunch
10am-3pm

5829 SE Milwaukie Avenue
Portland 97202
232-9440

Tuesday-Thursday
11:30am-11:00pm
Friday-Saturday
11:30am-midnight

13 COINS

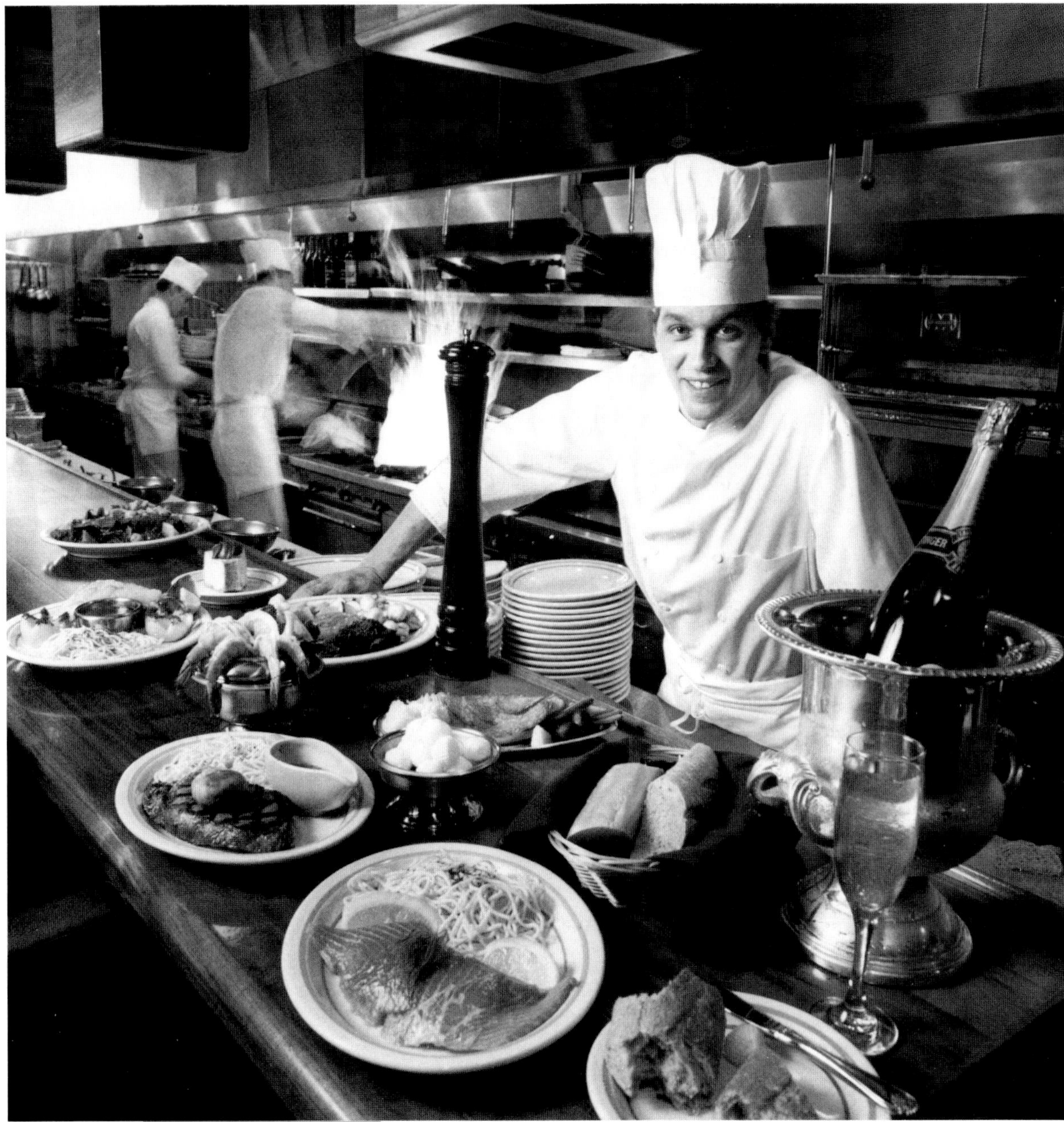

CAFES AND CASUAL DINING

Weekend twenty-four hour gourmet dining.

If mention of "24-hour restaurant" brings to mind a smoke-clogged freeway dive populated by creatures of the night, pay a 3 a.m. visit to 13 Coins Restaurant and you're in for a treat. Order the Australian rock lobster or filet of salmon or anything else from a menu with more than 160 entrees backed by service that just won't quit. 13 Coins resides in the sparkling Koin Center Building, a brick tower that itself is worth the trip. The restaurant features a piano lounge and dining room with high- backed booths and counter seating where you can watch the chefs at work. The focus is on Italian food and wine, and just a sampling of the menu looks like this: The pasta — smoked salmon fettuccine, tortellini dela casa and linguini with crab sauce; the seafood — trout, sole, oysters, halibut, salmon, frog legs and prawns; the steaks in the style of New York, filet mignon, T-bone and Salisbury; the veal scallopini, parmigiana and piccata; then there are several poultry dishes and omelettes of considerable stature. 13 Coins gets its name from a Peruvian folk tale where the coins represent undying love, care and concern; in the restaurant's case you can add a few more: service, style and selection, around the clock. Visa. MasterCard. American Express. Diners Club. Carte Blanche.

KOIN Center
213 SW Clay Street
Portland 97201
224-2646

Monday-Thursday
11am-4am
Friday-Saturday
24 hours a day
Closed Monday at 4am

Downtown
H24

THE GAZEBO GALLERY-RESTAURANT

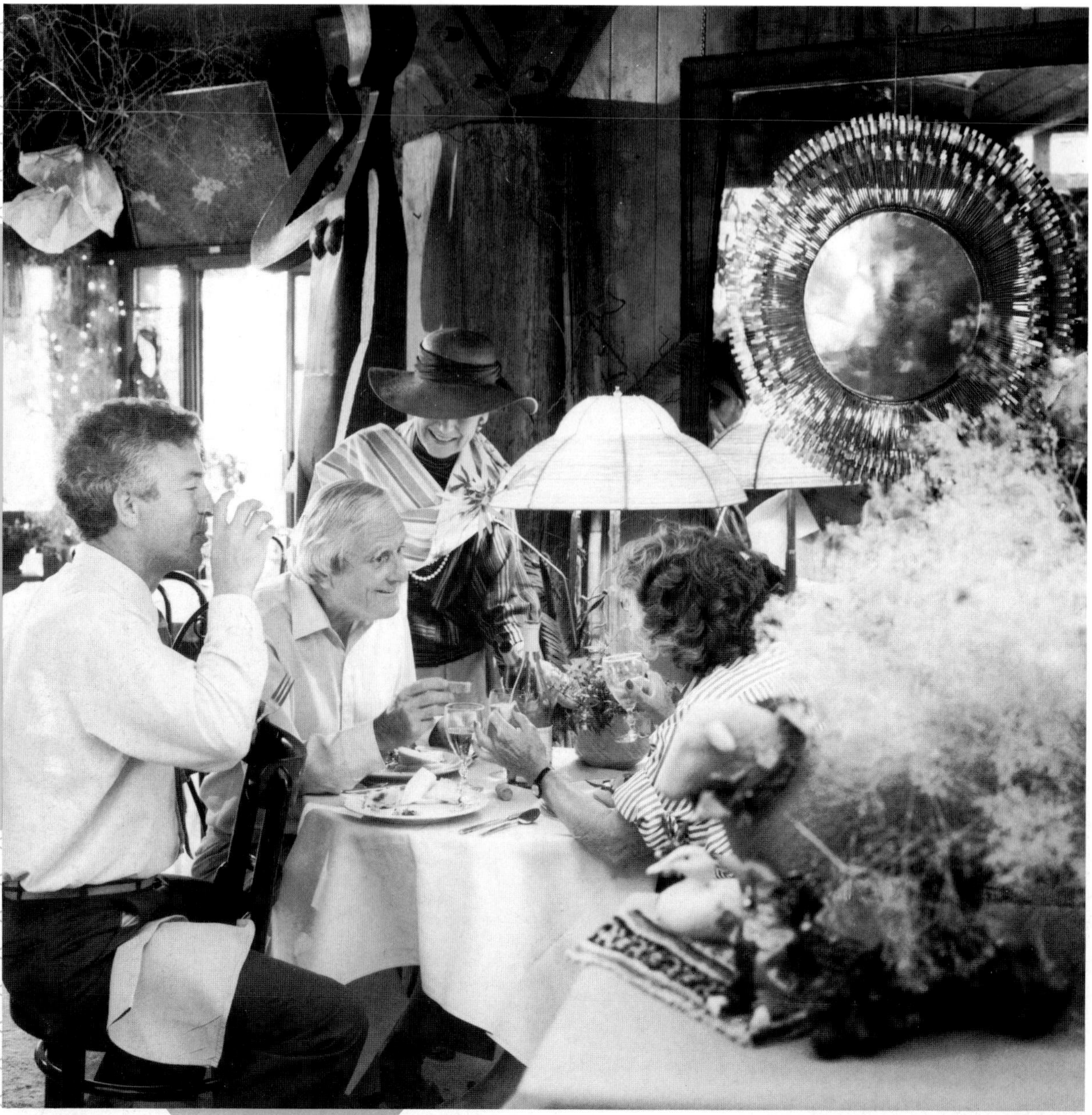

Art and food with a flair.

Lake Oswego/
Lake Grove

H4

The word Gazebo has happy connotations for Elizabeth Morrow, suggesting leisurely summer homes designed to maximize indoor space and providing views of the surrounding countryside. Her yearning for a venue expressing her very own sense of style and love of the visual beauty was realized some fifteen years ago when she recruited the services of her architect husband and the dream of the Gazebo was born — an airy, octagonal gallery-restaurant atop Mount Sylvania in Lake Oswego. She began by displaying the works of a small group of artists; when her taste in both art and cuisine appealed to her patrons, she added more — more art, more food, more hours. What stays the same at the Gazebo is Elizabeth Morrow's flair — her bright hats and personal touches, her eclectic passion and skill at integrating and harmonizing the ever-changing environment, and her commitment to providing fresh, delicious and creative meals with an international flavor to complement the atmosphere. A suggestion: before you go, put on something bright and expressive. After all, you're about to play a role in a dream come true. Visa. MasterCard. American Express.

Mountain Park
11 Mount Jefferson Terrace
Lake Oswego 97034
635-2506

Lunch
Tuesday-Sunday
11:45am-2:15pm

Dinner
Thursday-Saturday
5:45pm-8:15pm

BIJOU CAFE

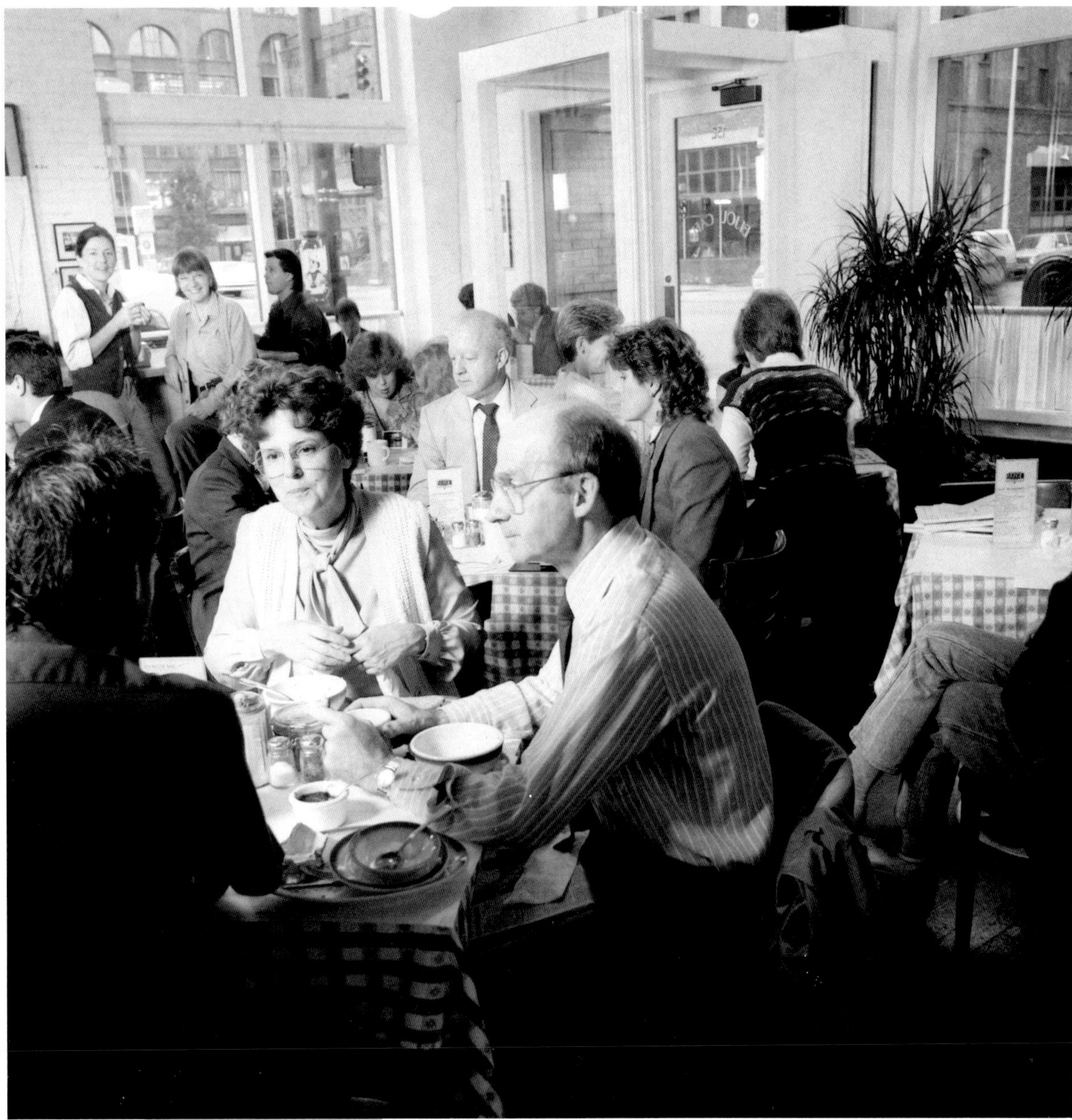

CAFES AND CASUAL DINING

Extensive menu, wholesome food, good value, quick service.

We'd let you in on a secret about the Bijou Cafe, but we're too late. Lots of food writers and other notables from Cuisine Magazine, United Airlines' magazine, Food Day, USA Today, Willamette Week, The Oregonian and others have written about the Bijou's extensive menu and wholesome food, or have published its recipes. Wolfgang Puck visited twice, and even Wally and Andre of "My Dinner with André" fame came by. The Bijou serves breakfast — all-day — and a hearty lunch at its Third Avenue location, with bottomless cups of coffee and an eclectic menu. A sample: the well-dressed classic known as the Caesar salad, roast beef hash (they roast it and dice it themselves), sumptuous latté and mocha drinks from the espresso machine, home-made salsa, Spanish rice, whole grain waffles and pancakes, burgers, milkshakes and more. The Bijou opened in 1978, and in 1982 owners Bonnie Allen and Kathy Hagberg more than doubled the dining area while increasing seating by only 20 percent to give the cafe a spacious, comfortable feeling. The cafe is elegant in its simplicity, with wood floors, blue-and-white-checked tablecloths, mirrors, high white walls and lots of natural light. It's a great spot — but it's no secret.

132 SW Third Avenue
Portland 97204
222-3187

Daily
7am-3pm

Skidmore Historic District

E25

CARO AMICO

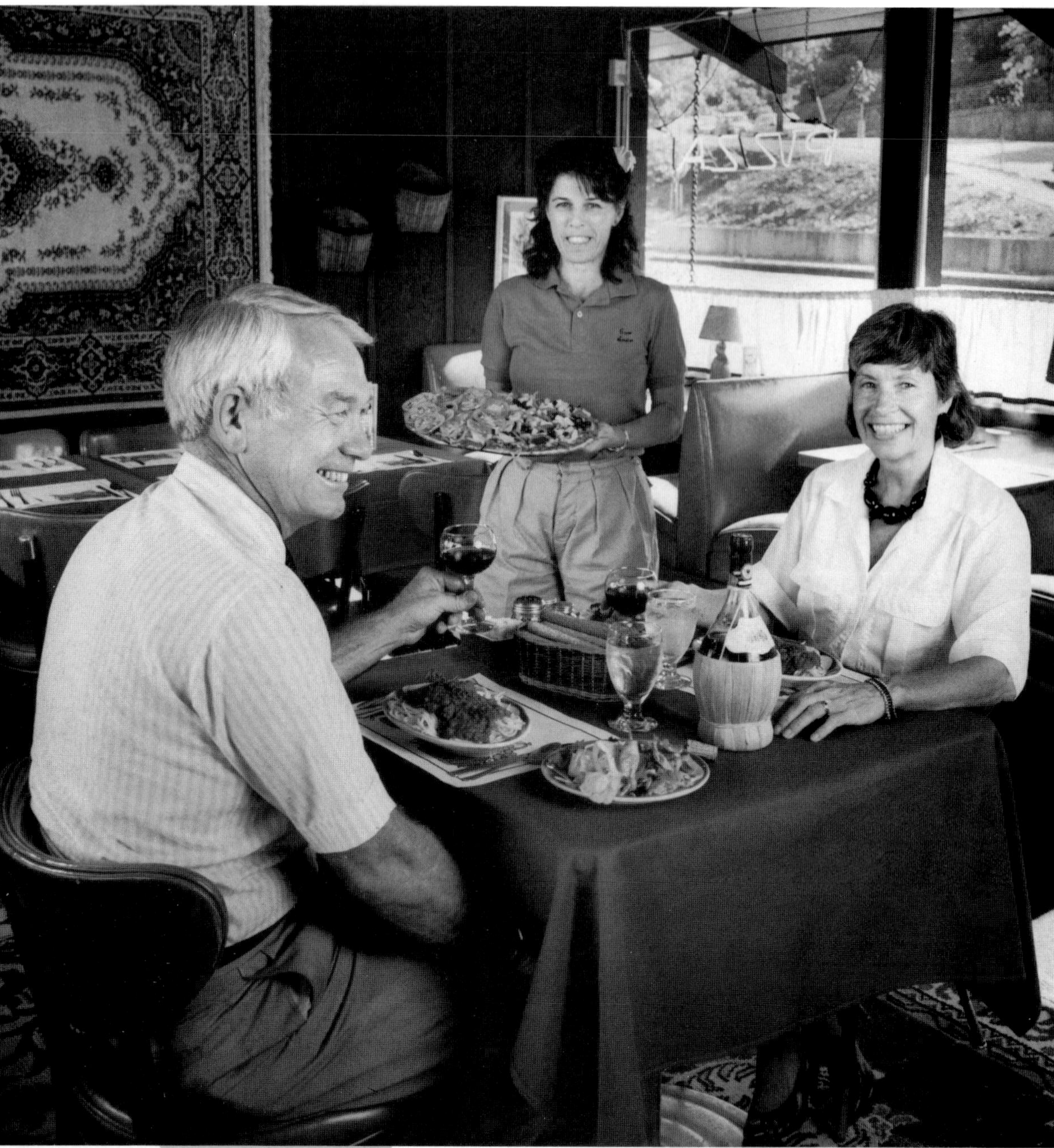

Pizza and Italian cuisine in a comfortable atmosphere.

Corbett-Johns Landing

F6

In a three-story Lair Hill Victorian Home, Portland restaurant patrons were first introduced to a quaint entrée called pizza. It was August 1949. Now, at a time when the average age of a pizza restaurant seems more like forty days than nearly forty years, Caro Amico lives on, more robust than a singing Italian waiter. Still owned by the same family, Caro Amico, which means "dear friend," continues to use recipes essentially unchanged over the years. And its oval, thin-crust pizza, cut in squares and served on a board, will convince you why Fred Baker's legacy is a Portland institution. Kenneth Baker and Elsie McFarland are the owners now, and they've left Caro Amico's interior basically unaltered since the 1960s, reasoning that cozy and comfortable tables and booths with tablecloths and fresh flowers are always in style. Caro Amico also offers Neopolitan style spaghetti and pastas; a full-service bar; wines from Italy, California and Oregon; bottled beers and Budweiser and Grant's Ale on tap. Every July, the restaurant's vitality is demonstrated with an anniversary celebration that erupts into a parking lot dance with bands, clowns, balloons and, of course, the only pizza good enough to earn a place in Portland's heart since 1949. Visa. MasterCard.

3606 SW Barbur
Boulevard
Portland 97201
223-6895

Tuesday-Saturday
5pm-midnight
Sunday 4pm-11pm

ROSE'S RESTAURANT

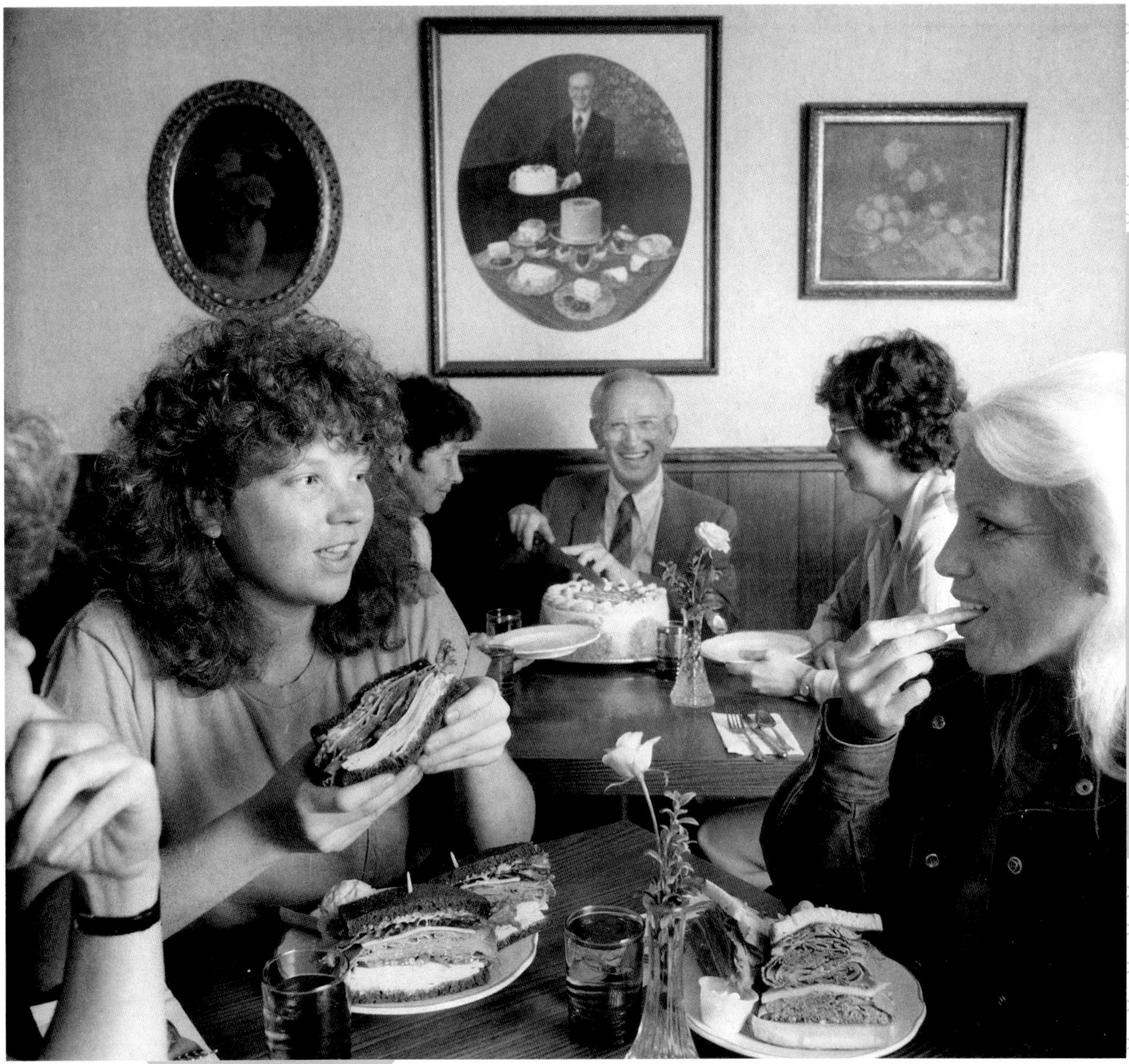

CAFES AND CASUAL DINING

Like going home for a meal.

If you're tired of restaurants that serve everything but food, try Rose's. Dining here is like going home for a meal, where mom fills your plate and says, "Eat up, it's good for you." The chef never scrimps on quality or quantity, whether it's the giant gourmet sandwiches (a meal in themselves); gigantic cakes, tortes and rolls, or the omelets, made from three large grade A eggs and filled to your heart's content. The Reuben sandwich may well be the largest on the continent — certainly there is none better. The chicken matzo ball soup and cheese blintzes are made right in the kitchen and the lox, cream cheese and bagel will not disappoint you. The extensive menu includes a complete selection for children, plus lunch and dinner specials for families and busy executives alike. Then there's the "Nascher's Delight", a splendid table buffet for two from the deli. Best of all, the prices are reasonable. Now more than thirty years old, the restaurant was named after its founder, Rose Naftalin. Owned since 1968 by Max Birnbach and junior partner Ivan Runge, the business has expanded to three locations, evidence that Portlanders know what's good for them. Visa. MasterCard. Diners Club. Carte Blanche.

315 NW 23rd Avenue
Portland 97210
227-5181

Monday-Thursday
7am-11:30pm
Friday 7am-12:30am
Saturday 8am-12:30am
Sunday 8am-11:30pm

Northwest Portland

I17

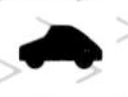

Menlo Park Plaza
12329 NE Glisan Street
Portland 97230
254-6545

same hours

Northeast Portland

D10

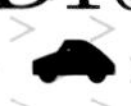

Beaverton Town Square
11995 SW Beaverton
Hillsdale Highway
Beaverton 97005
643-4287

same hours

Beaverton

E2

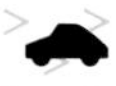

ALEXIS RESTAURANT

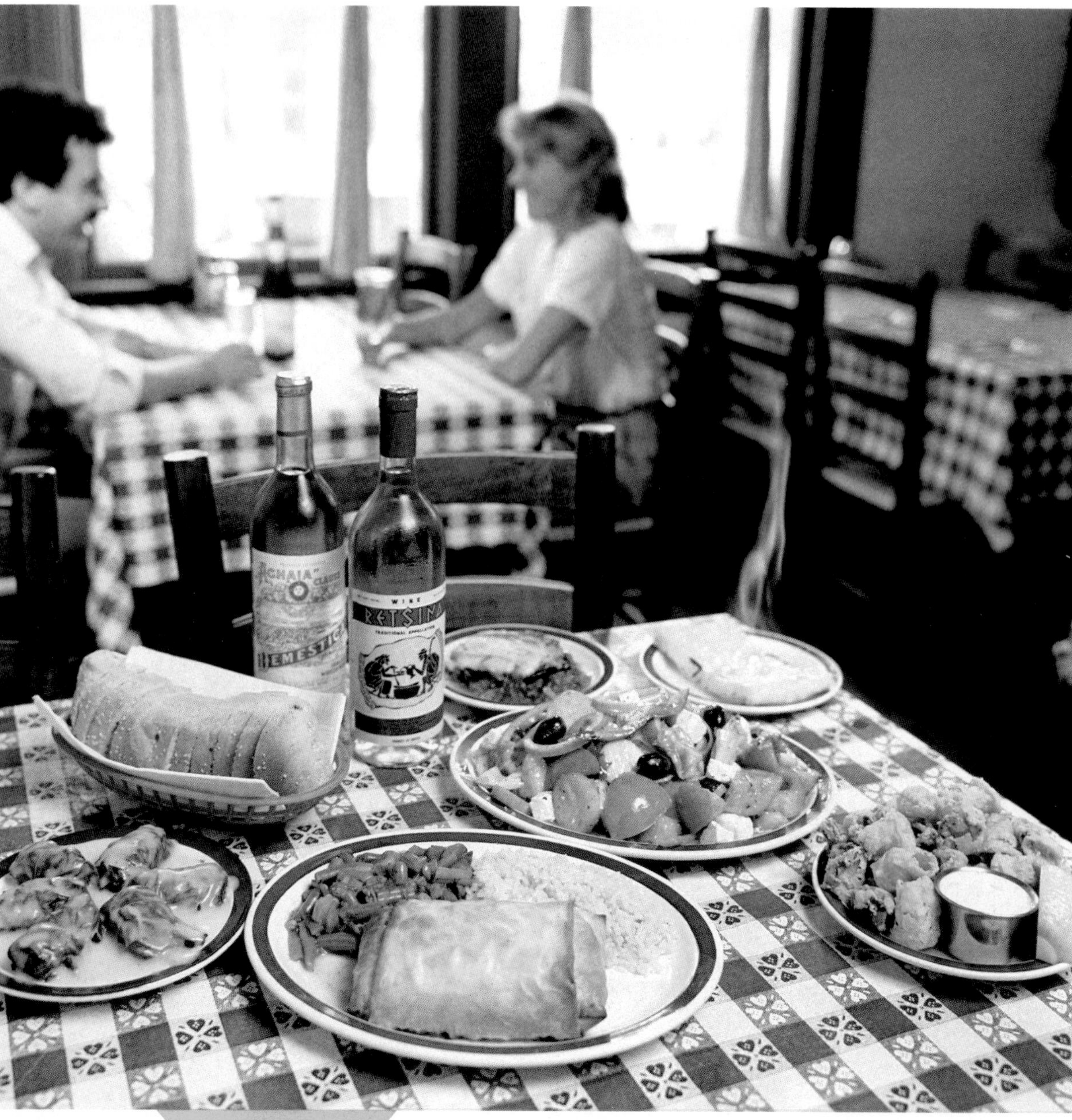

CAFES AND CASUAL DINING

Homemade Greek recipes, lively Greek atmosphere.

Old Town

E25

Drawn first by relics of ancient Greek glory, tourists now travel to Greece and the beautiful, blue Aegean Sea for the warm climate, equally warm hospitality, and the wonderfully creative cuisine. You can travel half way around the world for this experience, or go to the Alexis Restaurant, where Alexis Bakouros has transplanted a little bit of old Greece in the style of a friendly Greek taverna. This is a family business, and the whole family participates. Voula and Ilia Bakouros and Theodora and Gerasimos Tsirimiagos prepare and serve a fine variety of authentic Greek dishes. There's Moussaka, Greek Salad, Kalamarakia — fried squid, Souvlaki — a delicately flavored lamb shiskebob — and Dolmathes — grape leaves stuffed with a spicy meat filling; Kleftiko — buttery filo dough filled with lamb, mushrooms and cheese — and Saganaki, Kasseri cheese, flambé. For dessert, try the Boughatsa, a special custard and filo creation prepared from an old family recipe. Whatever savory dish you choose, you'll find Alexis a warm, festive place where the Ouzo flows freely, and the people serving you are as genuine as the dishes they set on your table. Zorba would approve. Visa. MasterCard. American Express. Diners Club. Carte Blanche.

215 West Burnside
Portland 97209
224-8577

Lunch
Monday-Friday
11:30-2pm

Dinner
Sunday-Thursday
5pm-11pm
Friday-Saturday
5pm-Midnight

COFFEE RITZ

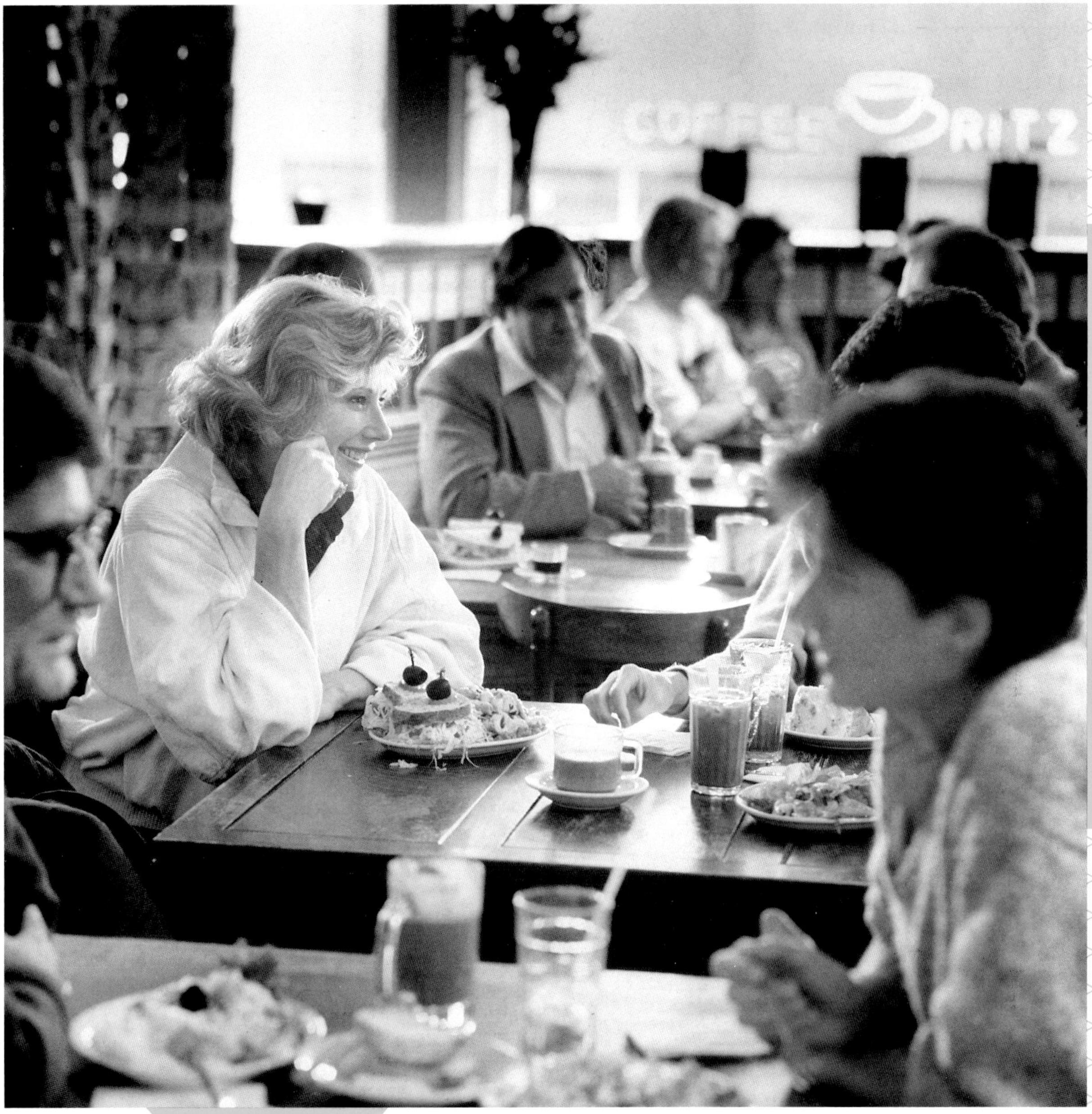

Where people meet.

Coffee Ritz is a small, centrally located, specialty restaurant with European flair. Designed to offer their customers a comfortable yet professional atmosphere, the restaurant has offered quality lunches, gourmet coffee drinks, cold beverages and delectable pastries to their ever-growing and loyal clientele for 10 years. The mixed aroma of rich gourmet coffees and fine pastries baking help create the perfect breakfast meeting place. A breakfast with croissants or bran muffins, cinnamon puffs with fresh squeezed orange juice and Coffee Ritz — a blend of espresso and Mexican hot chocolate — will start your morning right. For the business person, lunch offers a welcome break from the daily grind with an offering of savory homemade soups, such as rich French Onion with fresh grated cheese and homemade croutons, a wide variety of gourmet dishes such as their famous Caesar salad, Torte Rustica or the Baked Brie in Brioche. The Coffee Ritz is the perfect place for an afternoon's respite; the busy shopper will enjoy gourmet teas and scones. Splurge with espresso and chocolates or sample a variety of pastries that would satisfy the most fickle sweet-tooth. The same style and savvy that is associated with the cafe is now available from the Ritz Sisters creative catering service. Coffee Ritz is a tasteful way to take a break, plan your next party or simply relax and enjoy. Visa. MasterCard. American Express.

The Galleria
Second Floor
921 SW Morrison Street
Portland 97205
223-9649

Monday-Friday
7:30am-9pm
Saturday 8am-6pm
Sunday 11am-5pm

Downtown

F23

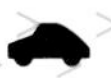

BUFFALO GAP SALOON & EATERY

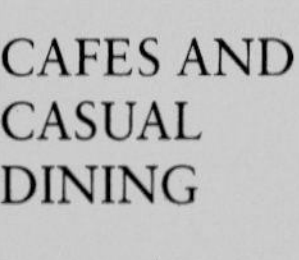

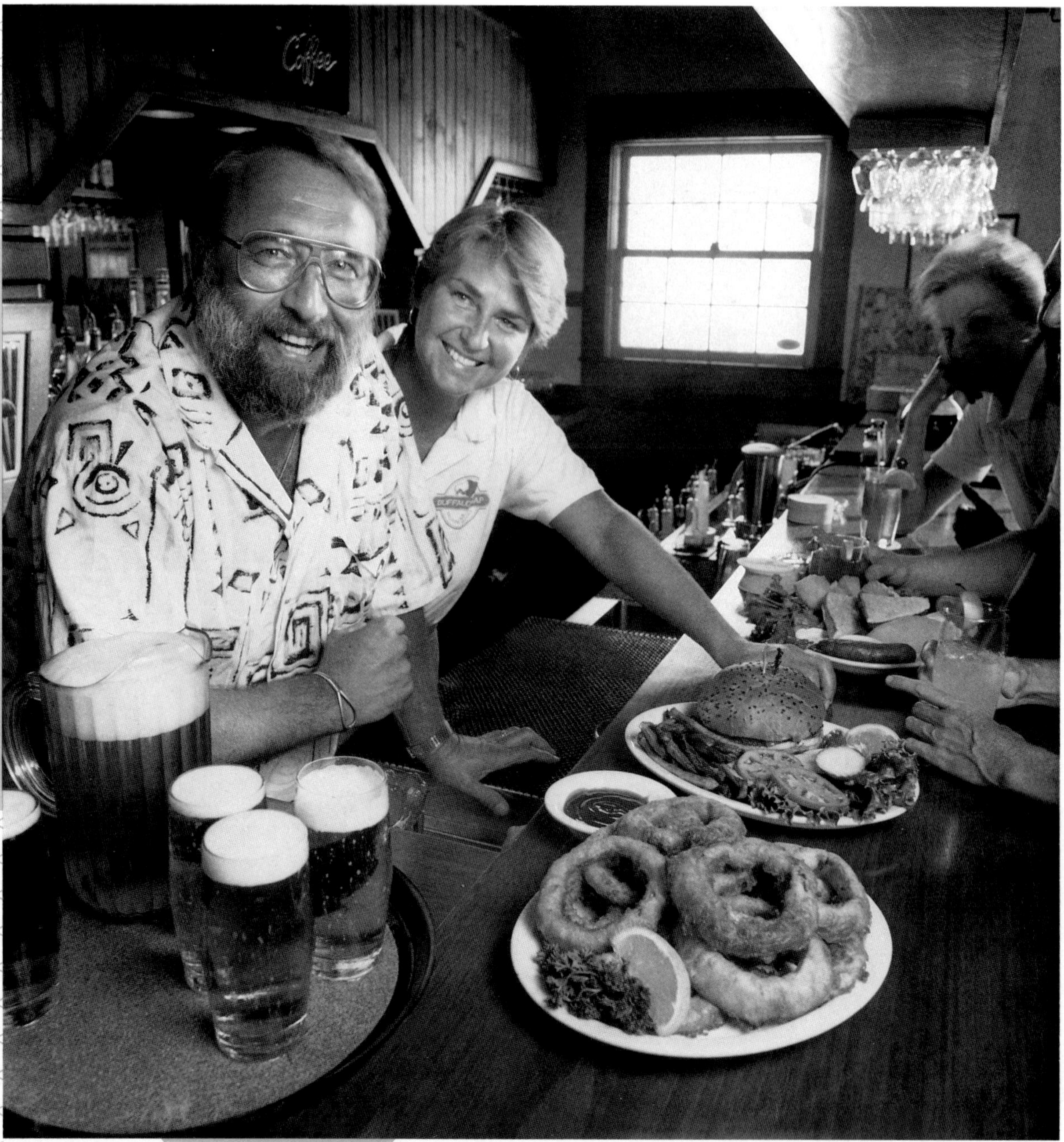

CAFES AND CASUAL DINING

Square meals and cocktails at people's prices.

Corbett-Johns Landing

F6

Part of Portland's architectural character derives from its large number of thriving businesses happily ensconced in renovated buildings. Among the most successful of such historical graftings is the Buffalo Gap, housed in a much-refurbished former brothel, which these days provides wholly licit pleasures. Serving a broad selection of comestibles for breakfast, lunch and old fashioned suppers, the Buffalo Gap specializes in "square meals and cocktails at people's prices" until 2:30 every morning. And we're talking two floors here, one of the few places in town where you can go dressed to the nines or in deckside attire. The pub-like main floor sports a large separate game room, including pool tables, pinball and videogames, while the "attic" upstairs features an outside deck to compliment its casual nightclub ambience. Customer accommodation is a founding principle. So while the menu offers over 75 printed choices, pizza, sandwiches and omelette combos are made to order for particular palates. Known citywide for its onion rings and pizza, the Buffalo Gap even provides hard-to-find live music, Monday, Tuesday, Wednesday, Thursday and Saturday nights. With such conviviality, it's no wonder the place is a favorite with discriminating restaurant workers and night owls. Visa. MasterCard.

6835 SW Macadam Avenue
Portland 97219
244-7111

Monday-Friday 7am-2:30am
Saturday 8am-2:30am
Sunday 9am-2:30am

METRO ON BROADWAY

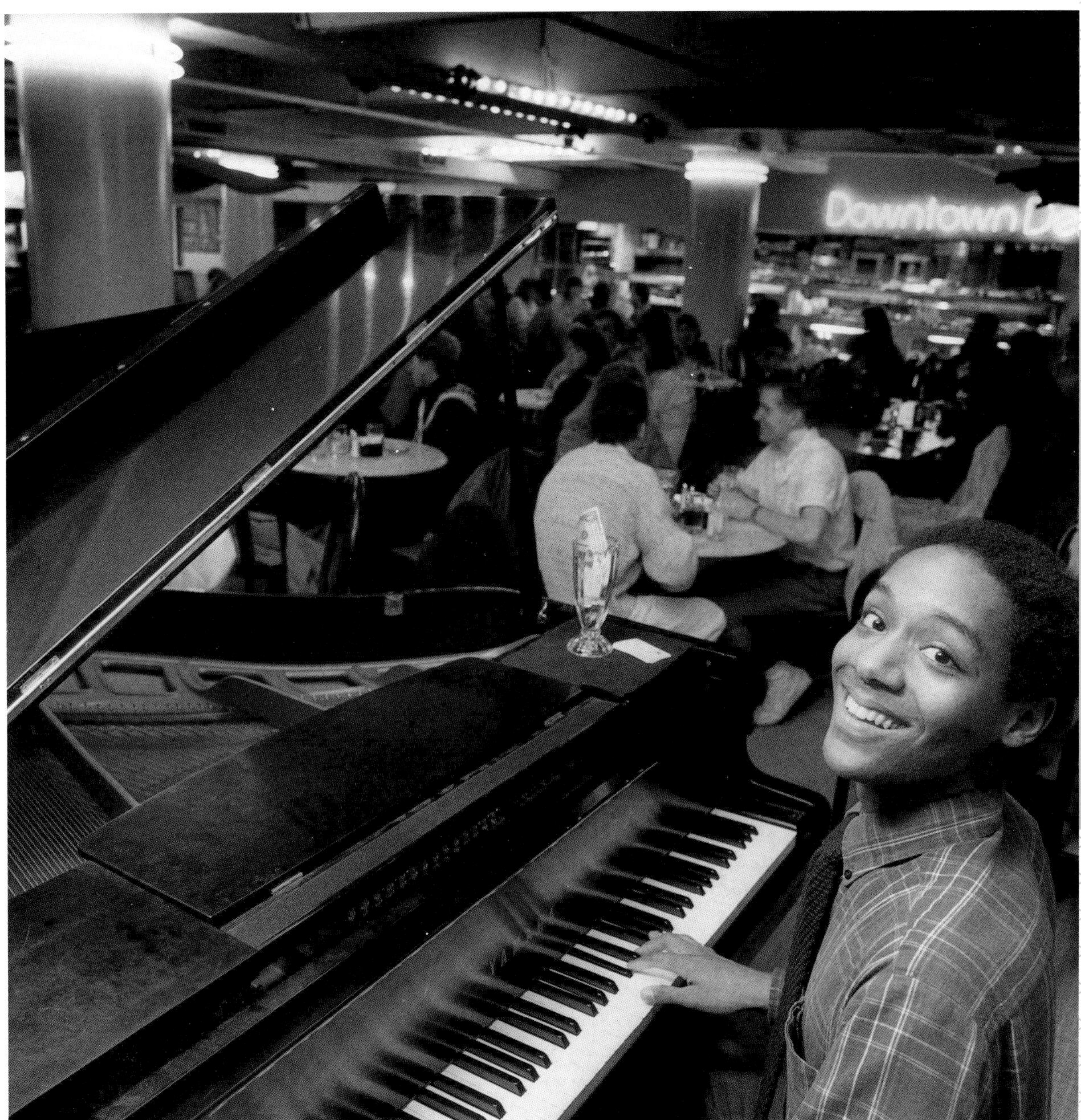

Restaurant-cafe with neon signs and ethnic cuisines.

It won't do to describe the Metro on Broadway as a sort of art-deco restaurant-cafe with neon signs and ethnic cuisines — but it's a start. It won't suffice to say that no matter what the weather, it's always festival time there. Or even to offer the information that six separate establishments serve everything from home fries to champagne, pizzas to crepes, and muffins to frozen yogurt, from early morn till midnight. And it's not enough to say it's a hangout for an assortment of Portland artistes, fashion-conscious bohemians of the 80's, or that you have to sit close to the piano to hear the jazz over a hundred semi-private celebrations. Nevertheless, all those things need to be said. There ought to be a word about the Metro's subterranean character, something more about the selection of cappuccinos, espressos, and coffees, the beers and decidedly potable wines which can be bought by the glass, the platter-sized cookies, and their daily offerings of what is one of the city's largest selection of gourmet desserts. Suffice to say that it's a warm, lively place to eat, meet friends, peruse a magazine over coffee, or just people watch. The next time you ride light rail downtown, visit the Arlene Schnitzer Concert Hall, catch a first run movie, or visit Pioneer Square, go see for yourself. It can't be described because it's different for everybody all the time. Visa. MasterCard.

911 SW Broadway at Taylor
Portland 97205
224-0835

Monday-Thursday 7am-11pm
Friday 7am-midnight
Saturday 9am-midnight
Sunday 11am-8pm

ABOU KARIM AUTHENTIC LEBANESE CUISINE

CAFES AND CASUAL DINING

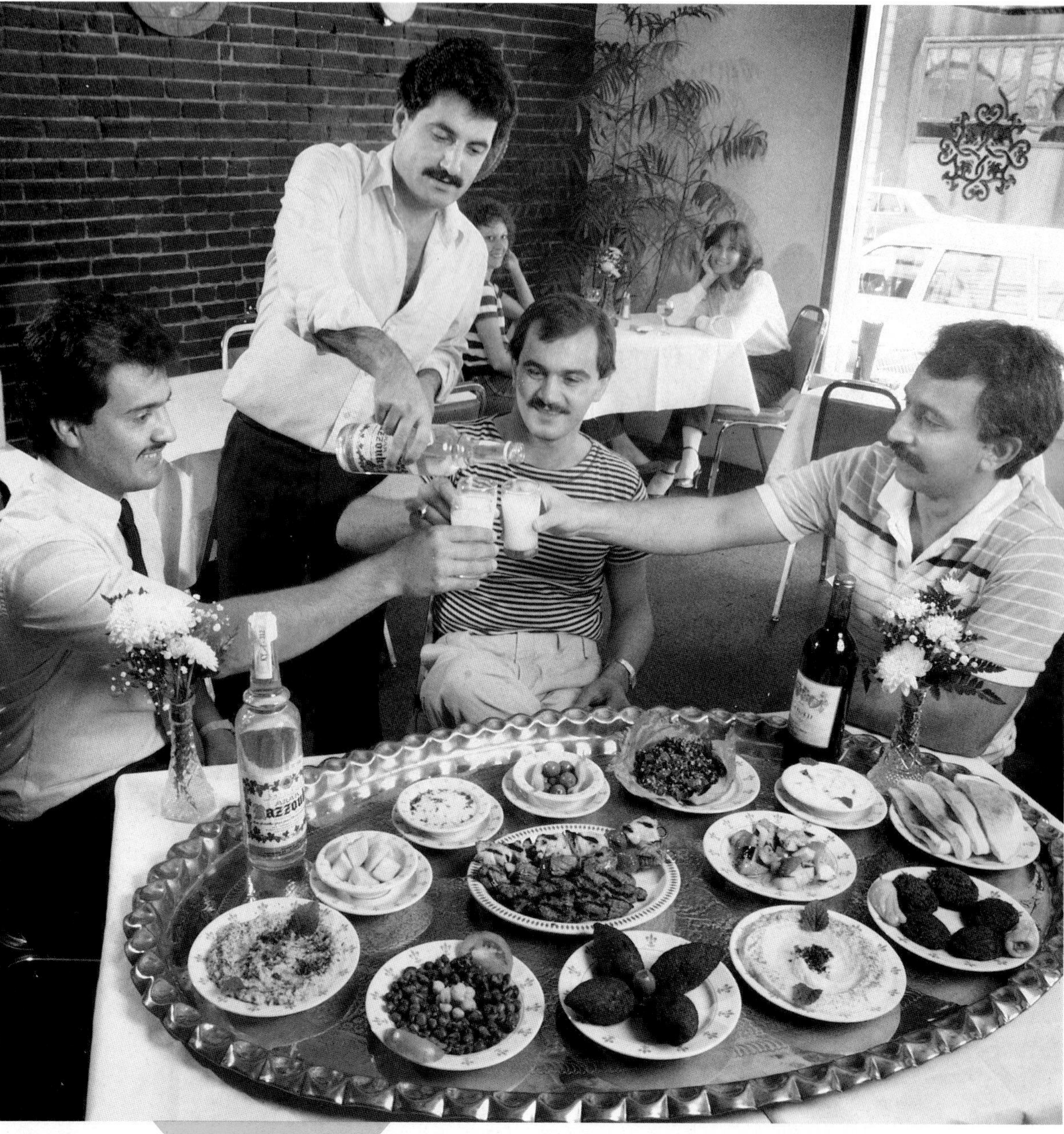

Fresh, healthy, authentic Lebanese cuisine.

Skidmore Historic District

E25

Secretly, we all yearn for an escape from our typical dining habits. When that mood hits, search out Abou Karim; you're in for a real treat. For more than ten years, owners Sami and Diane Alaeddine have helped Portland diners escape by serving them authentic Lebanese food and drink. This Middle Eastern cuisine is delicately seasoned, yet exotic, with lamb as the favorite. Try it flavored with cinnamon, ground and stuffed in cabbage rolls, skewered and broiled, roasted and spiced, or part of a delicious stew. There's chicken, lamb, or beef in kebabs or unusual pita bread sandwiches. All dishes are prepared with the freshest ingredients and over half the entrées are vegetarian specialties. Try the falafel, a deep-fried vegetarian sandwich made of ground garbanzo beans mixed with parsley, herbs and spices — or the mezza — a melange of exotic salads, stuffed grape leaves and kebabs. Health-conscious diners will appreciate another benefit of Abou Karim's menu: almost all items are approved by the American Heart Association. Ask about any item on the menu — remember, part of the enjoyment is to try new dishes. The atmosphere is seductive: Arabic music plays softly in the background, colorful tapestries hang on the wall. Abou Karim has catered to Saudi sheiks on private jets and, in Portland, it caters to you. To celebrate their tenth year in business Abou Karim added a brand new banquet room to the restaurant. Visa. MasterCard. American Express.

221 SW Pine Street
Portland 97204
223-5058

Tuesday-Saturday
11am-10pm

CASA-U-BETCHA

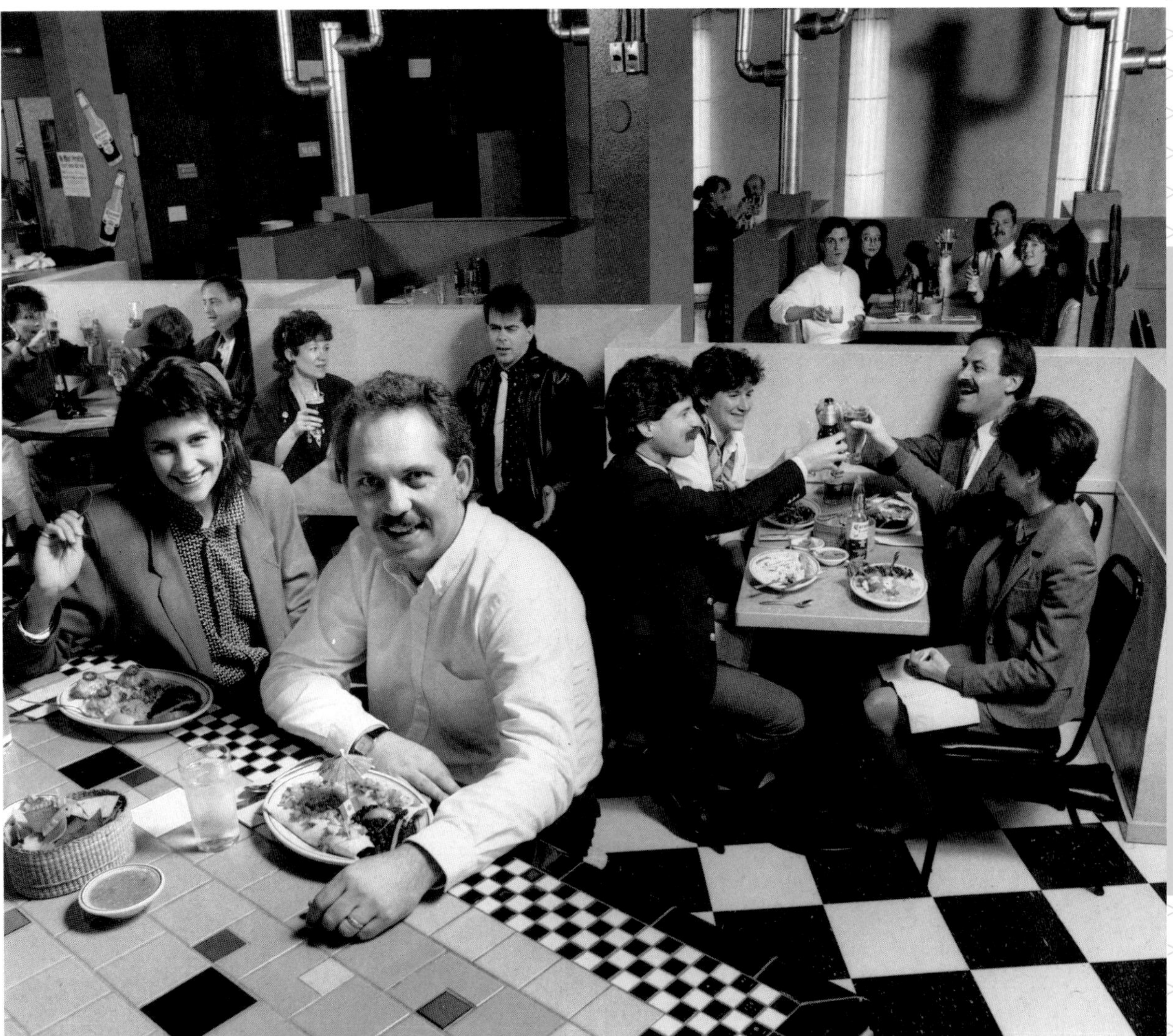

Casa-U-Betcha ...hot stuff.

Northwest Portland

I18

Explore the land of sheet-metal cacti, corrugated fiberglass clouds, and colors not found in nature and you'll discover Casa- U-Betcha — fastest-rising star in Portland's Mexican-food galaxy. The bizarre decor of this self-professed "Taco Club" is but an intriguing introduction to a restaurant known for its tasty variety of Latin cuisine. Owners John Stafford and Jeff Steichan describe their food as "delectibly homemade" and employ cooking techniques not found this side of the border to create memorable Mexican dishes. You'll notice something's different in addition to the decor as soon as your basket of chips and red and green salsas arrive at your table. The chips are blue corn and both salsas are incredible blends of fresh vegetables and spices. You won't want to stop there; try the pollo dorado (stuffed chicken breast) or choose from a variety of fresh seafood entrees: such as Chilean sea bass, lobster, razor clams or marlin. Most entrees are complimented by black beans or Mexican pastas. These side dishes are yet another indication of Casa-U-Betcha's commitment to quality and authenticity. Casa-U-Betcha also sports one of Portland's most "colorful" bars. You'll enjoy a wide array of beverages that include Mexican Hot Chocolate, Mexican beers and "Blue Margaritas." In its short time here, Casa-U-Betcha has become a gathering spot for artists, musicians and politicians drawn to Ethnic Row, Northwest Portland's collection of international restaurants. And while half the fun is joining them for lunch or dinner, if you can't get to Casa-U-Betcha, they'll cater your next party or meeting — and bring Mexico's best to you. Visa. MasterCard.

612 NW 21st Avenue
Portland 97209
222-4833

Lunch
Monday-Friday
11:30am-2:30pm

Bar
Monday-Thursday
11:30am-1am
Friday 11:30am-2:30am
Saturday 5pm-2:30am
Sunday 5pm-1am

Dinner
Sunday-Thursday
5pm-10pm
Friday-Saturday
5pm-11pm

HOT LIPS PIZZA

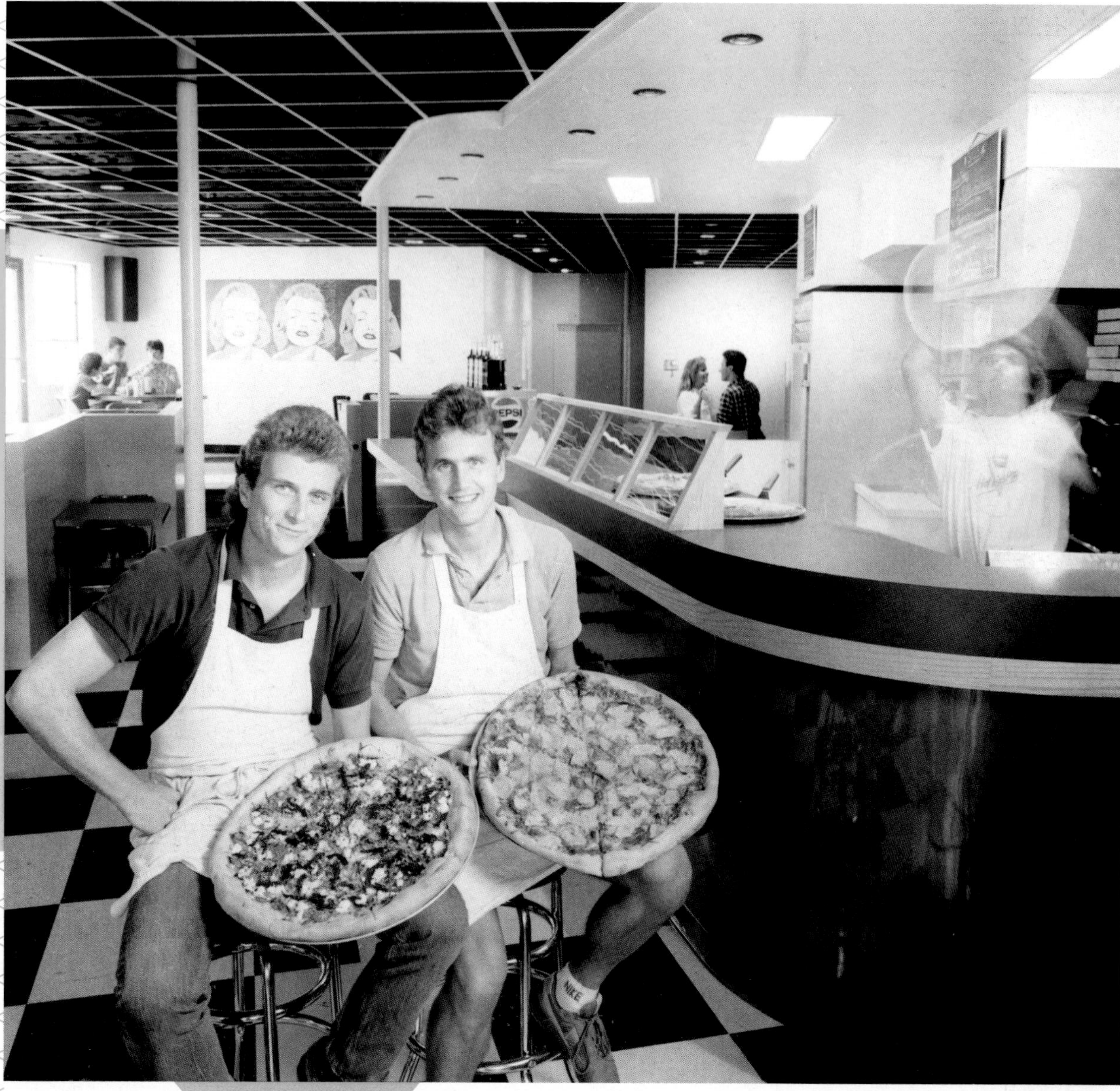

CAFES AND CASUAL DINING

Original pizza — by the slice/by the pie.

Downtown
F25

Downtown
I23

Southwest Portland
F3

If you're looking to sink your teeth into a pizza that opens the eyes, pleases the palate and wins the gold medal for originality, step up to the counter and order a Hot Lips masterpiece. Besides their totally tasteful execution of traditional varieties, Hot Lips adroitly combines unusual ingredients such as artichoke hearts, dried tomatoes and feta cheese to create some unusual pizza types — Tex-Mex, Greek and even Low-Cal, just to name a few. It's not that they ignore the tried and tested recipes to fabricate artsy but inedible items. Hot Lips is simply redefining the art of pizza making with inventions like the Waldorf, featuring such ingredients as green apples and walnuts. Hot Lips uses its own sauces and dough, imported and regional meats and cheeses, and savory toppings for pizza pies and slices good enough to win Oregon Magazine's "Best Pizza-by-the-Slice" award in 1985. Hot Lips' original establishment resides in the historic Postal Building, just a block from Waterfront Park. Inside, the atmosphere is lively, casual, colorful and comfortable — as well-suited to the five-minute gotta-run lunch as to the unhurried dinner.

222 SW Washington Street
Portland 97204
224-5477

Monday-Thursday 11am-9pm
Friday 11am-10pm
Saturday noon-9pm

PSU Campus
1909 SW 6th Avenue
Portland 97201
224-0311

Monday-Thursday 11am-9pm
Friday 11am-10pm
Saturday noon-9pm

Raleigh Hills
Fred Meyer Shopping Center
Portland 97225
297-8424

Monday-Saturday 11am-10pm
Sunday noon-9pm

MACHEESMO MOUSE

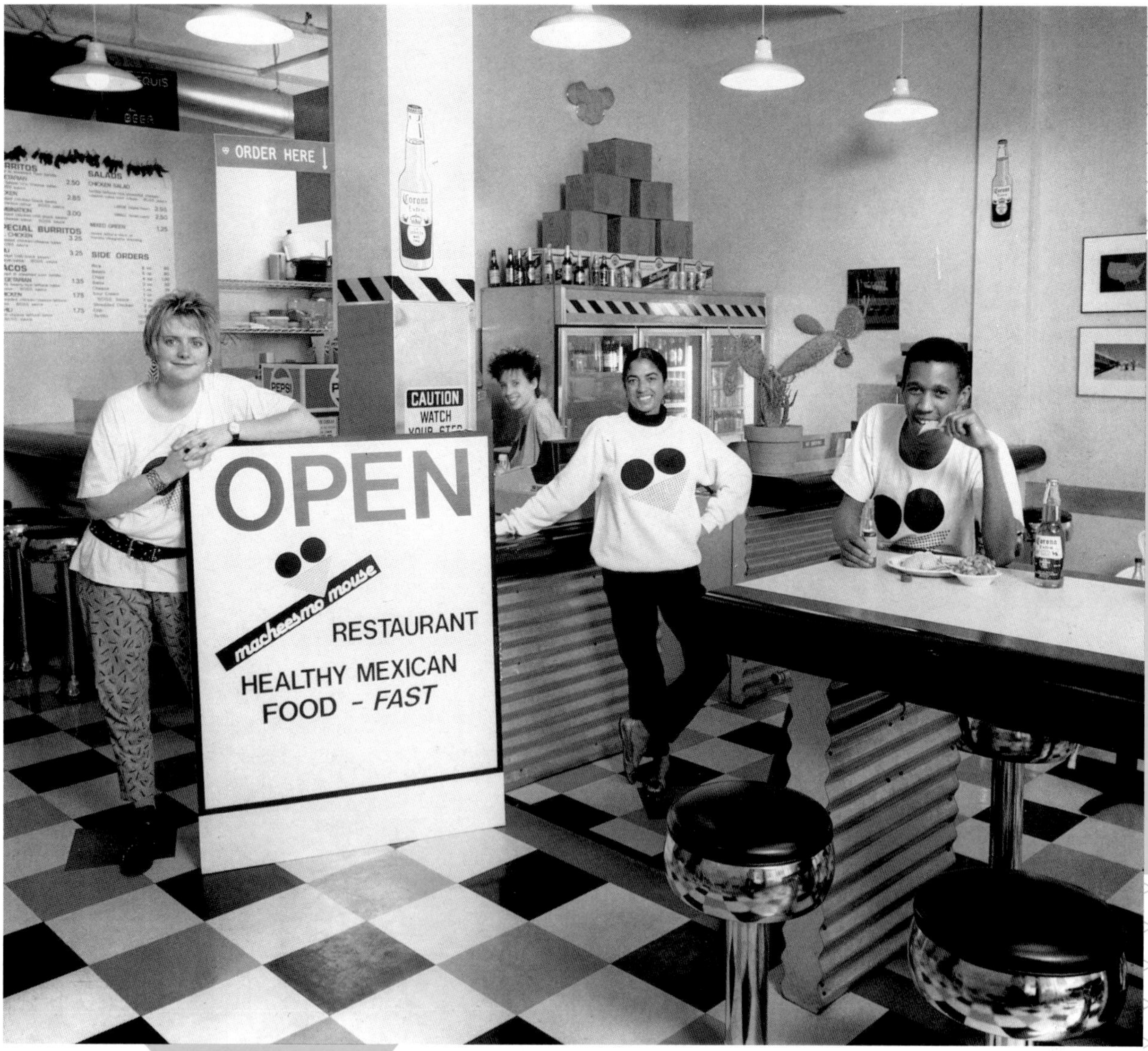

CAFES AND CASUAL DINING

Mexican fast food, fresh and healthy.

The food is healthy, authentic Mexican. The prices are benevolent. The decor is clean-camp. Featured in prestigious national publications such as Restaurant News Magazine, Oregon Magazine and others, Macheesmo Mouse has stirred up a roar of attention emerging as the new wave of the fast-food industry. Currently operating with four locations in Portland, the "mouse" expects to open several new stores to keep up with the current demand. Why are these little lunch/dinner spots so popular? Perhaps it's because of their distinctiveness inside and out. They pride themselves on, literally, a fresh approach to everything including the decor, which is as open and intriguing as the name on the door. Take note of the gridded lino floors — part of the trademark — and the counters with corrugated tin bases; you saw it here first. Refreshingly, the "mouse" spurns molded plastics as though it might contaminate the atmosphere. Equally pleasing is the food itself — no deep fried goo, here. It is meticulously made every day from the finest ingredients including always fresh produce, cilantro, spicy chili, and a variety of rich staples like brown rice and black beans. Their patented pledge reads, "we'll fuel you for high-mileage without weighing you down." Drinks include a delicious special house coffee, natural juices, sodas and a selection of imported beer. Don't forget that name: Macheesmo Mouse.

719 SW Salmon Street
Portland 97205

Monday-Saturday
11am-11pm

3553 SE Hawthorne Boulevard
Portland 97214
232-6588

Monday-Saturday
11am-11pm
Sunday: Special Hours

1200 NE Weidler
Portland 97232

Monday-Saturday
11am-11pm

811 NW 23rd Avenue
Portland 97210

Monday-Saturday
11am-11pm

Downtown
G23

Southeast Portland
D7

Northeast Portland
D6

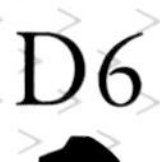

Northwest Portland
H17

FOOTHILL BROILER

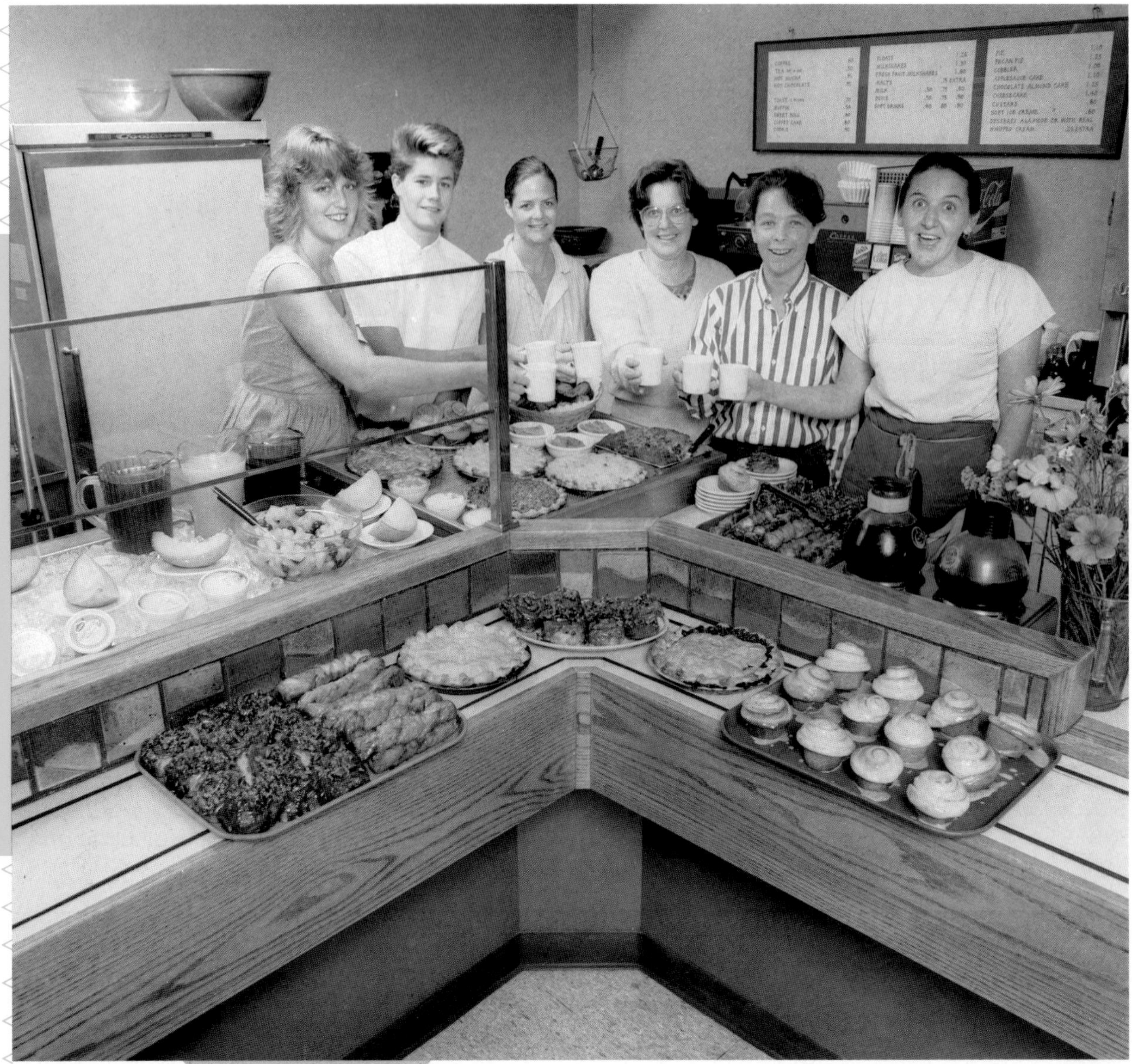

Friendly atmosphere for casual meals.

Northwest Portland

J17

Northwest Portland

J17

Newcomers to the Foothill Broiler are frequently astounded at the camaraderie which abounds here. Everyone — from the customers to owner Vida Lee Mick — seems to be on a first-name basis. The reason is simple — after one visit, no one stays away. This Northwest neighborhood establishment has been attracting Portlanders hungry for the Broiler's freshly prepared food for years. Their specialty — broiled, open-faced hamburgers, made from lean, high-quality beef — have been known to cause lunch-hour stampedes. Among the many tasty sandwiches offered, another long-time favorite is the tuna and cheese, made with solid white albacore tuna and served on fresh French bread. Breakfast specialties, such as homemade pecan rolls, cinnamon twists and bran muffins, entice neighbors daily to indulge that sweet tooth, have a cup of coffee and share the morning paper. During the holidays, desserts are particularly popular. In fact, baked goods, soups and salads are available for take-out and special order. This friendly, family-oriented gathering place, with its variety of choices, is certain to please. Another option for those looking for a comfortable casual eating experience is a Foothill annex located in the pharmacy directly across Burnside. Here you will find a bustling lunch counter serving a variety of breakfast items and tasty sandwiches and, of course, your good old Americana shakes and sodas.

Uptown Shopping Center
33 NW 23rd Place
Portland 97210
223-0287

Monday-Friday
7:30am-7pm
Saturday 7:30am-4pm

Pharmacy Fountain
2334 W. Burnside
Portland 97210
224-9226

Daily
8am-3pm

BOGART'S JOINT

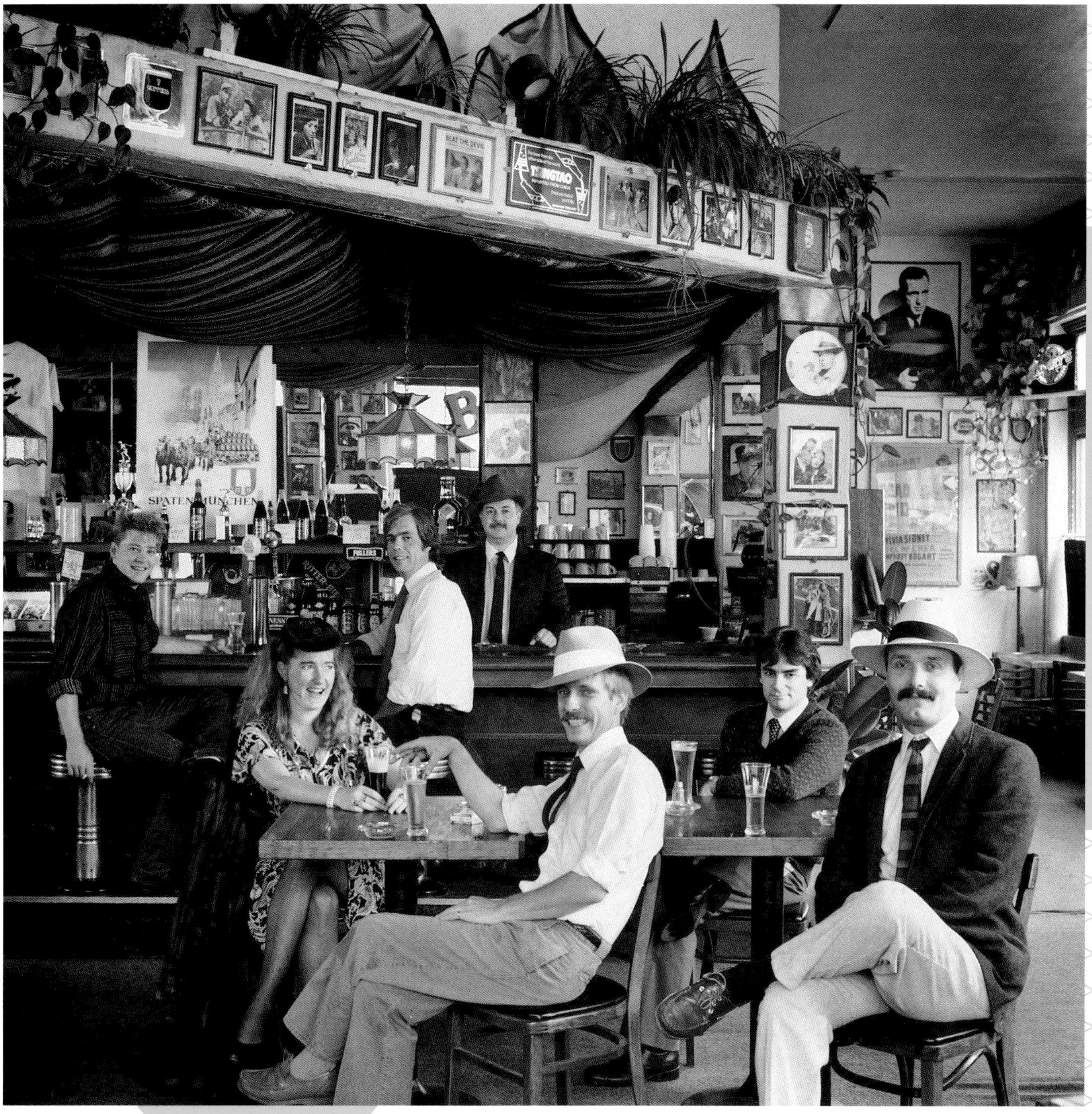

A nostalgic, exciting, warm, unique, happening place.

Jack Warner once asked who would ever want to kiss Humphry Bogart. Guess we all know the answer to that one. The oversize, foldout menu at Bogart's Joint is full of quotes by and about Bogie. "Of all the gin joints in all the towns in the world, she walks into mine." "Well, I ain't sorry no more, ya crazy, psalm-singin' skinny old maid!" And the atmosphere at Bogart's Joint is pure nostalgia. Walls are covered with Bogart memorabilia, ceiling fans give a "Casablanca" effect and a Maltese Falcon sits behind the bar. On weekends Sam plays — again — your favorite piano tunes from Bogie's era. Bogart's Joint serves 18 beers on tap and 200 kinds of bottled beer. The selection of imports is the largest in Oregon. Specialty soups are made daily, with generous sandwiches, salads, omelettes and burgers at great prices. Friday's clam chowder is a standout, as are the homemade chili and salad dressings. Bogart's will cater lunch, dinner or hors d'oeuvres for parties, events or meetings. Any item on the menu can be taken out. Oh, yes, those quotes were directed at Bergman in *Casablanca* and Hepburn in *The African Queen*; bet they could tell Jack Warner a thing or two about kissing Bogart. Visa. MasterCard.

406 NW 14th Avenue
Portland 97209
222-4986

Monday-Thursday
11am-midnight
Friday-Saturday
11am-1am

Galleria
921 SW Morrison Street
Portland 97205
224-3369

Monday-Friday
11am-9pm
Saturday 11am-6pm
Sunday noon-5pm

Northwest Portland

D5

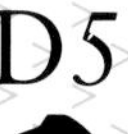

Downtown

F23

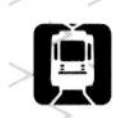

PARCHMAN FARM RESTAURANT AND BAR

CAFES AND CASUAL DINING

A Portland jazz club and restaurant.

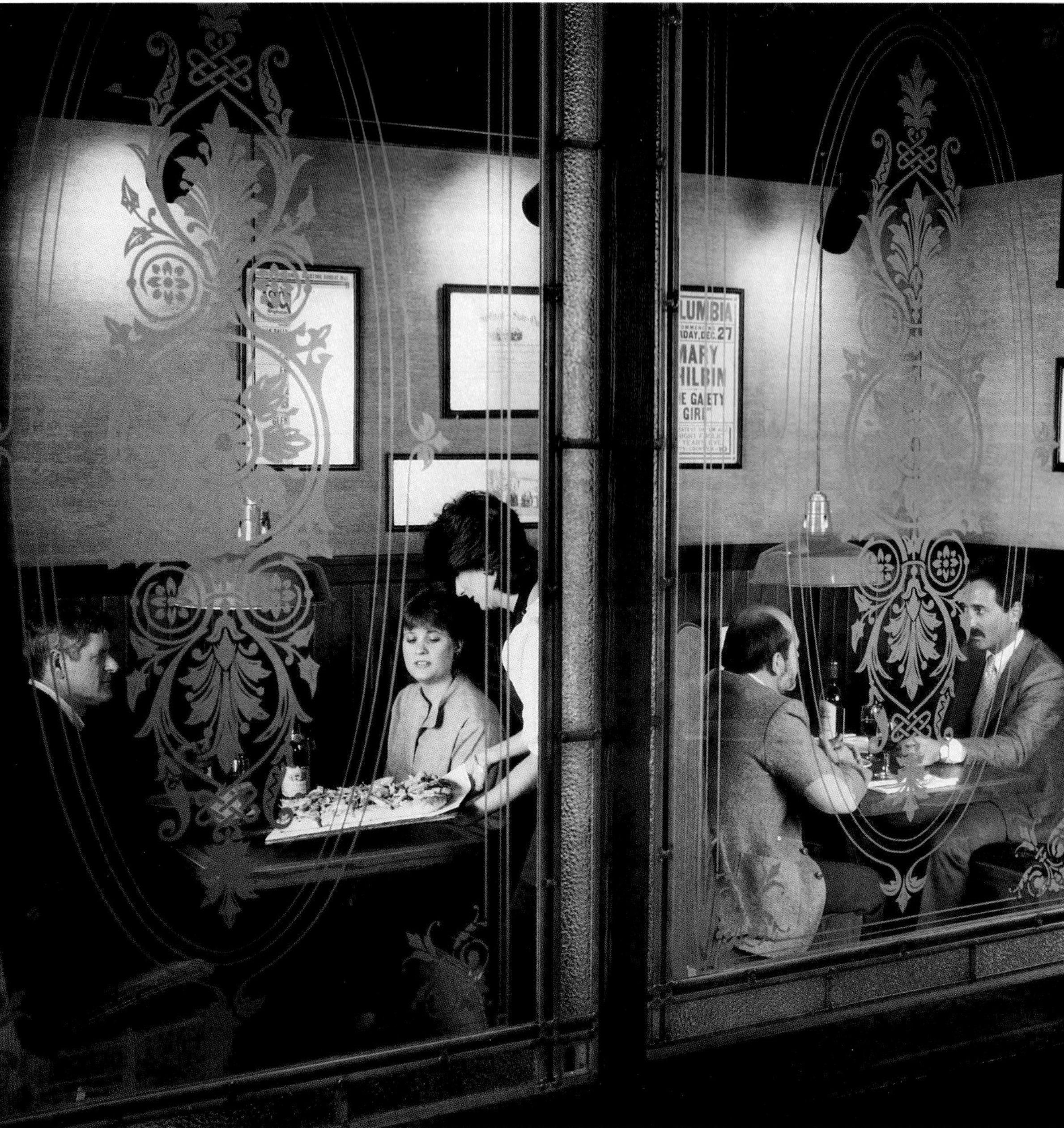

Southeast Portland

E6

Whether your taste runs to Stanley Turrentine, Mose Allison, Herbie Mann or Portland's own Dick Blake, there is no better spot in the city than Parchman Farm to soak up the music and indulge in good food. Behind its unpretentious exterior lies the heart and soul of jazz, six days a week. Parchman owners Rob and Marilyn Andersen are serious about their music, with a 1,000 plus record and tape collection always close at hand, and live musicians Wednesdays, Thursdays, Fridays and Saturdays. Equally close at hand are menu selections as tasty as a smooth saxophone lick. Start with the Italian style entrées that include nine varieties of Parchman's thick-crust, square-cut Sicilian-style pizza — and a create-your-own number with twenty toppings to choose from. Six to eight types of desserts, led by the popular chocolate truffle cake, are always available. And all this needn't be enjoyed only during the early hours — food is served late every night — until midnight weekdays and 1 a.m. Friday and Saturday nights. Now a decade old, Parchman Farm, like the best jazz, continues to improve with age. Its etched glass dividers lend privacy while maintaining a sense of spaciousness; low lights and tasteful wood detailing brew up an ambience that is traditional, not trendy. Visa. MasterCard. American Express. Diners Club. Carte Blanche.

1204 SE Clay Street
Portland 97214
235-7831

Monday-Thursday
11am-1am
Friday 11am-2am
Saturday 5pm-2am

THE VERITABLE QUANDARY

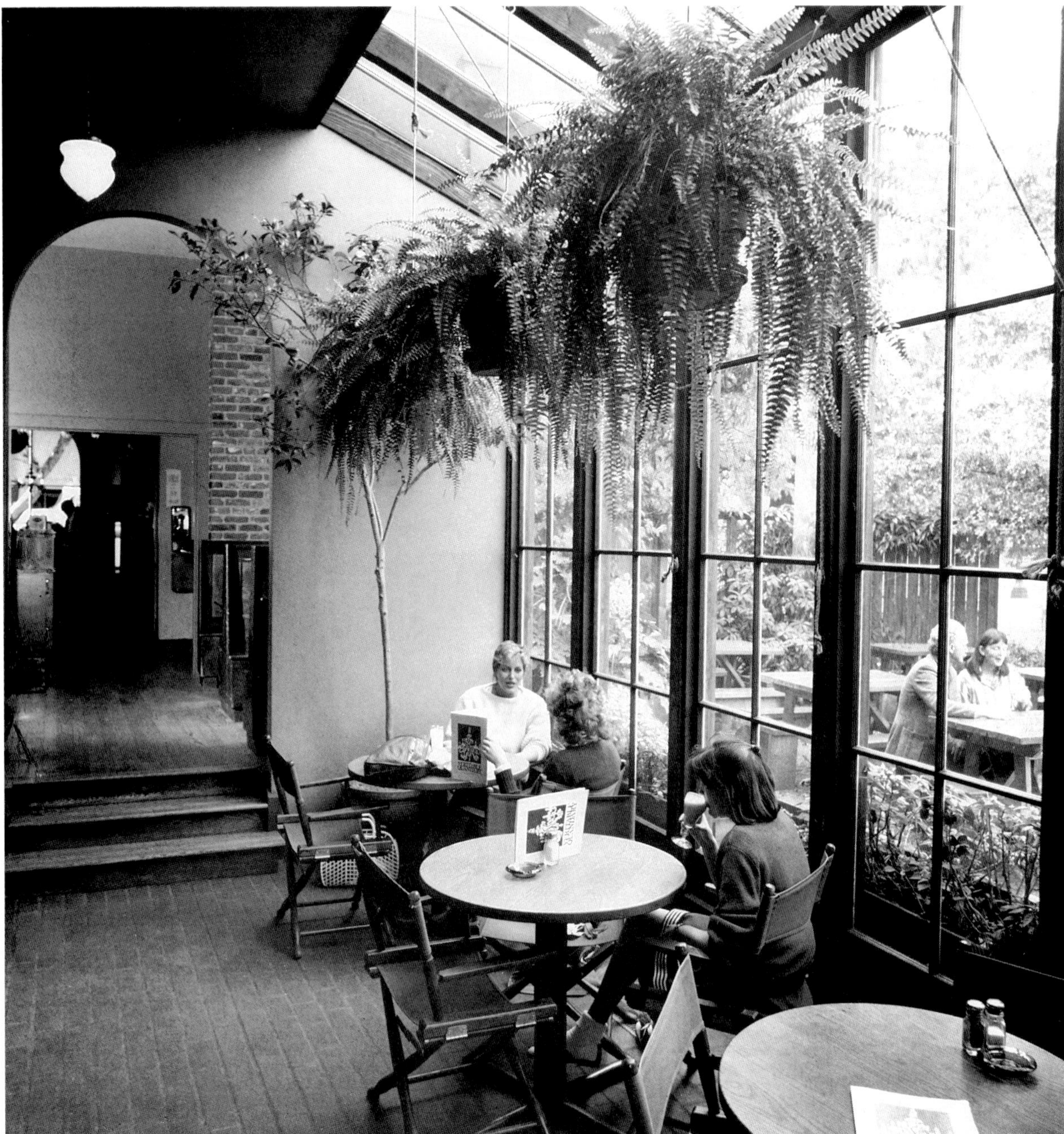

CAFES AND CASUAL DINING

Fun, eclectic clientele. Everything fresh from soups to seafood.

Perplexed about choosing a refreshment establishment for the evening? Dispel that feeling with a visit to the one-time oriental bathhouse, stonecutter's shop, small cafe, wartime rooming house and gypsys' residence — now affectionately known as the VQ. V for Veritable, Q for Quandary, together the name of what quite possibly is the city's best bar. How can that be, in a city that caters so well to those headed for a night on the town? Perhaps it is the sheer charm of its atmosphere, packed into a 15-by-100-foot-long building with a flower garden for outdoor eating, 22-foot mahogany bar and dining solarium for lunching in the airy light of day or supping under the stars. Perhaps it is the compact menu and regular specials, prepared by the city's hardest-working cooks in a postage-stamp of a kitchen. Maybe it's just the Shrimp Salad — a 15 year favorite — or specials that change daily, such as fresh homemade soup, fresh pan-fried fish, and pasta. Perhaps it's the Daily Oyster Shooters. Whatever it is, the VQ is "the" hangout for downtown bureaucrats, lawyers, theatre people, media types and other boulevardiers of all shapes and sizes. The dilemma of where-to-go now settled — on to the next quandary. Visa. MasterCard. American Express.

1220 SW First Avenue
Portland 97204
227-7342

Monday-Saturday
11:30am-2:30am

Downtown
H24

CATERING AND GOURMET FOODS

Personalized catering and classy take-out; wine tastings and cooking classes. The best sources for specialty foods from frozen yogurt to shiitake mushrooms to sushi makings. Fresh is the word.

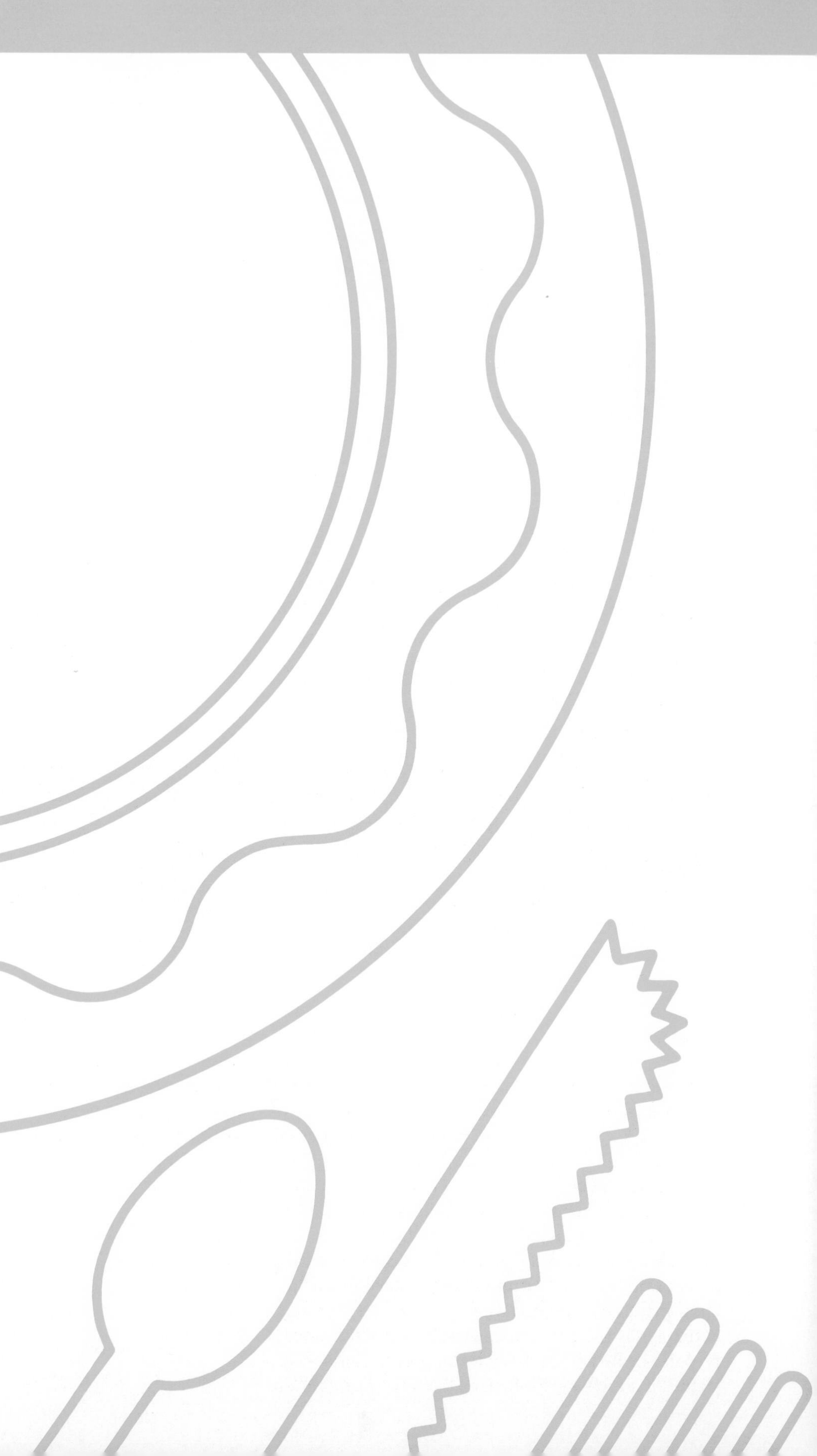

Anzen Oriental Foods and Imports *100*
Cloudtree & Sun and Main Street Grocery *94*
Coffee Bean *104*
The Coffee People *97*
Comella & Son & Daughter *91*
Cool Temptations *93*
Crane & Company *90*
Edelweiss Sausage & Delicatessen *99*
Elephants Delicatessen *96*
Executive Sweets, Desserts Etc. *106*
Great Harvest Bread Co. *102*
The Kobo's Company *235*
Le Panier Very French Bakery *98*
Nature's Fresh Northwest *103*
Pasta Cucina *101*
Pastaworks *89*
Paul Bergen Catering and Charcuterie *92*
Rose's Viennese Bakery *105*
Strohecker's *95*

PASTAWORKS

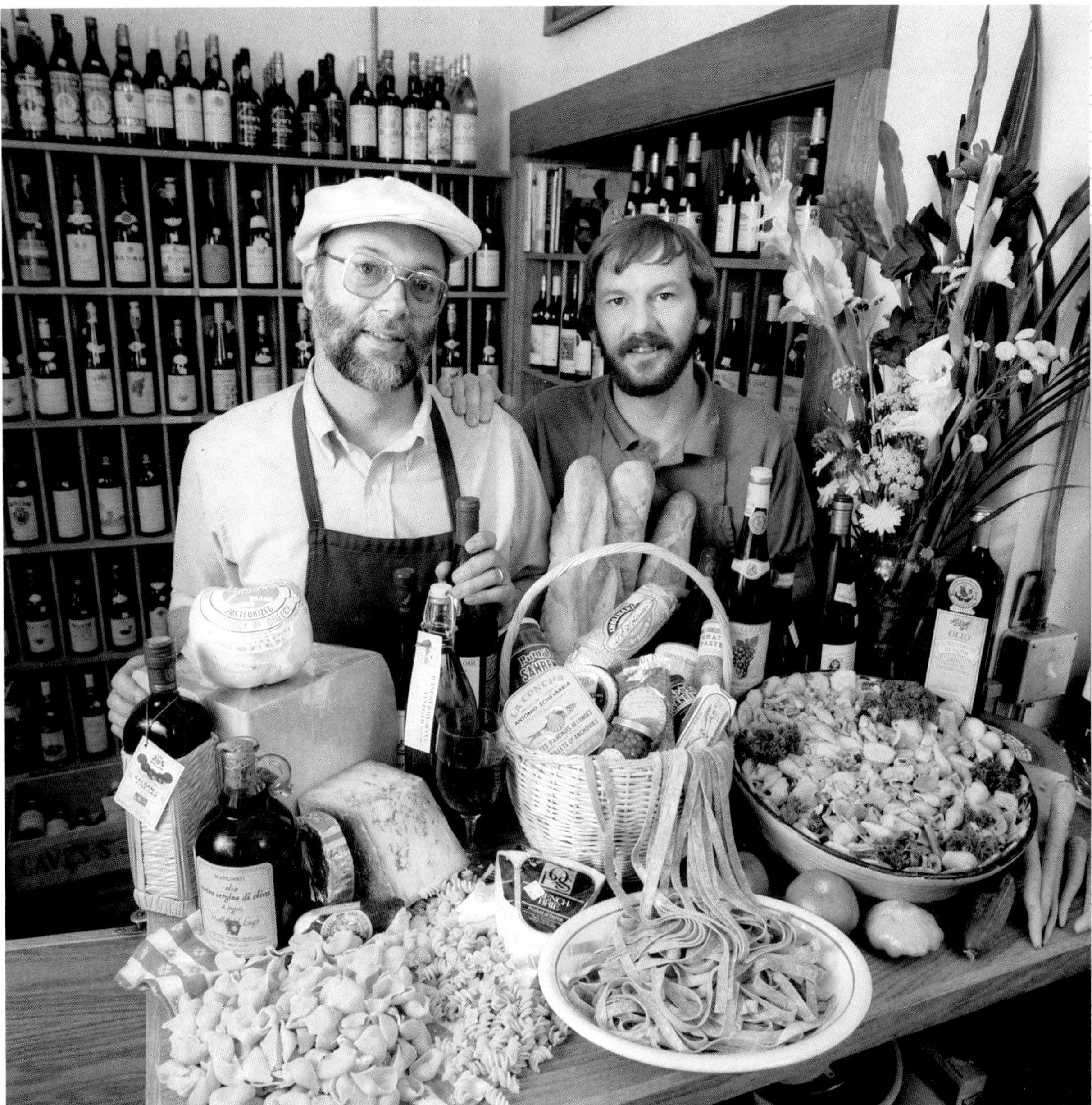

CATERING AND GOURMET FOODS

Purveyor of fine Italian food.

Southeast Portland

D7

If you're skeptical about superlatives, ignore the fact that Willamette Week called it the "best pasta in town," and try some for yourself. At Pastaworks, you'll be convinced. Their glorious pasta is made from scratch with nothing but fresh, high-quality ingredients. And the range of flavors — including traditional favorites such as egg and spinach and intriguing specialites such as chocolate, chestnut, and saffron — is only rivaled by the number of different types of pasta: fresh ravioli and fresh tortellini, sheet-rolled fettuccine and linguini, and seven shaped pastas, including rigatoni, shells, and orzo, which are extruded. Pasta, however, is not the only resource upon which this gustatory empire is founded. The deli is loaded with subtle goodies like extra-virgin olive oils, specialty vinegars, savory sun-dried tomatoes, Porcini mushrooms and Arborio rice, all of which will contribute to the special Mediterranean flavor of your dishes. Top the pasta with fresh, daily-made clam sauce or one of the pestos, add the cheeses — ranging from Mascarpone to Reggiano Parmesan — and your dishes will soar from the merely delectable to the nearly divine. Then complete your special combination with a favorite from Pastawork's excellent selection of Italian and Spanish wines and you'll begin to understand why Italians live to eat while the rest of the world only eats to live. So go ahead — be skeptical. You'll love the superlatives at Pastaworks. Visa. MasterCard.

3735 SE Hawthorne Boulevard
Portland 97214
232-1010

Monday-Saturday 9:30am-6:30pm
Sunday noon-5pm

CRANE & COMPANY FINE FOOD MARKET & DELI

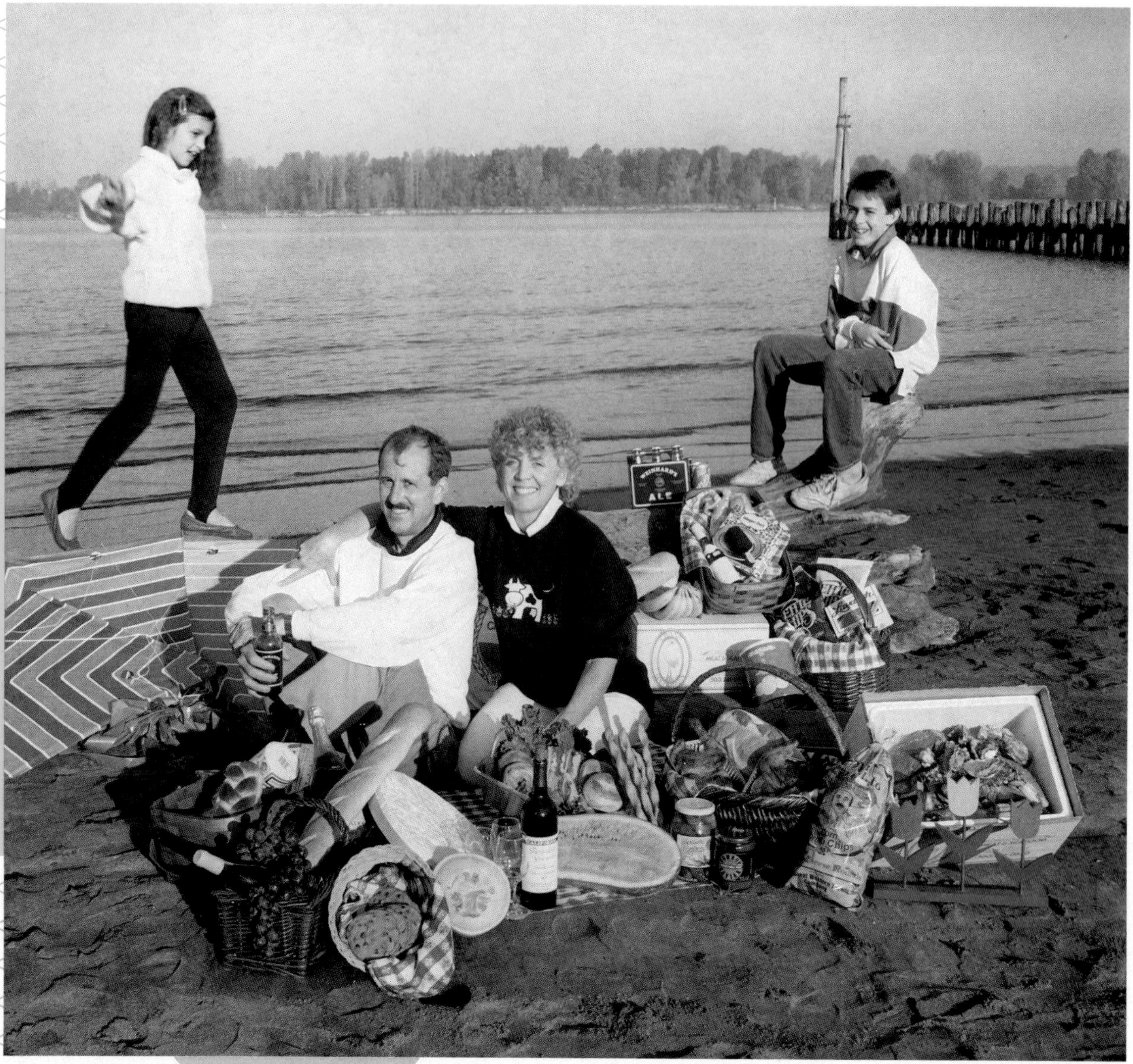

CATERING AND GOURMET FOODS

A tantalizing fresh food experience.

Southwest Portland

G5

Yamhill Historic District

G25

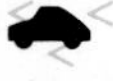

From simple beginnings in 1977, Crane & Company has evolved into a dazzling three location market business — a veritable cornucopia of gastronomic delights. Each location is unique with a variation in product offerings to meet the customer's needs. Crane & Company features superb seafood, magnificent meats, incredible condiments, delightful desserts, vin extraordinaire. The Terwilliger and Yamhill stores boast an extensive selection of fresh fish and meats, most recent additions being the new Country Natural lite beef and range fed poultry. Delicatessan enticements include imported and domestic sliced meats and cheeses, salads, desserts, fresh baked breads and pastries, prepared entrées and take-out catering. A hand picked selection of excellent wines and beers is available at the Terwilliger and Salishan stores, accompanied by an outstanding array of condiments, both imported delicacies and wonderful "made in the Northwest" products. The Yamhill location is an old-fashioned outdoor market, the Terwilliger store a cozy, friendly and fragrant place. The Salishan store has introduced a new standard of specialty food marketing to the Oregon Coast. Suffice it to say, all three Crane & Company locations offer an unmatched and delightful fresh food shopping experience. Visa. MasterCard.

8610 SW Terwilliger Boulevard
Portland 97219
246-4323

Monday-Friday 7am-7pm
Saturday 9am-7pm
Daily
Hours vary seasonally

Yamhill Marketplace
110 SW Yamhill Street
Portland 97204
293-3261

The Marketplace at Salishan
Gleneden Beach 97388
764-2316

Daily
Hours vary seasonally

COMELLA & SON & DAUGHTER

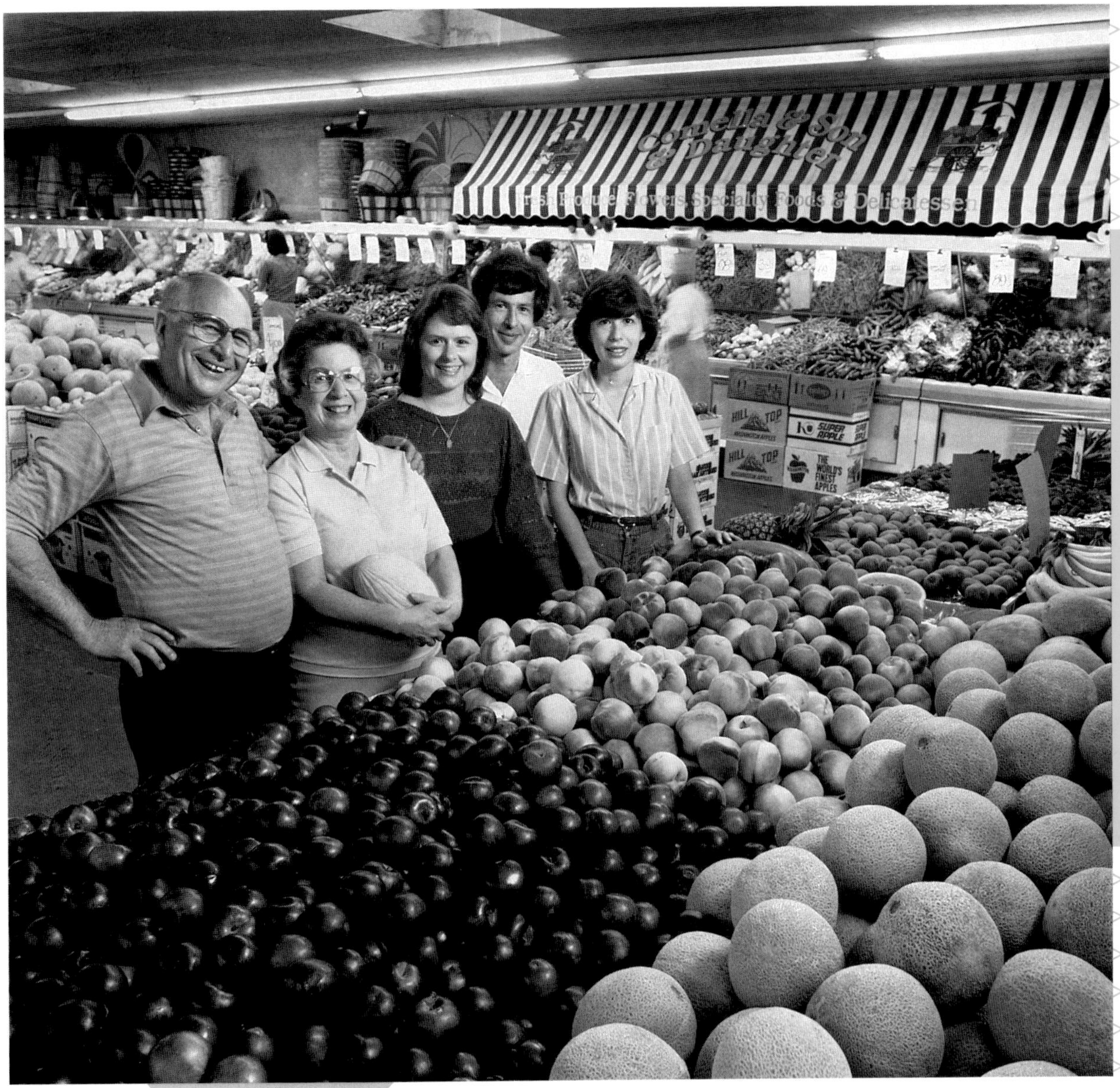

CATERING AND GOURMET FOODS

Fresh produce, flowers, gourmet foods and deli.

Fresh, ripe fruits and vegetables defy the logic that "if it's good, it isn't good for you", so when you stop by Comella & Son & Daughter fill your basket with a light heart. Shopping here is like shopping at an old farmers' market — except your range of choices is astounding. All the fresh produce, from familiar favorites to the most exotic fare, is picked to meet your most exacting standards. Quite often, platters of freshly cut fruit are offered for sampling — the pineapple, so sweet and juicy; the white peaches, simply fabulous! Comella's is a family affair: Frank and his son Steve started the business in 1978, and his daughter Cindy joined them a year later. You'll find Frank's wife Betty tending the books and flowers, Steve stocking the deli, Cindy in specialty and gourmet foods, and Frank — well, Frank is everywhere. As the resident celebrity and produce expert, Frank is a favorite guest on a variety of local TV shows. After choosing your produce, you can select bread and rolls from the bakery, pick your favorites from the old-fashioned bulk candy, and grind your own fresh coffee. The deli features gourmet specialties, meats, cheeses, and salads from their own kitchen. Comella's offers a huge selection of Northwest wines and imported beers. A new addition is a kitchen/classroom where Steve's wife, Audrey can fill your full catering needs, from a picnic for two to a reception for hundreds! Come for a visit — the Comella's promise you an unforgetable shopping experience. Visa. MasterCard.

6959 SW Garden Home Road
Portland 97223
245-5033

Monday-Saturday 9am-7pm
Sunday 9am-6pm

Multnomah/Hillsdale

F3

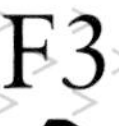

PAUL * BERGEN CATERING & CHARCUTERIE

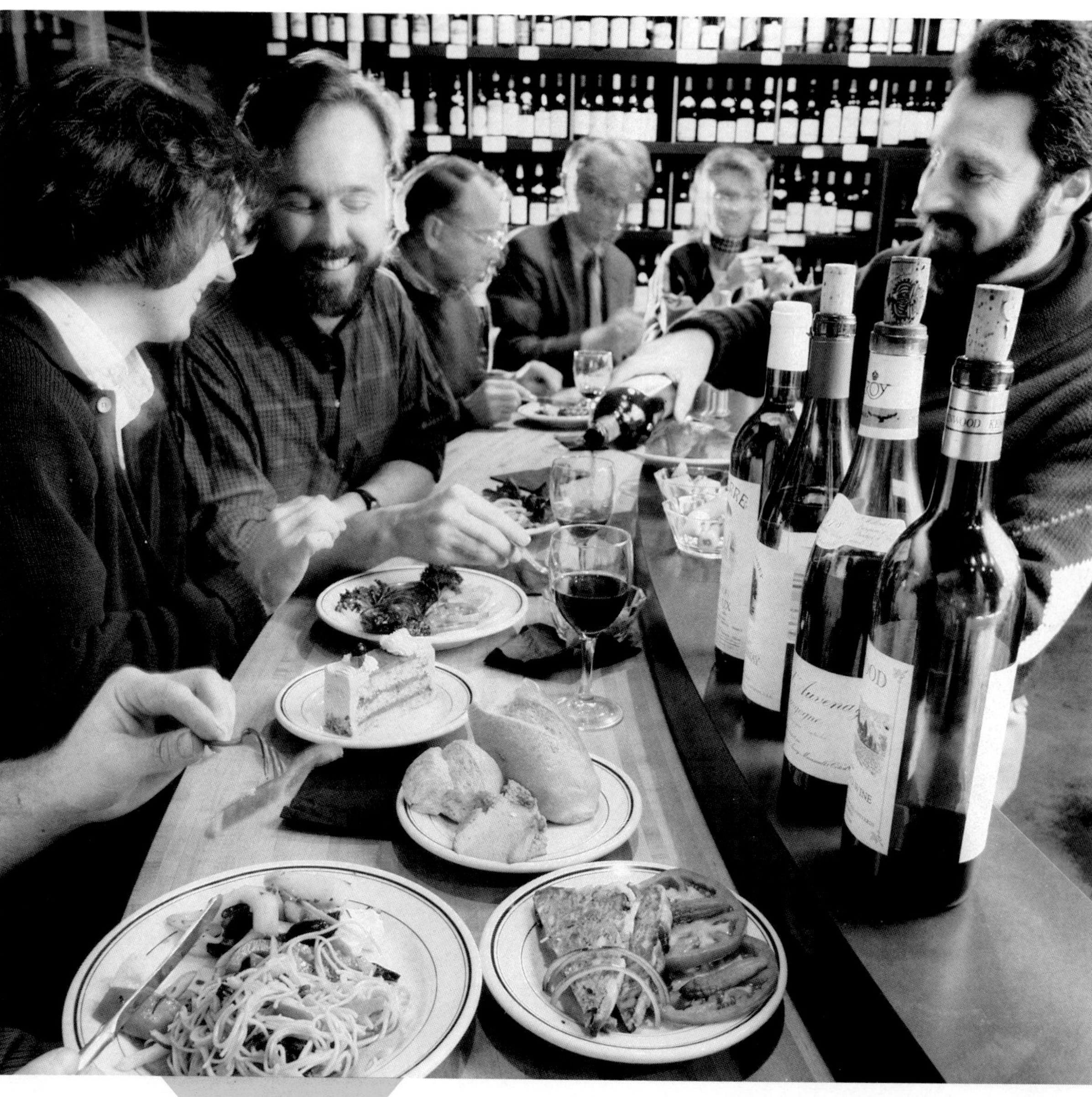

CATERING AND GOURMET FOODS

Delicious country-style food and intelligent wine.

Northwest Portland

I17

At Paul * Bergen, a catered event is a creative challenge where food, wine, service and environment are synthesized by owners Ron Paul and David Bergen. In recent months Paul * Bergen was commissioned to design a medieval feast for the visiting Magna Charta, to orchestrate a reception for an Arab cultural mission and to oversee an elegant birthday party for nine guests. What those accomplishments and the many other Paul * Bergen assignments share are imaginative solutions to the myriad details of each situation. Aided by the tremendous natural bounty of the Pacific Northwest, the staff listens, cajoles, suggests and samples until the ideal ingredients are assembled. But there is more, and it is suggested in the word charcuterie, a French specialty food store that displays fresh pâté, sausages, and entrées. Paul * Bergen is an inviting, unpretentious and sophisticated blend of charcuterie, cafe and wine bar. With talented employees and the freshest ingredients, Paul * Bergen produces luscious regional foods and fine, homestyle pastries. The cafe, serving lunch and dinner, features an outdoor grill, terrace and full espresso bar; every Friday night a Tapas bar bristles with Spanish appetizers. The fun's infectious! Visa. MasterCard.

Everett Street Market
NW 23rd & Everett
Portland 97210
223-2121

Monday-Thursday
9am-7pm
Friday-Saturday
9am-9pm
Sunday 10am-5pm

COOL TEMPTATIONS

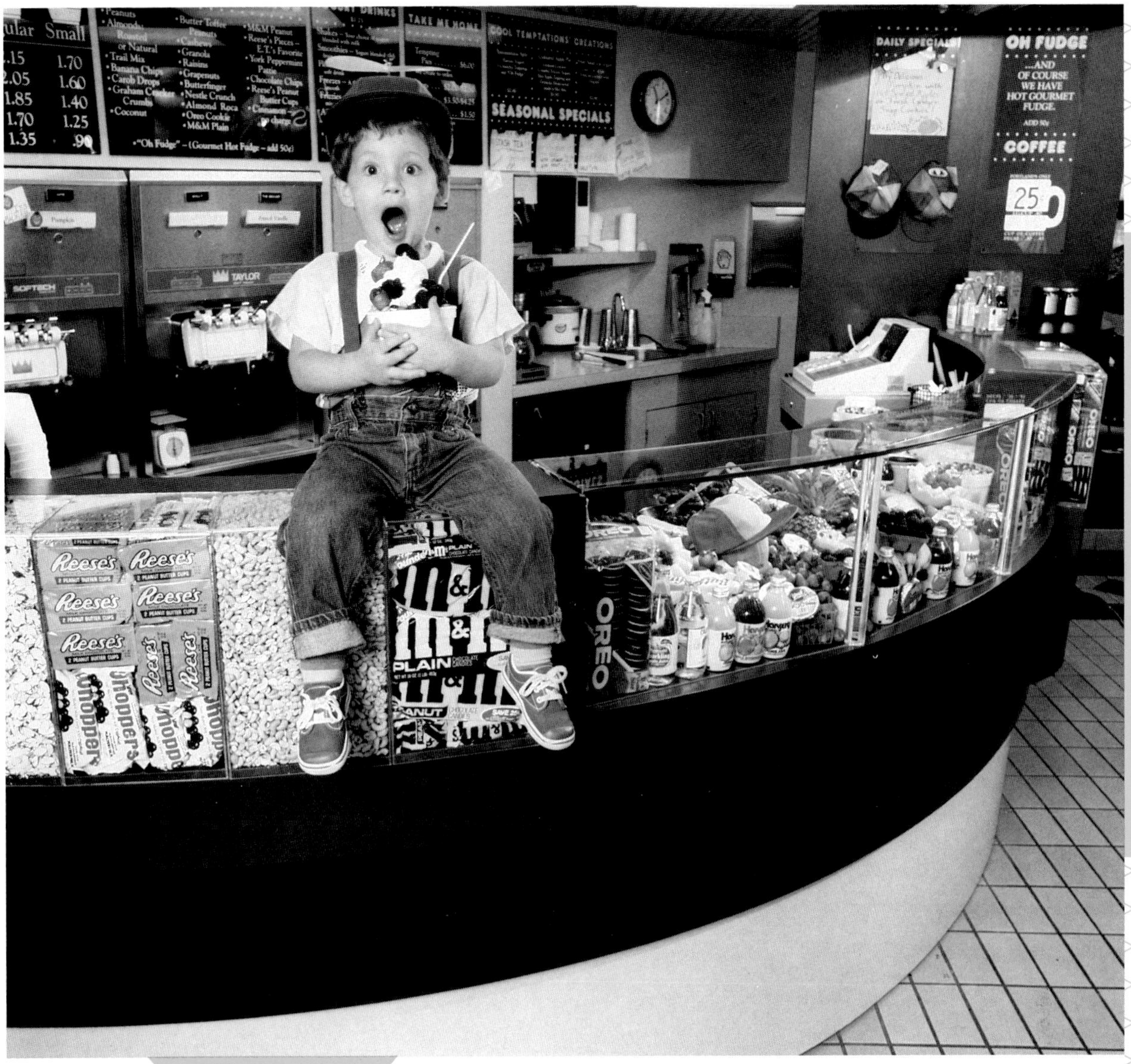

This isn't yogurt, this is divine.

When Stephanie Jewell abandoned her promising law career in 1985, it was to provide Portlanders with the essential fifth food group — frozen yogurt. Now, thousands of customers can testify that her upbeat, upscale, uptown and uplifting Cool Temptations shops are the best place to indulge in one of the most satisfying food experiences around. It won't take a subpoena to bring you to her court of first resort; frozen yogurt has half the calories, one-third the cholesterol and one-third the fat of ice cream. Add to that the huge selection of Stephanie's available flavors (among them Santa's peppermint stick, chocolate peanut butter — in a cup, very berry berry, strawberry colada, hazelnut amaretto, chocolate Grand Marnier and white chocolate macadamia nut) and you'll be sentencing yourself to sweet-tooth heaven. To those flavors are added selections from a huge array of toppings including Almond Roca, Reese's Peanut Butter Cups, Dilettante Gourmet Fudge. If you're looking for something unconscionably corrupt, examine an Almond Joy or Black Forest sundae, or hot berry cobbler. But don't delay: going without Cool Temptations' frozen yogurt is considered cruel and unusual punishment.

PacWest Center
504 SW Madison Street
Portland 97204
223-6322

Monday-Friday
9am-7pm
Saturday 11am-5pm

Everett Street Market
2310 NW Everett
Portland 97210
223-0863

Sunday-Thursday
11am-11pm
Friday-Saturday
11am-midnight

Mercantile Village
3972 SW Mercantile Drive
Lake Oswego 97035
636-7070

Sunday-Thursday
11am-11pm
Friday-Saturday
11am-midnight

Downtown
G23
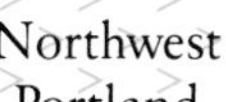

Northwest Portland
I17
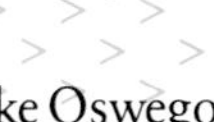

Lake Oswego/ Lake Grove
H4
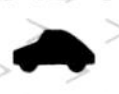

CLOUDTREE & SUN AND MAIN STREET GROCERY

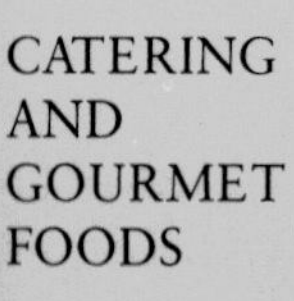

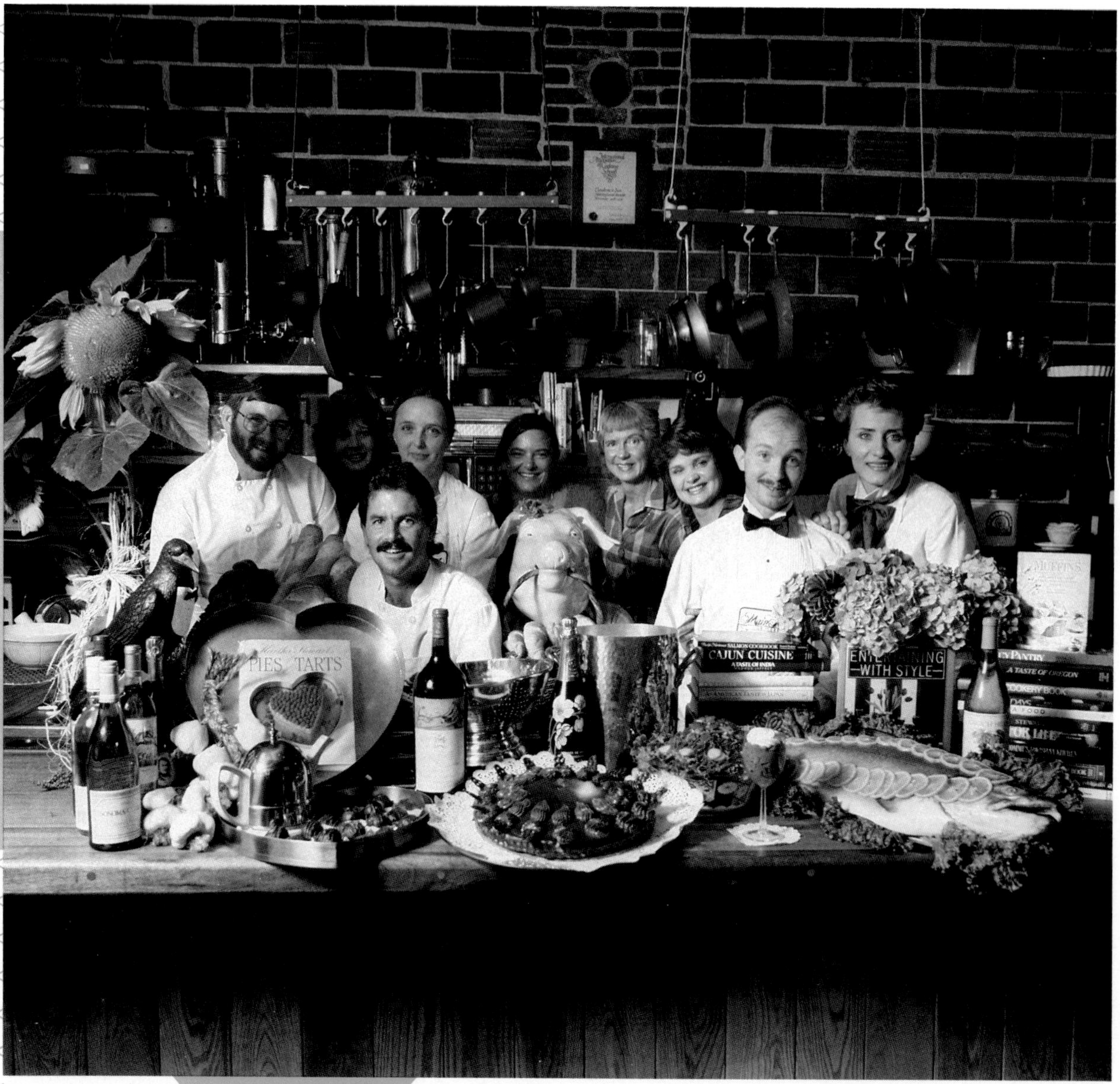

CATERING AND GOURMET FOODS

A joint food and culinary shopping adventure.

Gresham

E13

The next time you feel like a dinnertime escape to a quaint little restaurant with fresh flowers and white tablecloths — why not take a chauffeured ride? Board Portland's light rail and set off for Main Street Grocery in Gresham. Dinner is only one of many reason's to visit Main Street and its next-door neighbor, Cloudtree & Sun. Here you'll find no less than a restaurant, bakery, cooking school catering business, cooking equipment store, tabletop accessories section and seasonal gifts department. If that's not enough Cloudtree's cookbook array boasts more than 200 titles! In short, the two establishments provide a culinary shopping adventure unlike any in the region. Just one example of their exciting synergism is your option of buying dinner's wine from the grocery's superb retail section and, for a mere one dollar corkage fee, enjoying it with your meal. Cloudtree's renowned School of Cookery invites teachers and chefs from around the world to share their individual expertise. Their range of classes offers something for everyone — curious beginner, accomplished cook or aspiring professional. Visit Cloudtree & Sun and Main Street Grocery soon for a culinary adventure and inspiration. Call for directions or reservations. Visa. MasterCard. American Express.

Cloudtree & Sun
112 North Main Street
Gresham 97030
666-8495

Monday-Thursday
10am-6pm
Friday 10am-9pm
Saturday 10am-6pm
Sunday noon-5pm

Main Street Grocery
120 North Main Street
Gresham 97030
661-7877

Monday-Tuesday
7:30am-4pm
Wednesday-Saturday
7:30am-9pm
Sunday Brunch
10am-3pm

STROHECKER'S

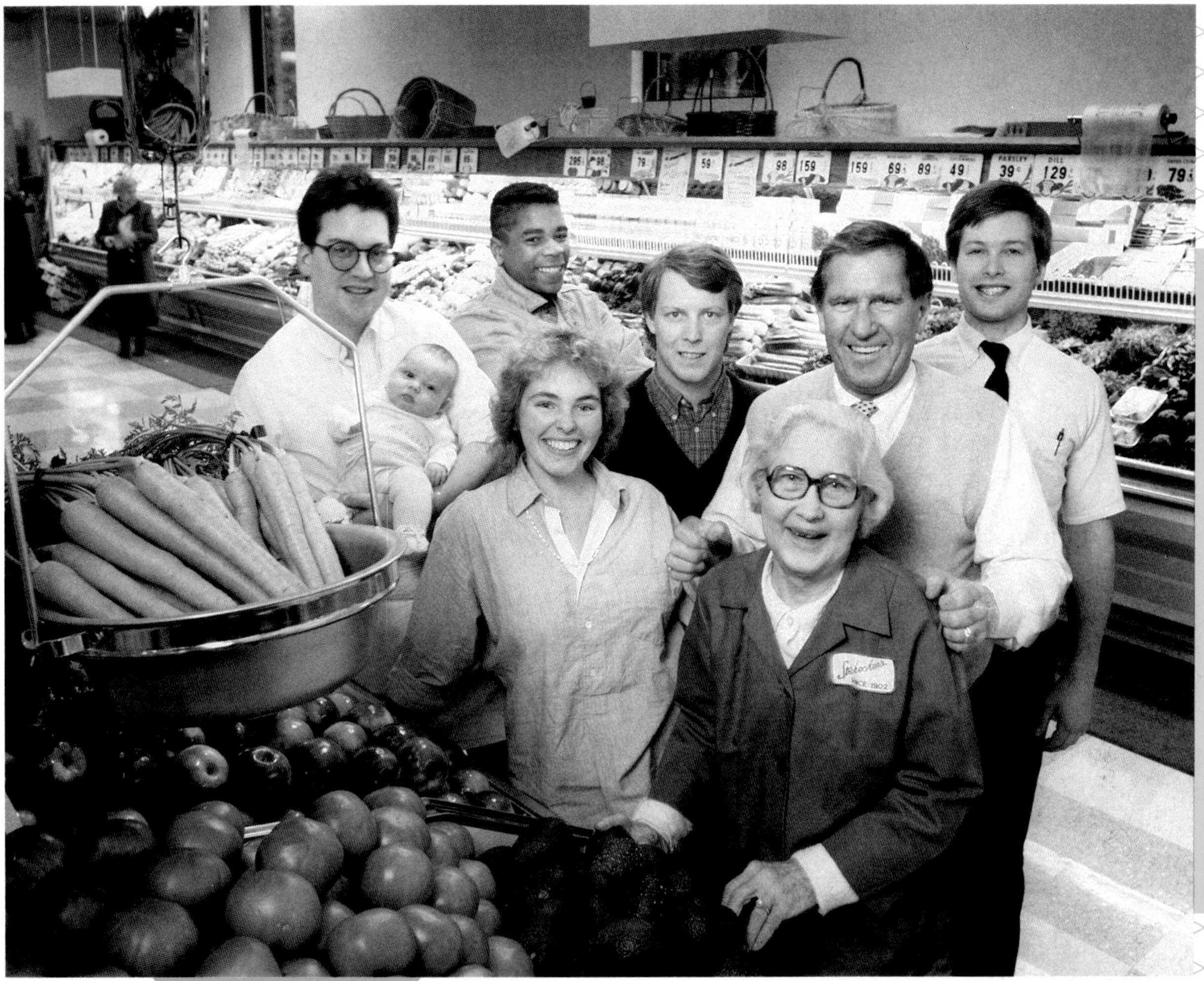

CATERING AND GOURMET FOODS

Gourmet food, vintage wines, surprising extras, wishes granted.

In 1902, when Portland Heights residents wanted a lamp chimney or buggy whip, they rang up Gottlieb Strohecker at the corner grocery store. Today, Portlanders still call on the Strohecker family for their everyday — and most exotic — grocery needs. Four generations of Stroheckers strive to live up to the family motto, "If we don't have it, we'll get it for you." Brothers Wayne and Keith and cousin Wes have brought together some of the finest specialty foods and services available under one roof. Great-grandfather Gottlieb wouldn't recognize that roof now. Expansion and remodeling have tripled the store in size and transformed it into what Wayne calls "the Nieman-Marcus of grocery stores." On the main floor, the custom cut meat department stocks well-aged meats and hand-selected seafood; the bakery carries the best from Portland's specialty bakers; the floral shop and full-service pharmacy are brand new. Downstairs, a delicatessen offers everything from sandwiches to complete catered dinners and serves as the headquarters for Strohecker's Cooking School. Wayne's legendary wine cellar displays vintages found nowhere else in Oregon. In this congenial atmosphere you'll appreciate the ultimate in service — your own charge account. Order a custom gift basket of gourmet foods — and use the basket again for your next shopping expedition to Strohecker's. Visa. MasterCard.

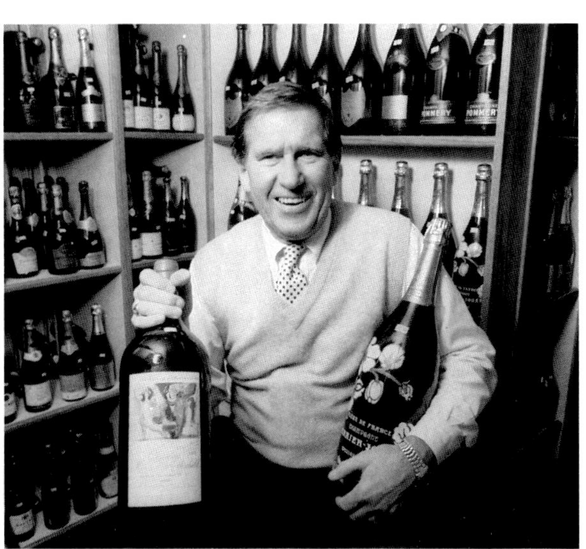

2855 SW Patton Road
Portland 97201
223-7391

Monday-Saturday
8am-8pm
Sunday 9am-8pm

Southwest Portland

E5

ELEPHANTS DELICATESSEN

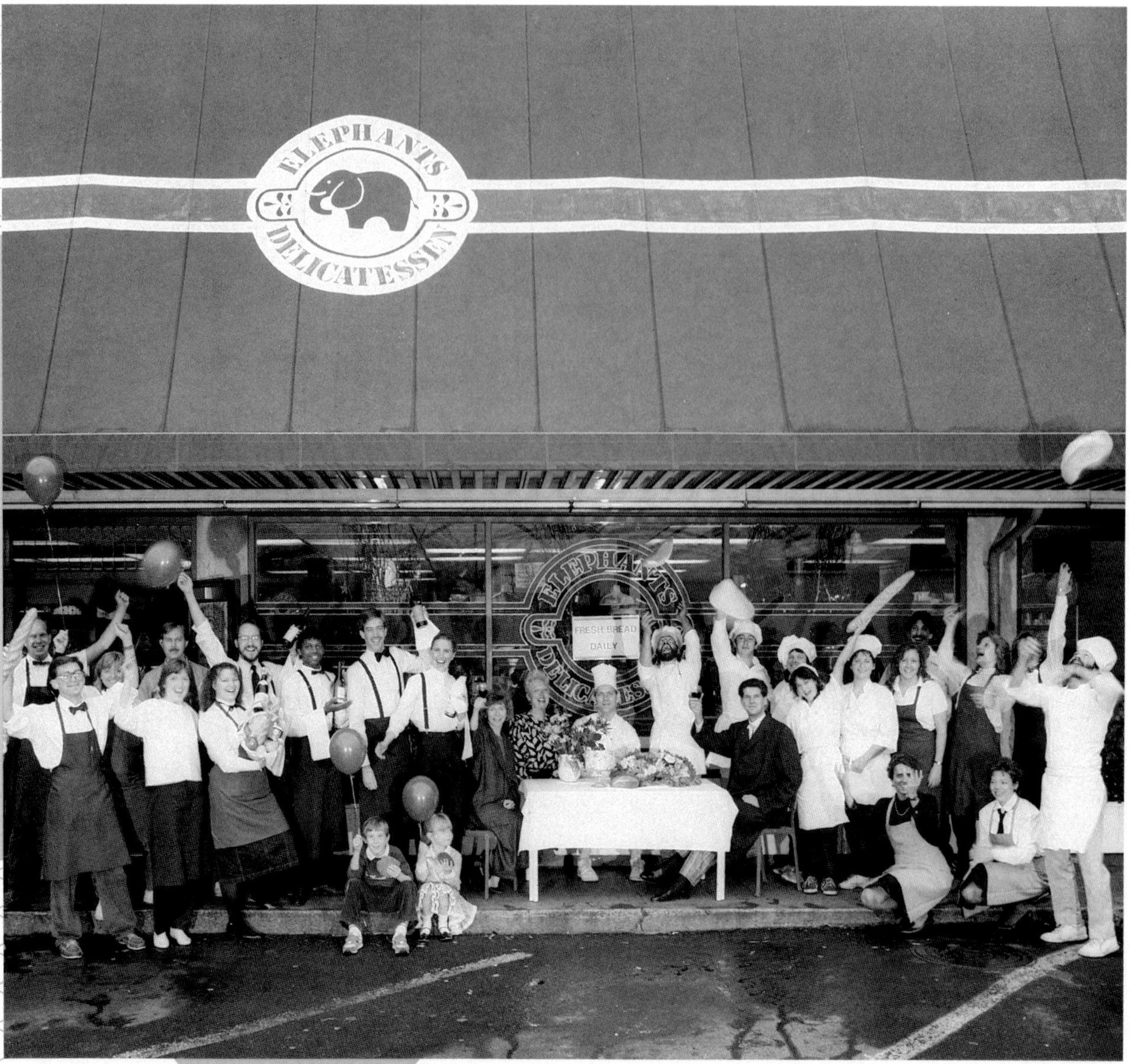

CATERING AND GOURMET FOODS

Portland's premier specialty food store.

Northwest Portland

J17

From coast to coast and border to border people come to experience Elephants Delicatessen. Like 20 stores in one, Elephants is loaded with items to tempt your senses and spark your imagination. From a gourmet-to-go section that's a boon to busy Portland palates come select salads, hearty stews, soups, roasted chicken, vegetables, savory tarts, gourmet gift baskets, and fresh pastas and sauces. Watch these specialties being created daily in Elephants' open kitchens. The delicatessen's box lunches are perfect for leisurely picnics or office meetings. One quick call will bring Elephant's mobile express van to downtown and the northwest community for delivery of tasty noontime meals. Elephants boasts crusty handmade breads baked in European steam ovens, scrumptious pastries, imported beer and wine and a huge assortment of cheeses from around the world. You can also enjoy pastas and grilled entrées, an array of daily specials and indulgences like espresso and fresh fruit pie. Their pizza has twice been named the city's best. Elephants caters too — to inspired tastes and busy schedules. Their expert catering staff will bring a complete meal into your home or office so you can relax and feel confident that all the details will be remembered. Treat yourself to the endless offerings. Visa. MasterCard. American Express.

Uptown Shopping Center
13 NW 23rd Place
Portland 97210
224-3955

Monday-Friday
10am-6:30pm
Saturday 10am-6pm
Sunday 9:30am-4pm

THE COFFEE PEOPLE

CATERING AND GOURMET FOODS

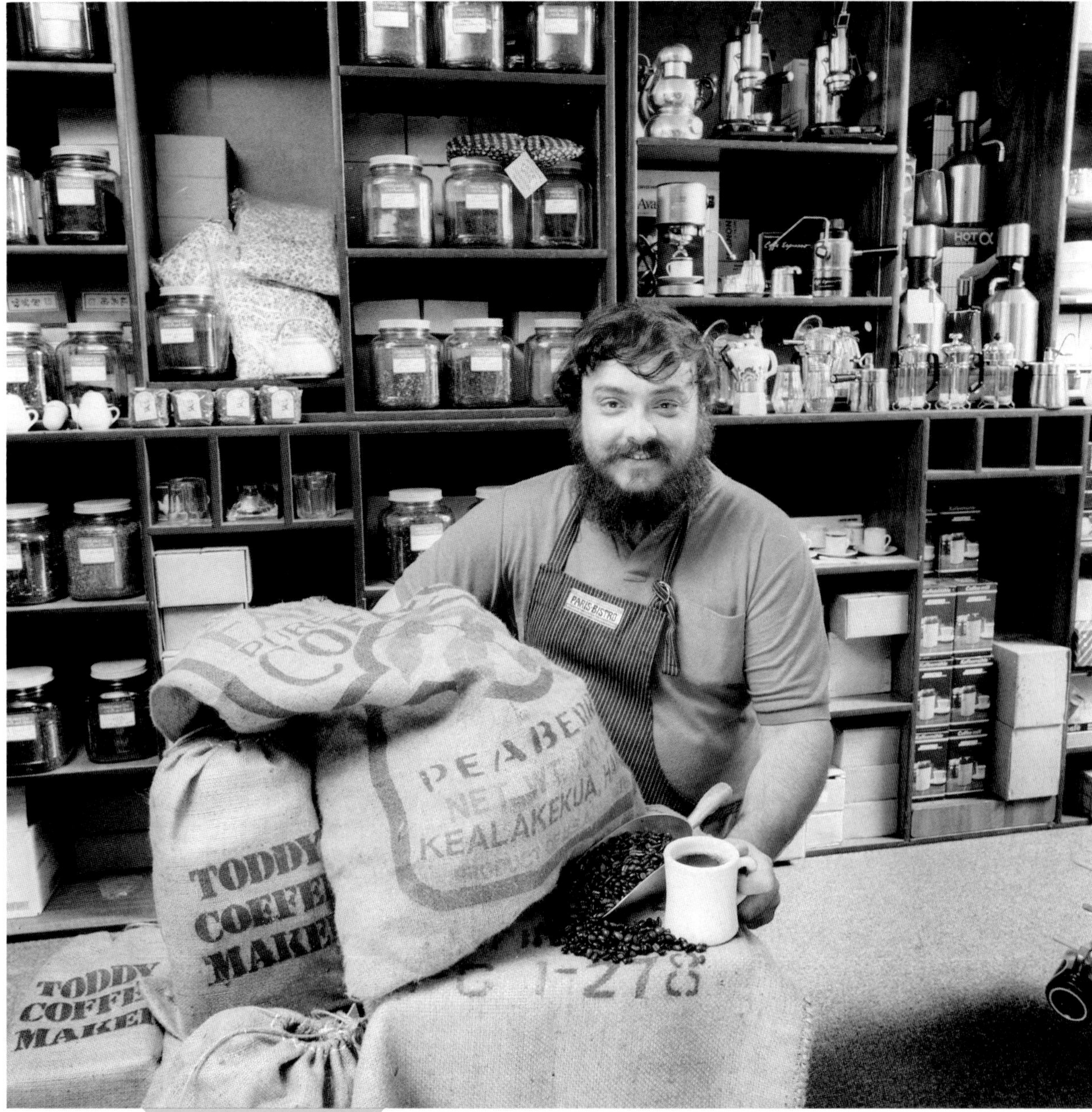

Fresh roasted variety of coffee beans — and much more!

Northwest Portland
H17

Meet Jim and Patty Roberts, operators of the coffee store that treats their product like fresh produce and their customers like special people. Jim knows this business from the grounds up, so to speak, and his commitment to his customers is first evidenced by a selection of more than 75 varieties of fresh-roasted European-style coffees and other varietal selections that emphasize the seasonal peaks and regional variations of beans produced within a given country. Because coffee from within a given producing country varies from month to month and batch to batch, well-known names like Colombia Supremo or Sumatra Mandheling are not always an adequate guide to cup quality. That's why Coffee People goes within the season to bring the freshest, zestiest coffees to their customers, selecting within the grades to find unique and exacting coffee experiences not available in supermarkets. "I take special pride in being able to make a recommendation that fits the individual," says Roberts, "and give them a coffee taste experience they're not likely to find elsewhere." The fruit of these efforts is a store densely packed with all manner of coffees and more than 40 varieties of bulk and packaged tea, including Coffee People's own famous Earl Grey Blend. You'll find brewing equipment by Jericho, Krupps, Braun, Hario and Melitta; espresso and cappuccino served outdoors by the cup; fresh cookies and muffins daily; and imported and domestic chocolates, toffees and a large selection of hard candies. Visa. MasterCard.

2275 NW Johnson
at 23rd Avenue
Portland 97210
221-0235

Monday-Friday
10am-7pm
Saturday 10am-5pm
Sunday noon-4pm

LE PANIER VERY FRENCH BAKERY

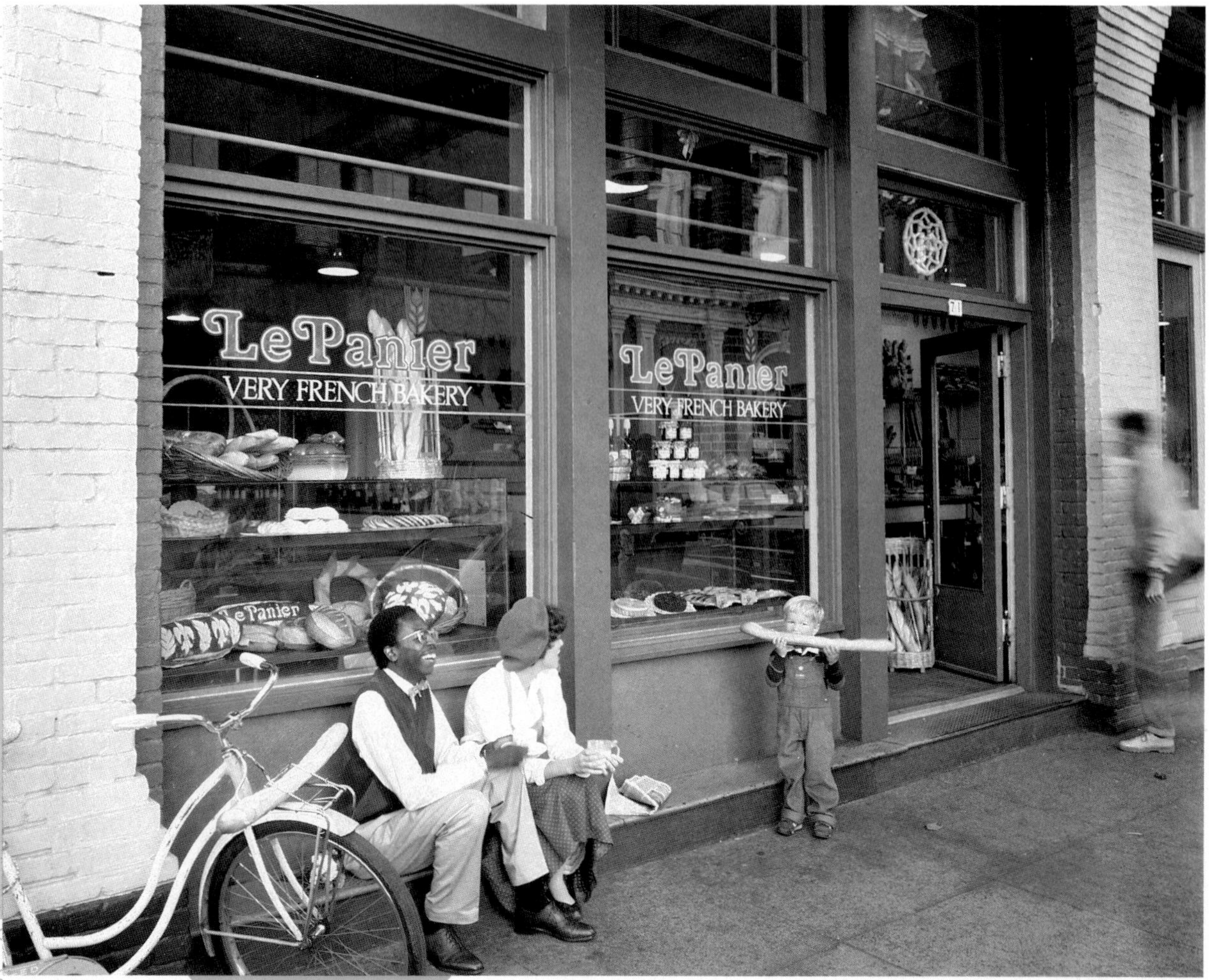

A bakery in the finest old world sense.

Quite possibly, even the European baking masters could learn something from a visit to Le Panier Very French Bakery. This is a bakery in the finest Old World sense...wood floors...the steam and heat of the ovens...patisserie displays...baskets of bread in a dozen shapes and sizes. All day, sophisticated French hearth ovens and skilled bakers are at work, turning out loaves wrapped in the crackling, crisp crust that is the very essence of French bread. Everything is authentic at this boulangerie/patisserie. At Le Panier, carrying on the finest traditions means that baguettes, country breads and parisians are made fresh daily without sugar and without shortening. And, of course, there is always a fresh supply of authentic all butter croissants and brioche. But there's more. An espresso bar that ranks among Portland's best. Pain Noel at Christmas. Couronne wreaths for holiday decorating. And even an original Le Panier creation, the Feuilleté, a square, open-faced tart filled with apples or Normandy-cream style sauce and chicken, gruyere cheese or vegetables.

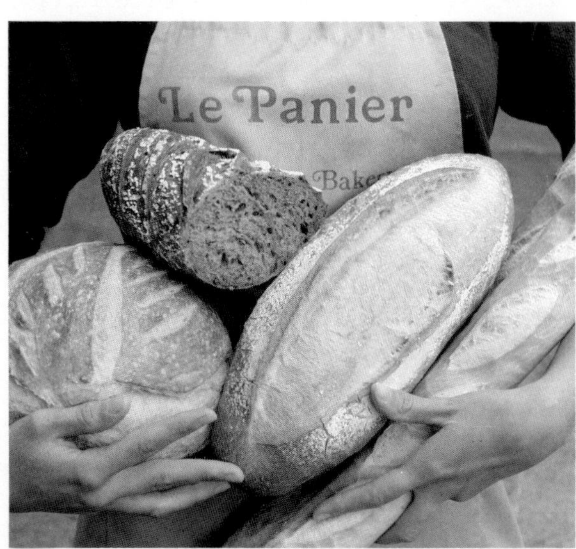

71 SW Second & Ash
Portland 97204
241-3524

Daily 7am-6pm

Clackamas Town Center
Portland 97266
659-5587

Monday-Friday
8am-9pm
Saturday 9:30am-6pm
Sunday 10am-6pm

Yamhill Marketplace
On Second Avenue
Portland 97204
241-5613

Monday-Friday
7am-6pm
Saturday 8am-6pm
Sunday 10am-6pm

Skidmore Historic District
E25

Clackamas Town Center
H9

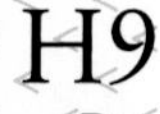

Yamhill Marketplace
G25

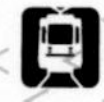

EDELWEISS SAUSAGE & DELICATESSEN

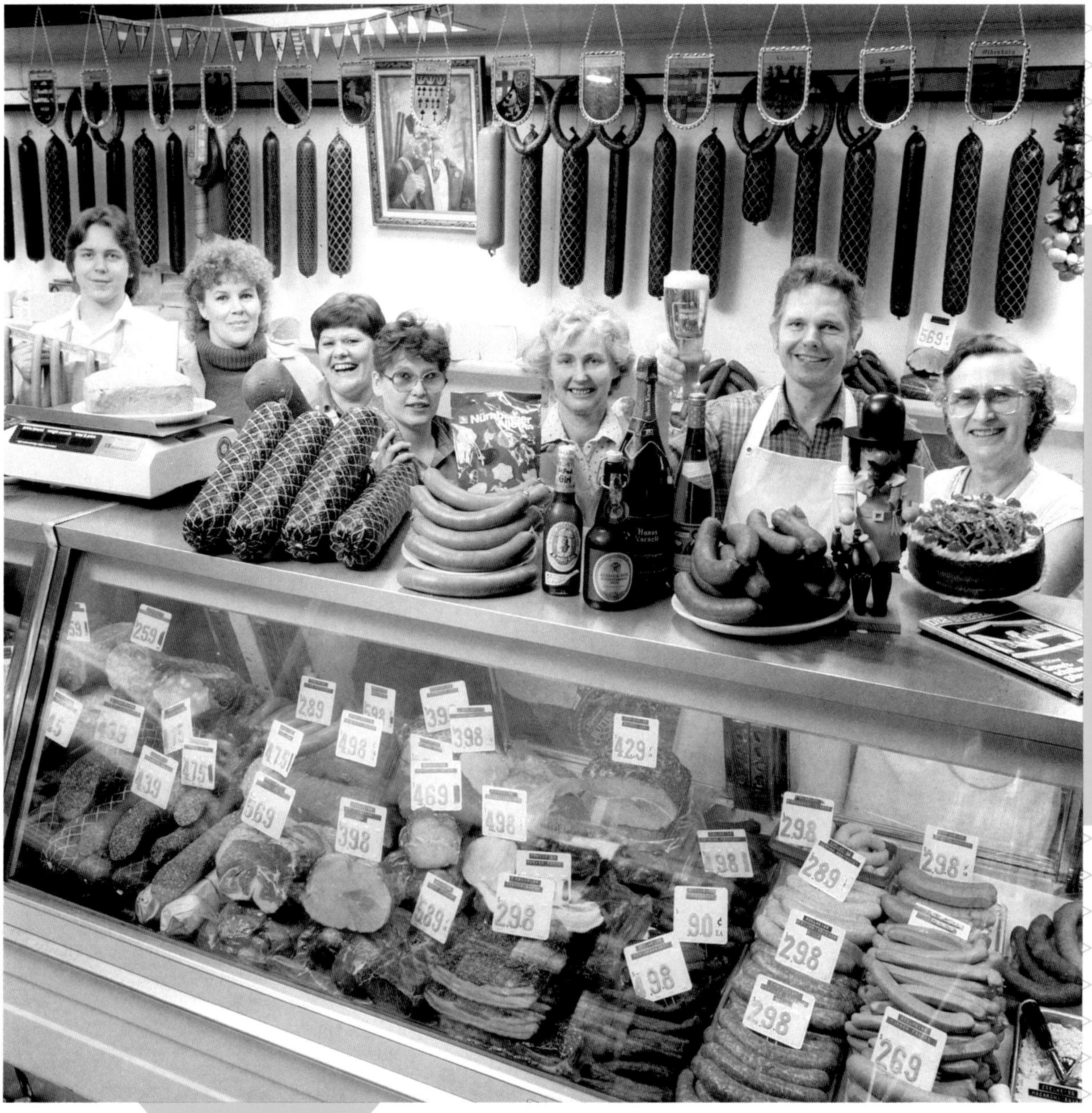

CATERING AND GOURMET FOODS

The complete German Delicatessen

If there's any delicatessen in Portland whose sausages could hang with pride in Hamburg and Frankfurt, Munich and Stuttgart, it's the Edelweiss Sausage & Delicatessen. Edelweiss offers eighty varieties of fresh, made-on-the-premises selections which you will smell cooking as soon as you step inside the door. If you can't wait to take yours home, the deli's eight-table eating area is an ideal spot for lunch, or coffee and a German torte. It takes more than salami, ham, bacon meat sausage and luncheon meats to make a world-class deli, however, and that's why George and Mary Lou Baier stock an uncommonly broad range of items. The Edelweiss features the finest European chocolates and cookies, including, come December, what might be the largest selection of chocolate Christmas tree ornaments in the city. If you're looking to recapture a romantic evening in the old country, the Edelweiss' German wines will spark the memory: there's also the imported jellies, juices, soups, cookies, breads, pudding mixes and a collection of rare cheeses. You'll even find some of the most popular German cosmetics, including creams, shampoos, soaps and mouthwashes. Good news for downtown Portland — Edelweiss now has a downtown lunchspot featuring a mouthwatering selection of their special delicacies. Visa. MasterCard.

3119 SE 12th Avenue
Portland 97202
238-4411

Monday-Thursday
9am-6pm
Friday 9am-7pm
Saturday 9am-6pm

1038 SW Morrison Street
Portland 97205
241-3354

Phone for hours

Southeast

E5

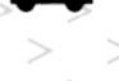

Downtown

F23

ANZEN ORIENTAL FOODS AND IMPORTS

CATERING AND GOURMET FOODS

The lure of the Orient beckons!

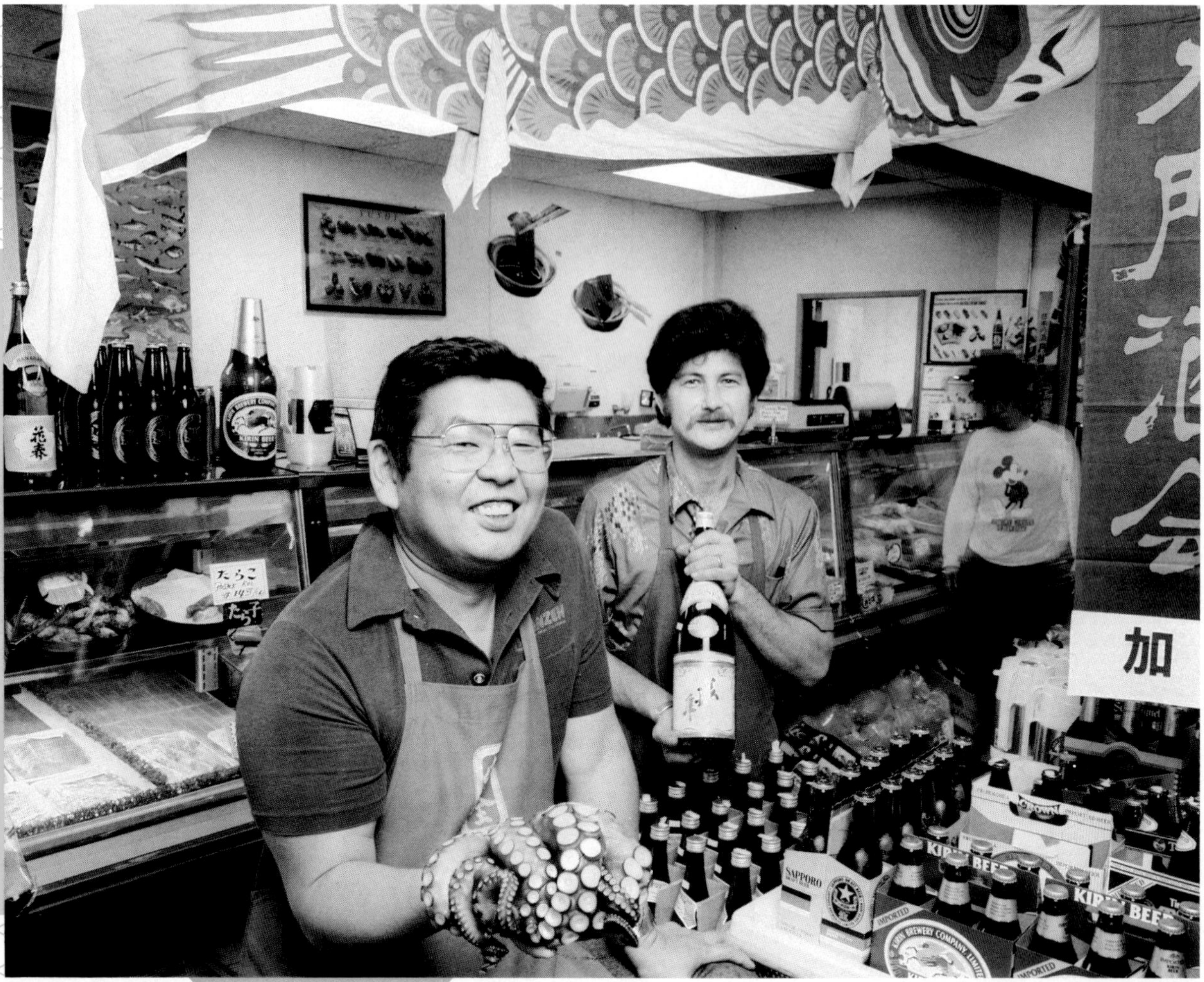

Welcome to a small reflection of Asia. Since 1902, Anzen Oriental Grocery and Imports has been a mainstay of Portland, serving the city with an ever growing and expanding inventory of Asian food staples, exotica and curiosities. Still going strong nearly 85 years later, Anzen is happy to provide customers with memories of home — as it does for its Asian customers, or new horizons — as it does for other Portland customers. While some customers arrive at Anzen's with definite shopping lists that can't be filled elsewhere, others come to browse for gifts, to sip free tea, and poke about among the well-stocked aisles. Whether you're in search of a very definite brand of hard-to-find soy sauce or sambal, banana leaves or fresh sushi, rare herbs or exotic sake, you'll find what you seek and then some. Once you've got your groceries, wander among the steamers, rice cookers, woks, cutlery or other kitchen necessities. A rack of books offers information on Asian history, cooking and a variety of arts. Jewelry featuring pearls and gold are on display, as are kimono, dishes, trays, futon — and bedding materials, ceramics and toys. Delightful gift ideas abound. When the lure of the Orient beckons, return to Asia — or discover it anew — at Anzen's. Visa. MasterCard.

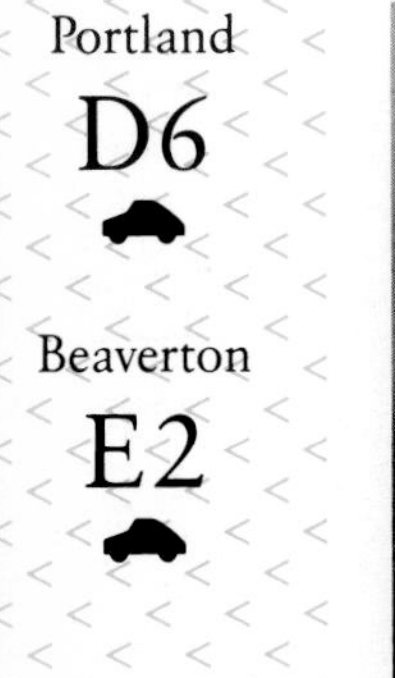

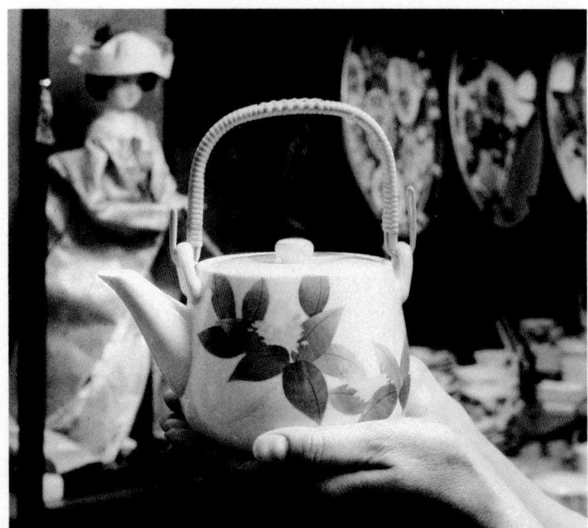

736 NE Union Avenue
Portland 97232
233-5111

Monday-Saturday
9am-6:30pm
Sunday noon-5pm

Canyon Place Mall
4021 SW 117th
Beaverton 97005
627-0913

Monday-Saturday
10am-6:30pm
Sunday noon-5pm

PASTA CUCINA

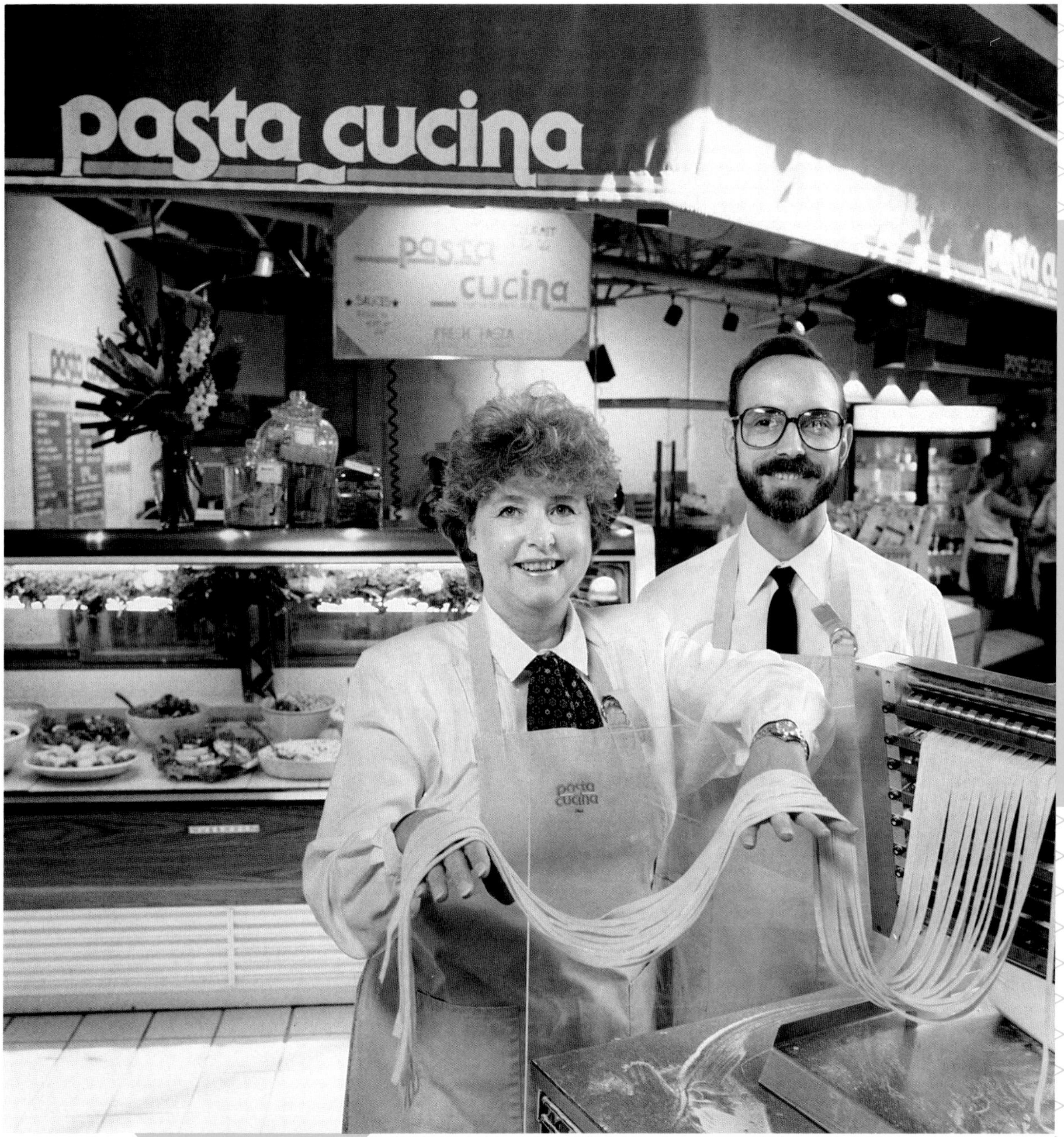

CATERING AND GOURMET FOODS

From our kitchen to yours.

For pleased Portland pasta patrons, canned spaghetti and meatballs is a thing of the past. At Pasta Cucina busy gourmets can take home a variety of freshly-made pasta and a mouth-watering selection of sauces. Fettuccine with Lover's Garlic Sauce (eat it only with someone who loves garlic as much as you do) or Fresh Lemon and Herb sauce can be yours to savor within moments of your arrival home. Each day, owner Judy Cooper and manager Gary McCutcheon offer five varieties of fresh noodles plus exceptional ravioli, and shaped pasta. Pesto, Garlic Herb, Marinara, Four Cheese and Spicy Artichoke are just a few of the delectable sauce offerings. If you've invited guests, but you're short on preparation time, ask the Pasta Cucina staff to help you prepare the dinner of your choice. Or sample the selection of take-out items, including Spicy Sesame Noodles, Marinated Vegetables, Pesto Fettuccine salad and fresh Lasagna. Pasta Cucina will prepare a delightful picnic—from entree to dessert. Cucina is the Italian word for kitchen—and pasta fans are treated to a full view of the home style "cucina" behind a tantalizing display case. Visa. MasterCard.

Yamhill Marketplace
110 SW Yamhill Street
Portland 97204
227-7515

Daily
10am-6pm

Yamhill Historic District

G25

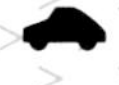

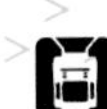

GREAT HARVEST BREAD CO.

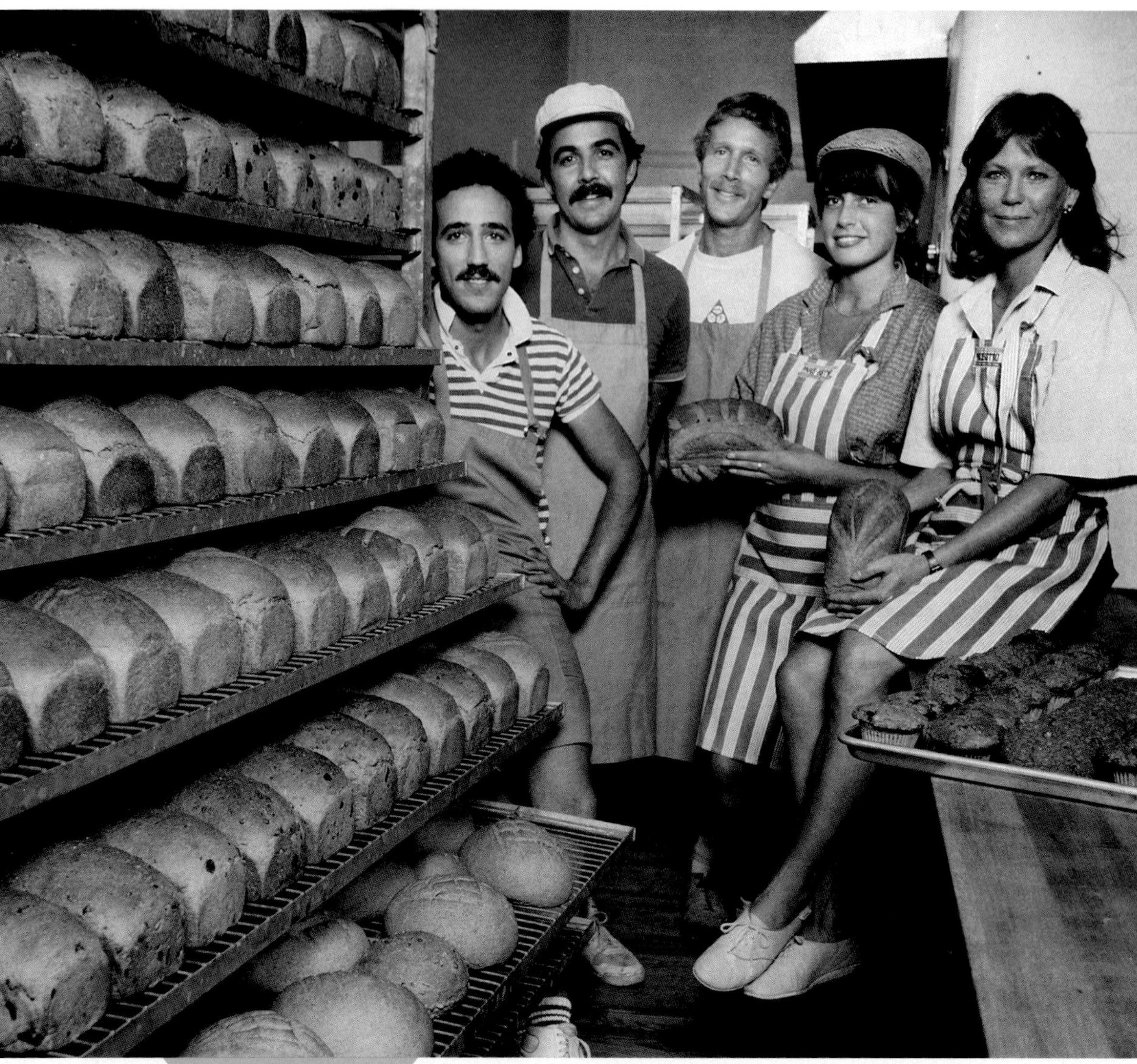

CATERING AND GOURMET FOODS

Premium Montana wheat, fresh milled and baked to perfection!

Yamhill Historic District

G25

Few advertising campaigns have the simple and direct success of the "Bread in Mouth" approach taken by Tim and Jane Hartfield, co-owners of the Great Harvest Bread Company. Each day, the Hartfields put out generous samples of their baked goods and let the aroma, texture, and eye appeal take care of sales. There are no pre-mixes or shortcuts in the preparation and baking of Harvest breads, cookies, rolls, muffins, and cinnamon rolls. In fact, Harvest's Premium Montana Hard Red Spring Wheat is personally selected and trucked to Portland. Ground fresh every day, organically sweetened, and kneaded by hand, this wheat becomes the foundation for an assortment of baked delectables that include six types of whole wheat bread and one rye, muffins chocked with walnuts, raisins, blueberries, blackberries, along with honey orange walnut and oatmeal raisin spice variations. Their cookies — oatmeal and peanut butter chocolate chip, and oatmeal raisin — have been touted by The Downtowner as the best in the downtown area. From this you might guess, their two varieties of cinnamon rolls and three kinds of dinner rolls are also masterpieces of the baker's art. It's said that a good bread travels well and Harvest's passes the test. Harvest's bread has been taken abroad to Germany to prove to skeptical parents that it's possible to get good bread in America!

837 SW Second at Taylor
Portland 97204
224-8583

Monday-Friday
7am-6pm
Saturday 8am-5pm

NATURE'S FRESH NORTHWEST

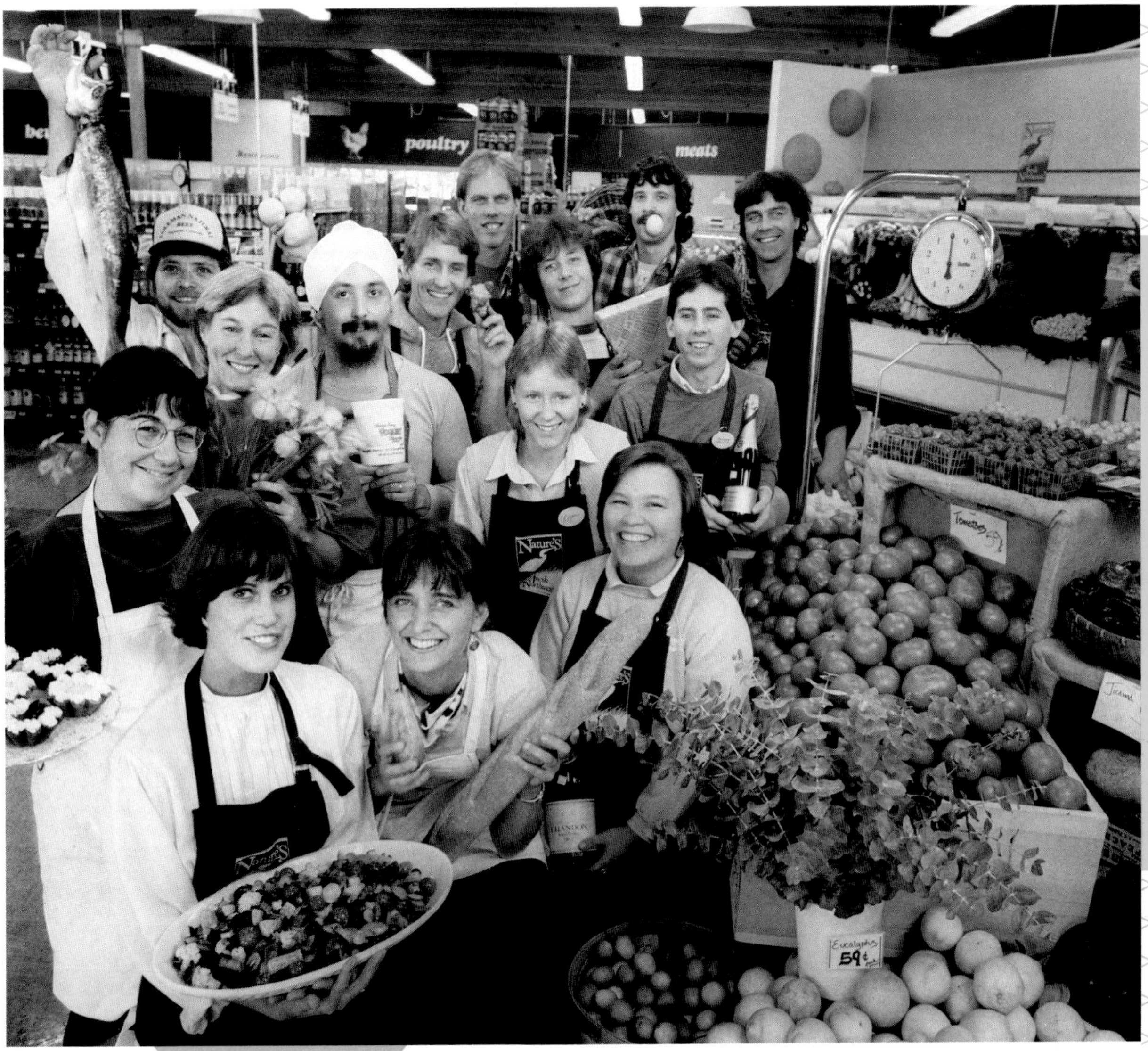

CATERING AND GOURMET FOODS

Where grocery shopping is an occasion.

Nature's Fresh Northwest is a one-of-a-kind grocery store. They offer the Northwest's largest selection of wholesome, honest, chemical-free foods. A fascinating place to do your basic grocery shopping, you don't just shop at Nature's — you explore. You can start your excursion with the produce department where you find fresh, seasonal mushrooms like shitakes, morels, and chanterelles, locally grown herbs, delicata squash and radiccio as well as artistic arrangements of more familiar produce, much of it organically grown. A trip to the bulk foods bins reveals 52 different grains including five kinds of rice, cous cous and an Andean grain called quinoa. There are also 78 serve-yourself herbs and spices at prices that put the little square tins to shame. The cheeses are an adventure in themselves; up to 150 kinds come from all over the globe — including Oregon. A selection of 450 wines and 90 beers should satisfy the most venturous epicure. A tour of the non-food items offers everything from the mundane (paper towels and dog food) to the exotic (delicately hand-carved gourds). The Fremont store carries very fresh fish and naturally grown chickens and the Beaverton store boasts an old-fashioned complete meat market of all chemical-free meat! When you're ready for a break, you can wind your way to the delicatessen at the Fremont and Beaverton stores and sit down with a snack or lunch and maybe take something home for dinner, too. Any one of Nature's three distinctive stores is a great place to spend a rainy day shopping.

4000 SW 117th Avenue — *Daily*
Beaverton 97005 — *9am-9pm*
646-3824

3449 NE 24th Avenue — *Daily*
Portland 97212 — *9am-8pm*
288-3414

5909 SW Corbett Avenue — *Daily*
Portland 97201 — *9am-8pm*
244-3934

Beaverton

E2

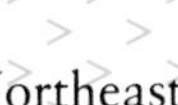

Northeast Portland

C7

Corbett-Johns Landing

F5

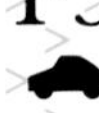

COFFEE BEAN

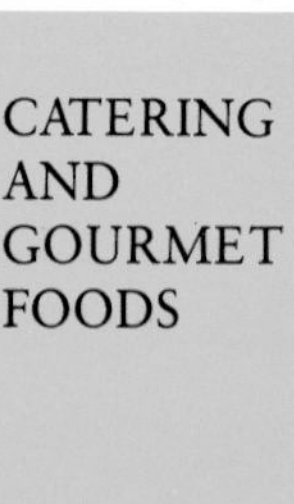

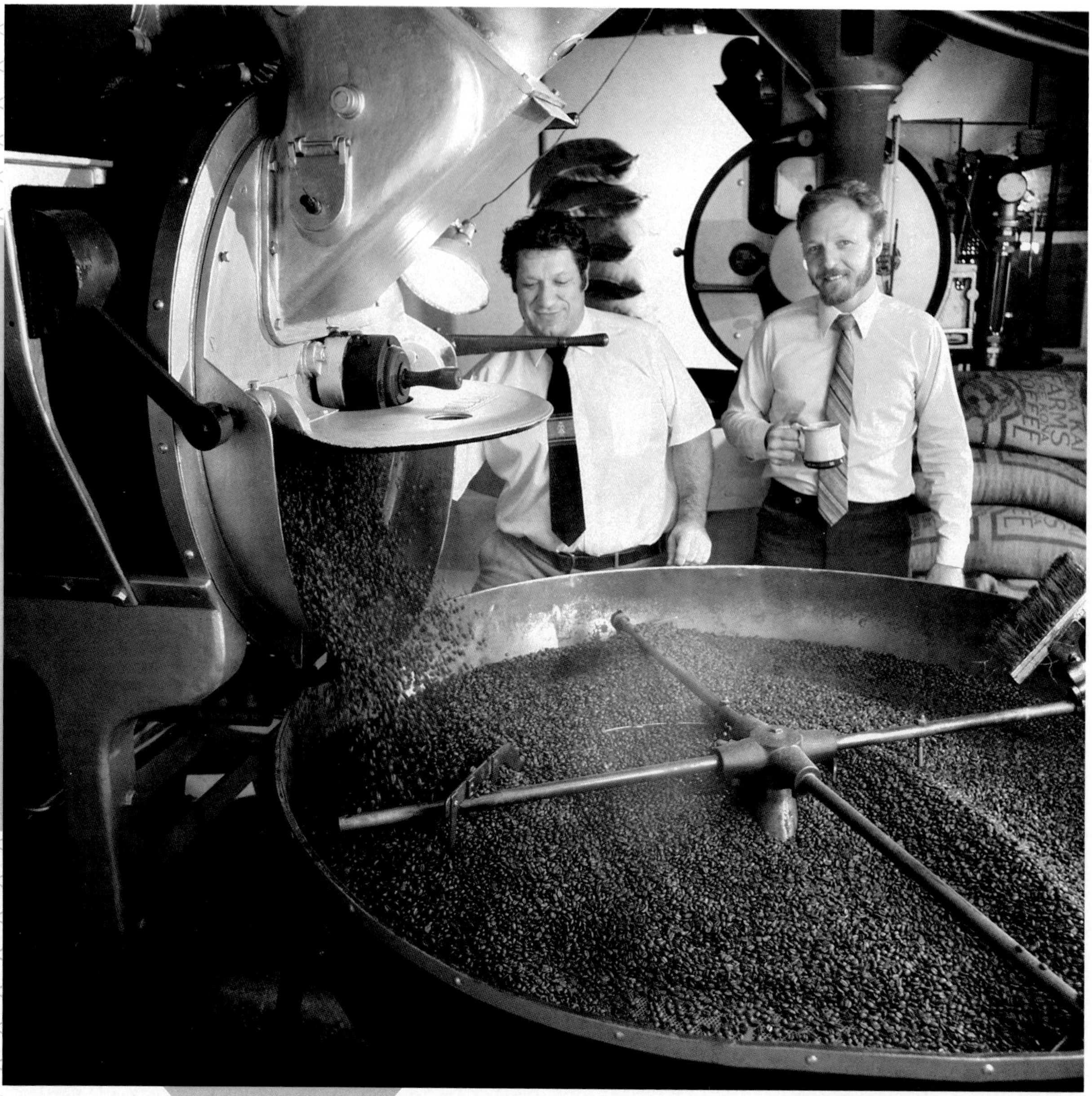

CATERING AND GOURMET FOODS

The Northwest's leading coffee roaster.

Beaverton

E2

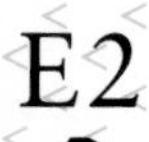

Like a pied piper, the rich, luxurious aroma of roasting coffee will draw you into the Coffee Bean. Since 1972, as the first and only Oregon coffee store to roast its own beans, the Coffee Bean has earned a reputation for unsurpassed quality. Now the Northwest's leading coffee roaster, Coffee Bean International provides some of the world's finest, most flavorful Arabica coffees. The beans are skillfully dry-roasted daily and "same- day" shipped from Coffee Bean's historic Northwest headquarters. Following an Old World European tradition, Coffee Bean roasts over 130 choice coffees under the direction of owners Gary Talboy and Jeff Ferguson. Fine restaurants in Oregon and Washington, such as the Couch Street Fish House, proudly serve their exquisite coffee. And many of the best coffee and tea stores nationwide rely exclusively on Coffee Bean International for their coffee and an array of other gourmet products. At the Coffee Bean Roasters, the retail location of Coffee Bean International, an expert staff will be delighted to assist you. They offer in addition to some of the best coffees available, exceptional blended teas, imported spices, superb chocolates and candies; tea brewers, espresso and cappuccino makers, "French Press" brewers, home roasting equipment; designer carafes, assorted cups, mugs and other delights. All of which awaits the true coffee afficionado in search of the perfect brew. Visa. MasterCard.

Canyon Square
4130 SW 117th at
Canyon Road
Beaverton 97005
643-3053

Monday-Friday
9am-7pm
Saturday 9am-6pm
Sunday noon-5pm

ROSE'S VIENNESE BAKERY

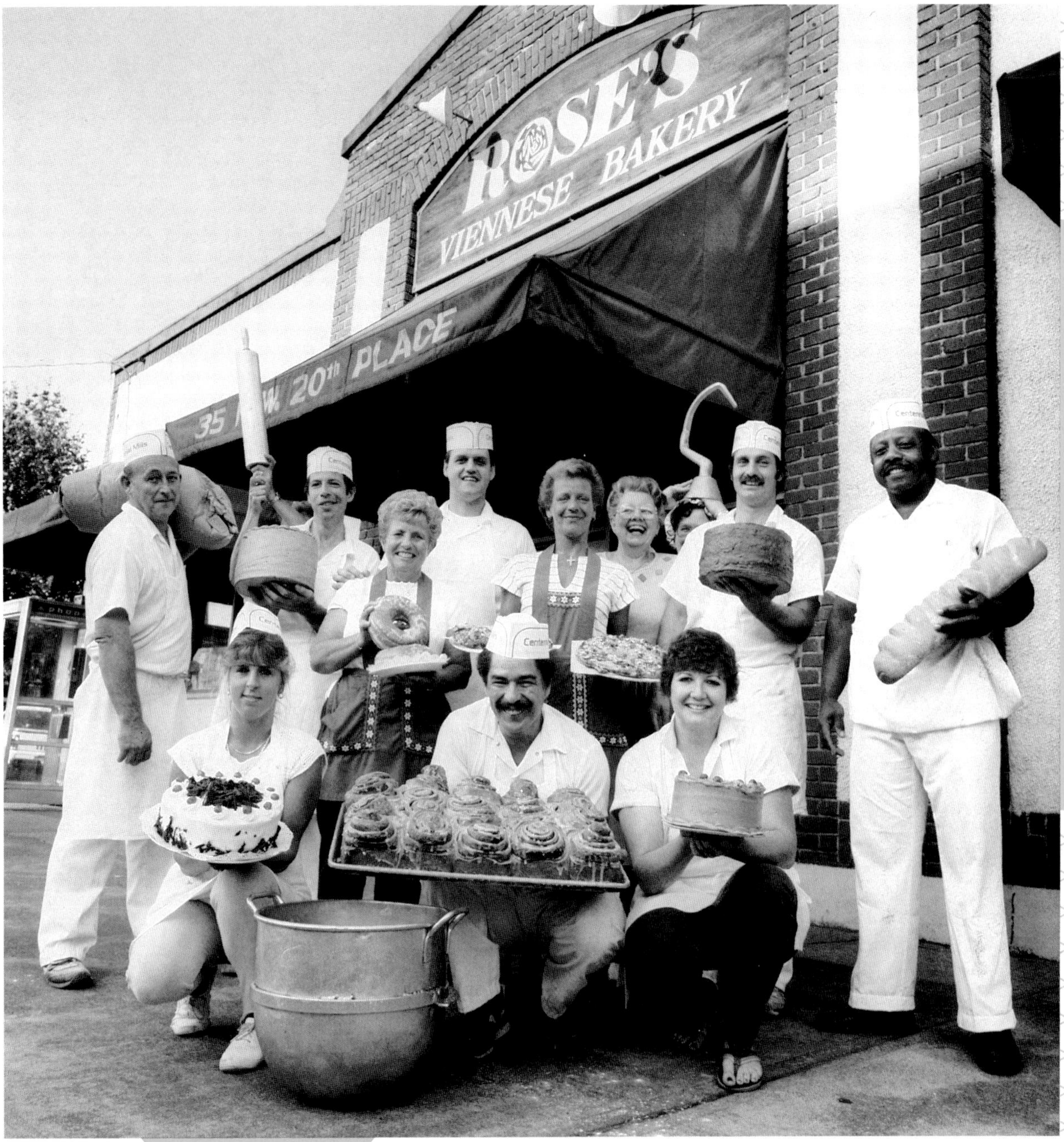

CATERING AND GOURMET FOODS

A unique Viennese bakery.

At a recent ceremony, Max Birnbach was awarded a silver medal from Austria for being, in the words of that country's consul in Seattle, "A first-class representative of Austria". Besides serving the memory of his homeland years after leaving, Birnbach and junior partner, Ivan Runge, have served customers of Rose's Viennese Bakery since 1968 some of the city's finest cakes and pastries. Old World Austrian specialities are created with aplomb here: apfel streudel, apfel streusel kuchen, gugelhupf, tortes, and eclairs are but a few of the many sweet delights contending for Dessert of the Day. Cakes for all occasions, especially weddings, are the specialty. Giant cinnamon, almond and pecan rolls will lure you from anyone else's. Russian and Bohemian rye breads will enclose sandwiches fit for the Czar himself. Chocolate lovers will be stunned by a pecan fudge cake so huge it almost needs a building permit. The bakery also supplies Rose's three restaurants, renowned for their generous servings and food in the best European tradition. Visa. Mastercard. Diners Club. Carte Blanche.

35 NW 20th Place
Portland 97209
227-4875

Monday-Saturday
7am-7pm
Sunday 9am-5pm

Northwest Portland

J19

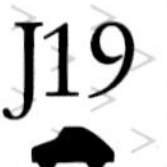

EXECUTIVE SWEETS, DESSERTS ETC.

CATERING AND GOURMET FOODS

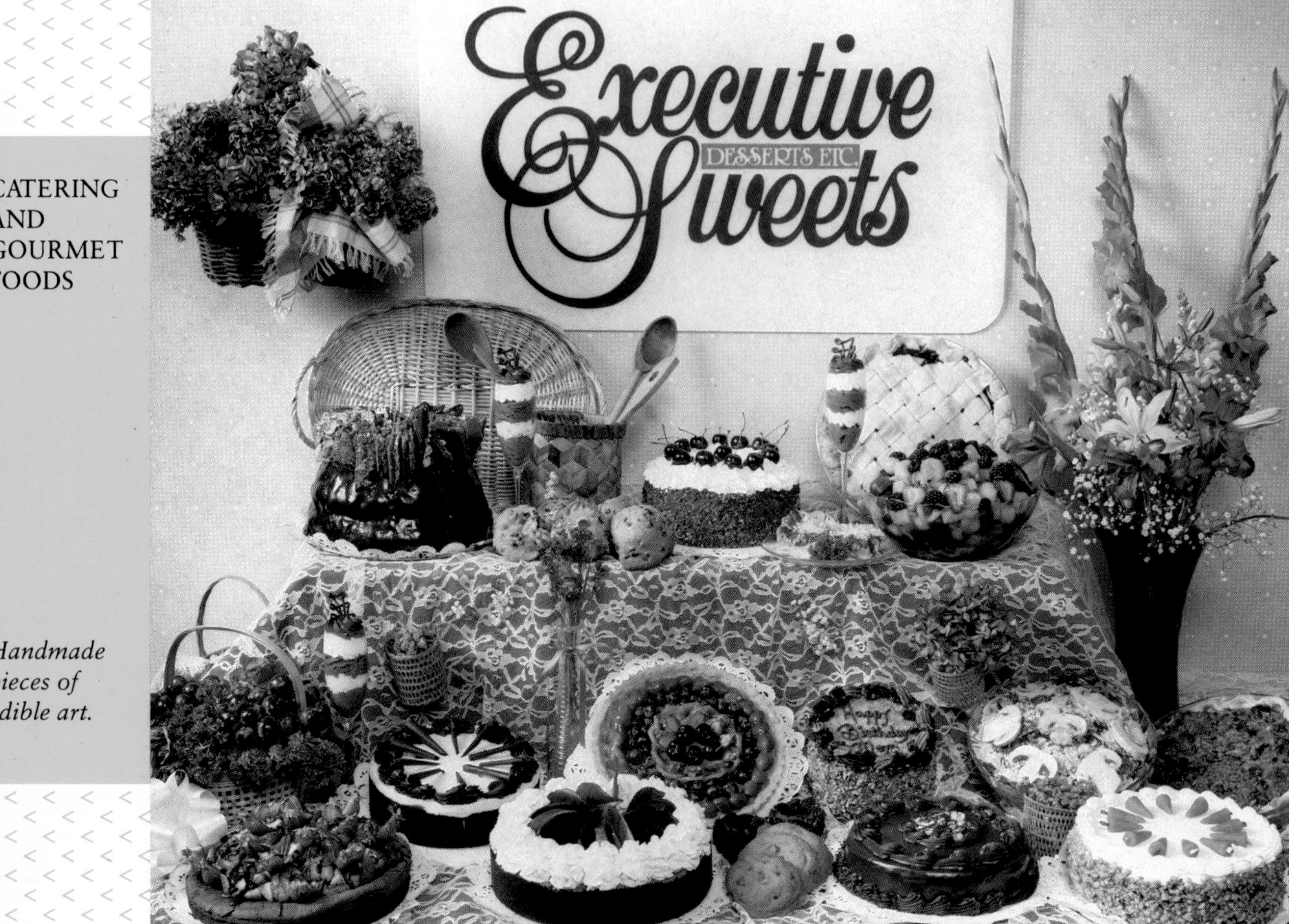

Handmade pieces of edible art.

Downtown
G24
Downtown
G22

As every connoisseur knows, objects worthy of recognition bear the unmistakable qualities that elevate them from ordinary to exquisite. At Executive Sweets the traditional cake and cookie have been transformed into handmade pieces of edible art, each one deserving the palate's praise. To create delicacies elegant enough to display in a museum, owner Jennifer Youngberg relies on handmade garnish, ribbons of fresh whipped cream and other highly perishable products. Besides a dessert-making style recognized throughout the city, she brings customers light lunches and stupendous salads, served in a casual, airy setting. Each day's chicken salad is filled with large chunks of breast meat whether it be Curried, Chinese style, Spicy with Peanuts, Tarragon style or Chicken Waldorf. Soups — among them Apple Chicken, Creamy Garden Bisque and Sherried Tomato — bring new style to an old favorite. Assorted muffins — blueberry, blackberry, raspberry, banana nut, pineapple and honey bran — help round out the list. But not to be forgotten is the Chocolate Mousse Pie, combining more than a pound of Guittard chocolate garnished with whipped cream and handmade chocolate leaves. And when the occasion arises: Custom wedding cakes and specialty desserts are a succulent sensation. Visa. MasterCard.

324 SW Taylor Street
Portland 97204
224-4222

Monday-Friday
7:30am-5:30pm

Retail/Wholesale Bakery
1201 SW Jefferson Street
Portland 97201
224-7228

Monday-Friday
7:30am-2pm

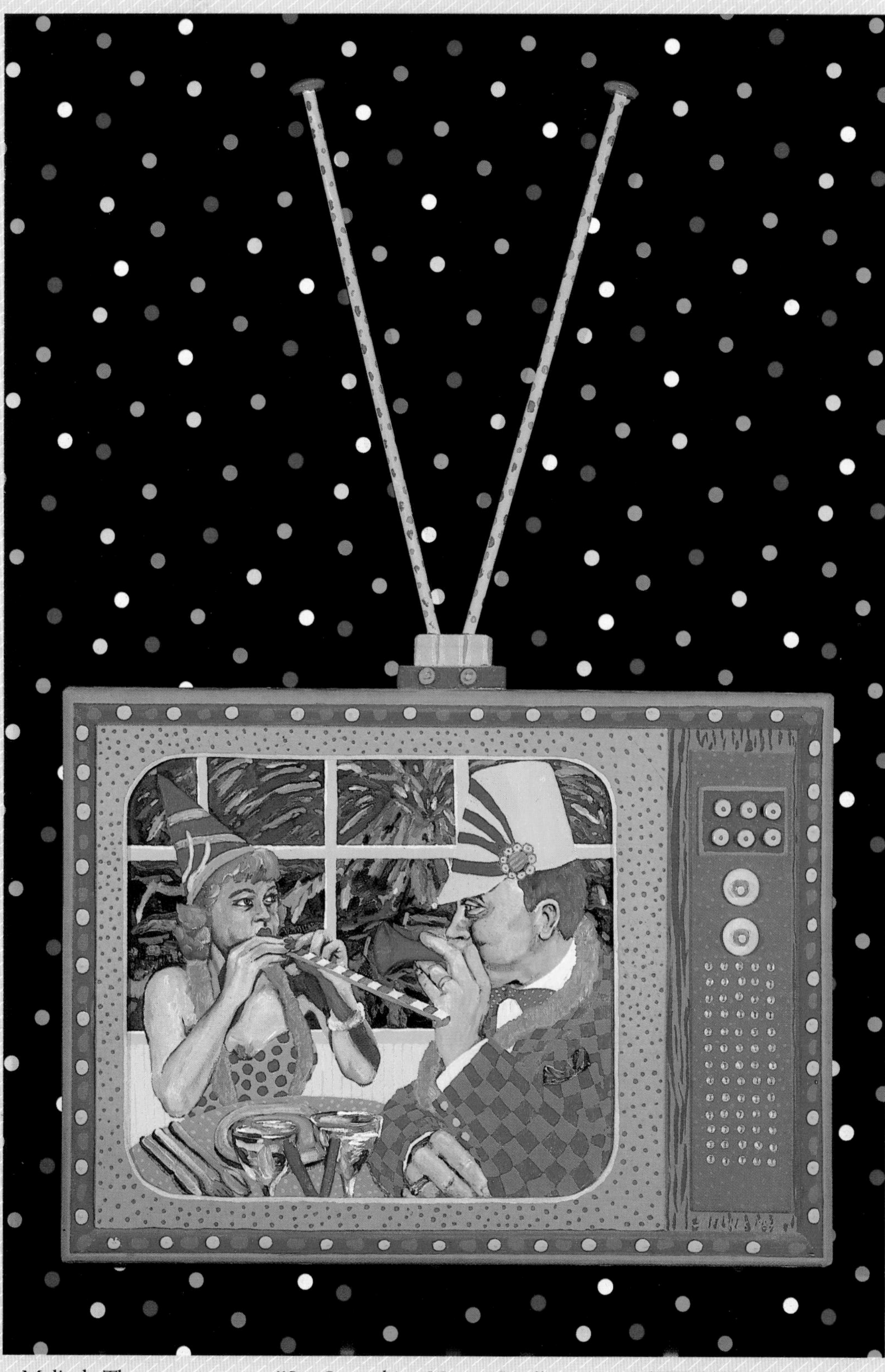

Melinda Thorsnes *"Say Something Mauna Loa"* LAWRENCE GALLERY

ENTERTAINMENT

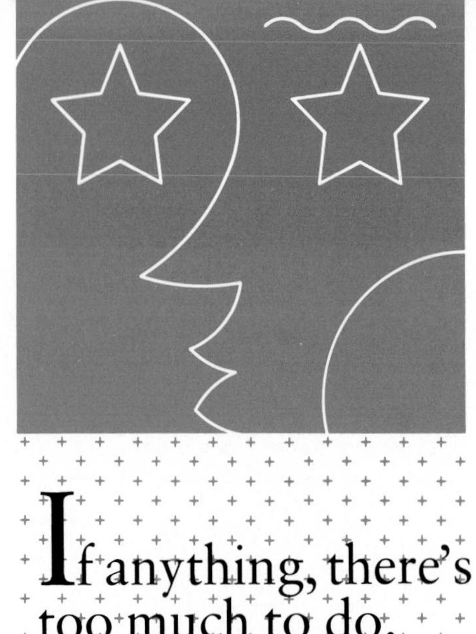

If anything, there's too much to do.

As our commissioner of Public Affairs, I guess I'm responsible. I'm certain that one morning I'll awaken to hear that headlines all over the country are screaming: "CITY OF PORTLAND INDICTED: POSSESSION OF IMPRESSIVE ARTS AND ENTERTAINMENT IN THE FIRST DEGREE!"

What can I say? Portland has always been one of the most enjoyable cities in the country and it is really time we were held accountable for it. It was bound to happen. For the last 30 years we've been quietly attracting a wealth of talented people who wished to join the native-born Oregonians in a well-kept secret. Well, we finally reached a critical mass and good times are bustin' out all over.

From St. Johns to Lents, from Argay to Bridlemile you don't have to look long or hard to see the creative, energetic and sensitive character of this city. You could start with the scores of parks we've had the presence of mind to create. Portlanders have demonstrated a spirit of cooperation rather than competition with nature. We have the largest municipal park in the country and we're proud of its miles of trails, wildlife, and flora. Our cityscape betokens a legacy of commitment to both greenery and urban development. It is a legacy Portland is prepared to improve upon and carry into the next century. However, if tonight is as far ahead as you want to look, Portland can more than accommodate you.

If anything, there's too much to do. Even before the sun sets a host of institutions offer enough childrens' activities to wear out the fittest parents, not to mention our myriad noontime and free weekend concerts. Four beautiful and completely different stages make up our new Performing Arts Center which hosts events that seat from 300 to 3,000 theater-goers. Great theater echoes from the stages alongside soaring symphonic music, electrifying jazz, outrageous comedy, country music, opera, dance and whatever else strikes the fancy of Rose City residents out on the town.

It is probably Portland's voracious appetite for the arts which has close to one hundred metro area nightclubs offering live music: there's somebody worth hearing every night of the week. Live music in Portland has reached its own critical mass. Whether you want to jam to Ghanian drums, mindboggling bebop, hibernian bagpipes, some of the best hardcore rock on the West Coast, or original instrument classical music, you can do it all in one night in Portland and never have to drive for much more than fifteen minutes. The devotees of the visual arts can keep themselves engaged for hours strolling through downtown galleries, ranging from the permanent and visiting collections at the Portland Art Museum, to those specializing in Native American work, or furniture as art, or the creations of Northwest artists. Even our sidewalks constitute an eclectic pedestrian sculpture garden.

Your stroll may take you down to the Saturday (and Sunday) Market under the Burnside Bridge, where you can peruse the booths and caravans of scores of craftspeople, overeat from far too many serious ethnic food stands, catch the intense mingling sounds of steel drums, strolling violinists, a fine hammer-dulcimer ensemble and watch, if you're lucky, the routines of the galaxy's most intelligent and professional multi-frisbee-catching dog.

Yes, there is a magic to Portland. Perhaps it comes from being nestled in a verdant valley at the confluence of two beautiful rivers. We do, indeed, have a superior cultural and recreational community. Our citizens have a holistic concept of "the bottom line." It includes food for the spirit as well as dollars in the bank. Our citizens don't just watch and support the arts, our citizens live the arts in our community theaters, art shows, bands, choral groups, and dance companies. We're talented, hardworking, and we're marvelous at enjoying ourselves. I can understand the rest of the country starting to sit up and take notice. It's the burden of being among the best.. We're Portland and we can handle it, with pleasure. *Mike Lindberg*

Mike Lindberg, *Portland City Commissioner, among many other responsibilities, is in charge of parks, recreation and the arts.*

Melinda Thorsnes *is an artist whose work is vibrantly colorful and whimsical, whether it be slouching cowboys or a penetrating self-portrait. Her oil-painted cut-out figures and acrylic-painted clay sculptures are "tongue-in-cheek" examples of "what makes people work." Widely exhibited throughout the Northwest, she is represented by the Lawrence Gallery.*

What's your pleasure? Handel on the river, Beethoven in formal attire, fireworks to Tchaikovsky, Satie in the round? From grand concert halls to blankets in the park, Portland's classical music scene offers much for musical palates from light to rich.

OREGON SYMPHONY ORCHESTRA

The Oregon Symphony's ever-popular Music Director and Conductor James DePreist pulls out all the stops each season, offering powerful classical music. Perennial favorite Associate Conductor Norman Leyden draws crowds with his entertaining Pops series. Symphony Sundays, meanwhile, provide relaxing, melodic fun for the entire family. The Oregon Symphony is the oldest orchestra in the West and can be counted on for consistently high quality entertainment. Music Max, the new ticket coupon system, offers a flexible season of enjoyment.

813 SW Alder Street
Portland 97205
228-4294
Tickets: 228-1353

Monday-Friday
10am-4:30pm

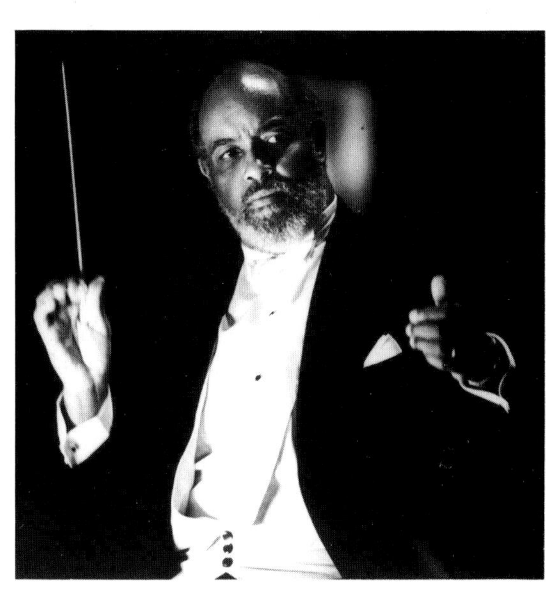

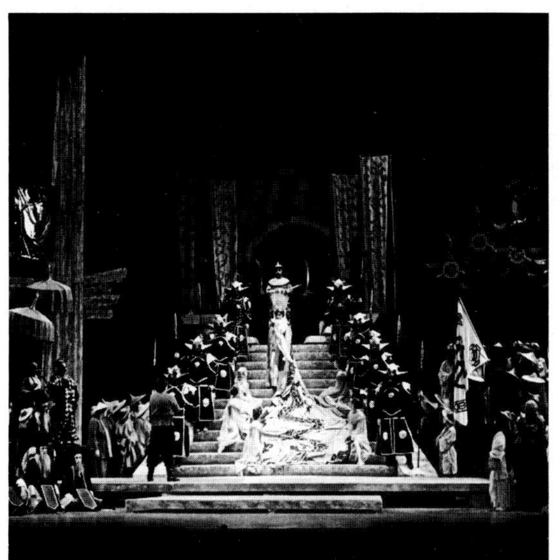

Rick Adams

PORTLAND OPERA ASSOCIATION

The 14th largest company in the country and one of the brightest cultural lights in the community, Portland Opera has grown steadily to its present stature as a fully professional, internationally-recognized opera company. With both traditional and innovative works in its repertoire, it accommodates a wide spectrum of tastes. The Opera's new young touring company — Portland Opera Players — introduces Oregon and Washington audiences of all ages to the magic of opera. This organization — worth its weight in C notes — offers the extraordinary.

1530 SW Second Avenue
Portland 97201
241-1407
Tickets: 241-1802

Monday-Friday
8:30am-5pm

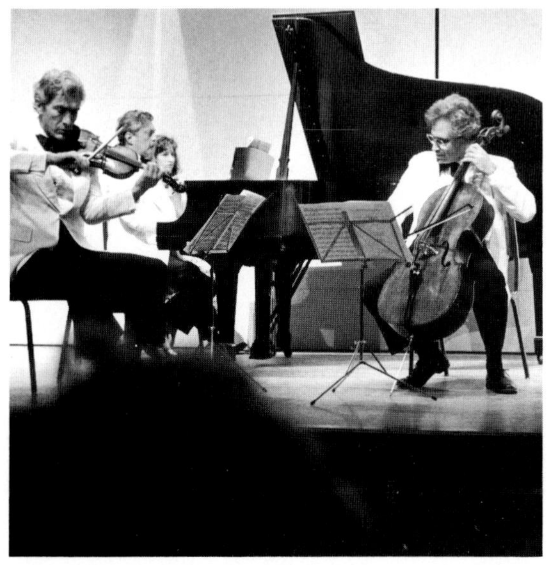

CHAMBER MUSIC NORTHWEST

From late June to late July Portland never worries about what to do on a pleasant summer evening. Hundreds happily pack picnic baskets and head toward a Chamber Music Northwest performance. It is easy to see how the popular pre-concert picnic tradition began ... the performances are held on the beautiful Reed College and Catlin Gable School campuses. Now a Portland classic, this nationally acclaimed summer music festival attracts some of the country's finest artists. The concert season offers refreshing informality, intimacy and musical excitement.

1421 SW Sixth Avenue
Suite 418
Portland 97204
223-3202

OREGON REPERTORY SINGERS

The Oregon Repertory Singers, under the direction of Gilbert Seeley, presents concerts of choral music at Lewis and Clark's Agnes Flannagan Chapel, as well as other locations around Portland. The choir, which recently toured Europe and was the recipient of a first place award at a prestigious music festival in Austria, is 60 voices strong and performs a four-concert season of varied repertoire. Talented and enchanting, Oregon Repertory Singers has brought a new dimension to choral music in the Northwest. Bach to Bacharach ... you'll hear it all.

P.O. Box 894
Portland Federal Station
Portland 97207
227-3929

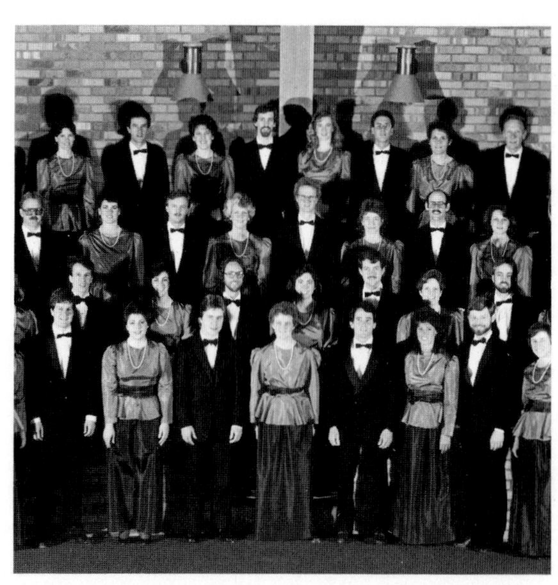

PORTLAND YOUTH PHILHARMONIC

Portland Youth Philharmonic is America's first youth orchestra and is generally acknowledged to be the finest in the country. Portland Youth Philharmonic performs a series of evening concerts in the Arlene Schnitzer Concert Hall and several special concerts a year. In addition, this orchestra was the first non-professional group asked to perform at the Waterfront classics. Under the brilliant direction of longtime educator and conductor Jacob Avshalomov, the Youth Philharmonic has had highly successful international concert tours.

1119 SW Park Avenue
Portland 97205
223-5939

Monday-Friday
9am-5pm

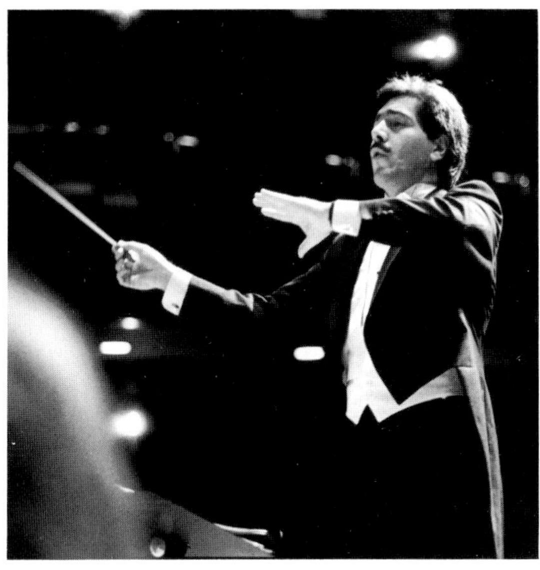

WEST COAST CHAMBER ORCHESTRA

The recipient of wide critical acclaim, the West Coast Chamber Orchestra, comprising thirty of the finest regional musicians, is the only professional chamber orchestra between Seattle and San Francisco. The small size and professionalism of the Orchestra provides the rare opportunity to enjoy classical music in the intimate setting of the Intermediate Theater at the new Performing Arts building. The Orchestra also participates in the Waterfront Classics series and special events in the spring and fall.

1615 SE Alder Street
Suite 504
Portland 97214
236-5537

Call for performance schedule

PORTLAND SYMPHONIC CHOIR

One of a handful of independent symphonic choirs in the country, the Portland Symphonic Choir is the oldest and largest independent choral organization in Portland. Over its history, the 130-voice group has performed world premieres and entertained at national conventions. It was one of three choirs honored to represent the United States at a prestigious European choral festival. The official chorus of the Oregon Symphony, the Symphonic Choir also presents a concert series of classic to contemporary works three times a year.

PO Box 1517
Portland 97207
223-1217

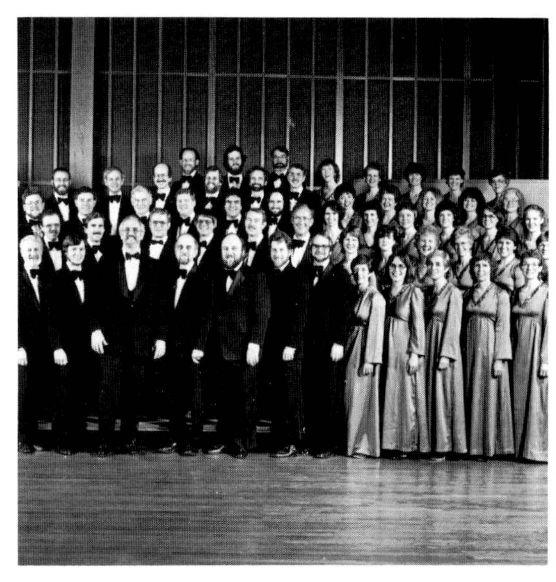

Rich Iwasaki

CHAMBER MUSIC SOCIETY

The Chamber Music Society of Oregon was formed in 1973 to show children and young adults that music is fun and to provide a happy way of spending time creatively. In a series of concerts and camps, beginning through advanced students receive instruction from fine local musicians and teachers. Scholarships and an instrument bank bring music instruction and instruments to many students who would otherwise never know the discipline, motivation and enjoyment that music provides. Help make this season successful — support these young musicians.

1935 NE 59th Avenue
Portland 97213
287-2175

Paul Blixt

THEATER

It's dark back there behind the curtains. The audience coughs, laughs, talks, makes noises with programs. They come expecting a miracle—transportation to a new world. The house lights dim, there is almost instant quiet, and the curtain begins to rise . . .

THE PORTLAND REPERTORY

The Rep is Portland's only professional equity theater which allows quality professional artists from across the nation to perform here. Their season of six major plays includes a blend of contemporary, modern and Oregon premiere productions. With the combined experience of founding director Mark Allen and artistic director, Brenda Hubbard, the Rep brings first rate artistic quality to Portland. The Rep boasts sell-out crowds, as theatergoers favor the comfortable seating and secured on-site parking in the beautiful Willamette Center.

25 SW Salmon Street
Portland 97204
224-4491

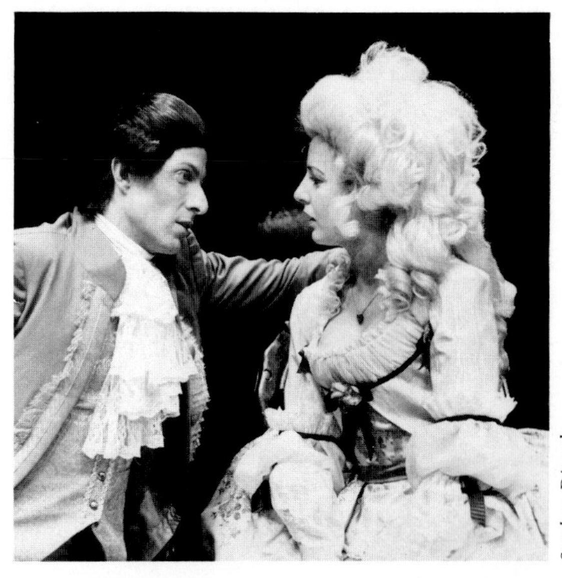

Stephen Dipaola

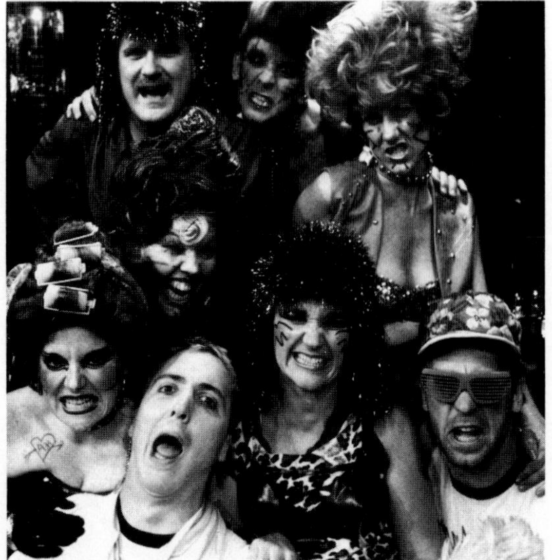

STOREFRONT THEATRE

Storefront Theatre is well known for its raw vitality, provocative visuals and sense of daring. Sometimes controversial, the theater provides original work and the Oregon premieres of plays such as "Angry Housewives," "Ma Rainey's Black Bottom" and "E/R Emergency Room." The theater, which has gained national recognition since its founding for exploring new elements of theater, now performs its regular season in the new Performing Arts building. Storefront is never dull. Season tickets guarantee seats for theater at the cutting edge.

Administrative office
615 NW Couch Street
Portland 97209
224-9598

Ticket office
224-4001

Rick Adams

PORTLAND CIVIC THEATRE

1530 SW Yamhill Street
Portland 97205
226-3048

Monday-Saturday
Noon-8pm
Sunday 5pm-8pm

Portland's oldest and largest live theater presents splashy Broadway musicals, drama and comedy in two separate theaters: the Mainstage for spectacular productions like "Sweeney Todd" and the intimate Blue Room arena for plays like "Requiem for a King" or "Greater Tuna." This year "Peter Pan" will be performed. Save money with season tickets for the regular season or the Summer Repertory Onstage (SRO) Company. Call for information on open auditions, volunteering, year round classes for children and adults, or ticket reservations.

THE NEW ROSE THEATER

The New Rose presents the classics, yet only those classics which are timeless in their message and speak to contemporary audiences. Actors are guided to place emphasis on the actor-audience relationship, which accounts for the feeling one gets of being part of the action when attending a New Rose performance. During its seven-play season, plays especially for children are also performed. This widely recognized theater performs in its own theater in the Masonic Temple, and in the new Performing Arts building's Dolores Winningstad Theater.

904 SW Main Street
Portland 97204
222-2487

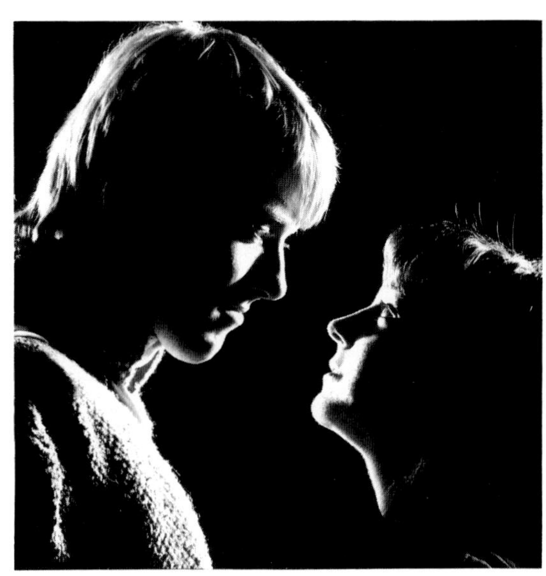

Rick Adams

ARTISTS REPERTORY THEATRE

Rick Adams

1111 SW Tenth Avenue
Portland 97205
242-2400

The Artists Repertory Theatre's "Off-Broadway" profile is stronger than ever. Audiences can look forward not only to excellent acting but to plays that always possess a different element or twist. Examples of some of the hits of recent seasons include "Sister Mary Ignatius," "Sea Marks," and "Quilters." A.R.T.'s intimate theater, located at the Wilson Center for the Performing Arts in the YWCA building downtown, is perfect for viewing some of the most satisfying adult and children's performance to be found in Portland.

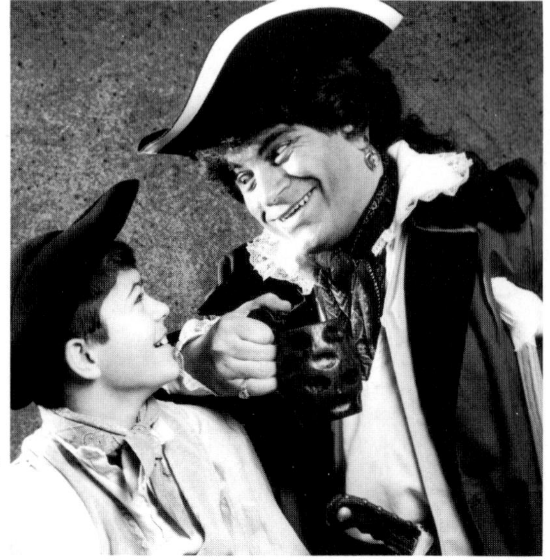
Owen Carey

FIREHOUSE THEATER

1436 SW Montgomery Drive
Portland 97201
248-4737

Monday-Friday
8:30am-4:30pm

Performances Saturday and Sunday

The Firehouse Theater building, constructed in 1901, was originally a fire station. In the mid-60's the Bureau of Parks and Recreation purchased and renovated the facility. Now celebrating its 22nd season in its 73-seat facility, Firehouse Theater annually produces four shows for adults and two for children. The plays range from comedy, farce and mystery to contemporary drama. As a community theater, the focus is on training. In addition to children's classes, courses in acting, dance and technical training are available to adults.

ECHO THEATER

Echo Theater, a movement and performance arts center, was created in 1983. At that time, the resident company, the progressive "Do Jump Movement Theater," renovated it to create usable space for dance and experimental works. The company offers innovative aerial, acrobatic dance and theater performances. Classes for kids and adults are available in tumbling, trapeze acrobatics and contact improvisation. The Echo Theater books performances by local, regional and national choreographers, features art films, performance art and special events.

1515 SE 37th Avenue
Portland 97214
231-1232

Monday-Saturday
9am-5pm

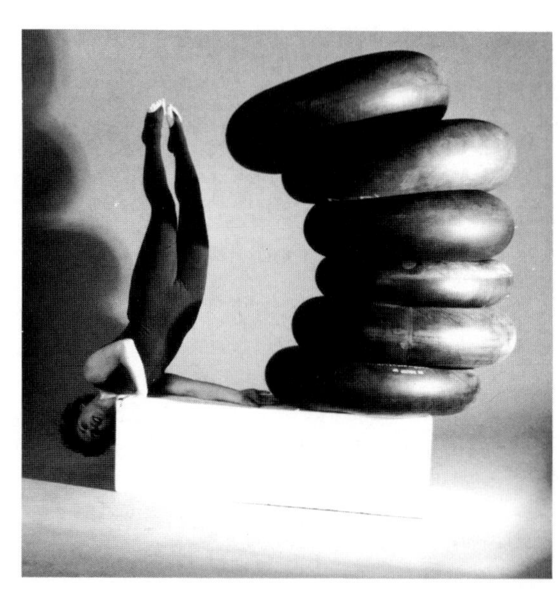

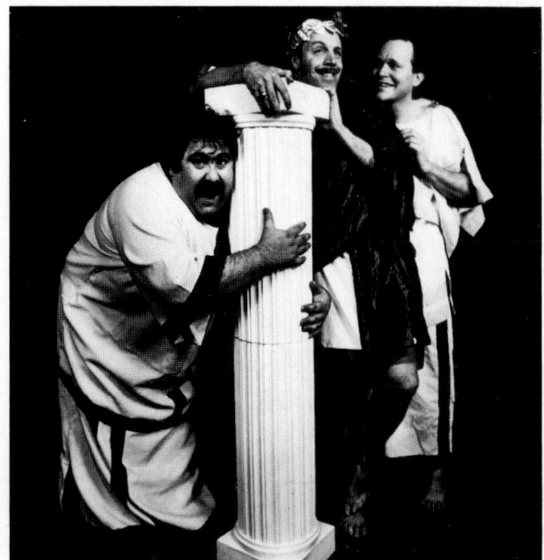
Duane Morris

THEATER WORKSHOP

511 SE 60th
Portland 97215
235-4551

Monday-Friday
9am-5:30pm

A program of the Portland Bureau of Parks and Recreation, Theater Workshop is the largest performing arts training program in the Pacific Northwest. Affordable classes in dance, mime, music, acting, and voice-training are taught by professionals from the theater community. The Musical Company, the performance arm of the Theater Workshop, produces four musical theater performances a year. Supported by ticket revenues and activities of its board, this non-profit theater performs its delightful musicals at the Eastside Performance Center.

The hush that falls over the audience just before the curtain rises on a dance performance is different somehow. Dance audiences in Portland know that they will leave a performance tingling...music, lights, costumes, movement swirl together in a mesmerizing magic.

BALLET OREGON

Under the artistic direction of Dennis Spaight, Ballet Oregon has a main season at the new Portland Center for the Performing Arts' Intermediate Theater. Known for its varied styles from neo-classical to modern dance and for its dynamic performances, the company has performed in such places as California, Idaho, Washington, New Mexico, Alaska and Japan. Ballet Oregon performs in over 100 Young Audience programs per year plus operates The Academy of Ballet Oregon, teaching and educating prospective dancers of all ages.

8500 SE 17th Avenue
Portland 97202
236-3131

Office:
8:30am-5pm
School:
9am-8:30pm

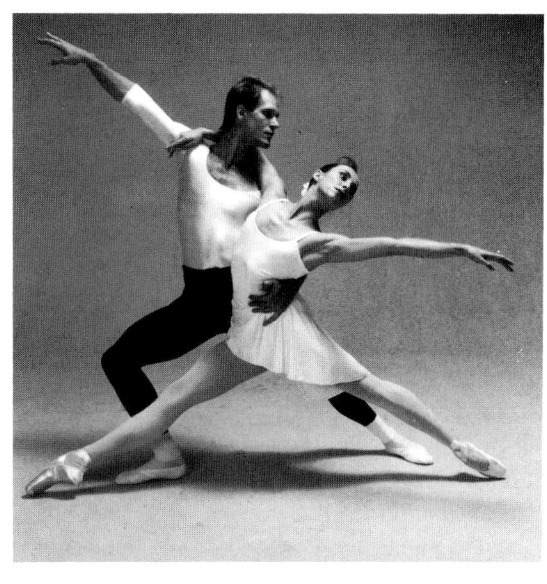

Michael Renfrow

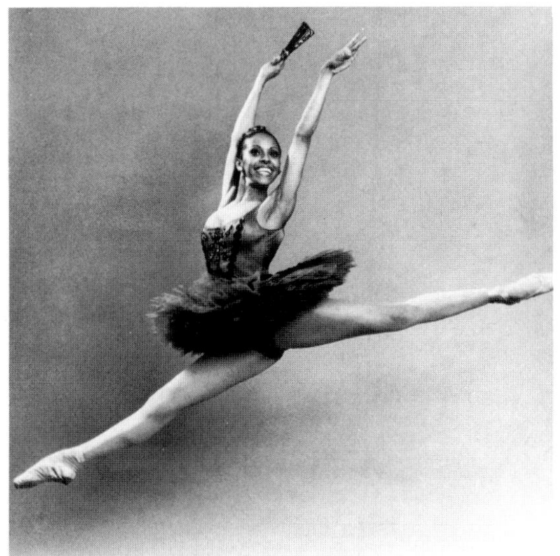

PACIFIC BALLET THEATRE

Pacific Ballet Theatre, the newest jewel in Portland's cultural crown, is bringing the excitement of dance to Oregon. Led by acting Artistic Director and Choreographer, Laurie LeBlanc and dancers from the Jeffrey Ballet and Dance Theatre of Harlem, the company has literally leapt to the forefront of the arts scene in the Pacific Northwest. The Pacific Ballet Theatre continues to attract recognized dancers from across the country. Its success story has made Portland one of the most desirable destinations for rising stars of the dance world.

1119 SW Park Avenue
Portland 97205
227-6867

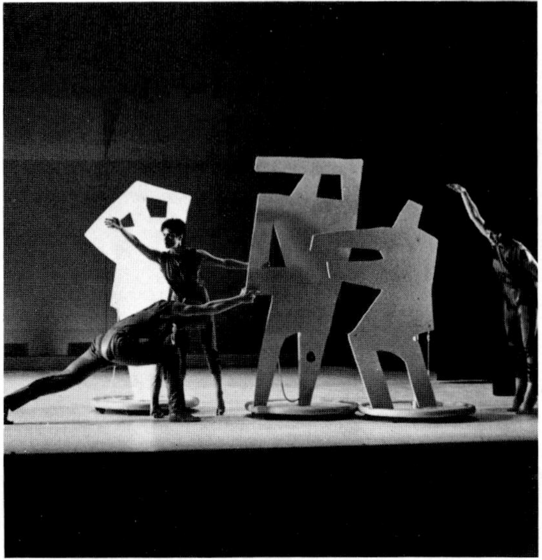

THE COMPANY WE KEEP

The Contemporary Dance Season
PSU Dance
P.O. Box 751
Portland 97207
229-3131

8am-5pm
Call for performance times and locations

The Company We Keep, in residence at Portland State University, creates performances of raw energy and startling imagery with a refreshing, thought-provoking, and independent style. Under the able direction of artistic director Judy Patton, the ensemble of dancers, choreographers, musicians and visual artists offer full-length formal theater, informal performance, master classes and workshops in multi-discipline collaborations. The company provides several performances each year that challenge the senses and broaden the arena of dance.

ELIZABETH ABTS DANCE COMPANY

The dance company prides itself on a number of scores: it is the only dance company in the area whose dancers all come from Portland; it successfully blends classic ballet training and jazz with the floor work that is so indigenous to the Graham technique; and it performs only original works. This delightful company has drawn its core from Elizabeth Abts School of American Contemporary Ballet. Their studio is light and airy ... a perfect place to watch youthful exuberance meld with rigorous discipline.

618 SW Park
Portland 97205
227-0911

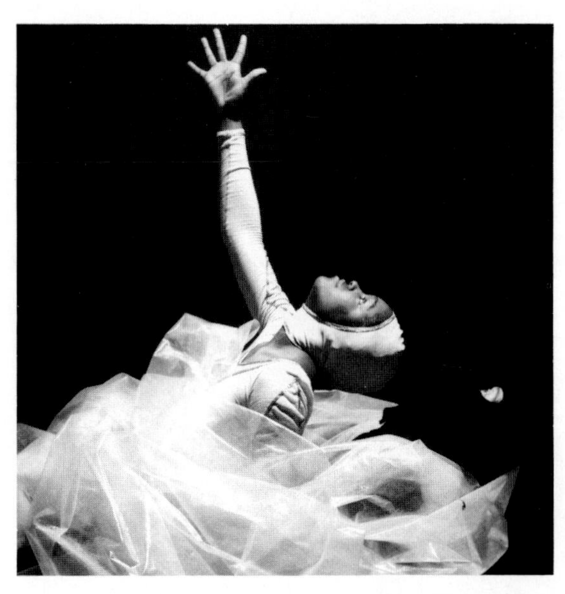

Michael Renfrow

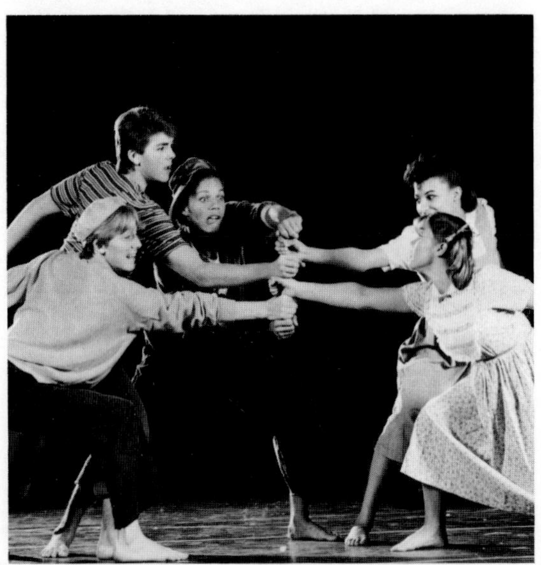

JEFFERSON DANCERS

Jefferson High School
5210 N Kerby Street
Portland 97211
280-5180

A special kind of excitement began several years ago when Jefferson High School became a magnet school for the performing arts. Since that time a kind of "Fame" atmosphere has taken the dance department by storm. So much so that the Jefferson Dancers developed a following that necessitated their move to the 3,000 seat Portland Civic Auditorium for performances. Their commitment to excellence brings in the best choreographers from around the country to train their students. The company performs several times a year to countless accolades.

The crowd is especially colorful tonight as they chat and drift back to their seats. The group on stage exchanges amusing remarks as they reassemble, surrounded by reflecting chrome and ivory. Absently twirling a swizzle stick, I think I could listen to these guys play forever.

CABARET

Darcelles XV, 208 NW Third Avenue. 222-5338. Portland's finest cabaret showbar features renowned female impersonators seven nights a week. Gourmet Dinner/Show package is available. Call for reservations. Entertainers available for private parties.

CLASSICAL

The Heathman, SW Broadway at Salmon Street. 241-4100. Page 50. The Heathman Lobby Lounge features a pianist playing classical and sentimental favorites on an ebony Steinway grand. Wood-burning fireplace, custom designed furnishings, quiet elegance.

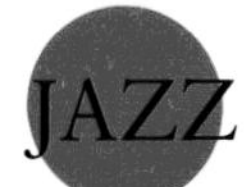

JAZZ

Brasserie Montmartre, 262 SW Park Avenue. 224-5552. Page 56. The art deco atmosphere is the perfect backdrop for some of the best jazz, seven nights a week. The Brasserie Montmartre also has a wandering magician on Friday and Saturday evenings.

Cafe Vivo, 555 S.W. Oak Street. 228-8486. Eclectic live jazz, featuring the Tom Grant Band and Italian cuisine make this one of Portland's favorite jazz clubs.

Crêpe Faire Restaurant & Bistro, 133 SW Second Avenue. 227-3365. Page 64. In this romantic candlelit setting, a couple can enjoy the music of classical and jazz soloists Wednesday through Saturday nights. A jazz pianist is an added attraction during Friday lunch.

DJ's Village Jazz, 500 SW First, Lake Oswego. 636-2024. Lake Oswego's most popular rendezvous features the best in local and national jazz Tuesday through Saturday.

The Hobbit, Corner of SE 39th and Holgate. 771-0742. Featuring some of Portland's highest quality live jazz on Monday, Friday and Saturday evenings. On other evenings, there's continuous taped jazz.

Jazz de Opus and **Opus Too,** 3 NW Second Avenue. 222-6077. Page 52. In the past Jazz de Opus has offered the greatest in live international jazz: Sonny Stitt, Red Holloway, Cal Tjader and Charlie Bird. Now it offers the finest in recorded jazz selections.

The Lobby Lounge at the Westin Benson, S.W. Broadway at Oak. 295-4282. Located in the hotel's magnificent lobby, the lounge is a favorite evening spot for downtown business men and women. Nightly entertainment features soft jazz.

Parchman Farm Restaurant & Pub, 1204 SE Clay Street. 235-7831. Page 86. Catch jazz Wednesday through Saturday evenings. Jazz trios provide a great way to spend a quiet evening with both good conversation and great music.

Remo's Ristorante Italian, 1425 NW Glisan Street. 221-1150. Listen to Portland's best jazz ensembles, nightly. There's gourmet pizza and light fare in the cafe-bar. On Sunday, Jazz musicians sit in.

Salty's, at the foot of SE Marion Street. 239-8900. Enjoy an unparalleled view of the Willamette River as you listen to live jazz from the bar or dance floor.

PIANO BARS

Alexander's, 921 SW Sixth Avenue. 226-1611. Enjoy a night with spectacular vistas and sophisticated ambiance located on the 23rd floor overlooking the Performing Arts Center. After-theater drinks and desserts accompany Portland's finest pianists.

Atwaters, 111 SW Fifth Avenue. 220-3600. Page 48. Atwaters, in the U.S. Bank Tower, commands a beautiful view of the Willamette River from 30 floors above. Enjoy the view, the Rack of Lamb or Salmon while you listen to Bill Hewitt at the piano Tuesday through Saturday.

Bogart's Joint, 406 NW 14th Avenue. 222-4986. Page 85. Live piano music from the eras of yesteryear. Bogart's Joint offers music from the 30's & 40's. The music runs the gamut from swing to blues.

East Bank Saloon, 727 SE Grand Avenue. 231-1659. Nothing fake here. From the kitchen-prepared food to the brick and wood interiors, you'll genuinely enjoy the casual dining. Thursday through Saturday catch Jeannie Hoffman on piano.

Hobo's Inn Old Town, 120 NW Third Avenue. 224-3285. Hobo's Inn has fine dining and a tasteful atmosphere to go along with live music nightly. A sing-a-long piano and light jazz on weekends keeps the mood bright and friendly.

McCormick & Schmick's Seafood Restaurant, 235 SW First Avenue. 224-7522. Page 54. With the richness of oak and brass, music wafts through the bar Wednesdays through Saturdays from 5:45pm.

RiverPlace Alexis Hotel, 1510 SW Harbor Way. 295-6166. Sit overlooking the Willamette River marina in the Esplanade Restaurant Wednesday-Sunday and enjoy some great jazz piano. Or savor Sunday Brunch with classical or contemporary guitar playing in the background.

13 Coins, SW Third and Clay. 224-2646. Page 71. Located in the Koin Center Tower, 13 Coins is the perfect choice for a late night snack or dinner. In the lounge listen to the music of pianists Joe Borland or Stan Davis.

Wilf's, at Union Station, 800 NW Sixth Avenue. 223-0070. Over the years Wilf's, with the stylings of Jim Schroeder, has become known as one of the best piano bars in Oregon.

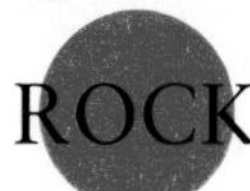

ROCK

BeBop U.S.A., 11753 SW Beaverton-Hillsdale Highway. 644-4433. BeBop is solid gold rock n' roll at its finest, seven nights a week. Art deco, chrome and neon compete with a live D.J. spinning 45's.

Eli's, 424 SW Fourth Avenue. 223-8688. Eli's is one of Portland's largest rock and roll clubs, 1/4 of a city block, three floors of jamming rock and roll, featuring Portland's most extensive video system.

Harrington's, corner of SW Sixth and Main. 243-2932. Harringtons offers Portland a taste of urban chic. Since its opening in December of '82, it was listed as one of the nation's Top 10 bars by *Esquire Magazine*. Enjoy a 50-foot Philippine mahogonay bar, high tech lights and sound system.

Key Largo, 31 NW First Avenue. 223-9919. Key Largo offers an amazing assortment of live music nightly. In its tropical atmosphere, Portland's finest bands perform while patrons enjoy exotic drinks. Key Largo offers jazz, rhythm and blues, rock, fusion and premieres top new musical acts.

River City Saloon, 1133 SW Jefferson. 224-2800. This contemporary saloon offers jazz, acoustics and rock n' roll Wednesday through Sunday.

Rusty Pelican, 4630 SW Macadam. 222-4630. Arrive early Tuesday through Saturday to enjoy the "bounty from the sea" at the noted Seafood Quarter Bar, then stay on and be part of the action with Top 40's and rock n' roll performed by local groups.

Satyricon, 125 NW Sixth Avenue. 243-2380. Underground music is alive and well seven nights a seek at Satyricon. You can hear national and local groups perform funk, rock, and jazz. You can view local artwork on display, listen to poetry readings and watch a fashion show.

Shanghai Lounge, 309 SW Montgomery. 220-1865. Page 62. Nine until closing seven nights a week hear Top 40's, rock n' roll and some original rock. Boasting the most sophisticated sound system in the Northwest and a large dance floor, this is the place to "boogie on down."

RHYTHM & BLUES

The Dandelion Pub, 31 NW 23rd Place. 223-0099. For a menu rich in rhythm and blues, stop by and sample live music Monday through Saturday. There's a full-service bar, menu and a casual atmosphere. Don't miss Blue Mondays!

The White Eagle, 836 N Russell. 282-6810. Established in 1905, this rhythm and blues club has inspired many songs. The White Eagle offers old-time atmosphere, the best rhythm and blues in town and room to dance.

TRADITIONAL FOLK

East Avenue Tavern, 727 East Burnside. 236-6900. One of Portland's few traditional music pubs, this tavern offers live music nightly. Music from around the world performed by internationally acclaimed bands from Irish to French and Flamenco to Bluegrass.

VARIETY

Buffalo Gap Saloon & Eatery, 6835 SW Macadam Avenue. 244-7111. Page 78. Buffalo Gap is more than just a tavern. There's outside dining in spring and summer and live music in the lounge all nights but Friday. At the beginning of the week you'll hear acoustic music. Toward the end of the week the music changes to jazz and blues.

Cisco & Pancho's, 107 NW Fifth Avenue. 223-5048. There's music Friday and Saturday evenings. Weekends offer a variety of music. Check for sports nights on the large screen.

Original Richards, 4534 SE McLoughlin Boulevard. 230-4845. Original Richard's features the best in local bands playing 50's and 60's music every weekend.

Pine Street Theater, 215 SE Ninth Avenue. 235-0027. This facility books acts such as Second City, Irene Loves Jezzabelle, Public Image Ltd. and David Crosby. Pine Street Theater has a dance floor and offers music from progressive to new wave.

Starry Night, 8 NW Sixth Avenue. 227-0071. Starry Night's 1,000 seat hall offers the best of blues, jazz rock, reggae and funk: from The Fixx, Spyro Gyra to Rita Marley, plus local bands. Its dance floor and balcony offer room to move.

The Long Goodbye, 300 NW Tenth Avenue. 227-1991. Jazz, rock and roll and late night-early morning music and breakfast is the specialty here.

COMEDY

The Last Laugh, 426 NW Sixth Avenue. 295-2844. The Last Laugh features national and local stand-up comedians seven nights a week with two shows on weekend nights.

MOVIE HOUSES

Clinton Street Theater, 2522 SE Clinton Street. 238-8899. The Clinton Street Theater brings the best of theater from around the world. Top American independents to prize winners from the Cannes Film Festival are on view.

Fifth Avenue Cinemas, 510 SW Hall Street. 224-6038. The Fifth Avenue is an intimate twin theater offering a wide range of art films. See the off-beat, controversial, the masterfully simple and up-beat.

KOIN Center Cinemas, SW Third and Clay. 243-3515. This state-of-the-art theater with a convenient downtown location boasts six auditoriums. The international flavor of the film fare is reflected in the concession stand which features espresso drinks and imported chocolates.

The Guild Theater, 829 SW Ninth Avenue. 226-0044. The best movies from the past are shown at the Guild, featuring festivals of great stars and directors from Humphrey Bogart, Alfred Hitchcock and James Bond.

The Movie House, 1220 SW Taylor Street. 222-4595. In the Portland Women's Club, modeled in art deco style, you enjoy the feeling of being a guest in someone's home. Major art films, classics and cross-over films offer entertainment for the thinking adult.

Northwest Film and Video Center, Berg Swann Auditorium, 1219 SW Park. 221-1156. The Center exhibits foreign, classic and independently made film and video. It's home for the Portland International Film Festival and the Northwest Film and Video Festival.

The Roseway Theatre, 7229 NE Sandy. 281-5713. The Roseway Theatre offers films of the golden age of motion pictures in a setting reminiscent of past cinemas.

MEMORIAL COLISEUM COMPLEX

Portland's Memorial Coliseum Complex has hosted some of the world's major entertainment attractions, from the Ice Follies to the Rolling Stones — and it's home for the Portland Trail Blazers. With three Exhibit Halls and eight Meeting Rooms, there's onsite catering facilities for 6,500 people and parking for 2,000 vehicles. Map D6.

Tickets/Event Info	239-4422
Meeting Arrangements	235-8771

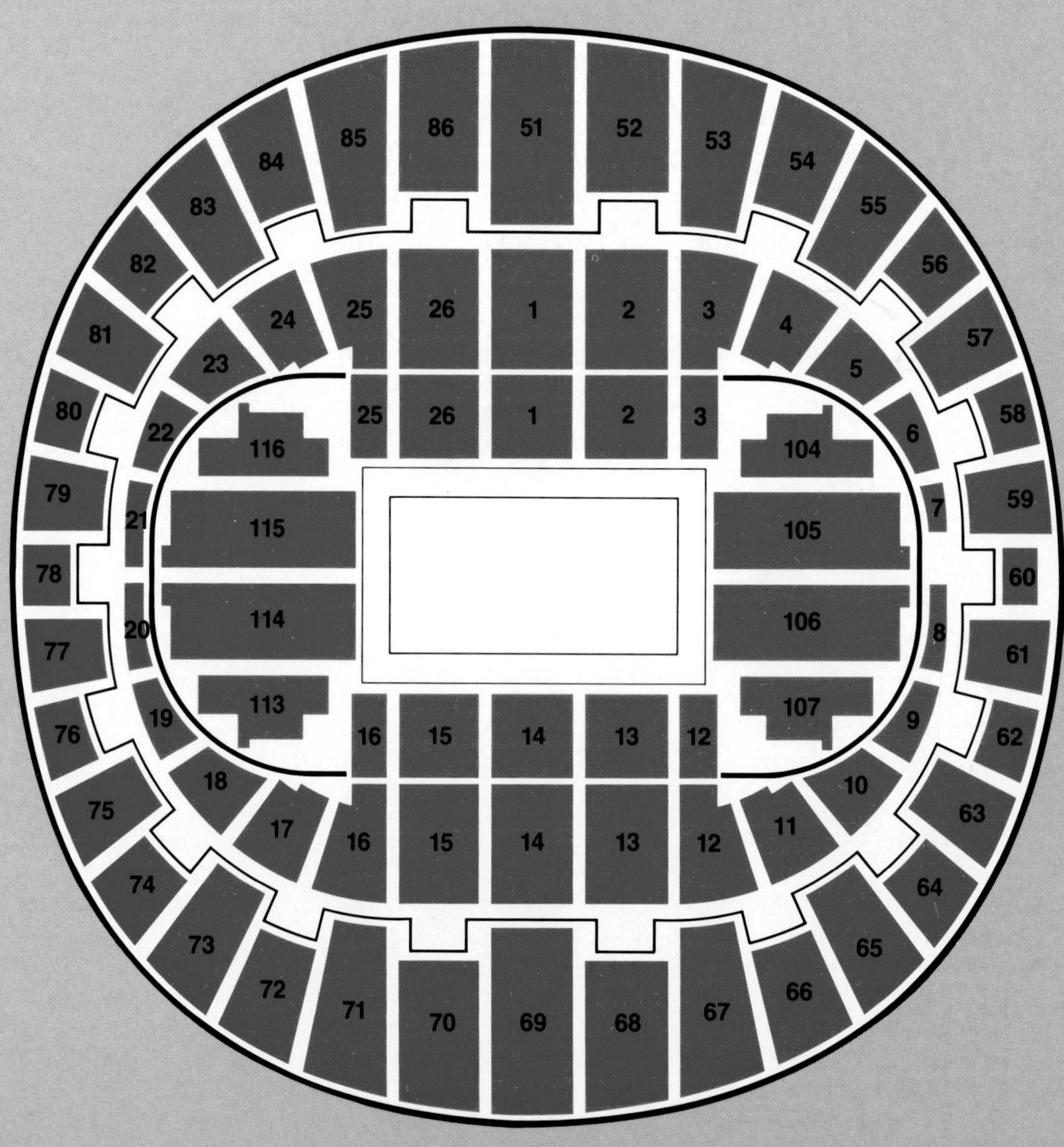

PORTLAND CIVIC STADIUM

Seating nearly 26,000, the Portland Civic Stadium, located at 1844 S.W. Morrison, offers renovated facilities with old time flavor for sports and entertainment. The home of soccer, football and baseball, Civic Stadium has also hosted entertainers Frank Sinatra, Elvis Presley, David Bowie and the Beach Boys. Map D5.

Tickets/Event Info 248-4345

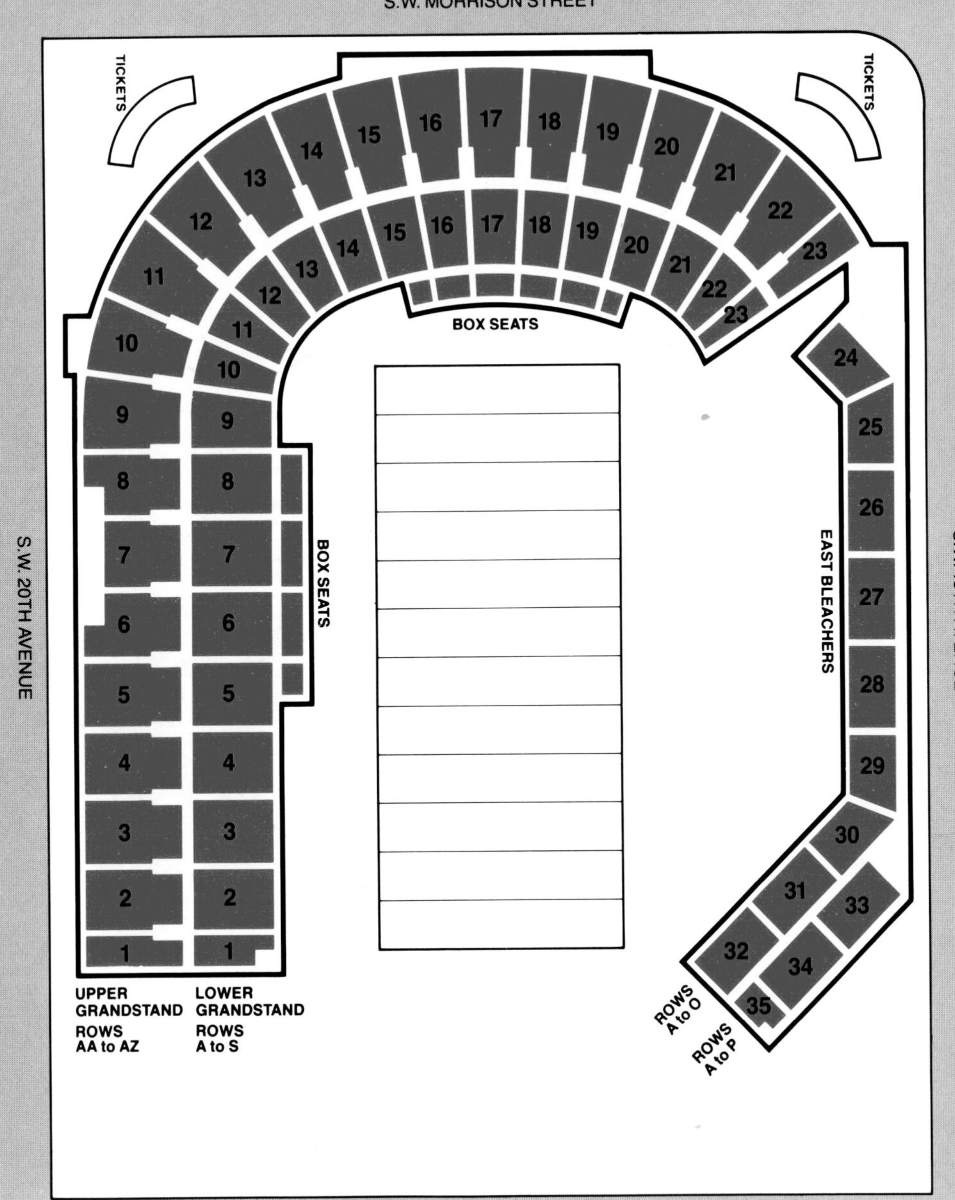

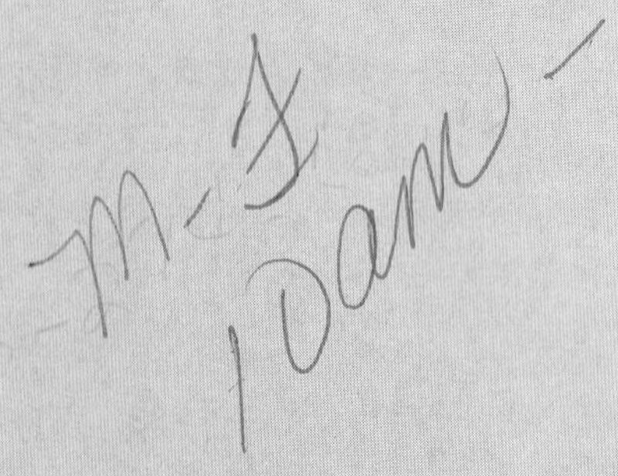

Located in downtown Portland, the recently completed Portland Center for the Performing Arts is a stunning four-theater complex consisting of the excellent and versatile Portland Civic Auditorium, the beautifully restored and renovated classic Arlene Schnitzer Concert Hall, and adjacent to "The Schnitz," the new design-award-winning Intermediate Theatre and the Dolores Winningstad Theatre.

ARLENE SCHNITZER CONCERT HALL

The beautiful Arlene Schnitzer Concert Hall, at Southwest Broadway and Main Streets, successfully combines the splendor of classic theater architecture with today's technology. It's home for the Oregon Symphony, the Portland Youth Philharmonic and stellar traveling productions. The auditorium is also used for touring Broadway productions, ballet, rock, jazz and classical music. Map G23.

Tickets/Event Info 248-4496

INTERMEDIATE THEATRE

Part of the new Performing Arts building across Main Street from the Arlene Schnitzer Concert Hall, the Intermediate Theatre is entered through a breathtaking grand lobby that is dominated by cherry wood and crystal clear, light-refracting glass. The 916 seats are positioned in traditional Edwardian theater style. The stage is an immense 79 X 44 feet. The seating area and stage are nearly equal in size, creating a dynamic relationship between the action and the audience. The space is designed to accommodate dance, dramatic and musical performances as well as lectures, seminars and films. Map G23.

Tickets/Event Info 248-4496

ARLENE SCHNITZER CONCERT HALL

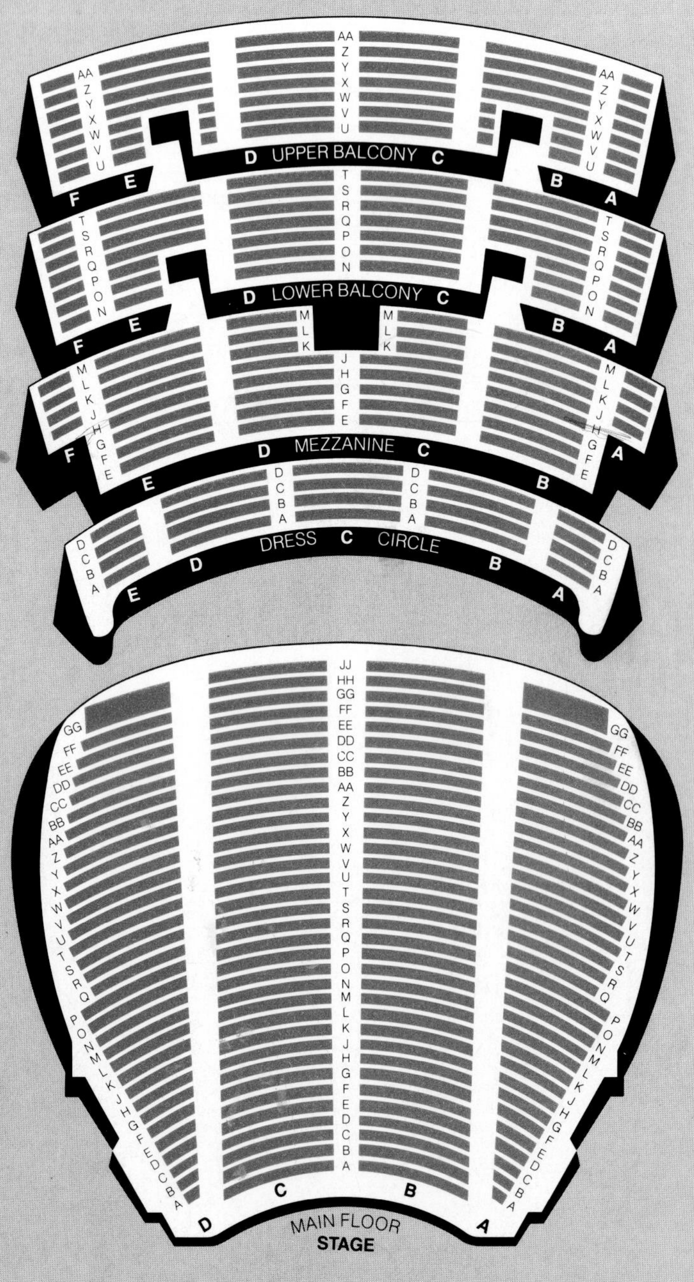

INTERMEDIATE THEATRE

SECOND BALCONY

BOX A BOX B

FIRST BALCONY

BOX A BOX B

ORCHESTRA

BOX A BOX B

STAGE

DOLORES WINNINGSTAD THEATRE

The "Winnie" as it is affectionately called, shares the new theater building with the Intermediate Theatre and benefits from the same award-winning design. An updated version of a Shakespearean courtyard theater, the versatile 360 seat theater can be set up in at least six different configurations. The stage and the orchestra floor are actually massive elevators that can be used at differing heights, or all at one level. Map G23.

Tickets/Event Info 248-4496

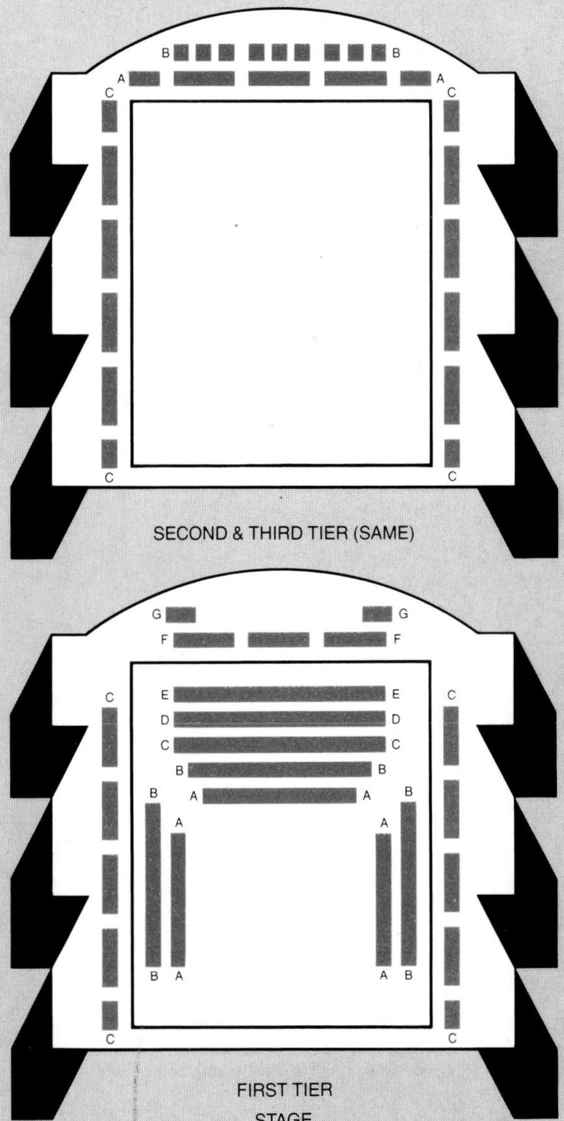

PORTLAND CIVIC AUDITORIUM

A 3,000 seat, first class production house, located at Southwest Third and Clay Street, our Civic Auditorium is one of the finest multi-purpose performance spaces in the nation. Acclaimed for its comfort, sightlines and acoustics, it is also one of the country's busiest. Events range from classical music, ballet, opera and drama to rock, jazz and country music. Map H24.

Tickets/Event Info ~~248-4496~~

SECOND BALCONY
E D C B A
K J H G F E D C B A
BOX E BOX A

FIRST BALCONY
E D C B A
H G F E D C B A
BOX 4 BOX 5 BOX 6 BOX 7 BOX 8 BOX 9 BOX 10 BOX 11
BOX 1 BOX 2 BOX 3 BOX 12 BOX 13 BOX 14

ORCHESTRA LEVEL
E D C B A
F-F E-E D-D C-C B-B A-A Z Y X W V U T S R Q P O N M L K J H G F E D C B A
PB PA

STAGE

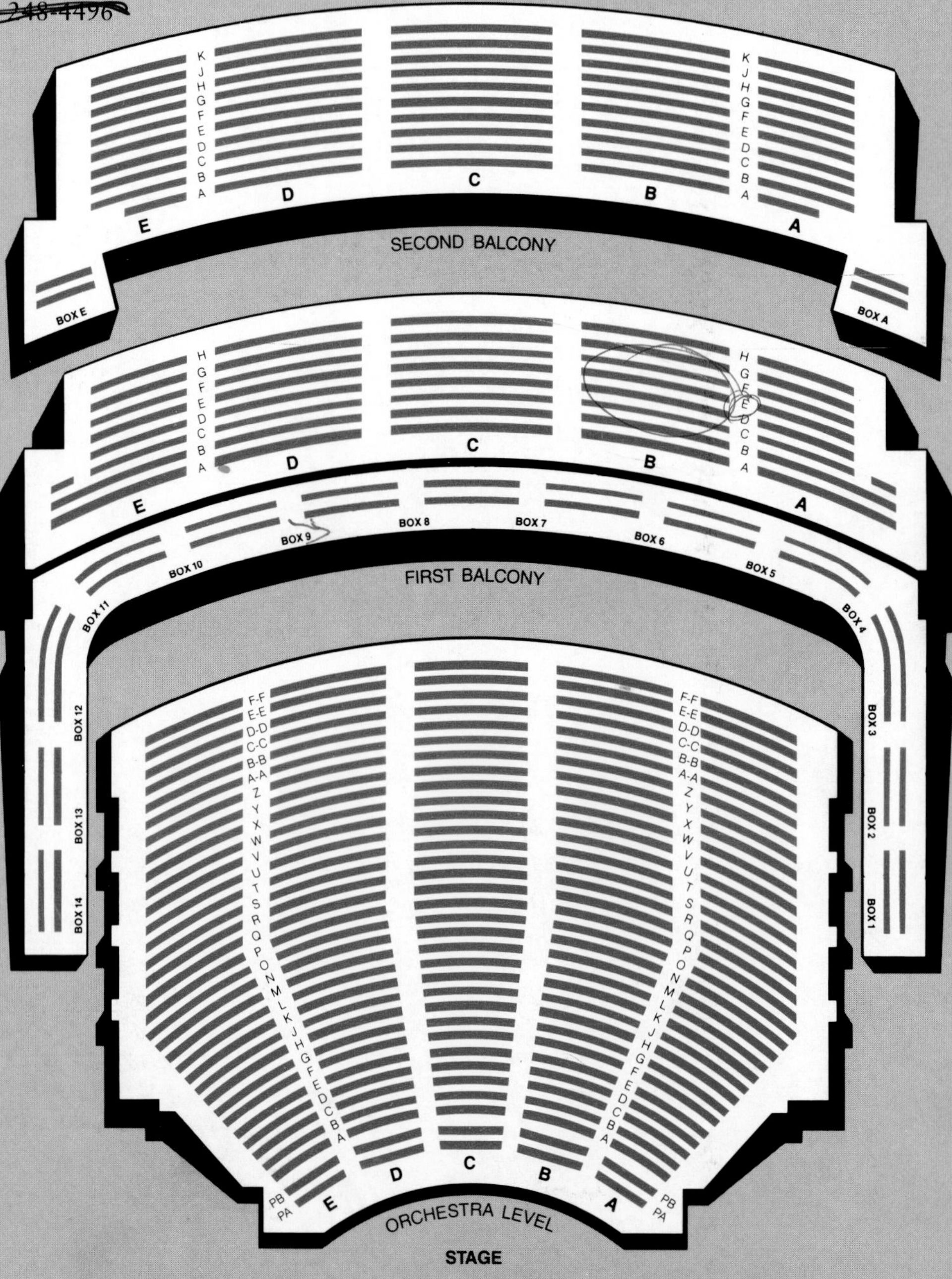

SEPTEMBER

All American Mutt Show, Sponsored by Oregon Humane Society, Lloyd Center Ice Pavilion 285-0644.

Antique Car Show and Auction, Memorial Coliseum 239-4422.

ArtQuake, Various locations 227-2787. Month long arts celebration for the whole family.

Beaverton "Good Neighbor Days, Schiffler Park, Beaverton 626-2486. Food, arts and crafts, antique truck show, 10 kilometer run, mutt show, and parade.

Composers' Festival, Pioneer Courthouse Square 223-1613. Pacific First Federal sponsors three new musical debuts.

Elegante '87, Hilton Grand Ballroom 234-9591. Parry Center benefit luncheon and fashion show.

Fall Century, Portland Wheelmen Touring Club 282-7982. Touring race, 100 miles.

Fall Plant Sale, Leach Botanical Gardens 761-9503.

Mt. Angel Octoberfest, Mt. Angel 845-9440. Ethnic foods, crafts and biergarten.

Octoberfest, Holladay Park, Lloyd Center 235-3138. Central Catholic fundraiser.

Oregon Art Institute Ball, 226-2811.

Oregon Road Runners Club, Duniway Park 635-9915. Duel Track Run. 10 miles on track solo or 2 person teams.

ORRC Portland Marathon and 8 Kilometer Run, 223-7867. 26.2 mile road race through Portland's neighborhoods.

Ping Golf Championship, Columbia Edgewater Golf Club 285-8354.

Reed College Music Matinee Series, Reed College Commons 777-7573. Sunday afternoon concerts series, September through May.

Ringling Brothers Circus, Memorial Coliseum 239-4422.

Senior Citizens Free Day at the Zoo, Washington Park Zoo 226-1561.

Wintering-in Festival, Oregon Historical Society, Sauvie Island 222-1741.

OCTOBER

A Wine Country Thanksgiving, Yamhall County 472-6196. Holiday wine and sales event.

Children's Halloween Safety Fair, St. Vincent's Auditorium 297-4411.

Classical Guitar Series, Lincoln Hall Auditorium, PSU, 229-4440.

Contemporary Dance Series, Lincoln Hall Auditorium, PSU, 229-4440.

Food Affair, Memorial Coliseum 239-4422.

Friends of Chamber Music Series, Lincoln Hall Auditorium, PSU, 229-4452.

Guild of Oregon Woodworkers' Show, World Forestry Center 228-1367.

Holy Trinity Greek Church Festival, 3131 N.E. Glisan 256-4640. Dinner, dancing, pastry shop, handicrafts and music.

Home Remodeling Show, Multnomah County Expo Center 249-7711.

Ladybug Theatre Opening, Multnomah Center 232-2346. Weekend performances for youngsters October through May.

Oh Fu Bonsai Kai, Japanese Gardens 223-4070. Bonsai exhibit.

OMSI Auction, Hilton Hotel 222-2828.

Piano Recital Series, Lincoln Hall Auditorium, PSU 229-4452.

Portland Gem and Mineral Show, Multnomah County Expo Center 632-6251.

Reed College Women's Committee, Fall Lecture Series 239-3557.

Swiss Weekend, Timberline Lodge 295-1827.

Verboort Kraut and Sausage Dinner and Bazaar, Visitation Parish, Verboort, Oregon.

Warren Miller Ski Film and Trade Show, Cascade Ski Club 248-4335. Portland Center for Performing Arts.

Washington Park Zoo Pumpkin Party, Washington Park Zoo 226-1561. Ages 3-11 perform tricks for treats at stations throughout Zoo.

NOVEMBER

America's Largest Christmas Bazaar, Multnomah County Expo Center 244-8338.

Bird Seed Sale, N.W. Cornell 292-6855. Fundraiser for Audubon Society.

Children's Museum's Toy Show and Exhibit, 248-4587. Display of best and worst children's toys.

Children's Book Week, Multnomah County Library 223-7201.

Christmas Tree Lighting Ceremony, Pioneer Courthouse Square. Holiday Concert and 75 foot Christmas tree lighting ceremony.

Christmas Tree Lighting, Lloyd Center Mall 282-2511.

Chrysanthemum Exhibit, Japanese Gardens 223-4070.

Great American Smokeout, American Cancer Society 295-6422. Event urging people to stop smoking.

Harvest Festival, Memorial Coliseum 239-4422. Craft Festival.

High School Soccer Play-Offs and Championship, 248-4345.

Northwest Film and Video Festival, Oregon Art Institute, Berg Swan Auditorium. Juried survey of new works by regional artists.

Northwest Fishing Show, Multnomah County Expo Center 636-9785.

Pray for Snow Dance, 295-1827. Timberline Lodge.

State High School Football Playoff Game, Civic Stadium 248-4345.

Valley Wine Tour, 357-5005. Washington County Wine Association.

Wild Birds in Wood Show, World Forestry Center 228-1367. Wood sculptures of northwest birds.

Wooden Toy Show, World Forestry Center 228-1367. Northwest toymakers display and sell creations.

WINTER

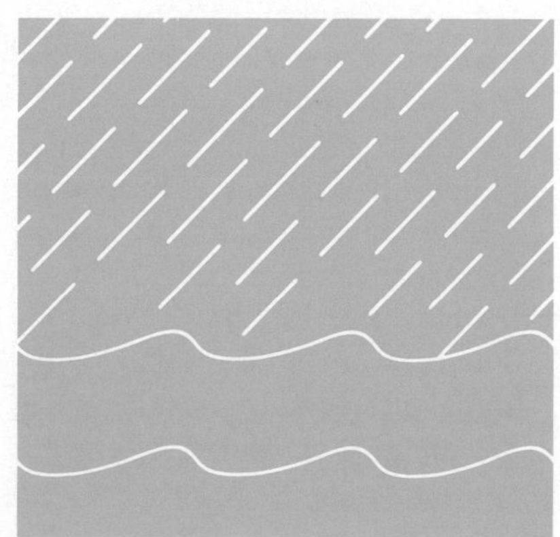

DECEMBER

62 KGW Resolution Run, Tom McCall Waterfront Park 223-7867. 8 kilometer run.

America's Largest Christmas Bazaar, see November.

Audubon Arts and Craft Sale, N.W. Cornell 292-6855. Wildlife artists display works for sale.

Children's Charity Ball, Joint fundraiser for Waverly children's home, Christie School and Parry Center. Features Les Brown Band.

Children's Free Day, Washington Park Zoo 226-1561. Ages 3-11. Special activities.

Christmas Ships on Parade, 222-4469. View elaborately decorated ships on Willamette River.

Christmas at Pittock Mansion, 248-4469. A different decorative theme annually.

Christmas Cheer and Author's Autograph Party, Oregon Historical Society 222-1741.

Christmas Vespers Concert, Chapel, University of Portland 283-7202.

Dog Show, Memorial Coliseum 239-4422.

Far West Classic Basketball Tournament, Memorial Coliseum 239-4422.

Festival of Trees, Memorial Coliseum Exhibit Hall. 230-6020. Providence Hospital's display of elegantly decorated Christmas trees, all for sale.

Holiday Woodcarving, World Forestry Center 228-1367.

International Christmas Tree Show, World Forestry Center 228-1367.

Messiah Sing-In, Buckley Center Auditorium, University of Portland 283-7202.

Messiah, Schnitzer Concert Hall 248-4335.

New Year's Eve Gala, Schnitzer Concert Hall 248-4335. Oregon Symphony Orchestra.

Pacrat Race, Sponsored by Portland Area Ski Club Council, Timberline Lodge. 295-1827.

Pre-Holiday Dry Run, Downtown 223-7867. 10 kilometer run.

Scanfest, Schnitzer Concert Hall 248-4335.

Sing Your Own Messiah, Civic Auditorium 248-4496. Portland Youth Philharmonic Orchestra.

State High School Football Championship Games, Civic Stadium 248-4345.

The Clock, Donkey, and Christmas, Schnitzer Concert Hall 248-4335. Ballet Oregon performance.

The Nutcracker Suite, Schnitzer Concert Hall 248-4335.

The Singing Christmas Tree, Schnitzer Concert Hall 248-4335.

Traditional Christmas, Timberline Lodge 295-1827.

Tryon Creek State Park Christmas Party, Lake Oswego 636-4559. Children decorate Christmas tree with bread cut out for birds and squirrels. Music and Santa.

Winter Wine Tasting, Oregon Wine Tasting Room, McMinnville 843-3787.

133

FASHION

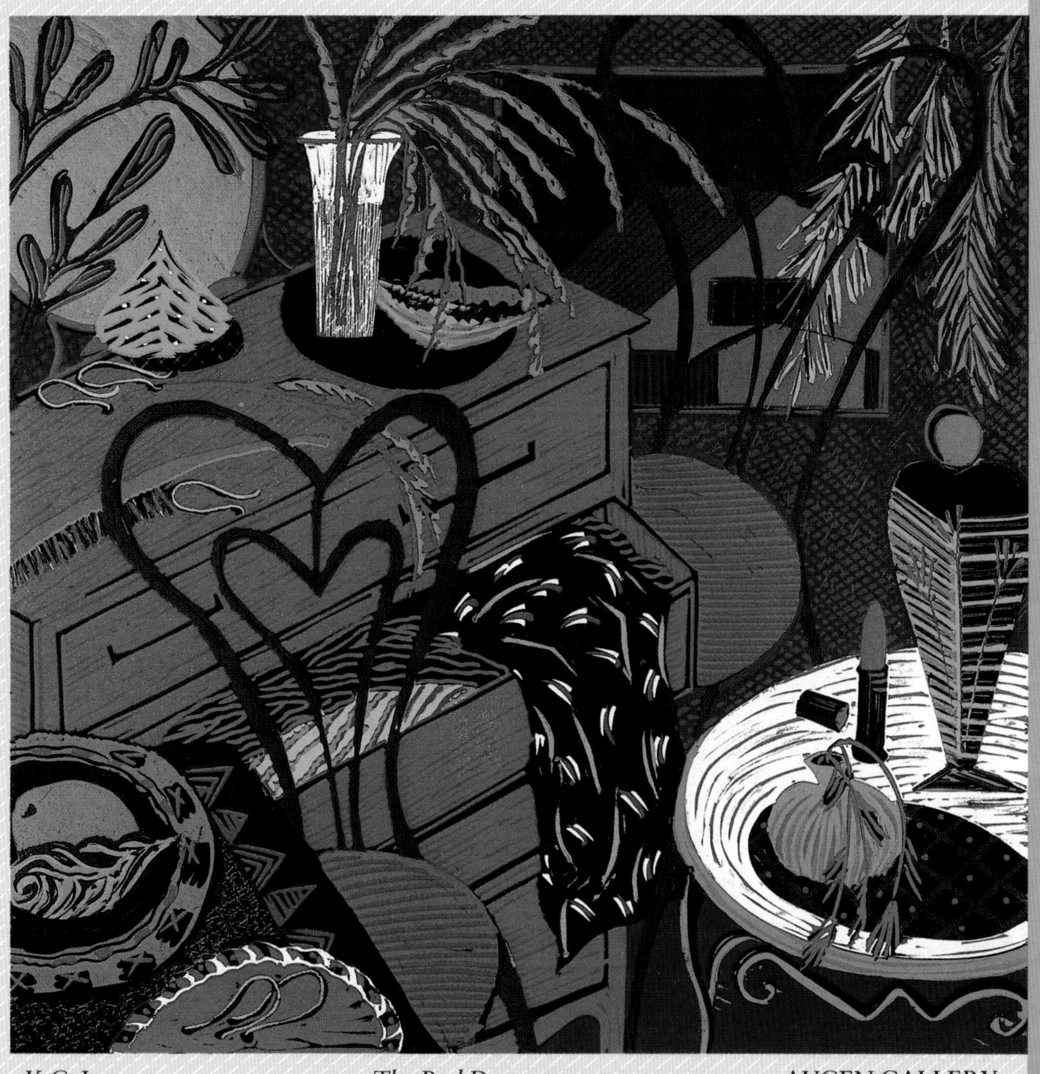

K.C. Joyce *The Red Dresser* AUGEN GALLERY

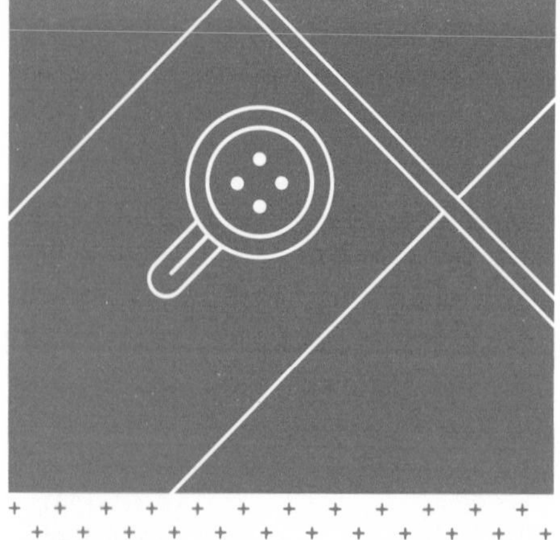

It's a great time to be wearing clothes.

OK, here's what seems to be:

One. In Portland, fashion is more a statement of individuality than it is a retreat from notice. Like the buildings we build, the laws we pass and the heroes we identify, difference makes the difference.

Two. People here, who have always performed more like dandelions than groomed grass, are just now realizing how unique their presentations have become... and what energy vibrates from them. Before, these things were simply taken for granted, like wet weather. Now, it's a wake-up call.

Three. Two basic forces drive most Portland fashion choices — function and authenticity.

Here are a few broad brushstrokes to illustrate:

• Earnest women in austere black and gray clothes emerge, after a moment's aside in a shop, sporting frankly artful pins and earrings. And continue as if nothing's changed.

• A core of working couples defend polyester blends. They're subdued, but they're not kidding.

• The khaki pant/duck shoe/polo shirt/60-40 jacket combination is a recreational uniform.

• With expenditures for running and biking uniforms second only to mortgage payments in household budgets, it's no surprise these clothes are also being pressed into general street service.

• Sneakers, twice-washed jeans and sweatshirts are appearing in executive suites on workday.

• Birkenstocks and hair are thinning but not gone. Street fairs, crusades and Grateful Dead concerts still generate fervor.

• Kenny and Freddy work the weekend bandoline on their hair, don jerseys and team jackets, and cruise east side roads.

• Shopping centers and downtown department stores enthusiastically outfit us in fresh, good-value professional and casual clothes that keep us safe and centered and discrete. So we can go as much without notice as we need to.

• Urban homeless and by-choice school-age commandos turn frayed hems, torn sleeves, and seams bound with bandannas into defiant, prideful statements that are so strong they make photographers and suburban kids itch.

• Even couture is more or less comfortable. Our share of select Armanis, Jayne Barnes, and Valentinos shine on the street. And local, more natural design efforts are finding that people are after what they offer.

Tim Leigh, *man-about-town, is a partner in the public relations and advertising agency, Bronson, Leigh, Weeks.*

K.C. Joyce *is a native Portlander who is one of the most innovative of Oregon's printmakers. Using a technique which Picasso invented but soon abandoned because of its complexity and time commitment, K.C. Joyce creates images which may involve up to 28 different color runs, and months to complete. She is represented by the Augen Gallery.*

A little of everything, right, all happening at once?

Right! and the thing is, people are liking it that way! The war of styles is cheered! The unconventional, independent spirit of Portland enjoys the tension and rif and color because it's a peek at reality and it feels like it belongs here. It's alive. It's our face. It's us. And we want to relish every piece.

As long as we can believe it.

Authenticity, not surprisingly, is the heart of Portland fashion. If we wear it because we do it, it's accepted and welcomed almost regardless of appropriateness. Or, even if it's something like Moroccan carpet leggings, if we wear it because we're sincerely trying to illustrate ourselves, that's OK, too ... in fact is usually worth a smile and a question.

But run something out that's phony or for-effect-only, and the reception immediately changes. Portland's truth-heat comes on, leaving us not only with a strong personal sensation of being off-base, but often with an audible "phooey" chasing us all the way home to the condo. Pretense just won't play well here.

So what?

Well, for the time being at least, this means Appearance Opportunity. Expediency and forced conservatism are relaxing. Merchants are discovering broader bands of apparel demand, and are filling them with imagination. Fashion, in an accelerating way, is becoming a result of our own choices... and not necessarily timid ones either. Personal style is picking up steam. We are changing from caterpillar to butterfly. And the process is producing a richness in Portland's palette we've never seen before.

It's a great time to be wearing clothes. *Tim Leigh*

FOR WOMEN

Clothing and accessories for every taste and occasion. European and American designers, maternity and petite sizes, plus wardrobe and image consultation.

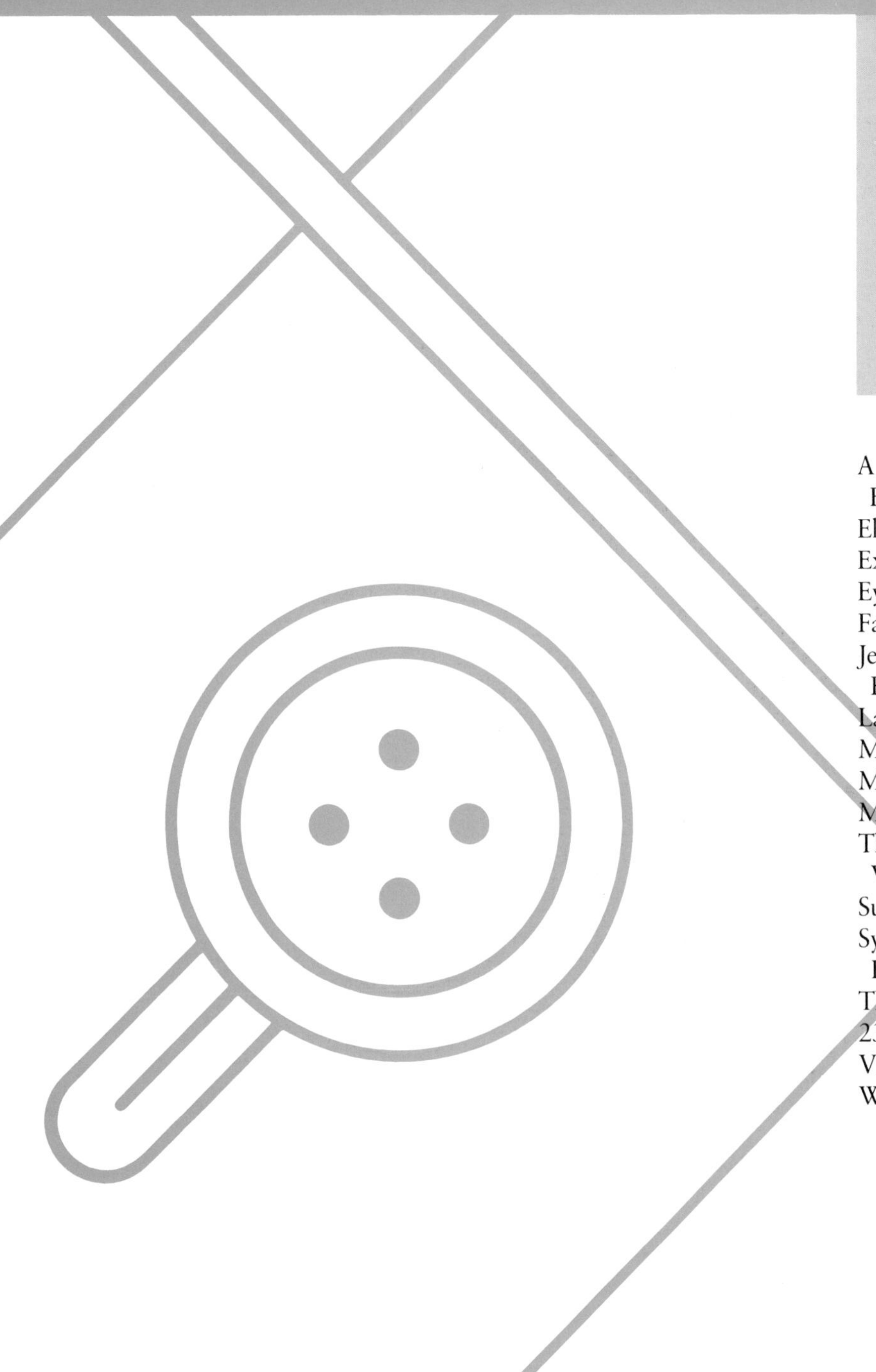

A Woman's Place Bookstore *280*
Elizabeth Street *137*
Expecting the Best *138*
Eye of Ra *151*
Faces Unlimited *141*
Jean-Marie Fine Lingerie *144*
La Paloma *143*
M. Willock *146*
Mario's For Women *142*
Mercantile *136*
The Petite Woman's Shoppe *147*
Suite 360 *148*
Sylvie, An Image Perfected For You *150*
The Towne Shop *139*
23rd Avenue Sweaters *140*
Victoria's *149*
West End Ltd. *145*

MERCANTILE

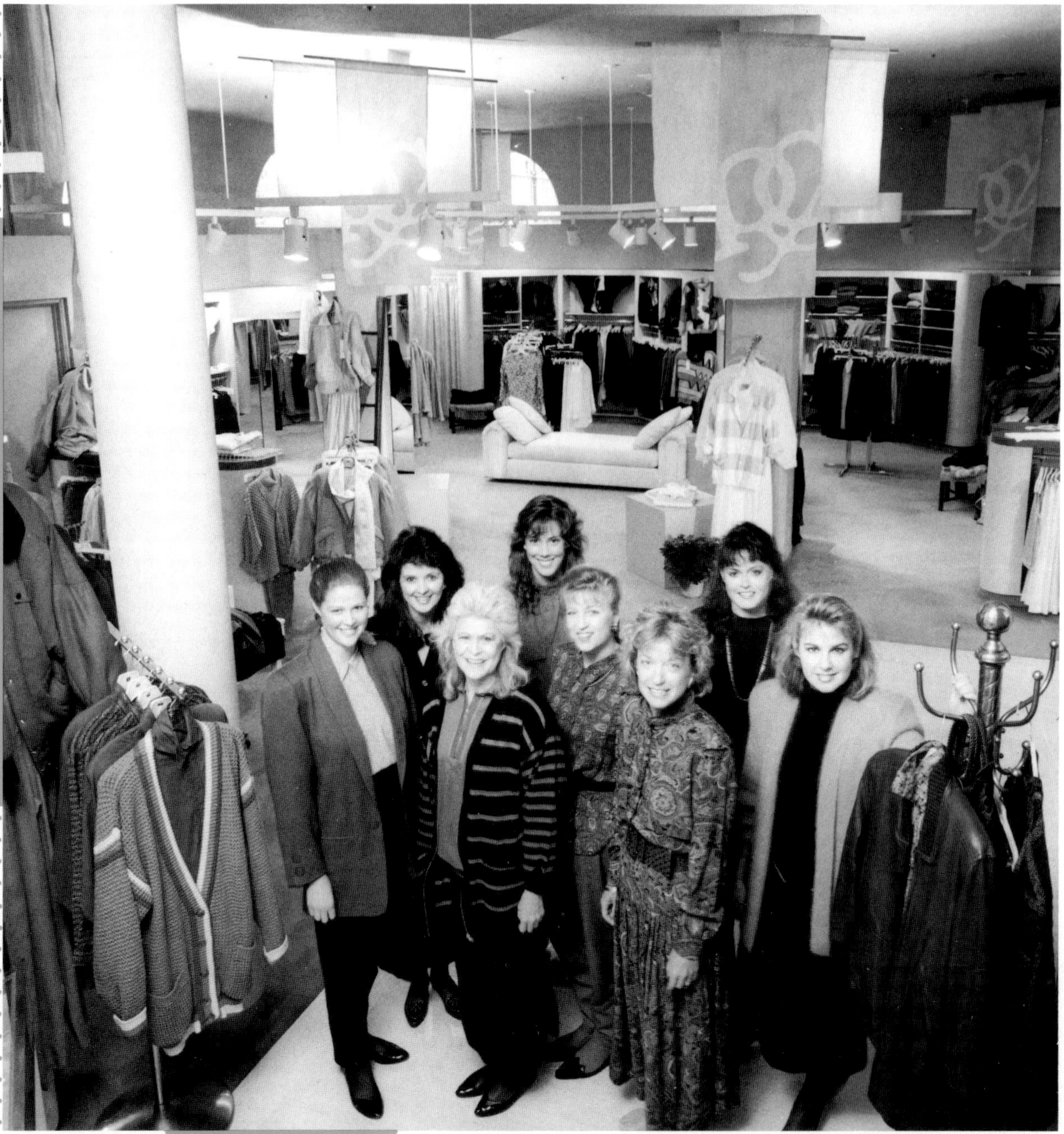

WOMEN

The season's newest and best — women's contemporary fashion.

Downtown

F23

Mercantile, located in the heart of downtown, is one of Portland's finest women's specialty stores. The 8,000 square feet of spacious interior provides a showcase for the exciting fashions of each season. The store was architecturally designed to create a comfortable environment focusing on dresses, designer sportswear and classic clothing. The dress boutique offers daytime, career, evening and special occasion dresses that have been carefully chosen as the season's best. Mercantile is well known for its exciting accessories — abundant with jewelry and belts — that have been hand selected to complement any fashion image. The Designer Sportswear area is filled with collections of European and American designers. The store also displays unique pieces in leather and suede, wonderful knitwear and one of a kind hand painted shirts. Over the years Mercantile has found that many of their customers want classic clothing with contemporary styling, so they have developed a special area to meet those customer's needs. J. G. Hook, Ruff Hewn, E. S. Deans, are just a few of the wonderful classic lines that are offered. Upon visiting Mercantile you will be greeted by a knowledgeable staff who pride themselves in giving individual attention. Visa. MasterCard. American Express. Discover.

735 SW Park Avenue
Portland 97205
223-6649

Monday-Friday
10am-6pm
Saturday
9:30am-5:30pm

ELIZABETH STREET

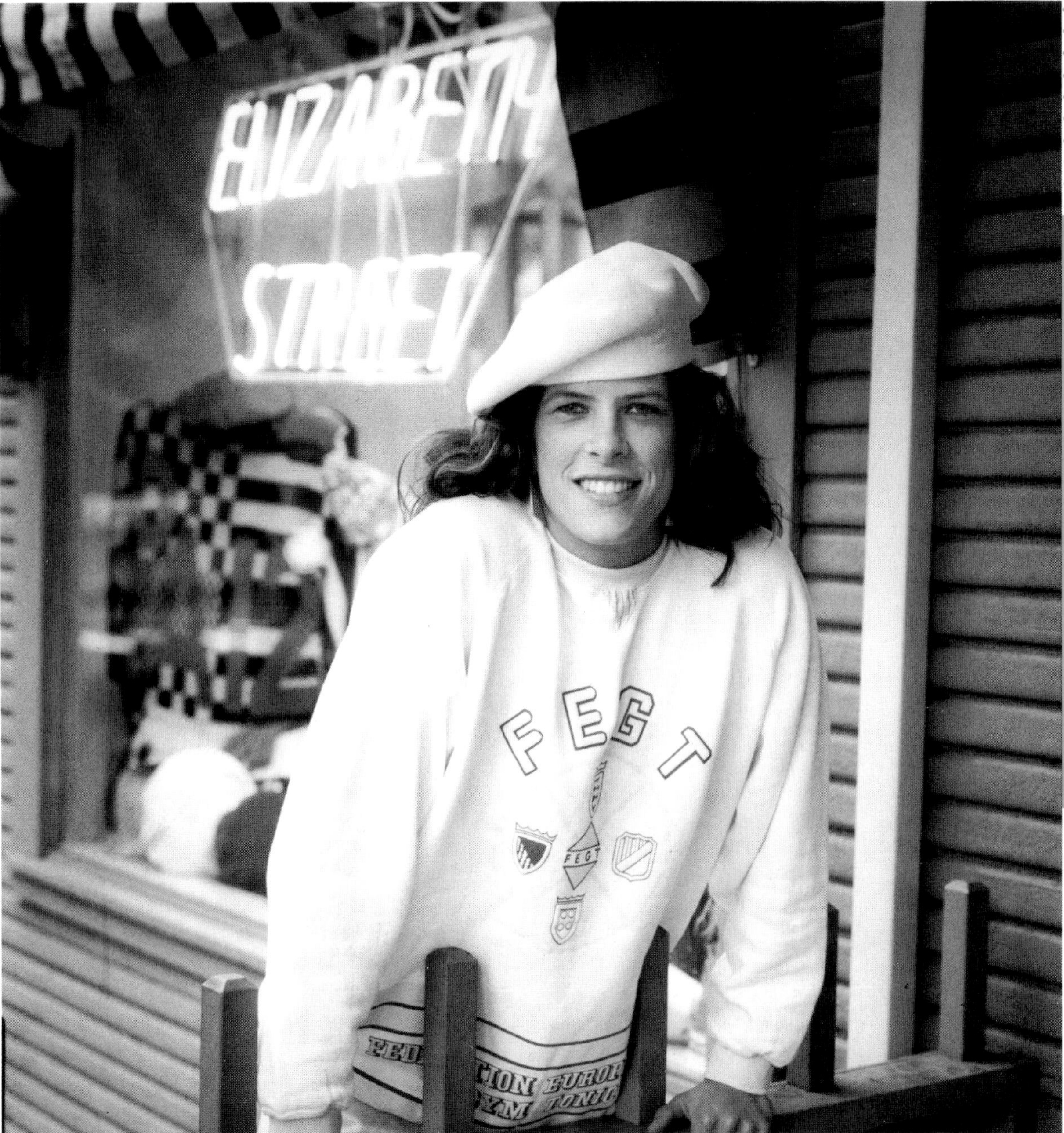

WOMEN

Casually elegant women's clothing.

Northwest Portland

H17

Years ago, Pat Morisky began designing women's clothes under the Elizabeth Street label. With their unusual colors, textures and fabrics, the pieces attracted a large following, substantial enough that in 1983 the Elizabeth Street store was founded. To her designs she has added a host of carefully selected, casually elegant clothing, eclectic jewelry and one-of-a-kind artists' pieces. The staff has the skills to coordinate the unusual to create an original and distinctly personal style. This is also a dazzling place to stop for a quick pick-me-up or an inexpensive fashion fixer, especially if the buyer is looking for a present that's just right. Baskets filled with goodies, nooks and crannies with something to offer, and decor highlighted with Pat's trademark attention to color, texture and form, all make the visit worthwhile. You'll find the simple, classic natural fibers from C.P. Shades; separates from OK Sam; Ruby Z's whimsical jewelry; British Khaki's wonderful fabrics and colors; and kicky clothing from Naf Naf and Triangle. Visa. MasterCard. American Express. Discover.

908 NW 23rd Avenue
Portland 97210
243-2456

Monday-Thursday
10am-5pm
Friday-Saturday
10am-6pm
Sunday noon-5pm

EXPECTING THE BEST

WOMEN

Fashions for the expectant mother and her baby to be.

Downtown

F24

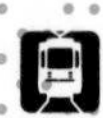

Beaverton

E2

Every woman deserves to expect the best from her wardrobe. Whether her particular lifestyle emphasizes career or sportswear, evening wear or casual, her clothing should be high-quality, flattering and stylish. Expectant mothers can now find clothes which meet these same standards in updated, contemporary maternity wear at Expecting The Best. Owner Andrea Warthen believes that there is no reason why mothers-to-be can't continue to dress in their same basic style. Whether the style of choice is tailored, flamboyant or elegant, there are fashions certain to meet every need at Expecting the Best. Andrea's staff specialize in wardrobe coordinating and consulting, and will take the time to determine what each client's lifestyle is, so that together they can create an attractive wardrobe for every budget. National designers represented here include fashions from Dennis Goldsmith, Belle France, Ma Mere and M. F. Fine. Local designers, such as Deux Amis, provide the most up-to-date looks with wonderful European fabrics. For the convenience of expectant mothers, the shop also provides beautiful infant wear, specialty infant gifts and baby shower registrations. To find a shop that truly reflects the fun and happiness of the most special time in a woman's life, visit Expecting The Best. Visa. MasterCard. American Express. Discover.

425 S W Morrison Street
Portland 97204
228-3407

Monday-Saturday
10am-6pm

Beaverton Town Square
11747 S W Beaverton
Hillsdale Highway
Beaverton 97005
626-3124

Monday-Friday
10am-7pm
Saturday 10am-6pm
Sunday noon-5pm

THE TOWNE SHOP

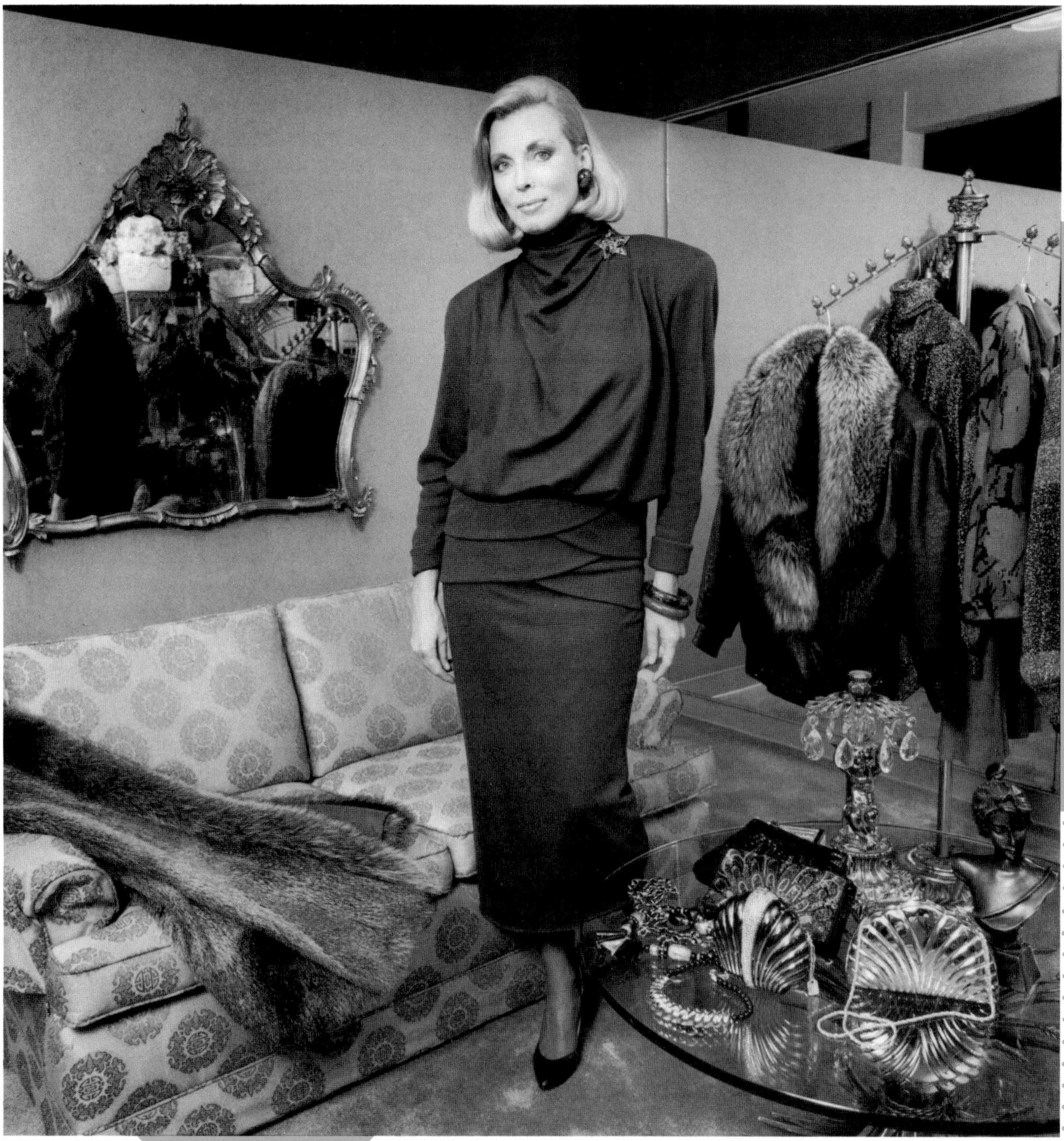

WOMEN

Distinctive fashions for discerning women.

Ann Klein, Geoffrey Beene, Calvin Klein, Bruestle, Levino, Yakko Leathers, Castleberry knits, Suzelle, Adele Simpson, Betty Hanson, Norma Walters — at the Towne Shop, an exclusive women's clothier since 1946, name dropping is easy. You'll find fine couture fashion, designer sportswear, cashmere and hand-knit sweaters, coats, raincoats, stunning hats, lingerie and loungewear, all of impeccable style and quality. The Towne Shop has recently focused on the rebirth of knit dressing and offer their customers a vast selection. Designer accessories; imported handbags, belts, scarves, fine and costume jewelry, are abundant. Margery O'Brien and her discriminating staff promise to spoil you — The Towne Shop is one of the few stores left where clothes are presented to the customer in a salon setting highlighted by an elegant decor and crystal chandeliers. In addition, there is a fabulous collection of hand-cut crystal, brass, porcelain, trays, pillows, and linen handkerchiefs, all wonderful ideas for gift giving. Wardrobe planning and informal modeling complete your shopping experience. And the Towne Shop presents an exciting exclusive to Portland and the west coast this year — Victoria Falls, a new designer line from the Soho District in New York. Visa. MasterCard.

Uptown Shopping Center
2328 West Burnside
Portland 97210
223-3420

Monday-Saturday
9:30am-5:30pm
And By Appointment

Northwest
Portland
J17

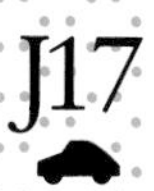

23rd AVENUE SWEATERS

WOMEN

Sweaters, sweaters, sweaters... and more.

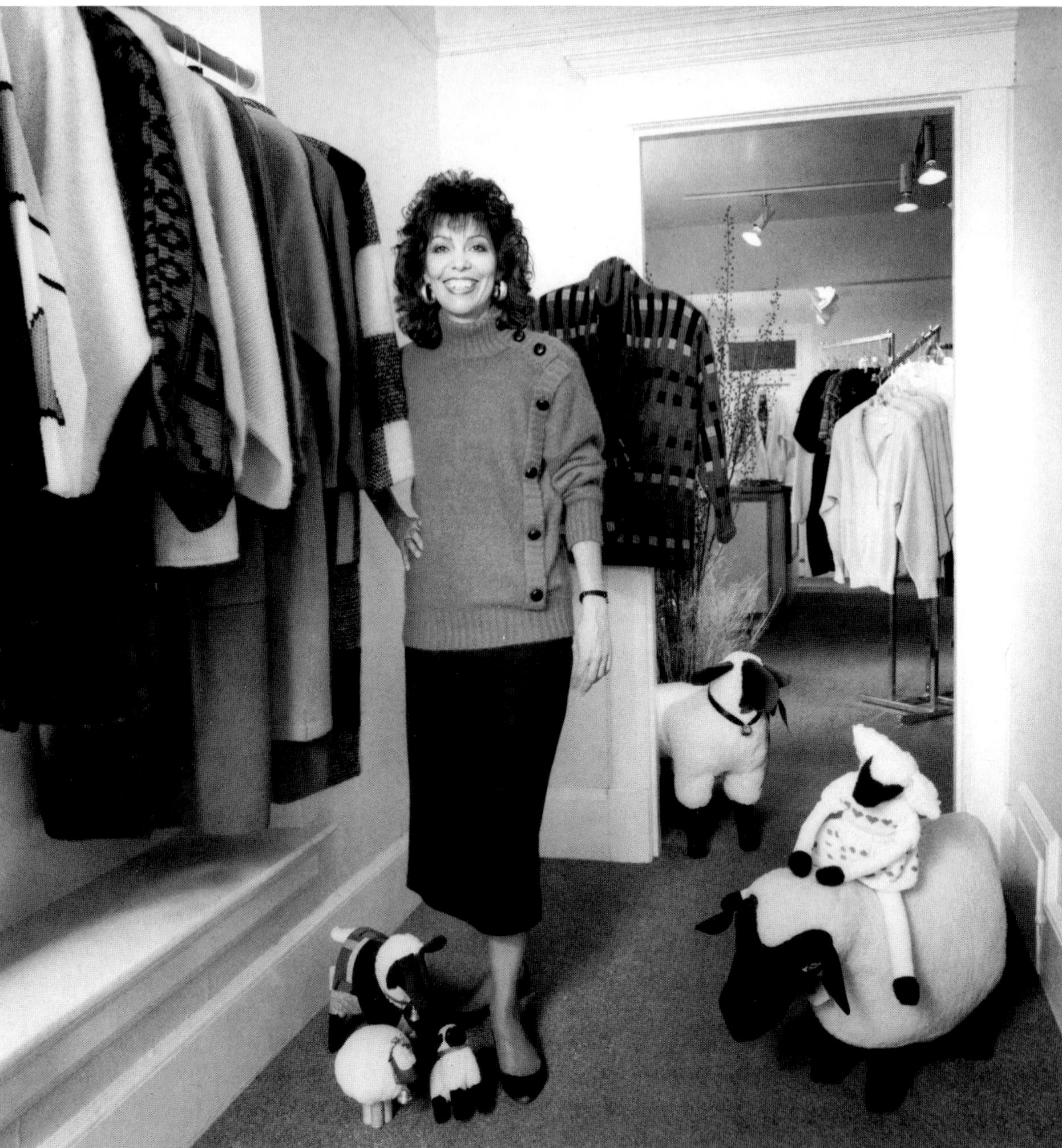

Northwest Portland
H17

Elegant, practical, comforting, individual. Nothing works wardrobe wonders like a sweater, and nowhere in Portland is there a better sweater fashion stop than Candy Grant's 23rd Avenue Sweaters. For any season and every reason, the skilled staff can help you choose sweaters. Sweater coats, dresses, knit skirts and pants of many natural fibers and blends. You'll find the works of I.B. Diffusion, Eagle's Eye, E.S. Deans, Outlander, Fia, Richard & Co., Jeanne Pierre, Catcher and Karen Kane, plus hand- knit sweaters from Mari Dembrow, Marlene Kerrigan, Sandra Brough, Julie Cherry, Sally Ford and Candy Grant herself. Novelty knitwear, hand-knit sweaters for infants and children, hand-woven scarves, knit hats and gloves, and sweater care products round out the list. All the fibers are here: Angora and wool with their rich feel, silk, and cotton. Styles run the gamut from comfortably classic to eye-opening contemporary; there are stunning imports and unusual styles knit right here in Oregon. But, most importantly, every customer earns the personal attention that sets 23rd Avenue Sweaters apart from the larger, multi-purpose retail stores and their less-inspired offerings. Visa. MasterCard. American Express.

738 NW 23rd Avenue
Portland 97210
226-0544

Monday-Saturday
10am-6pm
Sunday noon-4pm

FACES UNLIMITED

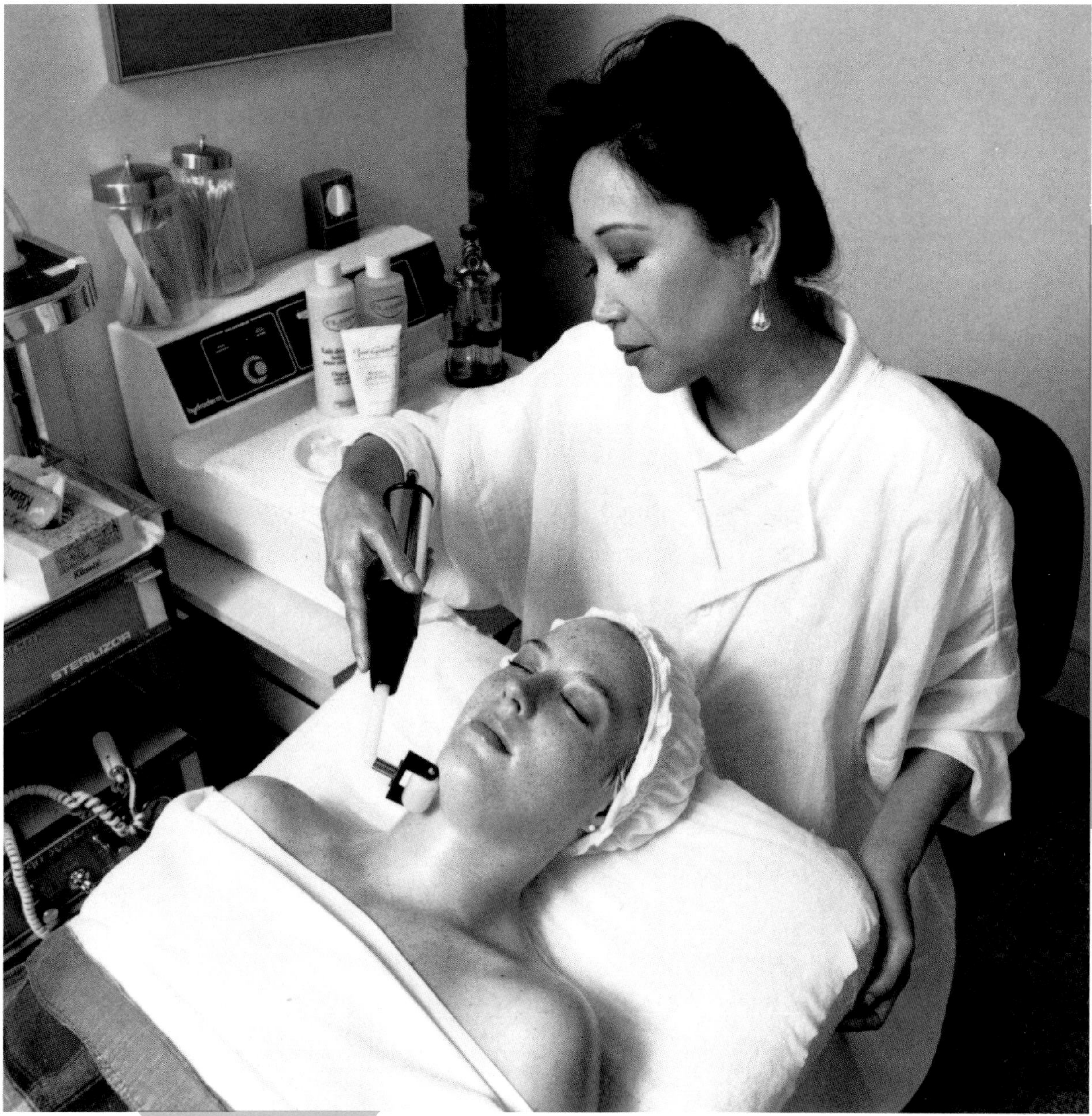

WOMEN

Take care of your precious skin — it has to last a lifetime.

The face that launched a thousand ships is not just a cliché at Faces Unlimited. Established in 1977 as the first independent facial salon in Portland, Faces Unlimited continues to be a leader in the art of make-up and skin care. Fashion model Pat Warren maintains a reputation as an innovator in the world of cosmetics and often appears on local TV as a beauty, skin care and fashion expert. Faces Unlimited has provided makeup artists for the Phil Donahue Show, for local television personalities and for Miss Oregons preparing for the Atlantic City pageants. Visiting celebrities drop in for that special bit of theatrical make-up or facials. Look for products from Payot, Rene Guinot, Stendhal, Clarins and Lancaster plus other internationally-acclaimed lines. Treat yourself at Faces Unlimited to a facial or a make-up application, or perhaps a luxurious special manicure or pedicure. Experts will tint your lashes and brows for a new and different look, or they can give you a facial or leg waxing. Faces Unlimited now offers an array of new services: two types of cellulite treatments, including intensive massage, can help you eliminate toxins and achieve your personal body goals. Make-up artists offer one-hour personal lessons, so that you can become your own make-up specialist. Treatments are offered in relaxed privacy by beauty and skin care experts. Let Faces Unlimited create that face of classic beauty. Visa. MasterCard.

911 SW Taylor Street
Portland 97205
222-4685

Monday-Saturday
9am-6pm

Downtown

F23

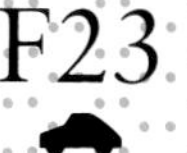

MARIO'S FOR WOMEN

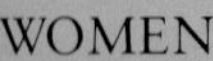

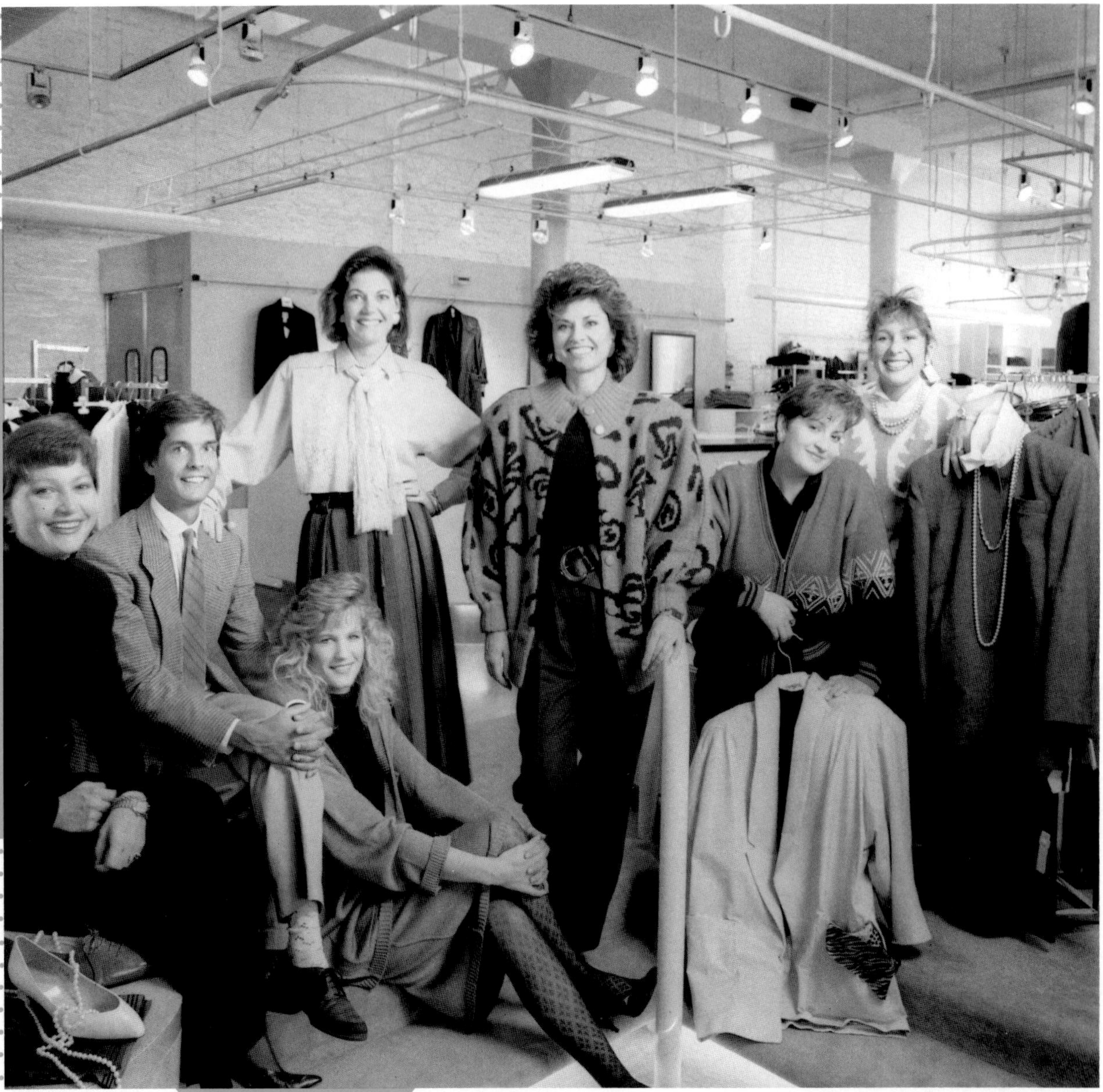

Lifestyle and investment dressing in a friendly atmosphere.

Downtown
F23

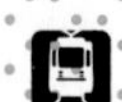

Some Portlanders may move away from home, but they never move away from their favorite shop — Mario's for Women. Such a loyal following is well-deserved. A few short steps inside Mario's for Women is like taking a shopping tour of the most fashionable designer showrooms around the world. It is immediately apparent— this establishment caters to women who desire to be impeccably dressed at all times. Buyers travel the world in search of the best contemporary "lifestyle" clothing from such designers as Byblos, Norma Kamali, XZEC, Joan Vass and Inwear. And the staff is ready to assist you in building a personal wardrobe. With your complete file at their fingertips, you'll learn instantly about suitable new arrivals. Your biggest dilemma will be choosing your latest look from these designers or Mario's own private LUNA label. Today, women play many-faceted roles personally and professionally and clothes must live up to their high expectations. Thank goodness, there's Mario's for Women. It's a trip around the world that's worth coming home for. Visa. MasterCard. American Express. Discover.

811 SW Morrison Street
Portland 97205
241-8111

Mario's for Men
921 SW Morrison Street
Portland 97205
227-3477

Mario's for Men
& Women
1513 Sixth Avenue
Seattle 98101
(206) 223-1461

Monday-Thursday
10am-6pm
Friday 10am-7pm
Saturday 10am-6pm
Sunday noon-5pm

LA PALOMA

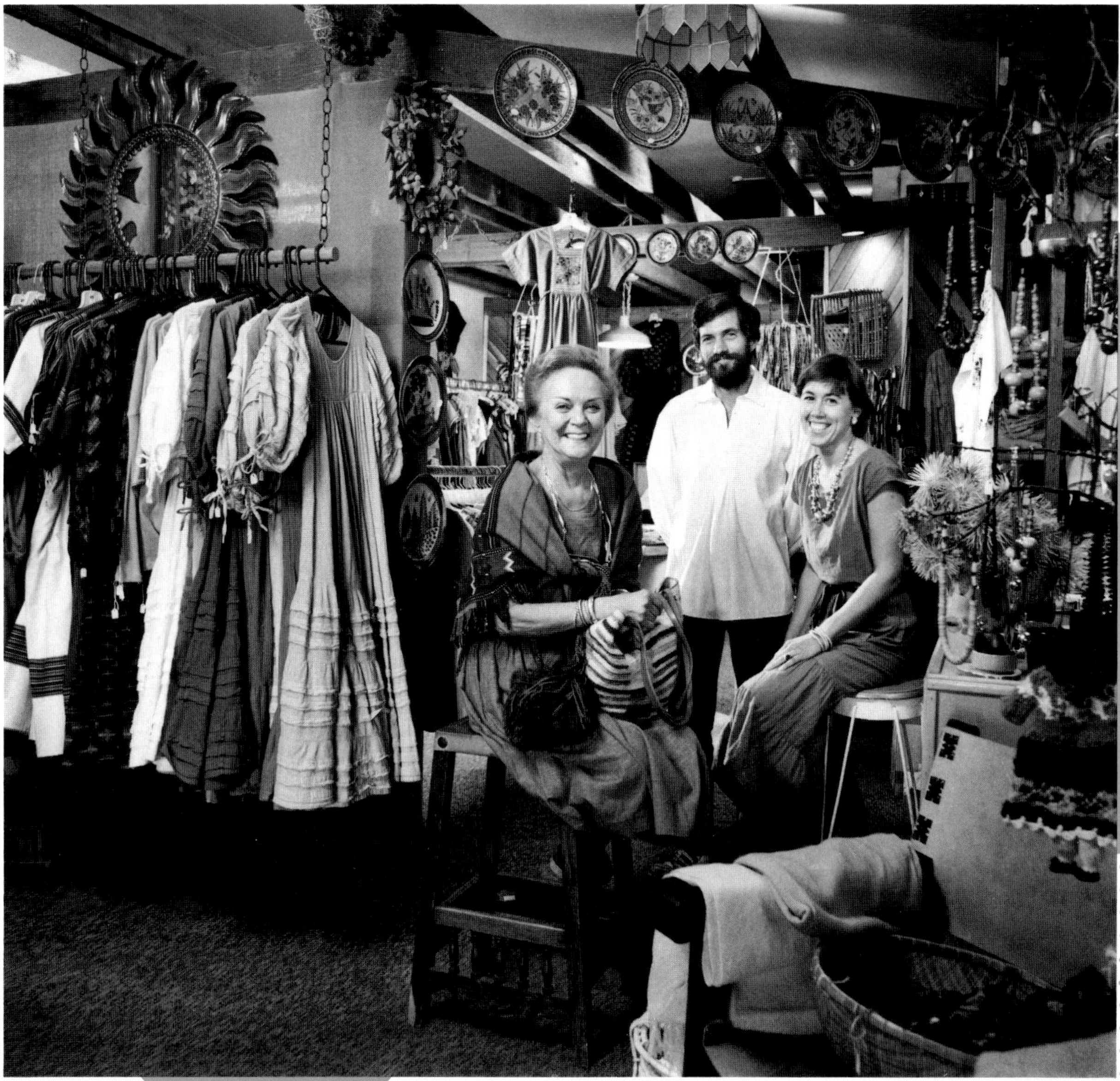

WOMEN

Natural fiber clothing and hand-crafted jewelry.

Multnomah/ Hillsdale

F5

Eight years ago, Mike Roach was exploring the old Benito Juarez Public Market in Oaxaca, Mexico, buying embroidered wedding dresses for this clothing and jewelry store owned by Mike and his mother Phyllis Roach. There he met Kim Osgood; their first date was a buying trip to a small village near the ruins of Mitla. Today, Kim and Mike are married and they operate La Paloma, offering natural fiber clothing, jewelry and folk art from 20 different countries, including the United States. Just as on Mike's trip to Oaxaca, your visits to La Paloma are certain to bring thrilling discoveries. In business for 12 years, La Paloma has an outstanding selection of dresses, a year-round supply of vacation and cruise clothes, contemporary jewelry and a world of other merchandise. Even globe-trotting customers find themselves returning frequently for the locally-made Alexa, George King, and Amber jewelry, the easy care domestic Color Me Cotton clothing, and the Skyr and Northern Isle cotton and wool sweaters. The staff specializes in maximizing your latest purchase or updating an old favorite with the perfect accessories. Travelers will also find the staff knowledgeable in suggesting just the right comfortable attire for your upcoming vacation. The focus at La Paloma is on fashions that have an enduring flair. Located in the Hillsdale Shopping Center, the shop is but 10 minutes from downtown and offers personalized service, easy parking, reasonable prices, and a relaxed, festive atmosphere. MasterCard. Visa. American Express.

Hillsdale Shopping Center
6316 SW Capitol Highway
Portland 97201
246-3417

Monday-Saturday
10am-6pm

JEAN-MARIE FINE LINGERIE

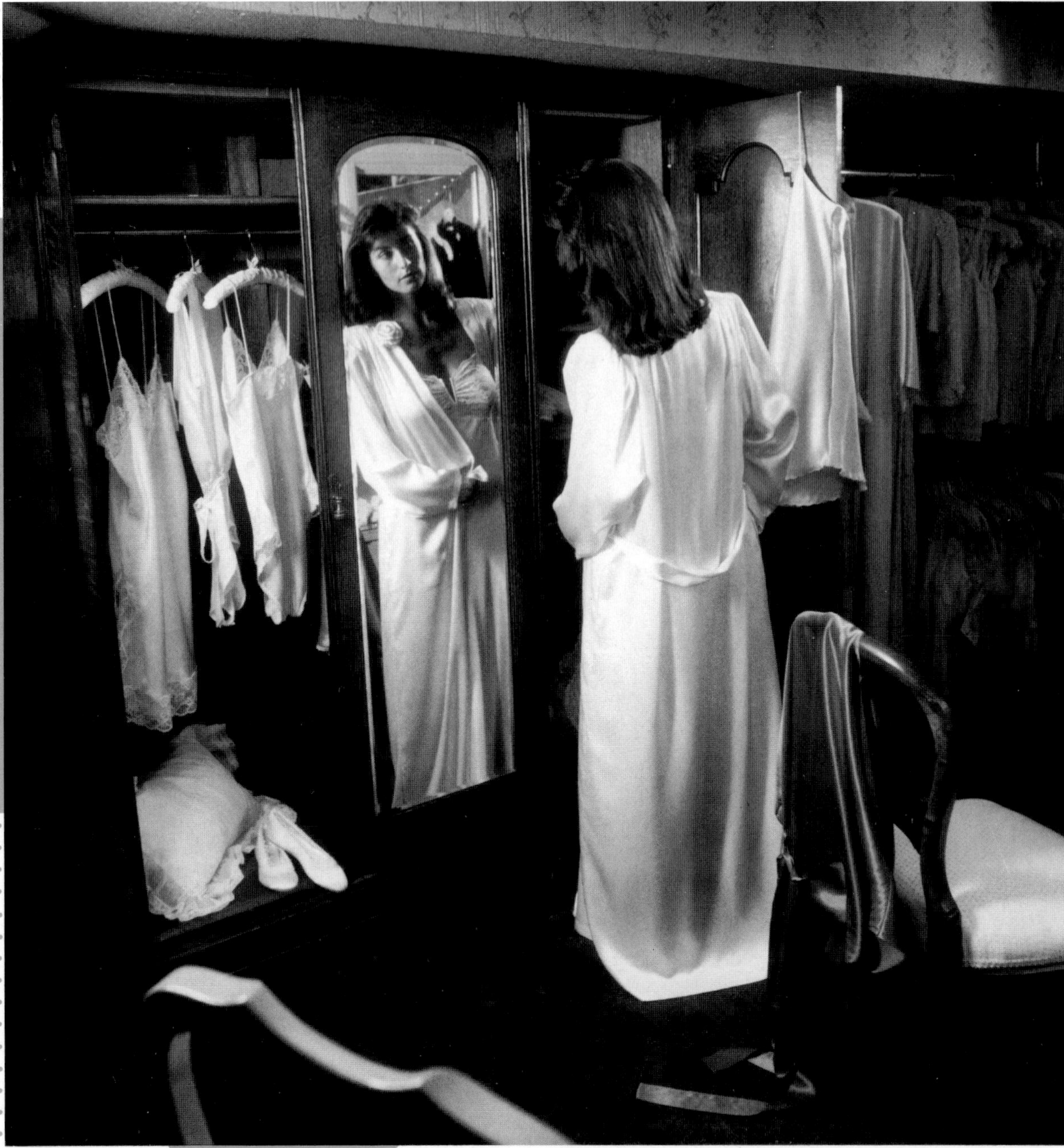

WOMEN

Specializing in Pacific Northwest designer fine lingerie.

Northwest Portland

J17

Fine fabrics and quality design are important to modern women, from their tailored jackets to their stylish shoes. And today, women apply the same standards to their lingerie. To fully serve quality-conscious women, Jean Hix opened Jean-Marie Fine Lingerie in Northwest Portland. The frame of a classic Victorian house opens onto a stylish shop which shows off the special product lines, including fine products by Pacific Northwest designers, as well as the finest lingerie from around the world. Jean Hix believes in personalized assistance — service that guarantees customers will love what they've purchased. If you don't find what you want, Jean will special order from an extensive network of lingerie designers and manufacturers. Enjoy the luxurious feeling of silk against your skin or the coolness of fine cotton on a hot summer day. Just visiting Jean-Marie Fine Lingerie can be a sensual experience — the colors and textures of quality lingerie make browsing a pleasure. And while you're there, remember that a gift from Jean-Marie can be the perfect present to make any woman feel best dressed. Visa. MasterCard. American Express.

2340 NW Westover Road
Portland 97210
224-4598

Monday through Friday 10am-6pm
Saturday 10am-5:30pm

WEST END LTD.

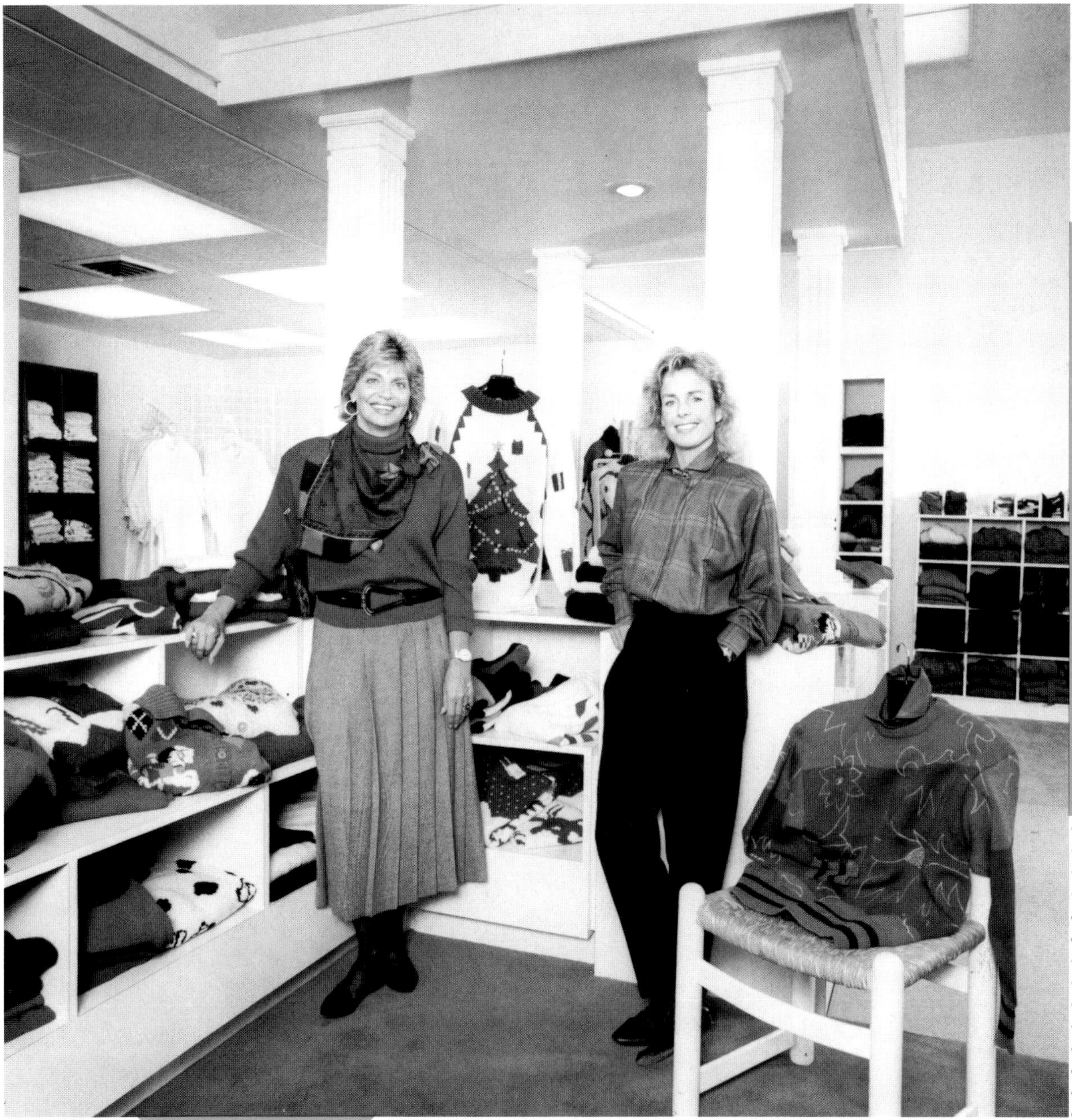

WOMEN

Full fashion wardrobing service.

If your criteria for a top-of-the-line women's clothing store include exclusivity, convenience, and special service, turn to the recently remodeled West End Ltd. The white, light, and spacious decor set a simple yet elegant stage for the distinctive clothing that is West End's trademark. West End's collection highlights carefully selected items not available everywhere. Distinctive hand-knit sweaters are featured and, reorganizing the luxury of natural fibers, West End has a wide selection of pants, skirts, and blouses in silk, cotton, wool, and ramie. Ensuring distinction for every occasion, West End offers cocktail, daytime, and professional dresses. Lingerie and play clothes from jeans to warm-ups, extend their collection to meet every need. All staff members have an unfailing sense of fashion and an uncanny ability to help you create a wardrobe distinguished by versatility and style. West End special services include at-home wardrobe consultation, notification of new arrivals of special interest and assistance in the selection of shoes, bags, and other accessories not available at the store. View their extensive collection during regular business hours, visit by appointment or attend one of West End's periodic fashion shows. An annual men's Christmas party helps men make their often difficult holiday selections. At West End, the customer's needs come first, making shopping a pleasant and productive experience. Visa. MasterCard. American Express.

22 NW 23rd Avenue
Portland 97210
224-2600

Monday-Friday
10am-6pm
Saturday 10am-5pm

Northwest
Portland
J17

M. WILLOCK

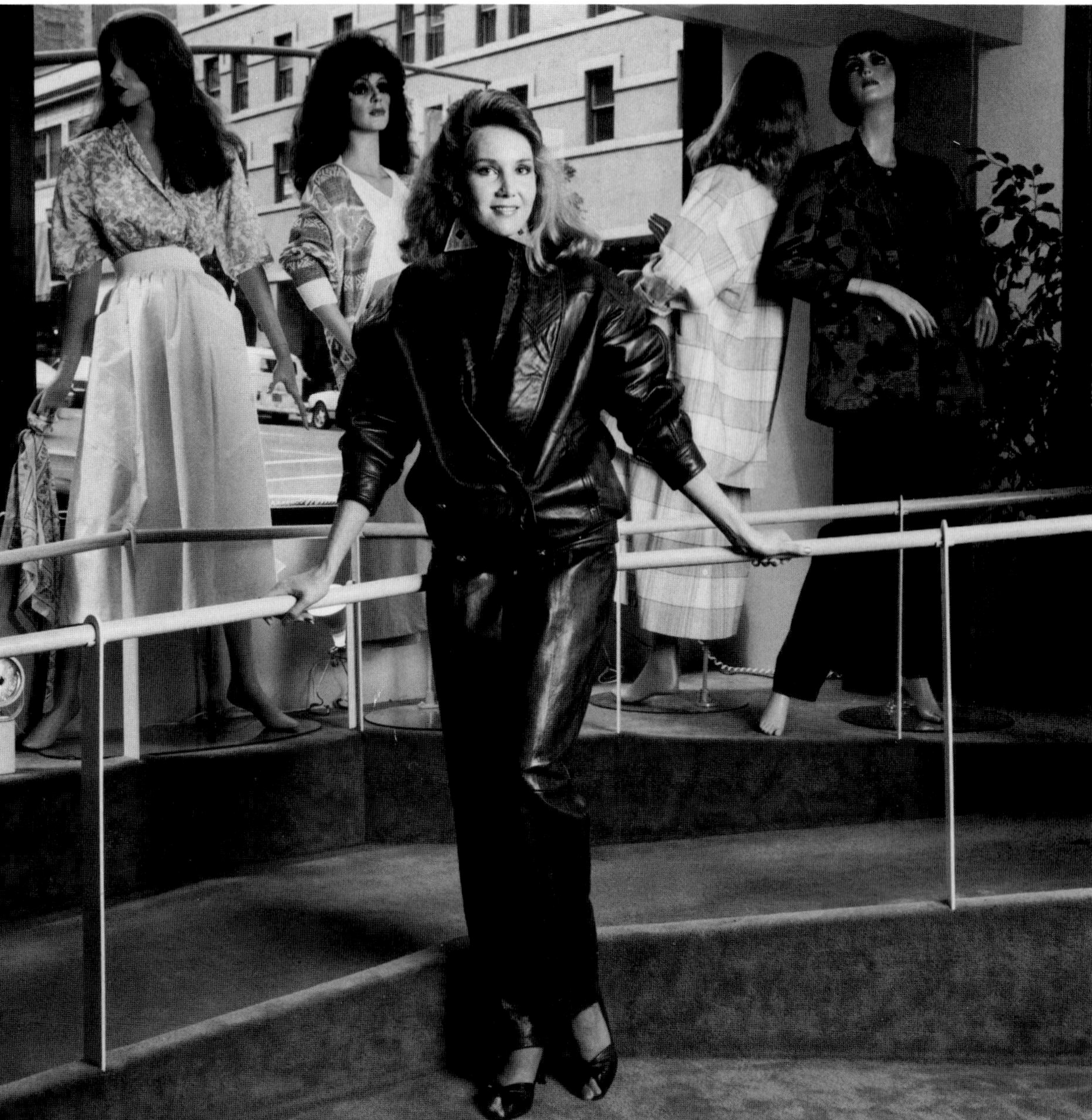

WOMEN

Investment dressing that's fun yet functional.

Downtown
F23

Maxine Willock has been around the world four times in the best of style. As a high ranking business executive, she's traveled to every continent, conducted business and met socially prominent people in situations where her personal fashion sense had to pass the most demanding scrutiny. Now, as owner of M. Willock, she shares her international experience in fashion and culture with her customers, offering them a superb selection of the finest merchandise, most of it unavailable elsewhere in the city. Mondi of American, and Brustela and Slendor, both branches of Mondi, are well-represented. Such sophisticated, refined clothes are considered investment pieces that can be worn and cherished for years. You'll find stylish sportswear from Bogner of American, the European manufacturer who has dressed skiers and tennis players beautifully for years. For real professional style, choose from Susie Hayward's limited collection of suits and slacks in lightweight wool, and elegant dresses and blouses. Joanie Char's dresses and blouses in soft, natural fibers are ideal for day-into-evening wear. M. Willock has recently added a special selection of separates from Geiger of Austria, which can be worn casually or to the most sophisticated affair. Leather belts, exquisite scarves and well-chosen jewelry complete the exclusive fashion statement that sets you apart — and at home — anywhere in the world. Visa. MasterCard. American Express. Diners Club. Carte Blanche.

860 SW Broadway
at Taylor
Portland 97205
226-3405

Monday-Saturday
9:30am-6pm
And By Appointment.

THE PETITE WOMAN'S SHOPPE

WOMEN

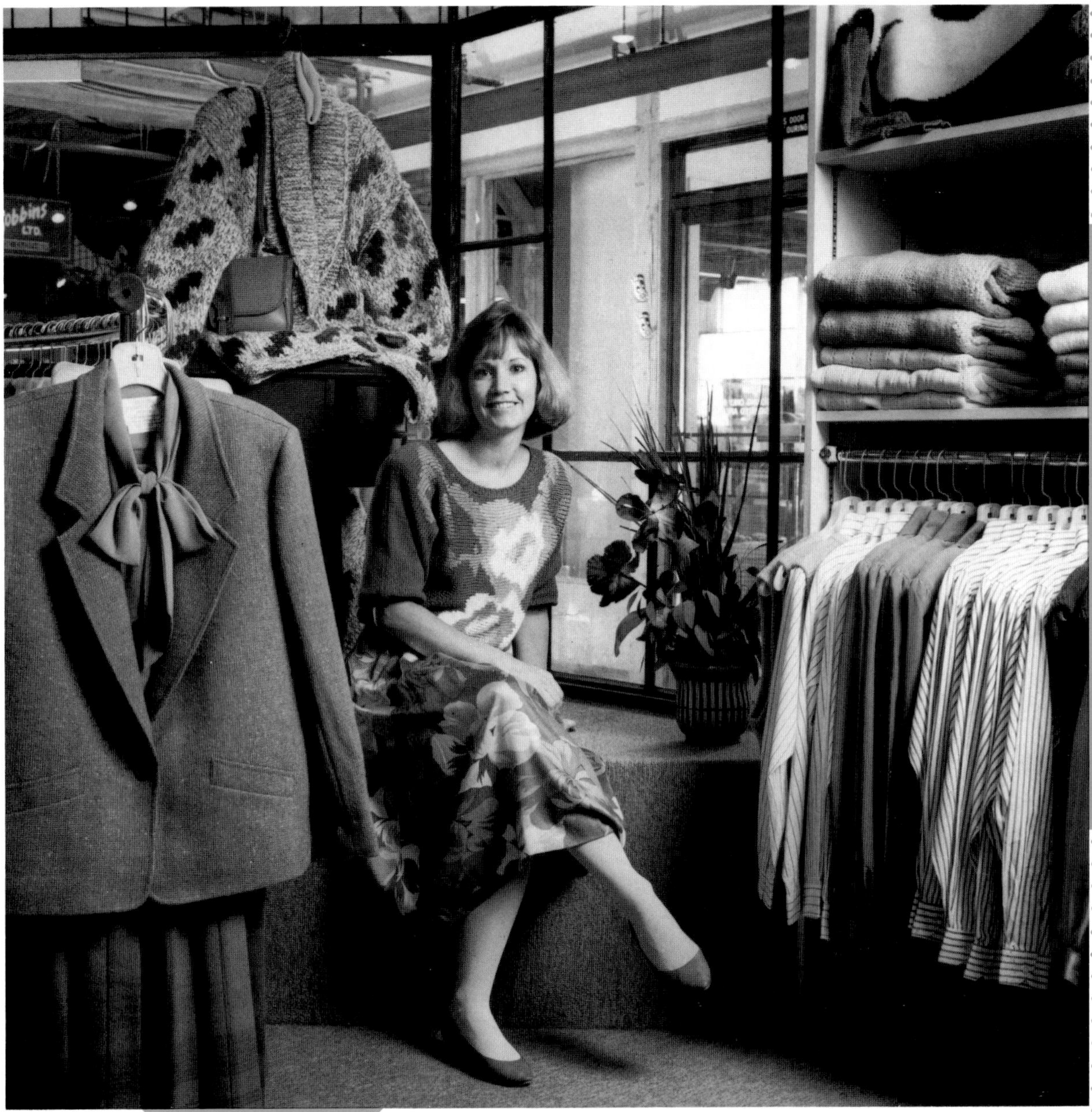

The original petite woman's shop in Oregon.

Corbett-Johns Landing

F6

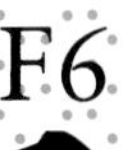

You've gone shopping and been frustrated again. Sound familiar? It seems that fashionable clothes are only for tall women. You're under 5'4 and look silly in all those bulky layers. Well, take heart. Trend setters like Nancy Reagan, Bo Derek, Linda Ronstadt and millions of American women share your problem. That's why The Petite Woman's Shoppe was begun. This sophisticated little store in historic Johns Landing features over 50 prestigious designer lines, including Albert Nipon, Ellen Tracy, Pendleton, Richard Warren and J.G. Hook. In sizes 2-12, all clothes are designed in proportions to fit women under 5'4". You'll find everything the impeccably tailored woman needs to go from home or office to a glittering evening on the town. And, because The Petite Woman's Shoppe feels that extra services are as important as the clothes they sell, monthly fashion shows, open houses, seminars and trunk showings are presented. Enjoy the personalized service and variety of wardrobe possibilities that this exclusive boutique provides. Everything they sell is made for petites. You can finally stop shopping in vain. Visa. MasterCard. American Express.

The Water Tower
5331 SW Macadam Avenue
Portland 97201
241-8595

Monday-Friday 10am-9pm
Saturday 10am-6pm
Sunday noon-5pm

203 Valley River Center
Eugene 97401
485-0072

Monday-Friday 10am-9pm
Saturday 10am-6pm
Sunday 11am-5pm

SUITE 360

WOMEN

A full circle of personal services.

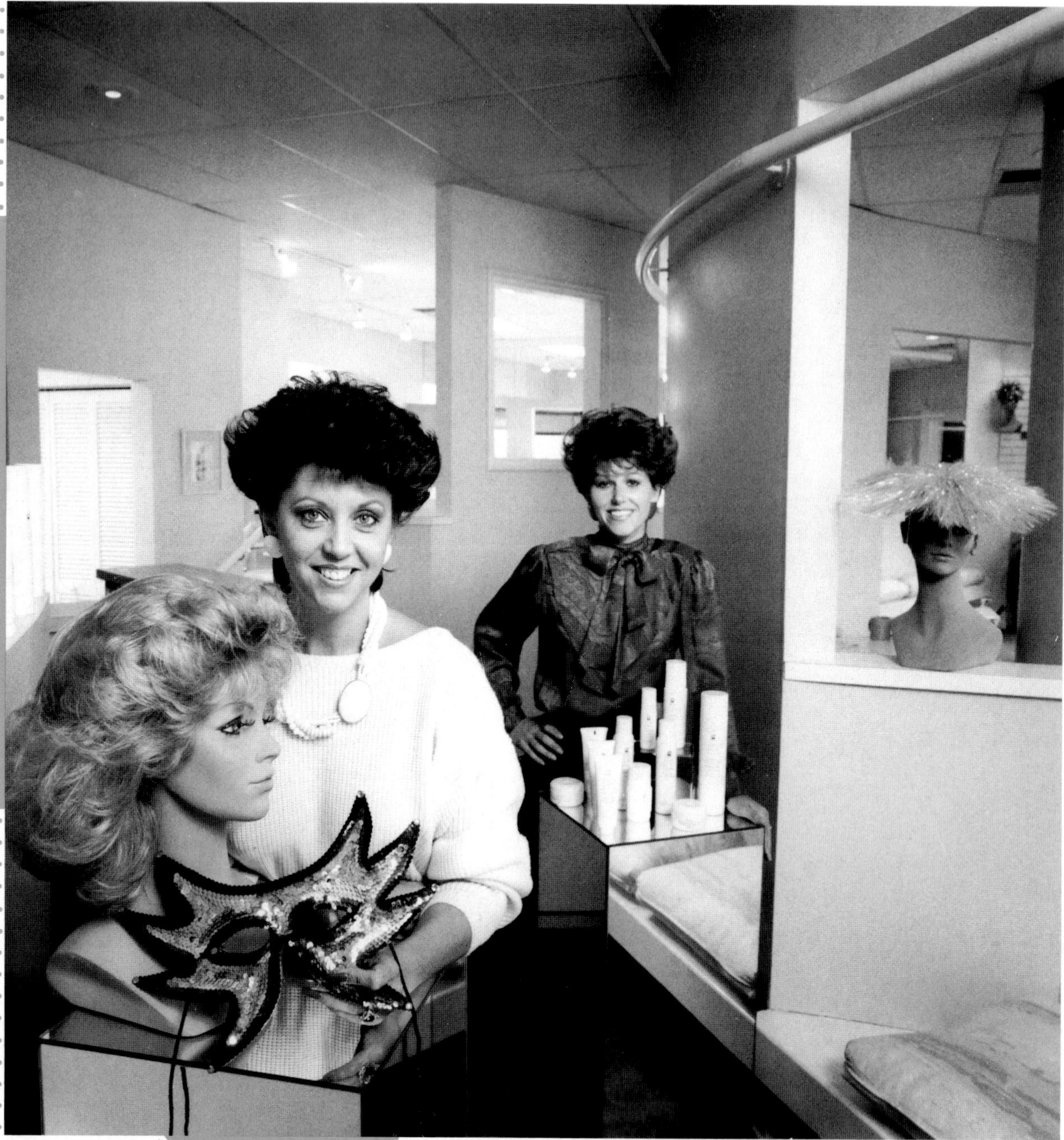

RiverPlace

125

Although Suite 360 just happens to be the RiverPlace address of Brenda Kay's comprehensive salon, it also effectively suggests the full circle of skin, nail and hair care services at this elegant setting. With her 20 years' experience in wig sales, Brenda also brings an important service to Portlanders: special assistance for the person who has lost hair due to medical treatment. With private fitting rooms, full services for wig care and one of the city's largest inventories of hairpieces, Suite 360 offers men, women and children a comfortable and complete way to be fitted with replacement hair until normal growth resumes. For other customers, the salon provides permanent waves, cutting, trimming and the latest in coloring for every conceivable look. Skin technicians assess your skin type and recommend skin care products, procedures and cosmetics. And pedicures, manicures and artificial or natural nail treatments are done at salon stations that all have a view of the Willamette River and other RiverPlace scenery. For that "other" you, Suite 360 has supplies (from mid-September to the end of the year) to turn your looks 180 degrees on special occasions: a large line of Halloween and Mardi Gras masks and what probably is the largest supply of holiday wigs in the city. Visa. MasterCard.

0315 SW Montgomery
Portland 97201
223-8092

Monday-Saturday
8am-6pm
Evenings by appointment.

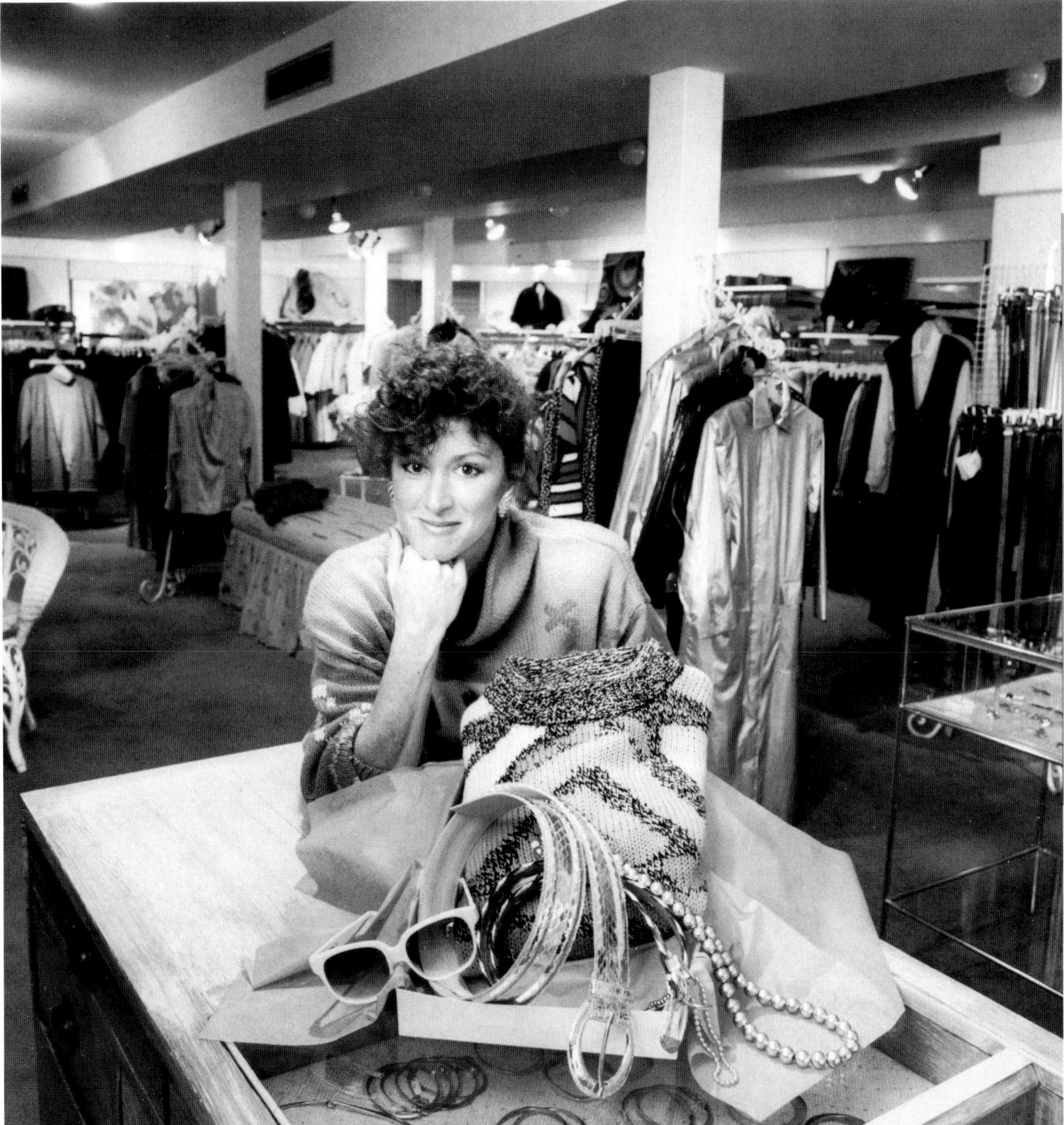

WOMEN

Contemporary and classic sportswear for women.

With its collection of refined classics and wonderful weekend separates, Victoria's city wide reputation has long been established. Perry Ellis, Ellen Tracy, Adrienne Vittadini, Dennis Goldsmith and Nicole Miller are just a few of the well known designers whose lines are available at Victoria's. Whether you're looking for classic pieces or the season's latest knitwear, you'll find that special fashion look that you will love to wear. In Victoria's comfortable and inviting interior, creative displays inspire even the most casual browser. A host of accessories — carefully selected lines of jewelry and belts — will give the perfect finishing touch to any outfit, from casually elegant sportswear to high fashion clothing. The amiable and thoughtful staff — experts in fashion sensibility — are standing by to assist and advise, whether you have a simple request or are looking for a complete wardrobe. And Victoria's tailor shop will always ensure the perfect fit. Visa. MasterCard. American Express. Discover.

Uptown Shopping Center
2362 West Burnside
Portland 97210
227-7882

Monday-Friday
10am-6pm
Saturday
9:30am-5:30pm

Northwest Portland

J17

SYLVIE AN IMAGE PERFECTED FOR YOU

WOMEN

Indulge yourself at Sylvie!

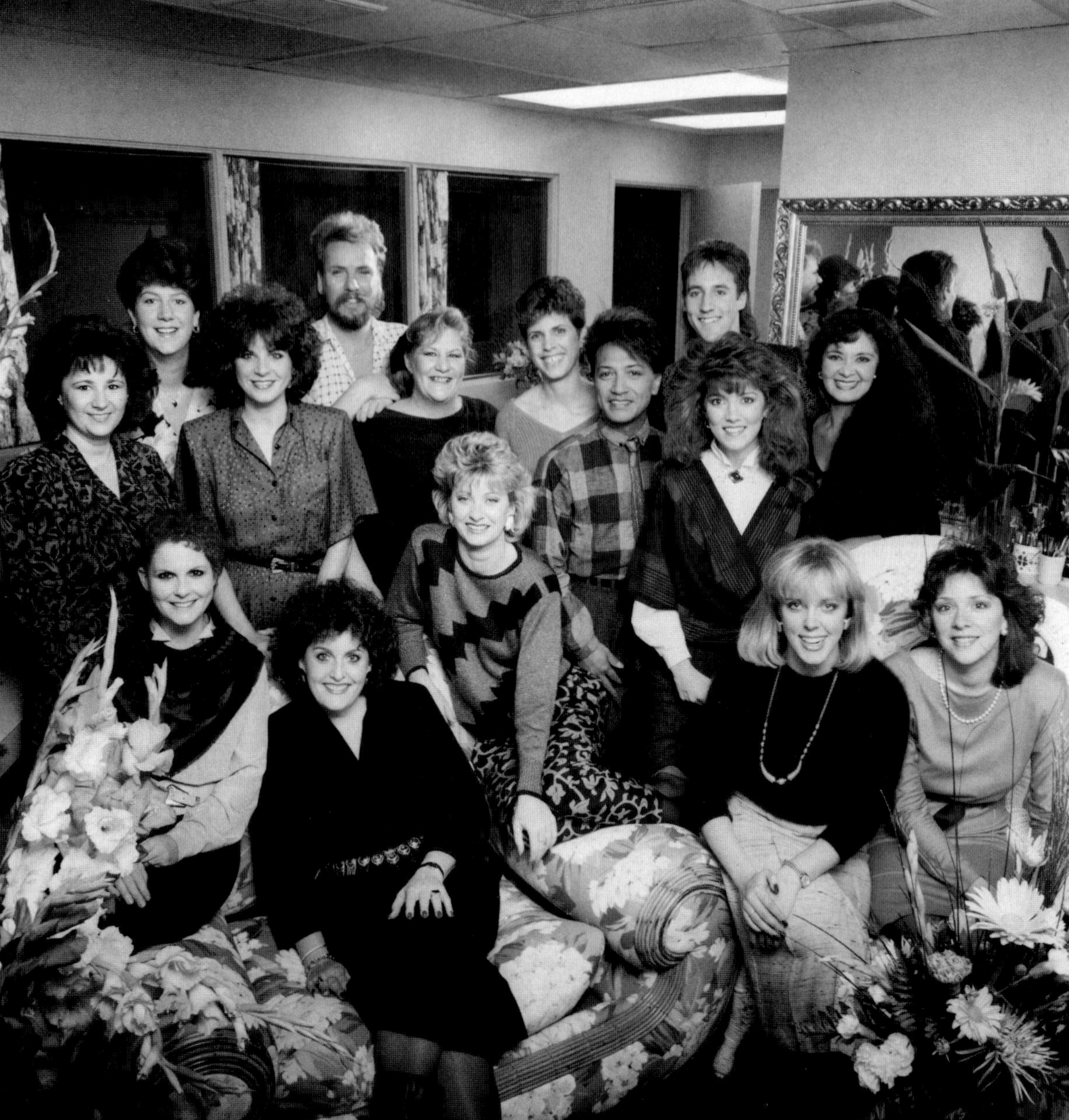

Northwest Portland

H17

It's only Tuesday and already you've had a hectic week. Why not forget the hassles and indulge yourself with a Swedish massage, European skin care treatment, pedicure, Juliette or silk nail wrap, or makeup consultation at Sylvie. In this warm solarium style retreat, professionals work to create an image perfected for you. Color analysis — with attention to line, texture and style — could include wardrobe consultation and coordination. And workshops for individuals or groups, in complete makeup instruction, feature skin care products by Sothys of Paris and Prescription Plus. If you would like to spend the day at Sylvie, there's limousine service from your home or office — or complimentary transportation from downtown hotels. The Swedish massage and European facial will be followed by a catered luncheon, color analysis and a luxurious pedicure and manicure. Sylvie also offers the ultimate in body waxing, as well as electrolysis, brow and lash tinting and of course a full service hair salon. If it's difficult for you to visit Sylvie during usual business hours, appointments can be arranged for your convenience. When you — or someone close to you — deserves a little pampering, remember Sylvie. One visit could change your whole perspective on the week. Visa. MasterCard.

2322 NW Irving Street
Portland 97210
222-5054

Monday-Friday
8am-6pm
Saturday 9am-5pm
Sundays & evenings
By appointment

EYE OF RA

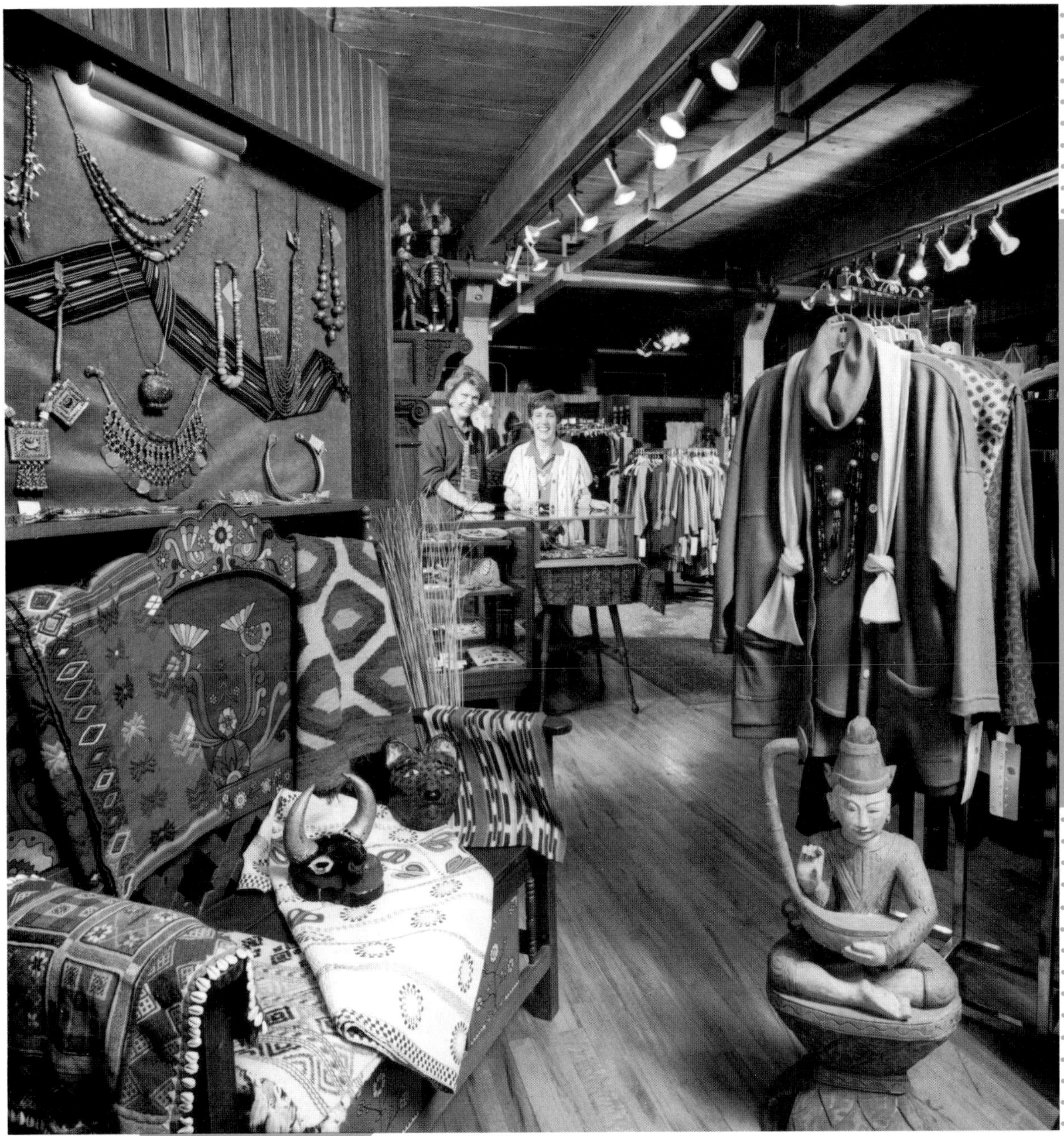

WOMEN

Folk Art, fine jewelry and fashion with an international flavor.

Images of exotic faces, famous ruins, priceless icons and faraway places spring to mind when you enter the Eye of Ra. Folk art, fine jewelry and fashion with an international flavor make this little shop irresistable. Renowned for elegantly ethnic tribal clothing — perfect for festive occasions — Eye of Ra also carries an exotic selection of contemporary imported clothing. Slip into a batik kimono, a casually elegant cutwork ensemble from Indonesia or beautiful raw silk from Cyprus. Wrap yourself in a Uruguayan ruana — a streetlength shawl made from hand loomed wool. Complete this eclectic fashion mood with antique jewelry and accessories from around the world for a look that is distinctly unique. Eye of Ra is known for unusual earrings — contemporary designs from well known Northwest artisans have joined the international collection of tribal pieces. The staff at Eye of Ra knows the histories of their merchandise, including the intriguing folk art that graces the shop — they'll help select the perfect piece for you or for that special someone. Discover the timeless, always contemporary, fashions of the world at Eye of Ra. Visa. MasterCard. American Express.

The Water Tower
5331 SW Macadam Avenue
Portland 97201
224-4292

Monday-Friday 10am-9pm
Saturday 10am-6pm
Sunday noon-5pm

Corbett-Johns Landing

F6

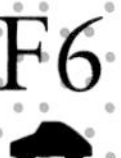

MEN & WOMEN

A distinguished selection of clothiers for men and those catering to both sexes. The finest in classic and contemporary, casual and formal, plus accessories and grooming sources.

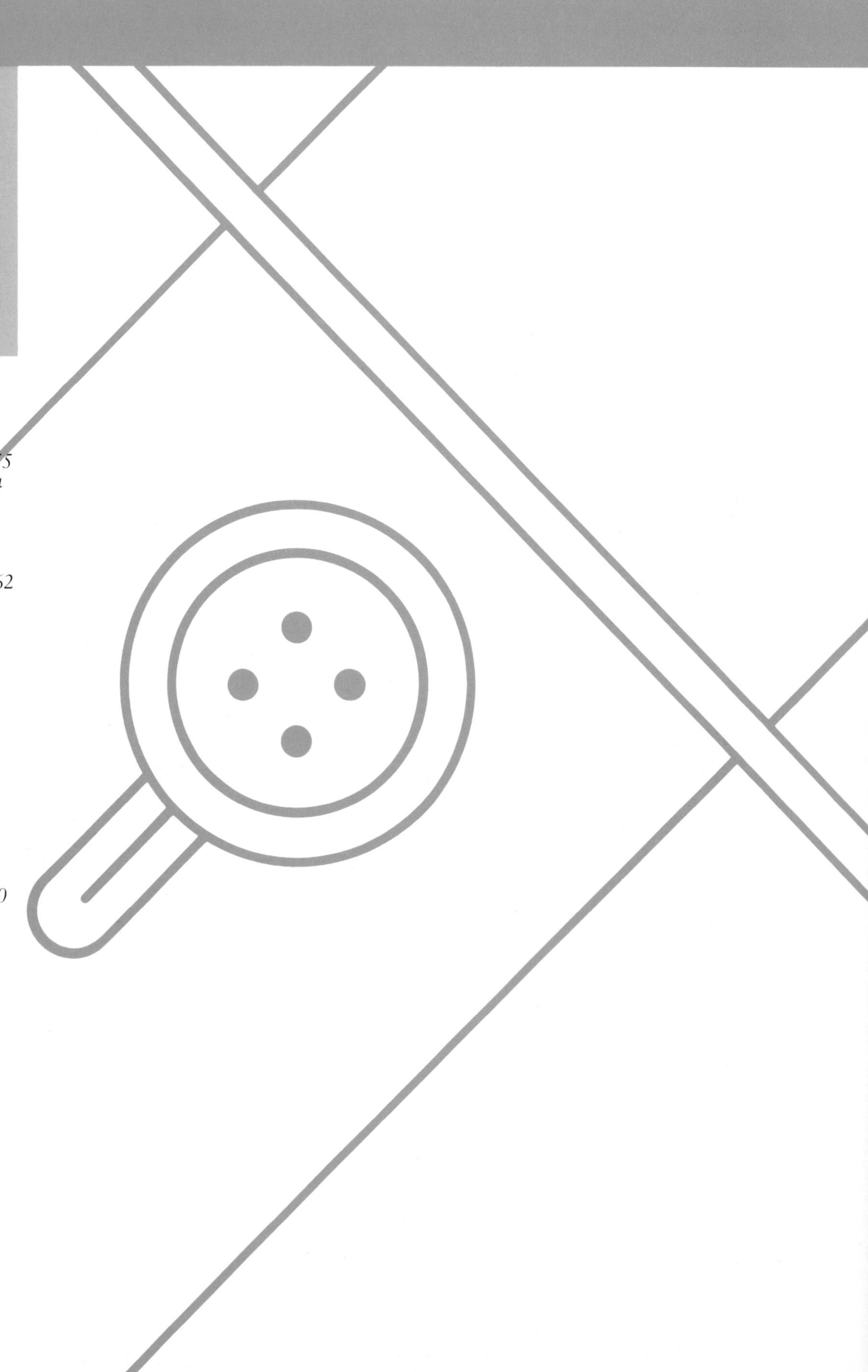

Alan Costley *161*
Alder West *165*
Cromwell Formal Wear *155*
Francesca's Fragrances *164*
Gary McKinstry Hair Design *159*
Gazelle Natural Fibre Clothing *162*
Hanna Andersson *179*
Harrington's Executive Clothiers *166*
Hickox and Friends *167*
Hot Cities *158*
Kids Hair Parlour *189*
La Paloma *143*
Mario's *154*
Mt. Park Pro Shop *206*
Nofziger *163*
Norm Thompson *157*
Northwest Passage Boots & Clothing Company *160*
Oregon Mountain Community *198*
Pacific Crest Clothing Co. *156*
Richard Ltd. *153*
Trade Secrets *168*

RICHARD LTD.

MEN

For fashion that lives on.

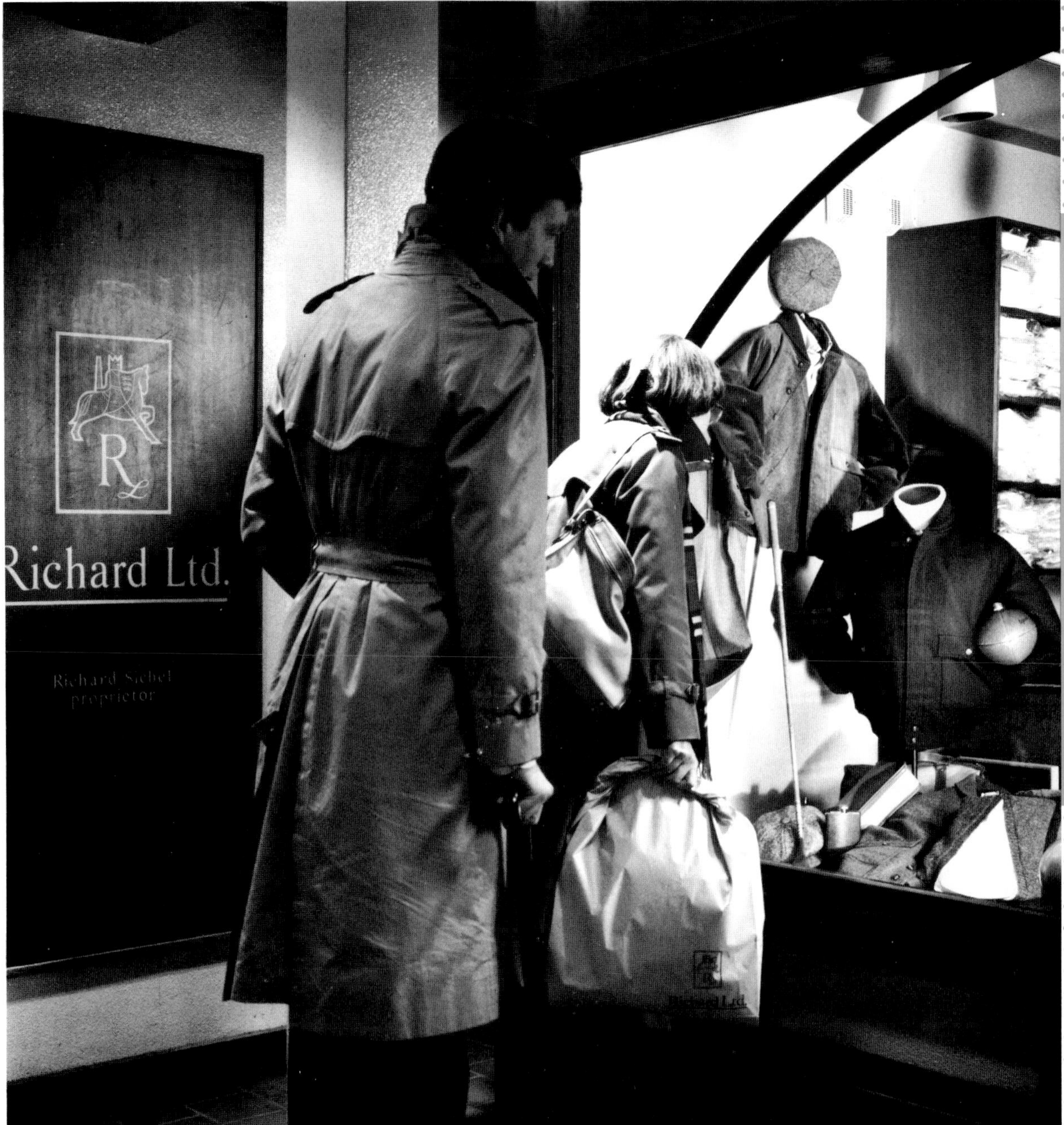

On any given day a small group of people can be seen standing in front of the windows at Richard Ltd., admiring some of the finest clothing ensembles available in the Northwest. Now more than two decades old, this shop has built a nationwide reputation for classic and updated traditional clothing, sportswear and accessories for men. The inventory here is replete with carefully chosen items, each created with exacting attention to detail and quality. Paired with timeless designs, that quality ensures a long, satisfying and stylish use for every article, whether it be a tie or suit. Richard Ltd. features such names in men's clothing and furnishings as Norman Hilton, Southwick, Arthur Freedberg, Corbin, Gittman and Sero, Tricot St. Raphael, Alan Paine of England and Pringle of Scotland, Robert Talbot, Polo and Ghurka. Naturally, the fabrics are nature's best: silk, wool and cotton. Richard Ltd.: for fashion that lives on. Visa. MasterCard. American Express.

725 SW Alder Street
Portland 97205
227-6601

Monday-Saturday
9:30am-5:30pm

Downtown
F23

MARIO'S

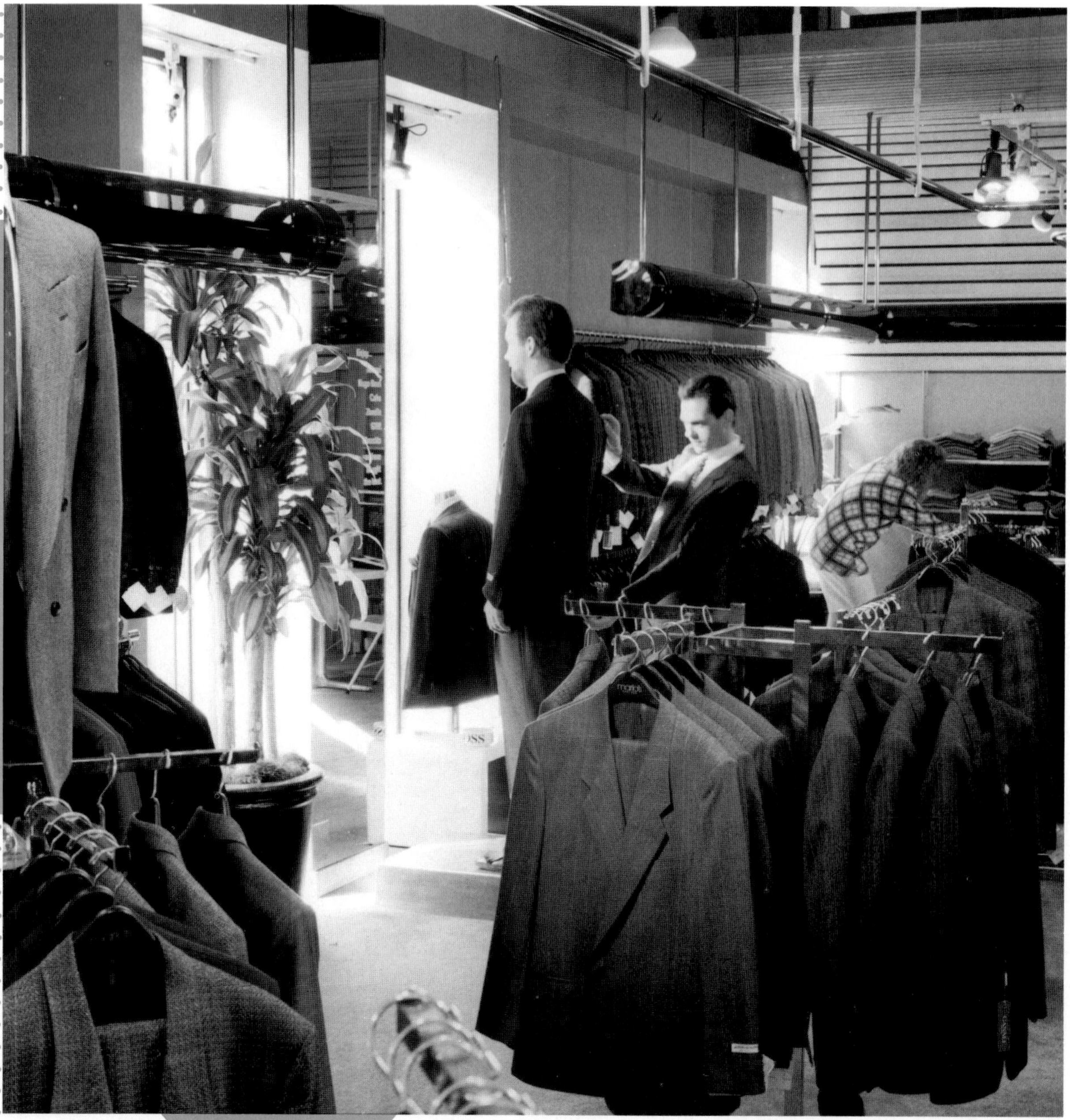

MEN

Lifestyle and investment dressing in a friendly atmosphere.

Downtown

F23

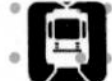

Menswear has finally come of age, and the evidence is right here in Portland, at Mario's. From casual sportswear to impeccably tailored suits, Mario's has been offering distinctive, contemporary clothing and wardrobe consultation for over 35 years. Whatever your clothing requirements, you can depend on Mario's knowledgeable staff to create a look that suits your unique lifestyle and coordinates with the garments that you already own. Along with classic favorites, you'll find the best designer names from all over the world, including Perry Ellis, Georgio Armani, San Remo, Hugo Boss, Jun, and Byblos. If you like, the staff at Mario's will keep a personal file for you, indicating your size, color preference, and wardrobe needs. You'll be informed when merchandise arrives that you might find interesting, and receive announcements for special events and spectacular sales. It's important to remember that the better you look, the better you feel. After a visit to Mario's, you're going to feel great. Visa. MasterCard. American Express. Discover.

The Galleria
921 SW Morrison Street
Portland 97205
227-3477

Monday-Friday
10am-9pm
Saturday 10am-6pm
Sunday Noon-5pm

Mario's for Women
811 SW Morrison Street
Portland 97205
241-8111

Mario's for
Men & Women
1513 Sixth Avenue
Seattle 98101
(206) 223-1461

CROMWELL FORMAL WEAR

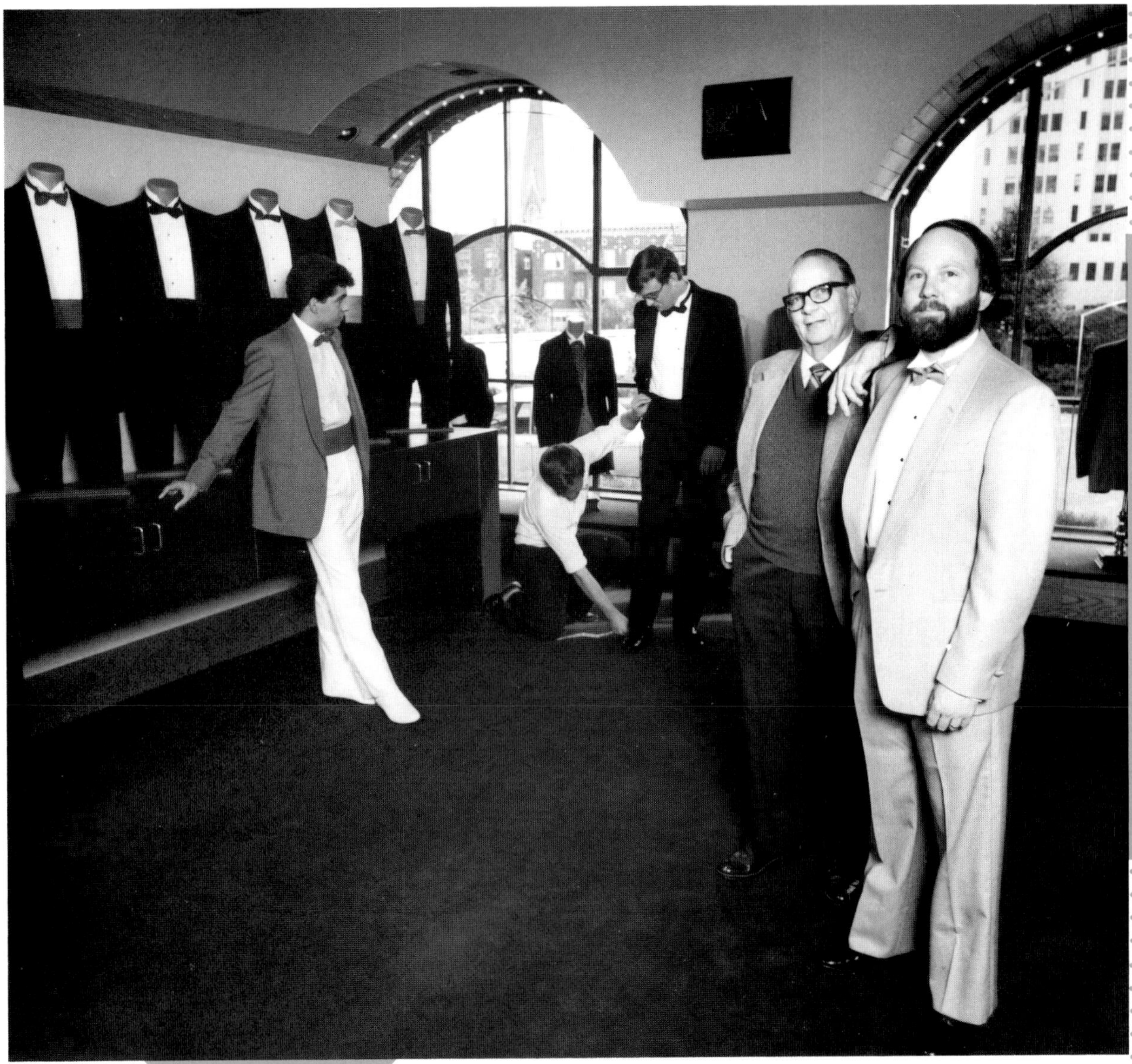

MEN AND WOMEN

Suitable for all your formal occasions.

More than a half-century ago, Cromwell began business as a custom tailor of fine men's and women's clothing. In the 1940s, formal- wear rentals were introduced; by the late 1960s the clothing was discontinued as the firm's destiny became clear: Cromwell Formal Wear would become the Northwest's major supplier of tuxedo rentals. Today there are two Portland-area retail locations, and more than 5,000 rental tuxedos from the sharpest lines in the industry: After Six, Lord West, Pierre Cardin, Bill Blass, Yves St. Laurent, Dynasty and Miami Vice. At the nucleus of the firm are George Sturgill and his son, Jim, whose combined experience at Cromwell's exceeds 70 years. That experience brings a high standard of quality and such made-for-the-'80s services as 30-minute tuxedo rental at the downtown location! And regardless of how pressing your requirements are, Cromwell maintains its personalized service, meticulous fitting and attention to detail that have been a company trademark since the Ford Model A was brand new. You'll find men's and boy's rental tuxedos in sizes 2 through 60, tuxedo sales, rental and sales of formal accessories, business suit rentals; consultation to determine the correct attire for weddings, proms, black-tie functions and women's tuxedo rentals. Prices are competitive, advice is unerring and, as always, the fit is more than suitable. Visa. MasterCard.

711 SW 14th Avenue
Portland 97205
226-4356

Monday 8:30am-9pm
Tuesday-Thursday
8:30am-5:30pm
Friday 8:30am-9pm
Saturday 9:30am-5pm

Canyon Place
3905 SW 117th Avenue
Beaverton 97005
644-0418

Monday & Friday
10am-8pm
Tuesday-Thursday
10am-6pm
Saturday 10am-5pm

Downtown
F21

Beaverton
E2

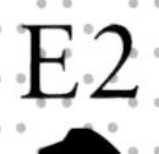

PACIFIC CREST CLOTHING CO.

MEN AND WOMEN

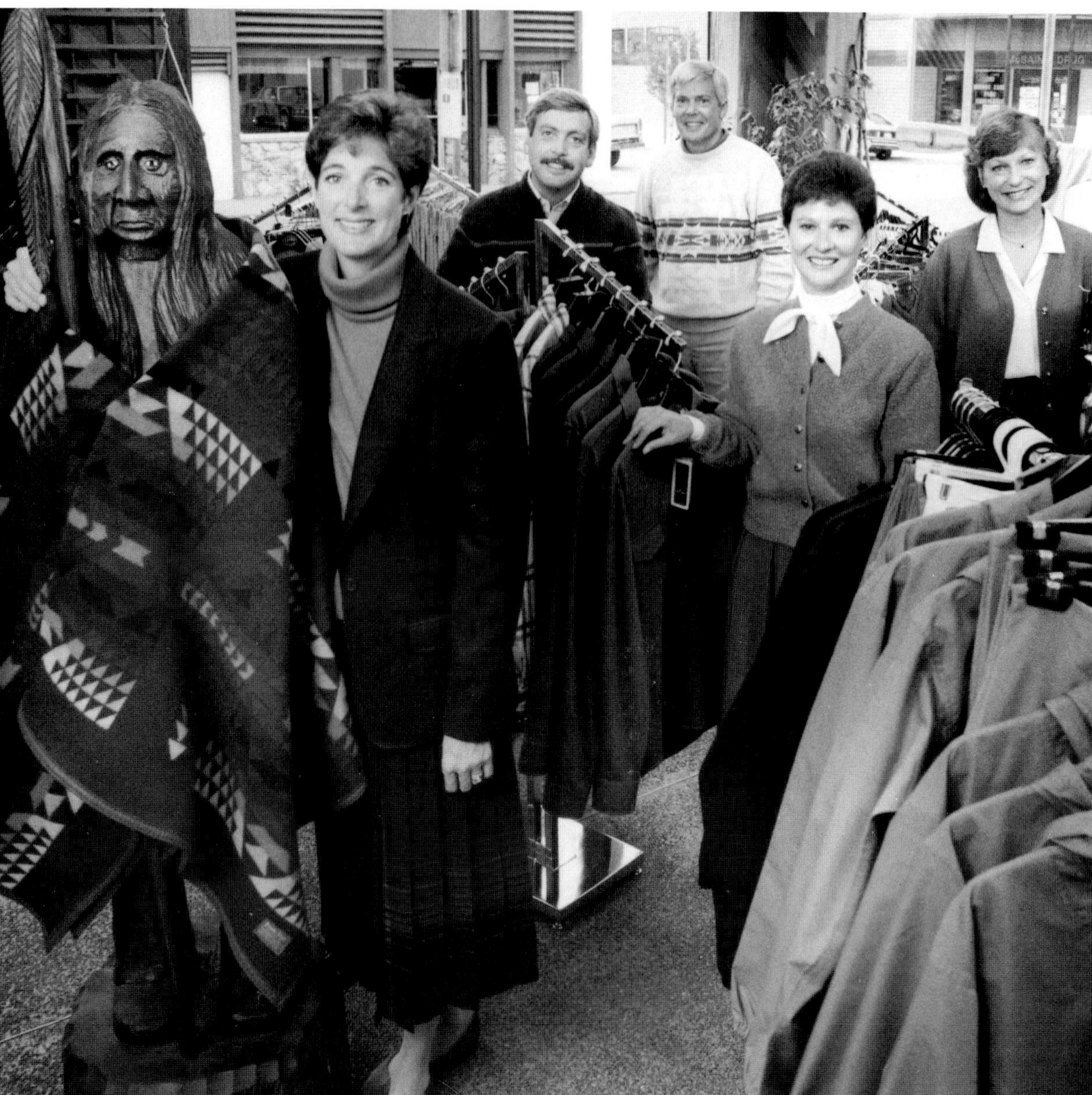

Classic clothing from Pendleton and Patagonia.

Gresham

E13

Perhaps no object, man-made or natural, embodies the spirit and individuality of the West Coast better than the Pacific Crest Trail. As it reaches from Canada to the Mexican border, the trail demands the utmost of its travelers, lays astounding beauty at their feet and suggests uncounted reasons to return. In a way, Pacific Crest Clothing Company is like that. Here is a store that salutes that uniqueness of spirit by offering clothes ready for the daily demands of Northwest life, whether they're worn on the ski slopes or at a casual dinner. The most savvy shoppers know that two lines more than any other are fit for the task: Pendleton and Patagonia. At Pacific Crest, the full Patagonia line for men and women is presented year-round, accompanied by Pendleton's clothing and the manufacturer's incomparable blankets. Other deserving lines earning a place here: J.G. Hook women's apparel; Dooney & Bourke leather goods for men and women; Byford sweaters for men and women; and Romika women's shoes. Pacific Crest's store, set in Gresham's renovated financial district, offers pebble floors, cedar walls, and leaded glass windows which — like the clothing — reflects the functional classic aura of enduring quality. Visa. MasterCard. American Express.

130 N Main Street
Gresham 97030
665-2701

Monday-Thursday
9:30pm-6pm
Friday 9:30am-8pm
Saturday 9:30am-6pm
Sunday noon-5pm

NORM THOMPSON

MEN AND WOMEN

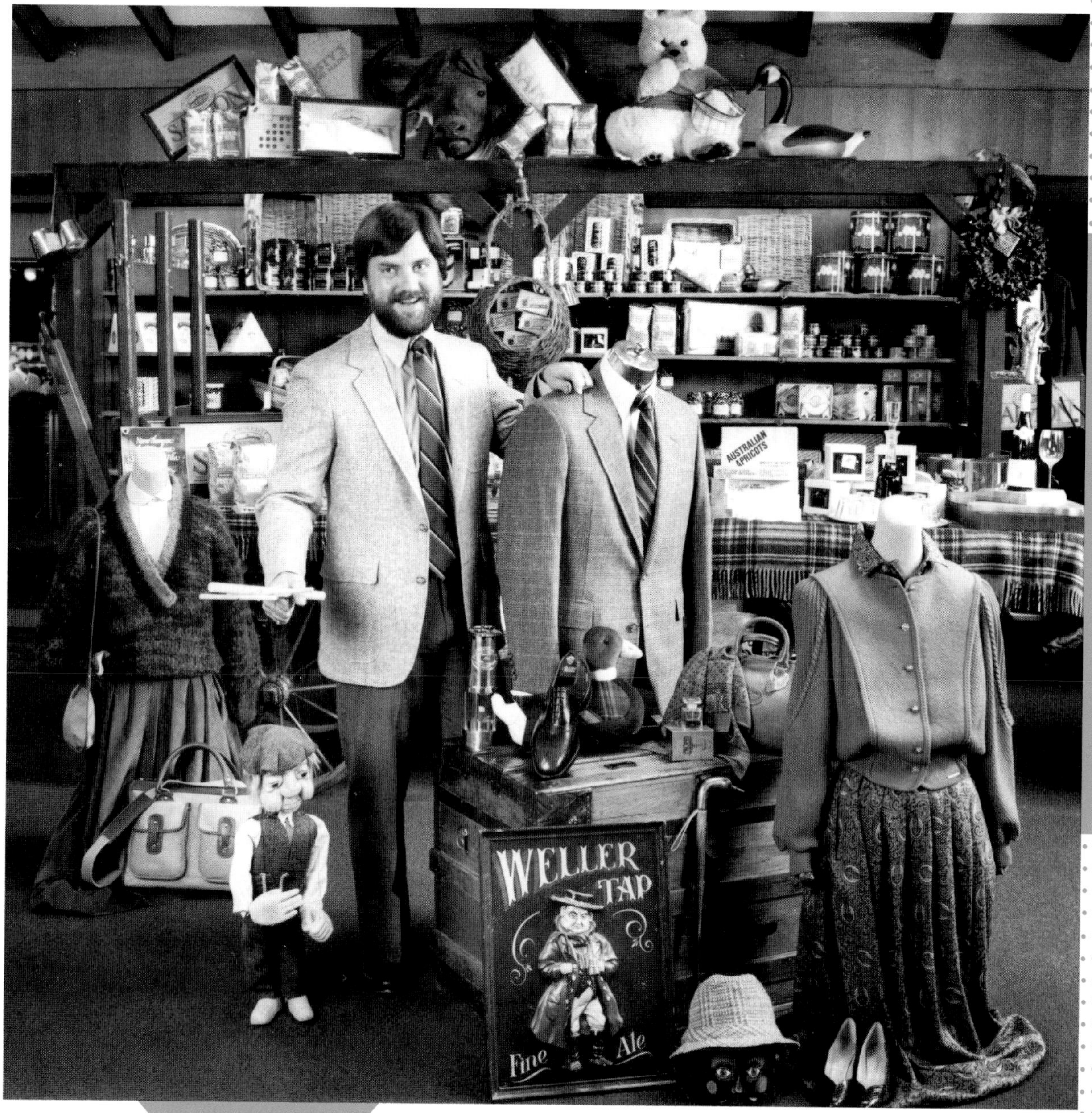

Escape from the Ordinary.®

Tired of hearing things like "limited warranty, usual restrictions apply" when you spend a princely sum for something? How about this instead: An absolute, unconditional guarantee for every product. Twenty minutes or twenty years after purchase — no questions asked. Norm Thompson's, "You be the Judge™", is their guarantee and one reason why this firm's patrons are among the most loyal anywhere. And why not? With its "Escape from the Ordinary® " philosophy, Norm Thompson offers its customers a superlative selection of imported gifts and clothing, whether they visit the stores or browse the mail-order catalog. Founded nearly 40 years ago as a sportsmen's supplier, Norm Thompson has greatly expanded its offerings never losing sight of patron satisfaction. If any one product symbolizes the firm, it is the Irish Country Hat, a go-anywhere item that survives the Northwest's roughest weather with aplomb. You'll also find hand-woven sweaters, Harris Tweed jackets and rare perfumes. For a special treat, there's gourmet food — smoked salmon, pickled asparagus, raspberry jam — and Flowers of Monet, seeds culled from the famous Giverny garden of Monet. Visa. MasterCard. American Express. Diners Club. Carte Blanche.

1805 NW Thurman Street
Portland 97209
221-0764

Monday-Saturday
9am-6pm

Portland International Airport
Main Terminal
Portland 97218
249-0170

Daily
6am-9pm

Northwest Portland
F20

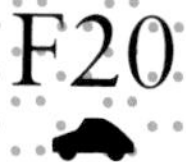

North Portland
A8

HOT CITIES

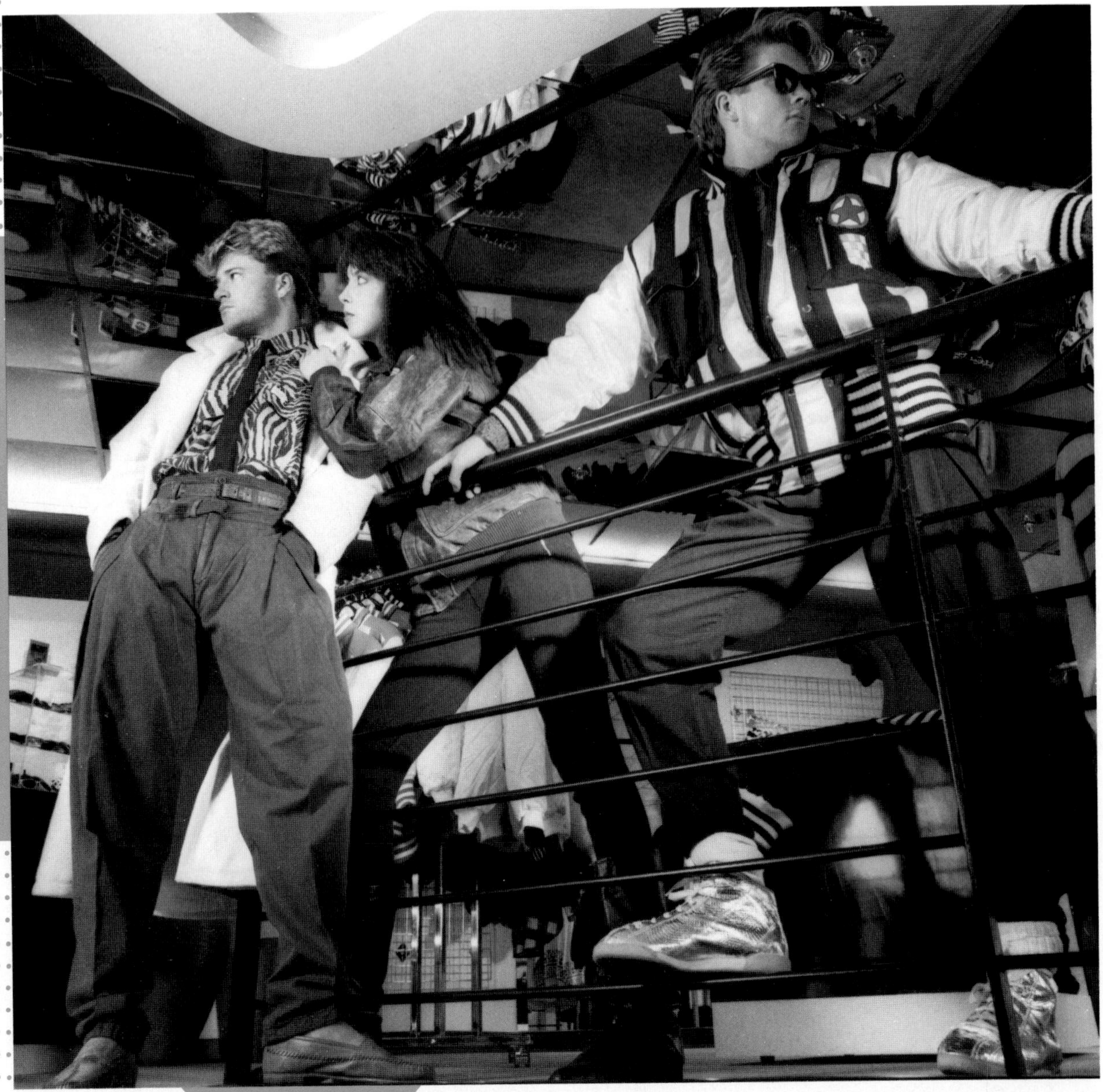

MEN AND WOMEN

An ultra-fashionable approach to clothing.

Downtown

F23

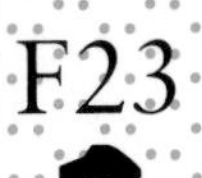

Step into this store and feel the pulse of the city follow you through the door. It may not be the pulse of the city of Portland that you feel, but if owner Jim Elmer has his way it may be soon. Climb the stairs, cross the neon-edged polished-metal floor, sip a complimentary glass of white wine at the wet bar and then look around. The sound system surrounds you with music; the environment is agreeably high-tech in grey, black, yellow and red. This place is user friendly; vitality oozes from every corner. You might as well check every rack, for each one begs to be inspected, examined and searched. Hot Cities is the brainchild of Jim Elmer, a longtime restaurateur who looked around and realized that Portland needed a clothing store with up-to-the millisecond fashions, a decor to match and salespeople who could make it all work. Although Hot Cities, like its inventory, is new, new, new, the sales staff has a combined 17 years' experience in fashion consultation. Hot Cities specializes in designer sportswear, displaying a broad range of merchandise that starts with casually elegant suits, performs great feats with footwear, turns heads with skirts and matching jackets and reaches out with retina- grabbing unitard bodysuits in leopard-skin designs. Need more? Slip on hand-painted socks, reach out with telephones molded into gonzo (Porsche and Mercedes, of course) automobiles and realize that now is the hour with Swatch watches. Names to watch for: M. Julian, Poco Loco, Blanc Blu, Revolution, Matinique. Turn on the fashion heat with Hot Cities. Visa. MasterCard. American Express.

722 SW Taylor Street
Portland 97205
227-2110

Monday-Friday
10am-9pm
Saturday 10am-6pm
Sunday noon-5pm

GARY McKINSTRY HAIR DESIGN

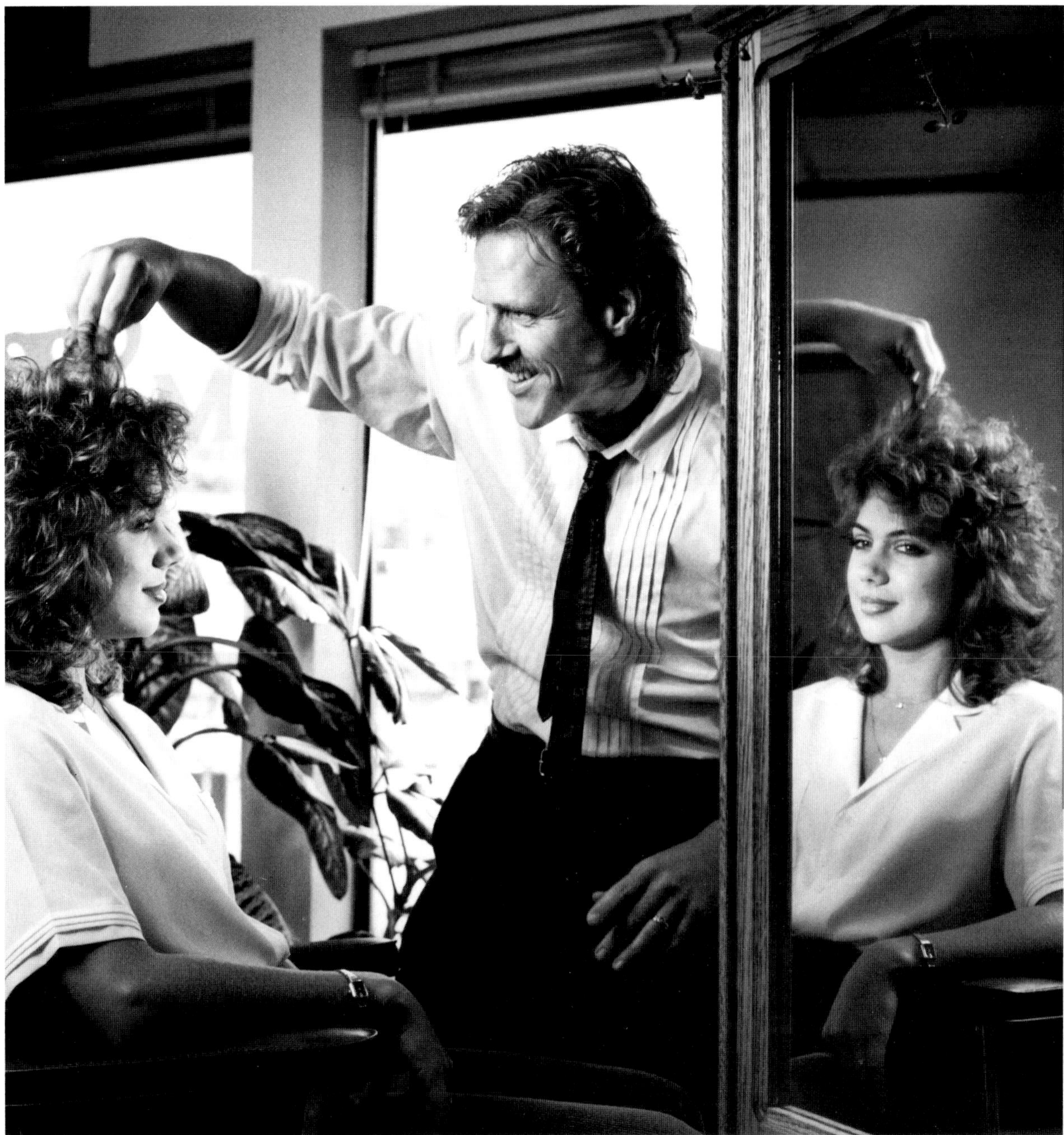

MEN AND WOMEN

Hair design that reveals your natural best.

Before Gary McKinstry lifts his scissors to your hair, he wants you to talk about yourself. Because every aspect of your life — from your occupation and personality to your features and footwear — create your own individual style. And your hair design should reflect it. Quality and consistency are the standards set by Gary for himself and the creative group he works with. That is the Gary McKinstry philosophy. Uncluttered open space, colors of forest green and warm peach, honey-colored oak, natural light and greenery: this is a setting where you immediately feel at ease. Whether your current cut needs shaping or you're in search of a whole new look, Gary McKinstry will find your natural best — there are no surprises. Individualized hair coloring, special permanents and quality hair care products are all available. As any man or woman would agree, the most difficult task is searching out the right hair designer. Luckily, the task is as easy as a trip to Gary McKinstry Hair Design. Visa. MasterCard.

West Slope
8835 SW Canyon Lane
Suite #201
Portland 97225
297-1766

Call for an appointment

Southwest Portland

E3

NORTHWEST PASSAGE BOOTS AND CLOTHING COMPANY

MEN AND WOMEN

Active outdoor clothing and footwear.

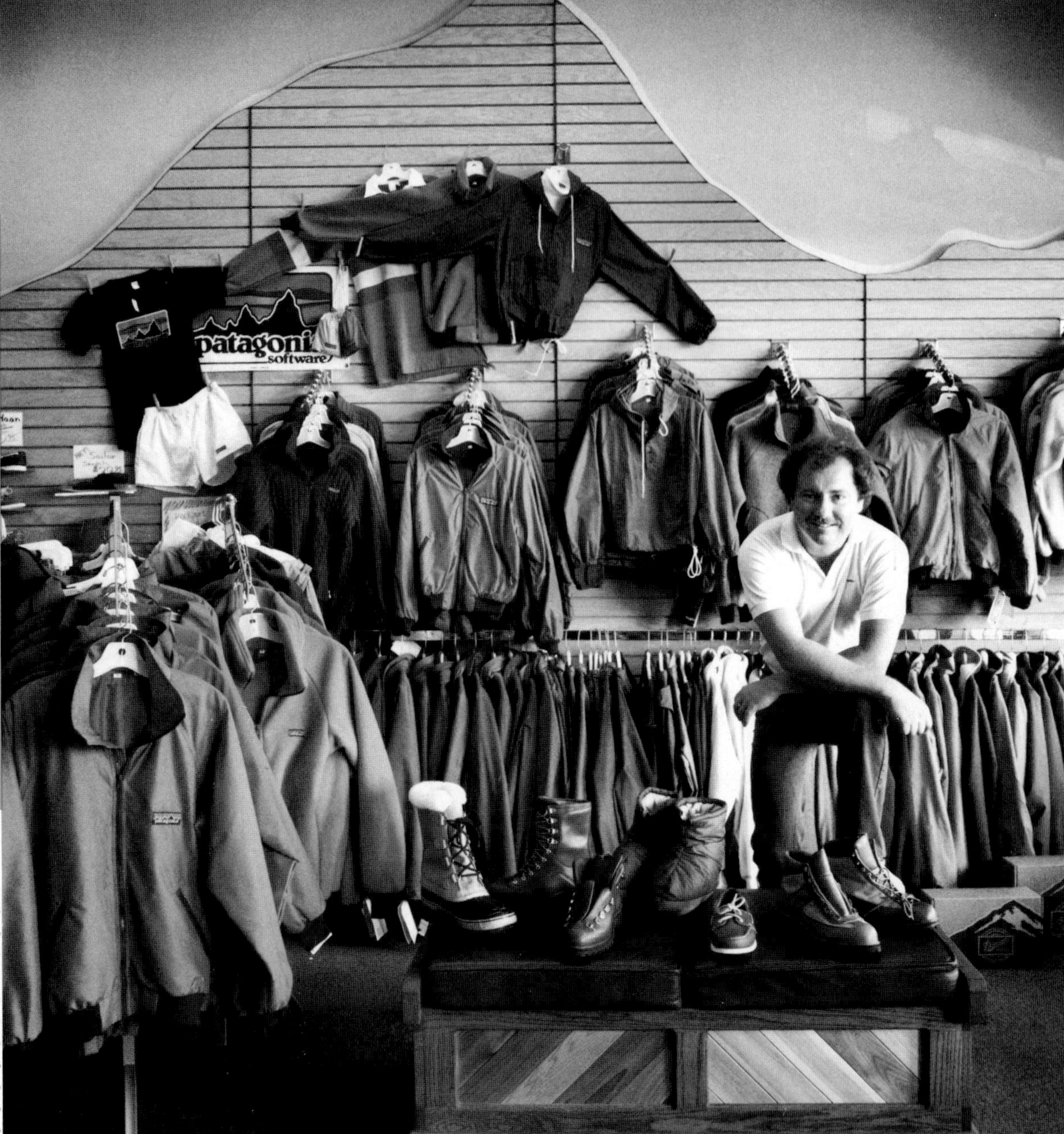

Beaverton

E2

In the early 1800s, stories were told about a waterway that crossed the northern U.S. and Canadian continent. But this legendary Northwest Passage wasn't explored until Roald Amundsen traveled it in 1906. Today's Northwest Passage Boots and Clothing Company aspires to be a legend among Portlanders and it's well worth exploring. Inside this model of a Canadian outpost, there is a boot for walking every trail from such renowned names as Danner, Rockport, Nike, Timberland and Sorel. Try on a pair and take them for a test climb on the in-store rock. This down-to-earth touch and hands-on knowledge comes from Peter Danner, owner and fourth generation bootmaker. Every article was chosen for its unequalled performance on the slopes, sea, trail and sidewalk. All around Northwest Passage Boots and Clothing, great outdoor and indoor wear abounds — baggy shorts from Patagonia; Gortex parkas from Helly Hansen, Columbia Sportwear and Wilderness Experience; day packs from Jansport; even Wigwam and Wickdry wool socks. City dwellers and wilderness lovers alike, will discover many treasures just by taking a short hike through the Northwest Passage Boots and Clothing Company. Visa. MasterCard.

Beaverton Town Square
11645 SW Beaverton
Hillsdale Highway
Beaverton 97005
643-3863

Monday-Friday
10am-9pm
Saturday 10am-6pm
Sunday noon-5pm

ALAN COSTLEY

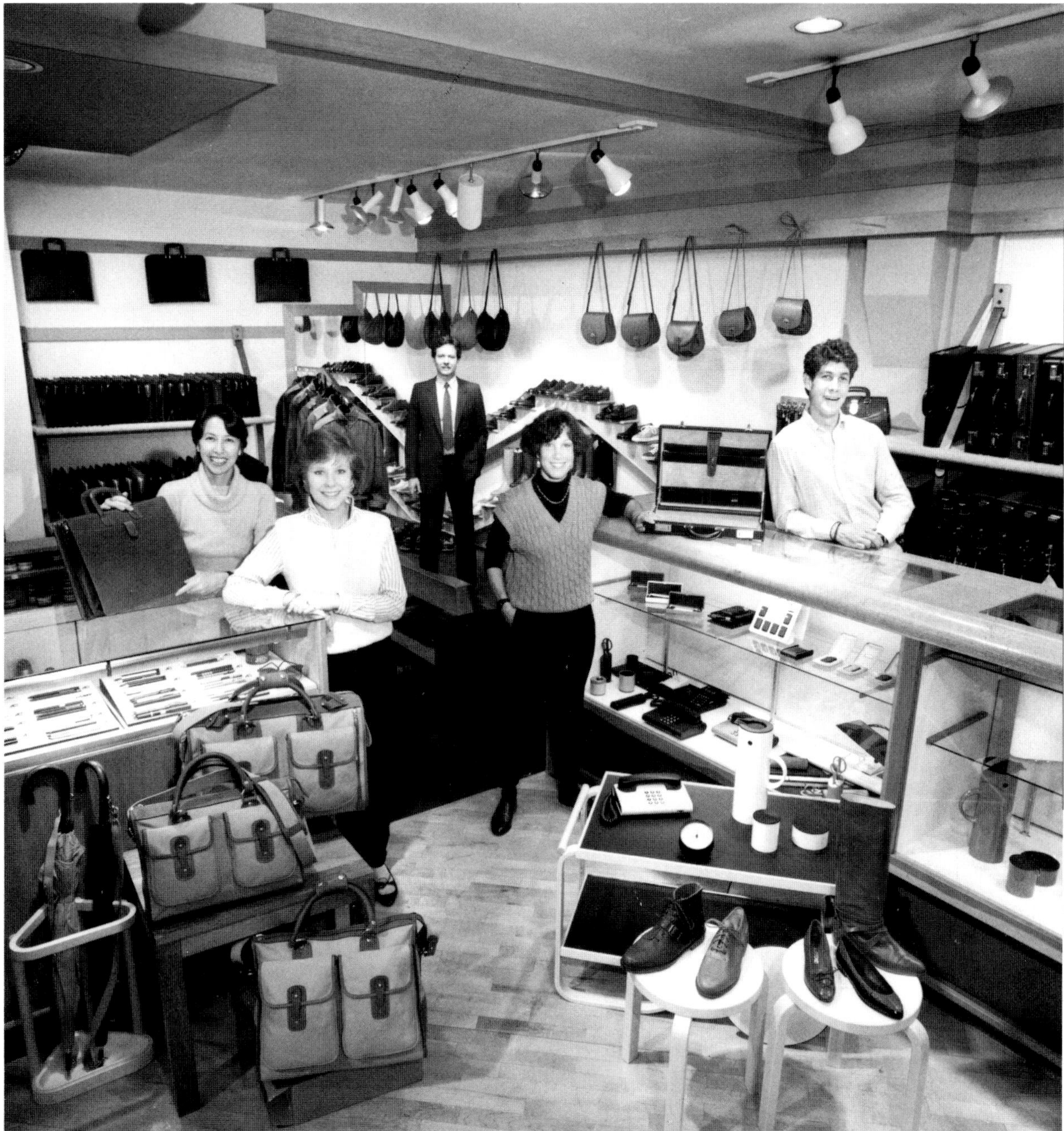

MEN AND WOMEN

Leather goods, footwear and accessories.

Alan Costley offers men's and women's footwear, business cases, personal accessories and a host of other items —in sum, an excellent cross-section of merchandise in a compact store. Founded in 1972 as the Cobbler's Bench, the name was changed in 1978 to reflect the broadening selection and continuing commitment to personalized service. "We wanted to make it apparent that this was a locally owned and operated business, not a corporate franchise," says company president Alan Costley, who had noticed that the oldest retail establishments routinely are named after a person, real or imaginary. Alan has selected the finest men's and women's shoes and boots, silk ties, wool scarves and handbags from Italy. Cole-Haan men's and women's shoes, Mont Blanc and Lamy writing instruments, Schlesinger Brothers business cases, Serengeti sunglasses, Robert Comstock leather jackets and many other lines provide customers with merchandise they can depend on. Whatever your selection, you'll find yourself in good company at this establishment. In fact, a real-life American Express commercial was acted out recently when world-famous pianist Keith Jarrett stopped by and no one recognized him until he produced his card! Visa. MasterCard. American Express.

816 SW Tenth Avenue
Portland 97205
222-2577

Monday-Saturday
10am-6pm
Sunday noon-4pm

Downtown

F23

GAZELLE NATURAL FIBRE CLOTHING

MEN AND WOMEN

Contemporary casual fashion in natural fibres.

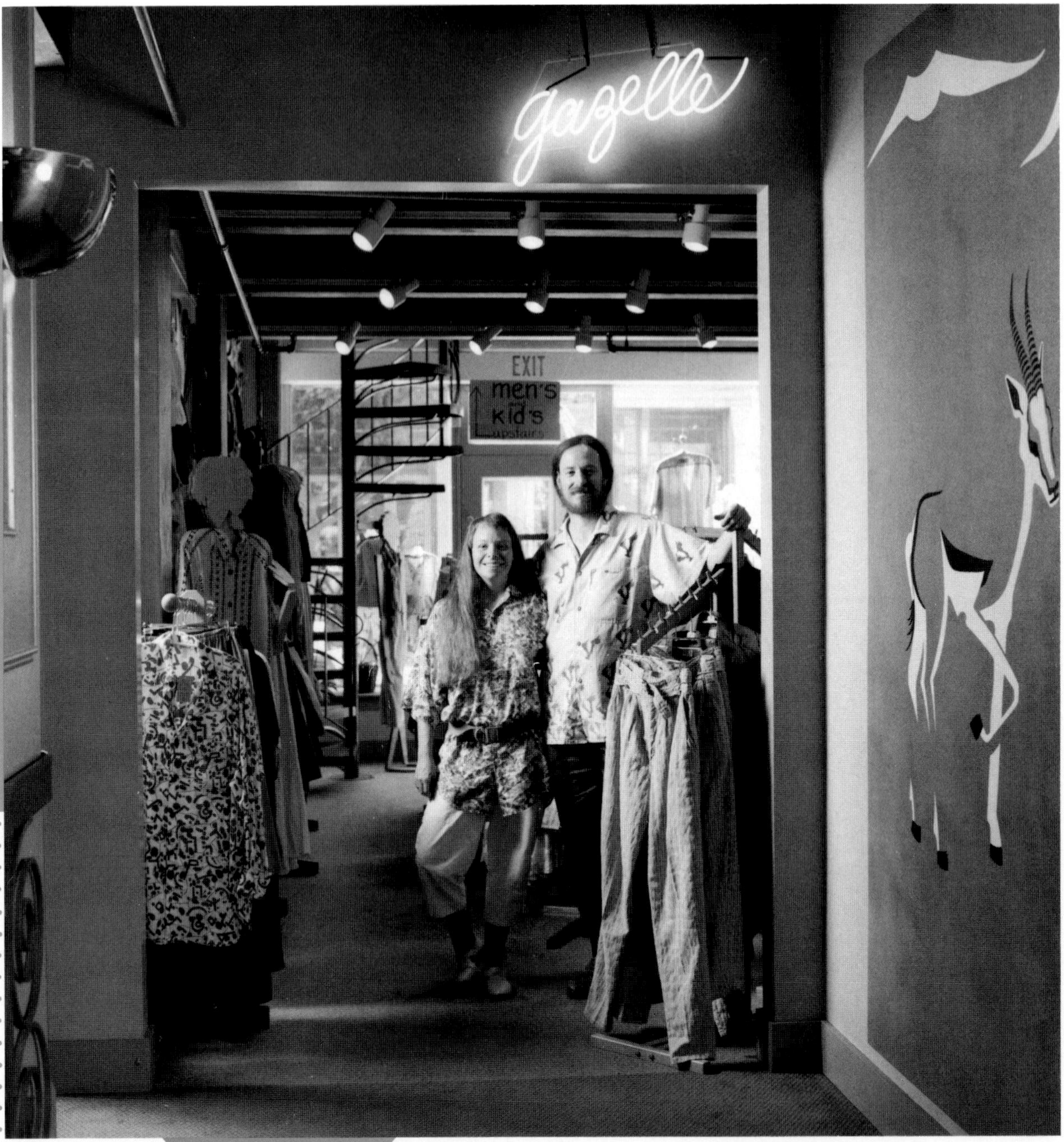

Skidmore Historic District

E3

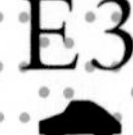

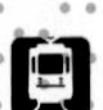

Gazelle owners Robin and Byron Ady have seen it happen time and again: a new customer walks through the door and instantly remarks, "This store is so different!" Robin and Byron are not surprised. Nestled in the stone of the century-old New Market West building, Gazelle's natural wood racks and beams give the shop a warmth and intimacy that appeals to all ages. Although the emphasis is on clothing of 100 percent natural fibers for women, men and children, the array of colors, pleasing prints and distinctive woven goods will first catch your eye. Gazelle's goal is to offer fashion not found in any other store, and Robin and Byron strive for a look that is contemporary but won't go out of style. "The secret of our success is buying what we like and not falling for trends," says Robin. "We concentrate on timelessness of fashion and quality of fabric and construction." To that end you'll find a display of scarves and sashes that is one of the city's most extensive, as well as selected children's clothing that includes sturdy basics and fun wear; and a host of truly contemporary fashions for men and women in cotton, wool, rayon, silk, ramie and linen. For quality at moderate prices and a timeless sense of style, Gazelle is the natural choice. Look for the annual Gazelle Jazz Hour concerts every May in the New Market Village. Visa. MasterCard. American Express.

New Market Village
54 S.W. Second Avenue
Portland 97204
228-1693

Daily
10am-6pm

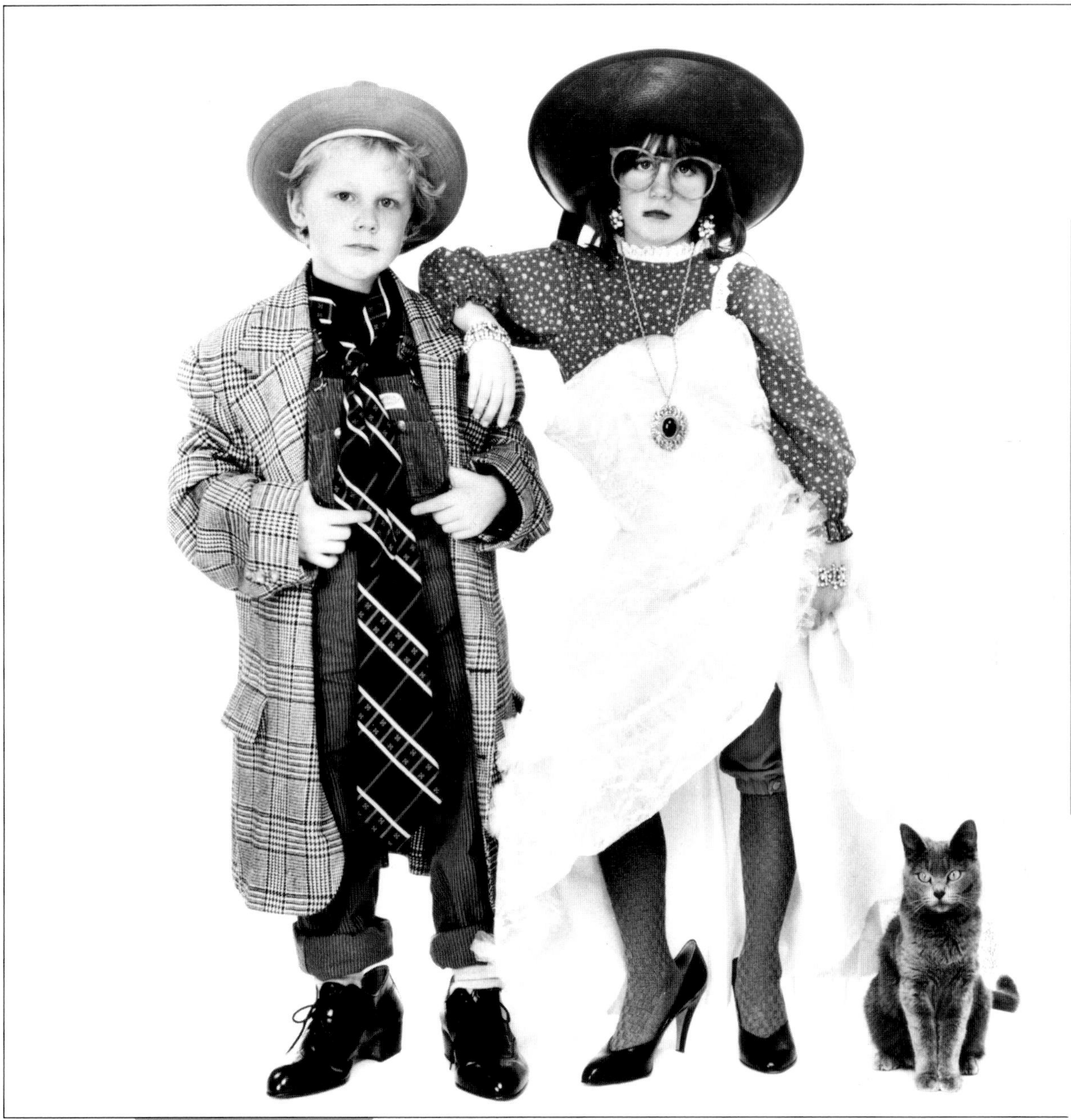

NOFZIGER

MEN AND WOMEN

Where everybody shops for shoes... eventually.

Most shoe stores are like supermarkets. They all sell essentially the same products, just arranged differently. Walk into Nofziger, though, and you'll immediately notice that it looks different. It might take a minute of two to realize why: special shoes, special styles and realistic prices. Elmer and Pansy Nofziger started the business in 1972 on a shoestring — no pun intended — and their perseverance has put them on Portland's shoe retailer map. Part of the reason is their uncanny ability to select shoes that are at the forefront of fashion which is of particular importance to their clientele. Services in short supply at some other stores are abundant here: skilled fitting, fashion counseling, tips on shoe care, displays arranged in an easy to examine manner, and friendly sales personnel make your shoe buying experience enjoyable. Visa. MasterCard.

The Galleria
921 SW Morrison Street
Portland 97205
226-6108

Monday-Friday
9:30am-9pm
Saturday 9:30am-6pm
Sunday noon-5pm

Downtown
F23

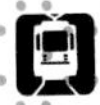

FRANCESCA'S FRAGRANCES

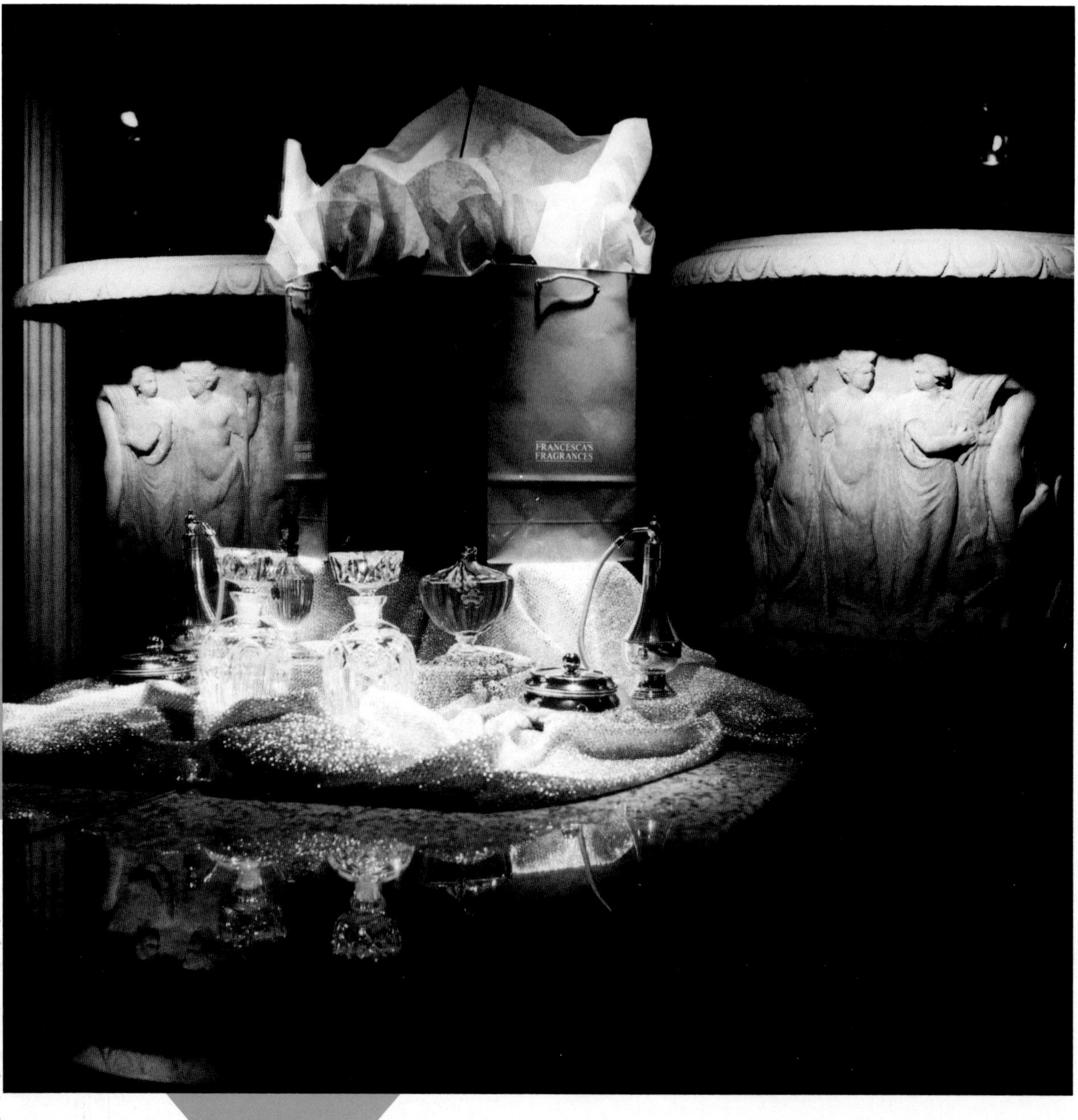

MEN AND WOMEN

Exclusive fragrance re-creations for men and women.

Corbett-Johns Landing

F6

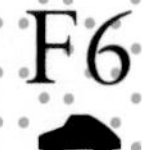

If the scent of a particular fragrance evokes memories of that first kiss, that special someone, that timeless moment, then expect to be enchanted with Francesca's Fragrances. The pure, clean, classic, European salon design combined with subtle harmonies of color and fragrances creates an extraordinary awakening of the senses. Francesca's Fragrances is a full service perfumery, specializing in exclusive fragrance recreations for women and men. Their house perfumes and men's colognes are blended in Paris, then manufactured in New York. Trained staff members conduct PH testing to determine, through body chemistry, fragrance compatibility thus assisting a customer in selecting a wardrobe of fragrances that match lifestyle, mood and profession. These long lasting re-creations offer the luxury of the world's greatest perfumes within your reach. Owners Leanora Stephanoff and Marilyn Beardsley carefully select one-of- a kind fragrance accessories, exquisite scent bottles, unusual European jewelry and other distinctive gift items that make shopping at Francesca's a rare and pleasurable experience. Signature tote bags, creative gift wraps, a search and locate perfume register, plus attention to detail completes the total concept of personalized service. Francesca's Fragrances believe that long after the perfume you have purchased is gone, the quality of their service will linger on. Visa. MasterCard.

The Water Tower
5331 SW Macadam Avenue
Portland 97201
274-5461

Monday-Friday 10am-9pm
Saturday 10am-6pm
Sunday noon-5pm

ALDER WEST

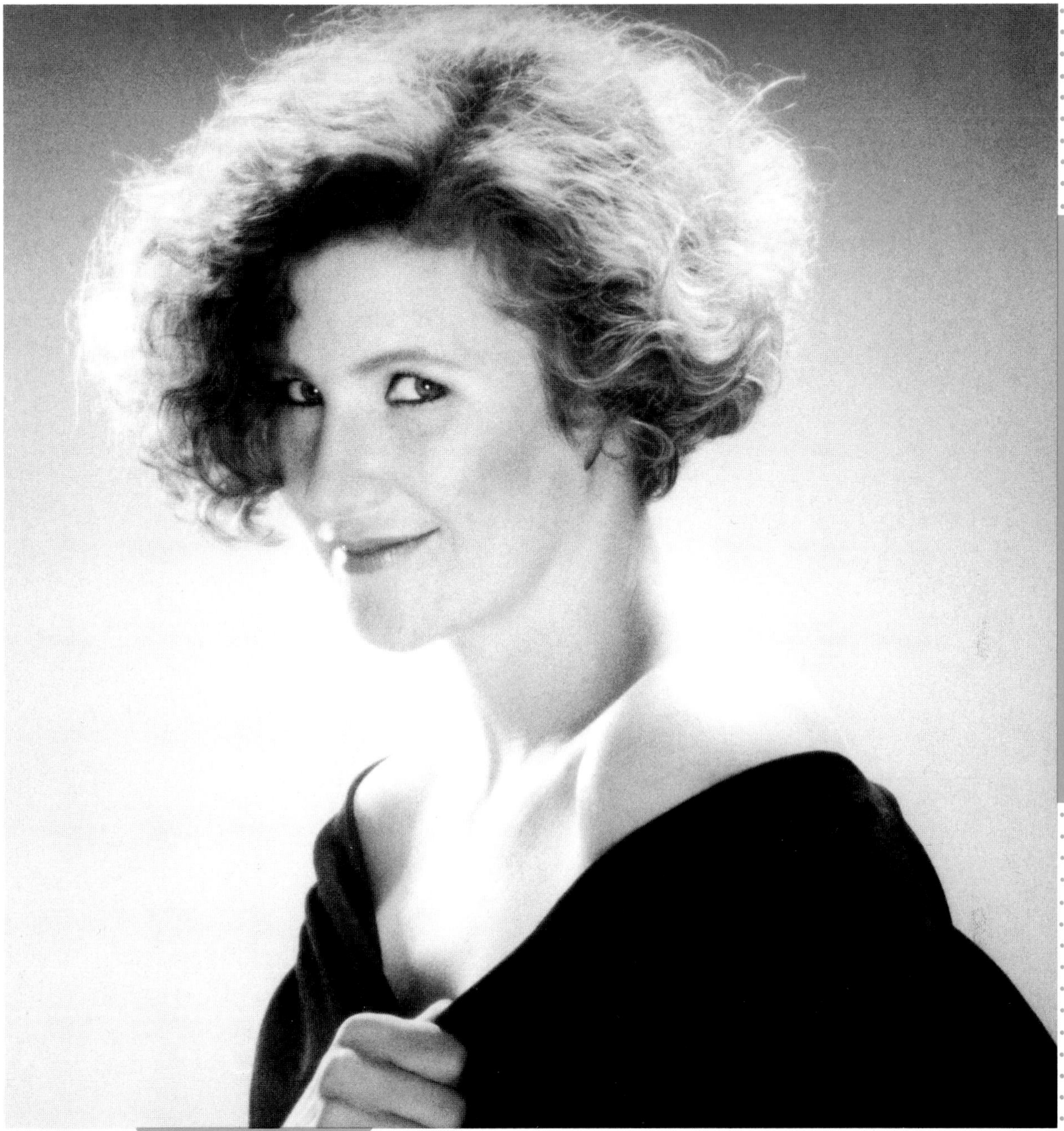

MEN AND WOMEN

Hair design reinforcing individual expression.

Downtown
E23

Throughout the past fourteen years, Alder West has won a reputation for its outstanding creativity in hair design, hair coloration, and directional perming techniques. The salon has the distinction of being a fashion leader in the Northwest. Salon emphasis on high standards and consistent quality of design was originally inspired by Dennis Dreiling, founder of Alder West. All salon creations are individually inspired by the client and adapted to their needs. The highly talented, distinguished staff seek to reinforce the client's personal style. Consequently, Alder West is the result of a collaborative dedication to artistic and technical advancements in hair design. Owner, Roxanne Mossman is respected throughout the Northwest for her innovative, educational contributions in hair coloring and is spokeswoman for three outstanding manufacturers: Mastey de Paris, Gefden International, and Focus 21. Within Alder West she has engendered an enthusiastic atmosphere where inventiveness seems to flourish. In salon products are exclusively, Mastey de Paris, Focus 21, and Gefden International. Visa. MasterCard.

1020 SW Alder Street
Portland 97205
227-5534

Monday-Saturday
8:30am-7pm

HARRINGTON'S EXECUTIVE CLOTHIERS

MEN AND WOMEN

High tech tailoring, old-world touch.

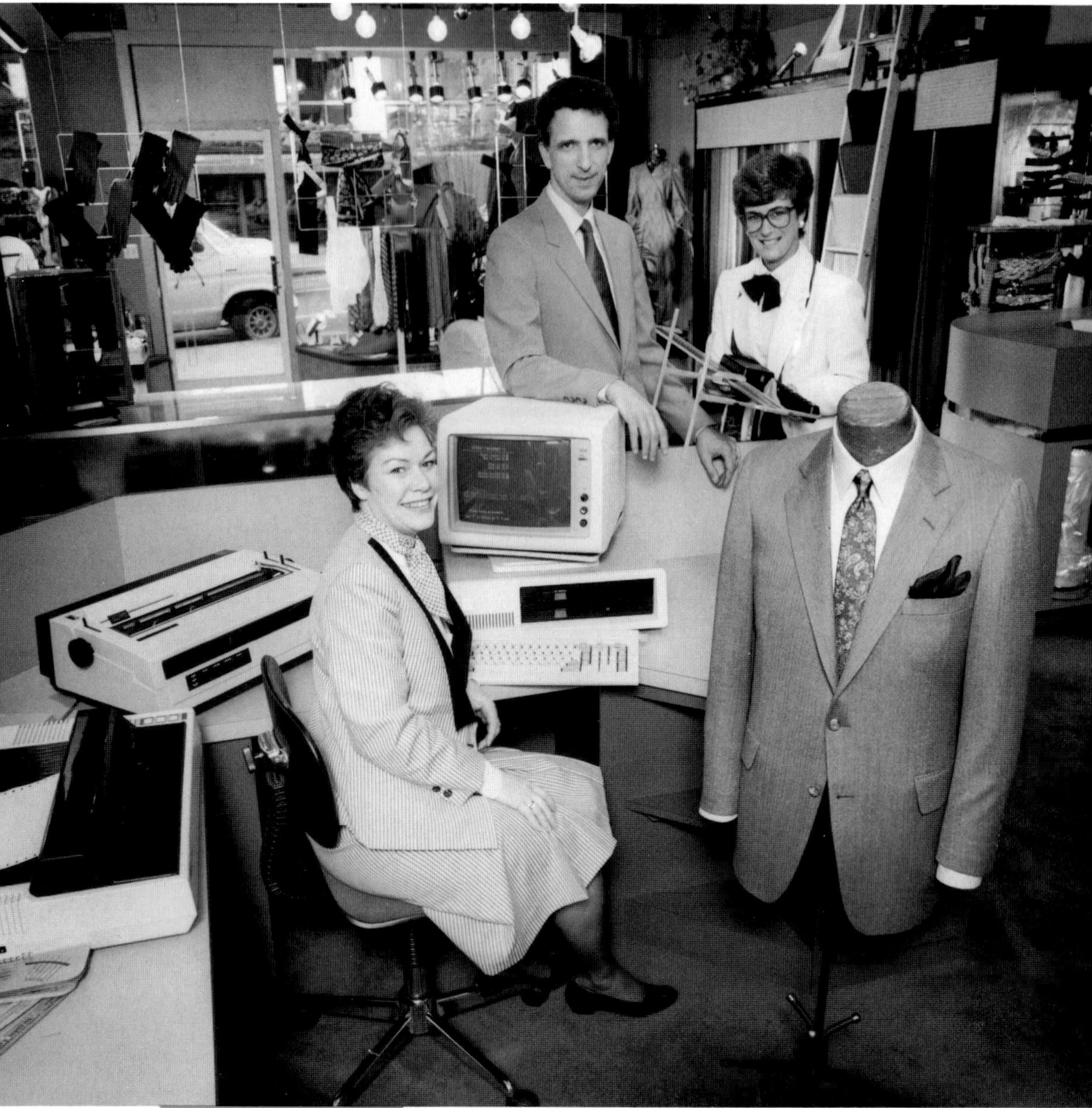

Downtown
G23

It was inevitable — the ubiquitous computer would find a niche in the world of custom clothing, bringing speed and precision to a time-honored art. And so it has at Harrington's Executive Clothiers, where computerized measuring means astounding fit, delivery in four to five weeks and prices that are comparable with ready made suits. Patented technology, exclusively at Harrington's, merges old-world craftsmanship and state-of-the-art technology. It works like this: customers are measured with special electronic devices — accurate to .001 inch — that sends electronic signals to an IBM PC. A printout verifies the measurements, which are then transmitted to a mainframe computer in the midwest. Material, selected at Harrington's, is then laser-cut, sewn by custom tailors, and returned as a finished product. The shop offers men's and women's clothing; custom-cut suits begin at $349 in blends and $389 in wools; hand-tailored suits start at $480. Custom shirts and blouses begin at $41; tailored dresses at $350. There's also men's and women's neckwear, gloves and hats and free wardrobe consultation. Company president Linda Harrington's philosophy is to provide every customer with clothing that will harmonize successfully with surroundings and profession. With that desire — and a background as an executive with a high-technology firm, it was only logical that she harness the power of a computer to give Portland clothes buyers a head start on the 21st century. Visa. MasterCard. American Express. Discover.

947 SW Broadway
Portland 97205
(503) 226-0305

Monday-Saturday
10am-6pm
or by appointment

HICKOX & FRIENDS

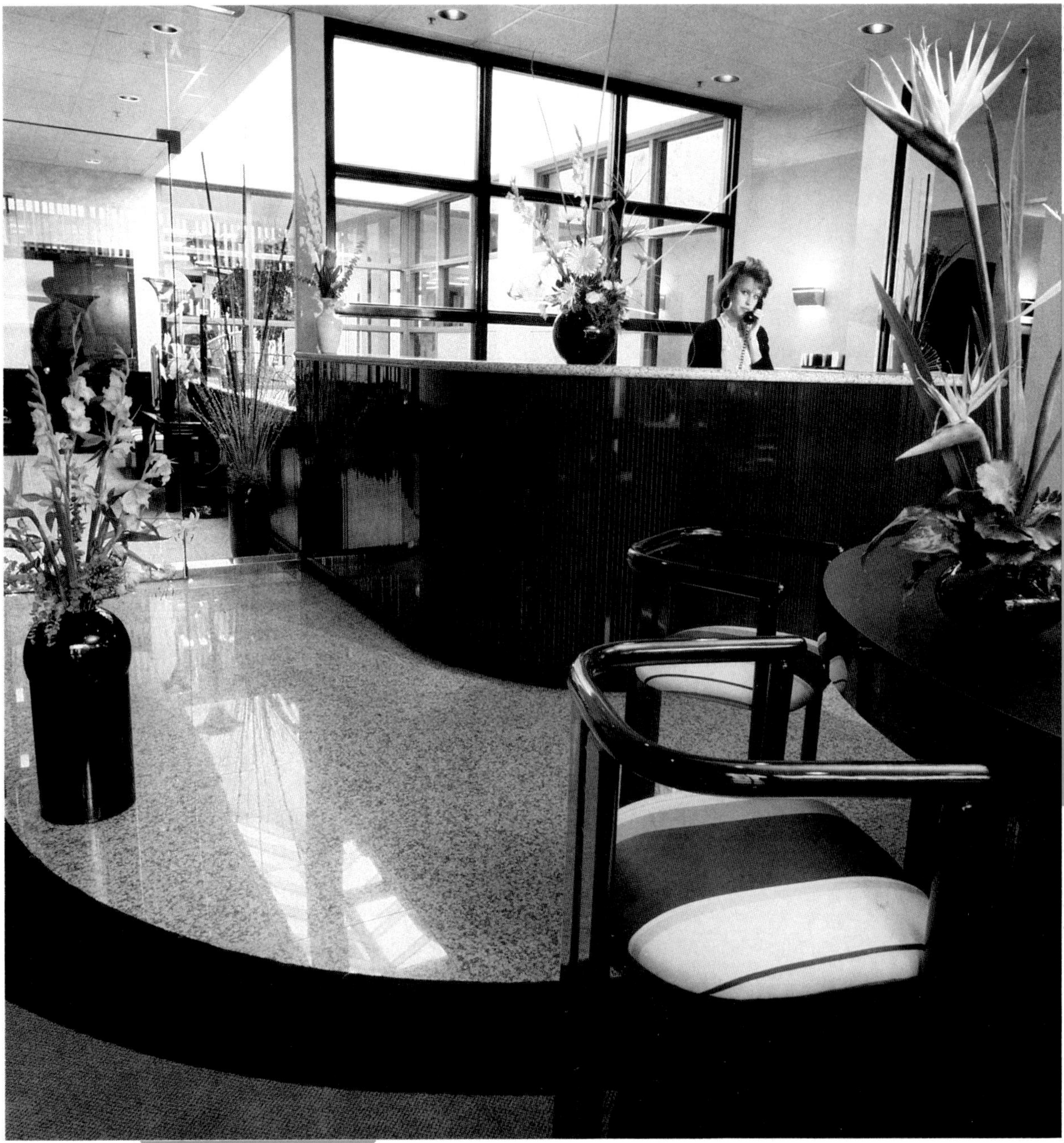

MEN AND WOMEN

Internationally inspired hair design.

Where in Portland can you visit a newly renovated Art Deco building on the National Register of Historic Landmarks and come away with a haircut that's sweeping the streets of Europe? At Hickox & Friends' new penthouse suite in the historic Charles F. Berg Building, a skilled staff of hair designers practice their talents in an immaculate new salon. Attention to refinements of form and function characterize the Hickox approach to haircutting as well. Both John and Sharon Hickox, co-owners of the salon, have studied with international artistic directors, whom they consider the best in the craft. They travel widely and often, attending shows in New York and Europe and bringing back current street styles, which they adapt as necessary to come up with the right shape for the right person. Over the years, John and Sharon and their highly trained staff have built a reputation for combining high fashion with unpretentious, functional, easy-care hair design. Their clientele includes so many media personalities that they have been dubbed "hairdressers to the stars." Now, in a downtown setting sparkling with '30's elegance, they carry on their tradition of gracious service and fine design. Visa. MasterCard.

The Berg Building
615 SW Broadway
Penthouse Suite
Portland 97205
241-7111

Monday-Friday
7am-5:30pm

Downtown
F24

TRADE SECRETS

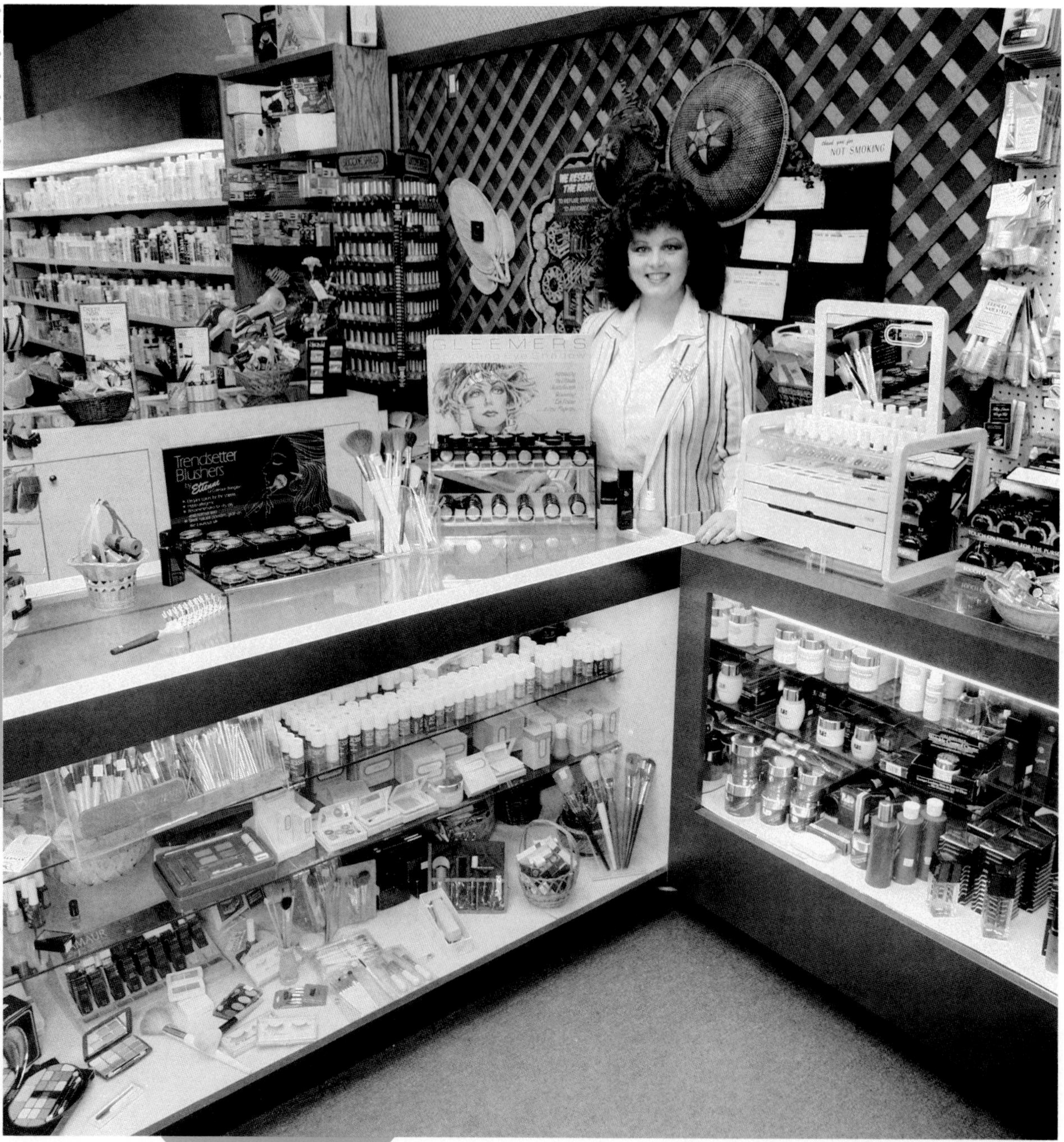

MEN AND WOMEN

Personal attention to your beauty needs.

Yamhill Historic District

G25

To the constant benefit of their customers, Virginia L. Bowen and Toni Schell have redefined the term "trade secrets." At this Yamhill Marketplace establishment, a trade secret is not closely guarded; it's either put on display for all to see or readily volunteered by the qualified staff. After all, the intent here is to achieve the best look possible by helping the client help herself or himself. And there are a multitude of ways, beginning with an extensive beauty products selection and a salon with two licensed hair stylists and a manicurist. Trade Secrets customers can choose from leading salon beauty products grouped conveniently in one location: among them Sebastian, Joico, Paul Mitchell, Tri, Mastey, KMS, Focus 21, Nexxus, Aveda, Gefden, La Maur and Redken. And shopping is enhanced by assistance that is at once friendly and professional. Perhaps in no other industry is the consumer confronted by such a bewildering array of products and claimed results; that's where Trade Secrets pays off. The personnel at Trade Secrets are ready to put their skills to work, ensuring that you'll always look your best. Visa. MasterCard. Discover.

Yamhill Marketplace
110 SW Yamhill Street
Portland 97204
241-5494

Daily
10am-6pm

JEWELRY

Designers of gold and silver jewelry, dealers in precious and semi-precious stones. Zsa, Zsa, eat your heart out! Special services include gem appraisals, repair and restoration.

Chris H. Foleen
Goldsmith *174*
Element 79 *171*
Equinox Fine Jewelry *173*
Goldmark Jewelers *170*
The Real Mother Goose *256*
Robert B. Eaton
Jeweler-Designer *172*

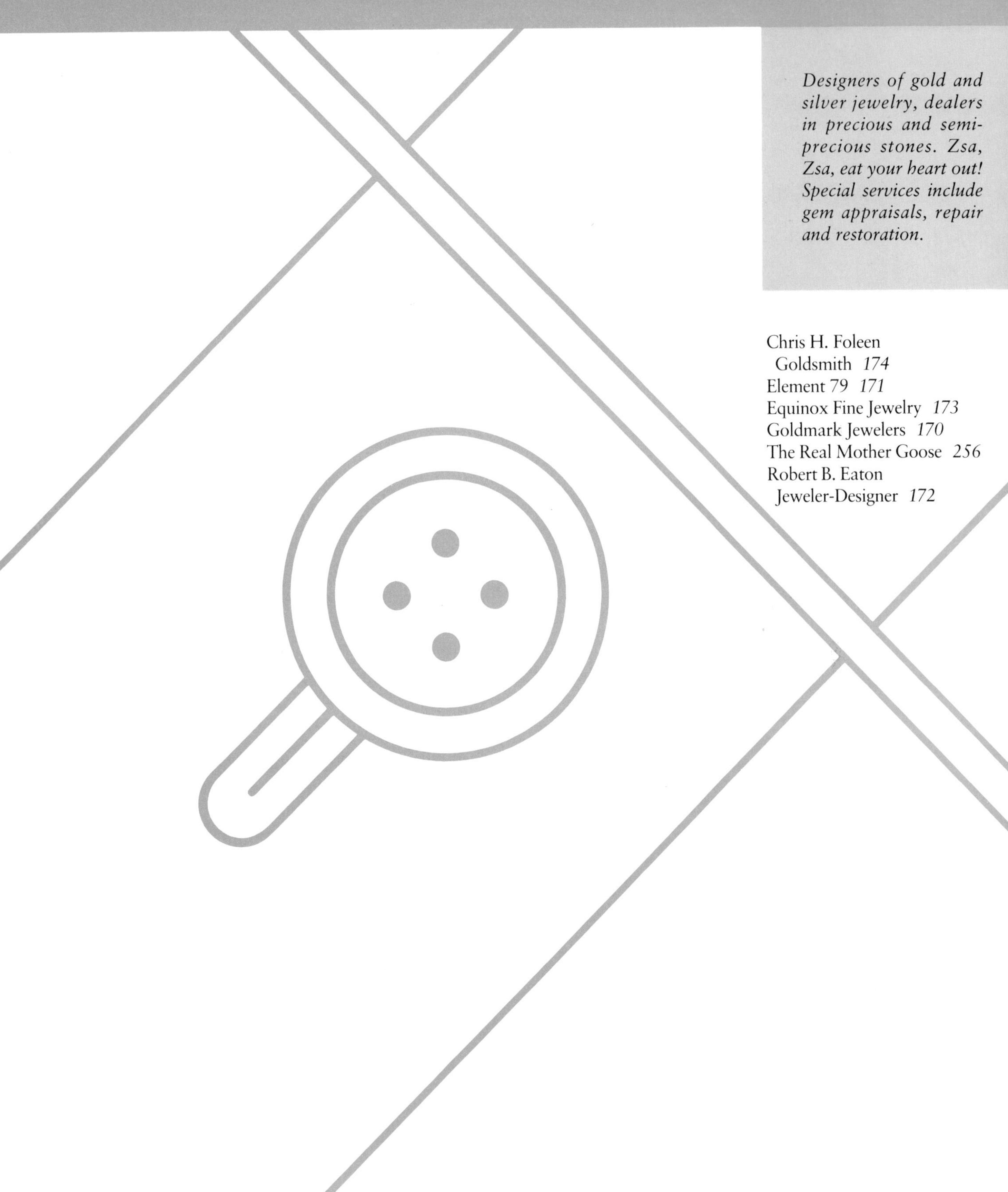

GOLDMARK JEWELERS

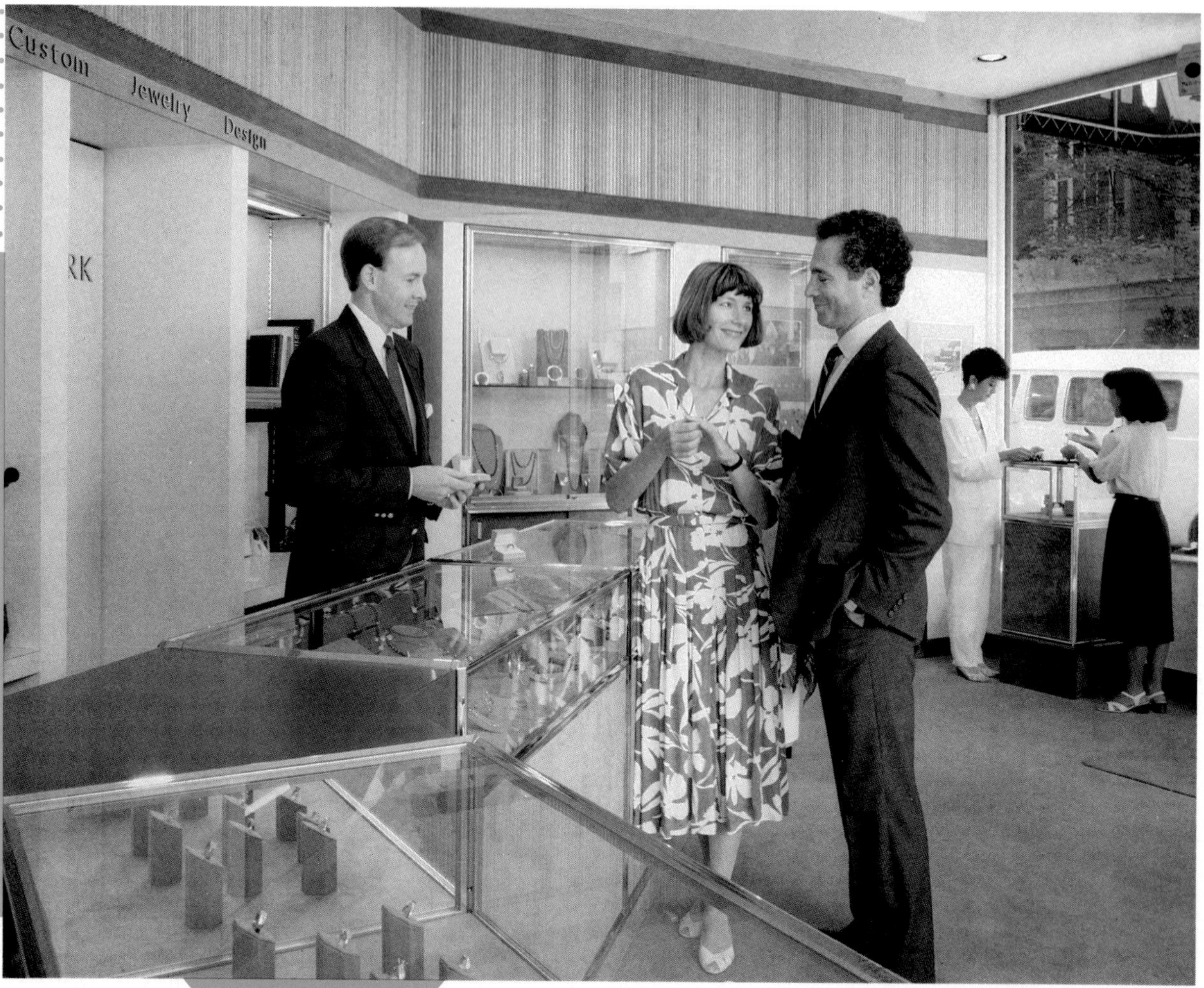

JEWELRY

Jewelry created exclusively for you.

Historically, a gold mark was a stamp of quality used by skilled European goldsmiths to signify their completion of an important piece of jewelry. In Portland since 1976, the stamp of quality is found at Goldmark Jewelers, specialists in the design and creation of fine one-of-a-kind jewelry — where you the client become a designer. Owner and designer/goldsmith Cal Brockman and his associates will work closely with you, sharing your ideas and desires as together you interpret your dreams into a unique piece of personalized jewelry. Your piece is then expertly fashioned in Goldmark's on the premises studio ensuring the strictest attention to every aspect of quality workmanship. One visit to Goldmark Jewelers' elegant glass-enclosed showroom will reveal a stunning collection of hand selected, ready-made jewelry, exhibiting contemporary designs as well as timeless classics that form the cornerstone of fine jewelry design. There, surrounded by rich woods, muted fabrics and fine works of art, customer and goldsmith alike are certain to bring their best creativity to task — and be rewarded with the lifelong satisfaction that uniquely personalized jewelry can bring. Visa. MasterCard. American Express. Discover.

Downtown
F23

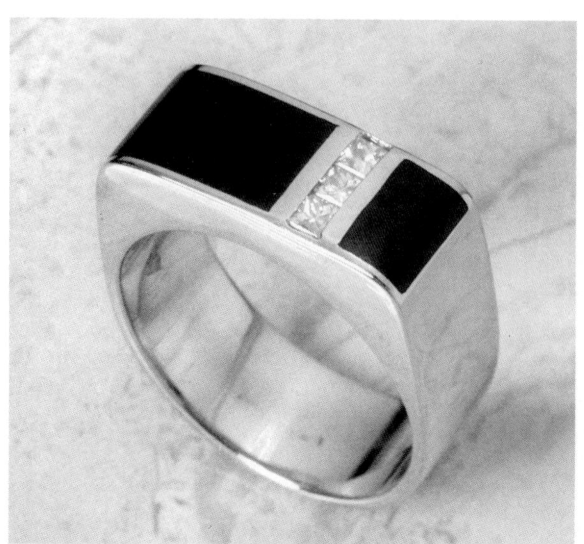

1000 SW Taylor Street
Portland 97205
224-3743

Tuesday-Friday
10am-5pm
Saturday 11am-3pm
And by appointment

ELEMENT 79

JEWELRY

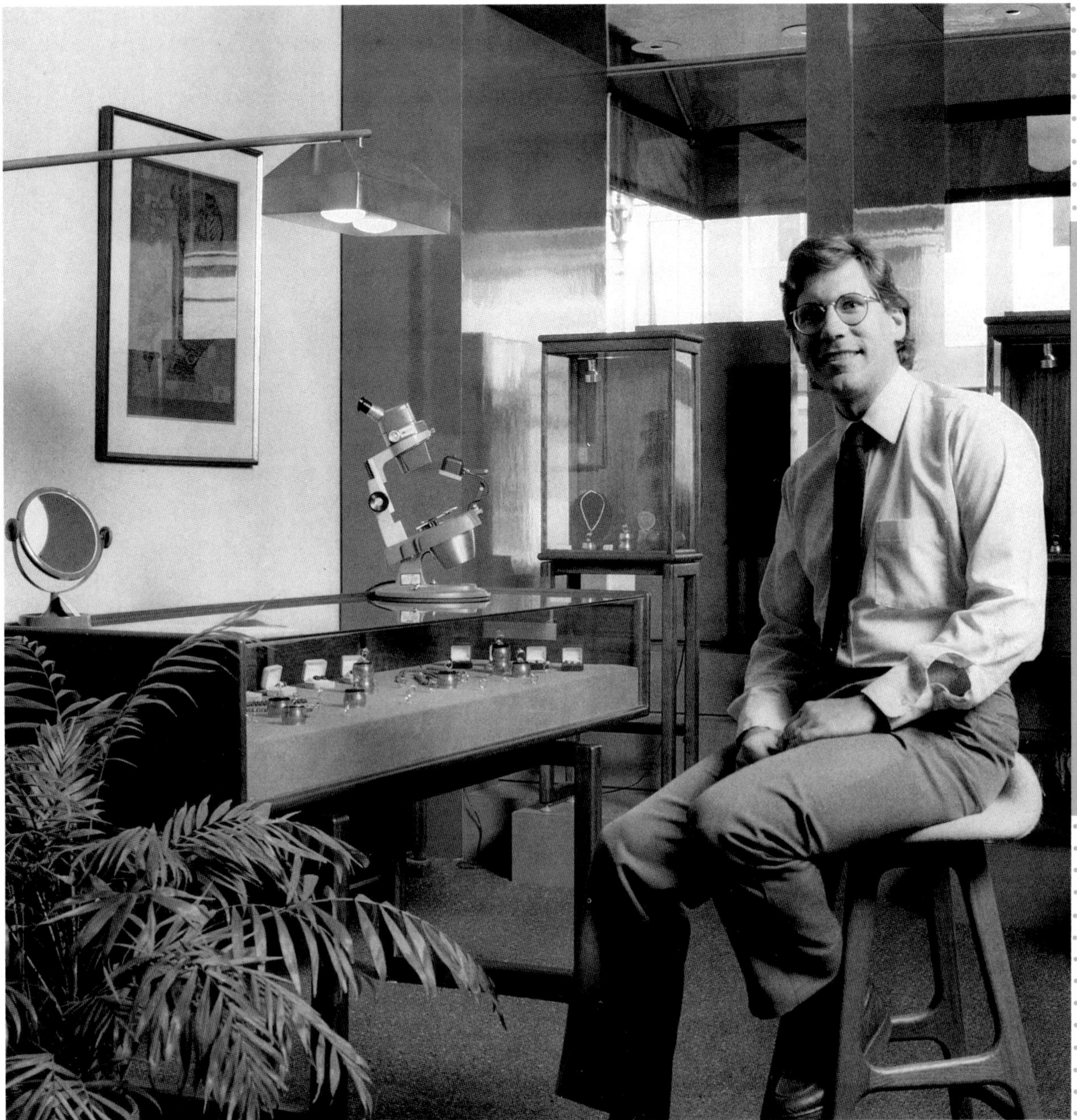

Contemporary designs in gold.

As an accomplished goldsmith, Thomas L. Jones captures the gleam of rare metal and the fire of gemstones for jewelry pieces that come with a special aura: the romance of having artwork created just for you. Thomas, owner of Element 79, specializes in limited-edition or one-of-a-kind pieces. Element 79's location, in the historic Pittock Building, is out of the way and hard to find, but it reflects Thomas' confidence that customers will seek his expertise and workmanship. He's right: they have done just that for more than a decade. In part, it may be because he operates on the simple principle that the selection of fine jewelry is accompanied by a unique set of emotions and motivations that often are reflected in the pieces themselves. To achieve that, Thomas is equally adept with gold and platinum, diamonds and gemstones. He also sells ready-made pieces in addition to his custom work and handles remounting. His artistic skill is readily witnessed: his knowledge and high standards are evidenced by his status as a Registered Jeweler in the American Gem Society. The title is confered on individuals who have extensive gemological knowledge and who adhere to the Society's rigid ethical code. Valid for only one year, registration must be renewed, based on continuing education and on sustained ethical business practices. Visa. MasterCard. American Express.

412 SW 10th Avenue
Portland 97205
223-6020

Tuesday-Friday
10am-5:30pm
Saturday 10am-4pm
And by appointment

Downtown
E23

ROBERT B. EATON JEWELER-DESIGNER

JEWELRY

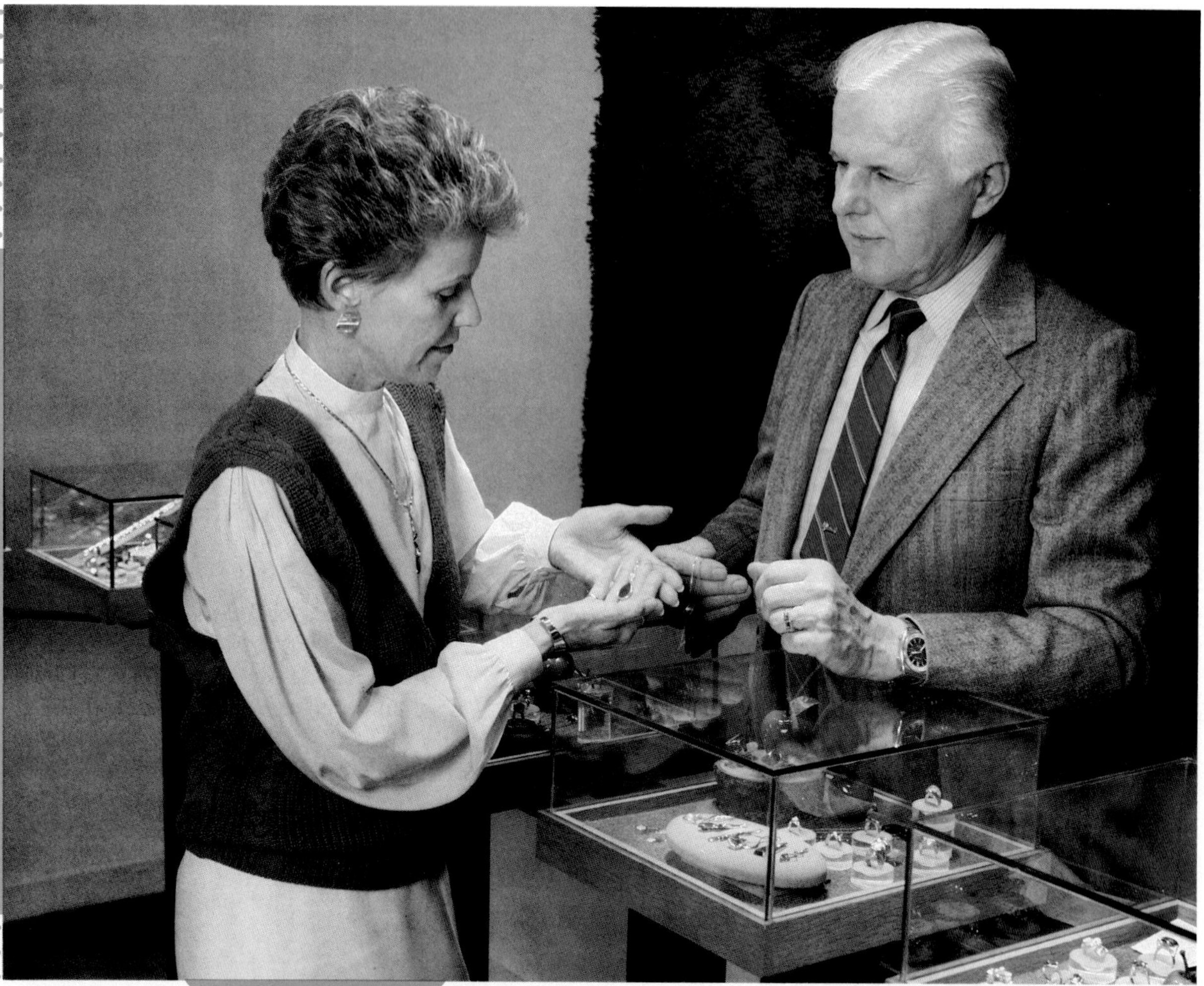

Special interest jewelry and designs in gold.

In the early 1970s, Portland Jeweler Robert B. Eaton became dissatisfied with the questionable quality and limited selection of jewelry then on the market. Following the adage, "if you want it done right, do it yourself," he turned to the creation of his own designs. That practice continues today in his shop in Morgan's Alley, where years of service have brought him such customers as Johnny Cash, Cliff Robertson and "Pappy" Boyington of Black Sheep Squadron fame. Mr. Eaton works only with 14 and 18 karat gold, precious and semi-precious stones. Most of his inventory is from his own designs; many are one-of-a-kind pieces, offering a welcome change from standard mass-produced fare. Mr. Eaton's practice is to work on a one-to-one basis with the customer, draw a sketch of the piece, create a wax model, cast it and finish it on the premises. He also handles the design and remounting of customer jewelry; produces unique wedding rings; incorporates aircraft, boats, sports, animals and other items into special-interest jewelry; and works with business logos and trademarks to form pins, tie tacks, pendants, service pins and other items. If your concept for a piece of jewelry can be sketched, cast in gold and decorated with fine stones, Robert B. Eaton Jeweler-Designer can do it. Visa. MasterCard.

Downtown

F24

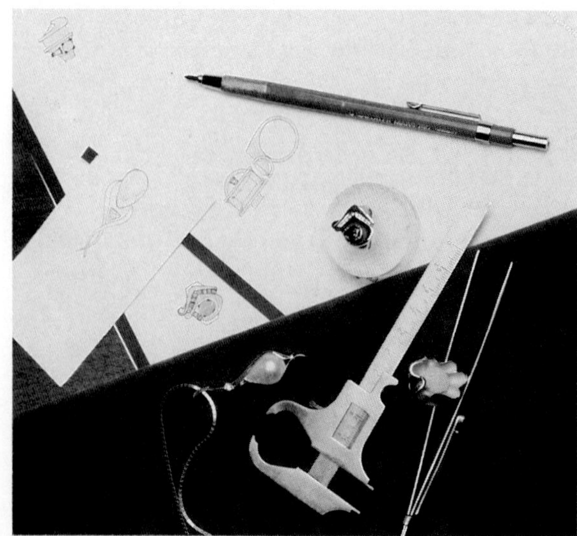

Morgan's Alley
515 SW Broadway
Portland 97205
224-9324

Monday-Saturday
10am-5pm

EQUINOX FINE JEWELRY

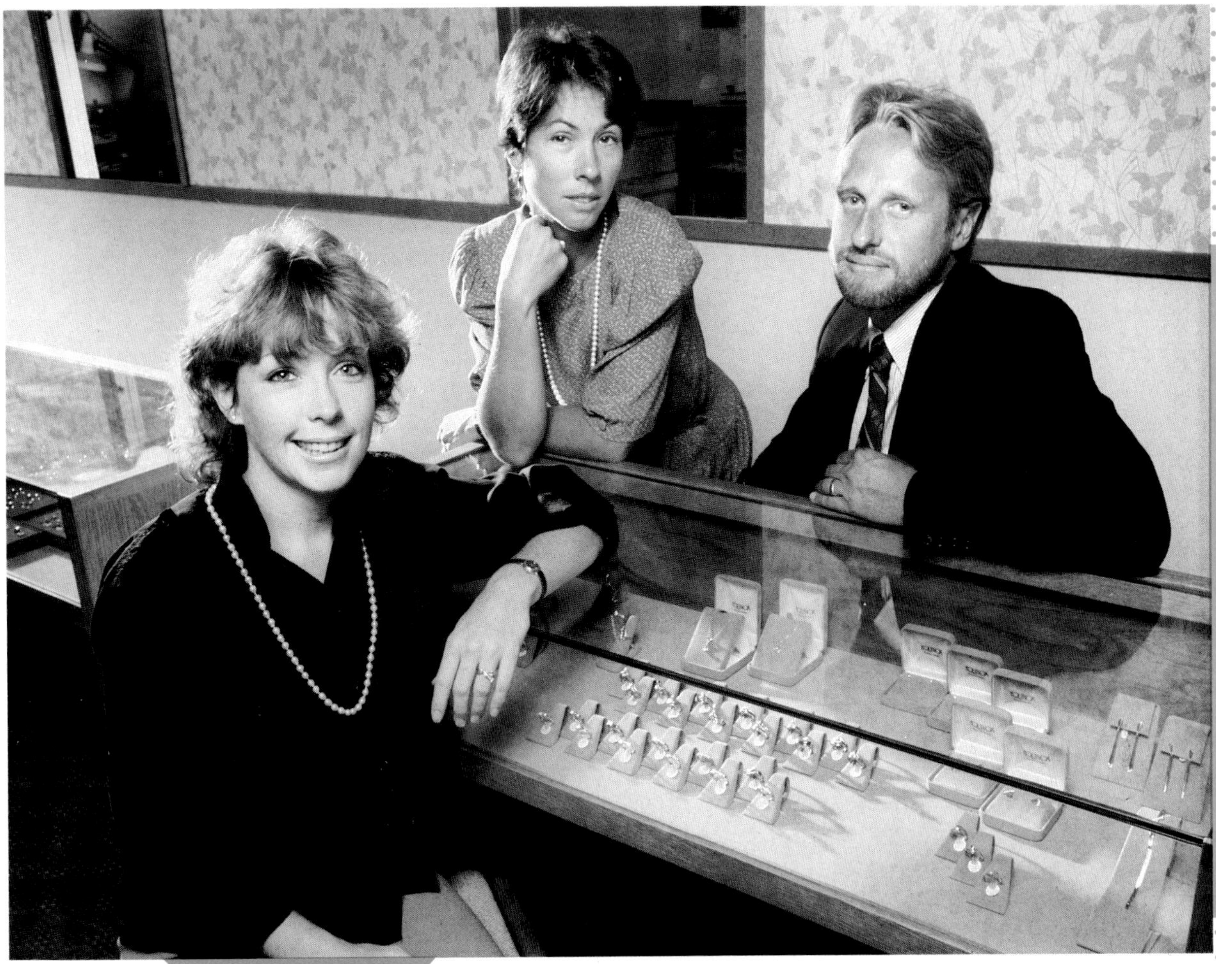

JEWELRY

Contemporary gold jewelry of distinction.

Children think of Equinox as the jewelry store with the fish tank. Many Portlanders think of it as the place they finally found that special wedding ring to symbolize their union. If you are fascinated by gems, browsing at Equinox and chatting with the knowledgeable staff should not be missed. Everyone who works at Equinox has an in-depth understanding of jewelry, because they are all actively involved in the conception and creation of the pieces on display. By discussing your specific jewelry needs and desires with you, they can help you decide on a ring, pendant or bracelet that will match your lifestyle and physique. If the jewelry on display is not exactly right, a special-order design may be just the thing. A particular specialty for the Equinox jewelers is devising updated settings for diamonds and other gems belonging to the client. Bead stringing, casting, stone setting and jewelry repair are also done on the premises. Precision-cut diamonds finished to the exacting ideal proportions are featured. Experience the dazzling array of colored gems from the fairy tale favorites such as ruby and sapphire to the rich excitement of tourmaline, tsavorite, tanzanite, andalusite and other extraordinary species. While you're visiting Equinox be sure to add your name to the mailing list to receive the Equinox Newsletter and notices of periodic gemstone feature displays. Visa. MasterCard. American Express. Diners Club. Discover.

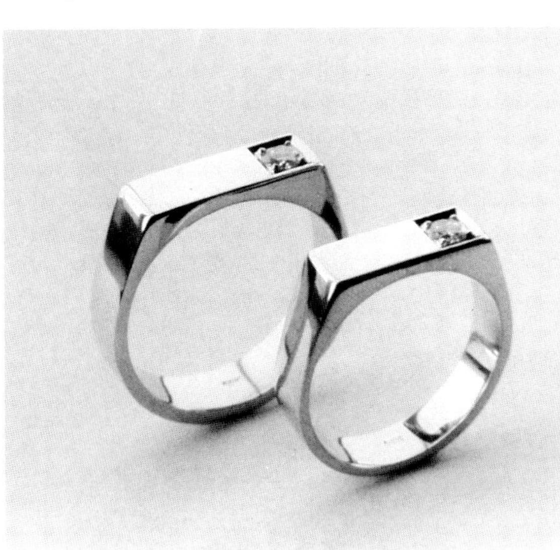

The Galleria
First Floor
921 SW Morrison Street
Portland 97205
226-3967

Monday-Friday
10am-8:30pm
Saturday 10am-6pm
Sunday noon-5pm

Downtown
F23

CHRIS H. FOLEEN GOLDSMITH

JEWELRY

Excellently crafted, elegantly designed jewelry.

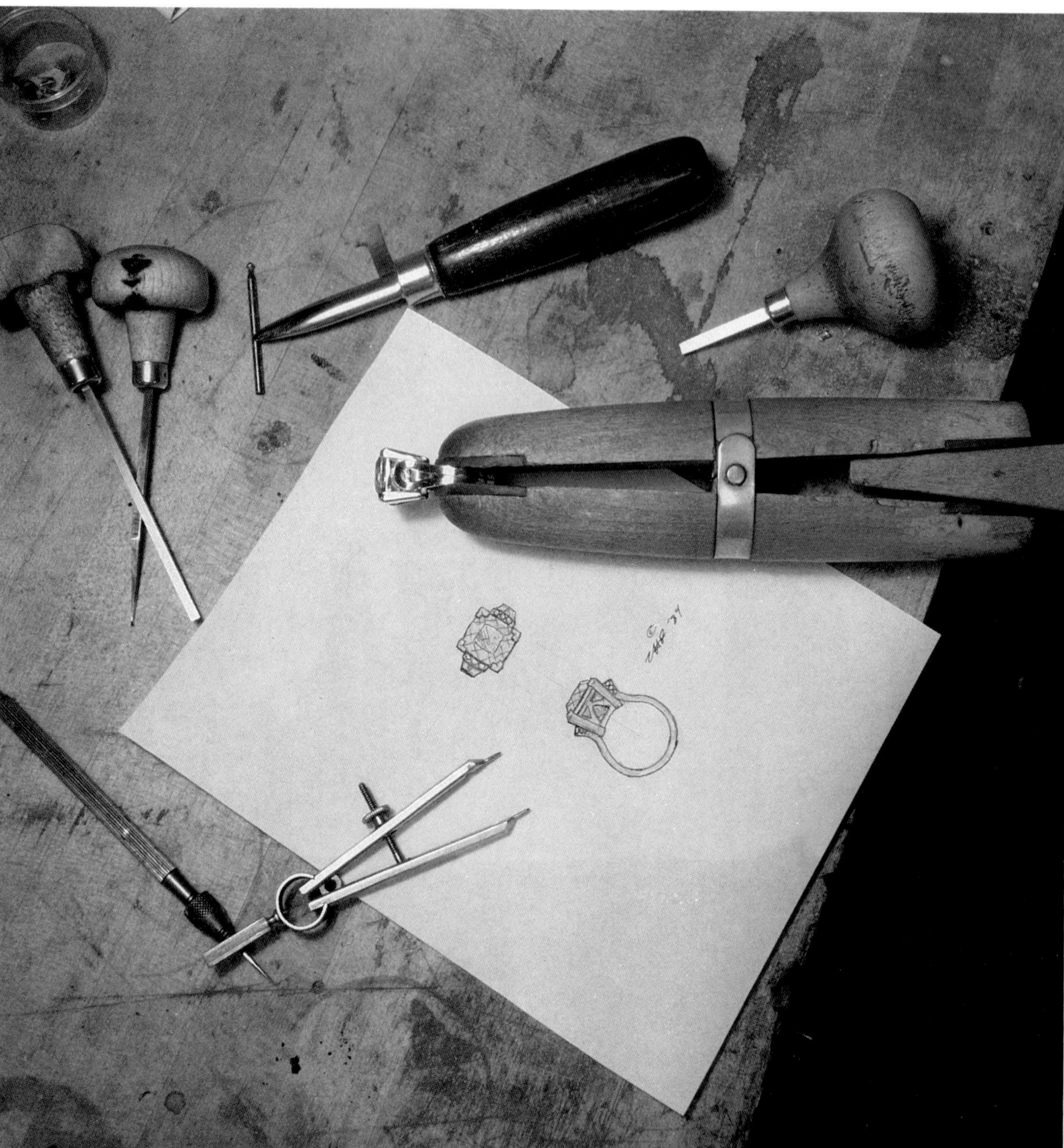

Southwest Portland

Chris Foleen, Goldsmith, completed his post-graduate studies in England and worked in the studio of C.F. Barnes, Master Engravers and Enamelists. He believes strongly in the consultation aspect of custom jewelry design. Through a cooperative process, involving you as much as possible in the drawing and designing of your custom piece, he is assured that the finished product will meet the highest expectations. Chris Foleen, Goldsmith works primarily in gold, but also uses platinum, and has a large variety of gems of especially fine quality and rare color, including diamonds in a wide variety of shapes, sizes, and facetings. You can bring him a sketch or just an idea, or have gems you already own mounted in a custom setting. You'll also find a limited number of custom pieces ready for purchase. In addition, your old jewelry can be restored to its former glory. Chris Foleen, Goldsmith does traditional hand-engraving on virtually any object from jewelry to guns; he is an expert in enamelling, the application of fine kiln-fired enamel to jewelry. Appraisals and gem identification are available. Visa. MasterCard. American Express. Diners Club. Carte Blanche.

P.O. Box 25162
Portland 97225
297-4257

By Appointment Only

KIDS AND TEENS

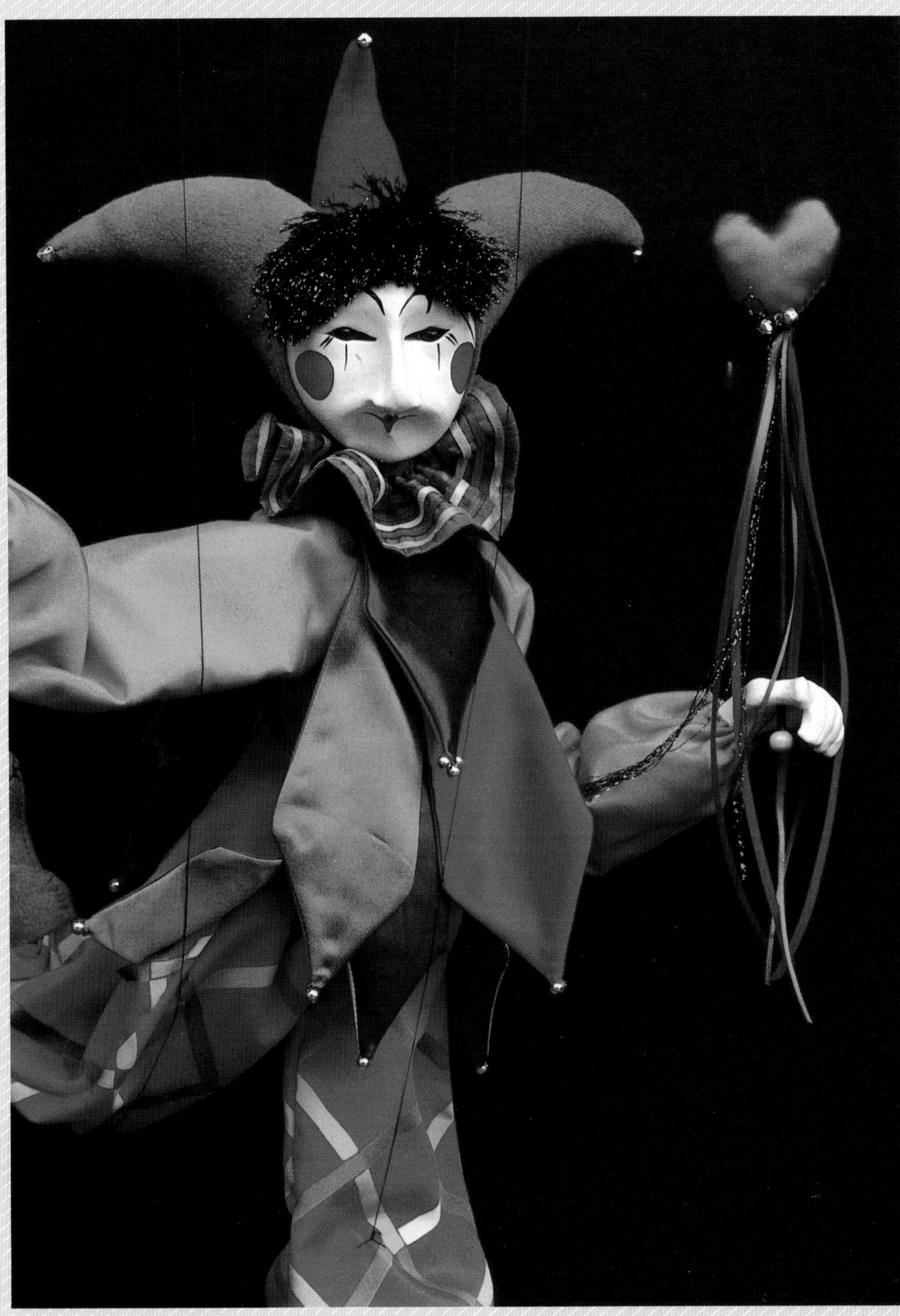

Louie Gizyn *Jester* CONTEMPORARY CRAFTS GALLERY

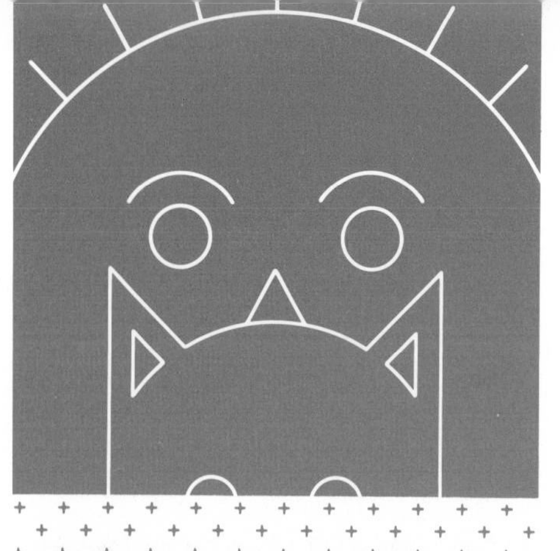

What, afterall, is more important than building forts with umbrellas?

It was raining. While considering the two blocks between me and the "important people reception" I surveyed, with some dismay, my open-toed patent leather pumps, the black silk dress, and the recently boofed head of hair. Like many Oregonians, I often shun raincoat and umbrella even during heavy showers, preferring to sprint or pretend it's not happening. However, this time, the umbrella.

Standing on the bricks before "Big Pink", the U.S. Bancorp Tower, I prepared to launch. In one well-practiced "swoosh" I raised the umbrella and popped it open. In a flash I was covered with sand. The umbrella had last been used by my young pal Will in a fort-building project at the beach on Sauvie Island.

If it weren't for Will, the inventive nine-year-old architect-in-training, I wouldn't have had the chance to do a "perspective check" on my life. What, afterall, is more important than building forts with umbrellas? Certainly not hanging out at another reception. Kids teach us what is important.

Not yet a parent myself, I probably need these reality checks more frequently than I get them. There we were at the art museum, seven year old Annie and I, studying (at different levels) a few fine Diane Arbus photographs. Diane Arbus is known for her alarmingly interior shots of people who are in some way bizarre, even if their oddness comes in the form of possessing an extreme case of the "ordinaries." Annie was transfixed, as were passersby transfixed by Annie. She had decorated herself for the museum by donning a pair of "deely-bobbers"... those things that look like head antenna that seem to take on a life of their own when worn. Diane Arbus is a fine artist, and yet I enjoyed watching Annie more.

I am blessed with intelligent, creative friends. Some of these creative friends have found themselves in the position of being parental units on a budget. They can't afford the fanciest, the coolest and the hippiest in toys and youth-wear. They keep it simple. Family projects, minor science and biology experiments with molds, paper airplanes, rockets, safety pin jewelry, bicycle trips, and tons of humor and laughter. There's a lot of love there.

In contrast I recall observing a tailored couple with groomed child in tow perusing one of Portland's swankest uptown delis. Mummie had little Bif pressed up against the chocolate and goody case. "Pretty expensive sweets for a kid," I thought. Sidling closer I realized that this exercise was not for the purpose of selecting sweets, it was to teach the agonized Bif French. "Can you say 'éclair'?"

In my years working with kids in the arts, I have witnessed all too often how we have drummed the creativity and spontaneity out of children by imposing adult priorities of status and control on the poor tykes. Fortunately, Portland offers a ton of fun, accessible, and spontaneous stuff for kids and families.

If, for example, you should ever tire of playing in one of Portland's beautiful and well-equipped parks, you can always take MAX (an adventure!) downtown to wander through the stores. I frequently resupply my stock of miniature rubber frogs and plastic ants at one of these fine establishments.

I always carry a supply of creepy-crawlies with me when visiting friends Ellie and Kevin. Their teenage kids and I have never outgrown the burning need to carefully plant little plastic bugs in the parental plates at dinner. I know Kevin and Ellie only tolerate this because I am, well, a friend, and appreciated for other more endearing traits. They understand that this is something that I think I can't do to my own dinner guests, so they allow me to engage their children in pranksterism.

Children are more insightful, intuitive, creative and resourceful than we sometimes appreciate. I admit, it is easier for me to gush because I do not currently live with children. I can have my quiet moments whenever I want them, causing some parents to regard my enthusiasm for children with slightly squinty eyes. I do value those special kid times, for the wit, the unexpected twists, the delight in discovery and, selfishly, for the learning and growing that I do in the company of children. *Catherine Windus*

Catherine Windus *is a board member and former president of Young Audiences of Oregon who taught art in a previous lifetime.*

Louie Gizyn *launched her career as an artist in 1978 and since then has travelled and exhibited her work across the country. "Creating marionettes and figured mobiles has become a full time passion. My work changes yet the medium of clay and cloth has remained the same." She is represented by the Contemporary Crafts Gallery.*

KIDS AND TEENS

European, Japanese and American designer clothing, special edition dolls, furniture that grows with you, toys, games and a very special hair dresser. Plus a gym and a museum especially for children.

A Children's Place *187*
Bambini's Children's Boutique *188*
Children's Country Store *180*
The Children's Gym *192*
Children's Museum *191*
Child's Play *186*
City Kids *185*
Dimples *184*
Early Childhood Bookhouse *182*
Expecting the Best *138*
Finnegan's *183*
Gazelle Natural Fibre Clothing *162*
Hanna Andersson *179*
Kid's Hair Parlour *189*
Le Papillon *178*
Mako *181*
Portland Family Calendar *190*
Teddy Bear's Picnic *301*

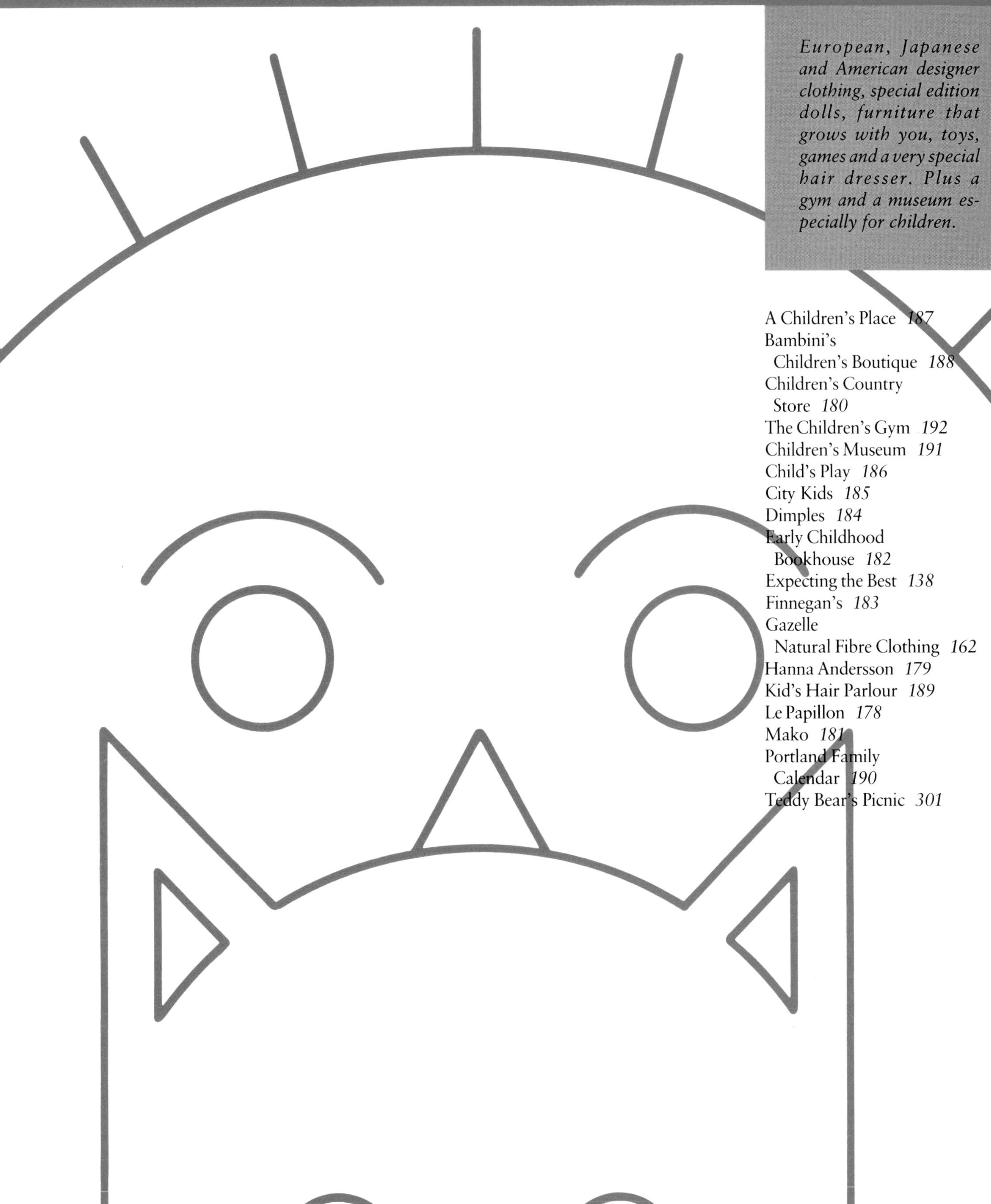

LE PAPILLON

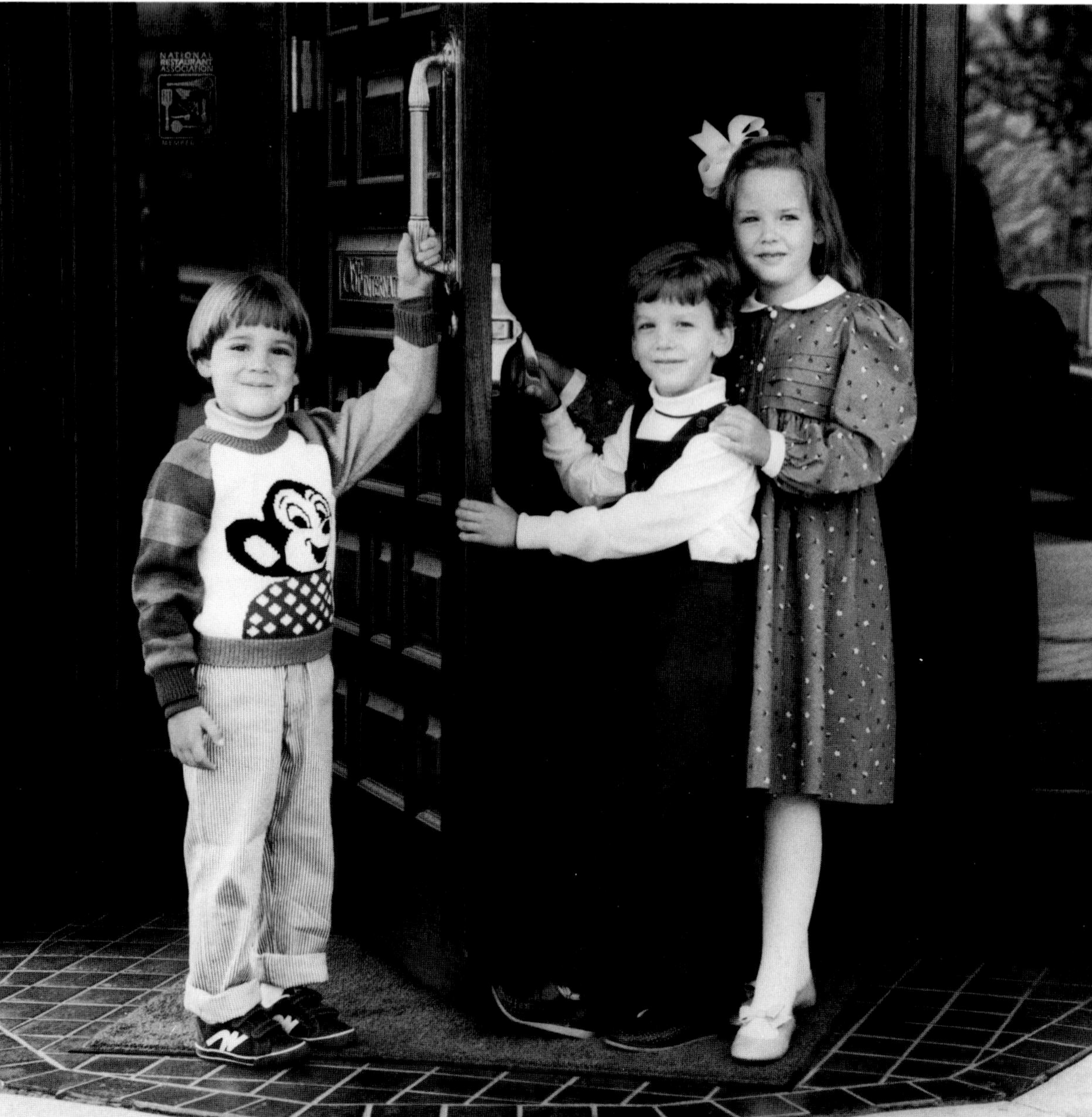

KIDS AND TEENS

Classic and avante-garde children's clothing.

Progress-Washington Square
G3

Like the dazzling white unicorn, "le papillon" is an enchanted creature who captures children's imaginations. You and your children will come under the butterfly's spell as you wander through this specialty store. From tots to teens, Le Papillon offers classic designs like those of Florence Eiseman and Imp as well as the fashion-forward creations from the best domestic and European designers. For preteen girls there are the exciting designs of Emanuelle and Italy's Scubidoo, for the young man the color and flair of Moustache. Whether it's party finery from Malley & Co. or OshKosh's newest ensemble you'll find it at Le Papillon. It is often said that accessories make the outfit; at Le Papillon it has never been so true. If it's the hair bow or the bow tie, you'll find just the right one, or their resident designer, Judy Johnson, will make one for you! For the infant, there are special layette and gift items; you'll find the traditional designs of Feltmen, the whimsical appliqués of Patsy Aiken and the avant-garde creations of Bibbity-Bobbity-Boo! Nursery accessories include Baby Bjorn's baby sitter, wooden nite lites from France and a complete palette of bedding accessories. There are treasures from around the corner as well as around the world; hand-painted tables and chairs, Brio trains and Corolle dolls. We all know that children are special...Le Papillon knows it best of all. Complimentary gift wrapping is available. Visa. MasterCard.

8772 SW Hall Boulevard
Portland 97223
641-6222

Monday-Saturday 10am-5:30pm
Sunday noon-5pm

HANNA ANDERSSON

Swedish quality in 100% cotton clothing.

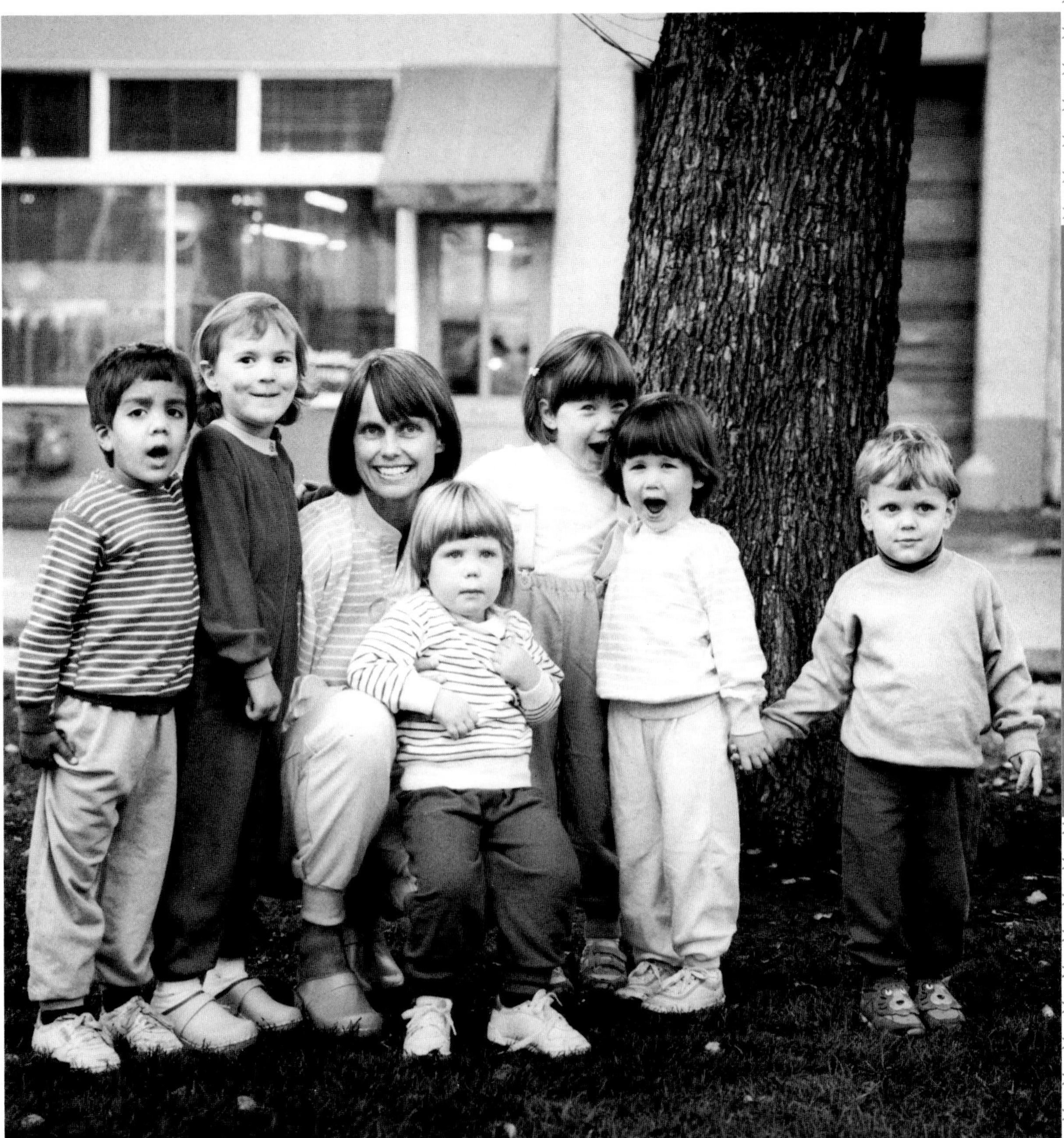

Basic quality is back with a vengeance. So Tom and Gun Denhart were not particularly surprised when friends showed such enthusiasm about a selection of children's clothes the couple had brought back from a trip to Sweden. Making use of Gun's Swedish contacts, the couple began an import business in childrens' clothes with the result that in three short years their inspiration, Hanna Andersson, has become one of the hottest mail order businesses in the Northwest. Named after Gun's grandmother, the venture deals almost exclusively in bright, 100% cotton clothing for children — washable, durable, and made in Sweden, a country known for its appreciation of function and quality. Launched initially from the family's garage, the business presently employs over thirty and is growing faster than the children they clothe. Recently they produced their eighth color catalog: forty-eight pages which showcase more than 1200 items and is mailed to over a million addresses annually. However they're sold, Hanna Andersson's clothes are backed with dedication to customer satisfaction, a commitment, which given the quality of their goods, remains all but invisible. Visa. MasterCard. American Express.

327 NW 10th Avenue
Portland 97209
242-0920

Monday-Saturday
10am-5pm
Toll Free outside Oregon: 1-800-222-0544

CHILDREN'S COUNTRY STORE

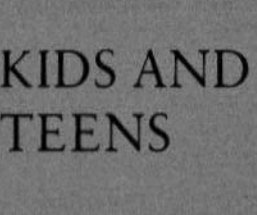

KIDS AND TEENS

Furnishing and decorating center for kids' rooms.

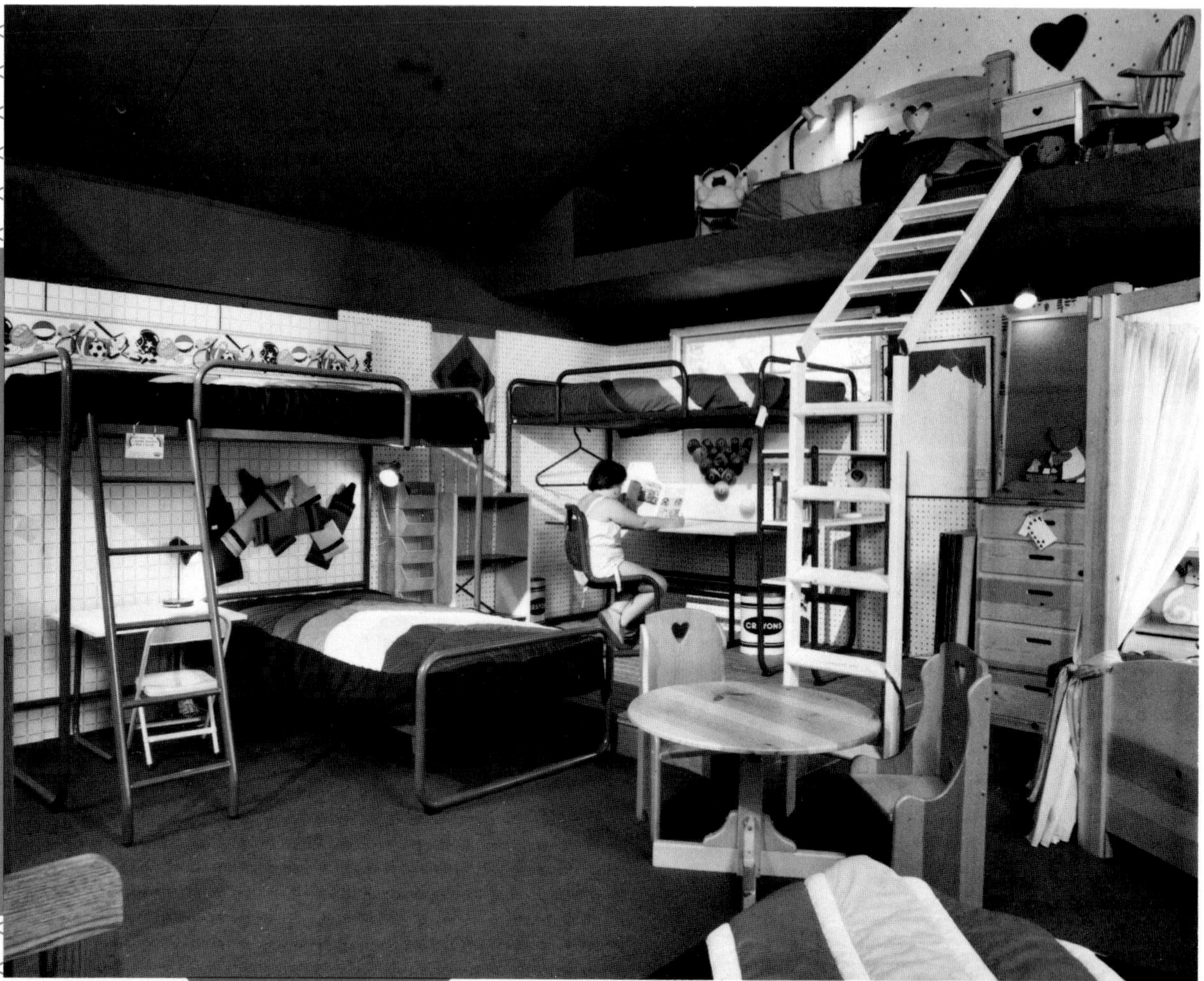

For the parent who believes a child's room deserves every bit as much attention to decor and furnishings as the rest of the house, Maude Caputo has the answer: her Children's Country Store. The store focuses its attention on the special surroundings which are so important to a youngster, but often neglected by businesses catering to the needs of the world's bigger people. By putting everything in one place, the Children's Country Store makes it infinitely more convenient and rewarding to create a room that your child will enjoy for years. Here you can wander through the building's cozy nooks and quaint alcoves, studying fully decorated room settings to gather ideas. You'll find wallpaper in patterns covering a range of choices from Walt Disney to Marimekko, quilts and bedding in wonderful colors and designs, and wall sculptures and hangings that challenge the imagination. The store offers a large selection of furniture: bunkbeds, twinbeds, dressers, desks in bright colored metal, natural woods or durable melamine — furniture that grows with its users and stands up to the task. Bring in color swatches or maybe just a pocketful of ideas, and come away with everything for a finished project. Don't you wish you had a room like that when you were a kid? Visa. MasterCard.

Beaverton

E3

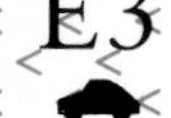

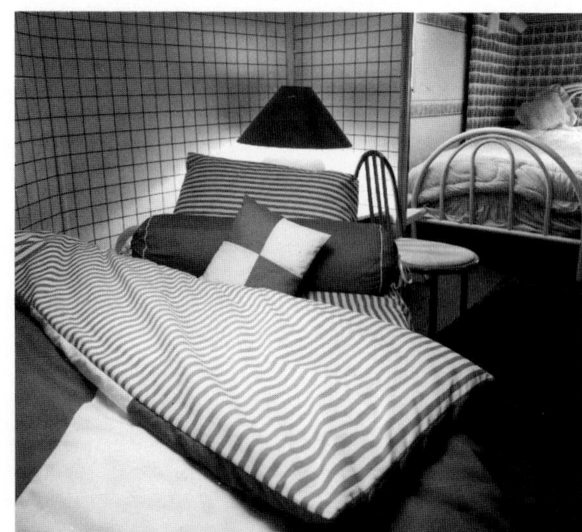

9955 SW Beaverton Hillsdale Highway
Beaverton 97005
644-3944

Monday-Tuesday 10:30am-6pm
Wednesday 10:30am-8pm
Thursday-Saturday 10:30am-5pm

MAKO

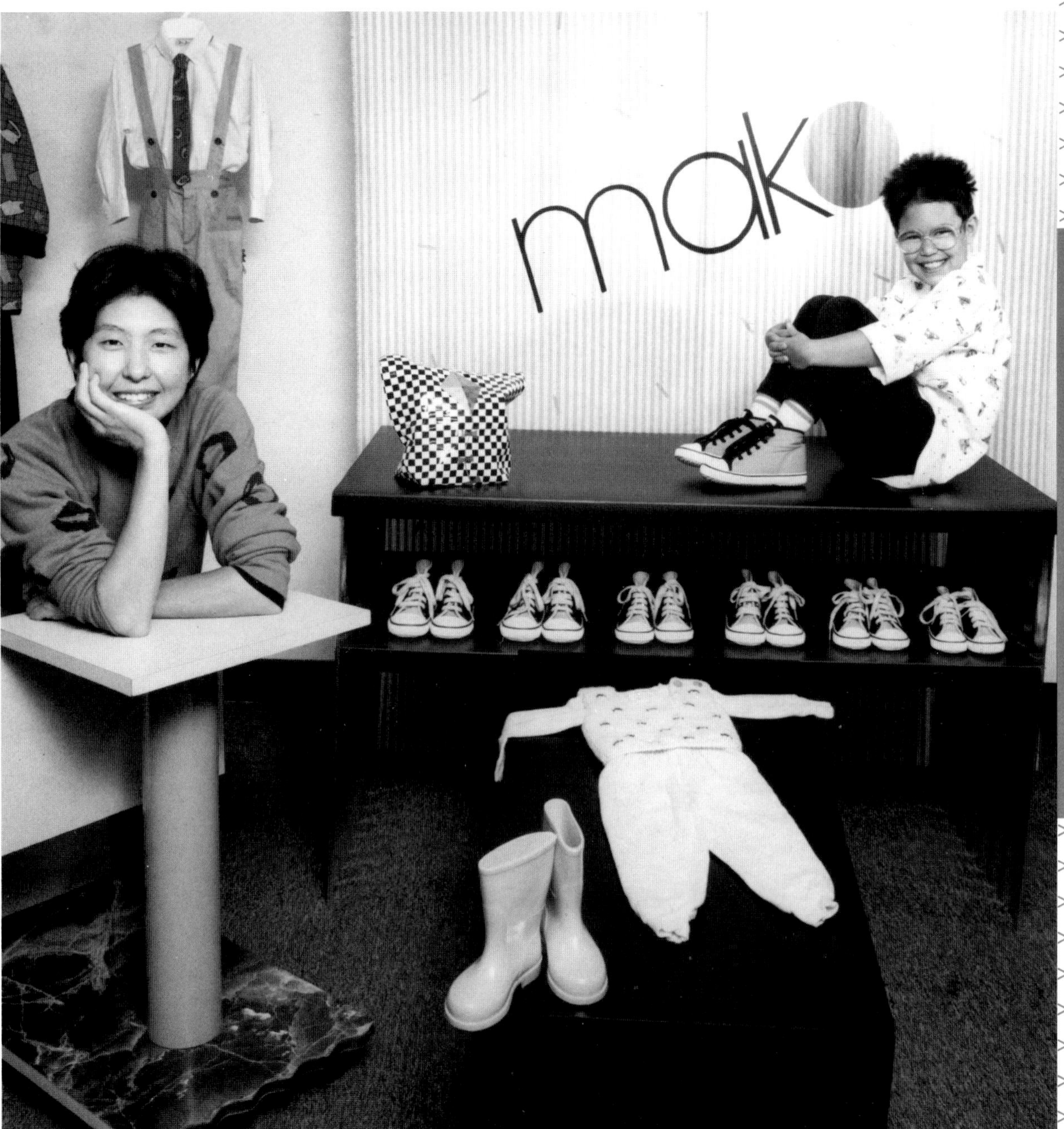

KIDS AND TEENS

Designed for little children by big children.

On any given day, walk into the singular shop for children's clothes known simply as *mako*, and you'll be greeted by Mako herself, the designer of the *mako* line known from New York to Honolulu. Or by her sister, Yoko, also a designer and holder of a Black Belt in Aikido. Or by her young daughters, Kent and Emi. Or even by her husband, Erik, an advertising executive. Kent will eagerly discuss the pros and cons of the leading edge Model D computer. And Erik will rhapsodise on the peculiar joys of British motorcycles: "The doldrums of the return run could often be relieved by trying to pick up the bits and pieces that had fallen off on the outward run." If you're thinking that *mako* is not the usual children's shop, you're not far wrong. From the knock-off Memphis furniture to the anti-retail use of open space, the *mako* concept is as boldly graphic as the original line of children's clothes that bears the *mako* label. "Too many children's clothes," says Mako "are designed to please parents. I design to please children." And yet, parents who wish to sport a *mako* original have been known to persuade Mako to design a silkscreened sweatshirt or a handknitted sweater for them. "Some parents never forget they were children once," says Mako innocently. Visa. MasterCard.

732 NW 23rd Avenue
Portland 97210
274-9081

Monday-Saturday
10am-6pm

Northwest Portland

H17

EARLY CHILDHOOD BOOKHOUSE

KIDS AND TEENS

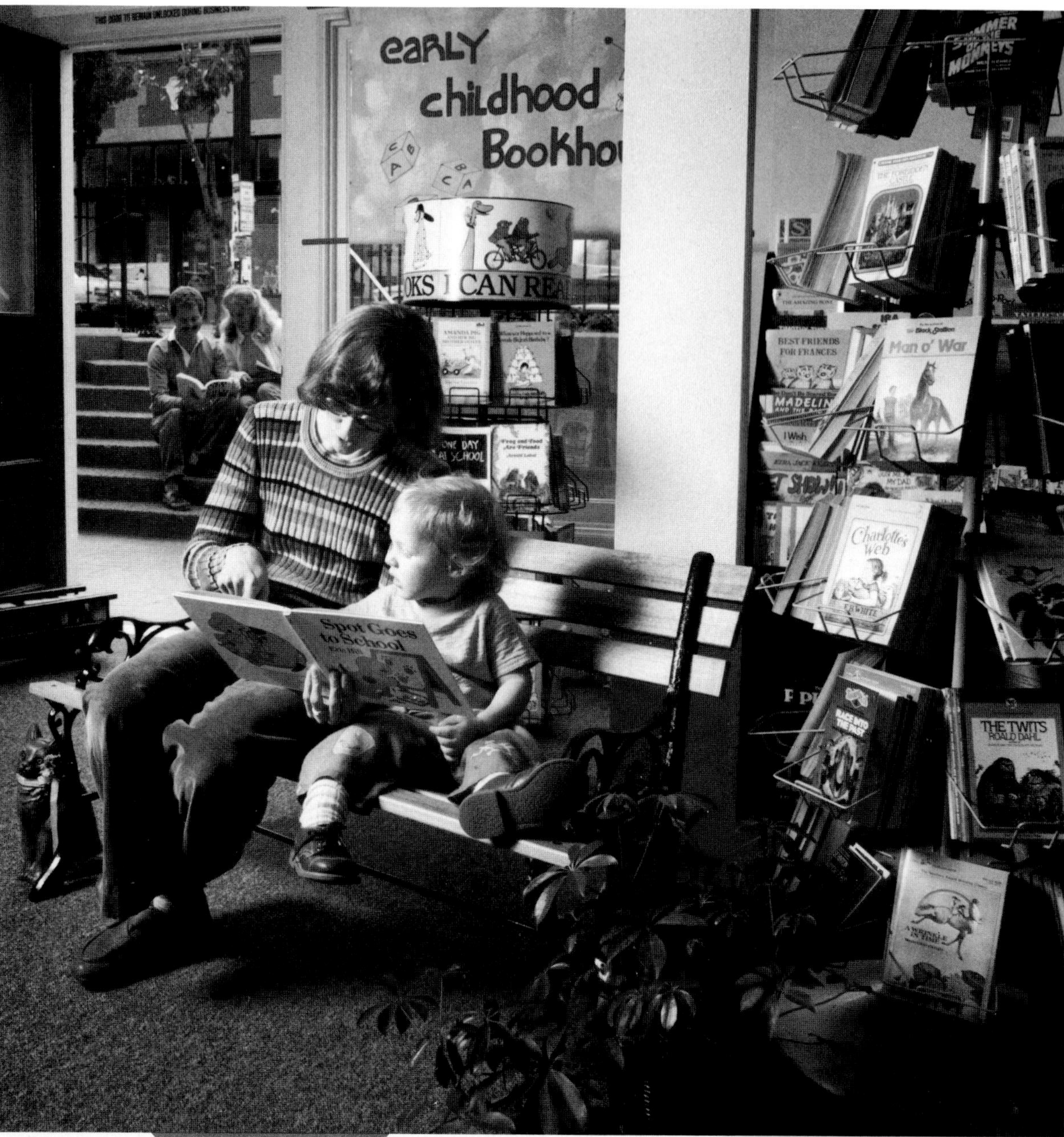

A Victorian house full of children's books and surprises.

Northwest Portland
H17

Beaverton
E2

How early should you introduce your baby to books? Experts agree reading to your child can start as early as birth. Because your baby can't tell you which books to read, try talking to Jeanne Lybecker, Keith Stangel or any of the parents and teachers at the Early Childhood Bookhouse. They'll show you colorful baby books made of bright cloth, shining cardboard and cushy, vinyl- covered foam. There are books that squeak and smell, pop and fold — along with children's records and tapes. But you don't have to be a child to enjoy a stroll through this comfortable, Victorian house complete with a park bench, backyard and lattice "secret garden." Parents and teachers will find volumes on problem solving, curriculum, cooking and games. And a variety of computer books and software are ready for a demonstration on the Bookhouse computer. Special orders are a specialty too. Parents from around the globe shop the Early Childhood Bookhouse through their mail order catalog and newsletter. But the best part of the Early Childhood Bookhouse are the puppet shows, story-telling events and spontaneous games. Come in for the fun of it. Visa. MasterCard.

724 NW 23rd Avenue
Portland 97210
224-6372

Monday-Saturday
10am-5:30pm

Book Barn for Children
4570 SW Watson Street
Beaverton 97005
641-2276

Monday-Saturday
10am-5pm

FINNEGAN'S

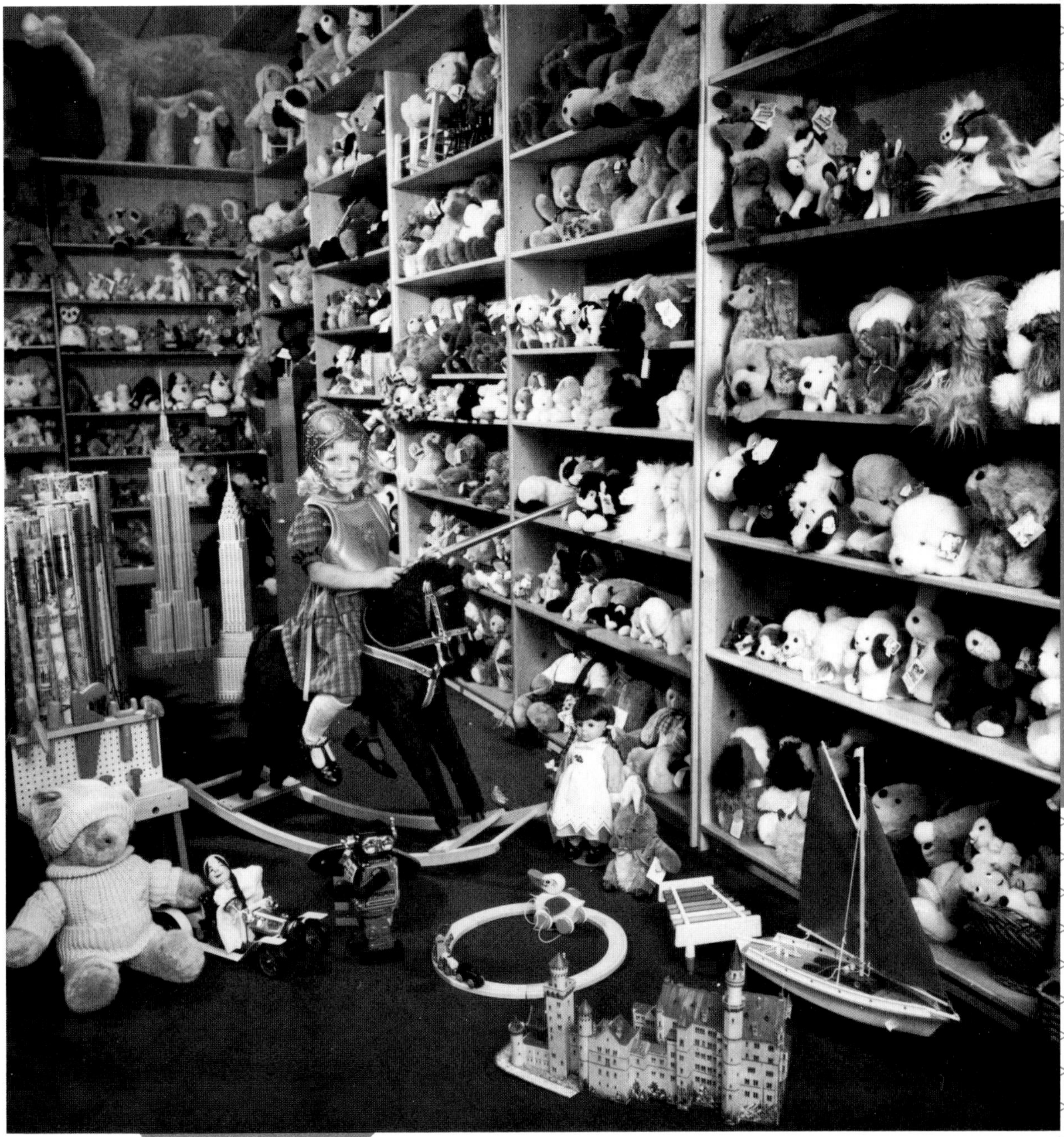

KIDS AND TEENS

Imported and American toys and gifts for children and adults.

There could be a leprechaun around any corner at Finnegan's, for surely a storybook assortment of toys and magic creatures inhabit this store. Marionettes and mobiles dance overhead while giant animals prepare to pounce from the highest shelves. Wee folk are beckoned by baskets of Whirl-A-Birds, Rubber Razzers, Insty Animals, and Magic Topsy Turveys. Future maestros learn to make music on brightly colored small-scale pianos, clarinets and xylophones. The largest assortment of wind-up toys in town includes a kangaroo that does somersaults and a bird that flies! Hand puppets keep kids — and grown-ups — entertained for hours. Finnegan's selects toys to suit all budgets and to please adult and child alike. One visit is not nearly enough to explore the over-flowing shelves, bins, baskets and racks. "Surprise" toys are a specialty at Finnegan's — cameras that are really water pistols, a coffee mug with a bear or frog inside, purses shaped like watermelons. Over 3,000 greeting and postcards offer hours of browsing, and a full line of Recycled Paper Products, rolls of gift wrap and bright stickers add to the colorful display. You'll never run out of wishes at Finnegan's — even if you miss the leprechaun. Visa. MasterCard.

922 SW Yamhill Street
Portland 97205
221-0306

Monday-Saturday
10am-6pm
Sunday noon-5pm

Downtown

F23

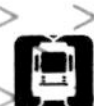

DIMPLES

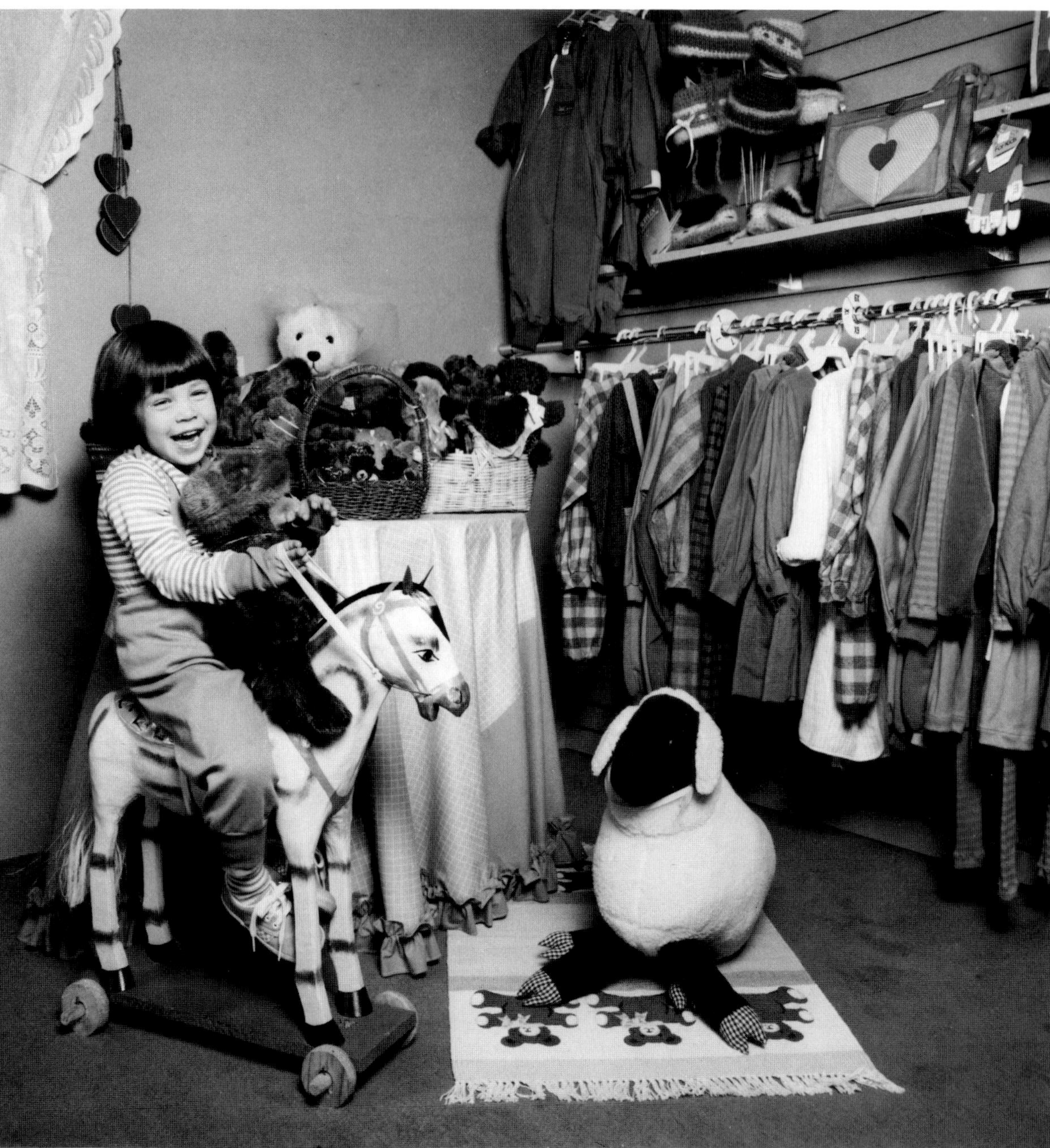

KIDS AND TEENS

Clothing, toys and gifts for the 6X and under set.

Northwest Portland

H17

Children are special, so why settle for the unrelenting sameness that chain and department stores offer today's child? If you're looking for a way to break the children's wear boredom barrier, have Mel Lee and Patsy Sweet at Dimples show you how. Dimples specializes in unusual and contemporary clothes for the little ones in your life, from just hatched to size 6X. Style and quality are paramount at Dimples, and that emphasis is evident everywhere, whether it appears in cottons from America, Europe and the Orient (for school, casual, camp or resort use), or in the fresh appeal of Northwest styles for the young owner. There's outerwear from American Widgeon and the Rat Rags collection from Seattle, with clear, simple lines that are as practical as they are attractive. But the selection at Dimples doesn't stop at clothing. Handcrafted items include sweaters, hand-painted clothing, dolls, teddy bears and other gifts. Mom is not left out either; gifts for her include jewelry, folk crafts, soaps, accessories, cards, antiques, baskets and collectibles. The store's interior, in shades of deep purple accented with hues of turquoise and salmon, is warm, inviting and whimsical. Special services make Dimples as appealing as a baby's smile — gift wrapping, free delivery to hospitals, package mailing and phone orders. Visa. MasterCard. American Express.

904 NW 23rd Avenue
Portland 97210
224-0428

Monday-Saturday
10am-5:30pm

CITY KIDS

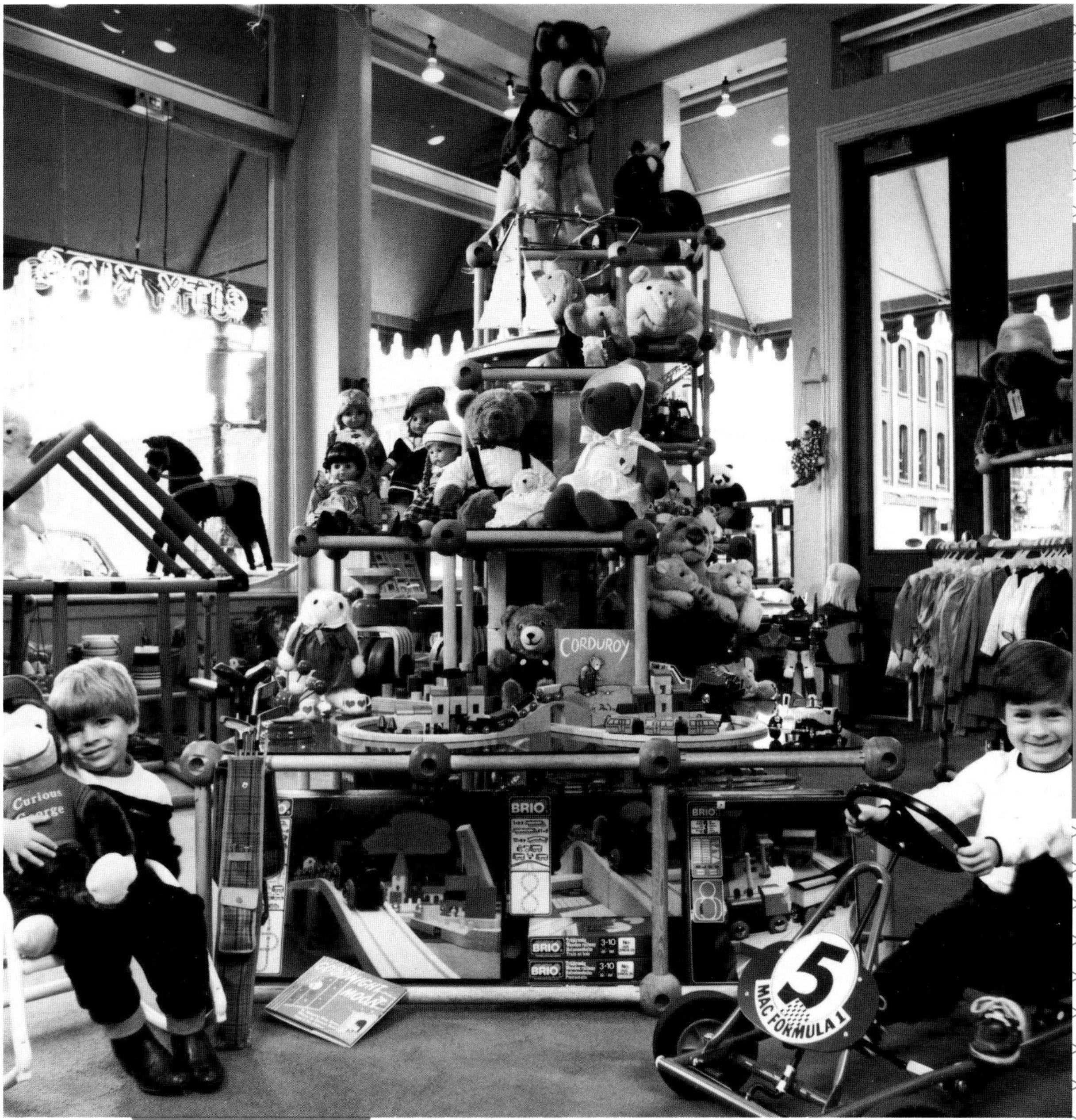

Special gifts for special imaginations.

Everyone has an imagination — that's why there's City Kids — a very special kind of store. City Kids has imaginative toys and unusual gifts for all kinds of kids, no matter how big they are. Vicki Morton and Linda Rucker, both former educators, have applied their knowledge and expertise to create a lively store where you will find just the right surprise — from books to games to little trains. City Kids has a wide assortment of the latest toys, cuddly stuffed animals, dolls, baby toys and gifts, including carefully chosen children's apparel, play structures and cards. In this special store you'll find the toys that help the mind stretch and grow. But you may come just to enjoy the special delights of childhood. That's why it's for everyone. City Kids has special gifts for special imaginations. Visa. MasterCard. American Express. Discover.

SW Second & Yamhill
Portland 97204
224-5784

Monday-Saturday
10am-6pm
Sunday 11am-5pm

Washington Square Too
Portland 97223
639-9300

Monday-Friday
10am-9pm
Saturday 10am-6pm
Sunday 11am-5pm

Yamhill Historic District

G25

Progress-Washington Square

G3

CHILD'S PLAY

KIDS AND TEENS

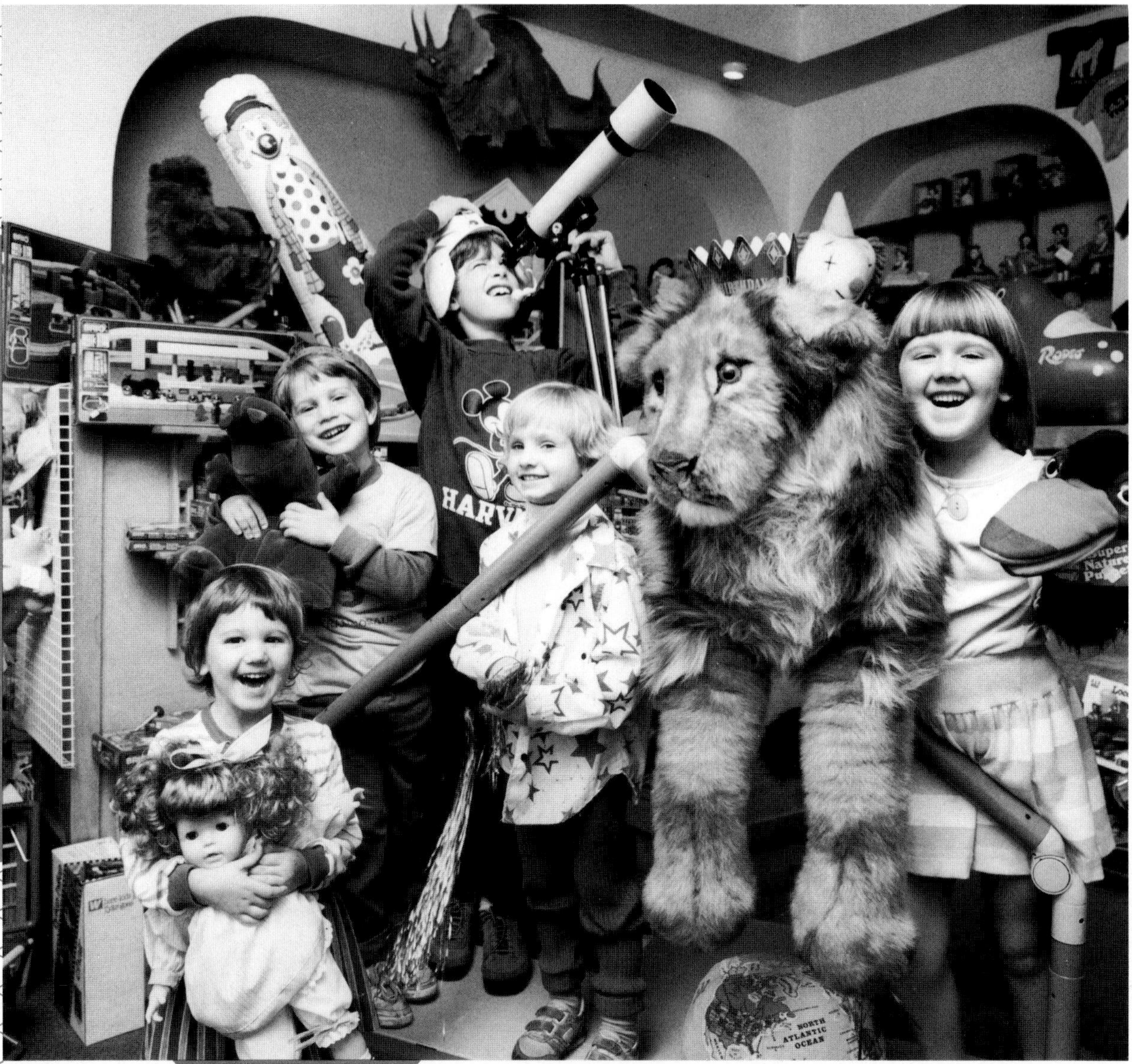

For creative play.

Northwest Portland

H17

It's widely known that play-things can have a dramatic effect on child development, and a growing number of parents are learning that a northwest Portland store is the area's most authoritative source for toys and advice. At Child's Play, television hype is discarded in favor of a close look at the play value and appropriateness of toys for the young owner. Parents will leave knowing that they made a well-informed choice on everything from dinosaurs to dolls, bath toys to blocks. The founders started the business in 1979 as the first Portland toy store with a developmental focus. Since then, Child's Play's reputation has grown to the point that parents frequently call with questions ranging from requests for play dough recipes to inquiries about what toys to take on vacation. Child's Play features sturdy, non-violent and "open-ended" toys in a wide price range, including many items priced from a dime to a dollar for "piggy bank" purchases. There are wooden toys for all ages, art supplies, animal models, infant/toddler toys, party favors and other paper goods, and doll houses. The store's soft "ice cream" colors provide a background for brightly colored toys and several play areas that enable kids to try out toys in a real test of user friendliness. Child's Play sends out a newsletter which provides customers with suggestions for suitable toys for different ages, and ideas for play activities. It also informs them of special events and workshops planned through the store for both children and adults. Visa. MasterCard. American Express.

715 NW 23rd Avenue
Portland 97210
224-5586

Monday-Saturday
10am-5:30pm

Call for Sunday and holiday hours

A CHILDREN'S PLACE

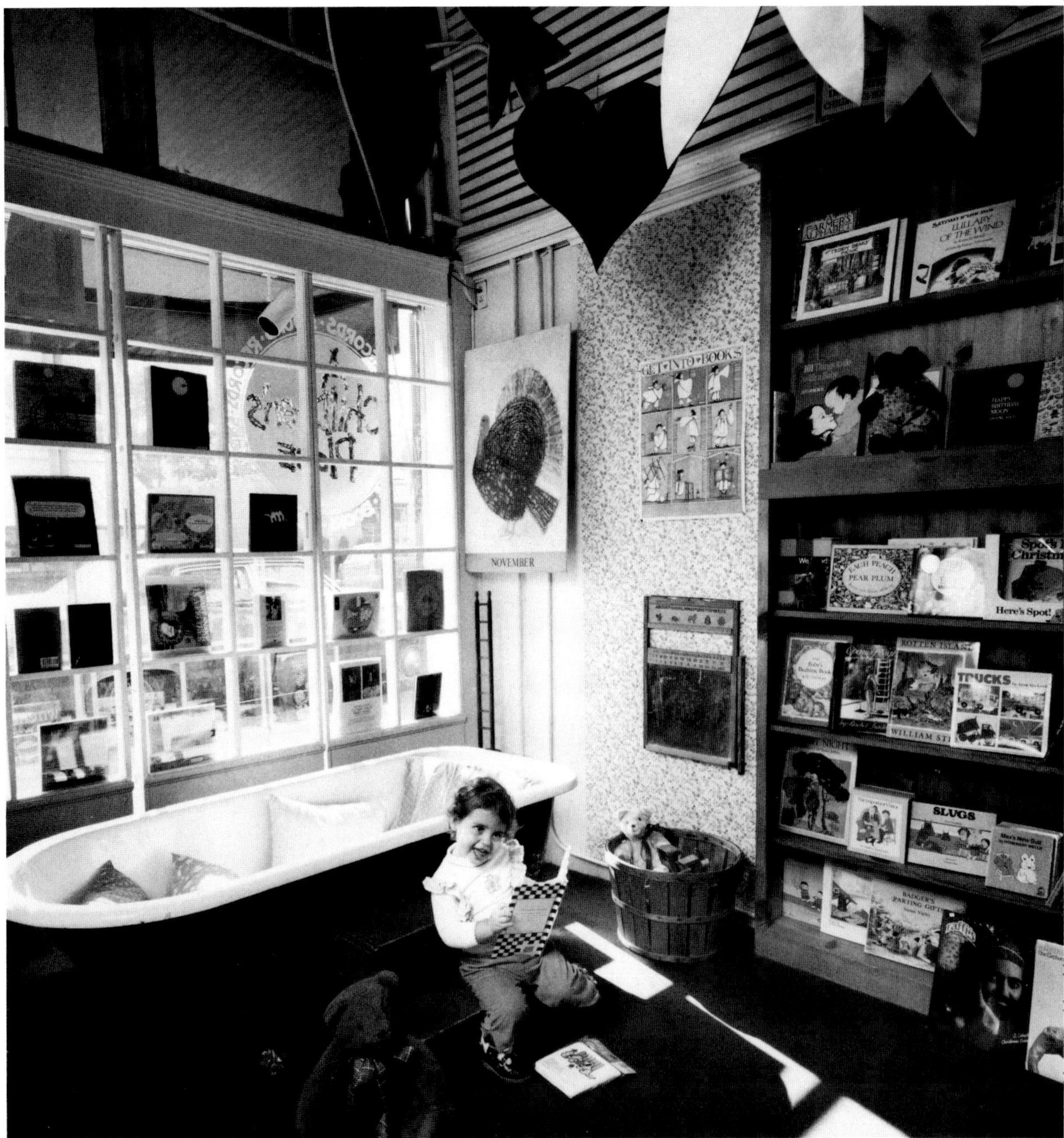

Encouraging kids to discover the wonders of reading and music.

Here is a special store, created specifically with children in mind. Encouraging kids to discover the wonders of reading and music is a challenge that owners Jan Bruton and Lynn Kelly thoroughly enjoy, and they do it with an admirable inventory of books, records and tapes. You'll find the widest selection of records and cassettes in town, ranging from lullabies and activity songs to stories and classical music by artists such as Raffi, Anne Murray, Pete Seeger, Ella Jenkins, Hap Palmer, Tom Glazer, Sharon, Lois and Bram, and Roshenshontz. A Children's Place is proud to be the first sponsor in the United States of concerts by Raffi, and they plan holiday and spring concerts for young music lovers. An extensive collection of hardback and paperback books for toddlers through pre-teens is a young reader's delight, with volumes chosen from major publishing houses and small presses. There are foreign language books, children's dictionaries, books for teachers, parenting books for mom and dad — and special appearances by authors throughout the year. This cozy, whimsical store, where kids can curl up with a book in the store's old pillow-filled clawfoot bathtub while you browse, is truly a children's place. Visa. MasterCard.

1631 NE Broadway
Portland 97232
284-8294

Monday-Saturday
10am-5pm

Northeast Portland
C6

BAMBINI'S CHILDREN'S BOUTIQUE

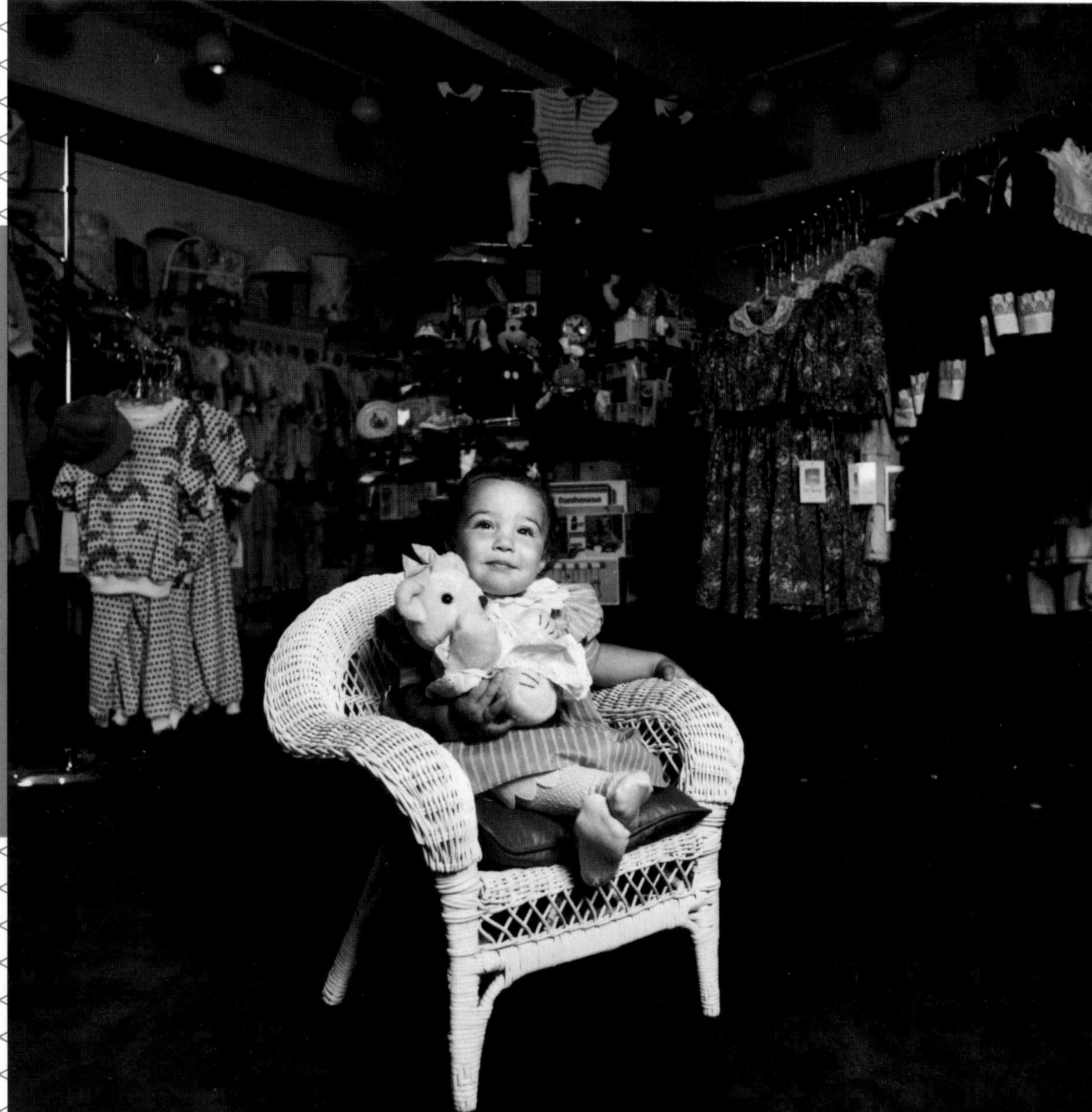

KIDS AND TEENS

European fashions, accessories and gifts.

Lake Oswego/ Lake Grove

14

Italians have a very special attitude towards children — warm, indulgent and affectionate. Bambini's Children's Boutique is suffused with this attitude in more than just its name. The open airy shop is filled with beautiful, bright and appealing children's clothing, accessories and gifts. The shop is well-organized with inviting displays — merchandise is easily accessible, not cluttered or overwhelming. There is a definite European boutique feeling in the unique selection with merchandise ranging from practical and durable every-day wear, to exquisite and fashionable outfits for special occasions. Owner Christine Rulli has created an atmosphere where ease and convenience in shopping is stressed in every detail. They offer such services as convenient parking, a play area for children, baby registry, clothing alteration and free gift wrap. Children's clothing in newborn through size 14 represents the fashions of Absorba, Creation Stummer, Bibo, Eagle's Eye, Merona, Choozie, Sarah Kent and many more quality European and American manufacturers. In addition to accessories and gifts, such as toys, jewelry, plush animals, room accessories and books; Bambini's offers infant bedding, communion and baptism outfits and accessories. Visit Bambini's Children's Boutique — you and your child will both enjoy the visit. Visa. MasterCard. Discover.

Lake Grove Shopping Center
16353 SW Bryant Road
Lake Oswego 97035
635-7661

Monday-Wednesday 10am-5:30pm
Thursday 10am-6:30pm
Friday-Saturday 10am-5:30pm

KID'S HAIR PARLOUR

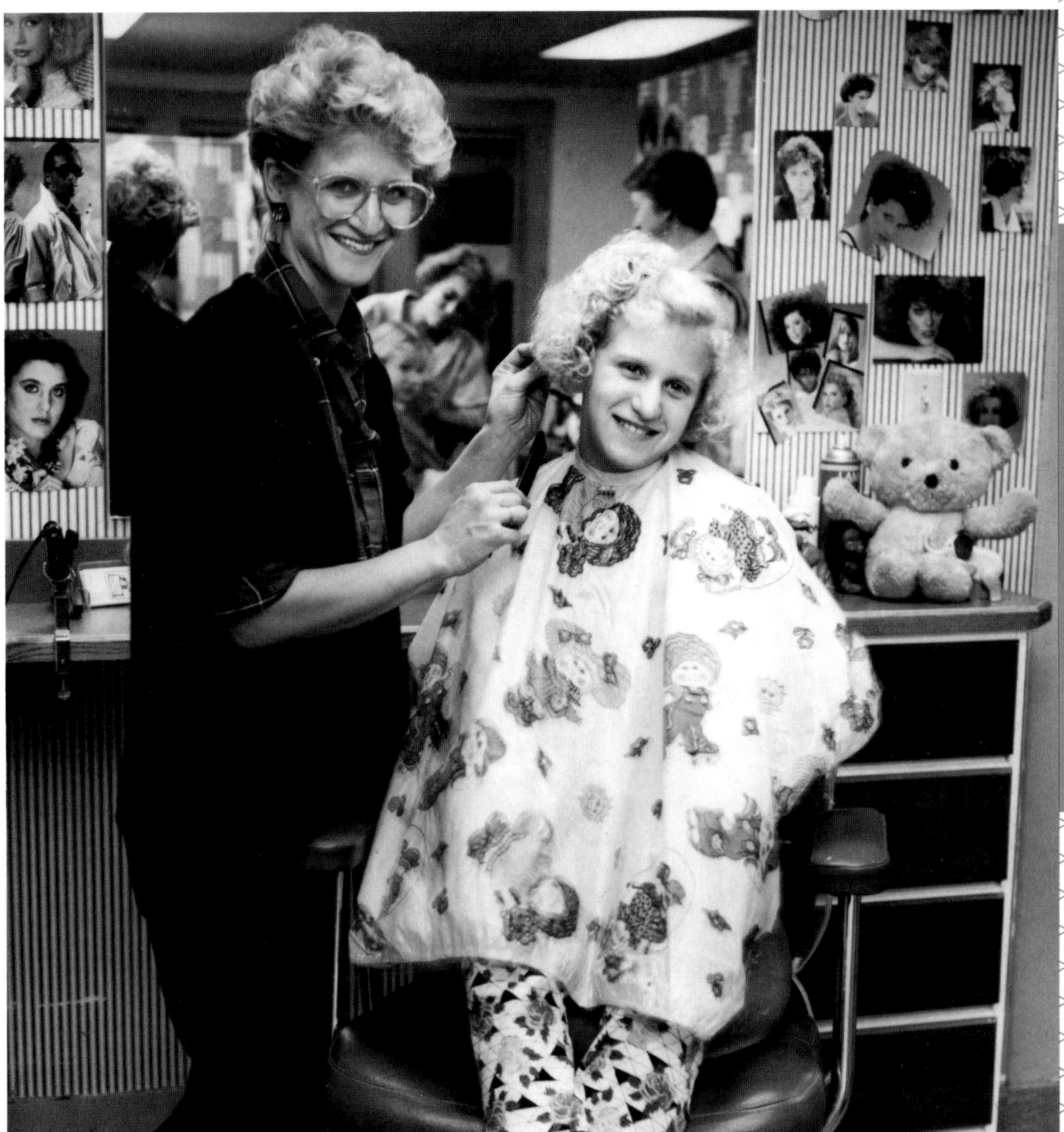

KIDS AND TEENS

Newborns to highschoolers are treated to the latest hair styles.

It's mom and dad's turn to tag along with the kids. Tiny tots, tomboys and teens are "number one" at Kid's Hair Parlour. Newborns through highschoolers are treated to perms, cuts, curls and the latest styles in a fun atmosphere that appeals to the young. You'll find Kid's Hair Parlour in Beaverton, one block east of Beaverton High School. The warm, comfortable Victorian house is filled with bean bag chairs, baskets of toys, children's books and a playroom with scads of good things to amuse the kids while they're waiting. Owners Connie Tygart and Vivian Engblom have a special knack for making sure kids have a good time, especially if it's their first visit. Only the finest KMS products are used to shampoo, condition and style hair. Kids can choose from a colorful array of barettes, combs, brushes, hair accessories, and earrings and they can get their ears pierced too! While children reign on the main floor, grownups relax upstairs at Adults Too, where fine hair care services are provided for "big people." Visa. MasterCard.

12795 SW Third
Beaverton 97005
641-9400

Monday-Friday
9am-5pm
Saturday 9am-4:30pm
Weekday evenings by appointment

Beaverton
F2

PORTLAND FAMILY CALENDAR

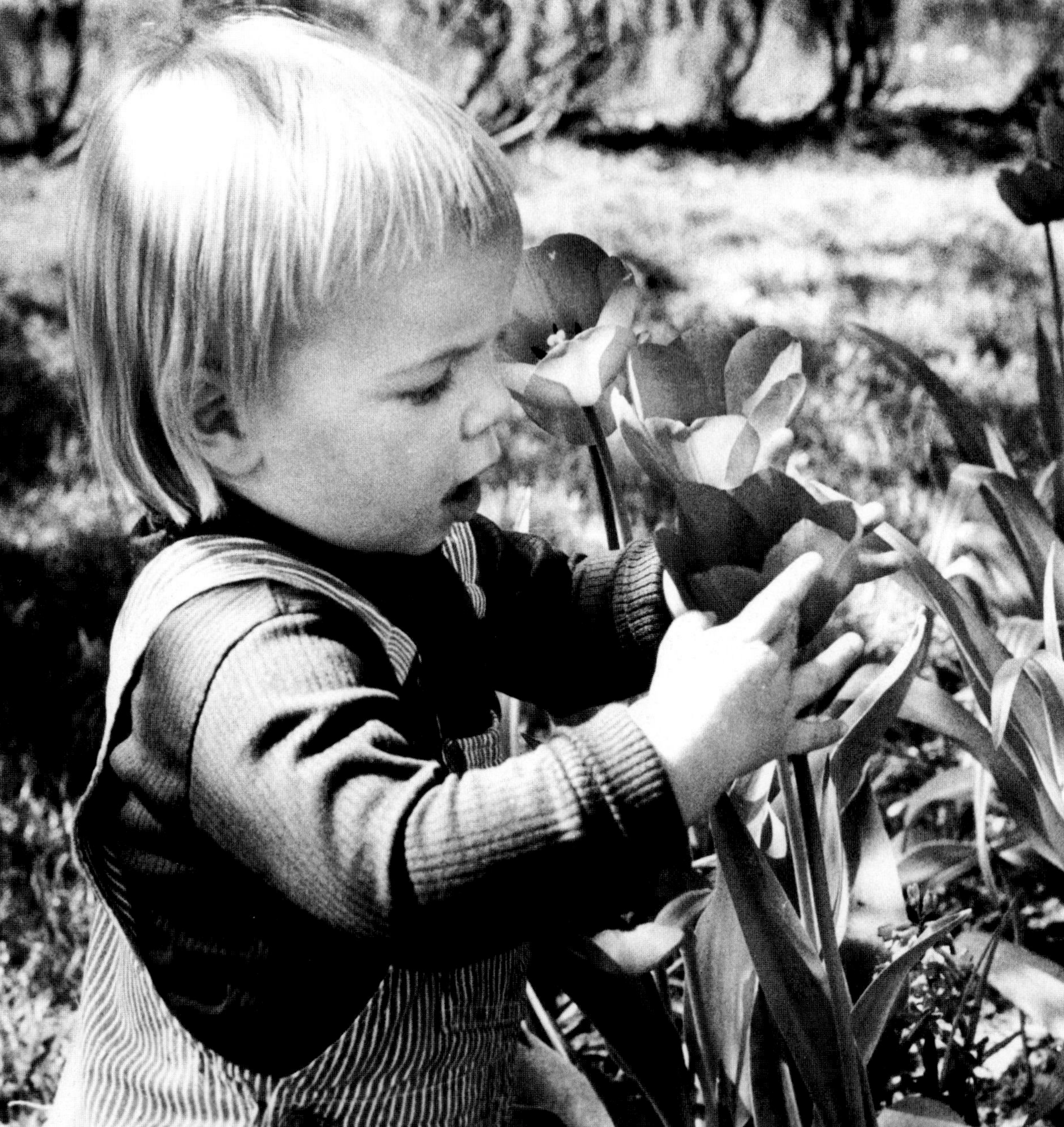

KIDS AND TEENS

A monthly guide for Northwest parents.

Northwest Portland

120

Portland Family Calendar is a monthly newspaper for parents with young children. It is also widely read and used as a resource by area professionals who work with families and children: teachers, doctors, counselors, and social service agency staff people. It contains listings of hundreds of activities, classes and resources each month. The listings include: arts and crafts activities and classes; film and theater events; health and wellbeing topics, such as clinics, classes and services for adults and children; music and dance activities and classes; parenting classes and support groups; prenatal classes and birth alternatives; activities and classes just for preschoolers, including indoor parks, toy libraries and co-ops; sports classes, events and physical activities; museum events and hours of operation; and a monthly listing of special events for families. It is the only comprehensive monthly guide to activities for families in the metro area. The paper also publishes articles on family life, health, books, outings, activities, crafts and entertainment for families, written by area professionals and free-lance writers in various fields. The articles emphasize parent-to-parent sharing of ideas and knowledge.

1819 NW Everett Street
Portland 97209
220-0459

CHILDREN'S MUSEUM

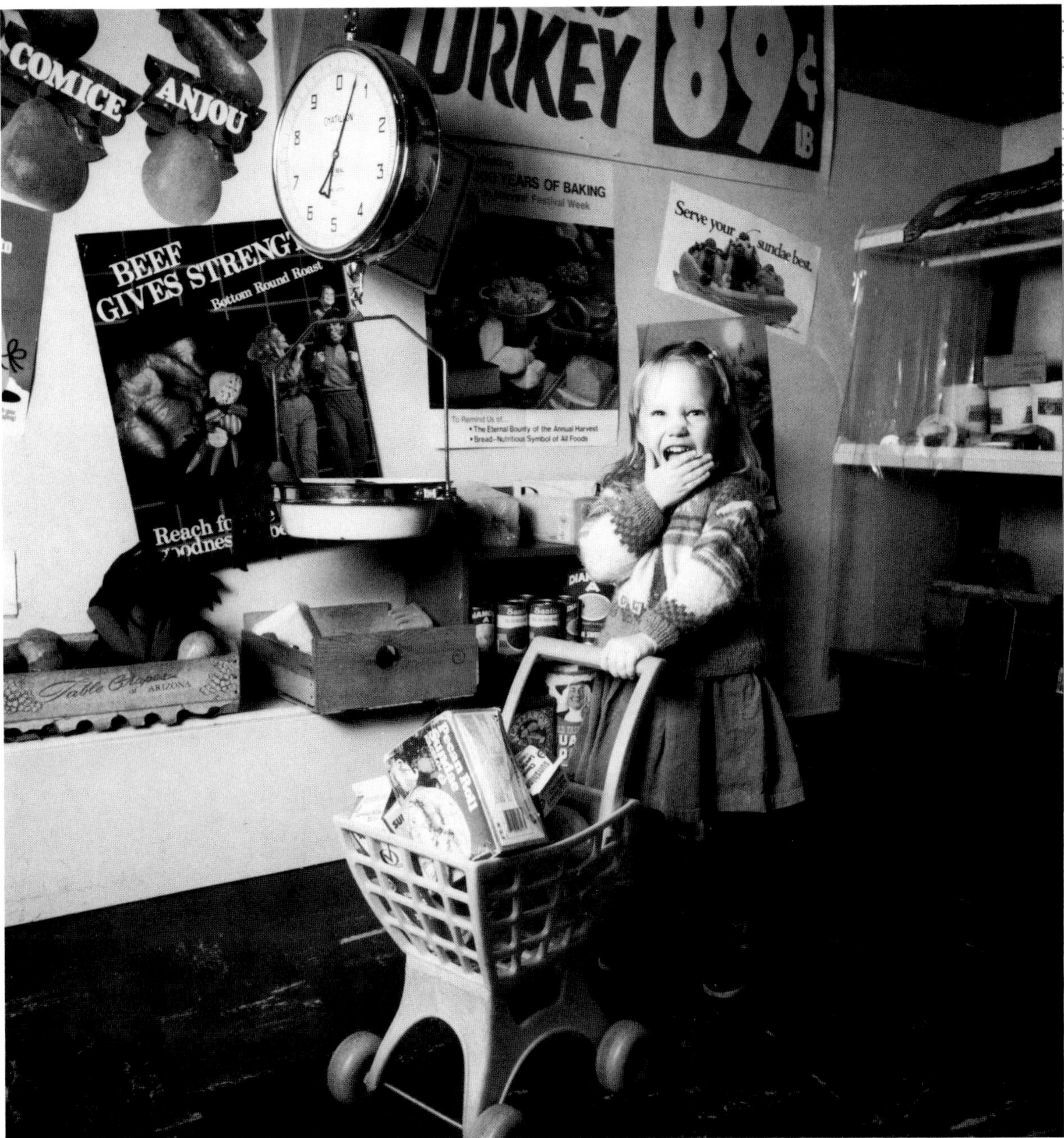

KIDS AND TEENS

Helping children grow into productive, creative adults.

Play shopper in Kidcity Grocery Store... beat on a slit drum in Zulu Village... let a baby play in a fancy playhouse in Baby Room... pet a zipperpillar... pound clay in Clayship. These play opportunities in the Children's Museum encourage age-appropriate developmental learning — helping children grow into productive, creative adults. The focus at the Children's Museum is fun — from holiday workshops to birthday parties built around Art By The Hour presentations in claybuilding and multicultural adventures. The Children's Museum currently offers over 400 classes in art and movement for children age six months to ten years of age. These classes encourage experimentation and inventive use of art materials. Memberships in the Children's Museum are available to individuals and families. Membership opens the door to special opportunities in classes, presentations, workshops and free repeat visits to developmental exhibit areas. Admission donations of two dollars per adult and one-fifty per child are requested. The Children's Museum is a facility of City Arts, a division of the Portland Bureau of Parks and Recreation.

Lair Hill
3037 SW Second Avenue
Portland 97201
248-4587

Tuesday-Thursday
9am-5pm
Friday 9am-8pm
Saturday 9am-5pm
Sunday 11am-5pm

Corbett-Johns Landing

F5

THE CHILDREN'S GYM

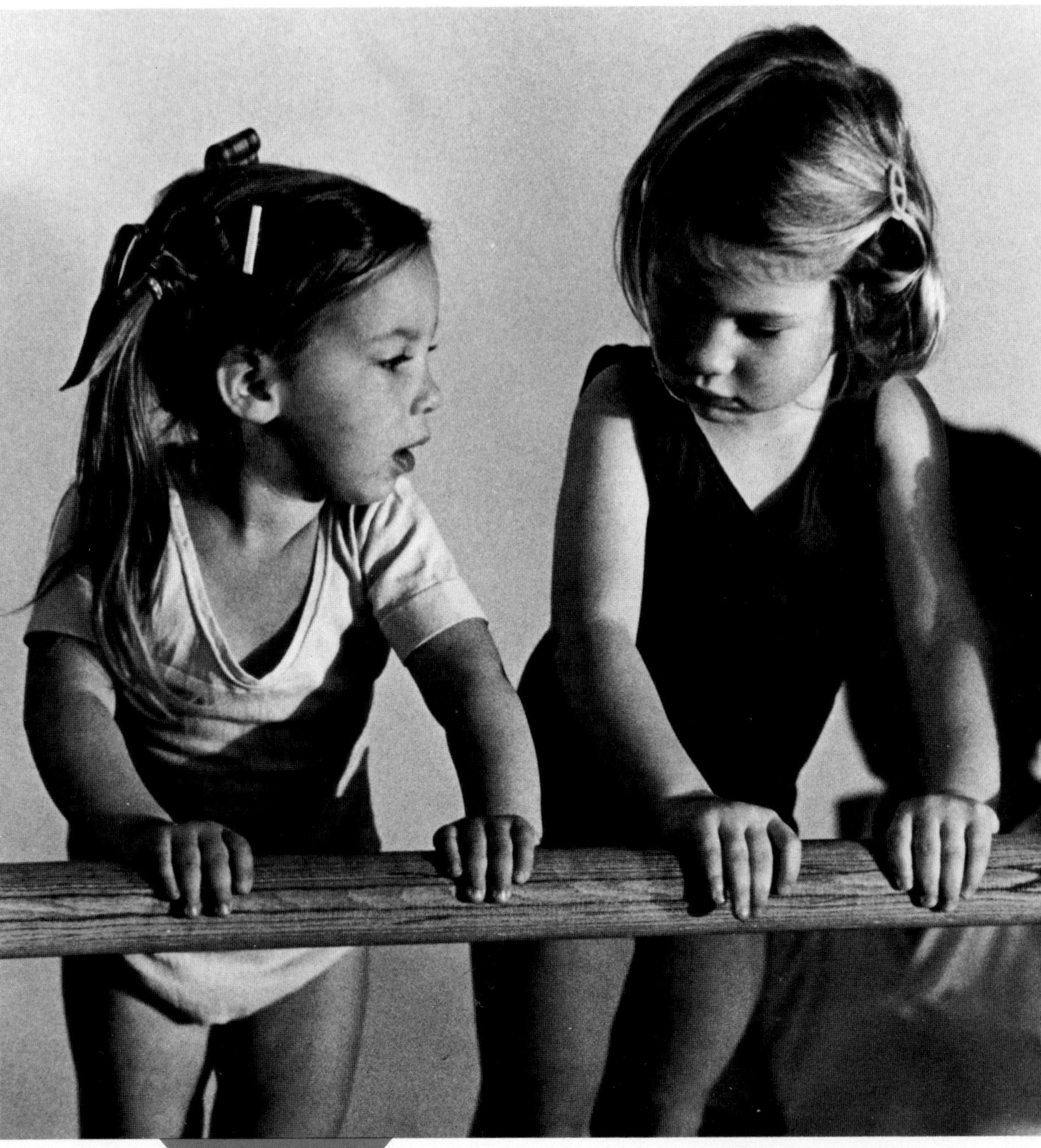

KIDS AND TEENS

Unique gymnastic training program for children.

Northeast Portland

C7

The Children's Gym offers a unique gymnastic training program for children from 18 months up to 12 years old. The environment is colorful and visually stimulating, the atmosphere is relaxed, the emphasis is on fun, the aim is to develop self esteem while training children in coordination and motor development. Expert instructors ensure that sessions meet the special needs of each child, with safety as the bottom line. In the Jumpmates class, toddlers from 18 months to 2 years, accompanied by their parents, enhance their flexibility in gentle stretching and exercises on the balance beam and trampoline. Kids from 3 to 5 years — the Tiny Tumblers — begin their classes with stretching followed by a creative musical warm up. Small groups move on to individual instruction on gymnastic apparatus. Special activities at the end of class leave children eager for their next lesson. Gym Dandies — kids 6 to 12 years old — continues motor development training and basic gymnastics. The keys to success at The Children's Gym are positive reinforcement and gentle encouragement to develop healthy minds in healthy bodies.

1825 NE 43rd
Portland 97213
249-JUMP

Monday-Saturday
9am-7:30pm

193

SPORTS AND RECREATION

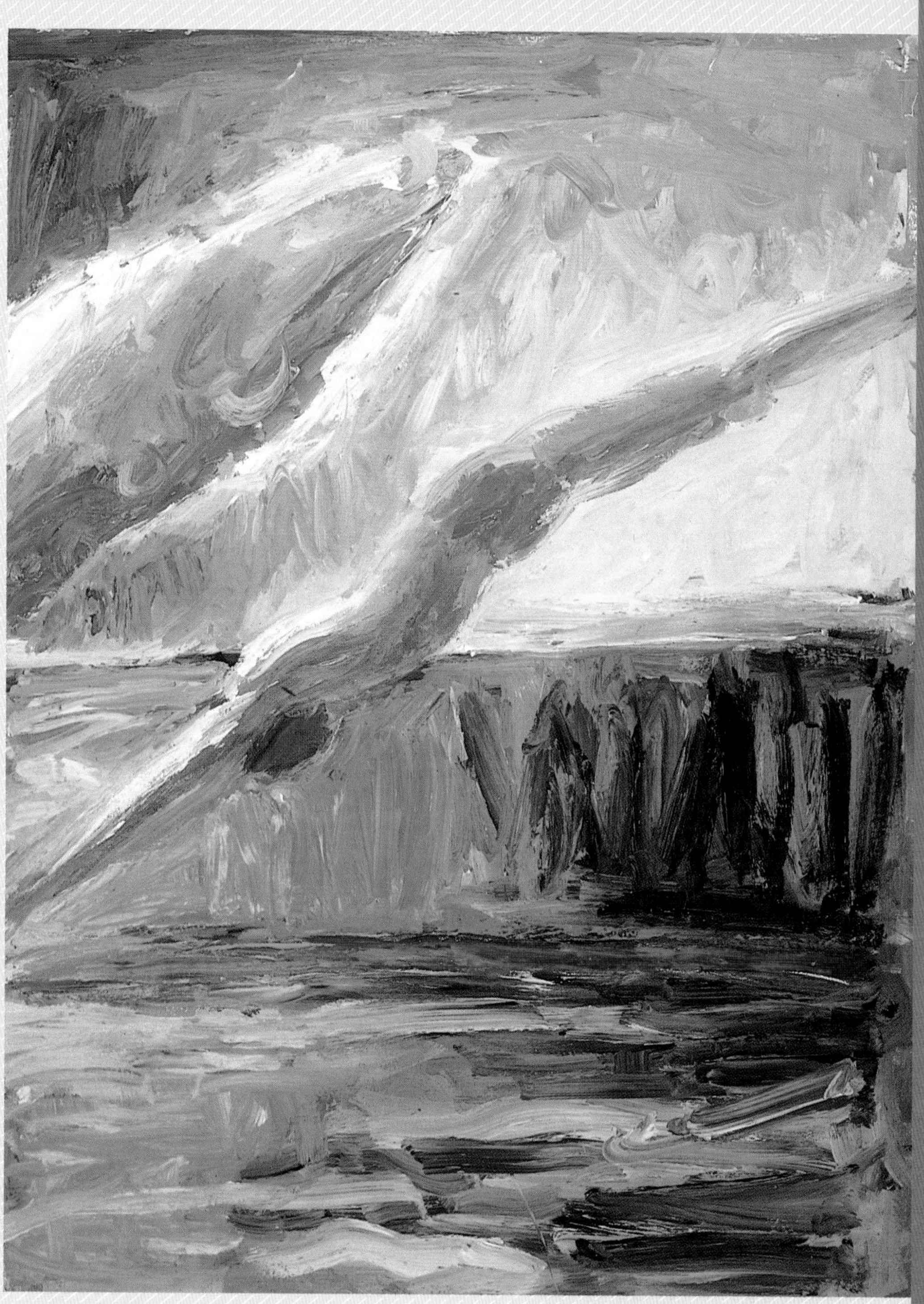

Laura Ross-Paul *Dive* ELIZABETH LEACH GALLERY

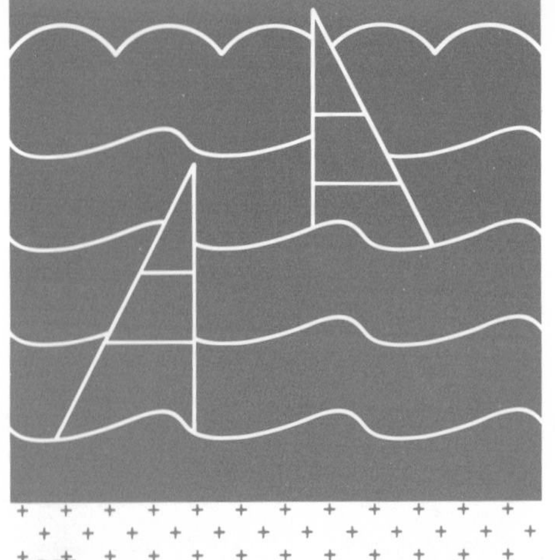

In very few places does sport come in as many forms as in Portland.

Forty-some years ago, the great Viennese philosopher, Ludwig Wittgenstein, changed the direction of modern philosophy with a simple observation: Many activities called games have nothing in common other than that they all fall under the name "game."

Had Wittgenstein written in Portland, Oregon, rather than in a small cottage in Galway, Ireland, (not a major sport center to my knowledge), he might have come by his theory of names sooner. If, like the rest of us, he'd spent a spring afternoon in the garage humping out the backpack, skis, kayak, fungo bat, football, fishing rod or ice ax, years of thinking might have crystallized in a single back-breaking afternoon. Then British analytic philosophy would be known as Oregon analytic philosophy. History ... go figure.

In very few places does "game"—more particularly "sport"—come in as many forms as in Portland. When thinking of the obvious, the basketball Trail Blazers come to mind. I have seen two Trail Blazer games in 10 years in the City of Roses. That, I think, makes me a typical Portlander. During the professional basketball season, the Trail Blazers headline the morning sports section, followed reverently statewide. And yet, let's not forget the 12,666. Should each of these ticket-holders to a Trail Blazer game give his or her ticket away ten times a year, less than a third of the population of the city would see a game at the Coliseum in any given year. So while the Trail Blazers stand at the pinnacle of Portland sport by some definitions, by others they're just another game in town. Wittgenstein came to such a realization... but, how much time he could have saved had he lived in the City of Bridges.

Back to the typical Portlander: myself. Even though I have been to few Trail Blazer games, there have been countless other times I've sat in the sun among the 222 (as a rough average) at Beaver baseball games, watching the likes of Alfredo Griffin, Tony Pena and Juan Samuel throw and hit their way to the Bigs, and el Tiante junk his way down. Little Al (Unser) won the only PIR Rose Cup that I spectated, sitting near the chicane and trying to beat the hundred degree heat with the local brew. In the cavernous Expo Center I rooted for Mike Colbert to win another shot at the title when boxing was still held at the Expo Center and Mike Colbert was still considered a contender.

Furthermore, I've backpacked enough to know that a freestanding dome tent is best when making camp in the pumice of Eastern Oregon or in snow. I've fished less than I've backpacked and, typically, never caught a steelhead. In fact, I've never caught a salmon either, unless my two seasons commercial fishing count—and in my birthplace in the East where fishing is never confused with work, they would. Rainbow and brown trout I came by easier, but then who needs fish on a high mountain lake when osprey plummet out of the trees across the way and the rising sun bathes the mountain in gold.

I've climbed the glaciers of Hood, the Sisters, and Rainier where the ice is blue in the afternoon and snowbridges over crevasses melt almost as you cross them. Sculling through the morning mist on the Willamette River behind Ross Island, I've used the excuse of tiredness to pull up my racing shell for a beaver duffing as it passed my bow, or to marvel at a big heron winging ponderously as a pterodactyl at treetop. I've huffed up Terwilliger hill during the Cascade Run Off. Fought traffic in town on my bicycle and fought the mountains outside of town. And I'm a writer. Think of what a real sportsman might accomplish in these parts.

I don't consider myself an athlete or sportsman and never have. Nor would more Portlanders consider themselves such than is average in a city this size. And yet, games and sport are so much a part of the woof and warp of Portland and the Northwest that without really thinking about it we play constantly.

Of course, if Ludwig would have played without thinking about it, he might never have written the Philosophical Investigations. So give him Galway. Call us the City of Games.
Chris Boehme

Chris Boehme *resides in Portland and can often be read in the pages of the* Oregonian's *"Northwest Magazine."*

Laura Ross-Paul *is well known throughout the Northwest for her watercolors, portraits and printmaking. "The two moments in life that interest me are the intimate and the heroic, which I seek to combine in my work." Active as an artist and teacher, Laura is represented by the Elizabeth Leach Gallery.*

The power of thousands of eyes focused on one point is intense. The oxygen saved by suspended breathing could serve a space station. The release of coiled muscle in the body of one man sparks the chain reaction. The response is deafening. What a game...can you believe it?

PORTLAND TRAIL BLAZERS

Portland Trail Blazers have sold out over four hundred consecutive games. That record is unsurpassed. Why do the fans come? Winning is the answer. But the Blazers pride themselves on community involvement; they run a class act, on and off the court. Over four hundred charities benefit each year from their association with the team. Blazer Coach Mike Schuler stresses defense and the great teamwork of his players. The Blazers' experienced and explosive lineup includes Kiki Vanderweghe, Sam Bowie, Clyde Drexler, Terry Porter and Steve Johnson.

700 NE Multnomah Street
Suite 950
Portland 97232
234-9291

Monday-Friday
8:30am-5:30pm

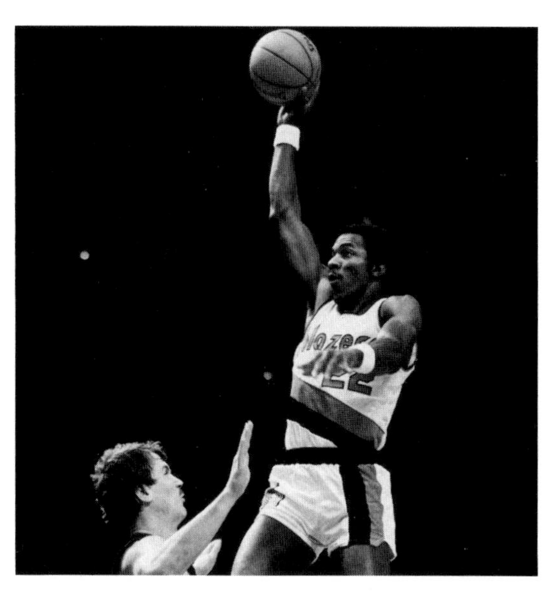

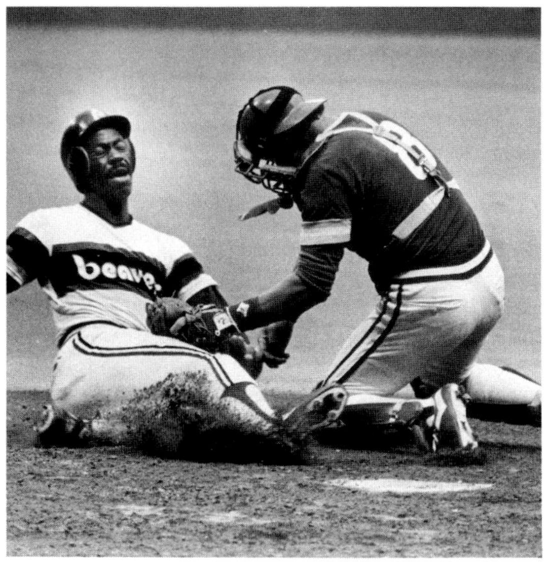

PORTLAND BEAVER BASEBALL

Mailing Address:
P.O. Box 1659
Portland 97207
2-BEAVER

Civic Stadium:
1844 SW Morrison Street
Portland 97208

The Beavers — top AAA minor-league affiliate of the Minnesota Twins and holder of the 1983 Pacific Coast League Pennant — celebrated their 80th anniversary in 1987. In the past, Portland fans have seen top-flight talent such as Tony Pena, Rick Rhoden and Lou Pinnella turn major league. Keep an eye on today's players: you might see tomorrow's stars! The 72-date home season features a yearly exhibition game with the Twins. Post game concerts featuring local and national acts will convince you this is the best family entertainment buy around.

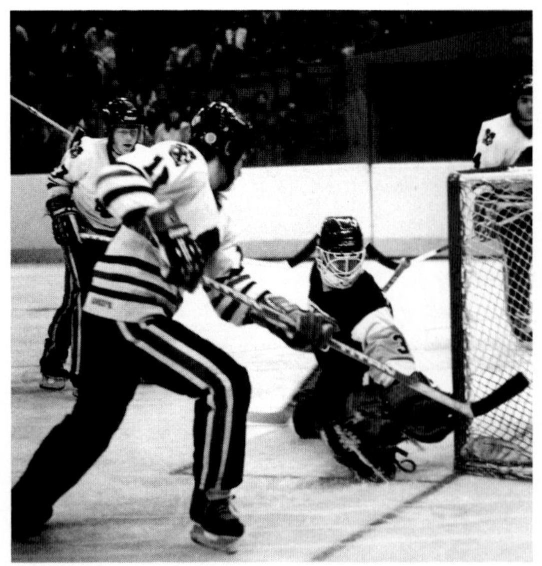

PORTLAND WINTER HAWKS

The Portland Winter Hawks brought its special brand of high speed, boardcrunching action to the United States in the fall of 1976. They have continued a tradition of excellence in hockey with 26 former players represented in the National Hockey League in the 1985/86 season. This is the highest number of professional hockey players ever produced by any amateur hockey team in the world. In 1986 the Winter Hawks became the only team to host the Memorial Cup Tournament twice. These young men have brought honor to Portland.

Portland Memorial Coliseum
1401 North Wheeler
Portland 97227
238-6366

Call for game times

PORTLAND MEADOWS

Portland Meadows, with its amazing sand track, provides the excitement of pari mutuel horse racing. Here, the Northwest's finest thoroughbreds and quarter horses compete for $2,000,000 in purse money in a variety of stake events. Always comfortable in the beautiful glass-enclosed facilities, which include the Turf Club, Clubhouse and grandstand-terrace area, spectators wager on major national races held throughout the U.S. Quality food and beverages are available from one of the country's most respected concessionaires.

1001 North Schmeer Road
Delta Park Exit,
Immediately off I-5
Portland 97217
285-9144

Season:
October-April
Fridays 7pm
Saturdays and Sundays
1:30pm

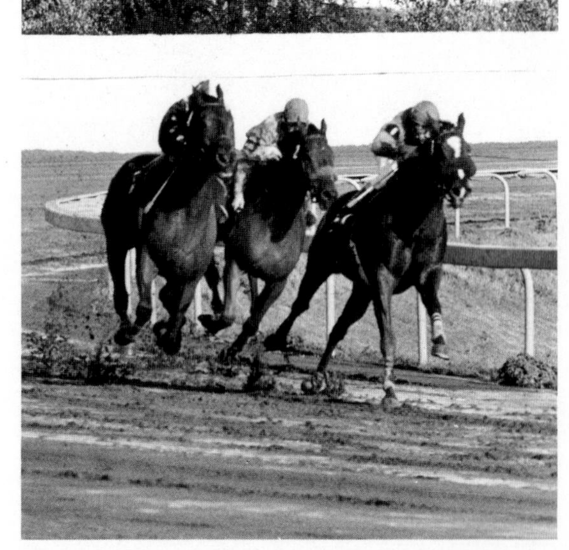

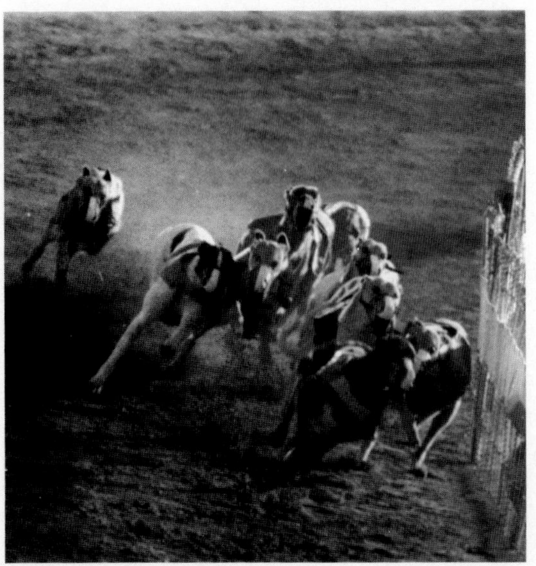

MULTNOMAH KENNEL CLUB

Thrill to greyhound racing at its finest and experience the excitement of pari mutuel wagering during the Multnomah Kennel Club racing season. You can get involved in the action close to the track with full concession services, or watch from free bleacher seats or reserved second floor deluxe box seats on the finish line. Comfortable table seating is also available on the third floor Fairview Terrace or in the fine dining facilities of the Club Skyview on the fourth floor. Acres of free and convenient reserved parking are available to all patrons.

Greyhound Race Track
P.O. Box 9
Fairview 97024
667-7700

Tuesday-Saturday
7:30pm Post Time
Saturday Matinee 1pm
May-September

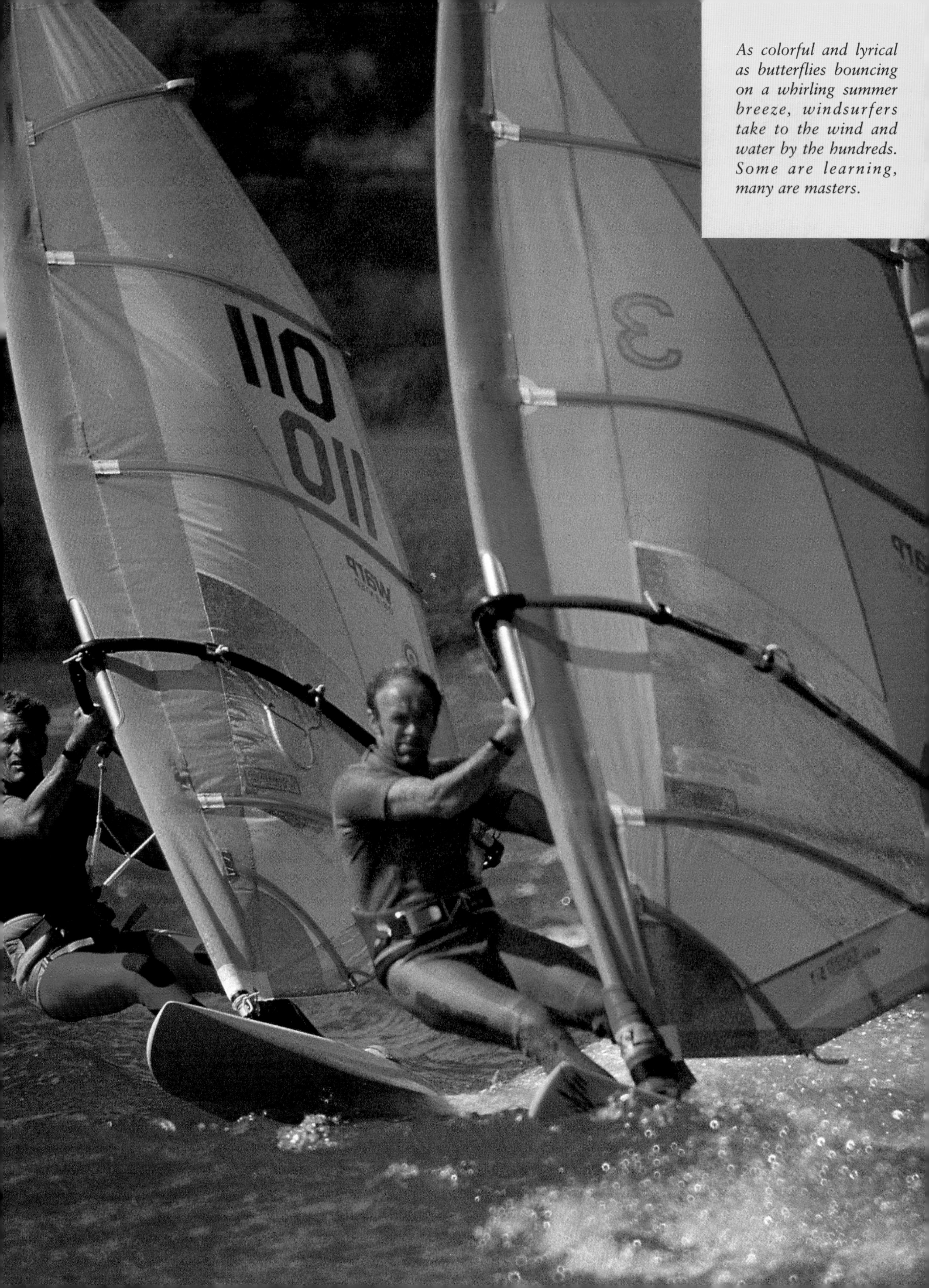

As colorful and lyrical as butterflies bouncing on a whirling summer breeze, windsurfers take to the wind and water by the hundreds. Some are learning, many are masters.

OREGON MOUNTAIN COMMUNITY

Outdoor equipment and clothing that performs.

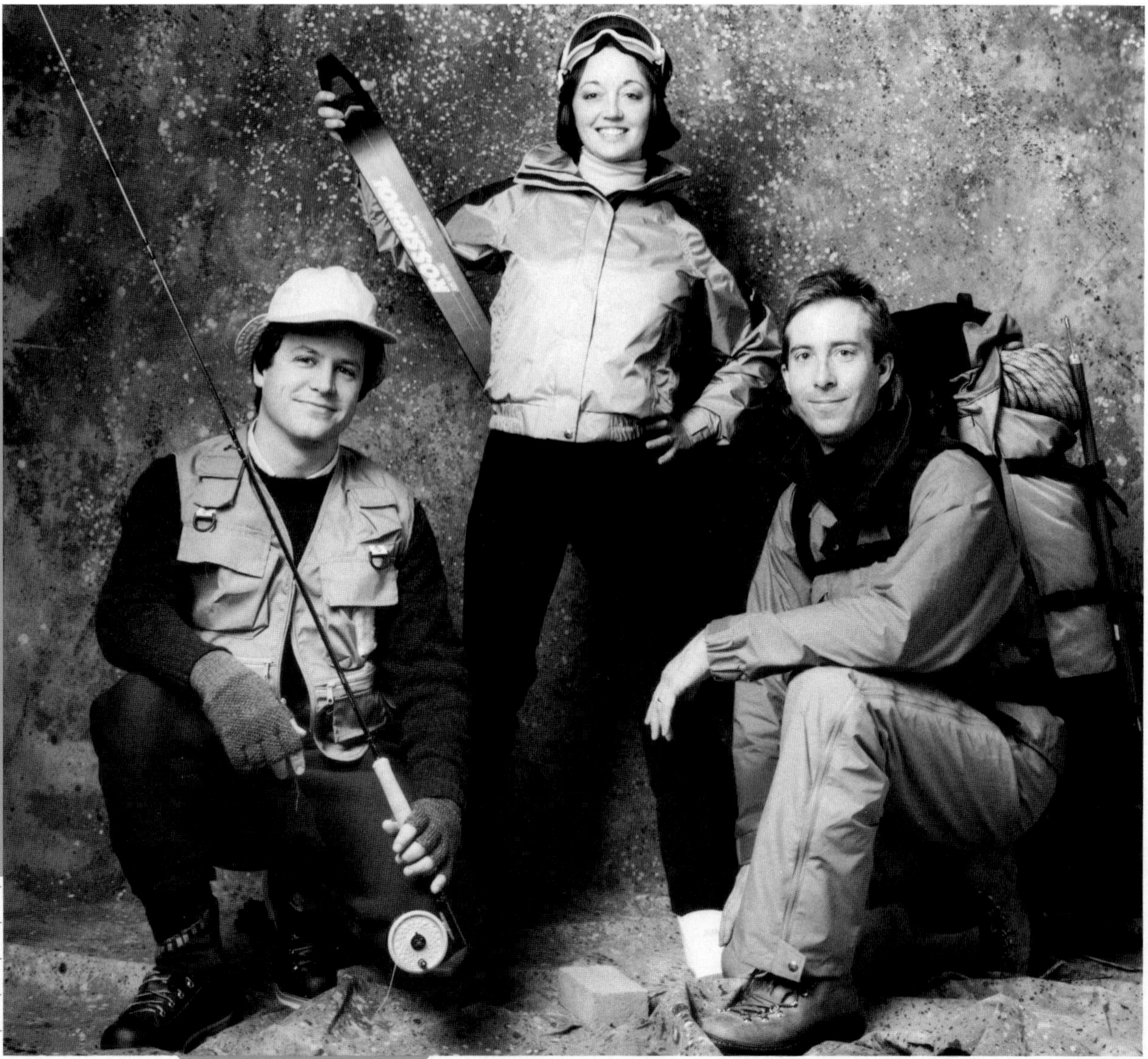

Whether you're bound for the Himalayas, or the city's rain-soaked streets, Oregon Mountain Community has the equipment for the occasion. Long a popular supplier for hikers, climbers, travelers and cross-country skiers, OMC has recently added high quality fly fishing, downhill skiing, and cycling goods to their inventory. And instruction in fly tying and casting are offered through OMC year round from an experienced instructor. There's clothing from The North Face, Patagonia, Marmot, Solstice, Woolrich and Skyr; back country equipment from Chouinard, Gregory, Lowe, Wild Things and Jansport; ski equipment from Rossignol, Fisher, Merrell, Lange, Salomon and Raichle; and fly fishing gear from Orvis, Winston, Simms and Scott. Since 1971, Oregon Mountain Community has helped Portlanders select outdoor equipment that performs well in the face of adversity. Visa. MasterCard.

Old Town

D25

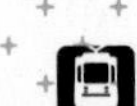

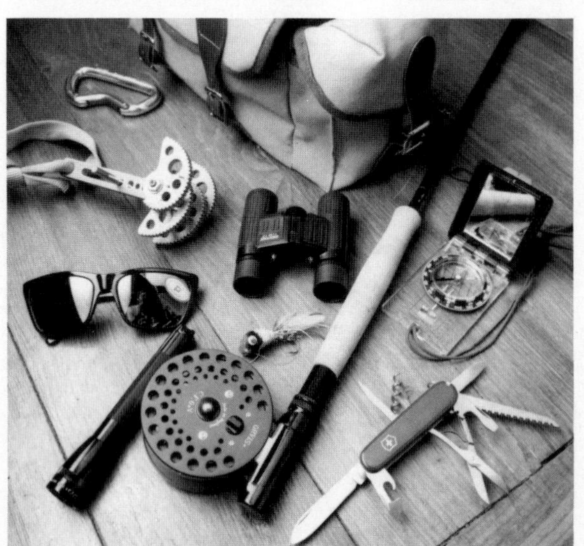

60 NW Davis Street
Portland 97209
227-1038

Monday-Thursday
10am-6:30pm
Friday 10am-7pm
Saturday 10am-6pm
Sunday noon-5pm

TAILWIND OUTFITTERS

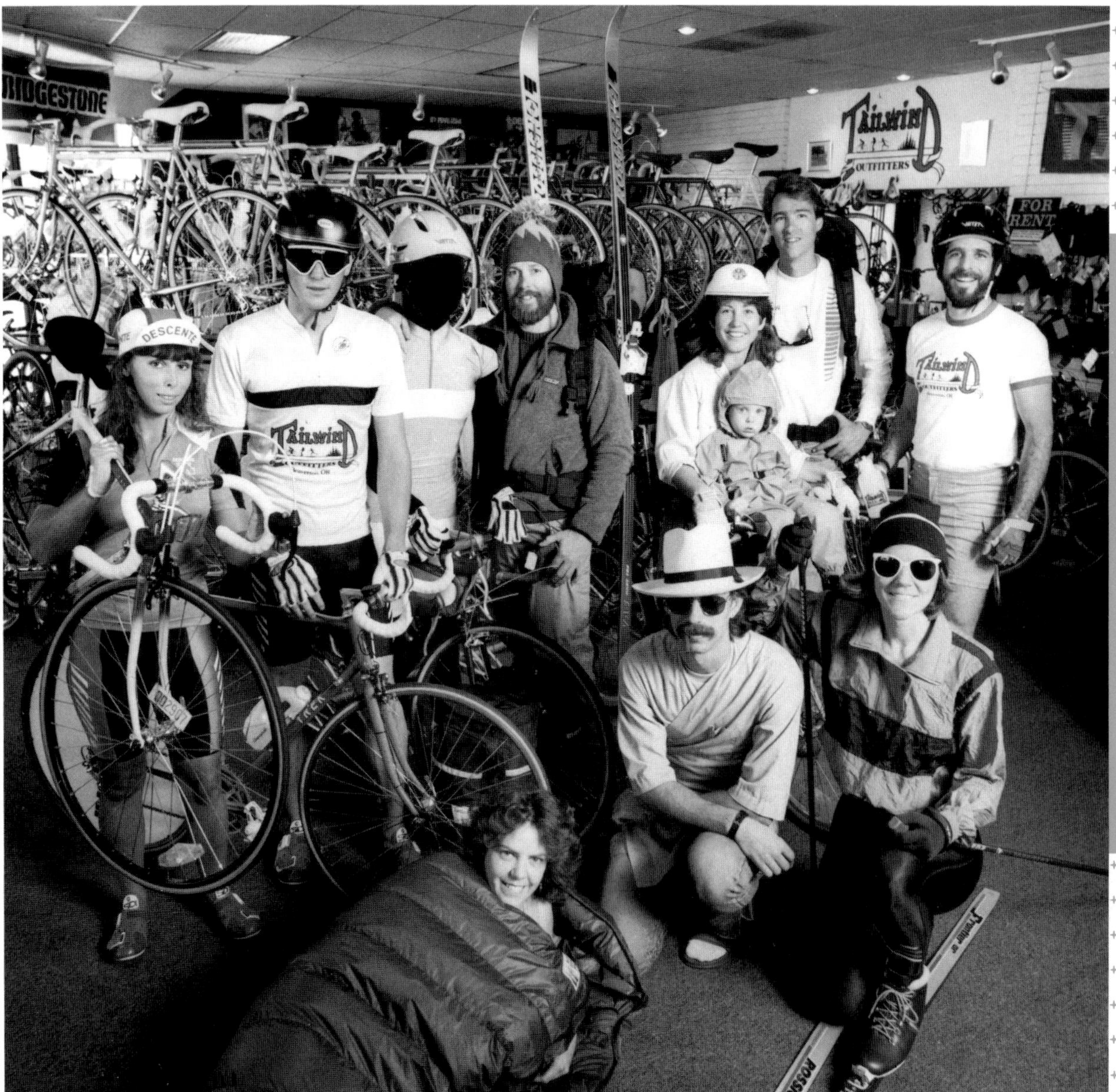

SPORTS AND REC

Home of Dr. Derailleur and Sally Sidecut, XcD.

For bicyclists, cross-country skiers and backpackers, life without Tailwind Outfitters would be as incomplete as a ten speed without pedals, skis without tips and a camp stove without fuel. Professionals and novices alike look for Tailwind (and tailwinds, for that matter) when taking to the outdoors, whether it's for a ride around the block or a cross-continent expedition. At the core of Tailwind's success is a sales staff of experts who routinely field test the equipment they sell. And they'll never react as if you had just rode up on Pee-Wee Herman's bike when you ask a basic question. Tailwind offers bike tours and classes, ski lessons, service for everything they sell, clothing and equipment designed for men, women and children, and rental equipment of the same uncompromising quality as what they sell, so you won't have to worry about breaking down in the outback. You'll find bicycles from Trek, Bridgestone, Specialized, Terry, Ciocc, and Vitus; cross-country skis from Rossignol, Karhu, Trak and Epoke; Gregory and Mountainsmith backpacks; specialty clothing from Patagonia, Marmot and Descente; and tents, bags and accessories from Vuarnet, The North Face and Sierra Designs. Tailwind is an active supporter of a host of non-profit outdoor clubs, and is also the home of Dr. Derailleur, tending to the needs of all those on the chain gang. Visa. MasterCard. American Express. Carte Blanche. Tailwind Outfitters Charge.

Canyon Road at 117th Avenue
Beaverton 97005
641-2580

Moving to a new location, Fall 1987.

Monday-Tuesday 11am-8pm
Thursday-Friday 11am-8pm
Saturday 10am-6pm
Sunday noon-5pm
Closed Wednesday

Beaverton
E2

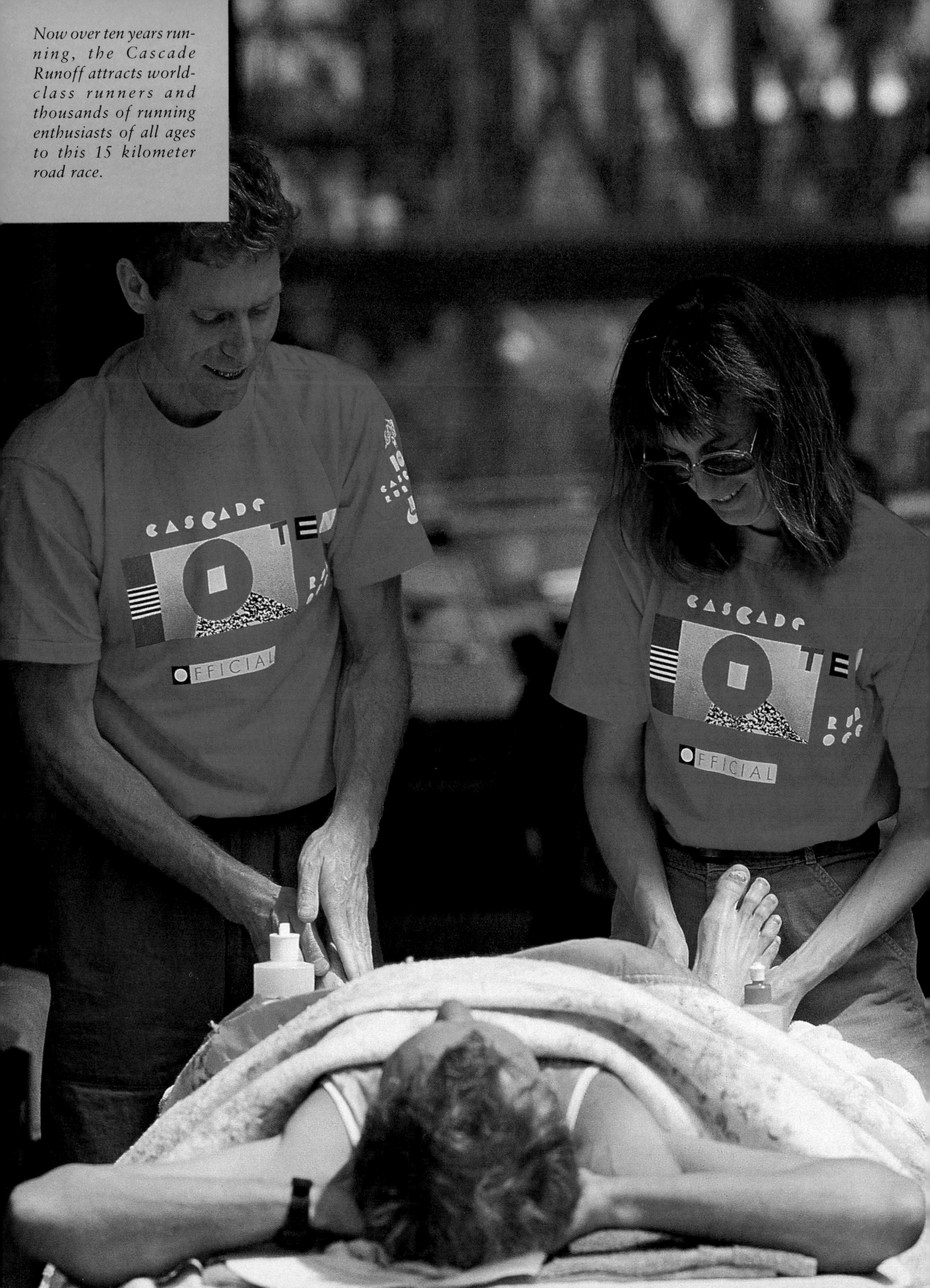

Now over ten years running, the Cascade Runoff attracts world-class runners and thousands of running enthusiasts of all ages to this 15 kilometer road race.

PHIDIPPIDES FITNESS CENTER

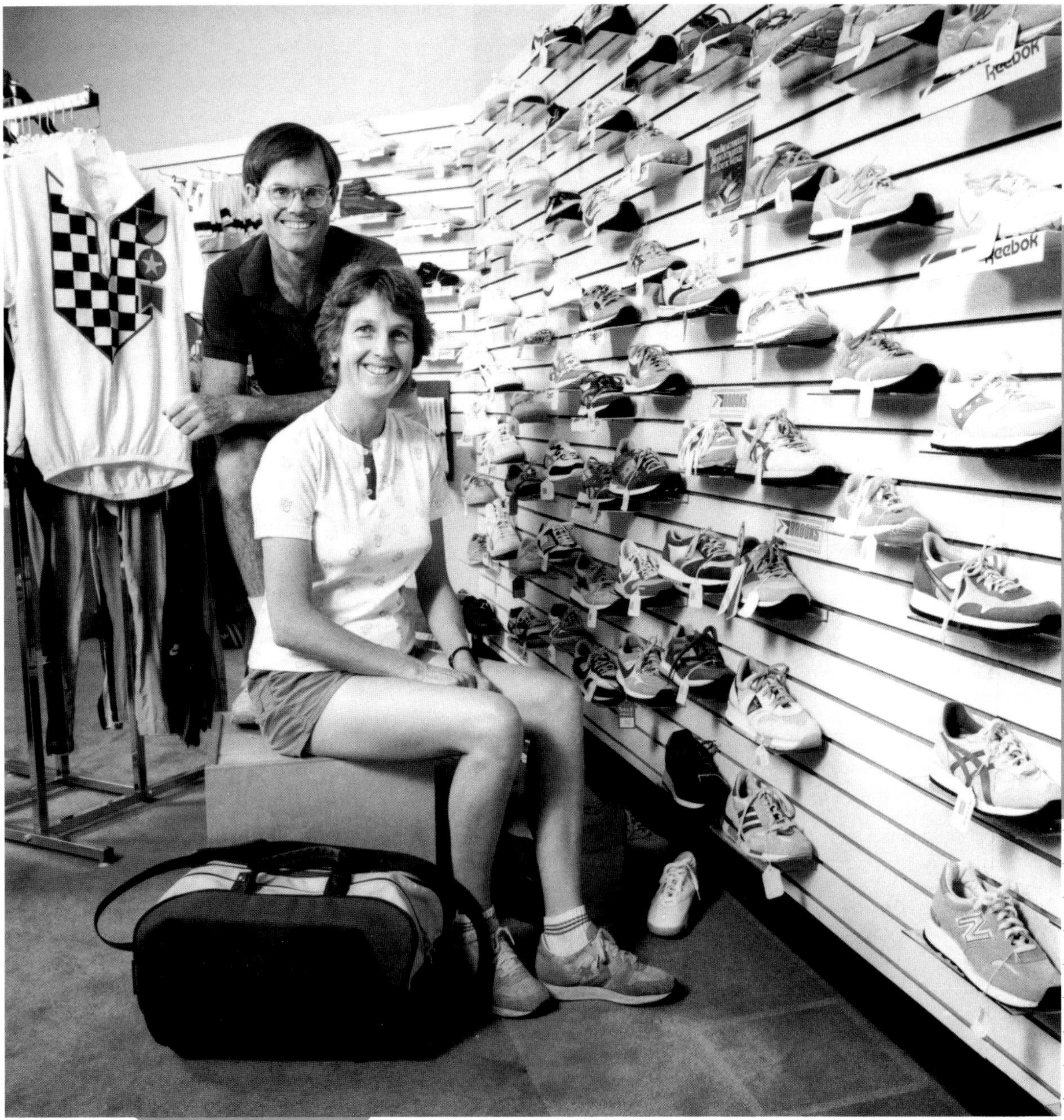

SPORTS AND REC

Running, aerobic, walking and court shoe specialists.

In 490 BC, the Greek messenger Phidippides was chosen to carry the news of Greek victory in battle about 25 miles, to Athens. It is from this legendary run that both the original marathon distance and the term "marathon" come, and this nationwide store, Phidippides Fitness Center, has chosen to adopt the runners name. Peter and Hilary Gilmore, former Bostonians and owners of the local Phidippides, believe that every person who visits their store should be properly educated in the selection of running, aerobic, walking, and court shoes and clothing, in training and racing techniques, and in aerobic conditioning. They offer a wide variety of shoes and clothing designed to fit well, look good and perform vigorously. You can even "road test" your shoes before you buy them. The staff at Phidippides are trained runners and fitness experts who understand your aches and pains, excitement and frustration, and want to help you achieve your fitness goals. They publish a bi-monthly newsletter, The Oracle, free to their customers which includes a road race schedule, fitness articles, and what's on sale in the store. You can join a Phidippides group for a fitness vacation to Vail, Tahoe, or Whistler every summer. Remember, at the end of his exhausting run, Phidippides said "Rejoice, we conquer." Visit Phidippides, and learn how you can, too. Visa. MasterCard.

333 South State Street
Lake Oswego 97034
635-3577

Monday-Friday
10am-7pm
Saturday 10am-5pm
Sunday noon-5pm

Lake Oswego/ Lake Grove

H6

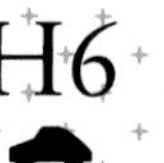

EBB & FLOW KAYAK CENTER

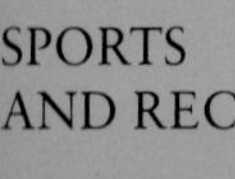

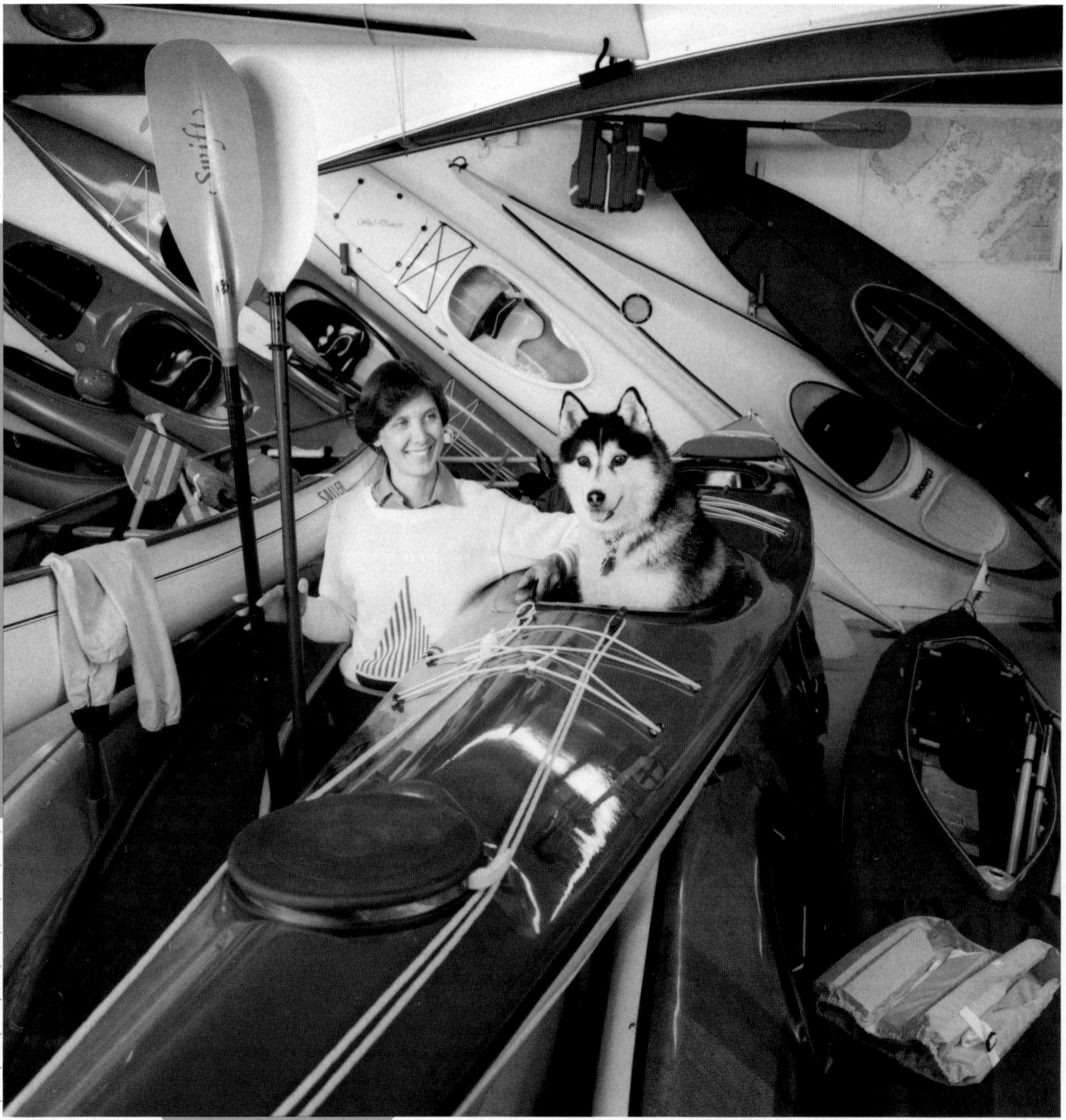

SPORTS AND REC

Kayaks, canoes for recreation, adventure, exploration.

Corbett-Johns Landing

F6

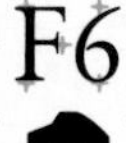

Whether you're paddling around Ross Island for the first time, doing the Inland Passage to Alaska or planning an Arctic expedition, Ebb & Flow Kayak Center can provide almost everything except the water. Paddling equipment is the year-round, exclusive focus of Ebb & Flow, the first kayak and canoe store of its type in the Portland area. The selection, quality and proven reputation of Ebb & Flow's gear is second to none, bringing the highest measure of safety and enjoyment to your efforts. Store personnel are expert practitioners who can provide instruction, discuss equipment selection and use, plus provide information on Northwest trips. After a warm welcome from Tashka (Siberian Husky) you'll be able to check out sea kayaks; folding kayaks from Klepper, Nautiraid and Feathercraft; whitewater kayaks from Perception and Prijon; Sawyer and Clipper canoes; paddle clothing, wet and dry suits, paddles, books, car racks and video tapes. A new boat or two will be displayed on the wall, books will reside in the fully stocked library, and club newsletters, charts and guide books will give you a canoe-full of ideas to plan your next outing. And when the urge overcomes you, Ebb & Flow's location at the entrance to Willamette Park makes it easy to take to the water. Visa. MasterCard.

0604 SW Nebraska Street
Portland 97201
245-1756

Tuesday-Friday
11:30am-6pm
Saturday 9:30am-5pm
Sunday noon-5pm
(Summer)

HOWELL'S UPTOWN SPORTS CENTER

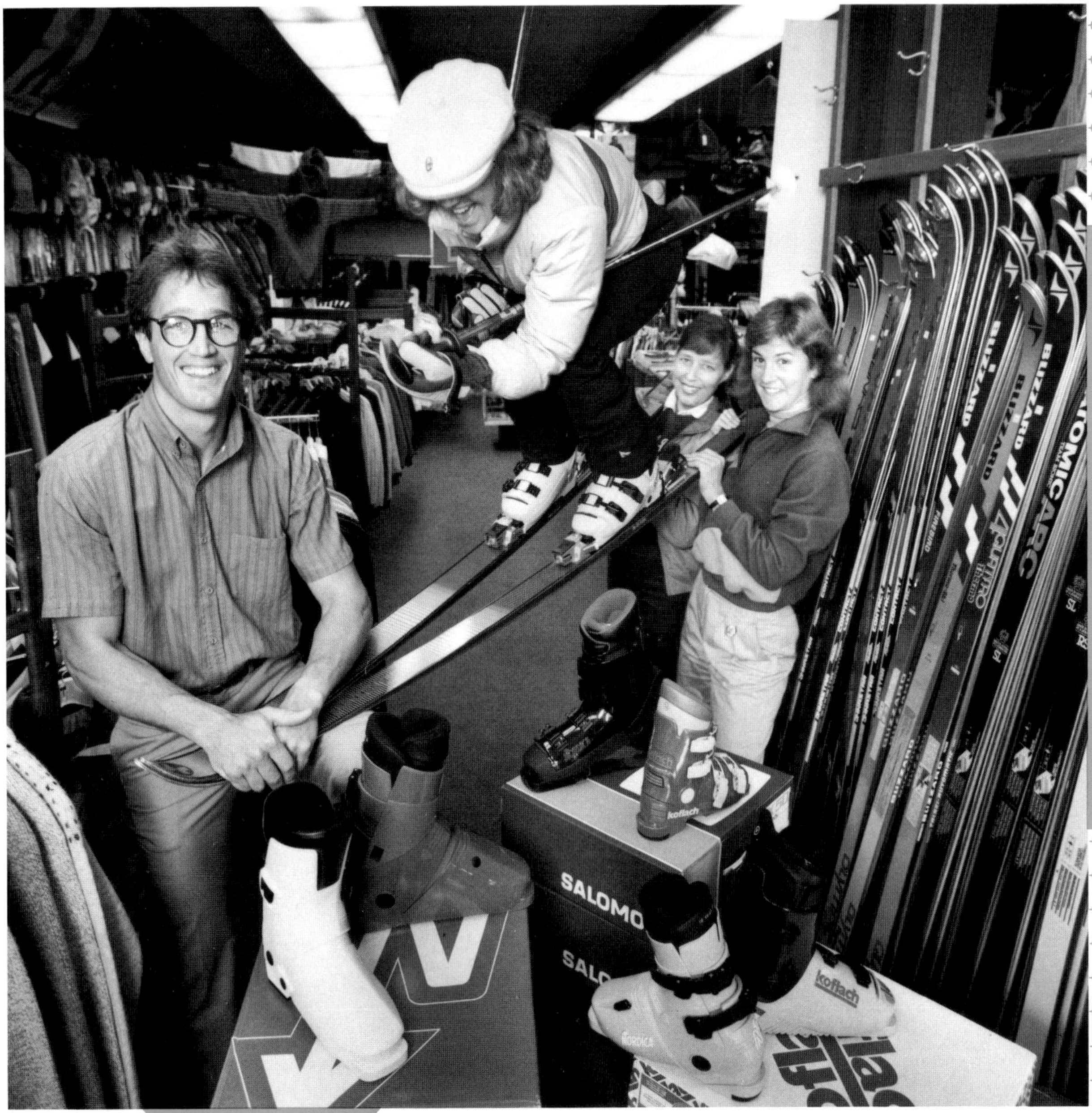

Winter and summer sport outfitters.

Each year, as Portlanders enjoy the last bit of Indian summer, the people at Howell's Uptown Sports Center are bundling up customers for the first signs of winter. Whether you're a hot-dogger or city stroller, Howell's can outfit you in the latest cold-weather clothing: indispensable Goretex, ski outfits from North Face, Patagonia's functional line, and quality styles from CB Sports. And those are but a few of the many ways Howell's can keep you dry and comfortable. If you want to add the latest in mountaintop fun to your list of wintertime toys, check out their selection of mono skis, an exciting option for slicing your way down the slope on one slat! Howell's can also help you get to all your sporting events on time with their large selection of sport watches from Town and Country and Innovative Time Company. When the temperatures turn milder, the shop sheds its wintry look and dons the latest in surf, turf, and tennis wear. And the selection is sensational: summer clothing from Raisen, Patagonia, and Maui and Sons; and a fine selection of Prince racquets. Howell's will string your racquet so you're always ready for the courts, and Vuarnet and Lacroix sunglasses are available even when the sun doesn't shine. Howell's Uptown Sports Center has supplied fun and functional attire to Portlanders for more than two decades, and you're certain to find both first quality gear and a receptive ear for every question. Visa. MasterCard. Discover.

Uptown Shopping Center
21 NW 23rd Place
Portland 97210
227-7910

Monday-Friday
9:30am-6pm
Saturday 9:30am-5pm

Northwest
Portland
J17

CICLO SPORT SHOP

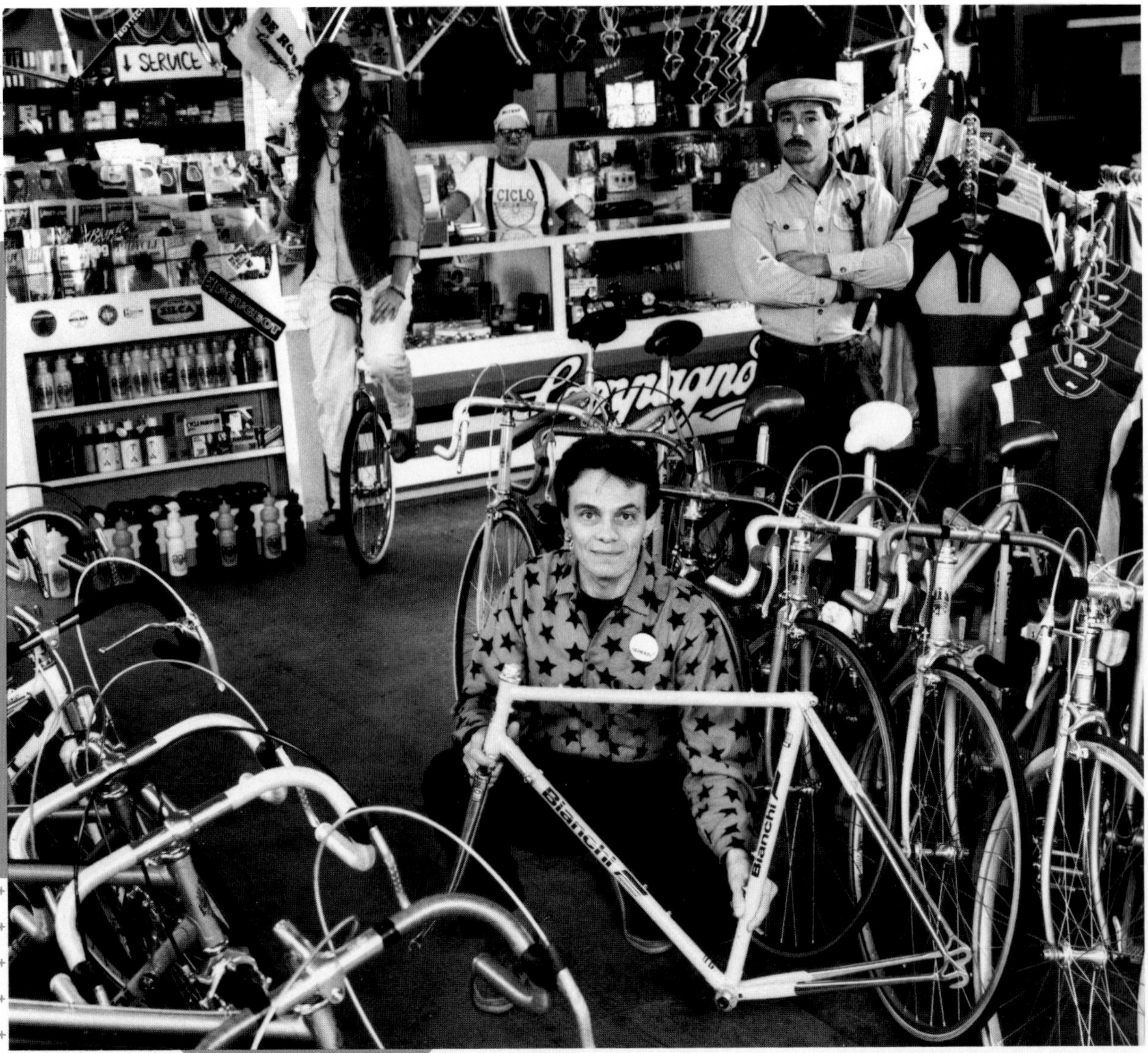

SPORTS AND REC

Bike cycling fun unlimited.

Old Town
D25

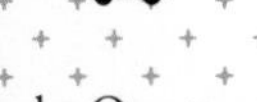

Lake Oswego/
Lake Grove
H6

In Italian, ciclo (say it chee-clo) means bicycle; in Old Town, Ciclo Sport Shop translates into "gateway to unlimited cycling fun." The shop specializes in European performance and racing-style bicycles, with an emphasis on mid and upper end state-of- art designs that leave nothing to chance. The store features Bianchi bicycles, from the century-old Italian firm known for its artistry, uncompromising quality and a unique color: celeste, a sort of aqua with a touch more green. Also to be found are France's Peugeots and Japan's Miyatas. Diamond Back, Tom Ritchie and Fat Chance supply Ciclo's mountain, or all-terrain bicycles. Ciclo also serves as the exclusive Portland representative for custom frames designed and assembled by Albert Eisentraut, the dean of American frame building. Starting off need not be expensive: there are also basic, practical bikes competitively priced, guaranteeing that the shop has just what you need for track, trail or street. Once Ciclo puts you on wheels (or repairs just about anything with two wheels and pedals), it supplies a broad range of clothing and accessories to keep you there, regardless of the weather. Everyone — racer, triathlete, tourist and commuter — finds something here. The store's selection of clothing, touring equipment and cleated bicycle shoes may be the best in the city; in winter Ciclo features long- sleeve jerseys, tights, arm and leg warmers, gloves, shoe booties and rain gear. When you'd rather not ride that storm out, Ciclo moves you indoors with wind trainers and rollers to keep muscles in tune. Visa. MasterCard. American Express.

35 NW Third Avenue
Portland 97209
227-3535

Monday-Friday
10am-6pm
Saturday 10am-5pm
Sunday noon-5pm

Village Shopping Center
91 S. State Street
Lake Oswego 97034
636-3521

Monday 10am-6pm
Tuesday-Friday
10am-7pm
Saturday 10am-5pm
Sunday noon-5pm

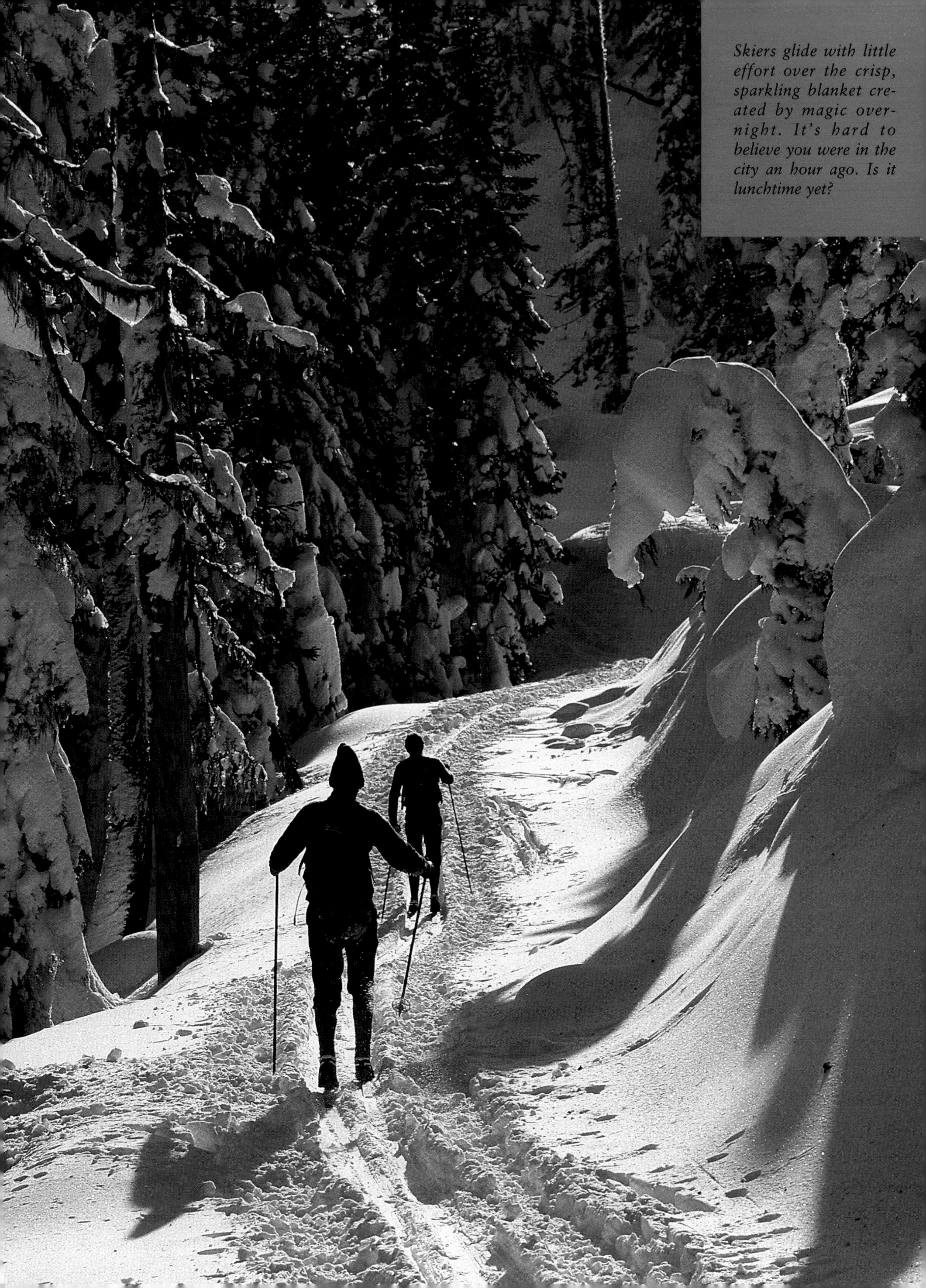

Skiers glide with little effort over the crisp, sparkling blanket created by magic overnight. It's hard to believe you were in the city an hour ago. Is it lunchtime yet?

MT. PARK PRO SHOP

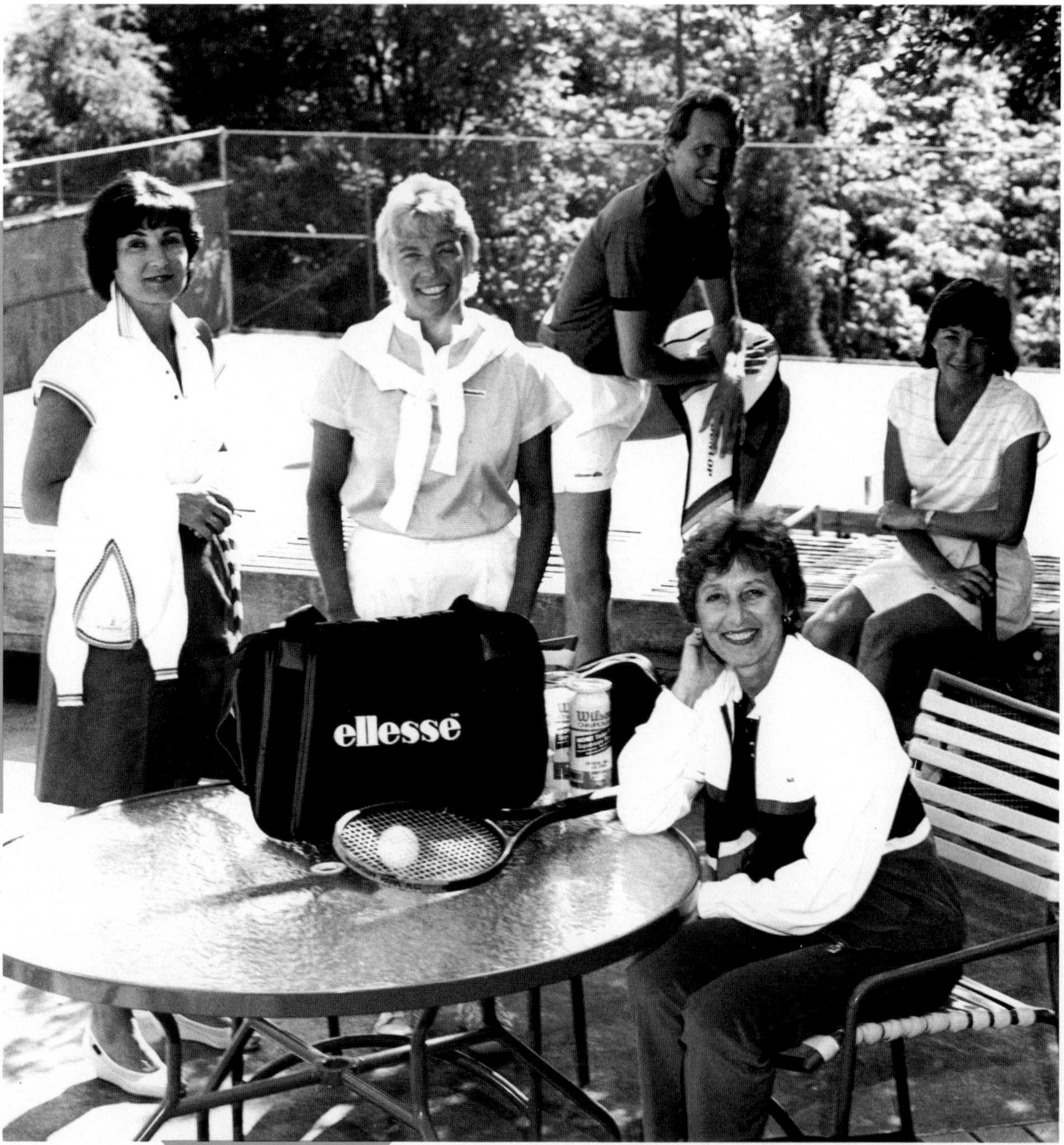

The little tennis shop with the big inventory.

Lake Oswego/ Lake Grove

H4

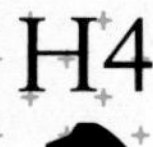

Every body is doing it! Getting fit, that is. If swimming, running, aerobics, tennis and racquet sports are your thing, Mt. Park Pro Shop is your place. Once a small convenience store for the Mt. Park Racquet Club, the shop now boasts an inventory of athletic apparel large enough for one California visitor to exclaim, "If you can't find what you want here, it doesn't exist!" Serious athletes and weekend sports fans alike will be appropriately attired by Fila, Ellesse, Le Coq, Sportif, Head, Ultra Sport and other famous suppliers of fine sportswear. Tennis and racquet sport enthusiasts in particular will be impressed by Mt. Park's inventory of apparel. If you are just starting out and aren't sure what you need, Mt. Park's professional staff will put you on the right track — they know and use the shop's products. Sporty fashion is the look of the 80's for homemakers, students, executives, hardcore athletes, senior citizens — everybody. Let Mt. Park Pro Shop dress your body for an active lifestyle. Visa. MasterCard.

3 SW Botticelli
Lake Oswego 97035
635-3776

Monday-Friday
9am-8pm
Saturday 9am-5:30pm
Sunday 11am-5:30pm

NIKE DOWNTOWN

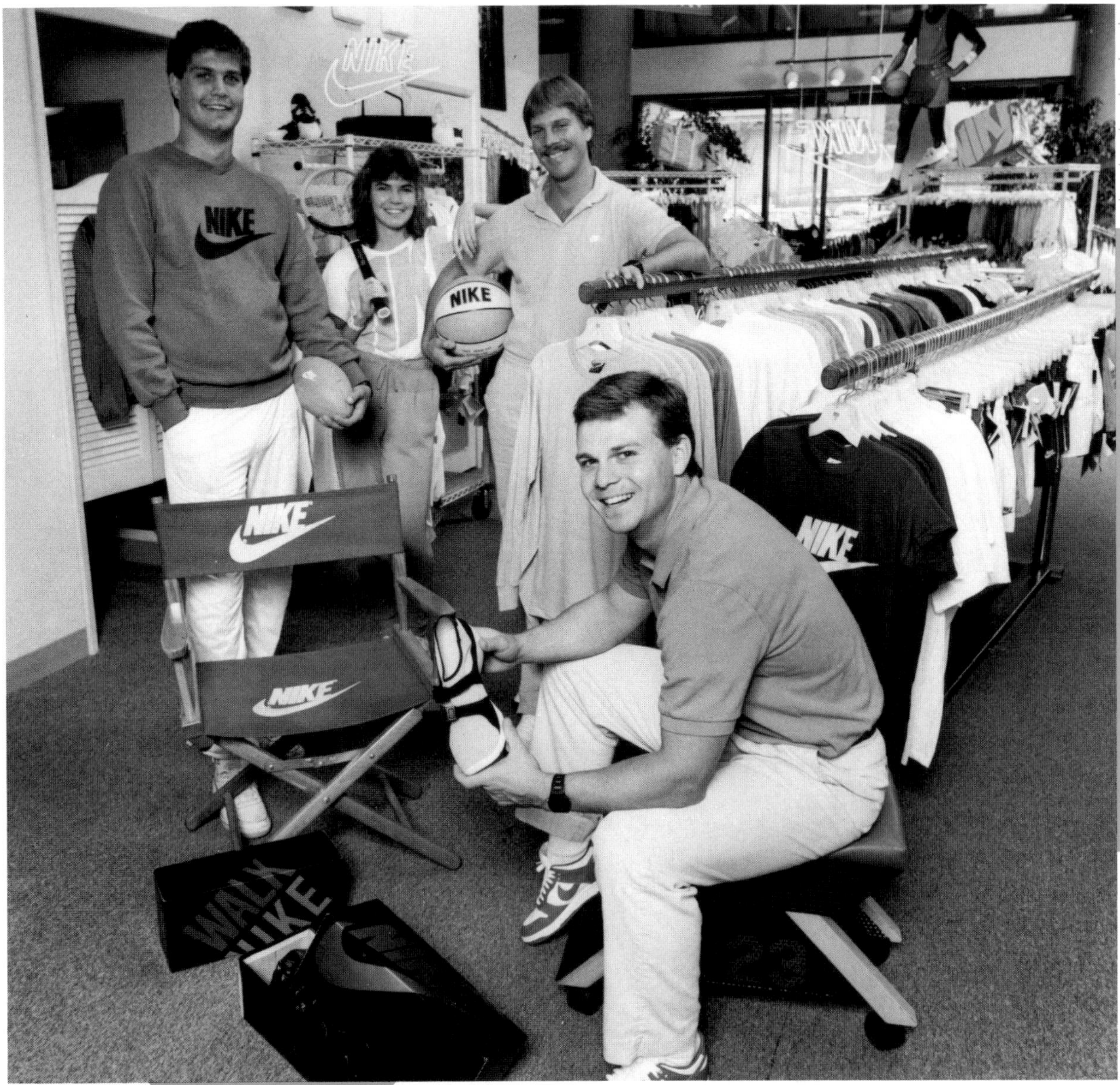

SPORTS AND REC

Authentic Nike athletic shoes and apparel.

For years, Portlanders have been partial to Nike. For runners and non-runners alike, the name is synonymous with casual and competitive footwear and athletic apparel. This enduring kinship may be due, in part, to Portland's pride in a firm whose international headquarters are here; it certainly is most significantly due to Nike's impeccable reputation the world over. But one of the special benefits of the firm's local presence is Nike Downtown, described best by the company slogan: "The Only Nike Only Store." Because it's 100 percent unadulterated Nike, the store can provide service, expertise and selection matched only by the firm's other retail outlets. The emphasis, as it always has been, is on fitness. Men's and women's running shoes and apparel are here in force, and the store is city headquarters for enthusiasts bent on registering for all major races, from the Cascade Runoff to the Portland Marathon and a host of other events. Shoes and apparel for aerobics, basketball, tennis, walking, golf and triathlon competition help round out the selection. If there's one Portland store that can claim to cater to body and sole, it's Nike Downtown. Visa. MasterCard. American Express. Discover.

341 SW Morrison Street
Portland 97204
241-2710

Monday-Saturday
10am-6pm

Factory Outlet
Union Square
3044 NE Union Avenue
Portland 97212
281-5901

Monday-Saturday
10am-6pm

99 West Tenth
Suite 104
Eugene 97401
342-5155

Downtown
F24

Northeast Portland
C6

MASTER CRAFT OF OREGON

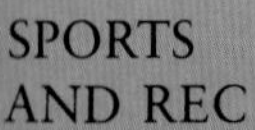

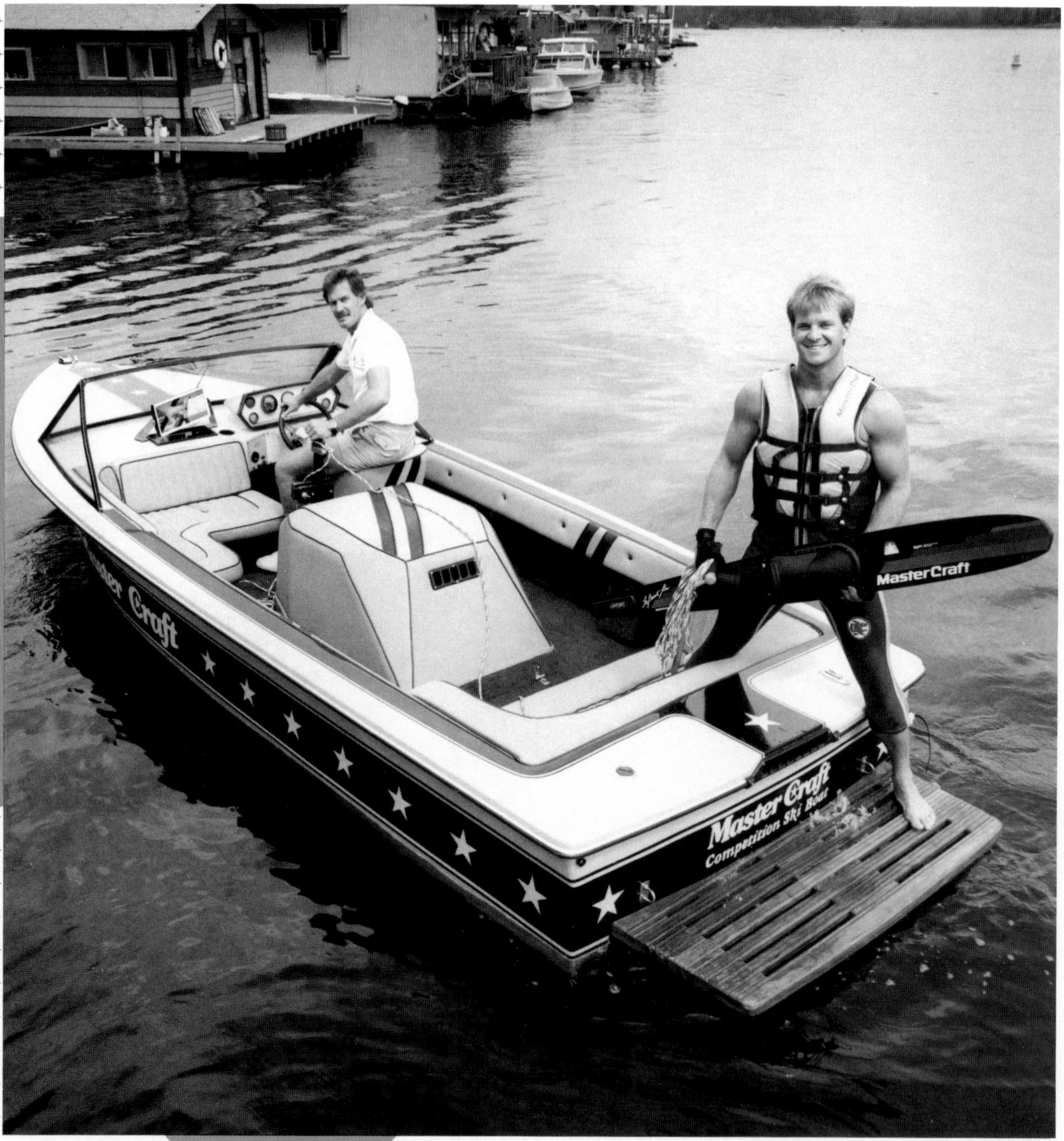

SPORTS
AND REC

Master Craft boats, skis, accessories.

Corbett-Johns Landing
F6

When you're out there on the lake or river, sliding over the water like a knife across frosting, it pays to have equipment you can trust. Serious water skiers turn to Master Craft, manufacturers of a line of boats that excels where others flounder. In Portland, there's a grand total of one outlet for Master Craft boats, a business that specializes in competition and family-oriented craft and deals only with water skiing equipment: Master Craft of Oregon. Specialization and expertise go a long way toward top performance, and Master Craft can meet the challenge. Master Craft caters to the beginner and expert alike with boats, skis and accessories (vests, ropes, gloves, hats); Dryflex Dry Suits that allow you to ski in the winter and keep the chill away; Eagle Wetsuits in barefoot, jump and shorty versions; and Vuarnet sunglasses, renowned for banishing the squints with technology and style. But Master Craft of Oregon, conveniently located in the Johns Landing area between Lake Oswego and downtown Portland, does more than just sell equipment. The firm has sponsored water ski shows in Portland and around the state; it's been featured on television shows, and can take credit for launching the first water ski school and Skiport, the first water ski team in the city. Visa. MasterCard.

7400 SW Macadam Avenue
Portland 97219
244-1355

Monday-Friday
10am-7pm
Saturday
11am-4pm

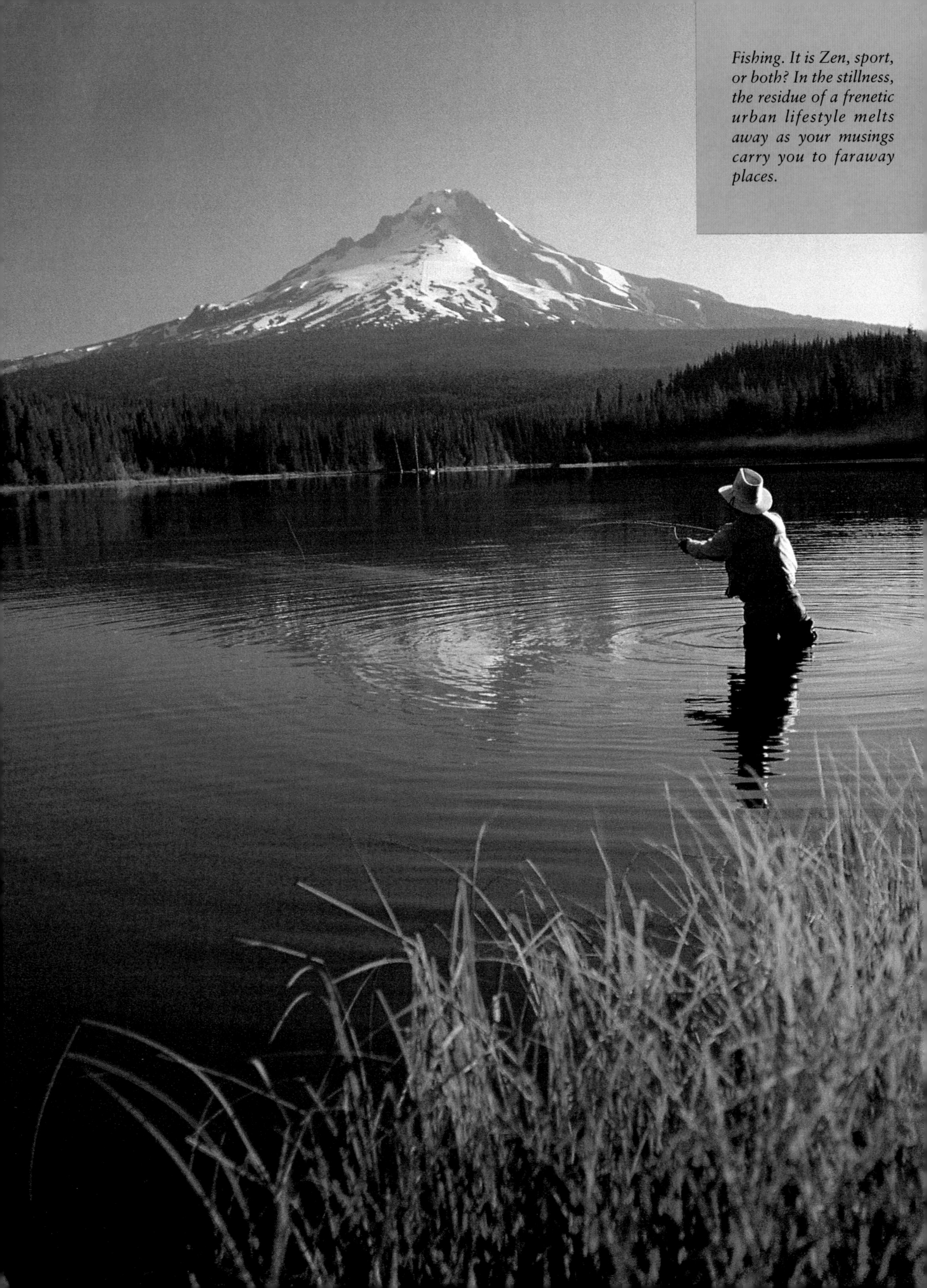

Fishing. It is Zen, sport, or both? In the stillness, the residue of a frenetic urban lifestyle melts away as your musings carry you to faraway places.

WOODMERE FARM

Equestrian training for the winning edge.

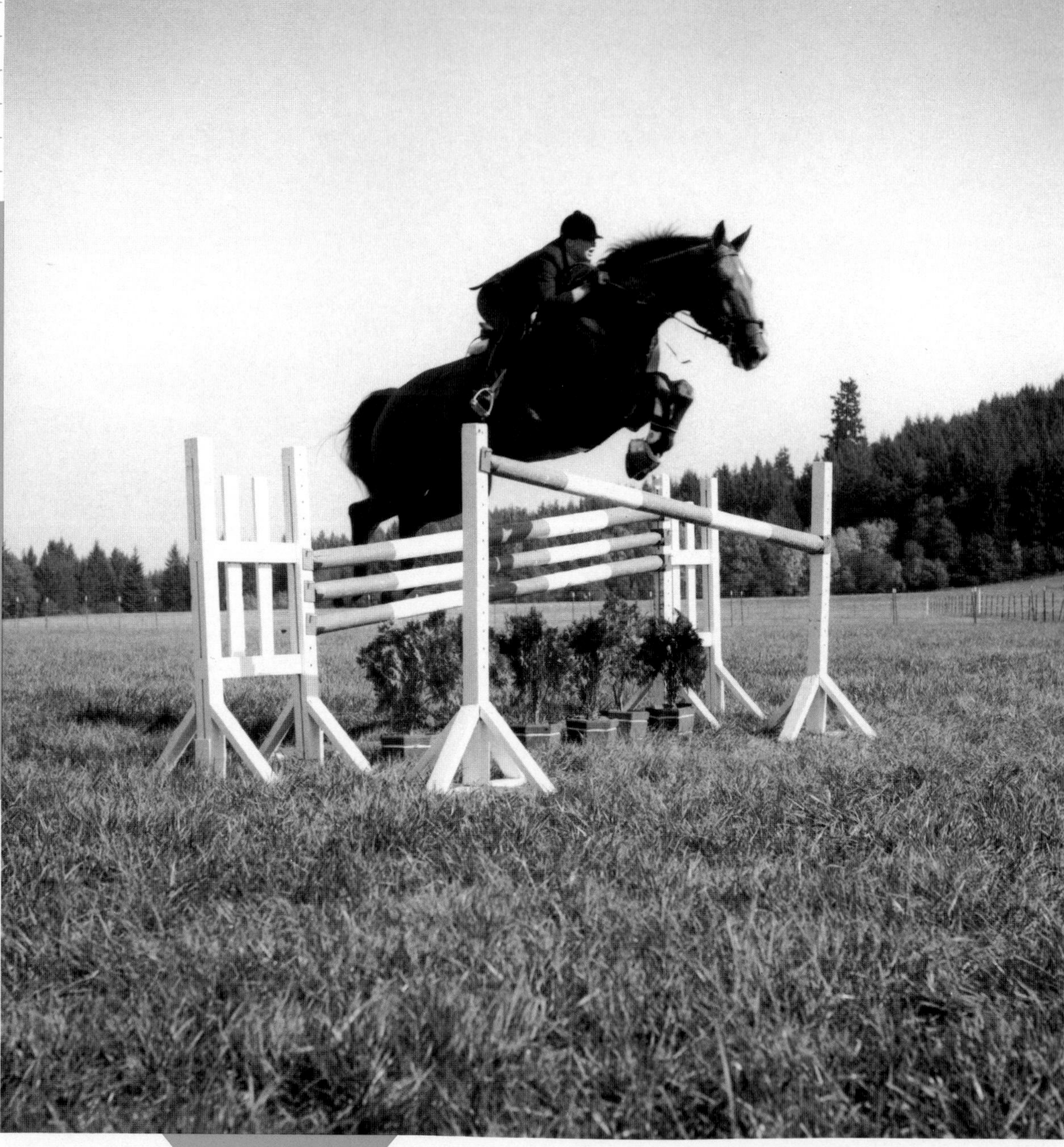

Beaverton

Woodmere Farm, just four miles west of Washington Square on Scholls Ferry Road, is a picturesque setting well known to discriminating horse owners. Woodmere brings an exceptional level of quality to the boarding and training of hunters and jumpers. They offer dressage fundamentals, huntseat instruction for intermediate to advanced riders, breaking and training of young horses, an evaluation/appraisal service for potential horse purchasers, as well as a selection of fine horses for purchase. The training staff is eminently qualified to prepare horse and rider for show competition in the hunter, jumper and huntseat equitation divisions — in any skill category. To further the rider's education, Woodmere hosts special events that include horse shows, a sports psychology seminar and semi-annual riding clinics by top trainers from the U.S. and Canada. And the facility is as complete as the staff is qualified. There are two arenas, an office/club room with heated viewing area, 50 roomy box stalls, an outside jump field, pipe-fenced paddocks and access to acres of wooded trails certain to delight riders of all ages. Whether you fancy equestrian competition or merely polished riding skills and the most conscientious care for your animals, Woodmere Farm is certain to meet your standards.

Route 1, Box 438
Beaverton 97007
649-1341

Tuesday-Friday
8am-8pm
Saturday-Sunday
8am-5:30pm

211

HOME

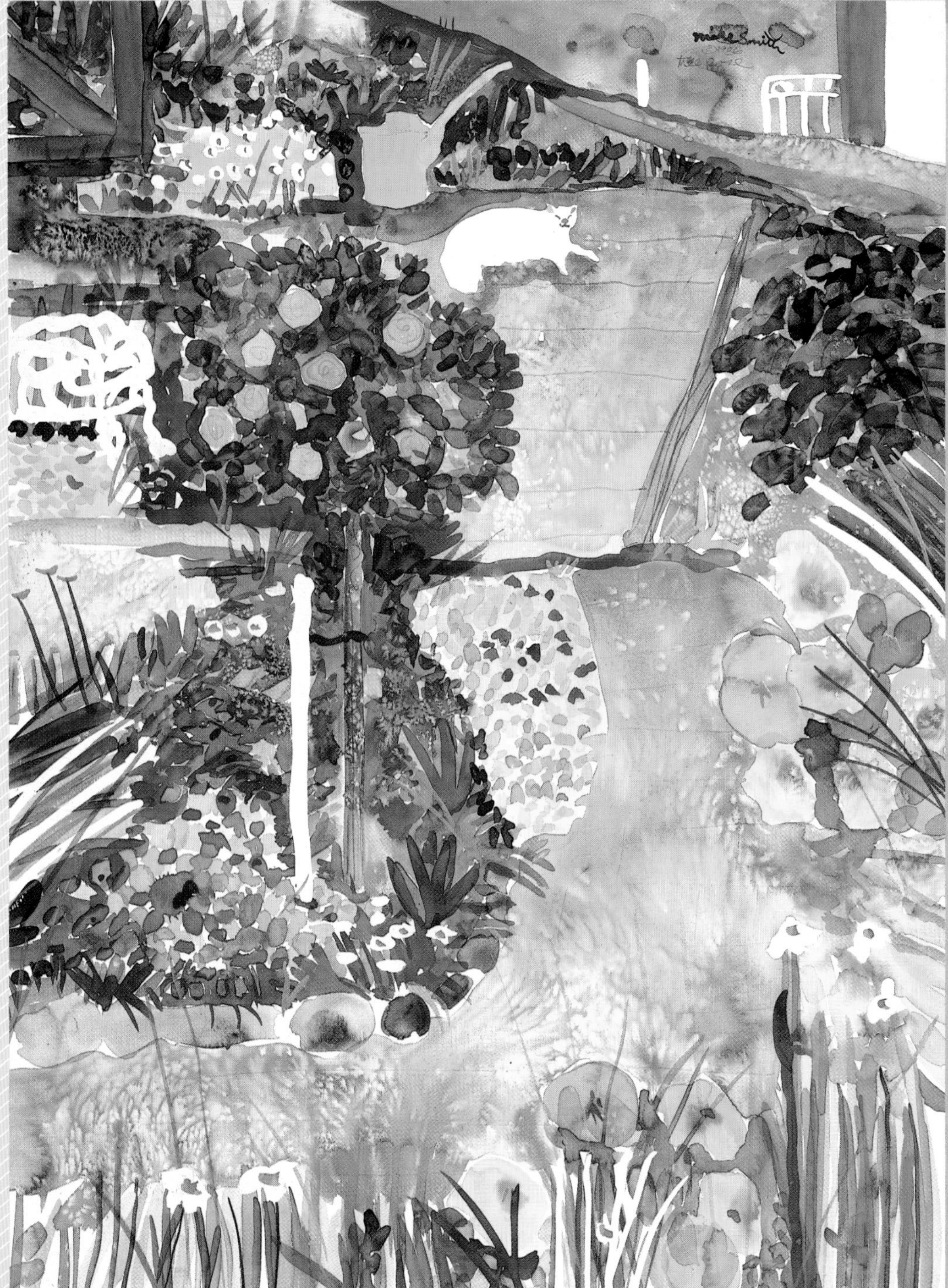

Mike Smith *Tree Rose* ATTIC GALLERY

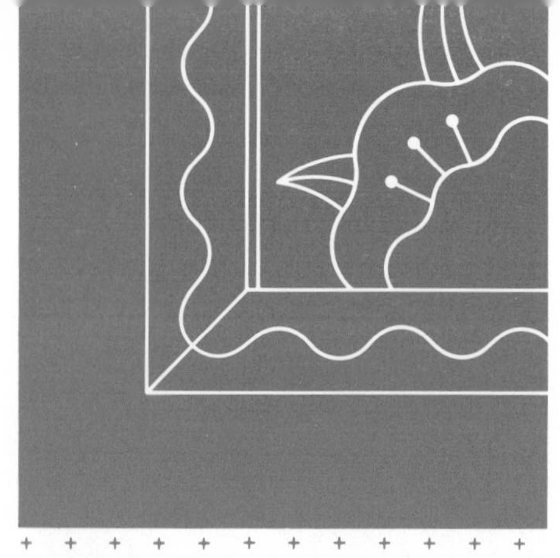

The way I see it, visitors should return home from my house instilled with good feelings toward me without really knowing why. My furniture should do that. My lamps, dishes, artworks, mantlepieces, rugs. They call it making a "statement." I've given a lot of thought to having my home make statements. Here is a statement I would like my house to make: "This is the first day of the rest of your life" or "We can do no wrong," something like that.

What a powerful tool this could be! But no, as far as home style goes, Northwesterners are more private and less graphic. The "statement" is implied; our lifestyle is fairly informal compared to other parts of the country. We are basically suburban and rural with a strong relationship to the land.

Here, home is where the heart is. We like our homes more than people do in other places, because we stay in our homes more than people do in other places. Maybe it all starts with rain, but there is this tendency to burrow in, hunker down and nest. Portland is the city where people mole into their homes and emerge with a condensed version of their unusual selves — traits that usually have to be pried loose to see, to know. Why else would we have the largest book store west of the Mississippi? Why else would home movies be so popular? Food? Compact discs?

And building the nest in Portland is, if anything, an adventure.

Most notable are all those estate and garage sales, which have an avid cult following. Portland is old enough to have a large population of aging houses and eccentric enough to harbor some of the finest kitcsh and art deco available, not to mention rare and priceless art and beautiful furniture. Those antiquities that do not end up in the home, often turn up as props in a local performance art, or adhered to a Rauschenberg-like artwork.

There is this tendency to burrow in, hunker down and nest.

And the searching uncovers the detritus of Portland home life in all its morbid and intriguing capacities. Some call it junk; other rare anthropological finds.

If you can't stand digging through layers of untold generations of use, there are all those antique and second-hand stores in Sellwood, on Hawthorne Boulevard, in Multnomah Village and Northwest Portland. An endless variety. It is from this market I received my favorite mod (circa 1955) creamer from none other than the hands of Sigrid Clark, now our city's first lady. The second-hand industry has provided me with dishes, table linens and placements, my favorite winter coat, and a sense of righteousness not only for money saved, but for recycling sentiment and material goods.

Beyond this level there are a multitude of design and furniture shops who offer sophisticated design products. I have simple demands, an even simpler salary and little patience for shopping, so I tend to beat paths to the same places. Northwest Futon Company is a dependable stand-by for a simple lamp or a cleverly designed couch/bed and Kitchen Kaboodle and The Kobos Company are great purveyors of kitchen and home utensils. Virginia Jacobs (linens), and Calico Corner (upholstery fabric), are others worth visiting, just to name a few of the deserving throngs.

And then there is shopping for art. There's a lot to be had here. Portland's art community offers great choices: Jamison/Thomas, Image, Elizabeth Leach, Blackfish, Augen, Lawrence, Northwest Artists Workshop, Quartersaw, Contemporary Crafts, Oregon School of Arts and Crafts' Hoffman Gallery, a gutsy new-wave hand-made furniture shop called Beyond Reason, and on, and on. What you can't buy you can contemplate.

Now furnished with the bare necessities, I'm saving my pennies for furniture made by one or two of the very skilled furniture makers and carpenters that Oregon attracts, and those delectable items sold in fine furniture stores. After a frustrated bout of attic renovation, I may even succumb to the talents of a designer who, I dream, will do all the shopping for me. Whatever the case, I can rest assured that I can make any "statement" I want in Portland. Everything I need is here.

Megan McMorran

Megan McMorran *is a freelance writer who has written features for local publications covering art and women's issues.*

Mike Smith *is a native Portlander whose works are found in collections around the world. His first years were spent in abstract painting and sculpture but his work has gradually changed to simply reflect his life and world near the studio. He is represented by the Attic Gallery in Portland.*

INTERIORS

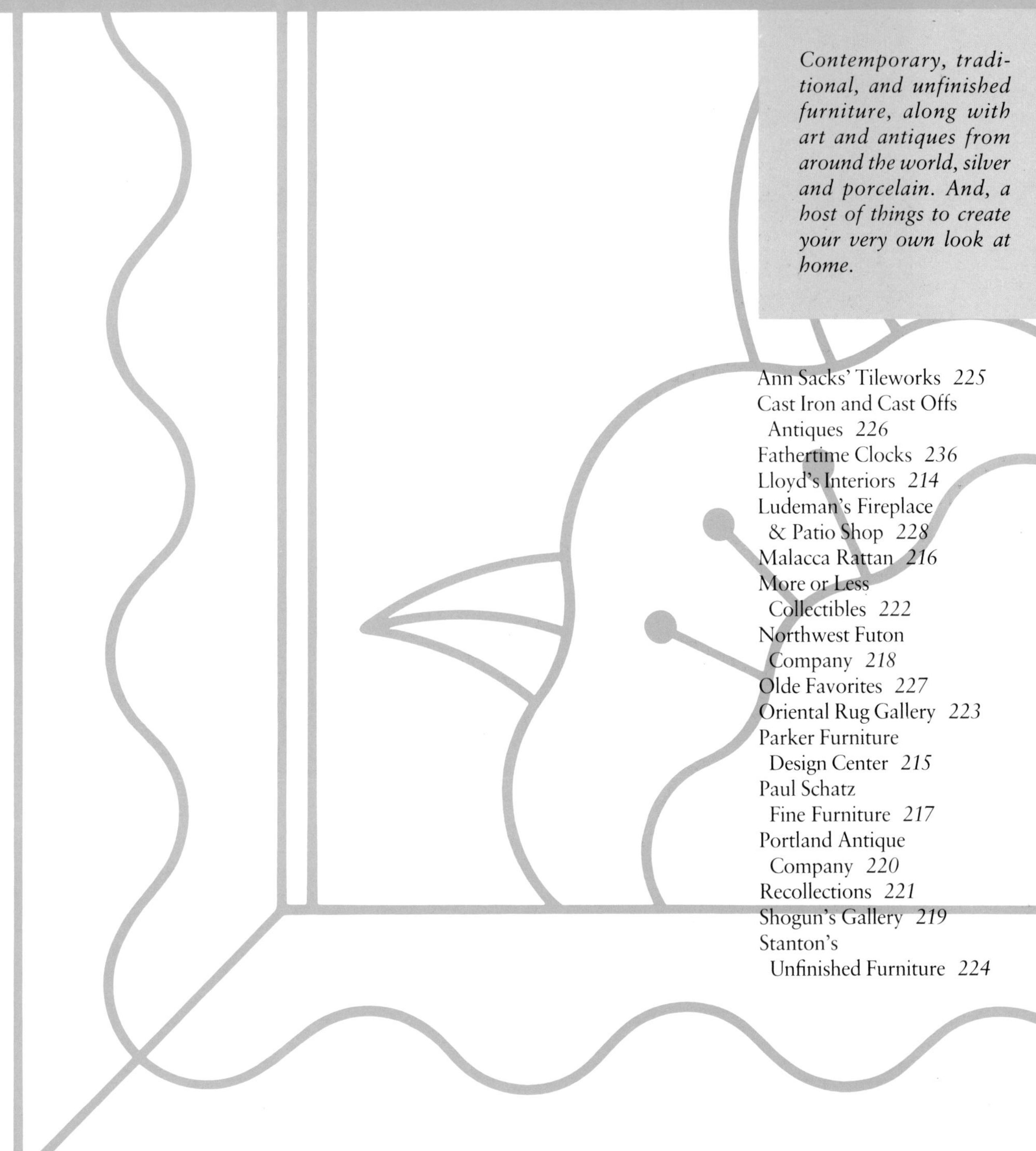

Contemporary, traditional, and unfinished furniture, along with art and antiques from around the world, silver and porcelain. And, a host of things to create your very own look at home.

Ann Sacks' Tileworks *225*
Cast Iron and Cast Offs Antiques *226*
Fathertime Clocks *236*
Lloyd's Interiors *214*
Ludeman's Fireplace & Patio Shop *228*
Malacca Rattan *216*
More or Less Collectibles *222*
Northwest Futon Company *218*
Olde Favorites *227*
Oriental Rug Gallery *223*
Parker Furniture Design Center *215*
Paul Schatz Fine Furniture *217*
Portland Antique Company *220*
Recollections *221*
Shogun's Gallery *219*
Stanton's Unfinished Furniture *224*

LLOYD'S INTERIORS

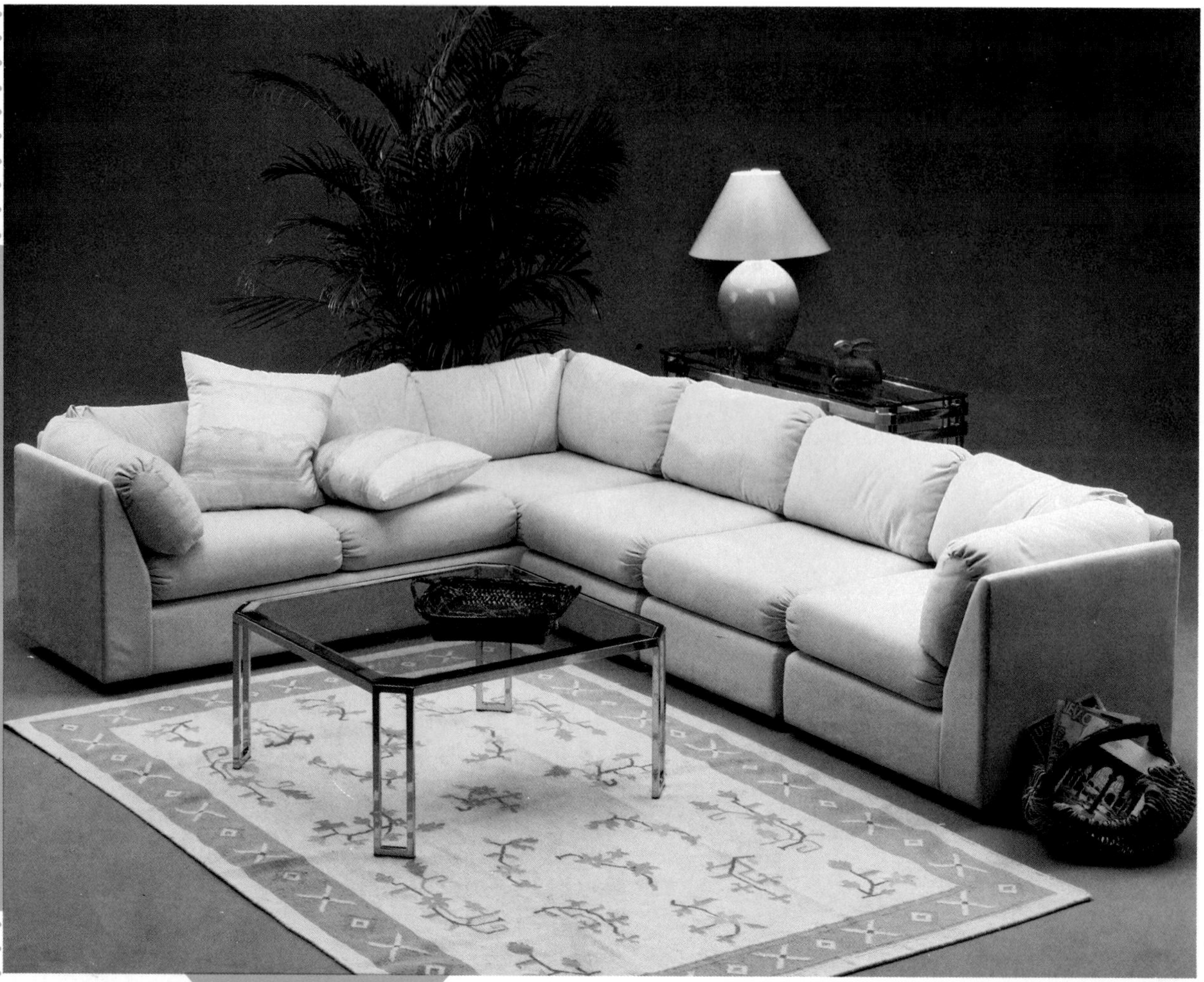

Fine contemporary furniture — professional design staff.

A beautifully appointed room has an elegant, effortless quality about it. It's easy to appreciate but hard to accomplish. The staff of professional interior designers at Lloyd's Interiors can help you achieve that rare ambience in your home or office, whether just one key piece is needed or you want to redesign an entire area. You'll find furniture, accessories, lamps and fabrics imported directly from Europe, as well as a fine selection of domestic pieces. Lloyd's trademark has always been its unique assortment of contemporary furnishings from modern pieces by Hans Wegner, Corbusier and Breuer to the more traditional pieces by Baker and Century. If you can't find the piece that's just right, Lloyd's designers will design and have built for you whatever is necessary to finish your room to perfection. Lloyd's also offers the largest stock of the Tech Line System in the Northwest. Come to Lloyds — your home deserves it. Visa. MasterCard. American Express.

Northeast Portland
C6

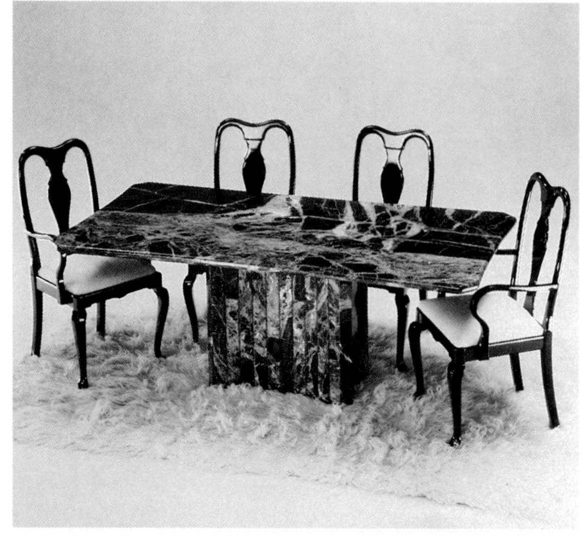

1714 NE Broadway
Portland 97232
284-1185

Monday-Saturday
9:30am-5:30pm
Sunday noon-5pm

PARKER FURNITURE DESIGN CENTER

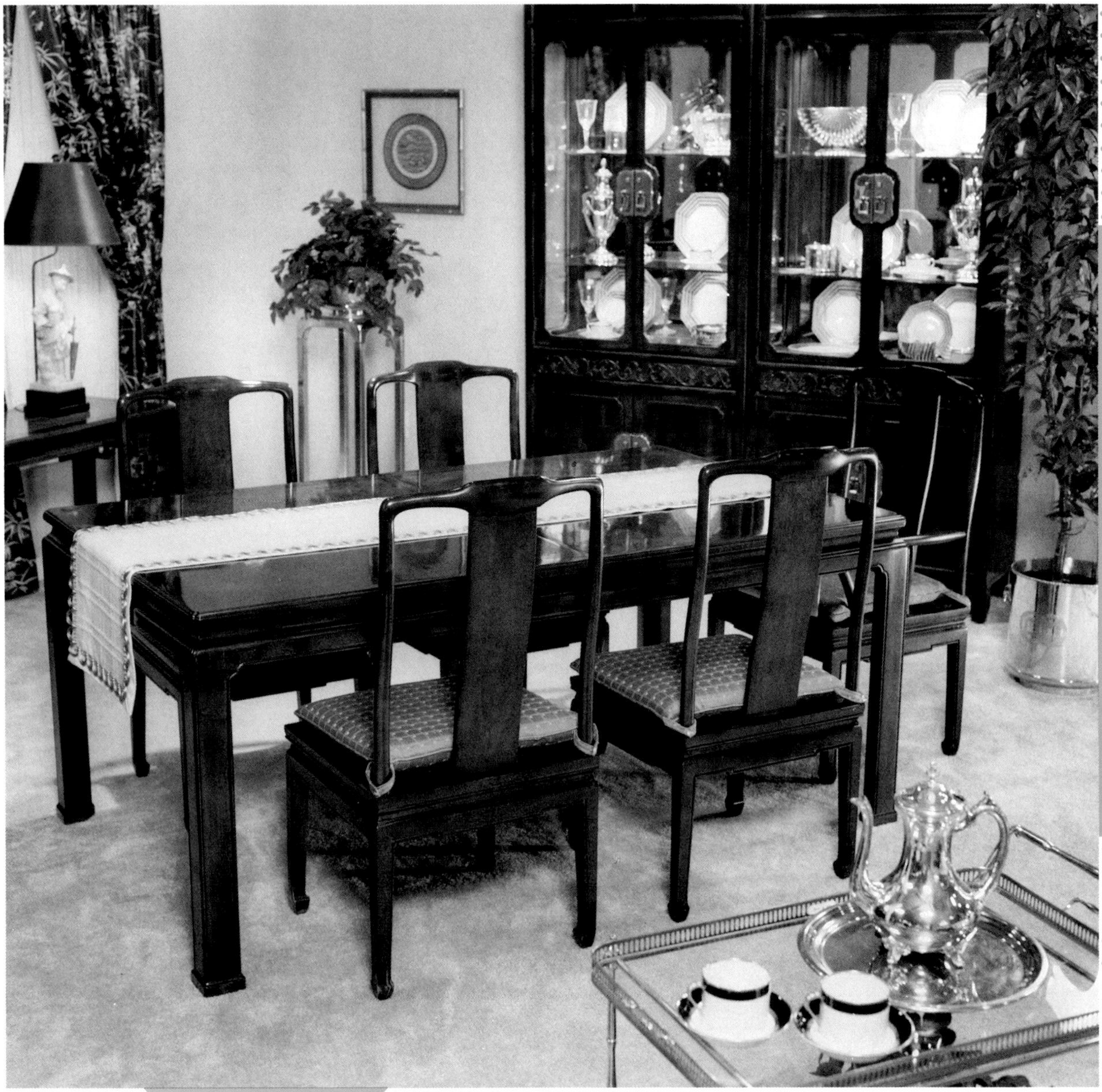

Contemporary and traditional furniture; carpeting and accoutrements.

To Louis, Betty, Gary and Craig Parker their watch-word, "Traditions in Excellence", extends beyond the walls which surround their more than one hundred thousand square feet of retail furniture and carpeting showroom. The motto, in fact, aspires to convey the Parker dedication to providing the very best — not only in furnishings, carpeting and accoutrements, but customer services. To begin with, the furniture. Here, in tasteful gallery arrangement, you'll find southern plantation reproductions by Baker Furniture, widely regarded as the finest cabinet manufacturer in the world. Also prominently on view are occasional pieces and dining room tables from Mastercraft, a standard-setting manufacturer with the only brass foundry of its type in the country. Other temptations include traditional and contemporary fine furnishings by Henredon, a selection of beautifully carved, hard-to-come-by pieces from White Manufacturing, and a tasteful assortment of affordably priced pieces from Thomasville and Weiman. Now, the design service. In the interest of maximizing customer pleasure at no extra cost, Parker advises and helps customers display their new acquisitions to the best possible effect inside their own homes. Three generations of Parkers are proud to support these traditions. Visa. MasterCard. Discover.

10375 SW Beaverton Hillsdale Highway
Beaverton 97005
644-0155

Monday-Saturday 9am-6pm
Sunday noon-5pm

6025 E Burnside
Portland 97215
232-2025

Monday-Saturday 9am-6pm
Sunday noon-5pm

Beaverton
E3

East Portland
D8

MALACCA RATTAN

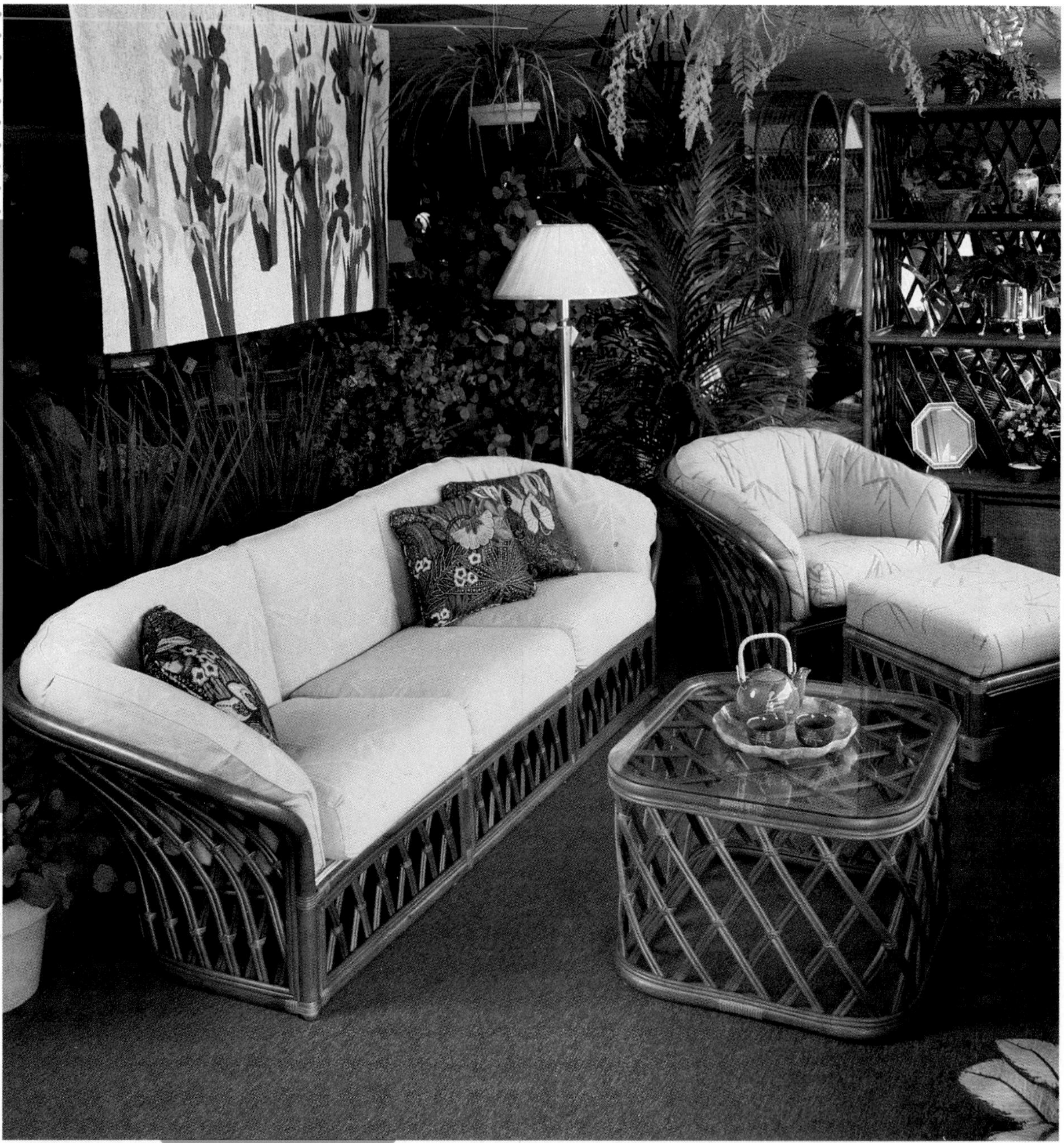

INTERIORS

Rattan and wicker furnishings for home, office and vacation hide-aways.

Progress-Washington Square

G3

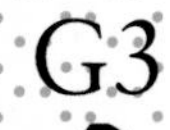

Steam the stems of the rugged, woody, climbing vine and it is transformed into some of the most intricate, graceful furniture to be found. The creation is a difficult process but, fortunately, the place to find such beauty in Portland is not. Simply walk into Malacca Rattan and sink into one of the many rattan and wicker sofas and chairs. Or sit at any of the tables, dining sets and bars. Then survey the vast collection of dividers, baskets, lamps and accessories. It may take a while to choose from among the myriad of beautifully designed pieces. But, whether your style is casual or sophisticated, rattan will elegantly naturally appoint any room in your home. Every cushion you see can be covered — or reupholstered — to coordinate with your colors by Malacca Rattan's own seamstresses; and draperies can be made to match. Malacca's decorator will assist you in choosing colors and pieces for your home, office and vacation hide-away. You could travel to the seaport in Malaysia that bears the name Malacca, but you won't need to book passage to find Malacca Rattan right here in Portland. Malacca Rattan — your headquarters for quality rattan and wicker home furnishings. Visa. MasterCard. Discover.

Greenburg Corners
9225 SW Hall Boulevard
Portland 97223
684-0591

Monday-Friday
10am-6pm
Saturday 10am-5pm
Sunday noon-4pm

PAUL SCHATZ FINE FURNITURE

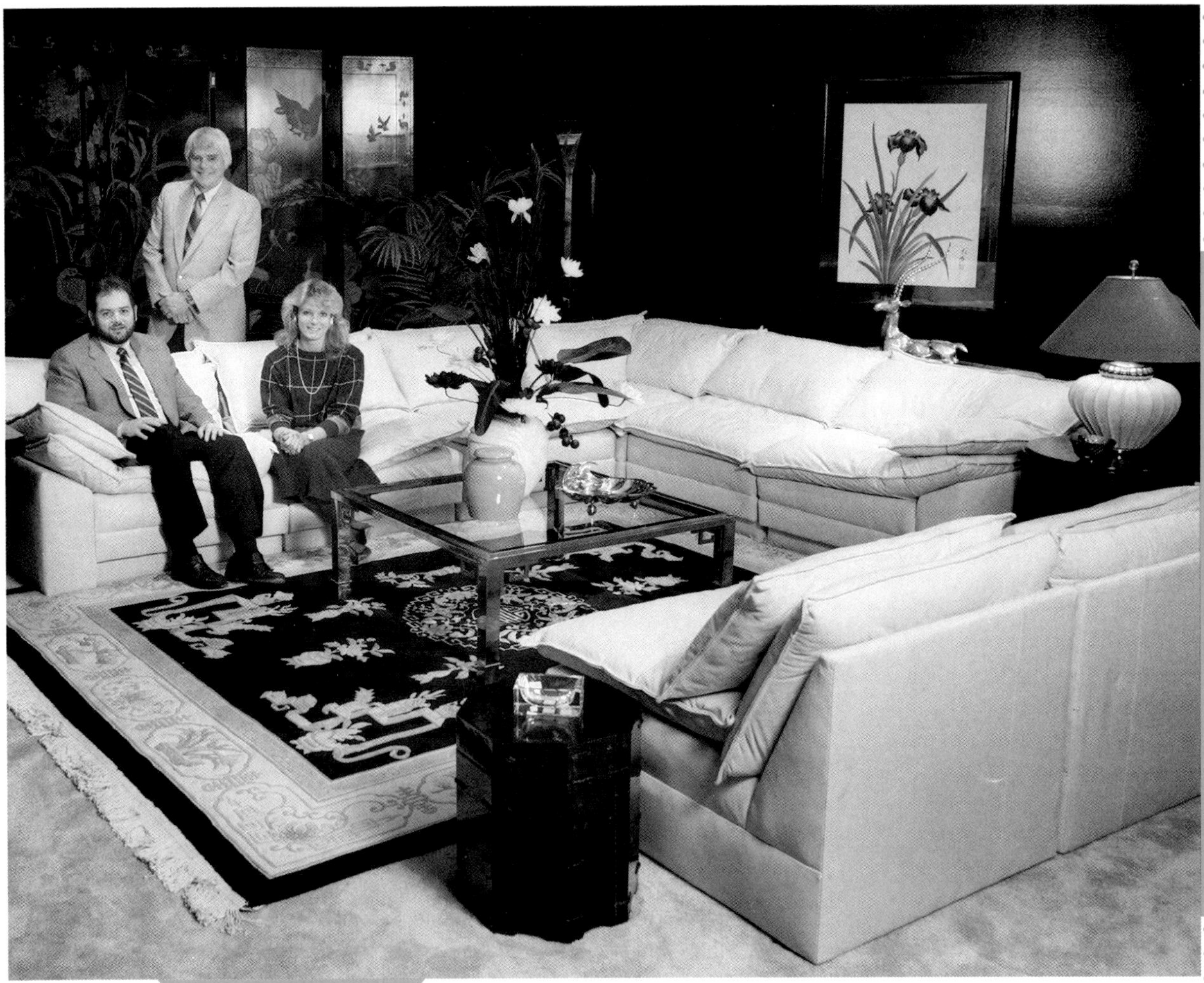

Distinctive home furnishings since 1919.

Paul Schatz Furniture takes pride in offering the very finest traditional and contemporary furnishings. And "Paul Schatz Pride" is backed by three generations of experience. Wander through the individual room settings; challenge the professional sales staff with your questions about furniture, carpeting, draperies, lamps and accessories. While Paul Schatz is the area's exclusive dealer for Drexel Heritage Home Furnishings, they also offer an exceptional selection of pieces in leather, wood, glass and brass from a variety of other sources. Both Paul Schatz locations offer complete design services to help you with room layout and color coordination. After you've made your selection, Paul Schatz painstakingly prepares each piece for delivery, backs it with a five-year limited warranty and delivers at no charge in Oregon and Southwest Washington. Drop by either of Paul Schatz's locations and see how a single visit makes life-long customers. Visa. MasterCard.

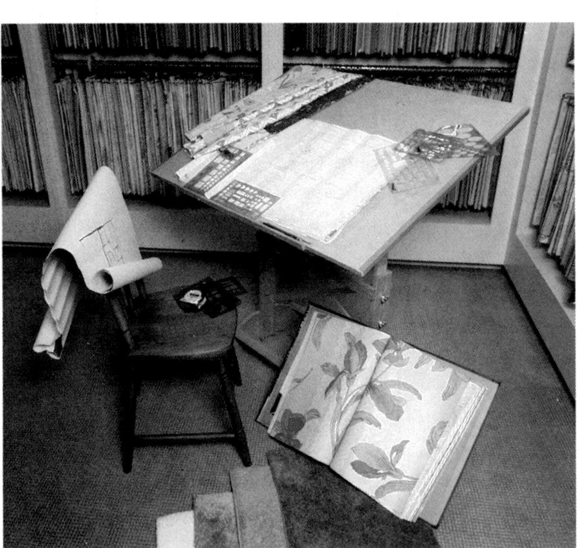

North Portland
A5
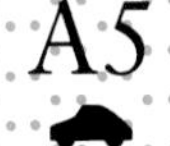

1223 N. Hayden
Meadows Drive
Portland 97217
285-4669

Monday-Thursday
10am-6pm
Friday 10am-9pm
Saturday 10am-6pm
Sunday noon-5pm

Southwest Portland
J3

7437 SW Nyberg Road
Tualatin 97062
692-1170

Monday-Thursday
10am-6pm
Friday 10am-9pm
Saturday 10am-6pm
Sunday noon-5pm

NORTHWEST FUTON COMPANY

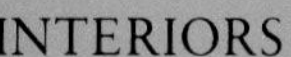

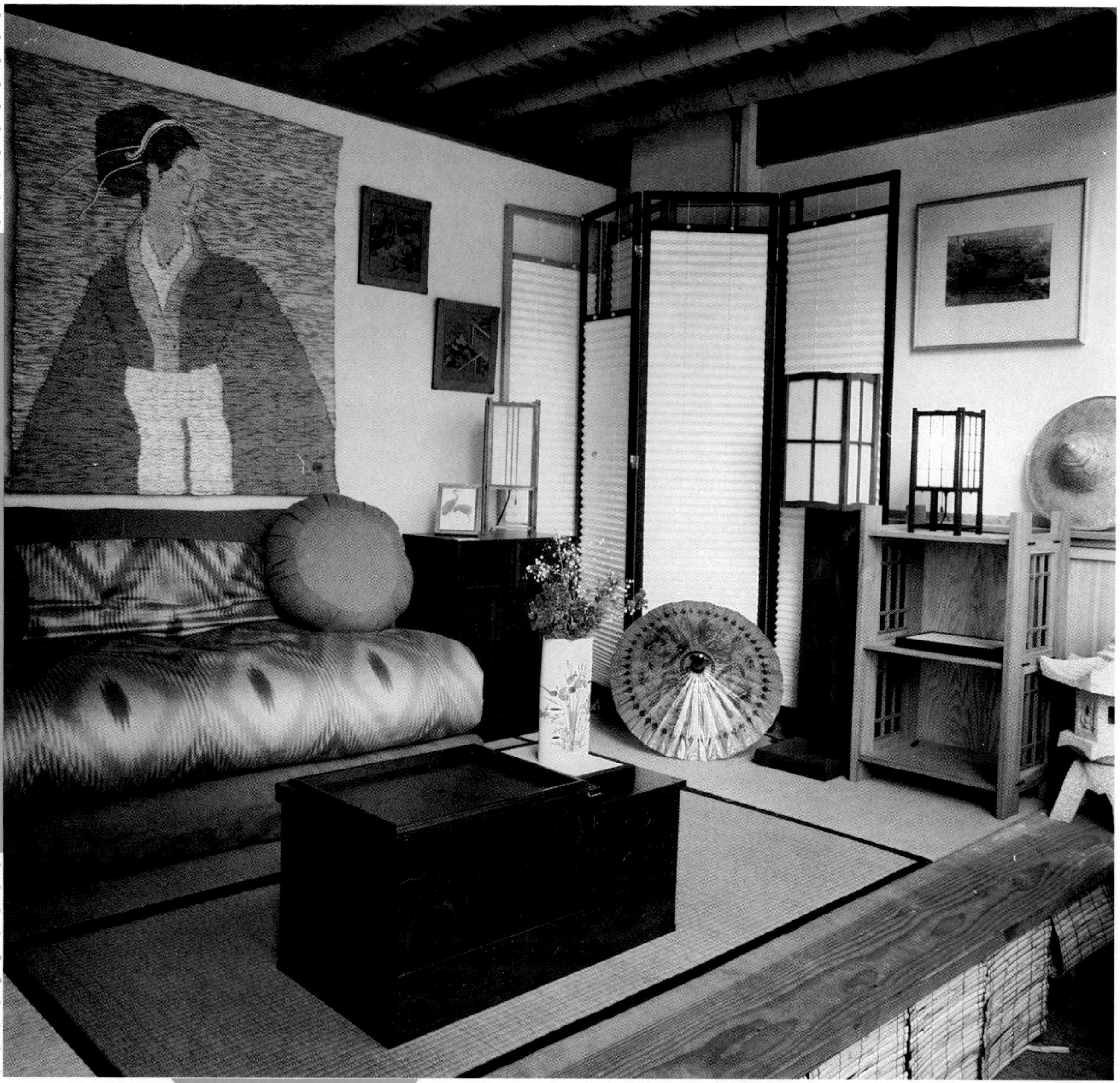

Portable, affordable, versatile and comfortable futons and more.

Yamhill Historic District
F25

Southeast Portland
D6

For more than 2,000 years, the Japanese have been treating themselves to the comforts of incomparable bedding: the futon. A traditional futon — pronounced footawn — is two inches thick and is laid out on tatami mats — made of rice straw — at night and rolled up during the day. Now, through a blend of cultures East and West, Northwest Futon Company creates for this country a beautiful and exquisite futon that departs from its traditional ancestor by providing thicker layers of cotton batting — raw cotton that is combed, cleaned and felted. The batting is encased in durable cotton duck and hand tied with linen thread to prevent shifting. Thus, sleeping on a futon is a simultaneously firm and gentle experience that offers great support for the spine. Even better, Northwest Futon manufactures its bedding right here in Portland, shipping nationwide to mail-order customers. Local shoppers, of course, have the chance to select their futon downtown, in a comfortable atmosphere where the mattresses are firm but the approach is decidedly soft-sell. In addition to futons, you'll find bed frames and convertible furniture, lamps and lighting supplies, tatami mats, shoji screens, wall decorations, kimonos and other natural fiber clothing. Stop by for a test rest in Northwest Futon's newly expanded store and discover comfort the Japanese have known for two millenia. Visa. MasterCard. Discover.

400 SW Second Avenue
Portland 97204
242-0057

Factory Outlet Store
105 SE Taylor Street
Portland 97214
239-4632

Monday-Wednesday
10am-6pm
Thursday 10am-7pm
Friday 10am-6pm
Saturday 10am-5pm

516 15th Avenue East
Seattle, WA 98112
(206) 323-0936

SHOGUN'S GALLERY

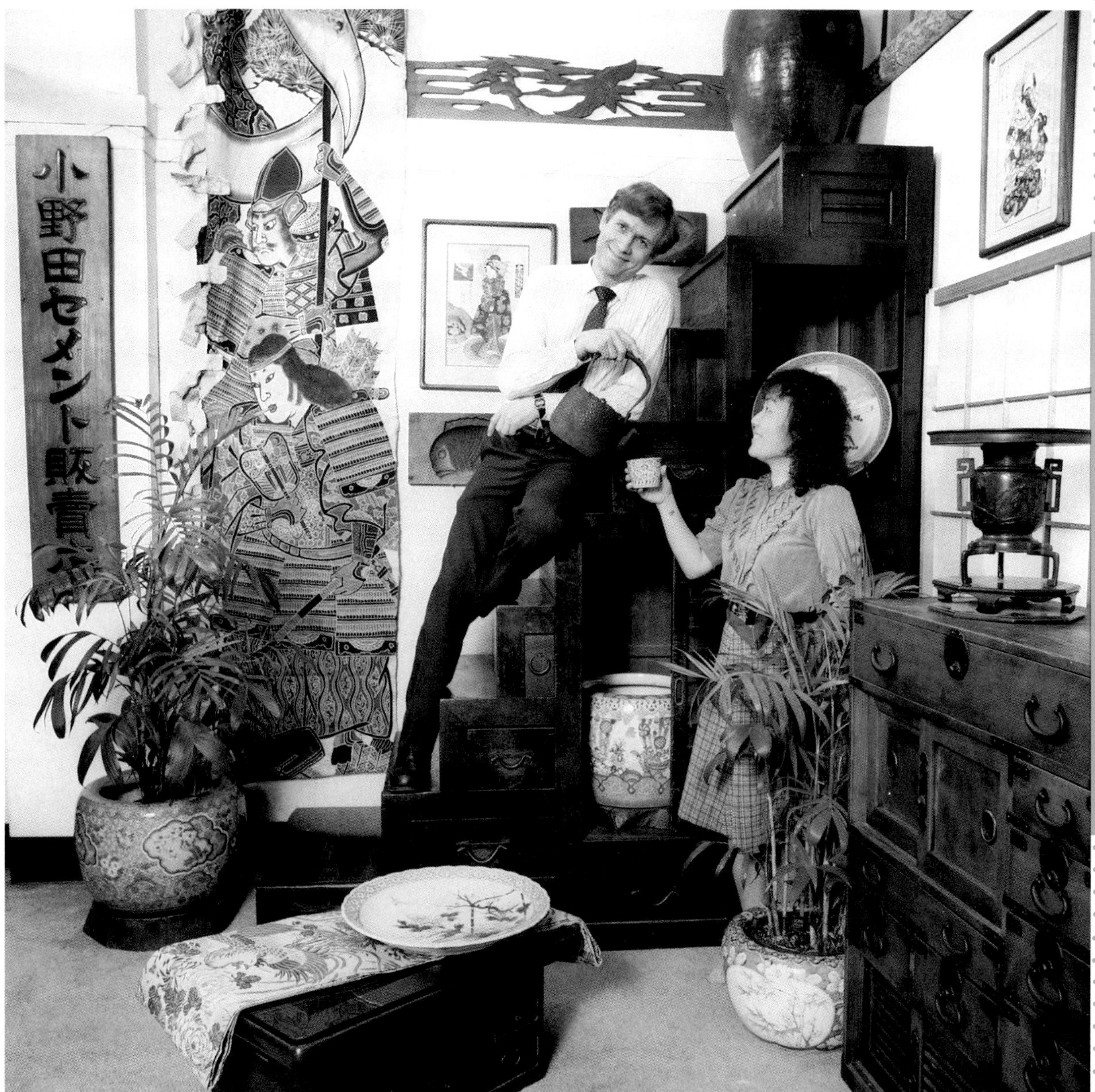

INTERIORS

Japanese art, antiquities and cultural items.

Perhaps now more than at any other time, Japan and the Pacific Northwest are inextricably entwined. Each day seems to bring another announcement of a major business venture that benefits the people of both countries. Japan's rich contributions to culture and art have not gone unnoticed, particularly by the owners and customers of Shogun's Gallery. For six years, the gallery has brought to Portland the finest Japanese arts, antiquities and cultural items. Simply put, a visit to Shogun's Gallery is a no-admission, museum-quality experience, six days a week. Owners Jim and Kimiko King started their undertaking in Japan, where they lived for eight years. At first they wholesaled their wares; then they opened a retail outlet in Portland. In Japan, they are licensed antique dealers; here they bring Portlanders the only store of its kind in the Pacific Northwest, with such delicacies as Tansu furniture, woodblock prints, Imiri ceramics, bronze ware, old fabric, Netsuke and bamboo ware. Because the Kings are licensed to do business in Japan, they can buy at exclusive license-only auctions there and return with unique wares. Prices typically are below those in Tokyo's retail stores, bringing Portlanders a shopping experience second only to a trip to the land of the rising sun.

1103 SW Alder Street
Portland 97205
224-0328

Tuesday-Saturday
10:30am-5:30pm

206 NW 23rd Avenue
Portland 97210
224-0328

Tuesday-Saturday
11:00am-4:30pm

Downtown
E23

Northwest Portland
J17

PORTLAND ANTIQUE COMPANY

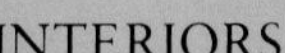

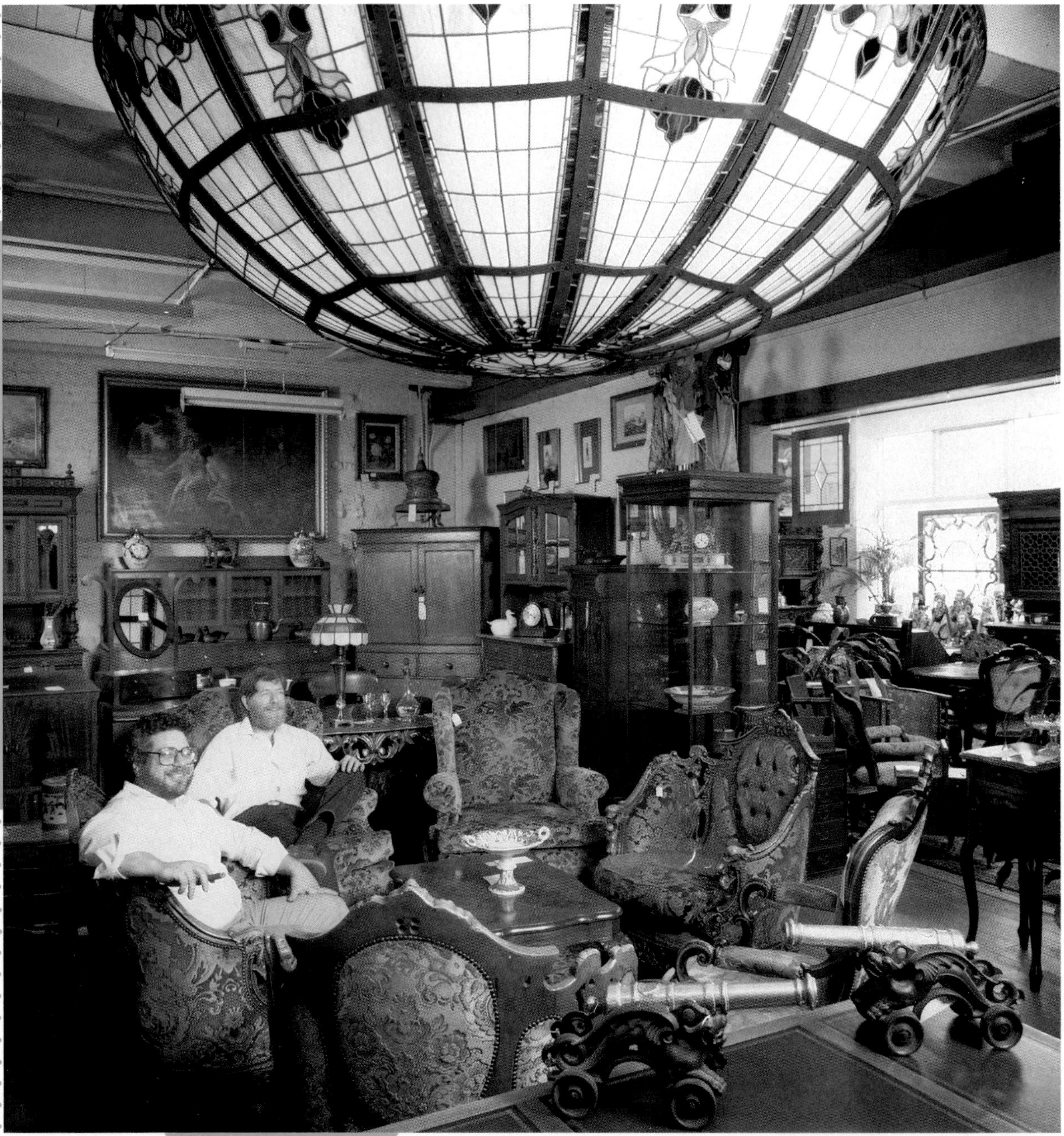

INTERIORS

Collections from andirons to zithers.

Northwest Portland

C22

Four or five times a year, Hank Langfus and Mat Laky travel to Europe and England to comb the countryside for the thousands of interesting antiques that they pack into their 15,000 square foot store. They collect everything from andirons to zithers in auctions, flea markets, dusty warehouses, private estates and even from gypsy junk dealers. Nothing interesting, unusual or of great value escapes them —they once bought a small three-wheeled Italian truck parked in front of their container in Rotterdam and packed it along with a Russian horse-drawn sleigh from the early 1800's. Each month two or three forty foot sea-going containers arrive at their dock loaded with bedroom sets, stained glass, country pine, living room sets, tables and chairs, glassware, dog carts, clocks, carpets, puppets and some fine 18th and 19th century furniture — something for everyone. All the furniture and thousands of small items are cleaned up and laid out with care on the three floors of their store; some items are left for the do-it-yourself refinisher. The wide variety and large selection is the result of Hank and Mat combining over 20 years' experience in the antique business in Portland. If you don't find what you're looking for, chances are it's in the next container at sea. Visa. MasterCard. American Express.

1314 NW Glisan Street
Portland 97209
223-0999

Daily
10am-6pm

RECOLLECTIONS

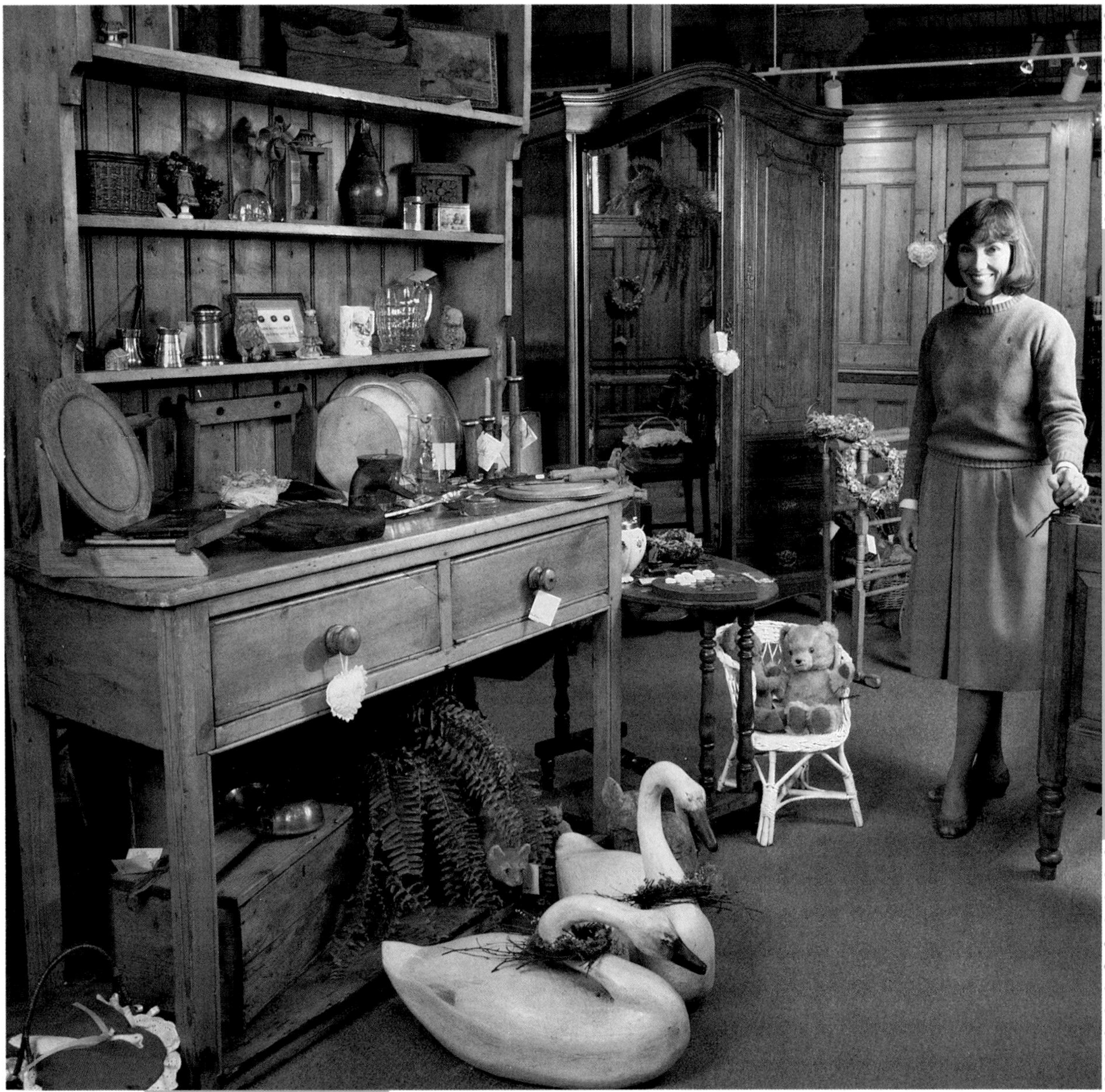

INTERIORS

Personally selected English and French antiques.

Looking for fine antiques for your home or office? Recollections proprietors Sandra and Thomas Miller have gone to great lengths to make sure that visiting either of their attractive stores is a rewarding experience. Recollections specializes in English and French antiques hand-selected in their native countries for quality and authenticity. Their acquisitions, artfully displayed in Recollections' homelike atmosphere, remind us that the work of craftsmen of years past deserves a secure place in our future. Items you will find include Queen Anne chairs, pine trunks, armoires, cupboards and chests; as well as walnut armoires and game tables. Upholstered new furniture rounds out the collection. Unusual pottery, elegant serving pieces and platters, lovely wall hangings, and English porcelain houses supplement the larger pieces. For special touches, Recollections also offers candles, baskets, dried flowers and potpourri. Whenever possible, the Millers attach a history to each antique and offer interior design consultation to help you select, arrange and display these items to their best advantage. Tom and Sandy believe that a home is a house where love dwells. They invite you to visit Recollections. Visa. MasterCard.

The Water Tower *5331 SW Macadam Avenue* *Portland 97201* *223-5966*	*Monday-Friday* *10am-9pm* *Saturday 10am-6pm* *Sunday noon-5pm*
2277 NW Johnson at 23rd Avenue *Portland 97210* *223-5005*	*Monday-Saturday* *10am-6pm*

Corbett-Johns Landing

F6

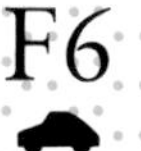

Northwest Portland

H17

MORE OR LESS COLLECTIBLES

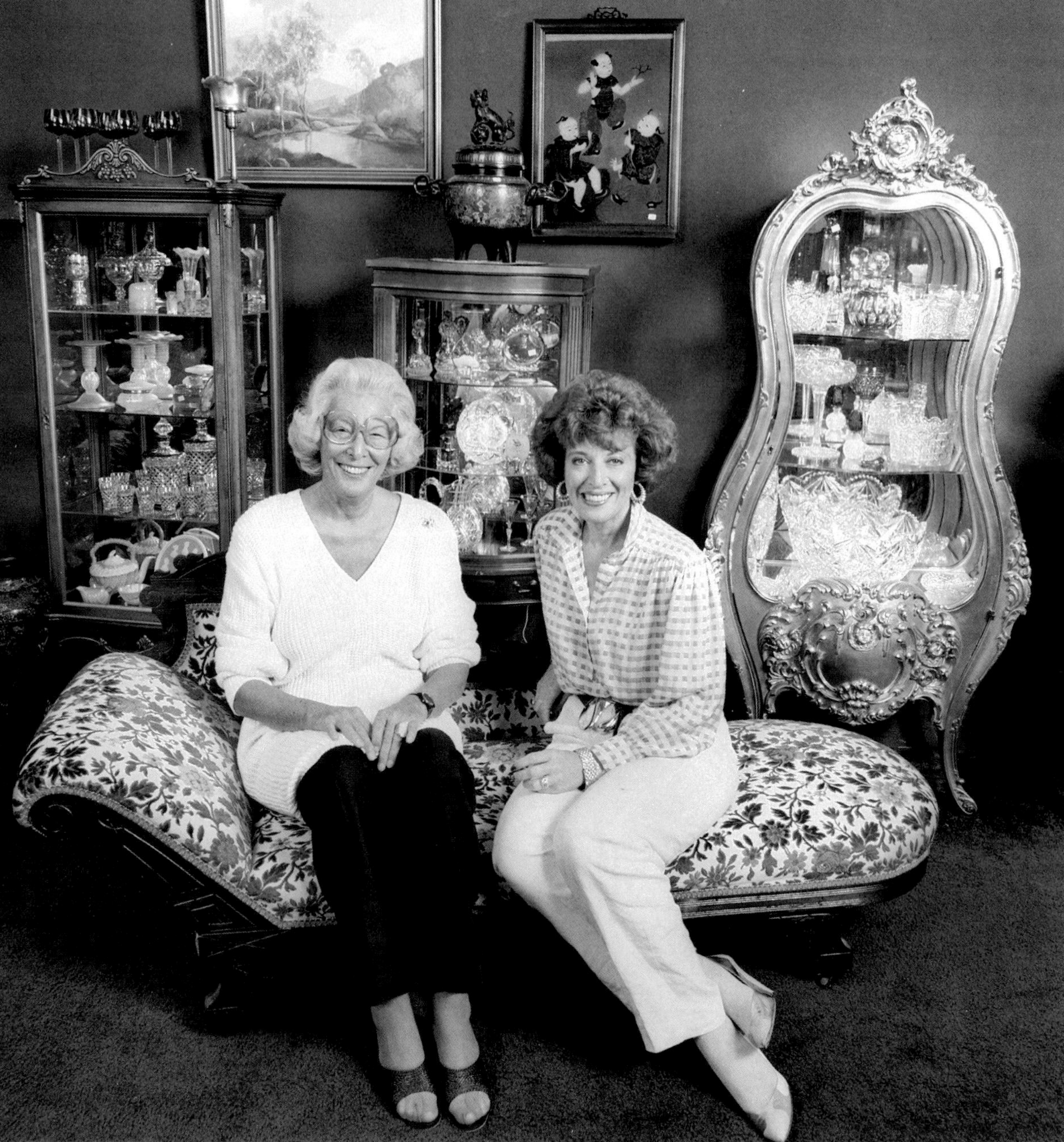

Fabulous glass, porcelains and oriental antiques.

Multnomah/ Hillsdale

F4

A jewel is tucked away in Multnomah Village. At More or Less Collectibles, the atmosphere is elegant with emphasis on quality and rare beauty. Owners Lillian and her daughter Leslie carefully hand-pick all items to offer only the finest cut glass, art glass, porcelain and orientalia. Whether you are a beginnner or an advanced collector, you'll delight in the beauty of pieces by Steuben, Tiffany, Victorian glass and fairy lamps, Royal Vienna, Dresden, and collectibles from Royal Doulton and Royal Bayreuth. Delicate Satsuma, cloisonné jewelry, bronzes and small pieces of accent furniture are also featured. The owners are experts in purchasing and appraising antiques; they pride themselves on knowing the history of each piece and make sure each item is in pristine condition. All merchandise is sold with a money back guarantee and will be shipped anywhere for you. Your purchases will be beautifully wrapped at no charge. The personal, professional touch of Lillian and Leslie shine in this exquisite, sophisticated shop. Visa. MasterCard.

7828 SW Capitol Highway
Portland 97219
244-9534

Tuesday-Saturday
11am-5pm

ORIENTAL RUG GALLERY

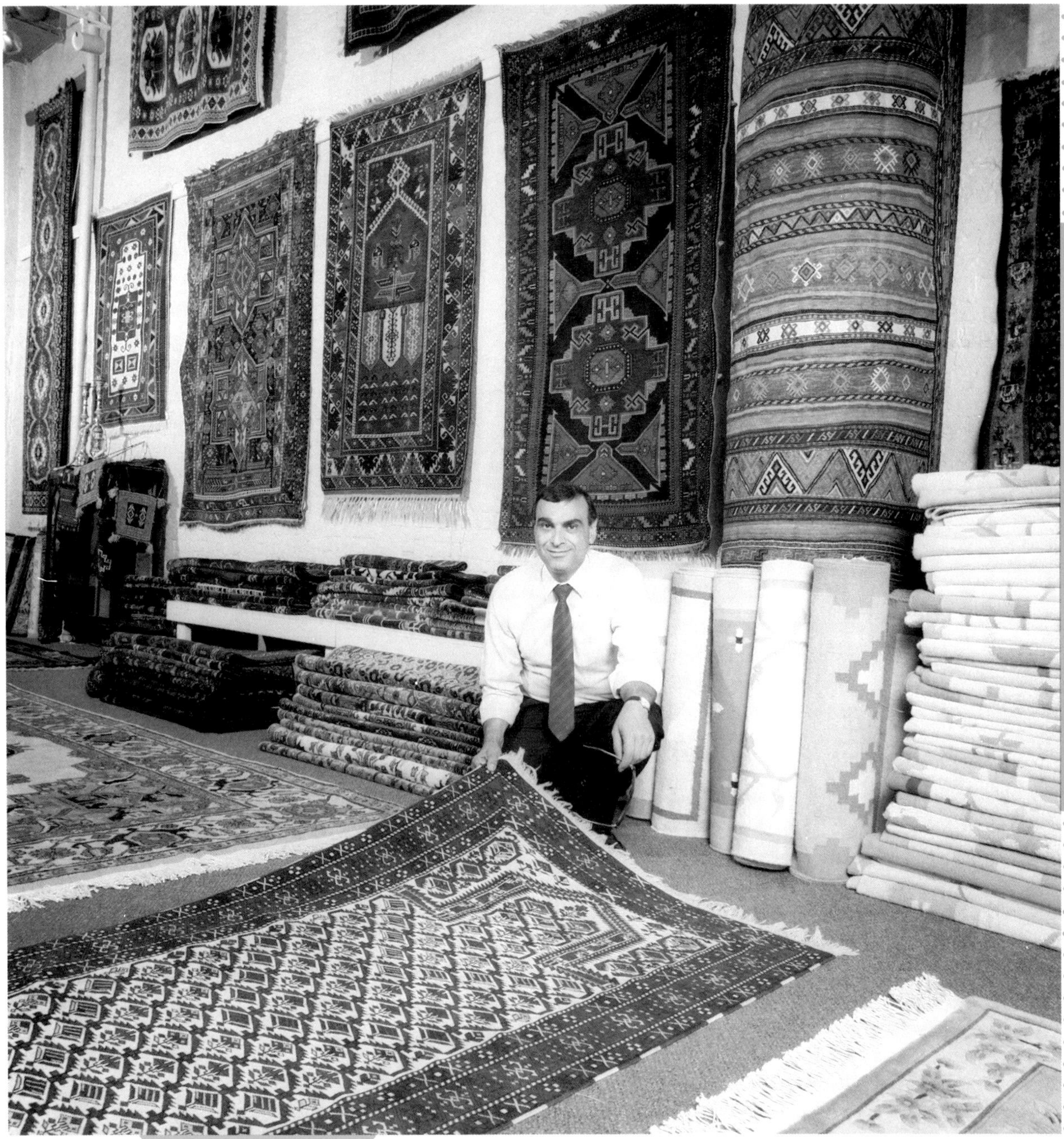

They shop the world for your rugs.

If you've recently admired magazine photographs of tastefully appointed rooms in the region, chances are you were looking at some of the Oriental Rug Gallery's superb selections. With that in mind, you'll understand why owner Hamid Maghbouleh's rugs have become favorites of Pacific Northwest interior designers. No photograph, however, can possibly equal the personal experience of seeing and feeling these rugs. Endowed with highly specialized and generously shared knowledge, Hamid stocks his downtown showroom with the broadest possible inventory of oriental rugs and kilims from around the world. Hamid is a third-generation rug merchant; he selects his inventory of city and tribal rugs — from Iran (Persia), Turkey, Afghanistan and India — during his travels around the world. As a result, his rugs are old and new collectibles that are at once good investments and affordable. His is a hands-on business, so when he's not admiring or explaining the different weaves and materials to his customers, Hamid will be arranging for the repairing, cleaning or appraisal of some of the finest rugs in the Northwest, if not the world. Visa. MasterCard. American Express.

220 SW First Avenue
Portland 97204
248-9511

Monday-Saturday
10am-5:30pm
Sunday noon-5pm

Skidmore Historic District

E25

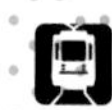

STANTON'S UNFINISHED FURNITURE

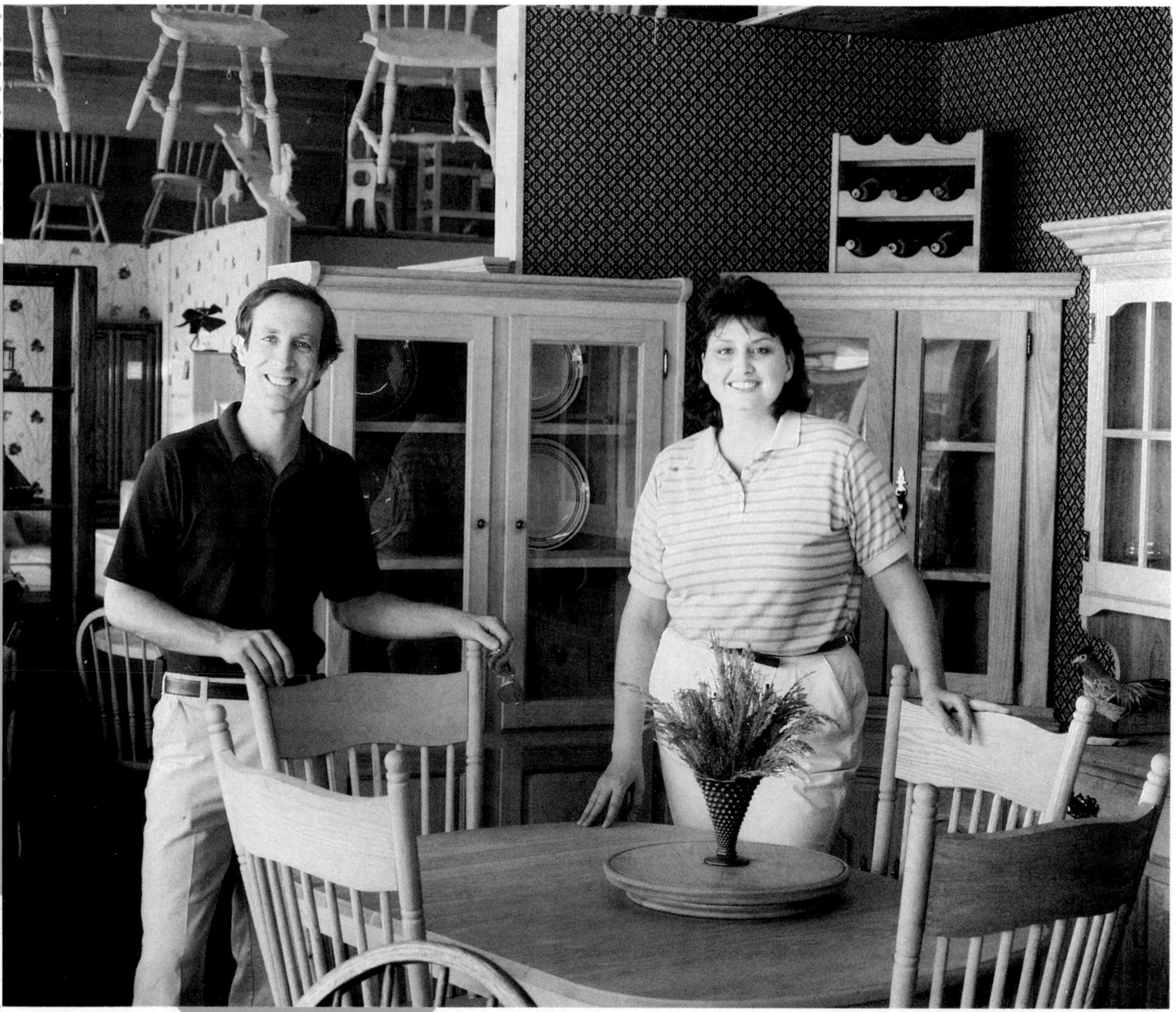

Oregon's largest selection of unfinished furniture.

Northeast Portland
D6
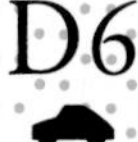

Southeast Portland
D8

Beaverton
E3

If for no other reason, step into Stanton's for the aroma. Open the door and inhale the fresh smell of a forest of carefully machined and assembled wood. Study the stacks of furniture, the innumerable designs and configurations. And realize that the simple motions of finishing will turn each item into pieces worthy of any home or office. Stanton's began life in a single Beaverton outlet of but 300 square feet nearly thirty years ago; today, there are three stores and Oregon's largest selection of unfinished furniture, bookcases and entertainment centers for stereo, television and VCR. By leaving the stain and protective oil topcoat from most of its inventory, Stanton's achieves two things: a handsome discount for the customer and the ability for the buyer, not someone in a far-off factory, to decide the precise color and intensity of each piece. Anyone who can hold a pencil can stain furniture. With the process comes the satisfaction of intimate contact with fine woods and the knowledge that the final step is your accomplishment. Stanton's can outfit almost every room with cribs, changers and cradles for baby; hutches, buffets, tables and chairs for the dining room; enclosures for electronic gear; more than sixty styles of custom desks for the office; and a bookcase selection guaranteed to do a Thoreau job of housing your library. Visa. MasterCard.

1712 NE Sandy Boulevard
Portland 97232
236-5428

Monday 10am-9pm
Tuesday-Thursday
10am-5:30pm
Friday 10am-9pm
Saturday 10am-5:30pm

10800 SE 82nd
Portland 97266
654-5282

Monday 10am-9pm
Tuesday-Thursday
10am-5:30pm
Friday 10am-9pm
Saturday 10am-5:30pm
Sunday llam-5pm

10175 SW Beaverton
Hillsdale Highway
Beaverton 97005
644-7333

Monday 10am-9pm
Tuesday-Thursday
10am-5:30pm
Friday 10am-9pm
Saturday 10am-5:30pm
Sunday 11am-5pm

ANN SACKS' TILEWORKS

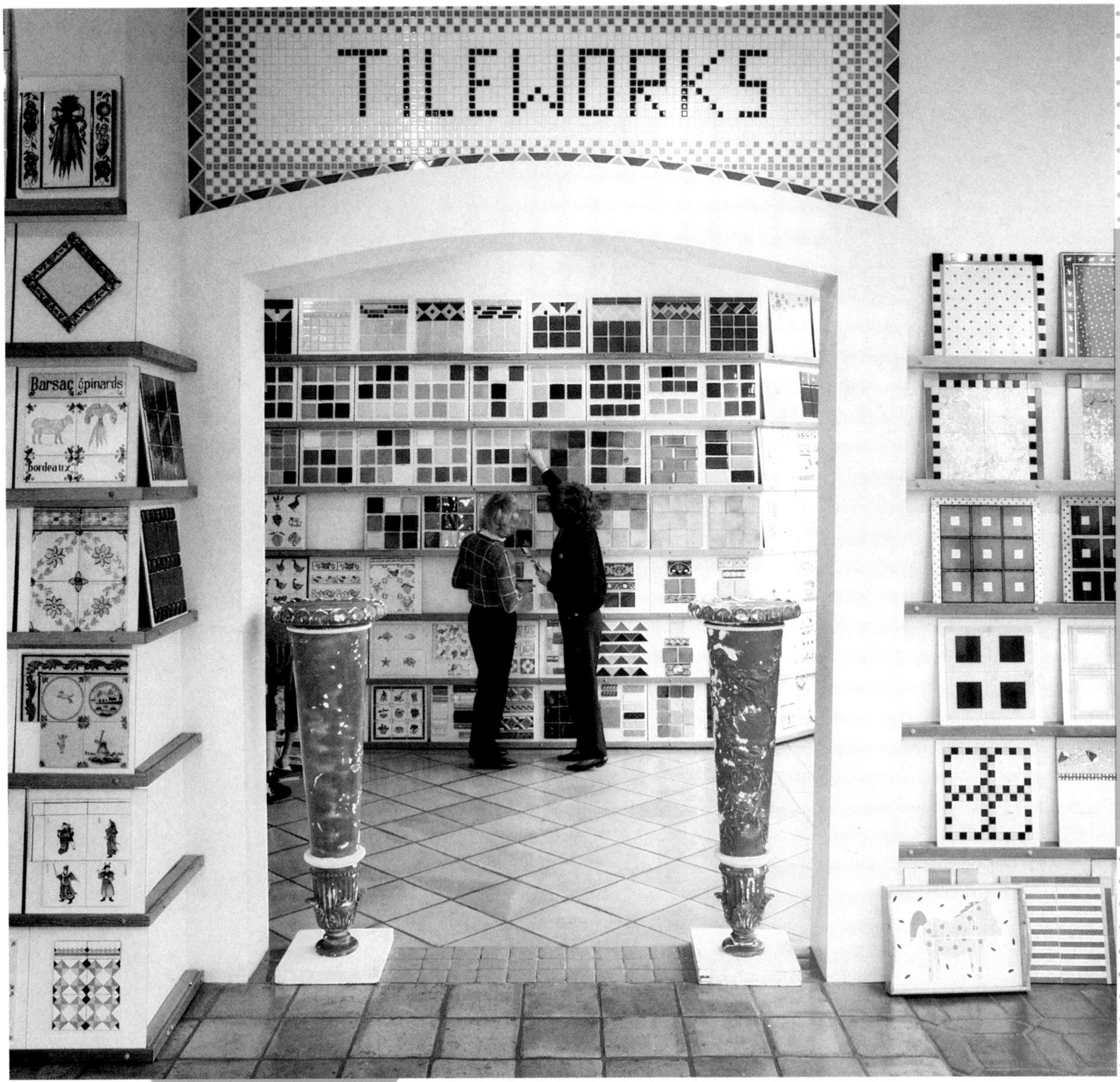

Exclusive tiles, marbles and granites.

No design materials combine the virtues of tile, marble and granite: almost unlimited styles, patterns, colors, and textures; suitability for hundreds of indoor and outdoor uses; and, perhaps best of all unsurpassed durability. When it comes to buying tile, marble and granite, selection and service are everything, and Ann Sacks' Tileworks scores high on both counts. Here, architects, designers and retail customers can find tile or stone that is aesthetically and technically correct, whether it be for the interior or exterior of a multi-story building or for a kitchen counter top and back splash. Ann Sacks' Tileworks manufactures its own beautiful line of tile and represents high-quality ceramics factories and marble and granite quarries from around the world. Tileworks' Custom Color Palette, with its rainbow of selections, includes trim pieces and accent borders. Also available are marvelous handpainted Country Floors tiles from Europe, the classical Italian look of Hastings Contemporary lines, and the finest selection of Mexican floor tiles, French terra cotta floor tiles, and handpainted sinks. In both Portland and Seattle, Ann Sacks' offers the Northwests' most exciting and competitively priced selection of marble and granite in both tile and slabs. Fabrication of slabs is available by their own craftsmen. Visa. Mastercard.

500 NW 23rd Avenue
at Glisan
Portland 97210
222-7125

Monday-Friday
8:30am-5pm
Saturday
Noon-4pm Winter
9:30am-noon Summer

115 Stewart Street
Seattle 98101
(206) 441-8917

Northwest
Portland

I17

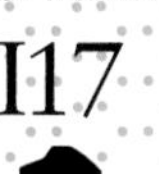

CAST IRON AND CAST OFFS

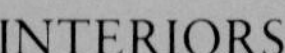

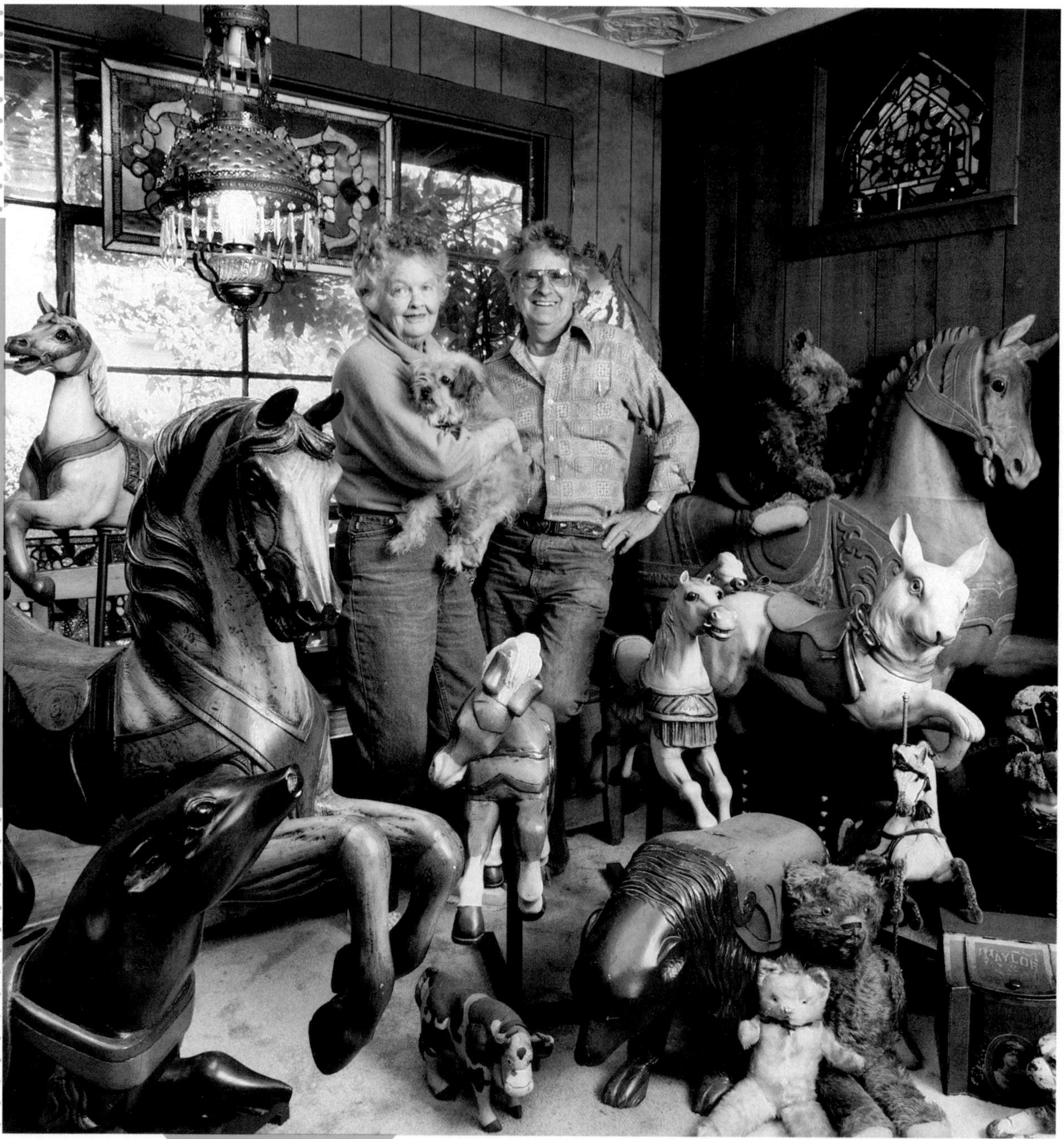

INTERIORS

Specializing in antique carousel horses for twenty years.

Oregon City

E8

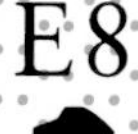

In a peaceful acreage located just outside Oregon City, Mary and Walter Youree are preserving a vanishing America. Cast Iron and Cast Offs is a treasure trove of collectibles and memorabilia. Displayed in this idyllic setting, our heritage is made tangible. Visitors from far and wide come to browse through the country furniture, old time store fixtures and antique brass cash registers. In a country barn shaded by century old maple trees, antique buffs admire the world famous collection of antique hand-carved carousel horses and other animal figures — and look on as the Yourees undertake the complex process of restoration. It's a rare treat to see these time worn relics of a bygone age carefully and lovingly returned to their colorful former glory. For over twenty years the Yourees have been performing their labors of love — bringing the past back to life. Visit Cast Iron and Cast Offs — and take home a piece of disappearing Americana. Visa.

14941 S. Henrici Road
Oregon City 97045
656-0193

Tuesday-Saturday
11am-5pm
or by appointment

OLDE FAVORITES

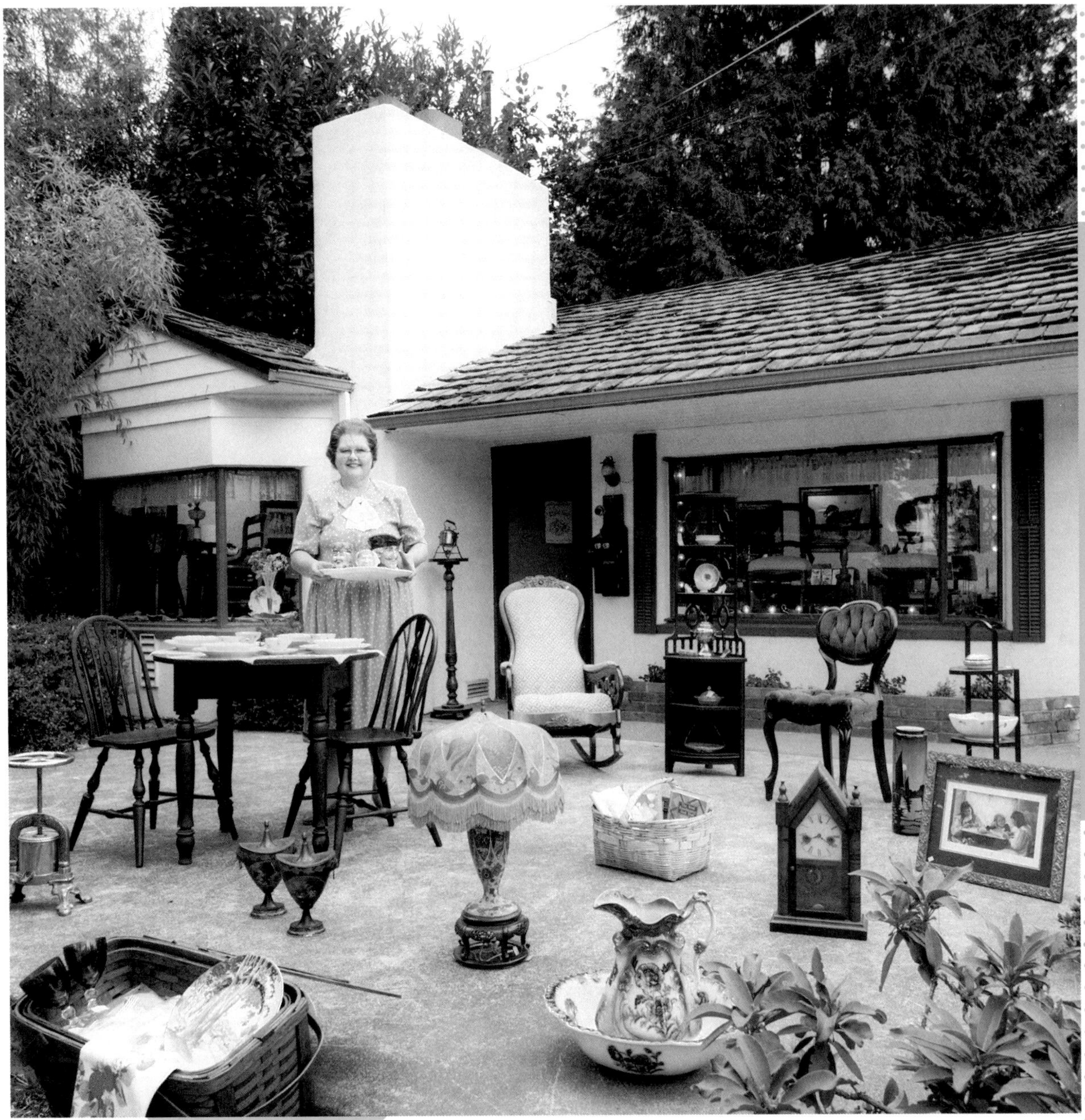

A cottage full of charming antiques and collectibles.

At the bend in the road on Scholls Ferry and Jamieson is a place Marilyn Brodie likes to call "the cottage on the curve." For her, Olde Favorites is the fulfillment of a lifelong dream. "I've been interested in old things since I was a teen-ager," she says, "and have collected things all my life." Now, with her family grown, she has gone public with her love for antiques. For customers, Olde Favorites is a place of discovery and charm, a cottage filled with Victorian, mid-20th century furniture of rich mahogany, American primitives and uncountable little items to enhance any home. This is no glitzy operation — Olde Favorites is the quintessential neighborhood shop, as inviting as afternoon tea in Surrey. (And you will probably be offered a cup!) You'll find such things as tables, chairs, desks, whatnots and chests in the Victorian style; pictures, lamps, glass and other antique accessories; a variety of primitive items; silver plate and china in older patterns; greeting cards and candles. Because the shop is compact and the front door none too big, the furniture pieces are smaller — which just happens to be ideal for 1980s rooms without 10-foot ceilings. "I don't have a dozen examples of each thing," says the unfailingly pleasant Marilyn. "Just one nice piece. Quality instead of quantity." Visa. MasterCard.

Raleigh Hills
5555 SW Scholls
Ferry Road
Portland 97225
297-6009

Monday-Thursday
11am-5pm
Friday closed
Saturday 11am-5pm
And By Appointment

Southwest
Portland
F3

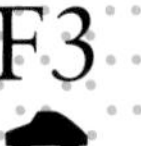

LUDEMAN'S FIREPLACE & PATIO SHOP

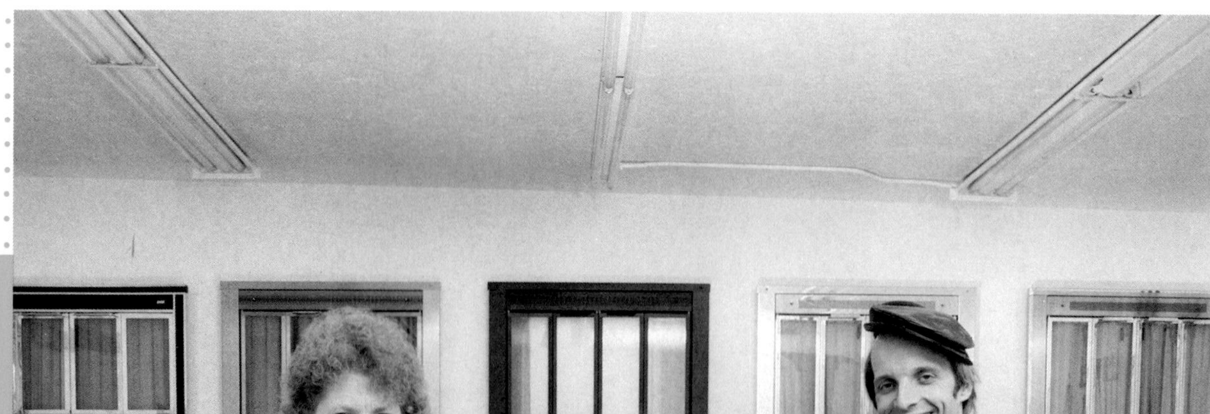

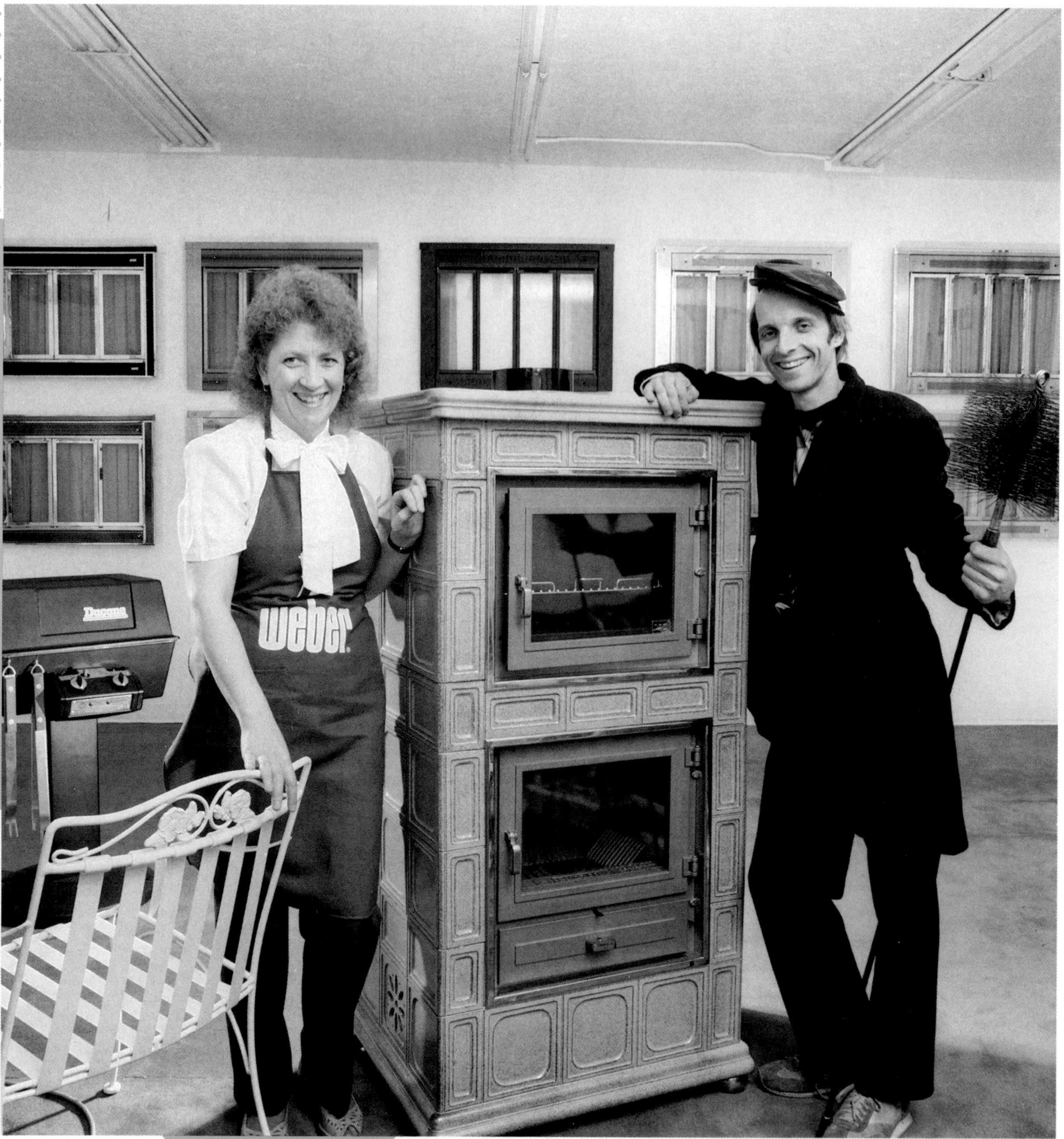

INTERIORS

Fireplace and barbeque equipment, installation and service.

Beaverton

E2

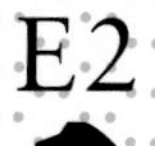

With six years' experience as chimney sweeps behind them, it might be said that Mark and Jennifer Ludeman know their business from the inside out. Furthermore, because Portland has both dry and hot, and wet and chilly weather, it could be said that few businesses address the pleasures of the Northwest seasons as exactingly as Ludeman's Fireplace and Patio Shop in Beaverton. All under one roof you'll find the outdoorsy pleasures of summer in the form of natural gas and propane barbecue equipment and parts, awnings and patio furniture, and then as the season turns, an inventory guaranteed to take the chill out of those crisp, damp nights. Nothing warms the heart like a fireplace, so whether your preference is for gas logs or wood from your own neatly chopped pile, Ludeman's has just what you need. For example, Ludeman's displays more than 20 glass doors in custom and stock sizes, plus at least 80 types of fireplace tool sets in solid brass, plated brass and wrought iron. For those with alternate heating arrangements, they stock a broad selection of woodstoves and inserts. Questions? Problems? Not to worry. As certified chimney sweeps, safety inspectors and licensed contractors, Ludeman's is fully prepared not only to sell, but also to install and service their merchandise. Let's just say they know whereof they heat. Visa. MasterCard.

126th & Canyon Road
Beaverton 97005
646-6409

Monday-Saturday
9am-6pm
Sunday noon-5pm

FINAL TOUCHES

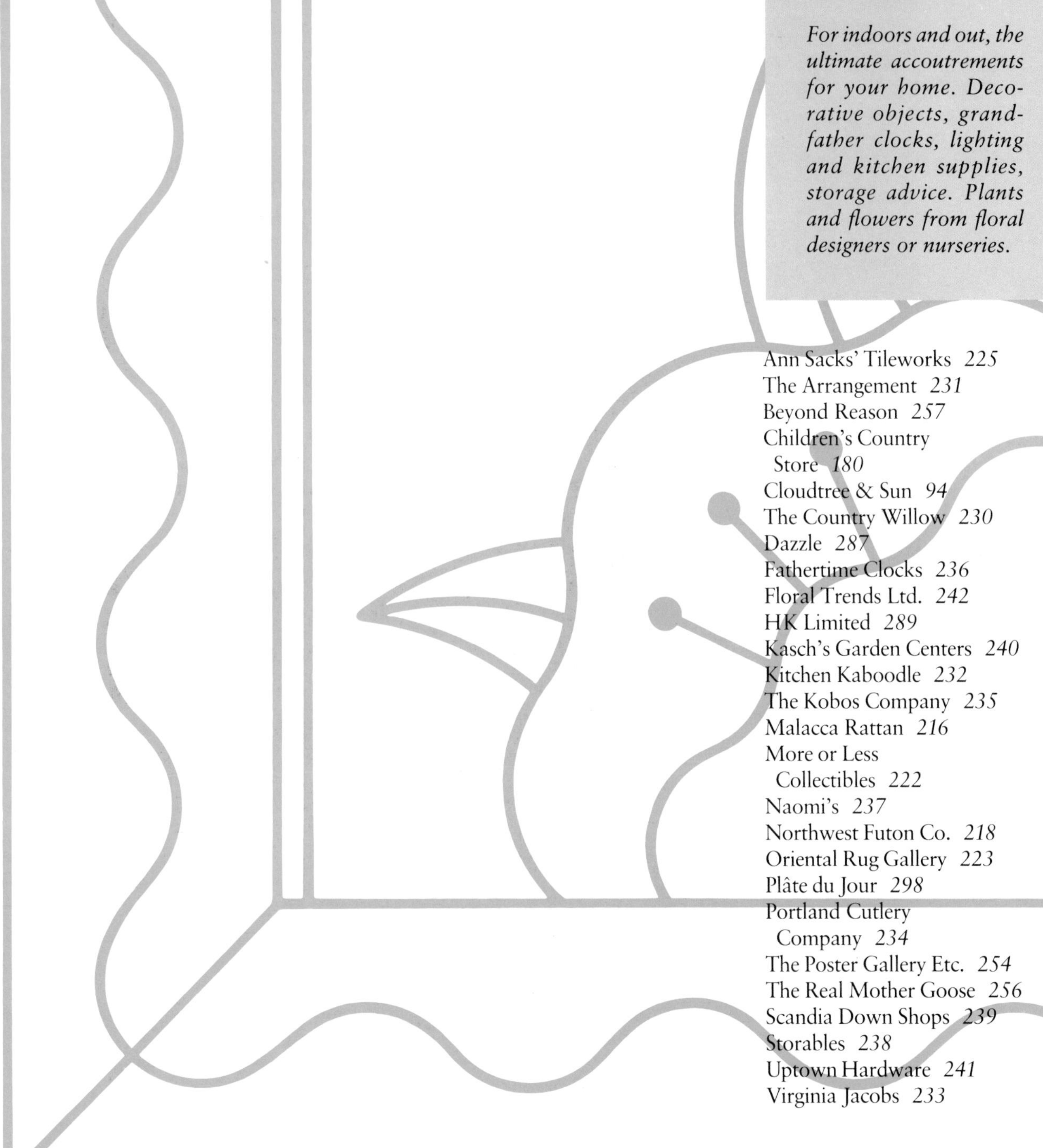

For indoors and out, the ultimate accoutrements for your home. Decorative objects, grandfather clocks, lighting and kitchen supplies, storage advice. Plants and flowers from floral designers or nurseries.

Ann Sacks' Tileworks *225*
The Arrangement *231*
Beyond Reason *257*
Children's Country Store *180*
Cloudtree & Sun *94*
The Country Willow *230*
Dazzle *287*
Fathertime Clocks *236*
Floral Trends Ltd. *242*
HK Limited *289*
Kasch's Garden Centers *240*
Kitchen Kaboodle *232*
The Kobos Company *235*
Malacca Rattan *216*
More or Less Collectibles *222*
Naomi's *237*
Northwest Futon Co. *218*
Oriental Rug Gallery *223*
Plâte du Jour *298*
Portland Cutlery Company *234*
The Poster Gallery Etc. *254*
The Real Mother Goose *256*
Scandia Down Shops *239*
Storables *238*
Uptown Hardware *241*
Virginia Jacobs *233*

THE COUNTRY WILLOW

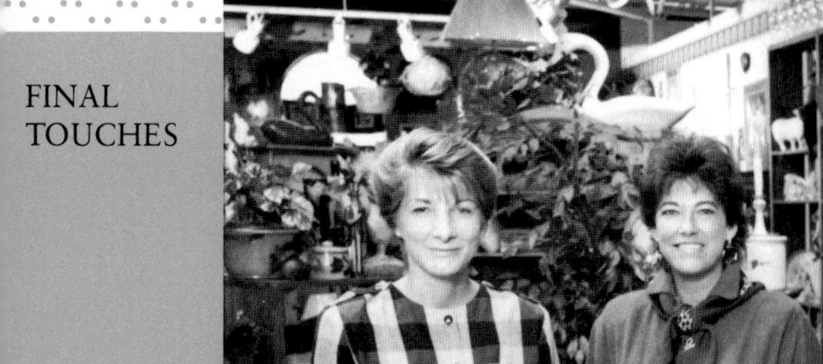

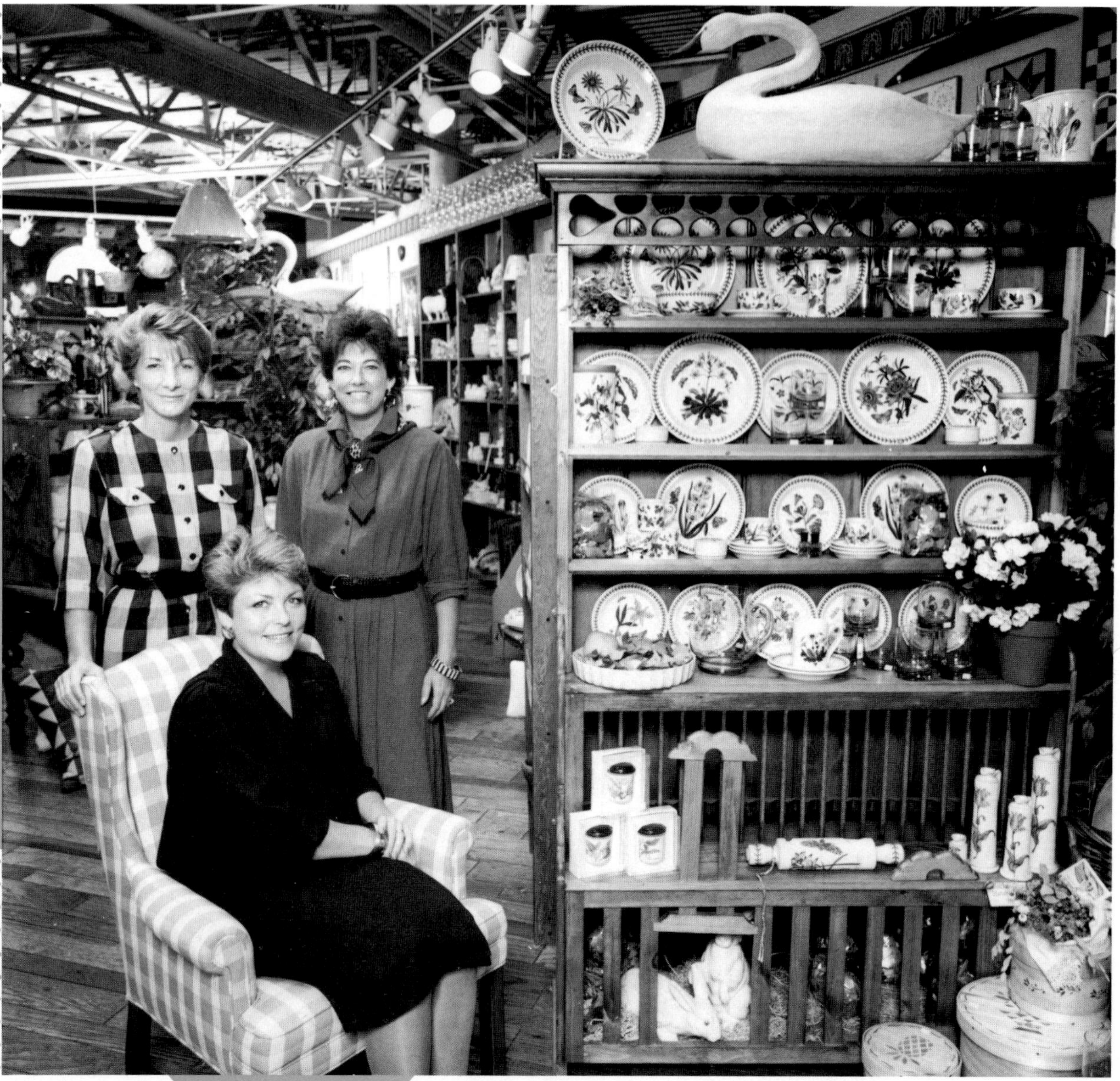

American by design.

Yamhill
Historic
District
G25

Life, it seems, is becoming colder and more impersonal with each passing year. Ask for a telephone number and you get a recording; bank "tellers" are becoming steel buttons with electronic personalities. A reaction, perhaps, to the world of chrome and glass is the rebirth of interest in country and traditional furniture and designs — a reawakening that sparked creation of The Country Willow. Joan Stockton, owner along with husband Steve, explains: "With the high tech and high stress of our society today, we feel that one's home needs to be a warm, personal refuge where you can be surrounded by the things you love." The store is in itself a refuge, offering a collection of Northwest, American and international gifts. There, the visitor can find American folk art by local and national craftspeople and custom furniture built locally to the customer's specifications. Ceramics — everything including Port Merion from England to the traditional salt glazed pottery from Rowe Pottery in Wisconsin — American and Italian brass items such as candlesticks and carafes — rag area rugs and imported Dhurries — are all here. And a "country collection" of placemats, napkins, and dishtowels are complemented by the subtle fragrances of one of the largest selections of bulk potpourri in town. Country Willow also showcases a classic selection of lace table runners, placemats, pillows and aprons. To help bring the kind of satisfaction with your surroundings that is as enduring as the finest traditional designs, The Country Willow also offers an interior decorating service. Visa. MasterCard. American Express.

Yamhill Marketplace
2nd Level
110 SW Yamhill Street
Portland 97204
222-6215

Daily
10am-6pm

THE ARRANGEMENT

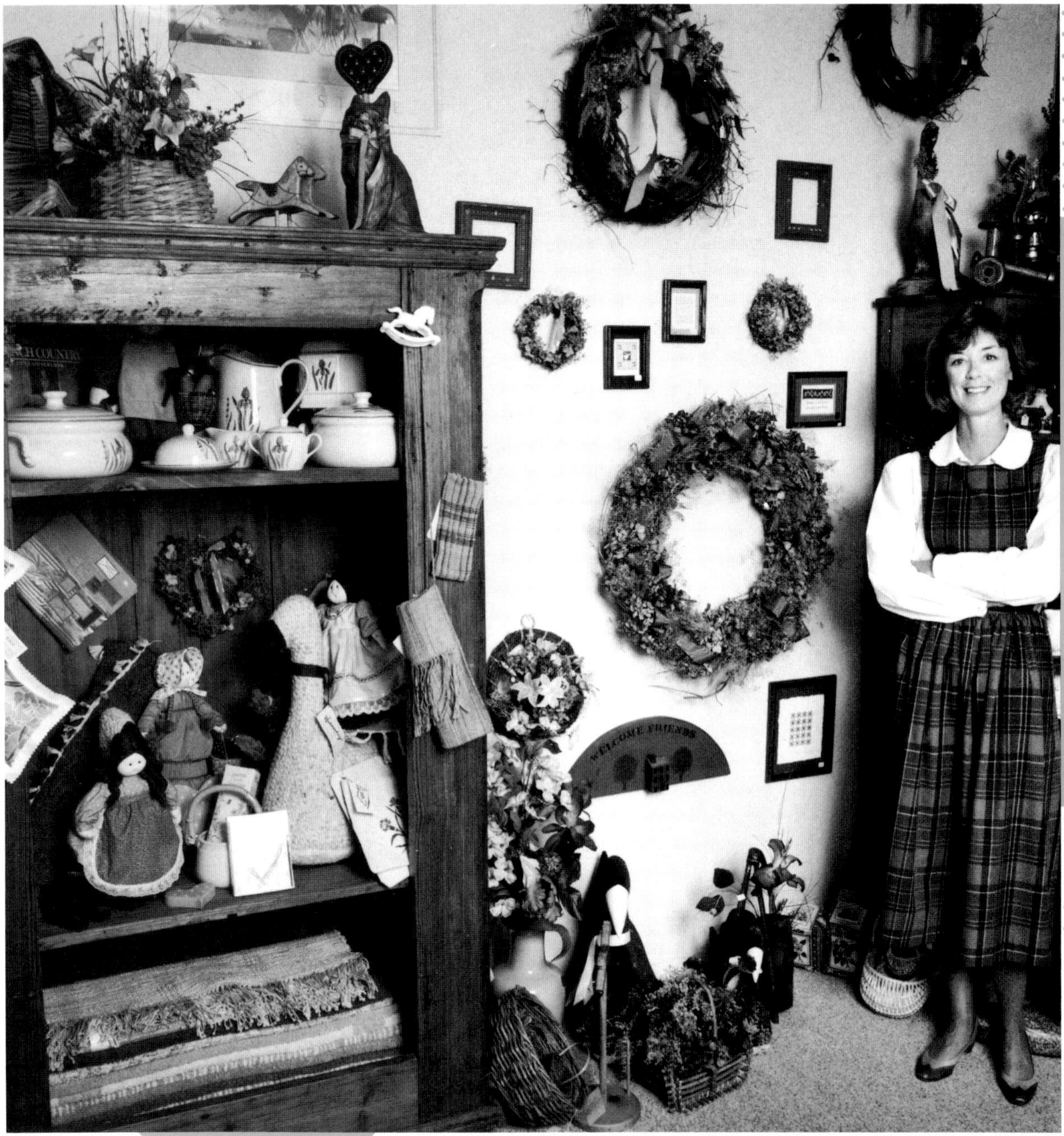

FINAL TOUCHES

Flowers, fashions and fabulous gifts.

Picture a brick-trimmed colonial building with grassy courtyard and brightly colored flower beds. Add to that an interior with pine hutches and white wicker brimming with American country items, and what do you have? The Arrangement, a gift shop with a new outlook on some cherished traditions. Originally built as a service station for the Beaumont neighborhood in 1925, the building was converted in 1983 to house The Arrangement. The shop still reflects its 1920's heritage with high ceilings, stucco-textured white walls and exposed weathered brick. Today's additions are handcrafted rugs, baskets, dolls, wooden Americana, and a selection of womens accessories — including a large selection of earrings, belts, handbags, and scarves. There is also an exceptional display of greeting cards and paper goods. But the real focus of the shop is owner Sue Mautz's floral arrangements. Dried and silk flowers, vine garlands, fresh seasonal flowers — they even do weddings — and a selection of colorful pottery provide The Arrangements special atmosphere. Holiday wreaths — custom shipped — and festive Christmas gifts and ornaments are a seasonal highlight. So come in anytime of the year to experience the natural charm of The Arrangement. Visa. MasterCard.

4210 NE Fremont
Portland 97213
287-4440

Monday-Saturday
10am-6pm
Sunday noon-5pm

Northeast Portland

C7

KITCHEN KABOODLE

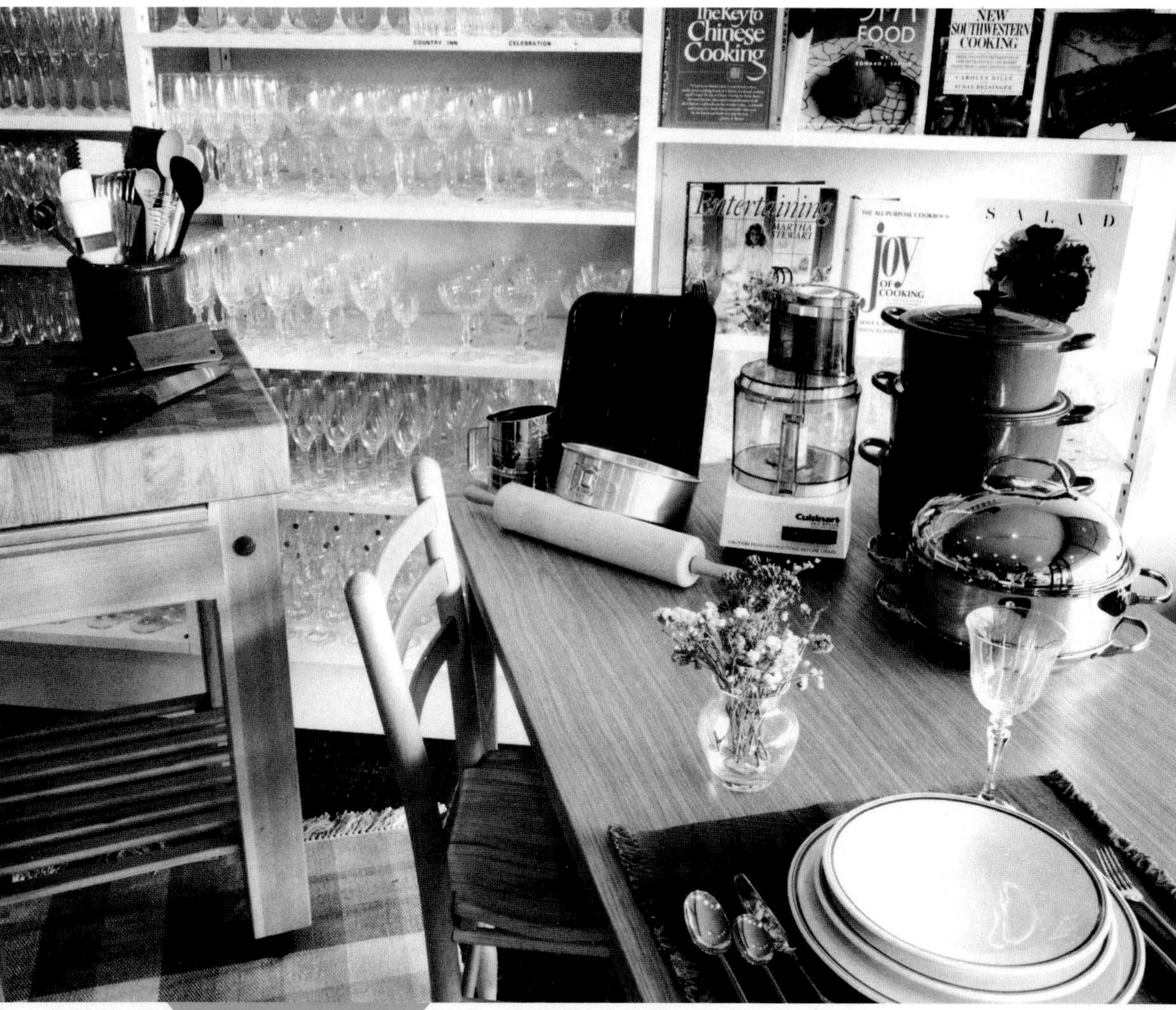

FINAL TOUCHES

We've come out of the kitchen.

Northwest Portland
I17

Downtown
F24

Progress-Washington Square
G3

Southeast Portland
H9

First they conquered the kitchen, and now the owners of Kitchen Kaboodle offer furnishings and equipment for every corner of the house. The name's the same ("Every Room Kaboodle" wouldn't sound quite right) and so is something else — the service and selection that made Kitchen Kaboodle the pre-eminent store of its kind in the Pacific Northwest. (Now, as always, Kaboodle customers are treated to products that are special, appealing and often not found in the mass-market stores.) If you're looking for what others will be selling tomorrow, chances are Kitchen Kaboodle has it today. Naturally, the basics are never neglected. (Likewise, if it's an esoteric gadget that others don't have — or have never heard of — Kitchen Kaboodle is a likely source.) Plus, you'll find more kit and kaboodle here than ever — leather sofas; dining tables of oak, ash and maple; oak beds; modular wall systems; children's bunk beds; home office and computer desks; closet storage systems; desk and pendant lamps — and lots more. Cuisinart's food processors and cookware, Henckel's exquisite cutlery, Krups's finely constructed small appliances, Taylor Woodcraft butcher-block tables, Porcelain D'Auteuil dinnerware and Elfa storage systems are but a small part of the inventory. Visa. MasterCard.

404 NW 23rd at Flanders
Portland 97210
241-4040

Monday-Thursday
10am-6pm
Friday 10am-9pm
Saturday 10am-6pm
Sunday noon-5pm

606 SW Washington at Sixth
Portland 97204
227-5131

Monday-Thursday
9:30am-6pm
Friday 9:30am-7pm
Saturday 9:30am-6pm
Sunday noon-5pm

8788 SW Hall Boulevard
Portland 97223
643-5491

Monday-Thursday
10am-6:30pm
Friday 10am-8pm
Saturday 10am-6pm
Sunday noon-5pm

Clackamas Town Center
Portland 97266
652-2567

Monday-Friday
10am-9pm
Saturday 10am-6pm
Sunday noon-5pm

VIRGINIA JACOBS

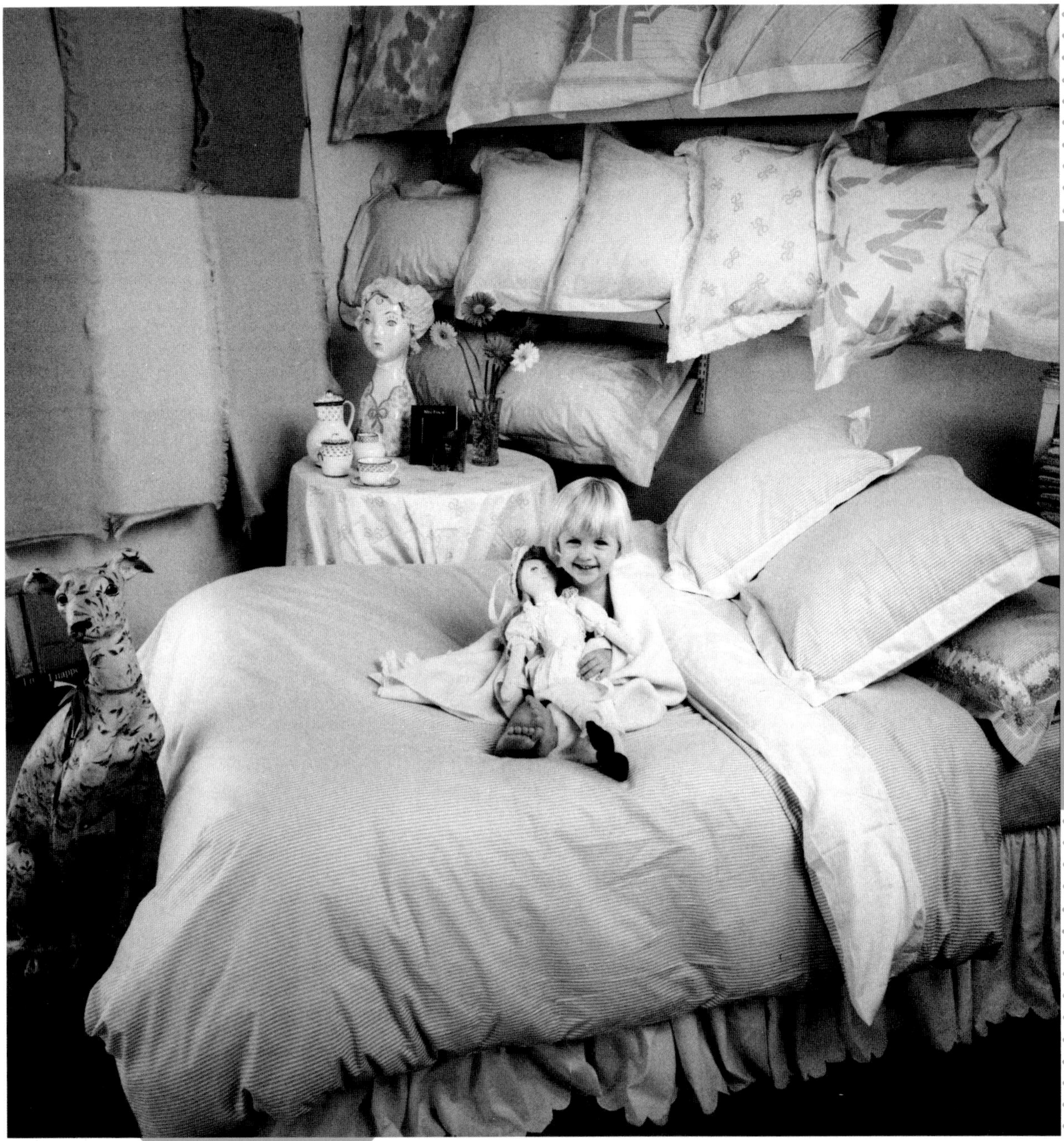

FINAL TOUCHES

Elegant, charming, a breath of fresh air.

You need only travel to Virginia Jacobs in Raleigh Hills to behold some of the finest linens that grace the boudoirs of Europe. A tour of this inviting, uncluttered store is like a European shopping trip: bedding, duvets and square pillows from France, table linens from Ireland, flannel sheets from Belgium and England. Owners Meg Virginia Finch and Sarah Jacobs Kingery combined their names and talents to provide Northwest residents with some of the most exquisite contemporary and traditional linens as well as custom bedcovers and monogrammed blanket covers. For those allergic to down and feathers, there are fine cashmere, mohair and wool comforters covered in 100% long stem Egyptian cotton ticking. European elegance need not stop in your bedroom. With Meg or Sarah's assistance, you can bring the discriminating taste of the continent to your table with hand painted French Faience and crystal glassware. Last minute entertainers and gift givers never need to lose sleep again — Virginia Jacobs even delivers to your door. Visa. MasterCard. American Express.

Raleigh Hills
4830 SW Scholls Ferry Road
Portland 97225
297-1882

Monday-Friday
10am-6pm
Saturday 11am-4pm

Southwest Portland

F3

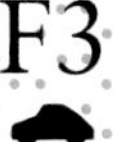

PORTLAND CUTLERY COMPANY

The sharpest shop in town.

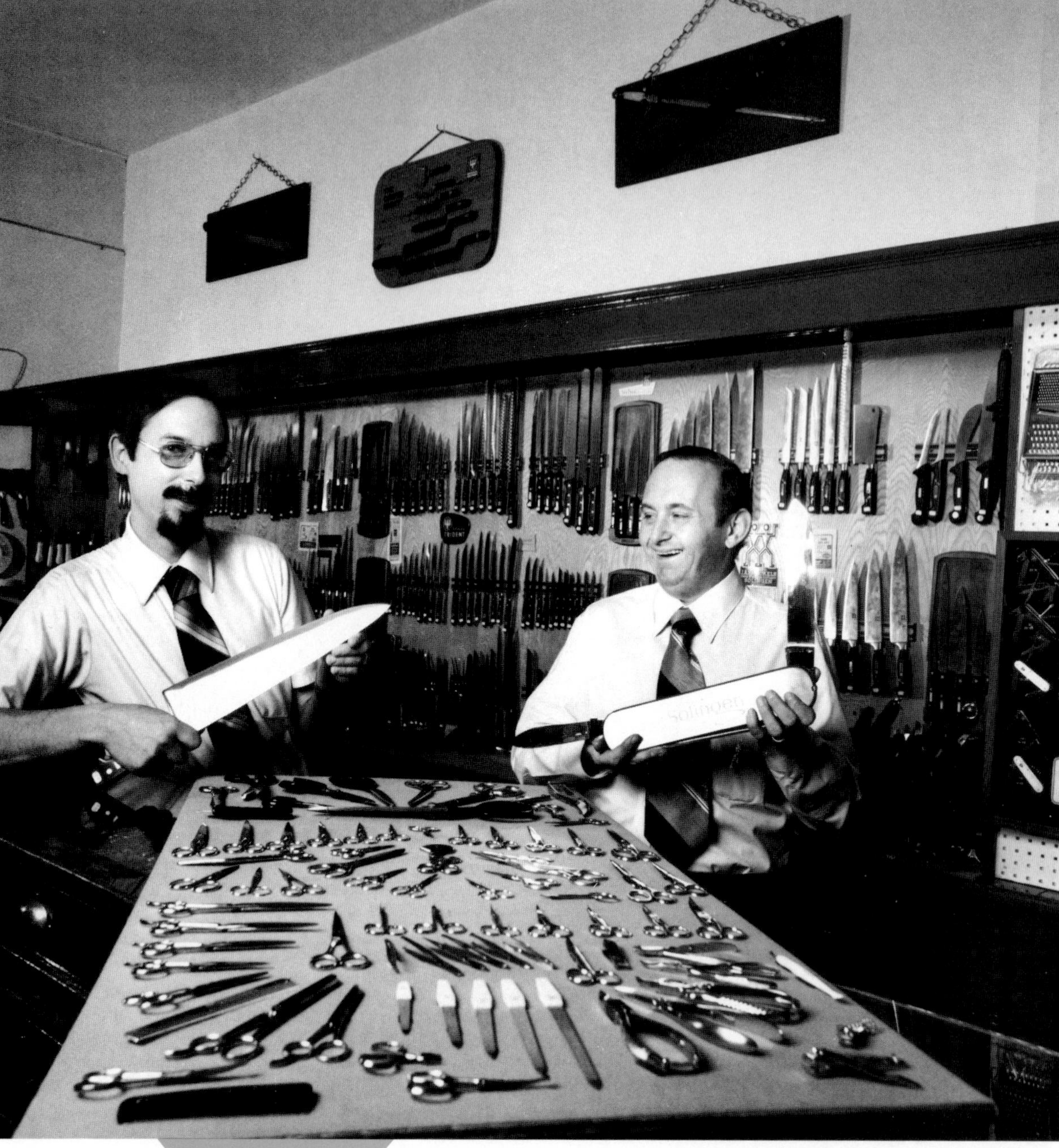

Downtown
F24

You can shop with confidence at the Portland Cutlery Company because proprietor Robert A. Steinmetz cares about cutlery. He won't sell any item he wouldn't be proud to own. Portland Cutlery Company has specialized in top quality tools since 1905. Kitchen knives; hunting and pocket knives; manicure and pedicure tools; scissors for crafts, sewing and barbering; tools for hobbies and gardening — the selection of cutting implements will fill your every need. In this pleasant atmosphere, staff members are helpful and well-informed. They can direct you to your special knife, as well as to a top-quality selection of shaving gear, weather instruments and magnifiers. Portland Cutlery stocks only the leading brands: J.A. Henckels Twinworks, Ed Wusthof Trident, Gerber Legendary Blades, Buck Knives, Kershaw Knives, Al Mar Knives, Wiss, Bausch & Lomb, Victorinox of Switzerland and Taylor, to name a few. With 80 years' experience you can count on the traditions of quality and service which have been honed to a fine edge at Portland Cutlery — "The Sharpest Shop in Town." Visa. MasterCard. Discover.

536 SW Broadway
Portland 97205
228-2030

Monday-Saturday
9:30am-5:30pm

THE KOBOS COMPANY

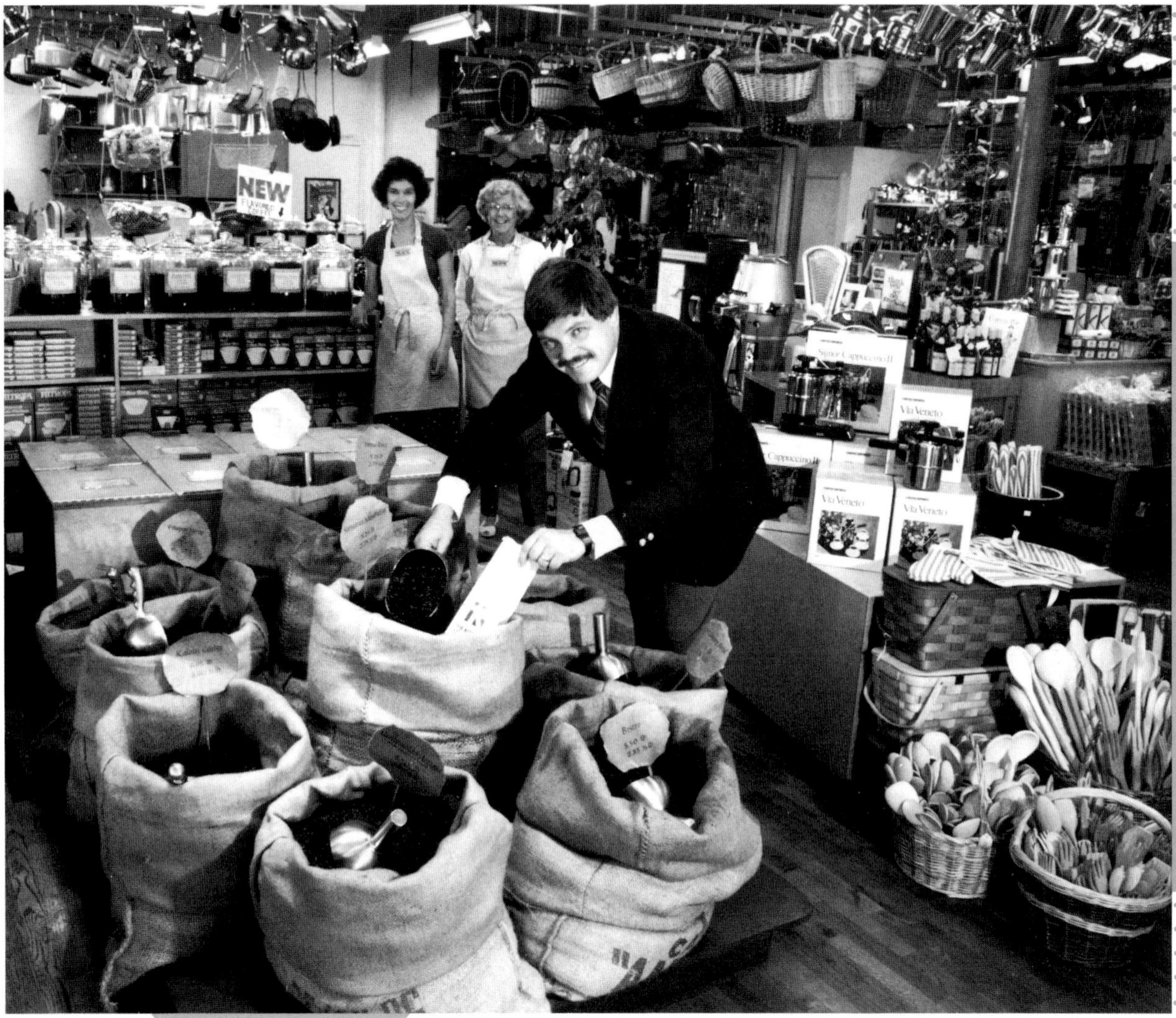

FINAL TOUCHES

Fine coffees, teas, spices and cooking utensils.

Step into a Kobos Company store and you will be assaulted — ever so nicely — by the heady aromas of open sacks of freshly roasted coffee beans, the rich smell of spices, and by the sight of a thousand kitchen tools, filling shelves and hanging from the ceiling. What began as a small venture by former teachers David and Susan Kobos in 1973, has grown to a four-outlet business catering to cooks of all skill levels, and coffee lovers who sip by the cup or buy by the pound. Coffee is the Kobos trademark: fragrant bags of it, waiting to be scooped up by the passing customer. At the Johns Landing store and the Kobos warehouse, all their coffees are fresh roasted, guaranteeing peak flavor. In the "chef's tools" department you'll find everything from can openers to Cuisinarts, cookie cutters to Feemster slicers, bread pans to Kugelhopf moulds. The fine knife selection and array of glassware and stemware round out the selection. There are occasional clinics and classes on coffees and teas, espresso and cappuccino, and personal demonstrations of most of the equipment Kobos sells. Plus, a knife sharpening service where it's all done by hand. Visa. MasterCard. American Express.

The Water Tower
5331 SW Macadam Avenue
Portland 97201
222-5226

Monday-Saturday 10am-9pm
Sunday noon-5pm

Corbett-Johns Landing
F6

Beaverton Town Square
11655 SW Beaverton Hillsdale Highway
Beaverton 97005
646-1620

Monday-Friday 10am-9pm
Saturday 10am-6pm
Sunday noon-5pm

Beaverton
E2

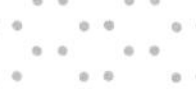

540 SW Broadway
Portland 97205
228-4251

Monday-Friday 7am-6pm
Saturday 9am-6pm
Sunday noon-5pm

Downtown
F24

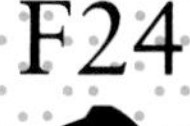

1321 Lloyd Center
Portland 97232
284-4832

Monday-Friday 10am-9pm
Saturday 10am-6pm
Sunday noon-5pm

Northeast Portland
D6

FATHERTIME CLOCKS

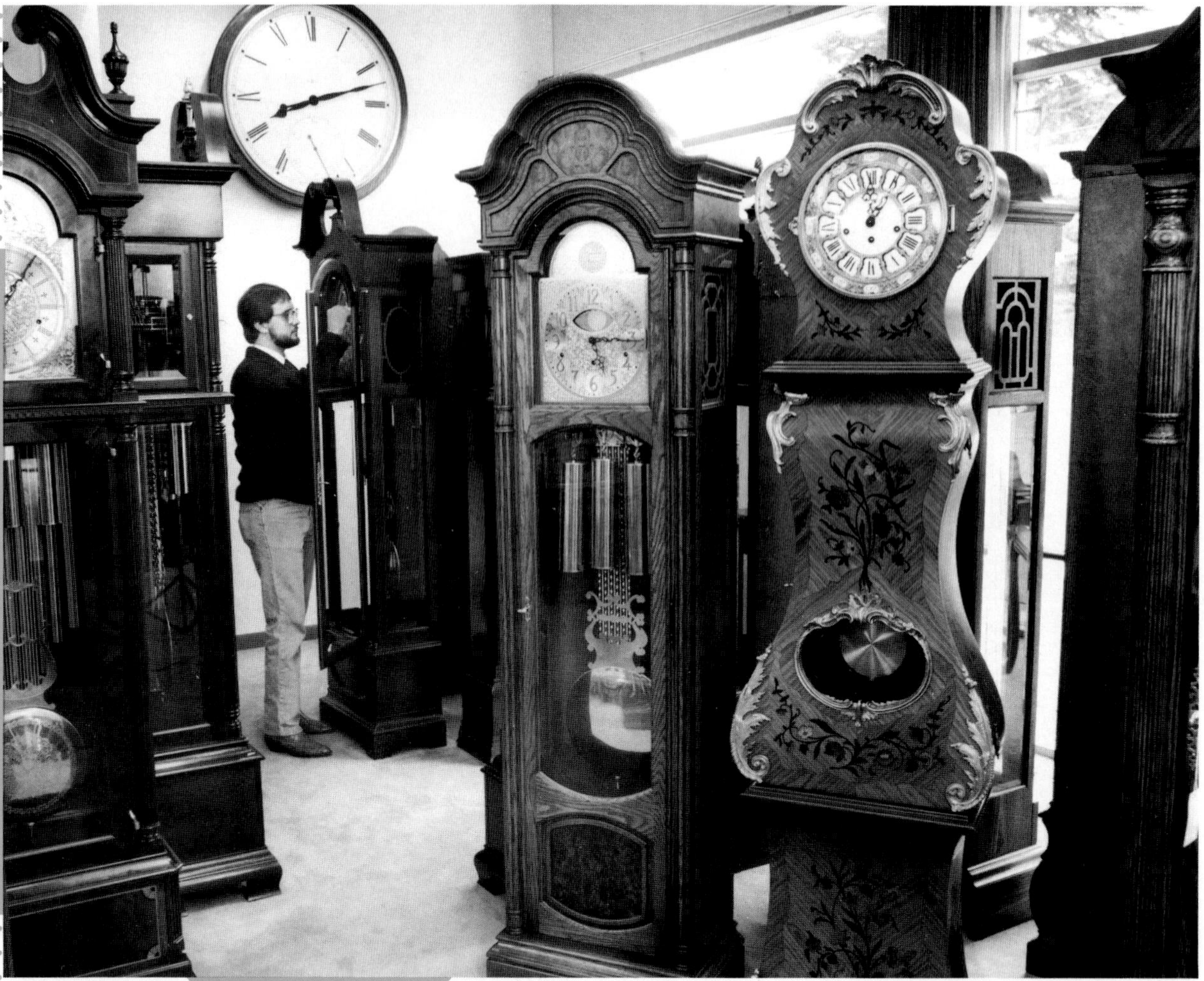

FINAL TOUCHES

Treasures in time.

For all its digitalized, miniaturized and computerized sophistication, today's technology has done nothing to outdo the sheer elegance of a grandfather clock. In a home or office, a grandfather clock transforms a room's feeling with calm tranquility. Grandfather clocks evoke memories of the past, and instill a sense of stability. Fathertime Clocks, with two stores in Portland and one in Salem, is the Northwest's largest clock store. Their specialty is heirloom quality grandfather clocks. Famous brand names offered include Howard Miller, Seth Thomas, Sligh and Ridgeway. Fathertime also displays a wide selection of wall and mantle clocks, barometers, hand inlaid music boxes, cuckoo clocks, pocket watches and globes. Their on-the-premises craftsmen also repair and restore all types of clocks. Trade-ins are accepted on grandfather clock purchases and appraisals for all purposes are provided. So visit Fathertime Clocks and step out of today's fast pace. Visa. MasterCard. Discover.

Southeast Portland
E7

Beaverton
E2

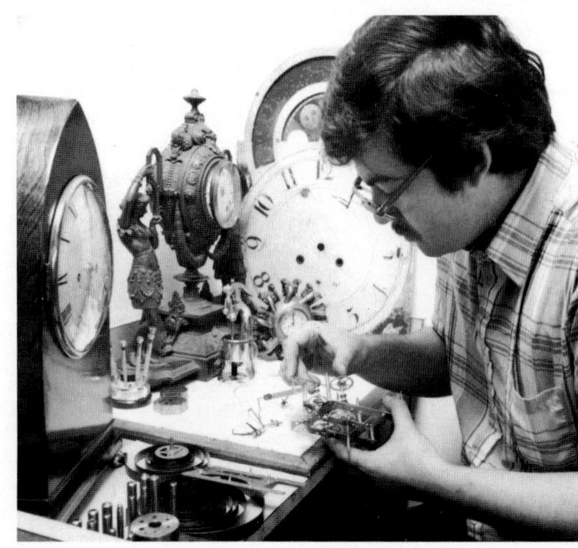

Eastmoreland
4451 SE 28th Avenue
Portland 97202
233-2161

Monday-Saturday
9:30am-5:30pm
Evenings by appointment

Beaverton Town Square
11739 SW Beaverton
Hillsdale Highway
Beaverton 97005
644-9910

Monday-Friday
10am-9pm
Saturday 10am-6pm
Sunday noon-5pm

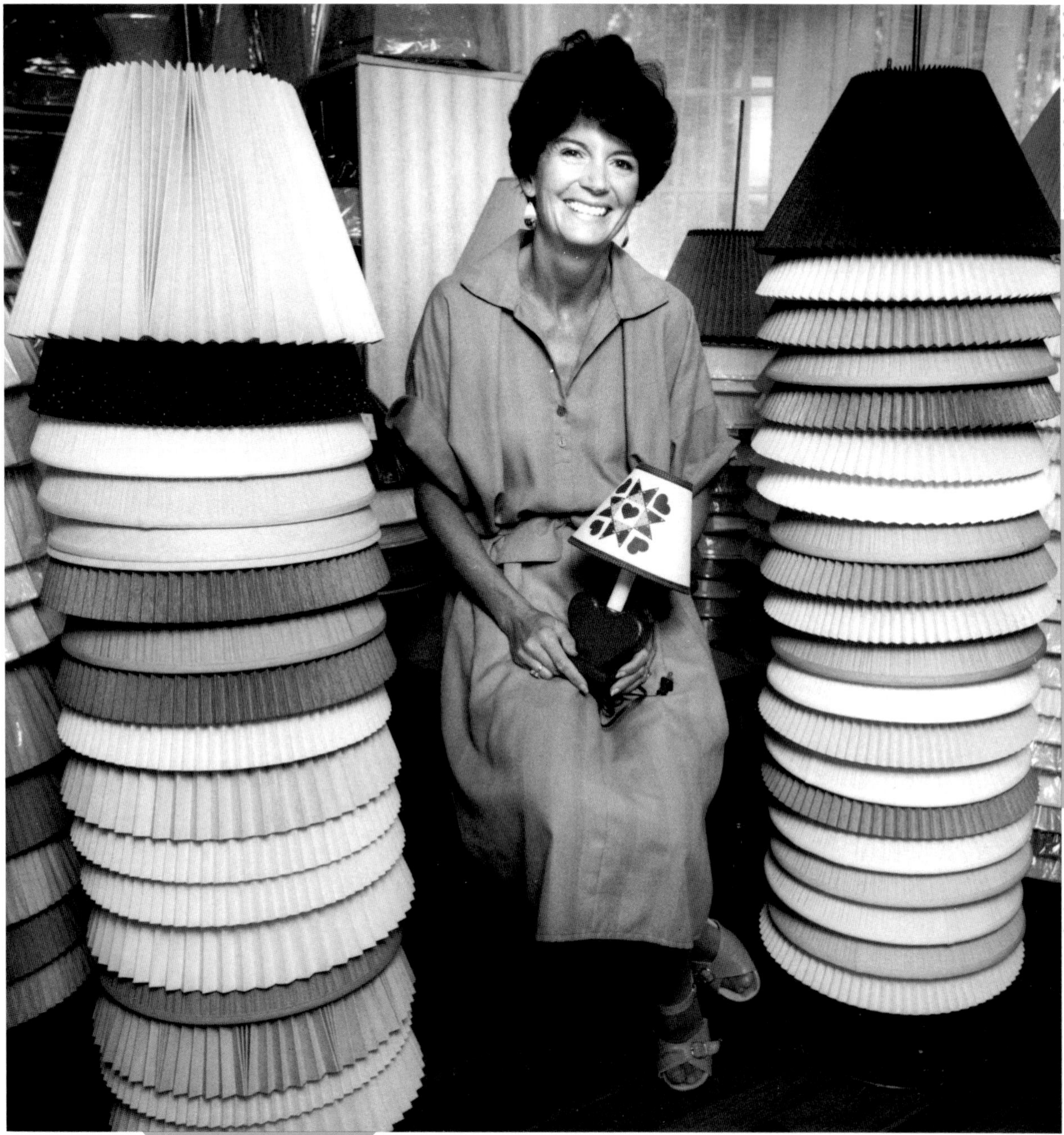

FINAL TOUCHES

The salvation of lamps everywhere.

When the renovators who transformed the old Paramount Theater into the Arlene Schnitzer Concert Hall came to the building's lighting fixtures, they faced a challenge — making the existing equipment deserving of its new, world class home. The task of breathing new life into those pieces fell to a business equal to the assignment: Naomi's Lampshades. For more than forty years, this store has been shedding its light on the repair, refitting and restoration of just about anything that wears a shade and holds a lightbulb. Remember that lamp with the tear in the shade that you turn to the wall so nobody notices? What about the lamp that works fine but needs cosmetic updating? Or the one that's nearly new but has a shade that doesn't quite fit the lamp's design or your room decor? Naomi's — the salvation of lamps everywhere — to the rescue. Besides keeping an inventory that numbers in the thousands, owner Linda Hannum can order any size in a splendid selection of fabrics and colors. So, to keep your lamps from migrating to a garage, attic, basement or closet before their usefulness is exhausted, consider Naomi's. As for objects that aren't exactly lamps now, but could be, Naomi's has the ingenuity and wherewithal to transform them too. Visa. MasterCard. American Express.

15942 SW Boones Ferry Road
Lake Oswego 97035
636-1884

Monday-Saturday
10:30am-5pm

Lake Oswego/ Lake Grove

I4

STORABLES

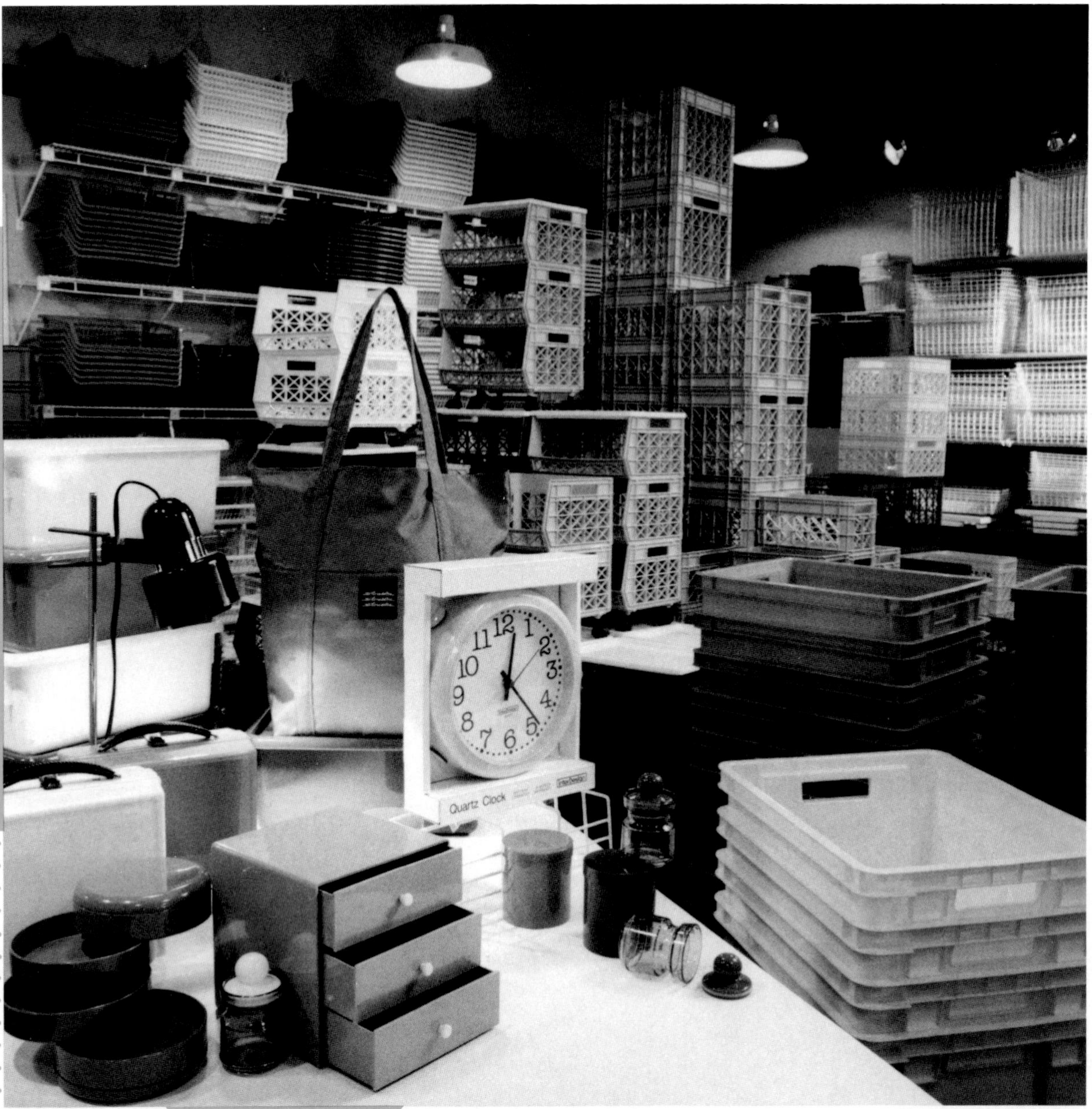

Stow it; stack it; store it.

Beaverton
E2

Downtown
F23

Corbett-Johns Landing
F6

Stow it, stack it, stuff it, store it with contemporary household organizers and storage systems from Storables. Choose from sweater boxes, shoe bags, tie racks, coat hooks, laundry hampers, coat hangers, underbed storage boxes, plastic storage jars, ventilated shelving, drawer systems, freezer baskets, garbage bag caddies, collapsible carts, travel toothbrushes, extension mirrors, market totes, briefcases, organizer grids, shoe stacks, swivel hangers, expanding hooks, stacking shelves, clip lamps, wine stemmers, divided trays, hinged boxes, key holders, shelves, dish racks, file carts, letter baskets, travel desks, mini carts, dishdrainers, organizer boxes, towel holders, adhesive hooks, magnetic mirrors, oval cans, belt anchors, shoe keepers, cassette drawers, tape dispensers, locker mates, roundabouts, pop-up washcloths, key tags, lunch boxes, log carriers, and lots of other fun things! Visa. MasterCard.

Beaverton Town Square
11685 S.W. Beaverton Hillsdale Highway
Beaverton 97005
646-2300

Monday-Friday 10am-9pm
Saturday 10am-6pm
Sunday noon-5pm

The Galleria
921 S.W. Morrison Street
Portland 97205
241-3300

Monday-Friday 10am-9pm
Saturday 10am-6pm
Sunday noon-5pm

The Water Tower
5331 S.W. Macadam Avenue
Portland 97201
227-4900

Monday-Friday 10am-9pm
Saturday 10am-6pm
Sunday noon-5pm

SCANDIA DOWN SHOPS

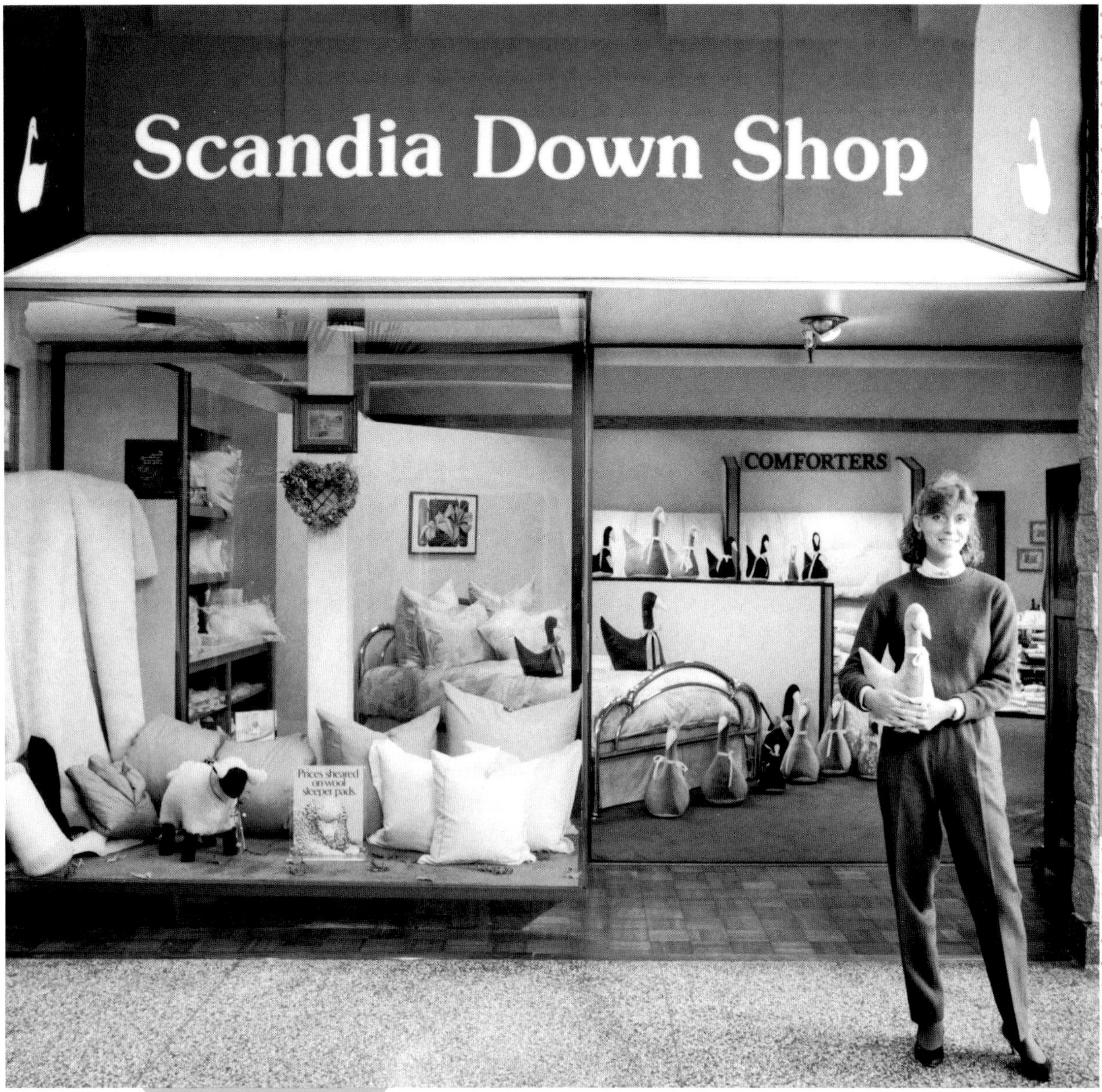

Down comforter outlet.

Just as man cannot fly unassisted, neither has science been able to duplicate that most marvelous natural material, down. There have been attempts, of course, but nothing to match the luxury and resiliency of down. In the bedroom, down brings unsurpassed comfort and coziness, whether it cradles your head or covers you from chin to toes. The advantages of down — warmth in winter, surprising coolness in summer — are significant, and so are the benefits of shopping at Scandia Down Shops. You won't be overwhelmed with department-store frenzy at Scandia Down; the stores are small shops filled with beautiful beds, special linen designs, down comforters, pillows and other items that will turn any bedroom into a sleep-time fantasy. Scandia has comforters of varying size and weight to fit every user, age group and price range, plus pillows filled with down, feathers or a mixture. Design linens are available in domestic and European patterns, the latter of 100% cotton. There also are brass beds by J.B. Ross and a custom sewing service that allows customers to bring in their own fabrics or choose from Scandia Down's large selection of colors and patterns. To make bedroom redecorating a breeze, Scandia's custom sewing center is at your disposal. Visa. MasterCard. American Express. Discover.

Yamhill Marketplace *110 S.W. Yamhill Street* *Portland 97204* *241-0545*	*Daily* *10am-6pm*
Washington Square *9510 S.W. Washington Square Road* *Portland 97223* *684-5112*	*Monday-Friday* *10am-9pm* *Saturday 10am-6pm* *Sunday 11am-6pm*

Yamhill Historic District

G25

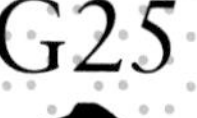

Progress-Washington Square

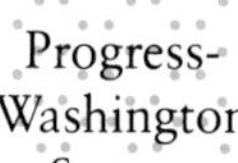

G3

KASCH'S GARDEN CENTERS

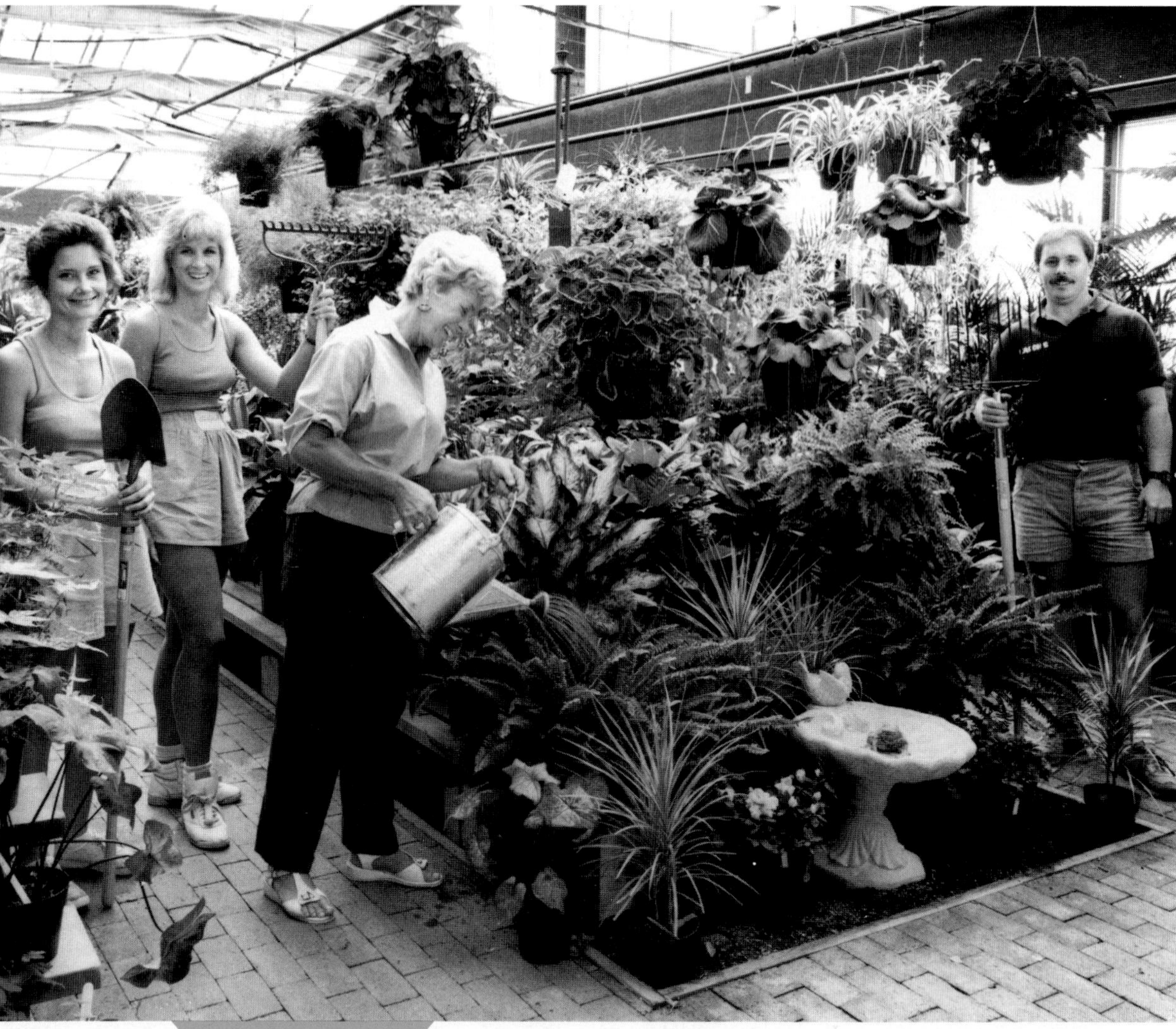

Everything that thrives on the good earth and sunlight.

Southeast Portland
F7

Beaverton
E2

Northeast Portland
D11

If it can be said that some folks have green thumbs, then surely the people at Kasch's Garden Centers have green arms. Day after day, they're up to their elbows in just about anything that thrives on the good earth and sunlight, from houseplants — minuscule to magnificent — to trees, shrubs and vines — dwarf to gigantic. The diversity of plant materials and garden supplies, fertilized by the knowledge of employees trained in plant selection and problem diagnosis, brings a bountiful year-round harvest to the customer. Kasch's, with more than forty years' experience, lays claim to the title of largest independent retail nursery in the Pacific Northwest. Their locations are within easy reach of wherever you are in the metropolitan area, and their inventory includes a constantly changing collection of interest to the very practical and the very particular gardener. There are annual and perennial bedding plants for every season, seeds, bulbs, supplies and plant care products, houseplants, dew-fresh cut flowers, and just about any green thing worth putting in a hole in the yard. Christmas is a special time at Kasch's as trees, lights, ornaments, cookies, fragrances and gracious employees offer a festive, welcome respite during a hectic season. Visa. MasterCard.

McLoughlin at Tacoma
Portland 97202
231-7711

Daily
9am-6pm
Xmas & Spring
9am-8pm

Cedar Hills Boulevard
Beaverton 97005
644-1640

Daily
9am-6pm
Xmas & Spring
9am-8pm

181st, North of Glisan
Portland 97230
661-5020

Daily
9am-6pm
Xmas & Spring
9am-8pm

Fourth Plain at 137th
Vancouver, Washington
98662
(206) 892-2258

Daily
9am-6pm
Xmas & Spring
9am-8pm

UPTOWN HARDWARE

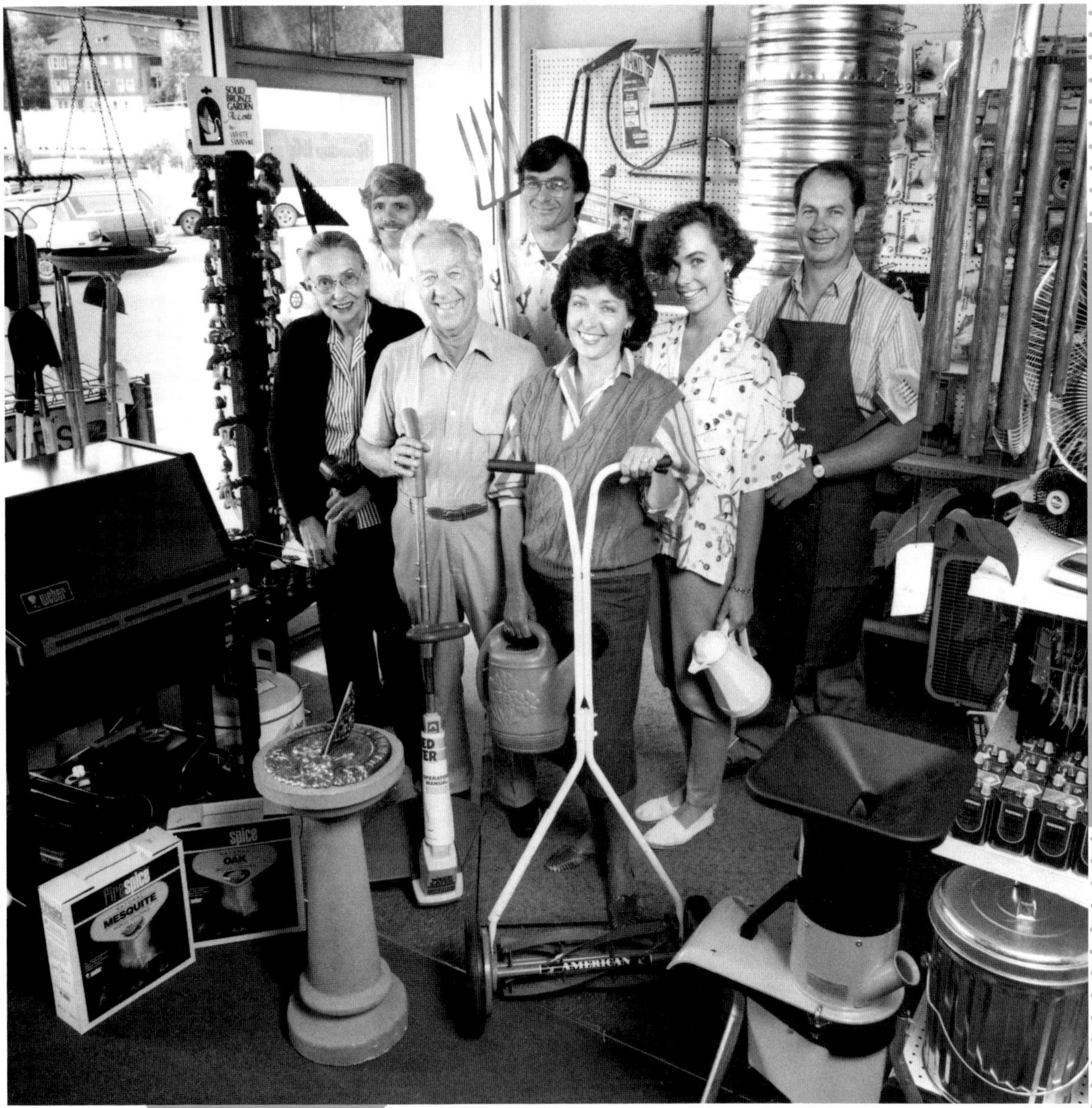

FINAL TOUCHES

Everything you expect from a hardware store...and more.

Northwest Portland

J17

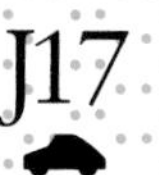

Some words just make you feel good. "Hardware store" has that solid, comforting feeling: it's tools for fixing stuff with dad, rummaging through bins of odd-shaped plumbing fixtures, nuts, bolts, screws; exploring aisles packed with everything you could ever need to do any job around the house. That's Uptown Hardware, home of the "uptown shuffle" where the stock is constantly changing to make room for the ever-fascinating, ever- increasing variety of gadgets and gifts. In addition to nuts and bolts you'll find intriguing items like decorative brass faucets, valves and bibs cast in the shape of birds and animals, weather vanes and sundials. There are hoses and all the usual garden tools; then there's barbeque equipment by Weber in a variety of colors and styles. For kitchen cooking, Uptown Hardware has every type of utensil imaginable, plus a complete line of houseware, bakeware and glassware. The Uptown Shopping Center is one of the oldest in Portland, and Uptown Hardware is one of its original stores. Started in 1950 by Ken McQuestion, Sr., the family business has built a reputation of putting the customer first. Ken has now retired but long-time customers still ask for "the grey haired gentleman who has helped us for so many years." Current owner and son-in-law Duane Cook is determined to carry on such family traditions. Good service has made good memories for customers at Uptown Hardware. Visa. MasterCard.

Uptown Shoppping Center
27 NW 23rd Place
Portland 97210
227-5375

Monday-Friday
9am-6pm
Saturday 9am-5:30pm

FLORAL TRENDS LTD.

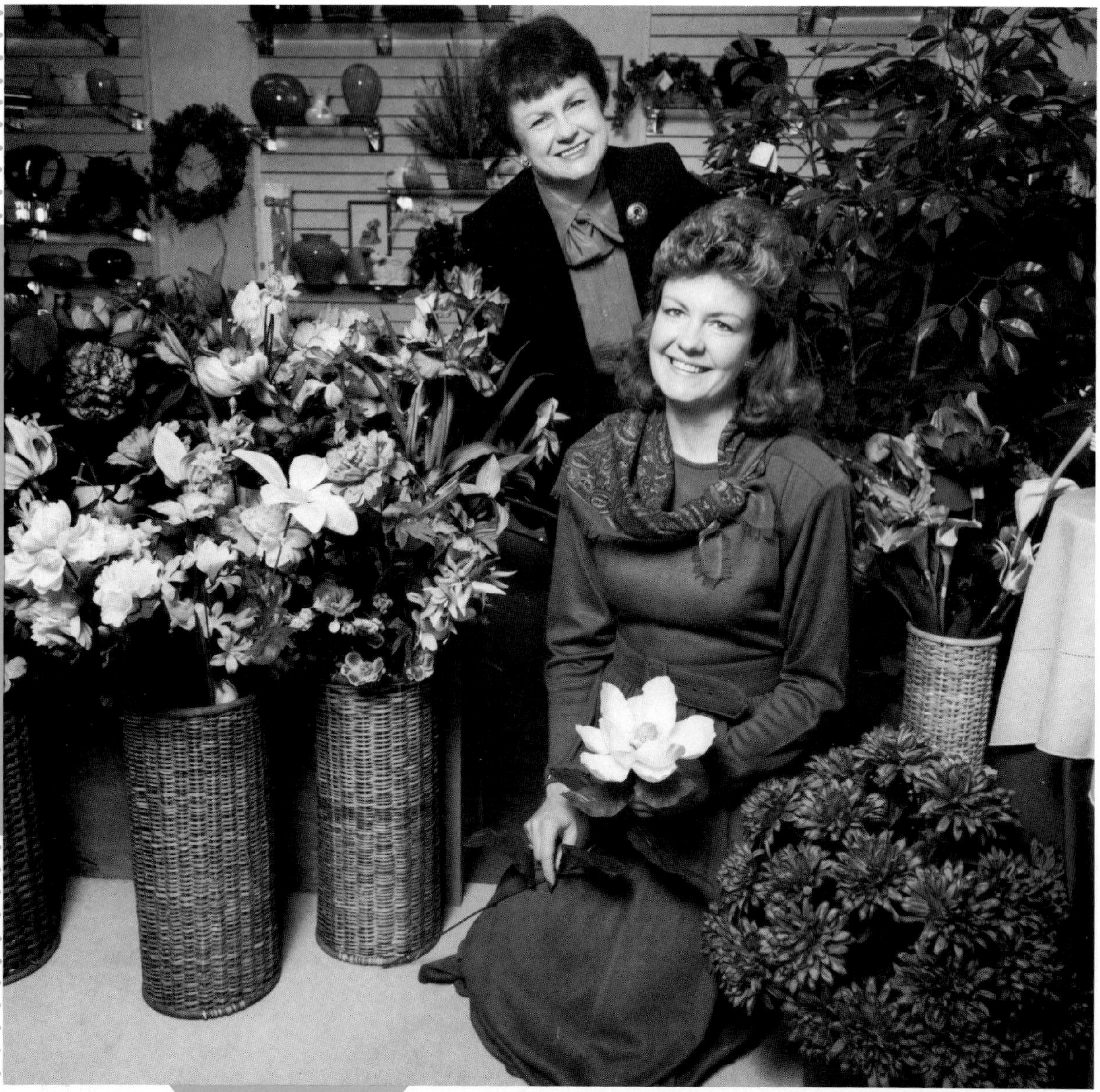

The shop with so much blooming imagination.

Beaverton

E2

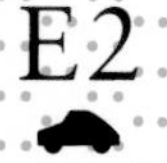

To classify Floral Trends as a florist shop is to describe a Stradivarius as a fiddle. Like the fine violin, Floral Trends is more elegant and sophisticated — like the virtuoso performer. The staff is exquisitely skilled with particular expertise in silk arrangements of all types. The owners, Margie Blair and Denise Sly and staff create designs that, like a fine musical instrument, have lasting value. As custom silk designers and certified floral designers, they specialize in home and office interiors. Their shop features a large selection of flowering stems, plants and trees in silk, but not to the exclusion of the real thing. Floral Trends also has specialists on staff for their fresh flower work. In just two years, the store has become known for its innovation and professionalism. The staff has supplied flowers for famous entertainers, beauty contestants, horse shows and pet poodles; they have decorated baseball bats, carburetors and made arrangements for many a practical joke. When it comes to home or office arrangements, Floral Trends will examine your interior textures and color samples to ensure floral design compatibility. On-site visits are the norm for multi-room projects, and the result, with its stylized European design, is a direct result of this painstaking effort. In its retail department, Floral Trends comes full circle, offering containers, balloons, Lenox candles and a variety of baskets. Wire services are available for world-wide delivery. Visa. MasterCard. American Express. Diners Club. Carte Blanche. Discover.

Beaverton Town Square
11677 SW Beaverton
Hillsdale Highway
Beaverton 97005
626-8437

Monday-Friday
10am-9pm
Saturday 10am-6pm
Sunday noon-5pm

ART AND CRAFT GALLERIES

Regional artists share the billing with established masters in art and fine crafts, contemporary and classic, national and international. Also find consultants, framers and sources of supplies.

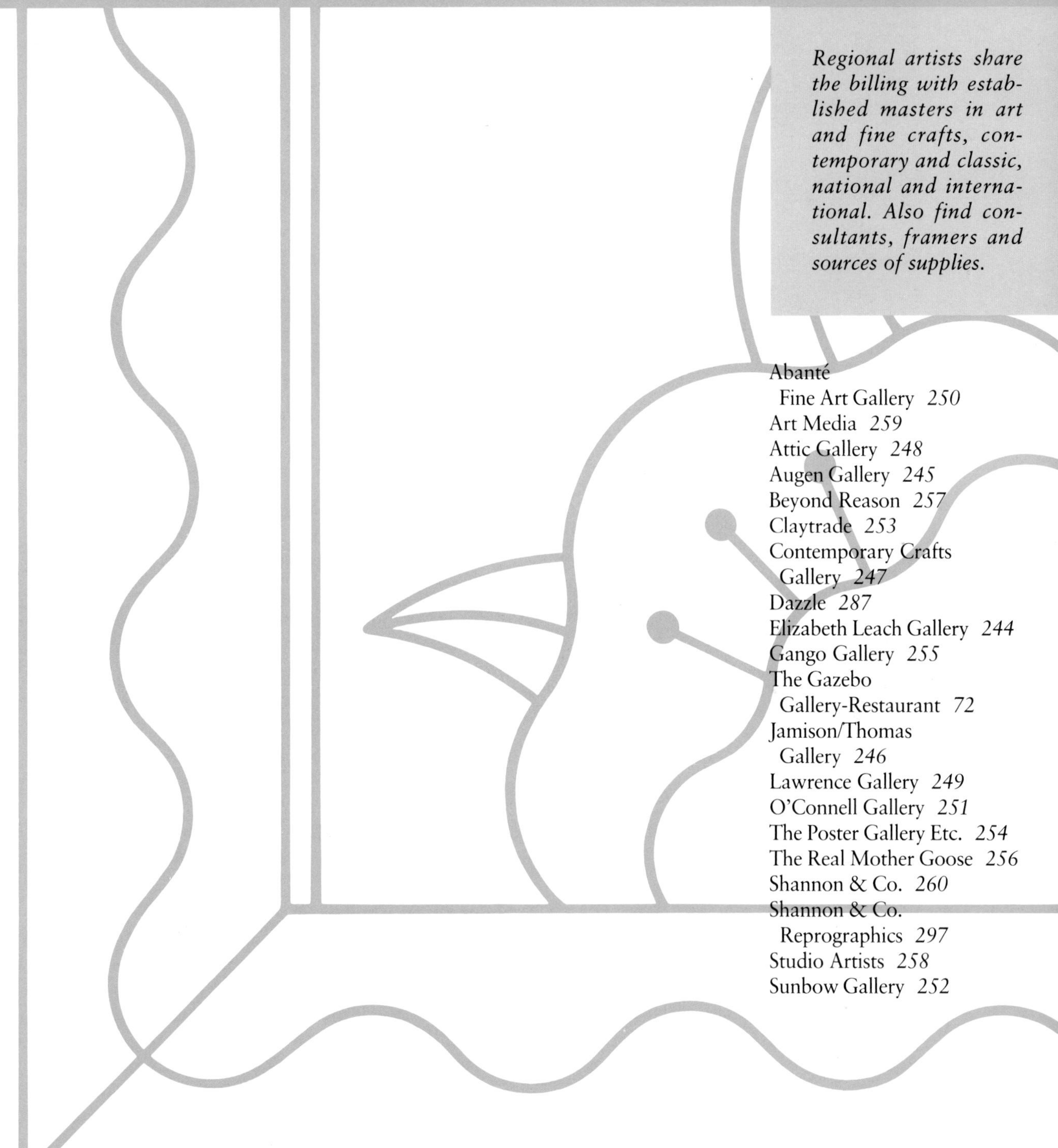

Abanté Fine Art Gallery *250*
Art Media *259*
Attic Gallery *248*
Augen Gallery *245*
Beyond Reason *257*
Claytrade *253*
Contemporary Crafts Gallery *247*
Dazzle *287*
Elizabeth Leach Gallery *244*
Gango Gallery *255*
The Gazebo Gallery-Restaurant *72*
Jamison/Thomas Gallery *246*
Lawrence Gallery *249*
O'Connell Gallery *251*
The Poster Gallery Etc. *254*
The Real Mother Goose *256*
Shannon & Co. *260*
Shannon & Co. Reprographics *297*
Studio Artists *258*
Sunbow Gallery *252*

ELIZABETH LEACH GALLERY

ART GALLERY

Contemporary fine art; paintings, sculpture, national prints.

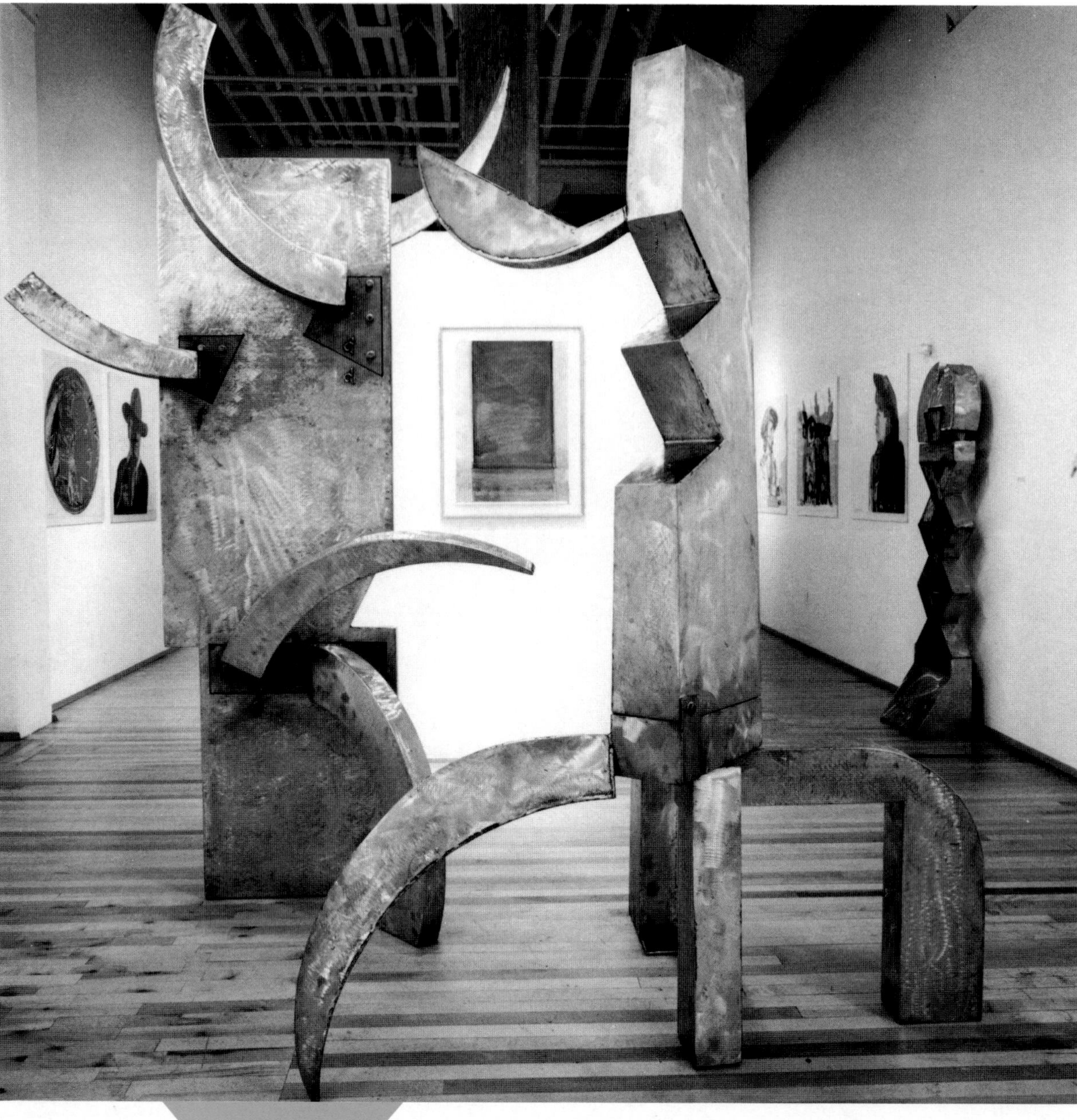

Skidmore Historic District

E25

High energy and dedication to the arts distinguishes the Elizabeth Leach Gallery. Each month new paintings, sculptures or recent national prints are featured in this downtown gallery located in the historic Haseltine Building. Exhibits highlight major blue chip artists like Wayne Thiebaud, Mark Di Suvero, Andy Warhol, Richard Estes as well as established regional talent such as Lee Kelly, Michihiro Kosuge, Laura Ross-Paul and Richard Gruetter. The gallery specializes in consulting with businesses and private clients to build collections of value. Elizabeth Leach worked as a consultant when it was determined to include original art in the Heathman Hotel's 160 guest rooms and public spaces. Other projects include Lee Kelly's sculpture commission for Cornell Oaks Corporate Center, a 40 x 50 feet stainless steel sculpture just off the Sunset Highway, and a special commissioned limited edition portfolio for One Financial Center. Elizabeth Leach has been nominated and accepted to the 1987 edition of Who's Who in American Art for her published articles about art and architectural history and curatorial work. She is currently organizing upcoming events for the Spring which include a tour of private homes featuring gardens landscaped with sculptural focal points, and in the Fall an outdoor sculpture exhibition at Yamhill Marketplace. Visa. MasterCard.

207 SW Pine Street
Portland 97204
224-0521

Monday-Friday
10:30am-5:30pm
Saturday 10am-5pm
First Thursday of each month until 9pm

AUGEN GALLERY

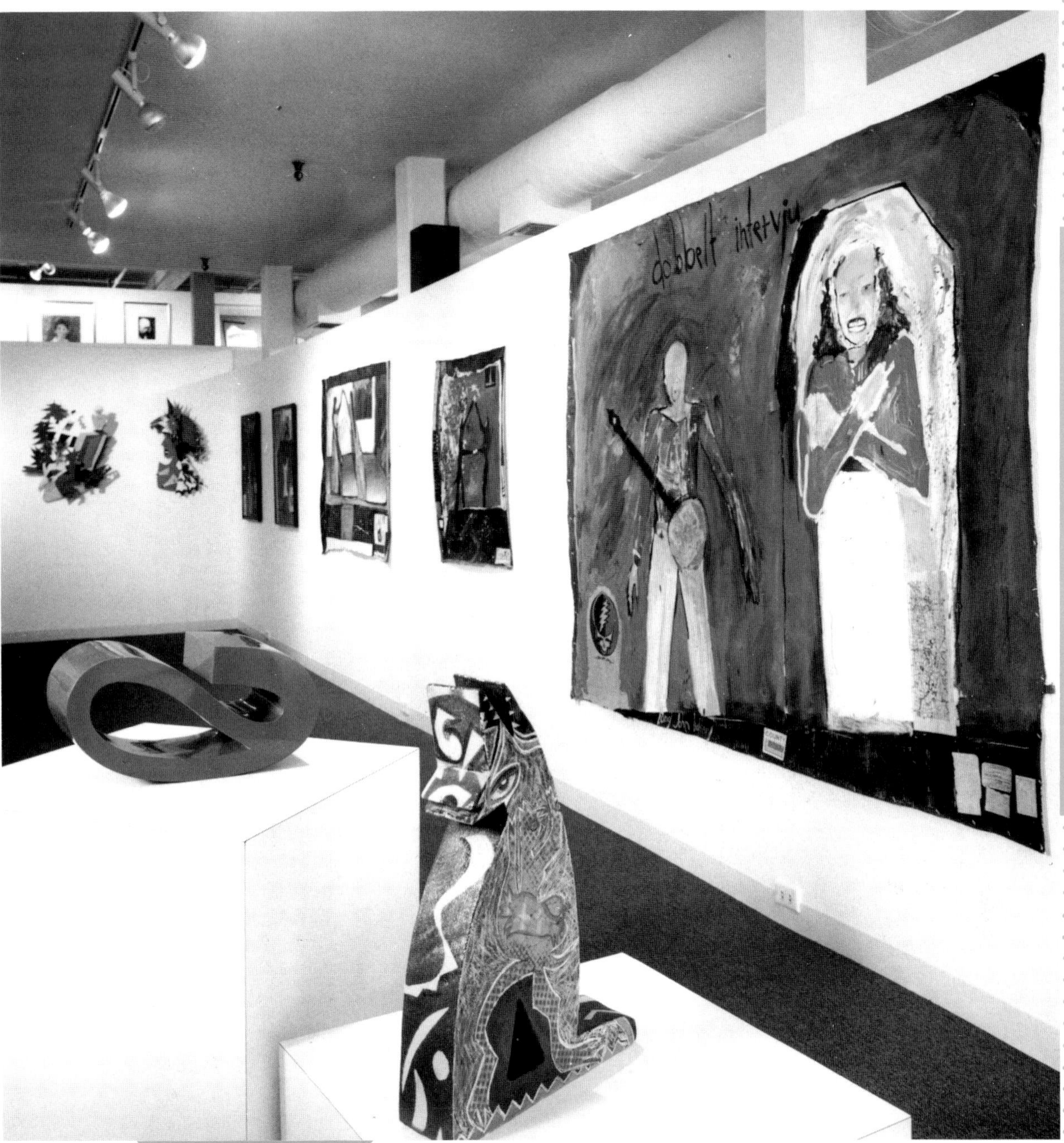

ART GALLERY

Displaying works of regional, national and international artists.

Among art connoisseurs, Augen Gallery is known both for its active publishing of handmade prints by Pacific Northwest artists and for its display of prints and other works of art on paper. In most cases, Augen Gallery is the only Portland outlet for important and exemplary works from a host of regionally, nationally and internationally known artists. Here, the collector will discover prints from Hockney, Lichtenstein, Stella, Wesselman, Motherwel and others. Take some time to discover the complex and colorful reduction linoleum block prints of K.C. Joyce, photographs by the Pacific Northwest's own Deborah Dewit, handprinted paper collage multiples from Daniel Goldstein and paintings by Royal Nebeker. Augen's custom and archival framing reflects their special expertise in preparing photographs and other works for collectors, businesses and the design trade. Recently Augen Gallery has moved to a new space directly across the street from Yamhill Marketplace on Second Avenue. Within 9000 square feet, Augen now offers more viewing space than any other private gallery in Portland. Visa. MasterCard. American Express.

817 SW Second Avenue
Portland 97204
224-8182

Monday-Saturday
10:30am-5:30pm
First Thursday of each month until 9pm

Yamhill Historic District

G25

JAMISON/THOMAS GALLERY

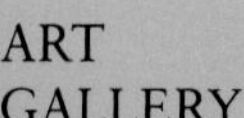

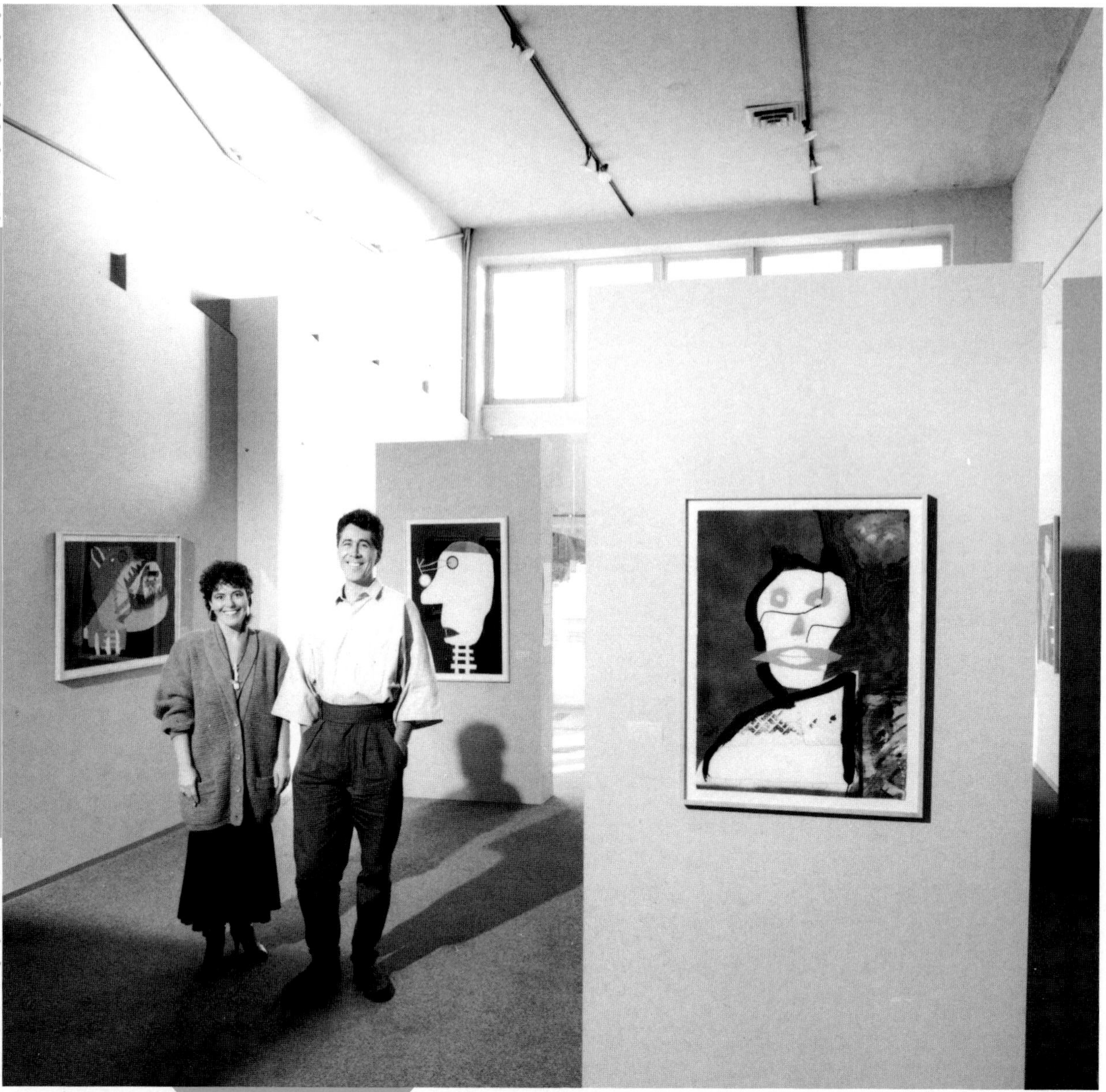

ART GALLERY

Representing West Coast folk, outsider and contemporary art.

Skidmore Historic Distric

E25

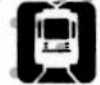

In 1980, William Jamison, a former college art instructor, founded the Folk Craft Gallery, dealing in handmade baskets and brooms, twig furniture and the art of Southeast Asian refugees. Soon he began to realize there were many self-taught artists in the region whose work deserved attention. Eventually, Jeffrey Thomas joined Jamison and Jamison/Thomas Gallery was born. The gallery represents fifteen West Coast artists, some self-taught, others academically trained. Artists whose ages range form 22 to 92 live as far away as Los Angeles and Seattle. Four of these artists are now represented by the Jamison/Thomas Gallery of New York, and will soon be joined by others. In Portland, works are displayed within space designed by Portland architect and glass artist, John Forsgren, who used 11-foot interior walls to bring a sense of intimacy to an 18-foot-tall space. Filling the gallery roster was far more difficult than calling up a handful of well known names; William literally spent days following up clues to locate the often-reclusive artists featured here. Many of the works are unusual, far-from-the-mainstream pieces, visitors will find paintings by Stuart Buehler, Jay Backstrand, Gregory Grenon, Ruza Erceg, Jon Serl, Eric Stotic and Rick Bartow; Debra Norby's ceramics; sculpture by Wally Warren, Mark Calderon and Mark Bulwinkle; and Martha Banyas' enamels. Visa. MasterCard. American Express.

217 SW First Avenue
Portland 97204
222-0063

218 Thompson Street
New York, NY 10012
(212) 995-0477

Tuesday-Saturday
10am-6pm
Sunday noon-4pm
First Thursday of each month until 9pm

CONTEMPORARY CRAFTS GALLERY

CRAFT GALLERY

...Where crafts become art.

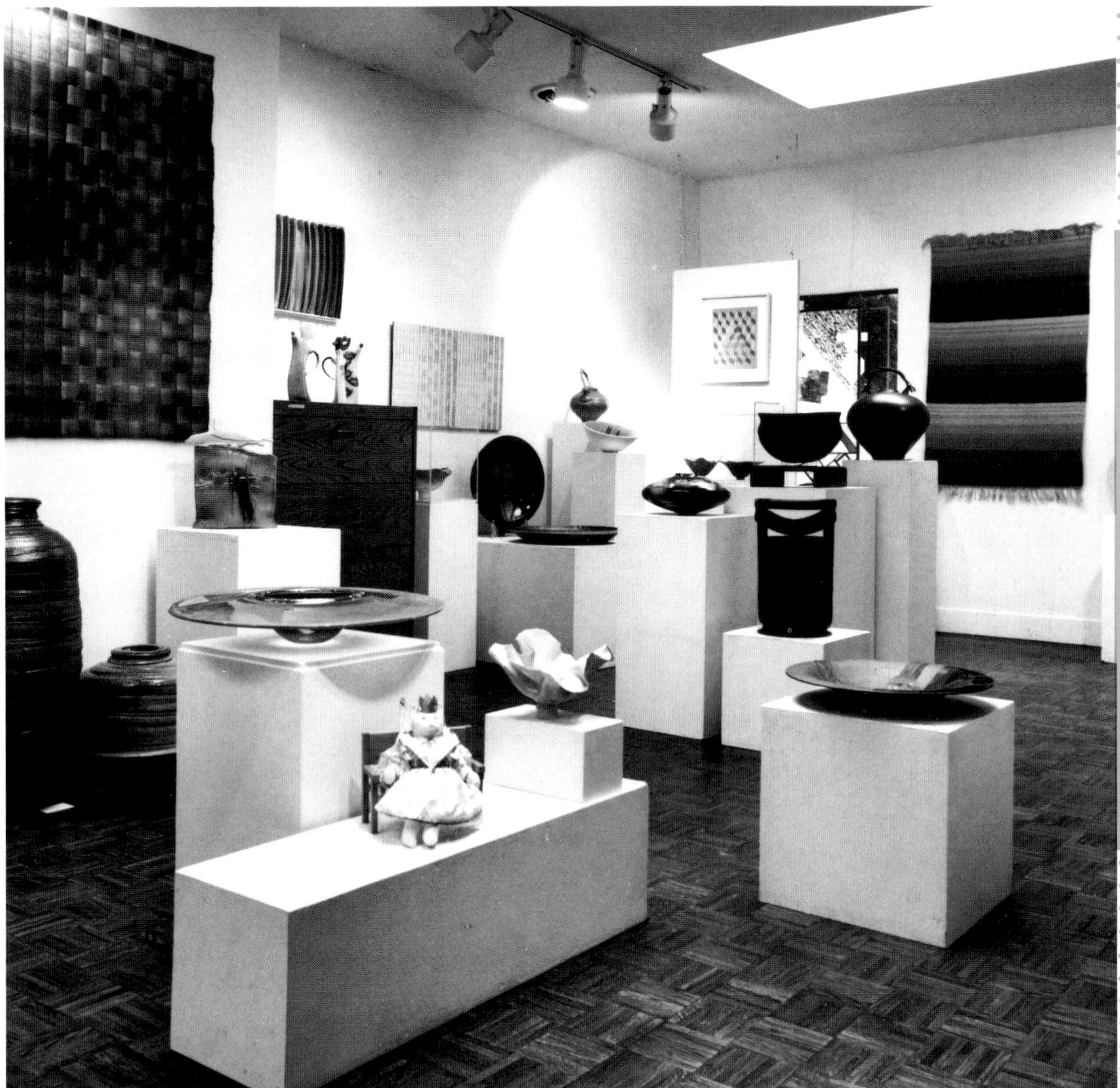

Founded in 1937, Contemporary Crafts Gallery is the oldest art gallery devoted exclusively to craft media in the nation. This non-profit organization displays the finest in all craft disciplines, specifically: clay, glass, wood, metal and fiber. Contemporary Crafts Gallery is celebrating its 50th Anniversary as a leader in diminishing the line between crafts and fine art. Its national reputation has attracted growing numbers of serious art collectors that recognize Contemporary Crafts Gallery as a vital center for creative expression in the Pacific Northwest. The Association maintains three exhibition spaces within the gallery, with shows changing monthly and coordinates an Artists- in-Education program in conjunction with area school districts. Contemporary Crafts Gallery traditionally features an unusual and unique Christmas/holiday exhibition sale beginning in late fall, sponsored by a core of gallery volunteers. Brochures — including maps — and catalogues of current exhibitions are available. Contemporary Crafts sets the aesthetic standards in terms of what is being currently created in the fine craft field, acting as the premier gallery in the Northwest for fine crafts in both the functional and non-functional area. Work displayed ranges from ceramics to jewelry to exquisite handmade furniture. Prices on items for sale vary widely, from below ten dollars to over a thousand. The gallery is free and open to the public. Memberships, which help support the association are available starting at $30 annually. Visa. MasterCard.

3934 SW Corbett Avenue
Portland 97201
223-2654

Tuesday-Friday
11am-5pm
Saturday noon-5pm
Sunday 1pm-5pm

Corbett-Johns Landing

E5

ATTIC GALLERY

ART GALLERY

Paintings, sculpture, ceramics, jewelry and prints by Northwest artists.

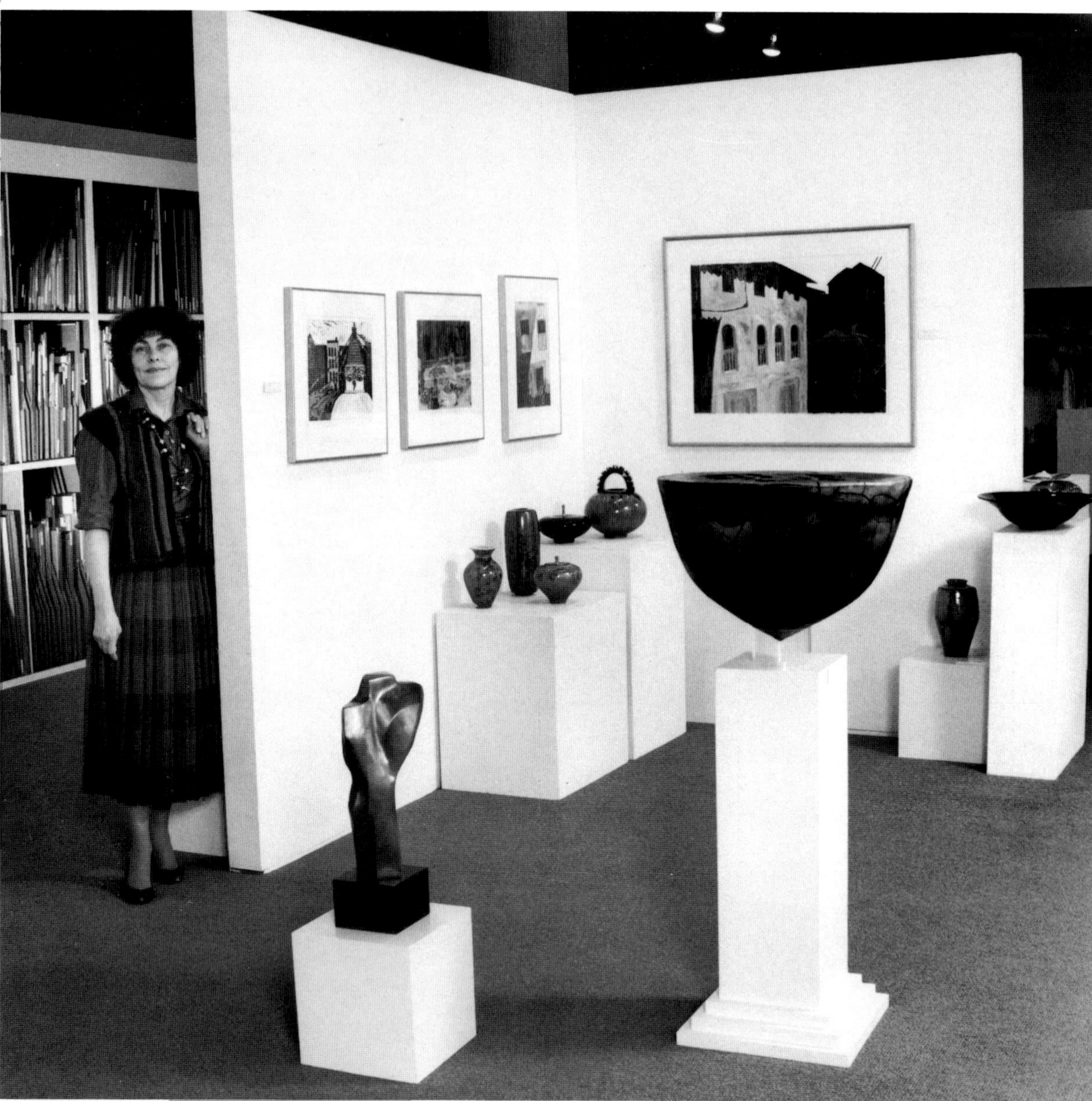

Skidmore Historic District

E25

The Attic Gallery had humble beginnings in an attic in Diana Faville's house on Sherwood Drive. The gallery has grown considerably since then moving to a more auspicious location downtown, with lofty ceilings and spacious surroundings to showcase the artwork. Located in one of the city's historic districts, Attic Gallery is now adjacent to Portland's light rail and is a part of "Gallery Row." Each month, the Attic Gallery has a reception spotlighting different artists, and the public is invited to attend, meet the artists, and view the exhibits. Pictured above are monotypes by Margot Voorhies Thompson and crystaline glazed porcelain and ceramic sculpture by Douglas Kaigler. The Attic Gallery represents over 75 artists and specializes in artwork by local Northwest artists, including watercolors by Elizabeth Brewster Rocchia, Arne Westerman, Sandra Jones Campbell, Kendahl Jan Jubb, John Maslen, and Mike Smith; mixed media paintings by Sidonie Caron and Joan Metcalf; pastels by Liza Jones; etchings by Christine Tarpey; acrylic paintings by Michael Ferguson and oil paintings by Sharon Engel and Loraine Balsillie. The gallery also exhibits ceramics, sculpture, prints, and jewelry. Diana Faville acts as an art consultant to many corporations and private collectors. There is a delivery service that will also assist in hanging of the artwork. A visit to the gallery offers an opportunity to browse through their extensive racks. Artwork may be taken out on approval, and payment plans are available. Visa. MasterCard. American Express.

206 SW First Avenue
Portland 97204
228-7830

Monday-Saturday
11am-5:30pm
Sunday noon-5pm
First Thursday of each month until 9pm

LAWRENCE GALLERY

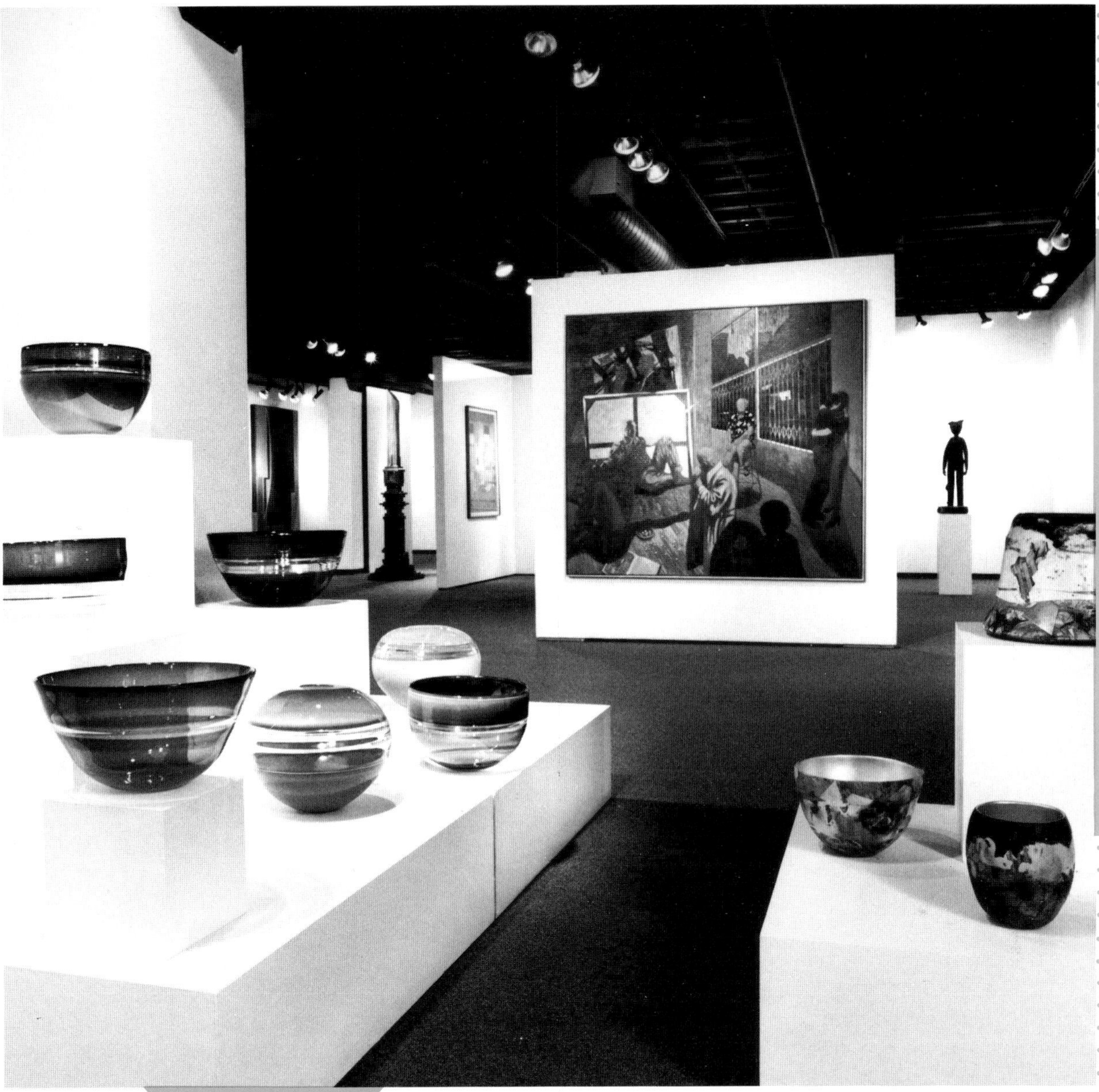

ART GALLERY

Art for the discriminating collector.

A dramatically lit glass-block entrance provides an enticing hint to the art awaiting you at Lawrence Gallery. Clean, contemporary white surfaces, complemented by a turn of the century stone wall, create an inviting setting for collectible art of well- established as well as emerging artists. Here, at one of three Lawrence Galleries in the state, two-dimensional work from Northwest artists and three-dimensional pieces from throughout the country are the focus. Styles range from photo realism to abstract expressionism in paintings, prints, sculpture, glass, ceramics and fiber. Captivating art is, of course, the gallery's raison d'être. Lawrence Gallery provides a full line of services for the private or corporate collector such as deliveries and professional installations for home or office, appraisals, and shipping to any destinations. Working with designers and architects or directly with individuals and businesses, the gallery also offers skilled corporate art consultation. The first Thursday of each month, special evening hours — until 9 p.m. — are the ideal excuse for a long, thoughtful look at some of the region's finest art. Visa. MasterCard. American Express.

842 SW First Avenue
Portland 97204
224-9442

The Marketplace at Salishan
Gleneden Beach 97388
764-2318

Highway 18
Sheridan 97378
843-3633

Monday-Friday
10am-5:30pm
Saturday noon-5pm
First Thursday of each month until 9pm

Yamhill Historic District

G25

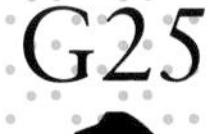

ABANTÉ FINE ART GALLERY

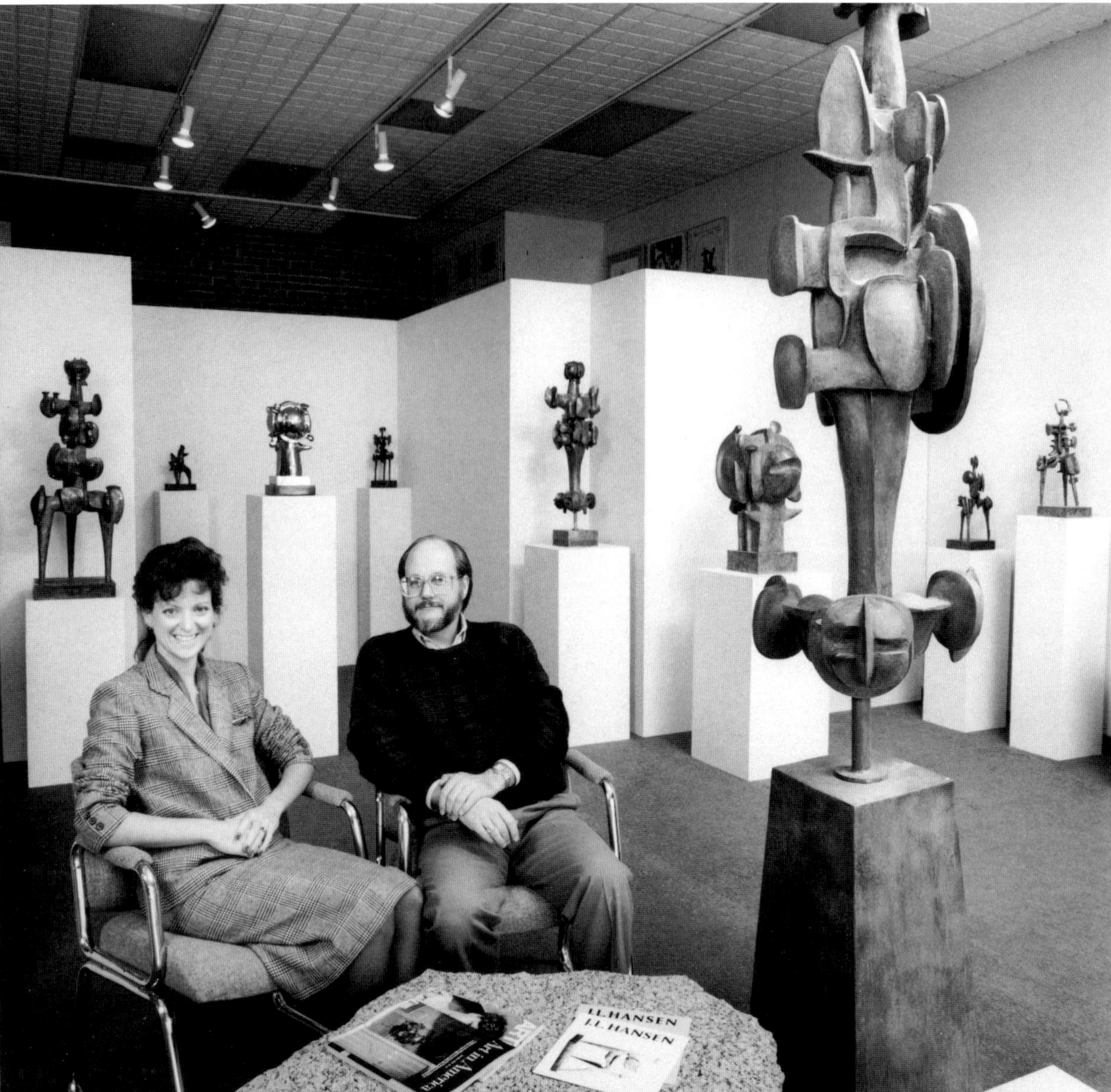

ART GALLERY

Featuring internationally known artists of the twentieth century.

Yamhill Historic District

G25

Abanté is Latin for a "leader in one's field," and Abanté Fine Art Gallery lives up to its name. Terrée Fiala and Rudi Milpacher, Abanté's directors, display an extensive collection for buyers in search of 20th century works by internationally known artists. Such modern masters as Picasso, Chagall and Miro are represented here; Abanté also is the exclusive international outlet for work by sculptor James Lee Hansen. But providing a comprehensive selection is only the most visible of Abanté's services. An extensive resource inventory system covers galleries and artists in the United States and Europe, enabling Terrée and Rudi to track down a particular piece or locate the gallery where an artist's work can be found. Art work of such high caliber as that which Abanté features deserve a fine setting, and the gallery's location, in the 1878-vintage Franc Building, lives up to your expectations. The gallery's large picture windows, densely hung brick walls, grey tones, ever- changing moveable walls and approximately 1,000 square feet of gallery space serve notice that this is a place for the serious art collector. As a brokerage, Abanté finds buyers for your pieces; as an appraisal service it ensures that their value is fully recognized. Assistance in the development of corporate and private collections also is offered. For Light Rail riders, Abanté's location near the Yamhill stop means the gallery is readily accessible to all those who appreciate fine art. Visa. MasterCard. American Express.

124 SW Yamhill Street
Portland 97204
295-2508

Tuesday-Saturday
10am-5:30pm
And by appointment
First Thursday of each month until 9pm

O'CONNELL GALLERY

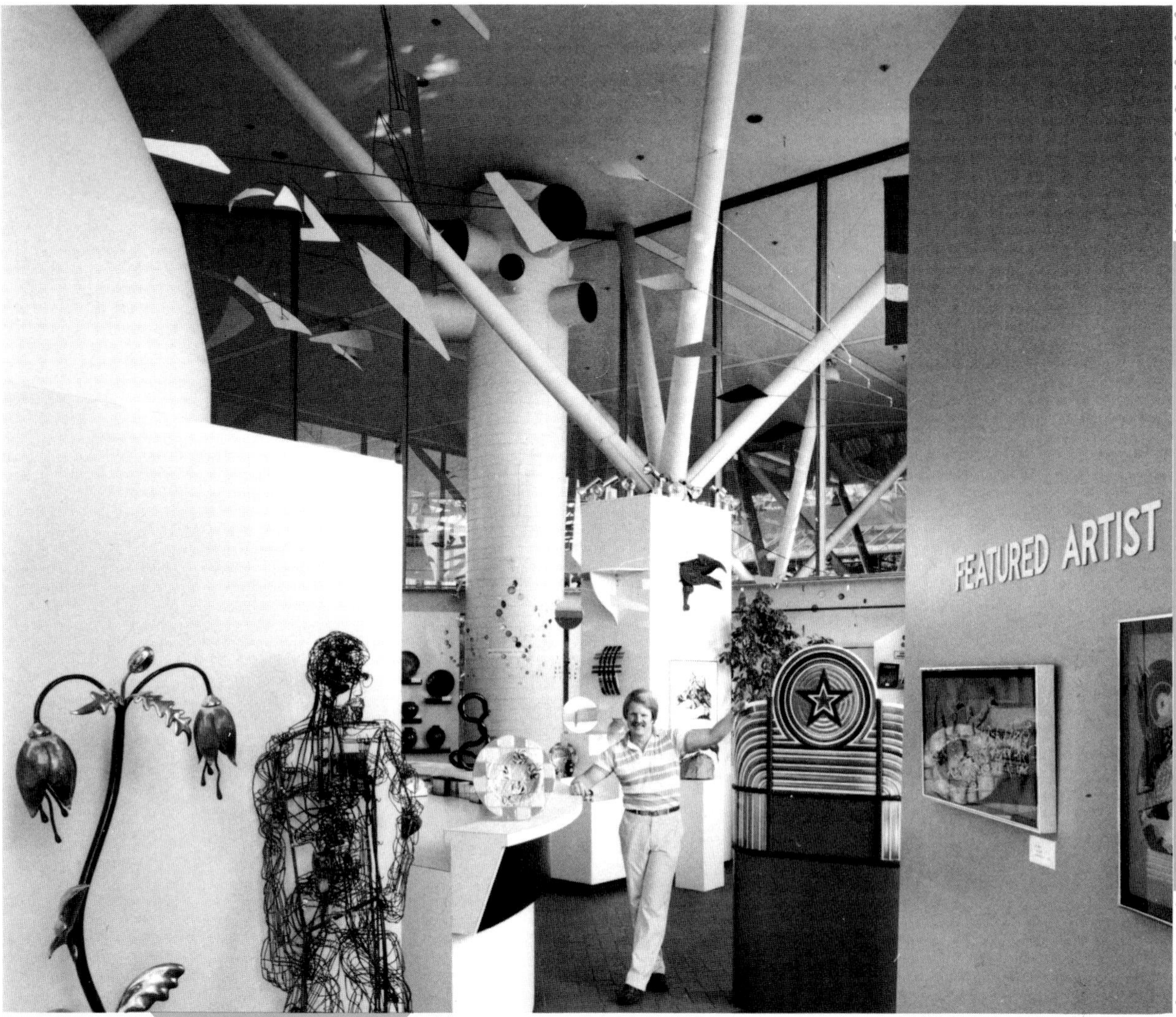

ART GALLERY

The Northwest's affordable, fun gallery for all ages.

O'Connell's is an art gallery with a difference. It operates on the premise that art at its best should titillate the imagination and tickle the funny bone — as well as touch the spirit. The gallery resides in an all-glass structure next to a working antique carousel and museum. Directly across the street from Waterfront Park and the new ferry dock, this airy and dynamic gallery displays all kinds of intriguing art — kinetic and other — from top Northwest artists and craftsmen. Colorful mobiles of metal, cloth and plastic dance overhead while the more earth-bound treasures compete for the eye's favor. Mt. St. Helen's hand blown glass vases, eggs and assorted ornaments; etched, fused and leaded glass pieces and pottery are found here. There are paintings in oils and watercolors; and sculptures of metal and stone. Spend your lunch hour enthralled by the kinetic ball gravitrams while you listen to the gossamer symphonies of the wind chimes and bells. There's a bonus for out-of-towners — free tourist information is available at the Gallery. Visa. MasterCard. American Express. Discover.

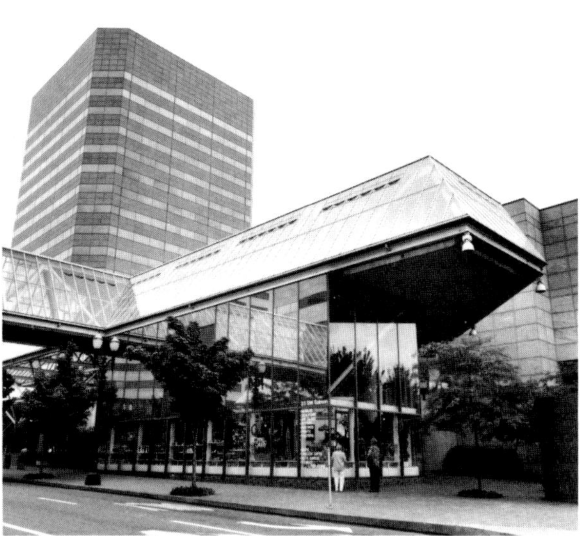

25 SW Salmon Street
Portland 97204
220-0330

Monday-Friday
10am-6pm
Saturday-Sunday
11am-5pm
First Thursday of each month until 9pm

Yamhill Historic District

G25

SUNBOW GALLERY

CRAFT GALLERY

Find the perfect gift in five seconds or less!

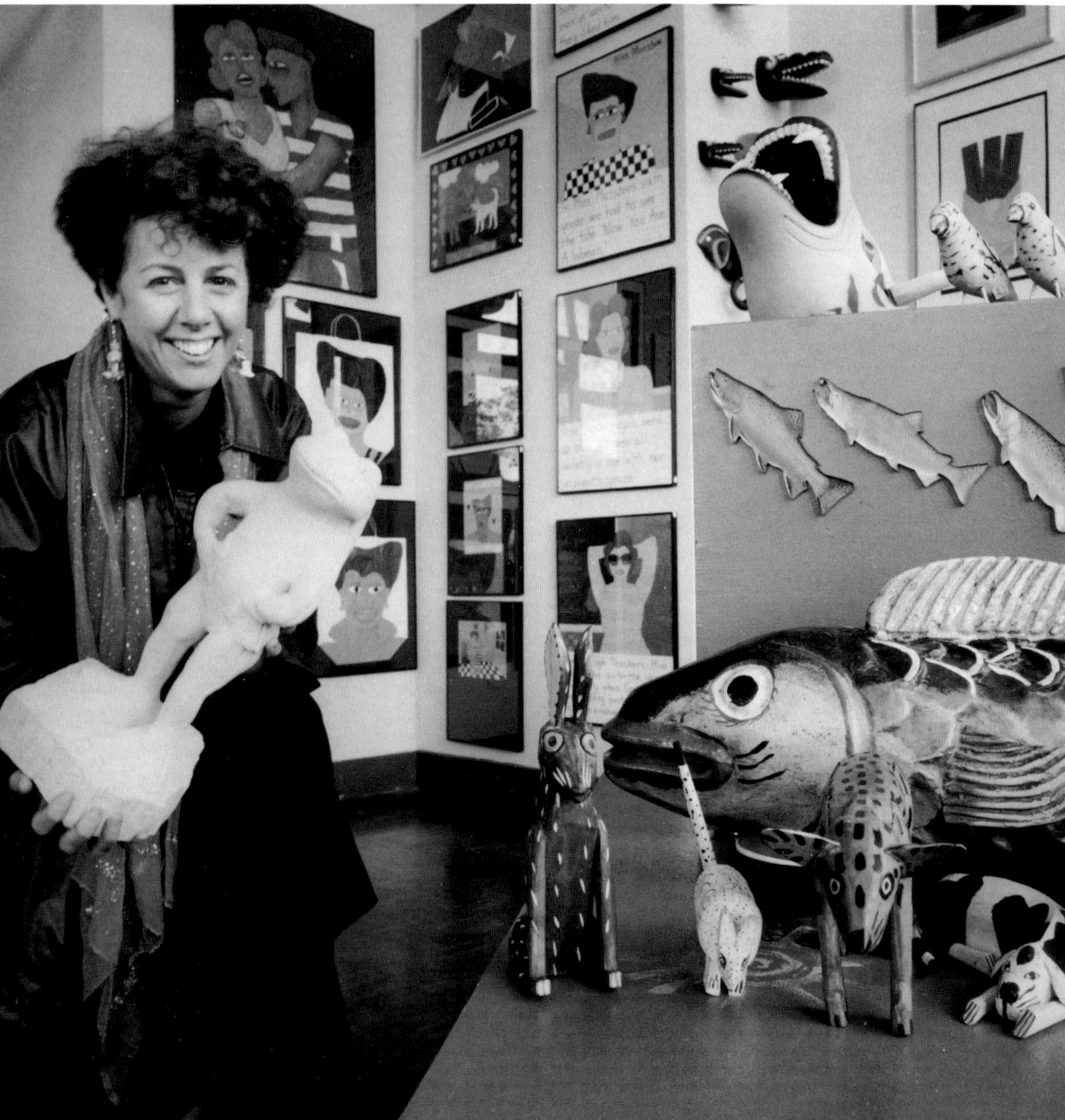

Yamhill Historic District

F25

Northwest Portland

H17

Seen too many art galleries that make you want to yawn, crawl into a corner and go to sleep? If you think art should be fun, and more interesting than a pile of bleached canvas, then Sunbow Gallery should be your next stop. Sunbow specializes in one-of- a-kind art and craft pieces that will make you smile. Laughing out loud is allowed at this gallery, where the challenge is to walk by the windows and not be lured inside by the light, airy, comfortable and inviting atmosphere. Owner Faviana Priola thrives on the customer enthusiasm evoked by contemporary jewelry; a collections of primitive carvings from Mexico, Guatemala, Sri Lanka, the Phillippines and Thailand; and enchanting 3-D fabric Arpilleras from Peru. Sunbow shows the paintings of Mar Goman, Chris Tarpey's etchings and glasswork by Sherry Shuster. Best of all, everything's at prices that won't move you to tears or require a second mortgage on your house. No wonder, that after all these — 11 — years, Sunbow customers are still laughing and asking for more! Visa. MasterCard. American Express.

206 SW Stark Street
Portland 97204
221-0258

Monday-Saturday
10am-5pm

Dazzle
709 NW 23rd &
"Papa Haydn"
Portland, 97210
224-1294

Zany Grey
115 Stewart
Seattle, WA 98101
(206) 448-8508

CLAYTRADE

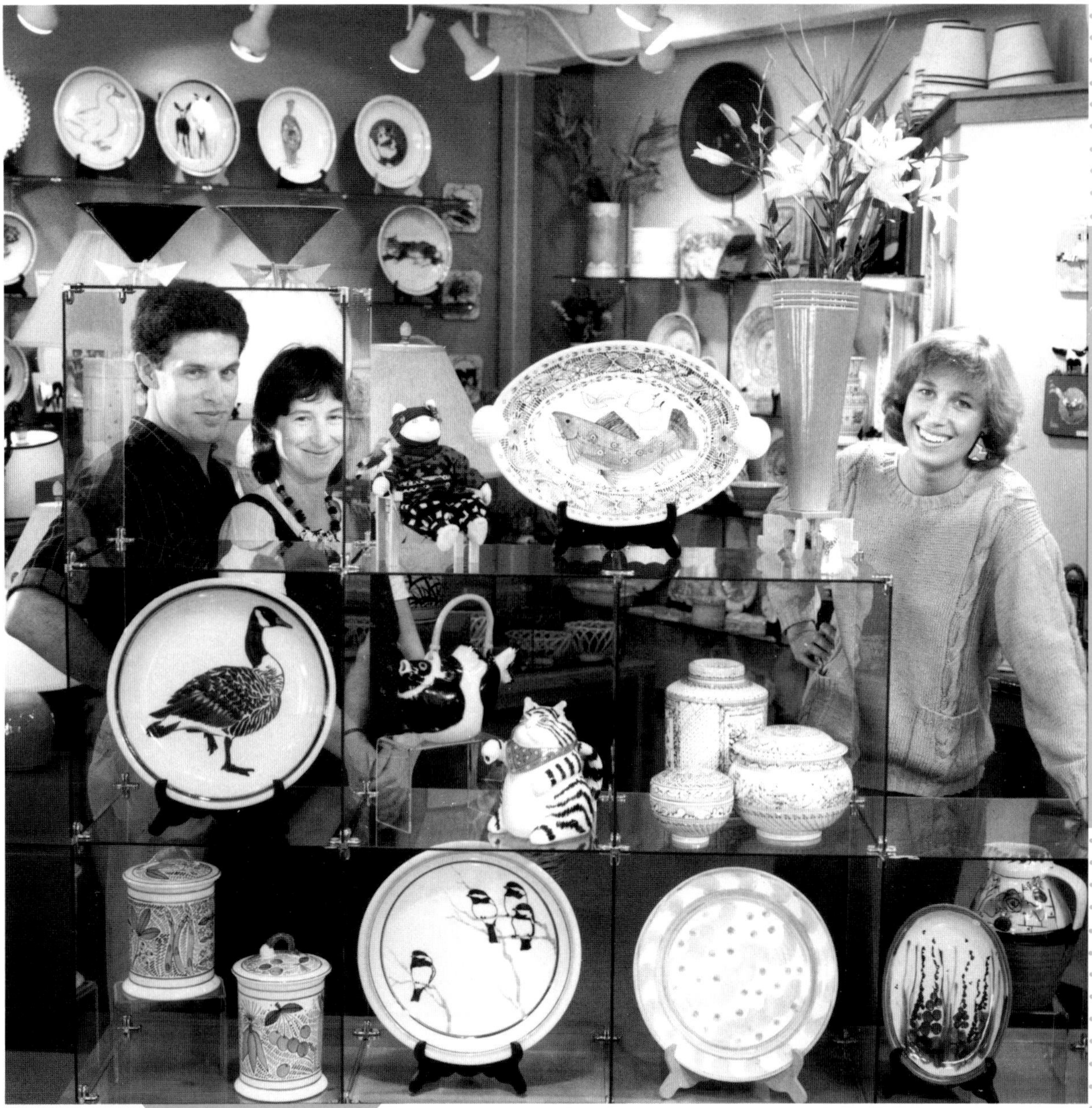

CRAFT GALLERY

Functional and decorative handmade ceramics and jewelry.

The Claytrade is a place you can get all fired up about. The wide range of functional and decorative handmade ceramics priced from three dollars to five hundred dollars features the works of Oregon artists. But other nationally known artists, some of whom use the Claytrade as their exclusive outlet, are also represented. What this all means to the customer is a substantial and affordable selection of works which are the bright and colorful, decorative and usable. Owners Paul Schneider and Lauren Eulau have put their individual artistic backgrounds to good use, choosing original works that reflect their own tastes and bring what many customers describe as a 'gallery' feel to the store. Paul is a potter himself, with 18 years behind the wheel. Paul and Lauren's many trips to collect ceramics and discover new crafts have paid off in unusual, creative works for the store. Ceramic jewelry also gets its share of attention at the Claytrade, which boasts the largest selection in the state at prices for every buyer. For those special occasions, the Claytrade creates custom dinnerware, personalized plates and bowls to commemorate weddings and births and such handmade items as lamps, tiles and bowls. Visa. MasterCard. American Express. Diners Club. Carte Blanche.

Cascade Plaza
8775 SW Cascade Avenue
Beaverton 97005
626-8931

Monday-Friday
10am-9pm
Saturday 10am-6pm
Sunday 11am-5pm

5th Street Public Market
296 East 5th
Eugene 97401
342-8686

Progress-Washington Square

G2

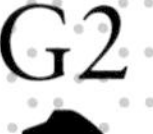

THE POSTER GALLERY ETC.

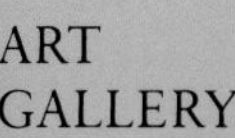

ART GALLERY

Posters and a whole lot more.

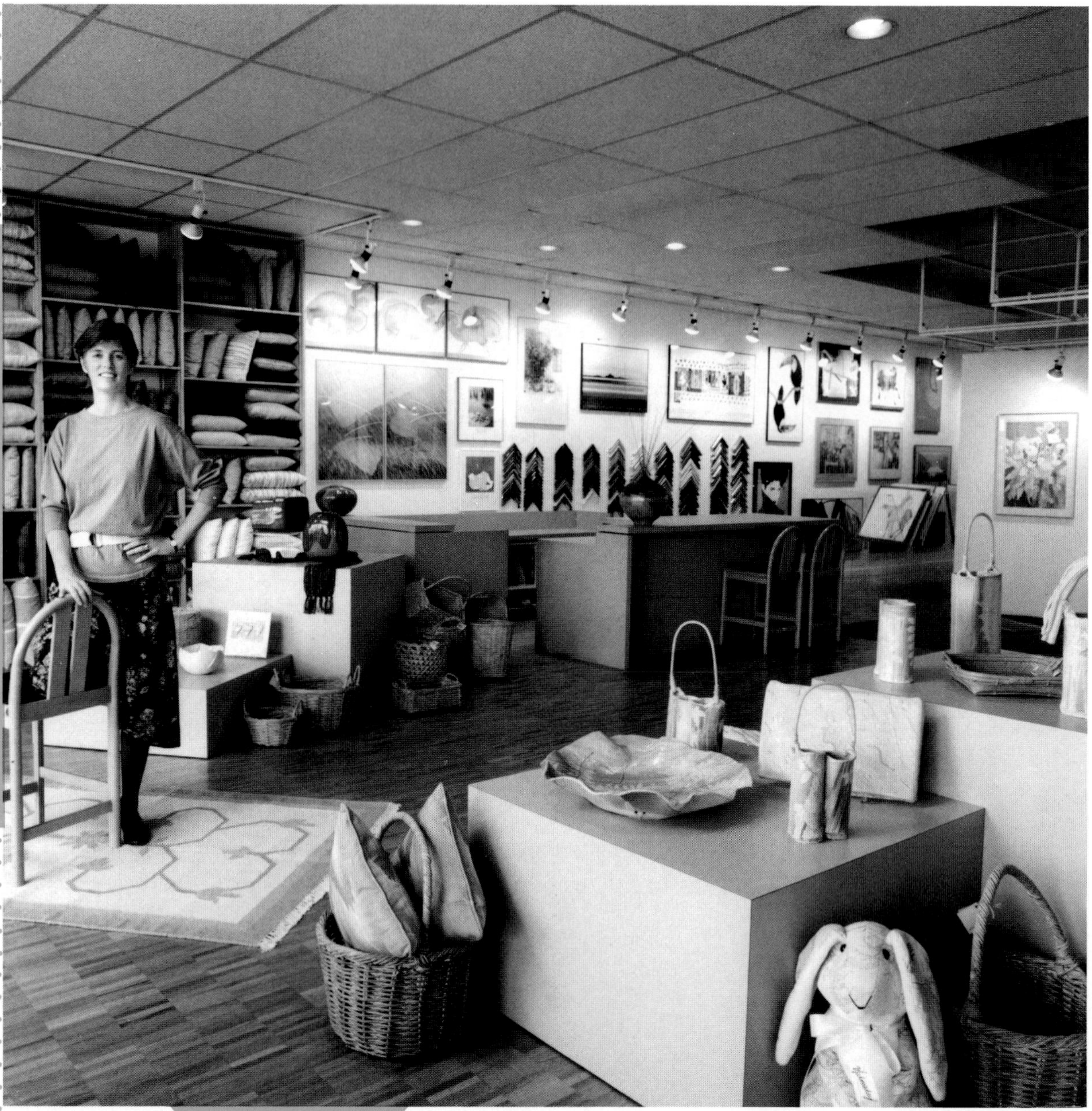

Skidmore Historic District.

E25

Progress-Washington Square

G3

On any one day, browsing through The Poster Gallery Etc., you might find exciting colorful, contemporary plates from New England, a display of unusual jewelry and scarves, handwoven textiles — silk pillows, whitewashed baskets, lacquered baskets, soapstone carvings and antique chests. On another day everything might be different. Owners Jackie Gango and Debi Gango-Teschke lavish tender care and their own unique style on the selection and display of an inventory that is comprehensive and eclectic, unique and inventive. As the name implies, The Poster Gallery Etc. is posters, more than 800 of which are framed and hung at the two galleries. Each one is fine art, an example of the world's most stunning poster work. But there is much, much more: a selection of original art from Northwest artists, custom framing, fine rugs — such as wool dhurries from India, and fabulous wall hangings. The work of Carol Grigg, one of Portland's best-known watercolor artists, is prominently displayed. Many of the items are the makings of fine collections and all will add that undefinable special touch to your home or office. Best of all, check the prices. You won't need to be an oil sheik to afford gifts from The Poster Gallery Etc. Visa. MasterCard.

205 SW First Avenue
Portland 97204
223-1712

Monday-Saturday
10am-5:30pm
First Thursday of the month until 9pm

8748 SW Hall Boulevard
Portland 97223
643-5586

Monday-Saturday
10am-5:30pm

GANGO GALLERY

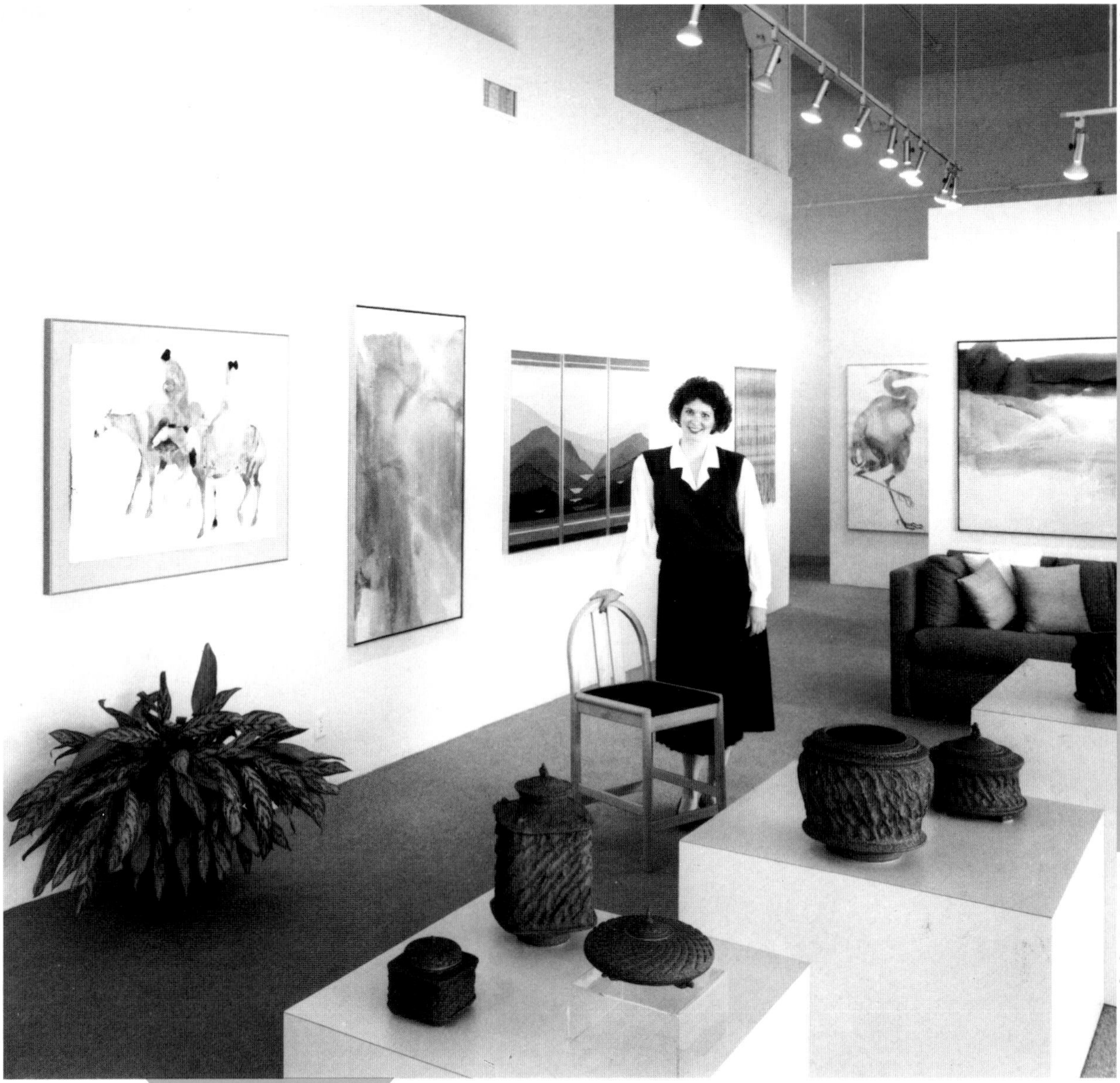

ART GALLERY

Original works by Northwest artists.

The Gango Gallery, winner of a national award of excellence, provides a lively and elegant art experience in each of its two locations. The scope of the Gango Gallery encompasses nearly all media, including watercolor, oil, acrylic, pottery and prints. The gallery feaetures an impressive selection of the kind of art you'd enjoy having in your home or office. In this warm and friendly atmosphere, you will enjoy Carol Grigg's nationally known watercolors and lithographs. Carolyn Dewey's work emphasizes seascapes and landscapes. Tish Epperson's two styles tend toward whimsey and cubism. Michele Taylor Hayakawa, also nationally known, does impressionistic gardens and florals in oil. Joan Metcalf's watercolor landscapes depict Northwest scenes. Ann Munson's colored pencil drawings portray charming animals, while Sharon Smith does bright watercolor florals reminscent of a Northwest garden. The gallery also features Debra Olson's handmade paper, Chris Rutledge's monoprints, and Lila Girvin's lyrical abstracts. Also included in this eclectic collection is pottery by Charles Gluskoter, Roberta Lampert, Gerald Wansoo Hong, Claudia Hoffberg and Kathy Bolin, and whimsical animal ceramics by Sandy Visse. To make difficult decisions easy, the Gango Gallery offers an art consulting service and custom framing. They will ship anywhere in the United States. Visa. MasterCard.

205 SW First Avenue
Portland 97204
222-3850

Monday-Saturday
10am-5:30pm
First Thursday
of the month until 9pm

8748 SW Hall
Boulevard
Portland 97223
643-5586

Monday-Saturday
10am-5:30pm

Skidmore Historic District

E25

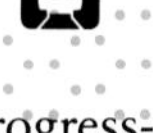

Progress-Washington Square

G3

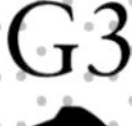

THE REAL MOTHER GOOSE

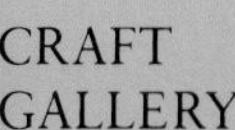

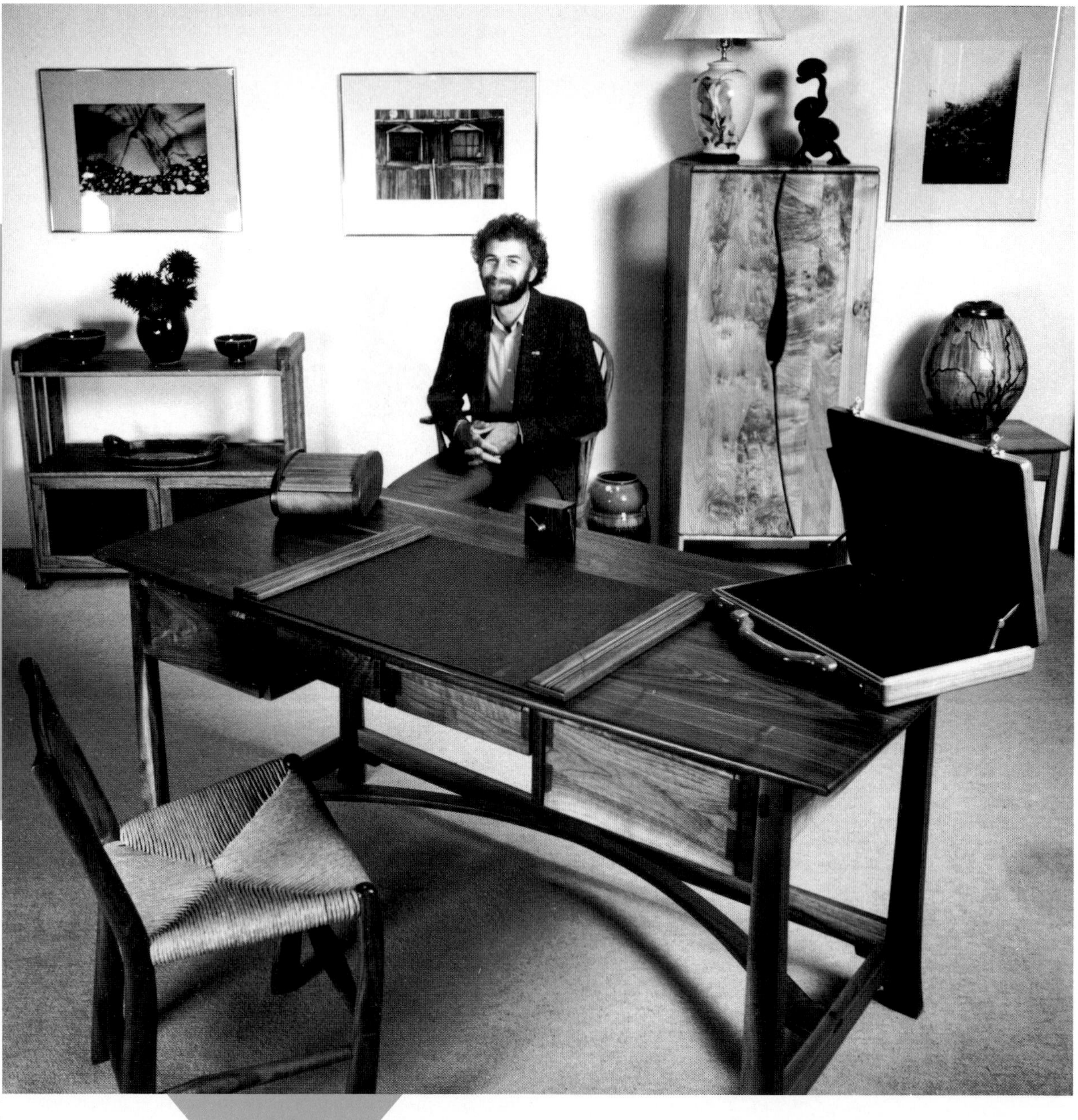

CRAFT GALLERY

A shop and gallery showcasing fine American craft and art.

Downtown

F23

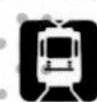

Progress-Washington Square

G3

Does the thought of searching for one more special gift fill you with despair? Relax! The Real Mother Goose is ready to brighten your day. With one of the largest selections of American crafts in the country, this shop offers one-of-a-kind pieces you won't find anywhere else. Owners Stan and Judy Gillis are justifiably proud of the nationally-known artists represented at the gallery. And their reputation as a source for high quality merchandise has grown steadily over the past sixteen years. In their shops you'll find custom designed furniture and specialty items, unique sculptural and functional ceramics, and delicate blown-glass pieces. Opulent, strokable textiles serve as visual or wearable art. Exquisite custom jewelry and glittering gems add to the shop's attraction. When a very personal piece of jewelry is in order, a resident designer and goldsmith will work with you to create an enviable original or redesign a family heirloom. At The Real Mother Goose monthly shows spotlight individual artists, so enter your name on their mailing list and learn about new artwork that's arriving regularly from across the country. When your imagination is in need of recharging, visit The Real Mother Goose. Visa. MasterCard. American Express.

901 SW Yamhill Street
Portland 97205
223-9510

Monday-Thursday
10am-5:30pm
Friday 10am-6:30pm
Saturday 10am-6pm

Washington Square
Portland 97223
620-2243

Monday-Friday
10am-9pm
Saturday 10am-6pm
Sunday 11am-6pm

BEYOND REASON

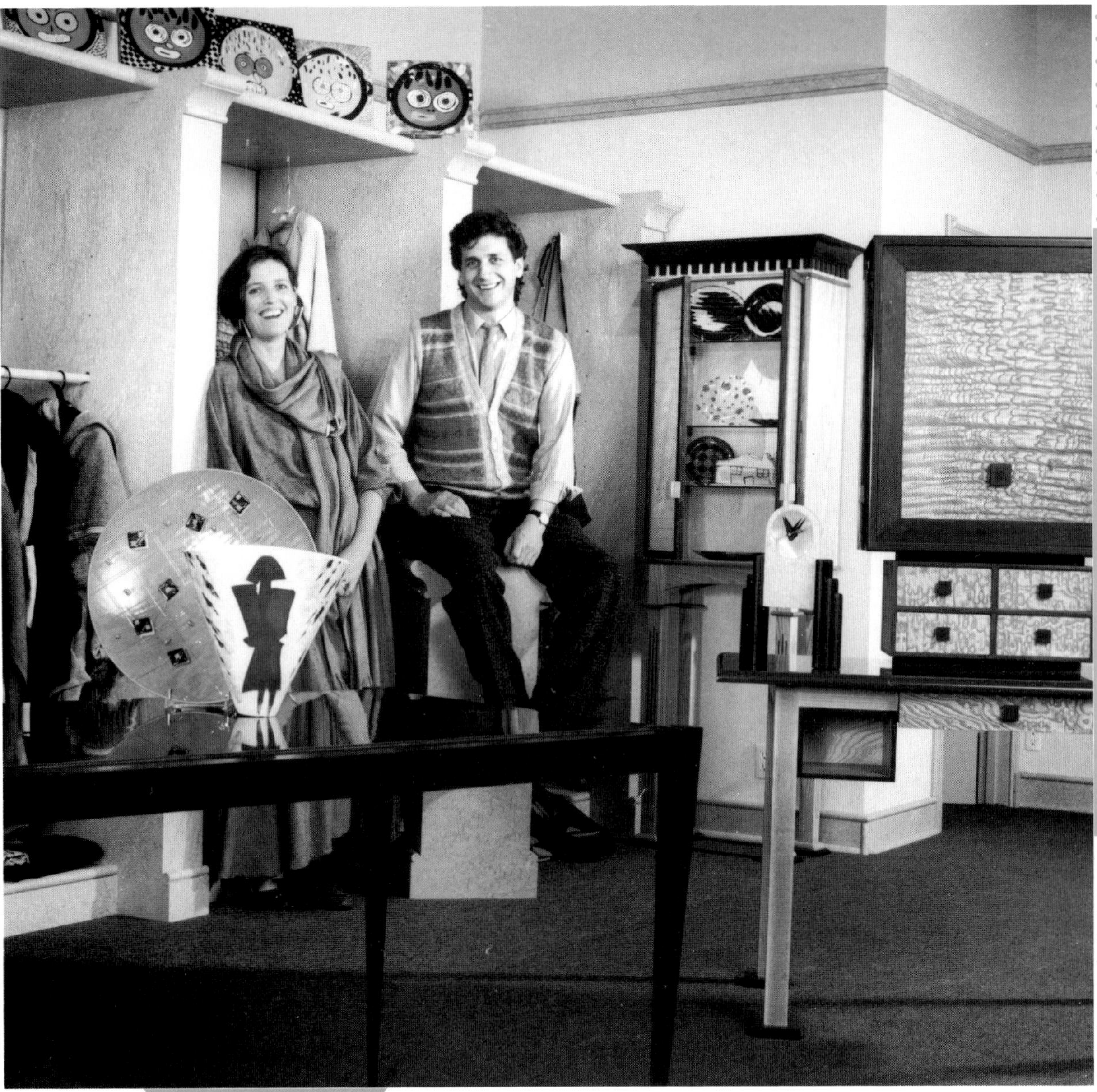

CRAFT GALLERY

Art from fantasy to function.

Northwest Portland

H17

When David and Sara Dochow recently returned to Portland after living in New York City for ten years, they discovered that although the art community was more alive than ever, something was missing. Beyond Reason, their youthful undertaking, provides that missing link — a forum for a growing number of regional artists working in highly specific crafts. Function is paramount at Beyond Reason, where the motto is, "Objects to use and incorporate into your life." The gallery's spatter-painted columns and pedestals, alcoves for display of single pieces, pink halogen spot lights, grey industrial carpeting and large front windows are a soothing setting for avant-garde, often colorful pieces. A focal point is sleek, unusual furniture from Northwest artists, which includes some of David's work. Both Sara and David relish mixed-media in the designs, such as the sand-blasted glass often incorporated by Tom Freedman and Beth Yoe, and furniture with a twist, like a Tinker Toy table — with interchangeable components — from David Simon and Bill Toney. Beyond Reason also has ceramics, glass, linens, woven goods and other household accessories; sweaters, painted silks, jewelry, hats, scarves and other clothing; fine art that includes painting, handmade paper and photography; and store fixtures. As a design consultant, Beyond Reason can assist with interiors and custom furniture for residential or commercial work. As for the gallery's name, "Opening an art gallery with three small children, a limited budget and being the new kids in town is 'beyond reason,'" says Sara. Visa. MasterCard. American Express.

2305 NW Kearney Street
Portland 97210
274-2029

Tuesday-Saturday
10am-6pm

STUDIO ARTISTS CAROLE HENNESSY-SMITH NANCY COFFELT & STAN SMITH

ART

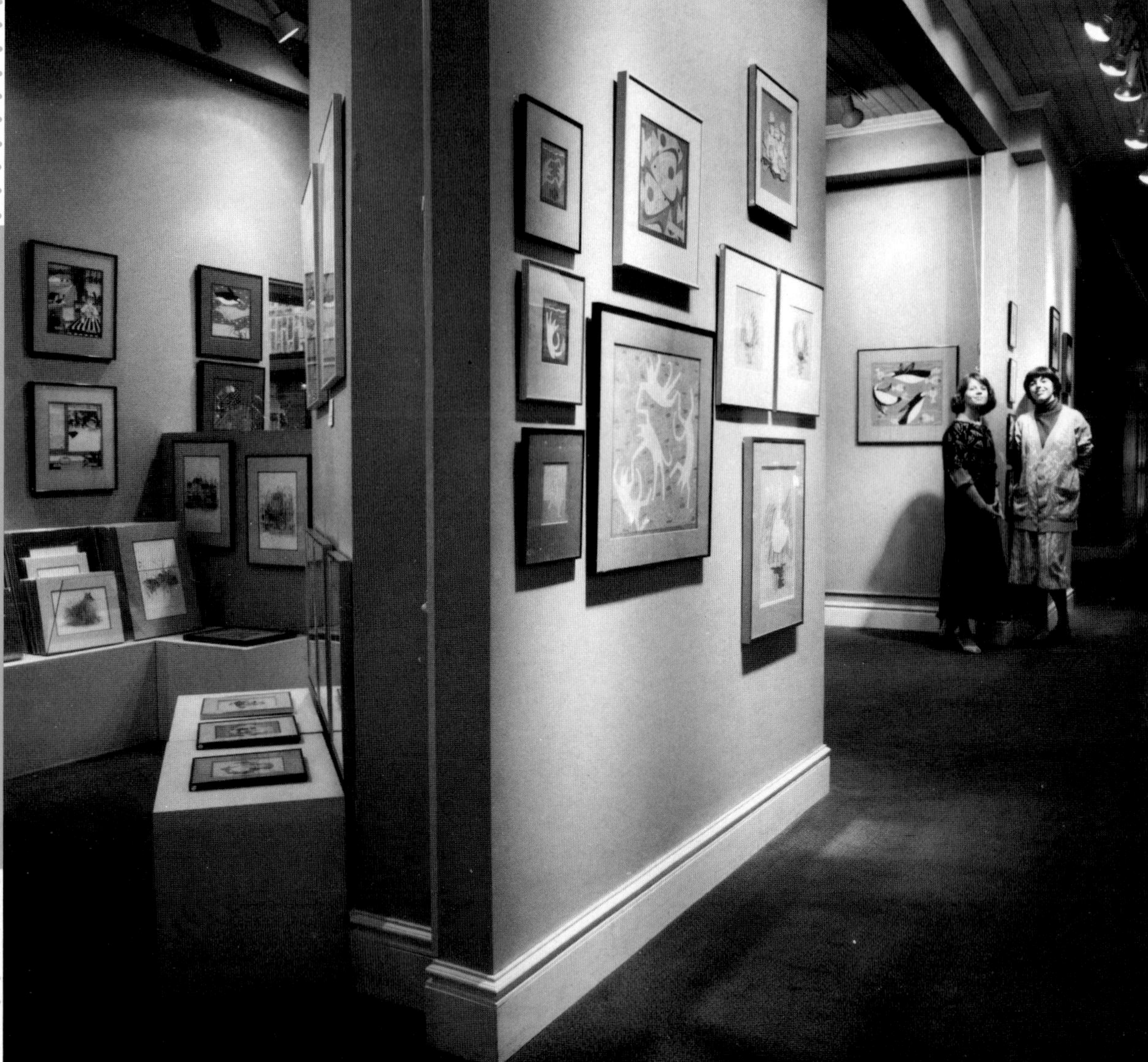

Watercolors, collage, oils, pastels and pen and inks.

Skidmore Historic District

E25

Carole Hennessy-Smith and Nancy Coffelt met in 1984 while selling their original works at the then newly renovated New Market Theater. Carole, Nancy and custom framer Stan Smith ran one of the cities' liveliest galleries, The Loft, as an open working studio. Carole, a graduate of the University of Oregon's Fine Arts program, works in an innovative collage technique using quality handmade rag papers with watercolor. Along with watercolor portraits, she has an ongoing series of Portland street scenes — recently purchased for Tri-Met's art collection. Nancy often works with playful themes — bad animals and crazy chefs — for simple pastel drawings that are bright and lively that reflect her sense of humor. They contrast with her detailed color pencil and pen and ink renderings of other subjects. Stan frames their pieces and does custom framing for customer art through his Oriole Art Service, and on Saturday and Sunday from April to Christmas he and Carole tend a gallery-booth display on the New Market Theater Plaza — adjacent to Saturday Market. Early 1987 brought change and transition for all three partners ending their shared work environment, but certainly not their working relationships. Carole has relocated to a private studio in the nearby Hazletine Building and is currently working on new watercolors and collage pieces to be placed with the Gango Galleries. Nancy moved her studio to her home in Southeast Portland, and her current works may be found at Portland's Augen Gallery. Visa. MasterCard.

Nancy Coffelt
232-8693

By Appointment Only

Carole Hennessy-Smith
Studio
133 SW 2nd Avenue
Suite 200
Portland 97204
227-0383 or
281-3924 (Oriole Arts)

ART MEDIA

ART SUPPLY

Tools and materials for fine and graphic arts.

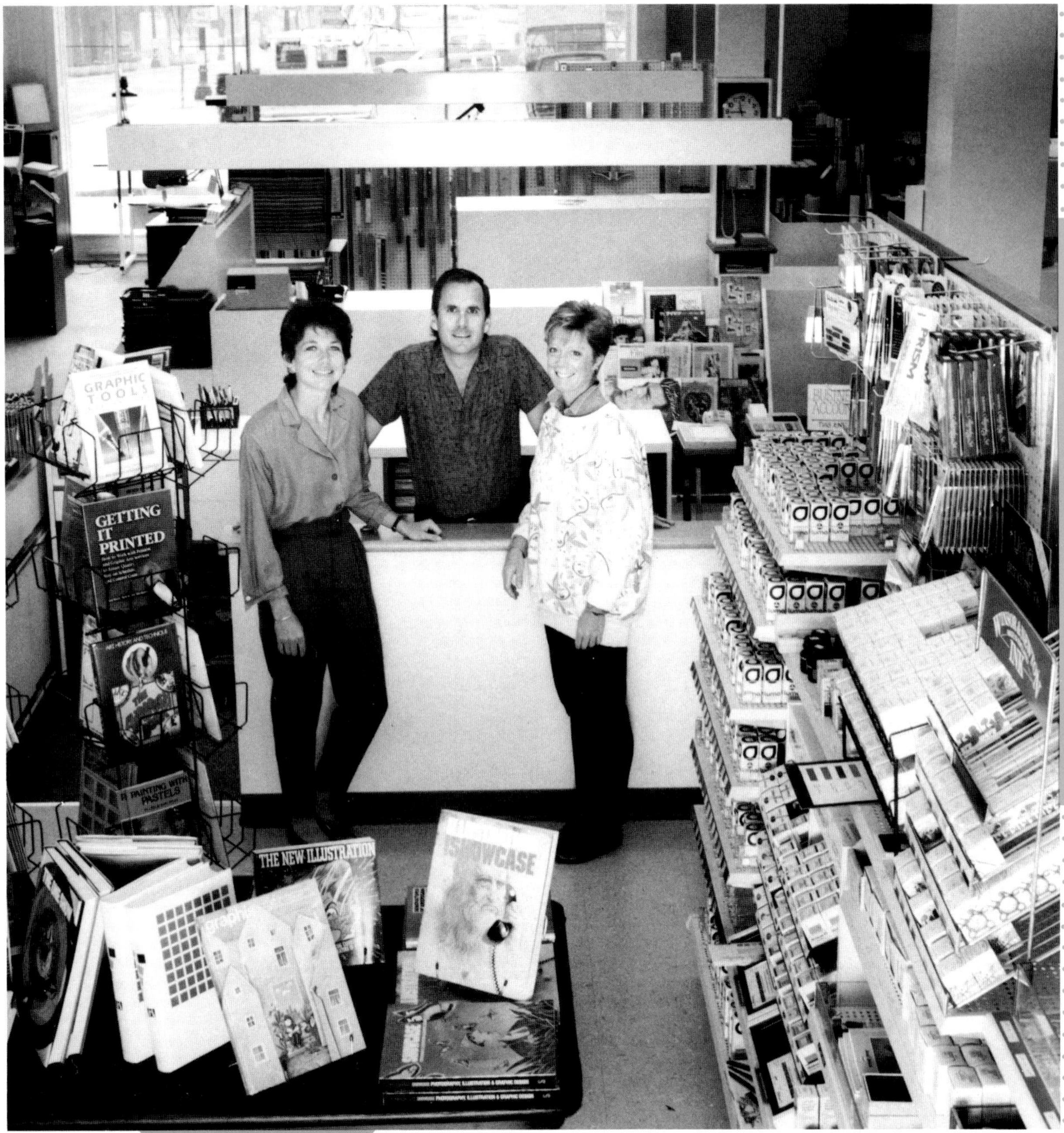

No one understands the needs of professional artists and art students better than one of their own. That is precisely why former art students David Mosher, Gail Vines and Kathleen Christian started Art Media. Just celebrating their 12th year in business, Art Media is a haven for discriminating artists in search of quality supplies. The product knowledge which all three owners brought with them at the store's inception has grown enormously over this decade of progressive business experience. The result is a well-organized, complete art supply store. It's hard to imagine a more pleasing environment in which to find the quality tools, materials and paper you need to create beautiful watercolors, oils and drawings. The precision graphics tools and supplies which can make or break a career can be found at Art Media. The staff here are able and willing to answer — or find the answer to — all questions about supplies — and art techniques in general. As an added bonus for their clientele, Art Media has started a delivery and sales service for larger company personnel who may not have the time to shop downtown for their art needs. Come in to Art Media for browsing, for facts, or for that necessary tool to begin your creative process. Visa. MasterCard. American Express.

902 SW Yamhill Street
Portland 97205
223-3724

Monday-Thursday
9am-8pm
Friday-Saturday
9am-5:30pm

Downtown
F23

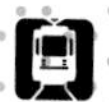

SHANNON & CO.

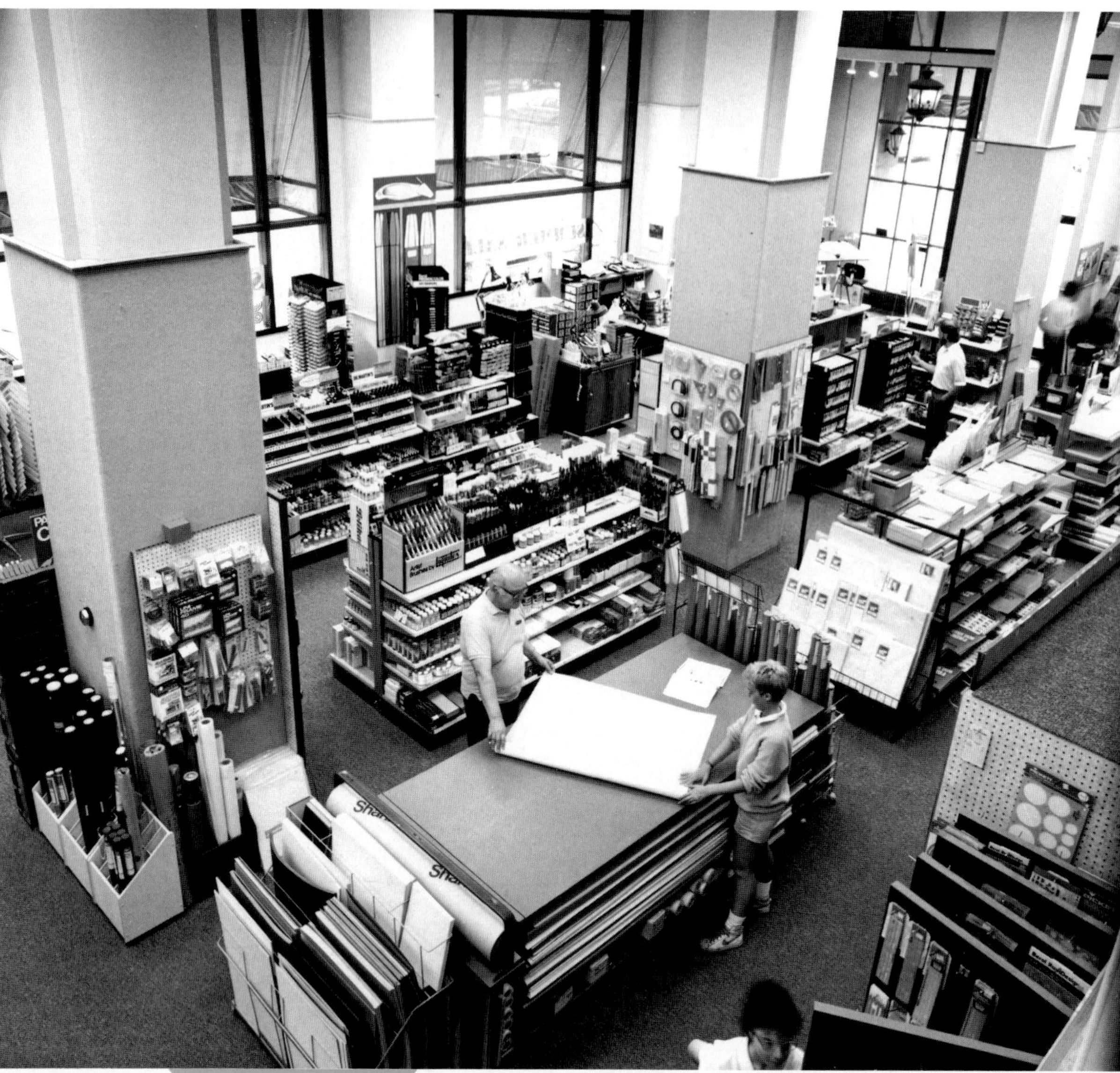

ART SUPPLY

Art, engineering and architectural supplies.

Downtown
E23

For more than 50 years, Portlanders in search of fine art, graphic art, architectural and engineering supplies have sought out Shannon & Co. for its wide selection and large inventory. In addition to the outstanding selection of quality art products, professionals, as well as amateurs, can count on sound advice from Shannon's seasoned sales staff. Together, their 75 years combined experience is a welcome asset and trusted resource to customers. Shannon & Co. carries such leading fine arts brand names as Winsor/Newton, Grumbacher, Liquitex, Arttec and much more. In the graphic arts category, Letraset, Pantone, Design Art Marker, Prismacolor Markers, X-acto, Crescent and Bainbridge Boards, Alvin Artograph, Planhold, and 3-M tapes and sprays are just the beginning of the store's comprehensive product offerings. Students and professional artists will find airbrushes, parts and supplies from Badger, Iwate, Paasche. And for everyone from professional to weekend artist to business person, the store offers a huge selection of pens, pencils and papers ranging from standard favorites to the unusual. In addition, Shannon offers drafting and art tables, stools and chairs, as well as a wide variety of lamps for any purpose. Shannon & Co. Reprographics Center, now a separate location, has expanded to carry supplies for graphic arts and drafting. In addition, the Reprographics Center now carries picture framing,, emphasizing metal frames in fantastic colors and finishes. The prices are "do it yourself", but Shannon does all the work. And, if you're downtown, they deliver. With its downtown location, Shannon & Co. is easily accessible from any part of the city. If it has to do with art, Shannon & Co. has it. Besides, its a fun place to shop. Visa. MasterCard. Commercial Accounts.

901 SW Washington Street
Portland 97205
228-6237

Monday-Friday
9:30am-5:30pm
Saturday 11am-4pm

SPECIALTIES

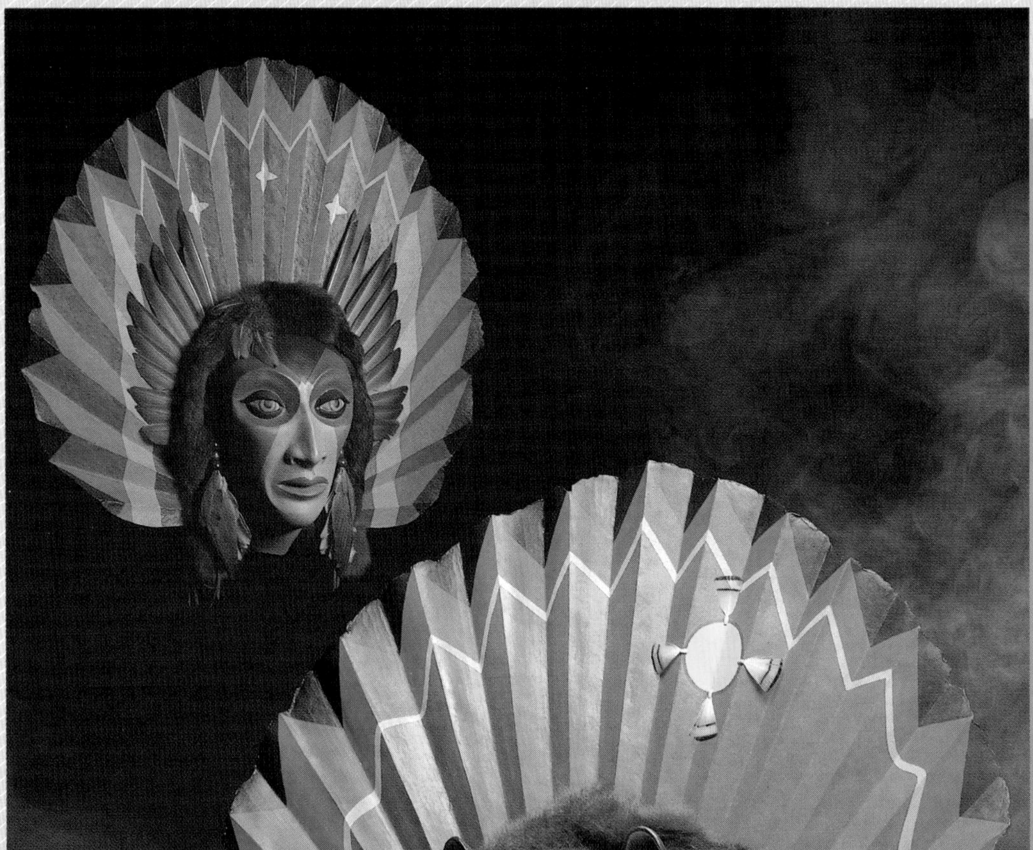

Marty Hart | *Wolf Fan* | THE REAL MOTHER GOOSE

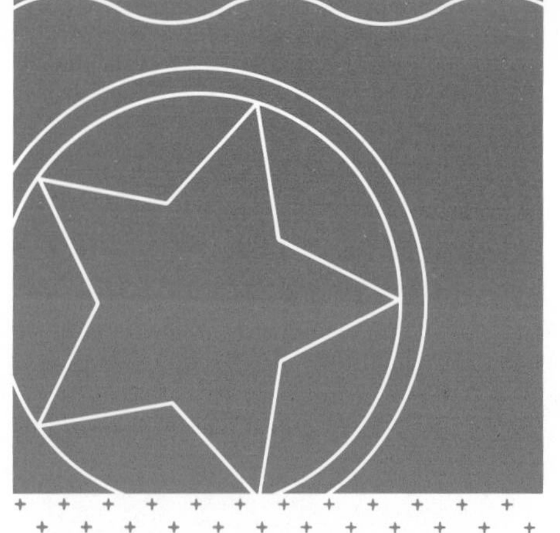

When it comes to Hanging Out, there are two kinds. There's Hanging Out Together. Which sounds like gangs of youths loitering on street corners, making lewd remarks to passersby, but there's little of that nowadays. Hanging Out Together is a new tribal ritual, young people evidently inviting one another to accompany them, on what used to be called Dates, thus: "Hey. Uh. You wanna Hang Out Saturday? Or wut." Dreadful.

Real Hanging Out, on the other hand, is a sort of solo, self-directed outing, where you just go Be Somewhere Else. You don't have to talk, and you don't have to spend money unless you feel like it, and you don't have to do anything but just Be ... sounds a little bit like Existentialism, but it's a lot easier.

My favorite place for Hanging Out is Newberry's, usually the Lloyd Center one where I preside over the end of the snack bar and drink Diet Coke and write letters and talk to the waitresses. Lynda, who is calm and given to saying things like, "I hear what you're saying." Betty, who just got married. Jan, who calls everybody "honey" and "dear." The downtown Newb's is a pretty good place for Hanging Out, too, but it's a carnival midway, a parade of folk washing up on the shore of the snack bar. It's too easy to get caught up in their stories, too hard to write letters.

Well, I'm from the Midwest, and I like touchy-feelies where I Hang Out. Fabric. Funny, bright colors. The Daisy Kingdom's good for a serious wallow in fabric and ribbons and serious, intense seamstresses. The Galleria's splendid for an afternoon's worth of Hanging Out, too. The Paper Parlour has good stuff. Bright colored paper for wrapping presents and for writing letters. You can have pencils fixed up with someone's name While-U-Wait. There are hundreds of cards that make you feel like writing to someone, anyone. Stickers. Rich-colored manila envelopes. Coffee Ritz is good to sit in and watch people, and wonder about them. Josephine's Dry Goods has lengths of cloth to make the seamstress' heart lurch in her chest. I have a length of filmy stuff with flowers blooming against a black ground, flowers the likes of which spring from no earthly soil. I got it at Josephine's, and I'm saving it to stitch into something wonderful, squirreling it away, taking it out every few months to stroke and admire, like shining, secret jewels.

It depends on what kind of mood you're in, this Hanging Out business. And whether your aim is to stay in that mood, or vamoose out of it, if you know what I mean.

One of the best hangouts around town is Powell's Bookstore, but I'm not telling you anything new, am I? For my money (more of which gets spent in there than is reasonable) the secret of the success of Michael Powell's cavernous establishment is that the man respects the off-kilter sensibilities of we who don't even regain consciousness until noon or so. When you've got an aching need to do a spot of Hanging Out at 10 at night, Powell's is there. It's better than being in a library, partly because there's something very satisfying about knowing you can own any of these books, and never worry about due dates. You don't have to be so hush-hush, a pretty tall order for some of us. Tucked away in the corner, Anne Hughes Coffee Room is perfect for plopping down for a cup of tea, maybe with someone you've run into and haven't seen for ages.

I once heard a flustered elderly lady call Bill Kloster's and Katie Radditz' Looking Glass Bookstore "The Laughing Gas." By mistake, I think. While smaller than Powell's — but then so's the Pittock Mansion — the Looking Glass is a joy, a rich source of offbeat discoveries with its wealth of science fiction and weird underground comic books and magazines found nowhere else. It has a nice, cozy feel, and they'll leave you alone, or help you out. Your choice.

Which is what Hanging Out is supposed to be all about, right?

Susan Stanley

It depends on what kind of mood you're in, this Hanging Out business.

Susan Stanley *is an essayist whose personal reflections are often seen in the* Oregonian *and a number of national magazines.*

Marty Hart *is an Oregon artist who designs and creates fans, masks and ritual objects in papier-mache incorporating organic materials such as fur, shells, feathers and grasses for accent. Each design is created as a limited edition. Marty is represented by The Real Mother Goose.*

BOOKS & MUSIC

Literary specialists for fiction classics, travel, foods, feminist concerns, holistic health, international magazines and periodicals; audio systems, video libraries and pianos new and restored.

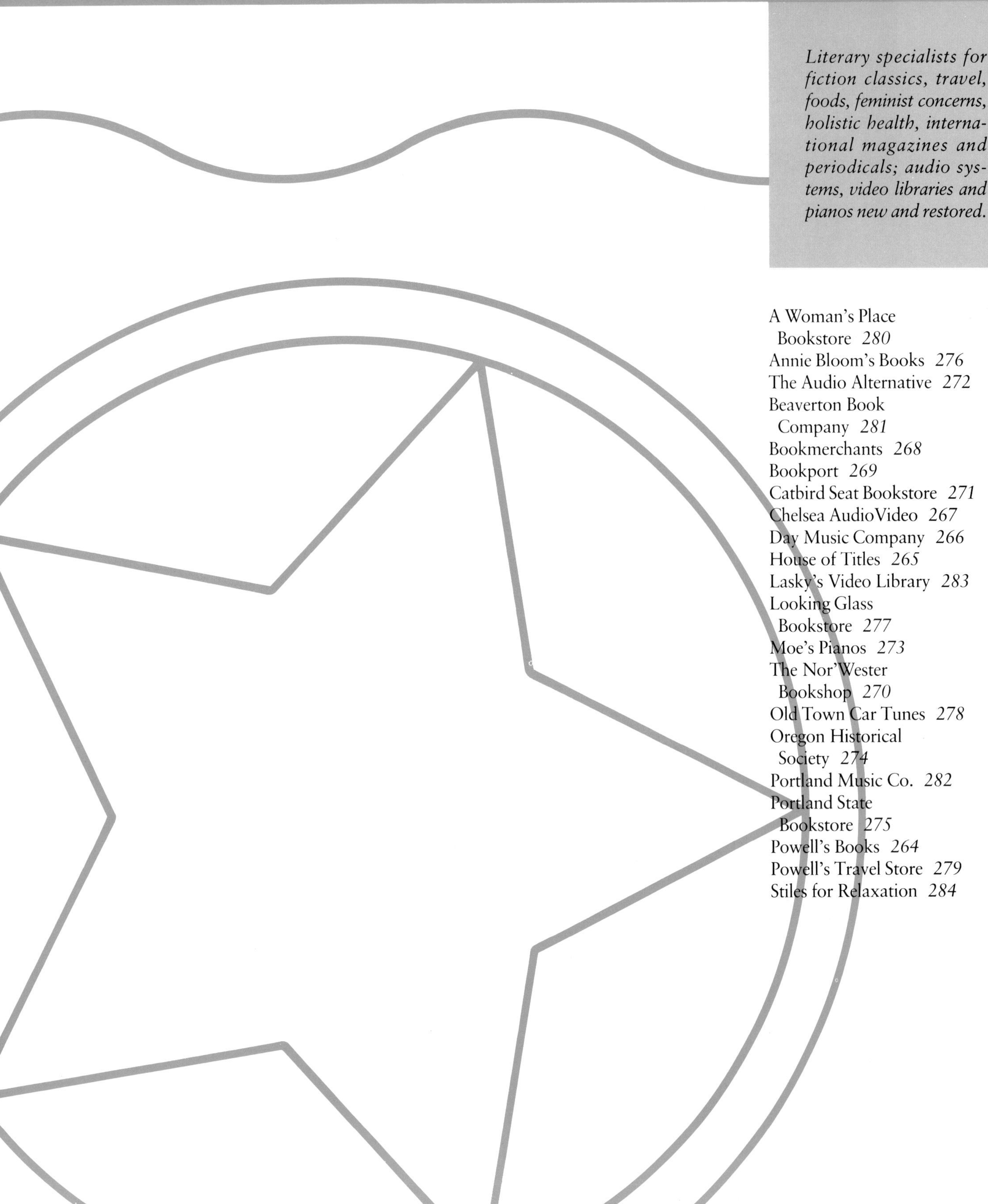

A Woman's Place Bookstore *280*
Annie Bloom's Books *276*
The Audio Alternative *272*
Beaverton Book Company *281*
Bookmerchants *268*
Bookport *269*
Catbird Seat Bookstore *271*
Chelsea AudioVideo *267*
Day Music Company *266*
House of Titles *265*
Lasky's Video Library *283*
Looking Glass Bookstore *277*
Moe's Pianos *273*
The Nor'Wester Bookshop *270*
Old Town Car Tunes *278*
Oregon Historical Society *274*
Portland Music Co. *282*
Portland State Bookstore *275*
Powell's Books *264*
Powell's Travel Store *279*
Stiles for Relaxation *284*

POWELL'S BOOKS

BOOKS

New and used books by the thousands.

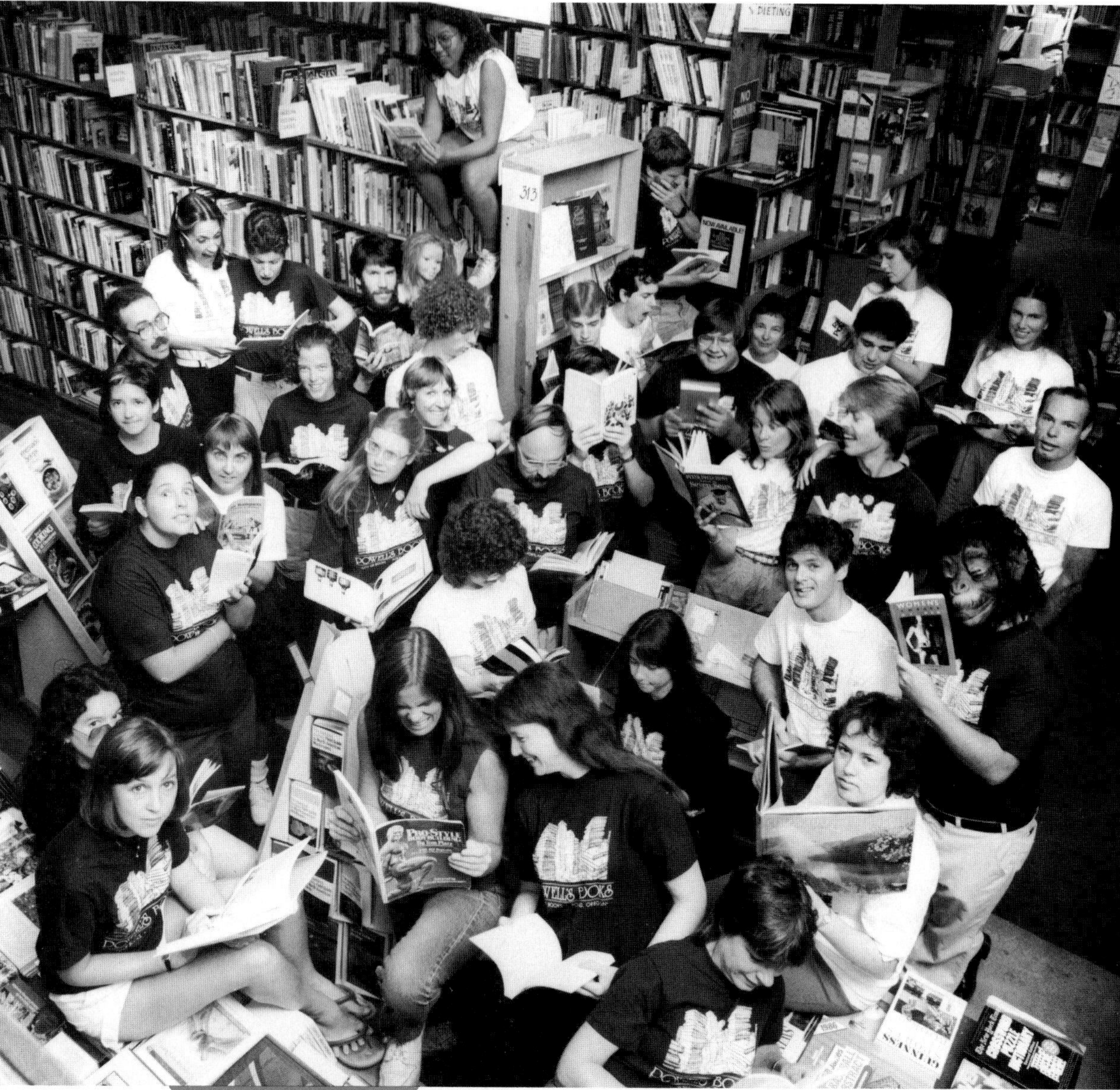

Downtown
E23

Progress-Washington Square
G2

To be a book lover in the Portland area and not know of Powell's Books is unthinkable. This is a store whose function for the reader is as crucial as verbs, nouns, periods and commas are to the English language. Now taking up floor space that covers an entire city block, Powell's Books is home to 700,000 books, new and used, on all subjects. Its shelves, reaching for the ceiling, seemingly go on for miles in all directions, and visitors without a sense of direction can become joyfully lost, wandering from Steinbeck to sailing and Nietsche to needlepoint for days on end. (They have maps for the less adventurous.) Besides books, Powell's stocks new magazines, books on audio tape, video tapes, cards and postcards. Its huge inventory — the largest on the West Coast — makes it the logical first stop for anything in or out of print, whether you're searching for a used dictionary or a first edition of "Gone With the Wind." Although literature, children's books and cookbooks are a specialty, the store has such an extensive selection in just about every subject that no visitor will be disappointed. In fact, two long-time customers had special cause for celebration recently; they were married in the store and instead of exchanging rings, they exchanged books. If you're thinking along the same lines, though, better hurry: the store is becoming, ah, all booked up. Visa. MasterCard.

1005 West Burnside
Portland 97209
228-4651

Monday-Saturday
9am-11pm
Sunday 9am-9pm

Cascade Plaza
8775 SW Cascade Avenue
Beaverton 97005
643-3131

Daily
9am-9pm

HOUSE OF TITLES

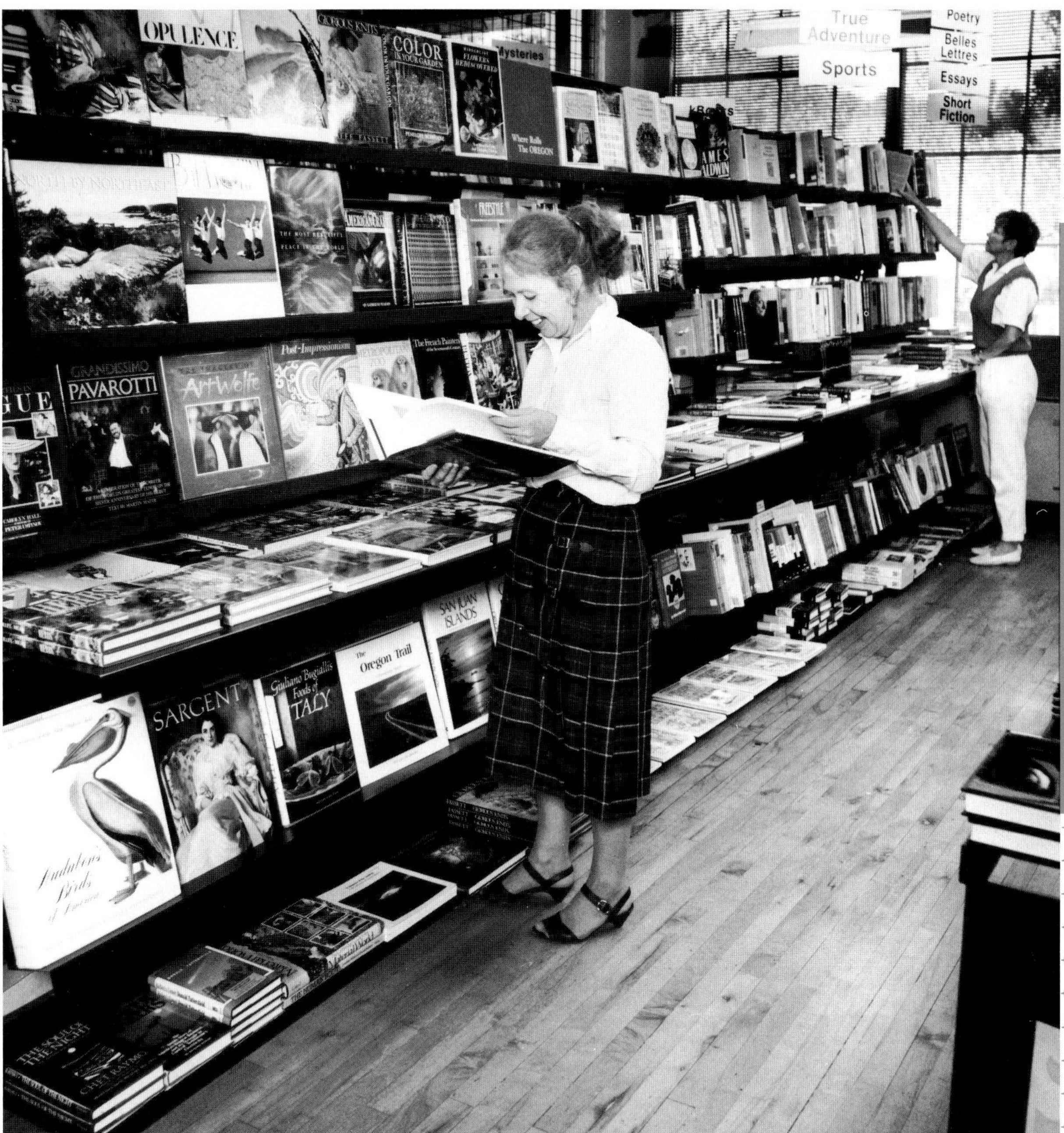

BOOKS

Beautiful books to buy for yourself or as gifts.

The space is bright and uncluttered, with room for the browser to study long expanses of cover-out titles. Copies of the New York Times Book Review are free; fashion magazines from Italy, France, England, Germany and Australia are close at hand and the gift book selection is unparalleled. Sound familiar? The enlightened quickly will recognize the House of Titles, a rising star in Portland's book world. Owner Liz Schenk bought the business in 1983 and has worked hard to provide the local literary community with more than ever before. Her efforts give every book lover the excuse to spend hours creeping from shelf to shelf, immersed in hardbound books covering a galaxy of subjects. There's something for everyone here: Calendars, cookbooks, children's titles, history, fiction, classics, travel, crafts and best-sellers. Also to be found is a splendid selection of elegant, hard-to-find books on art, architecture, photography and design, plus a stunning array of volumes for the Anglophile. The service is friendly and personal, and anything in print cheerfully will be specially ordered. When books beckon, consider yourself entitled to the House of Titles. Visa. MasterCard.

The Water Tower
5331 SW Macadam Avenue
Portland 97201
228-0290

Monday-Friday 10am-9pm
Saturday 10am-6pm
Sunday noon-5pm

Corbett-Johns Landing

F6

DAY MUSIC COMPANY

MUSIC

Portland's only full-service music store.

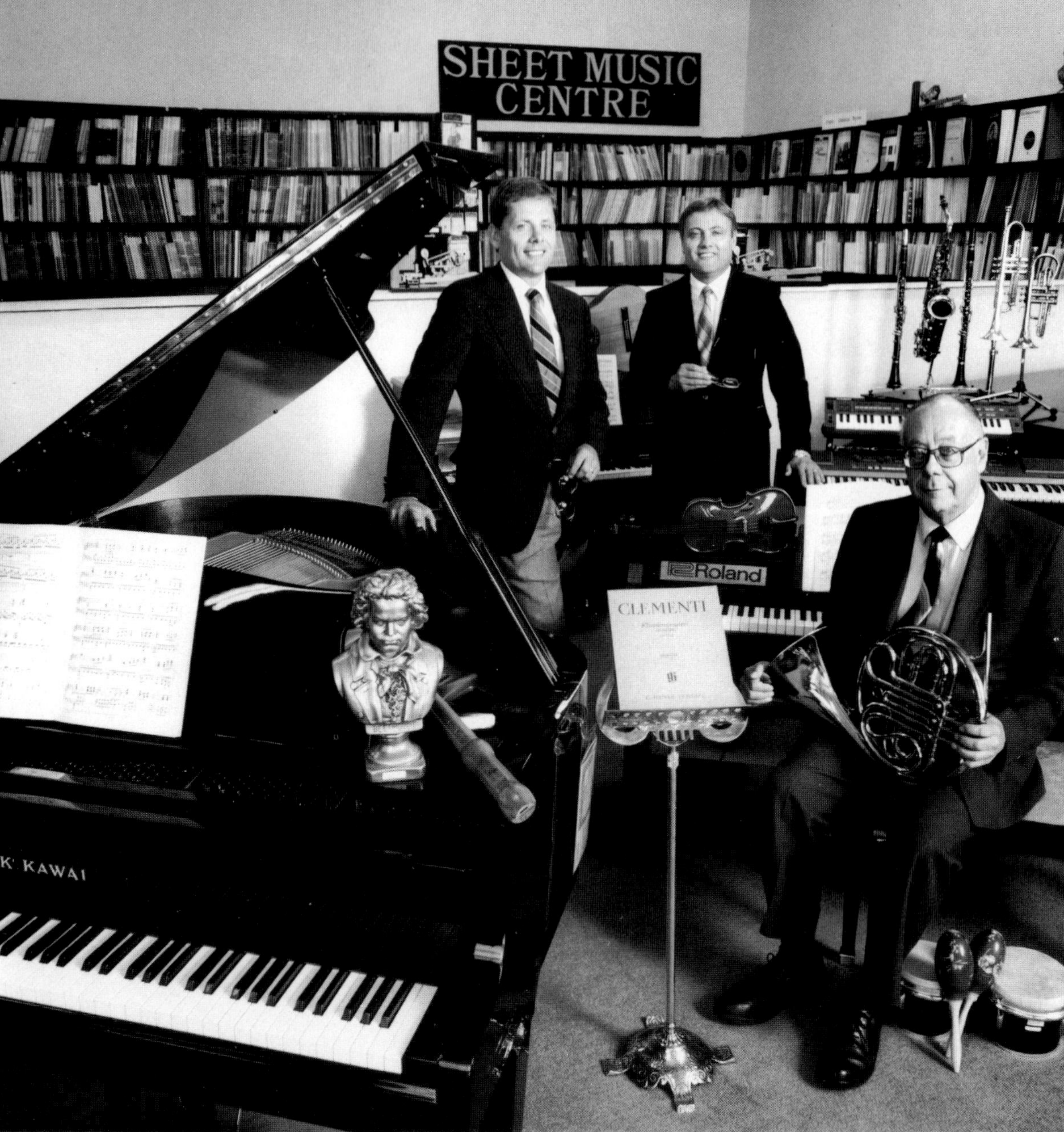

Southeast Portland

E8

In 1923, founder L. Carroll Day opened the doors of his new music company. His idea was to provide the city with its only full service music store — pianos and other instruments, sheet music, instruction, education, performance and endowments. More than sixty years later, the notes of his intention continue to reverberate in Southeast Portland. Naturally, inventory is a bit different these days — Allen digital organs and Roland digital pianos have joined the Kawai and Chickering acoustic pianos — but the selection of finely reconditioned used pianos, guitars, amps, band instruments, accessories and the vast sheet music department is second to none. Knowledgeable instrument reconditioning, expert advice, and community involvement are watchwords here. Day Music not only sells fine pianos, they sell and service most other instruments as well. The expert staff provides a wealth of instruction, administers the Day Music Scholarship Fund, and makes their 230 seat auditorium available for teachers and students. At Day Music, find all your musical needs orchestrated in one store. Visa. MasterCard. American Express. Discover.

5516 SE Foster Road
Portland 97206
775-4351

Monday-Friday
10am-7pm
Saturday 10am-6pm
Sunday hours vary

CHELSEA AUDIOVIDEO

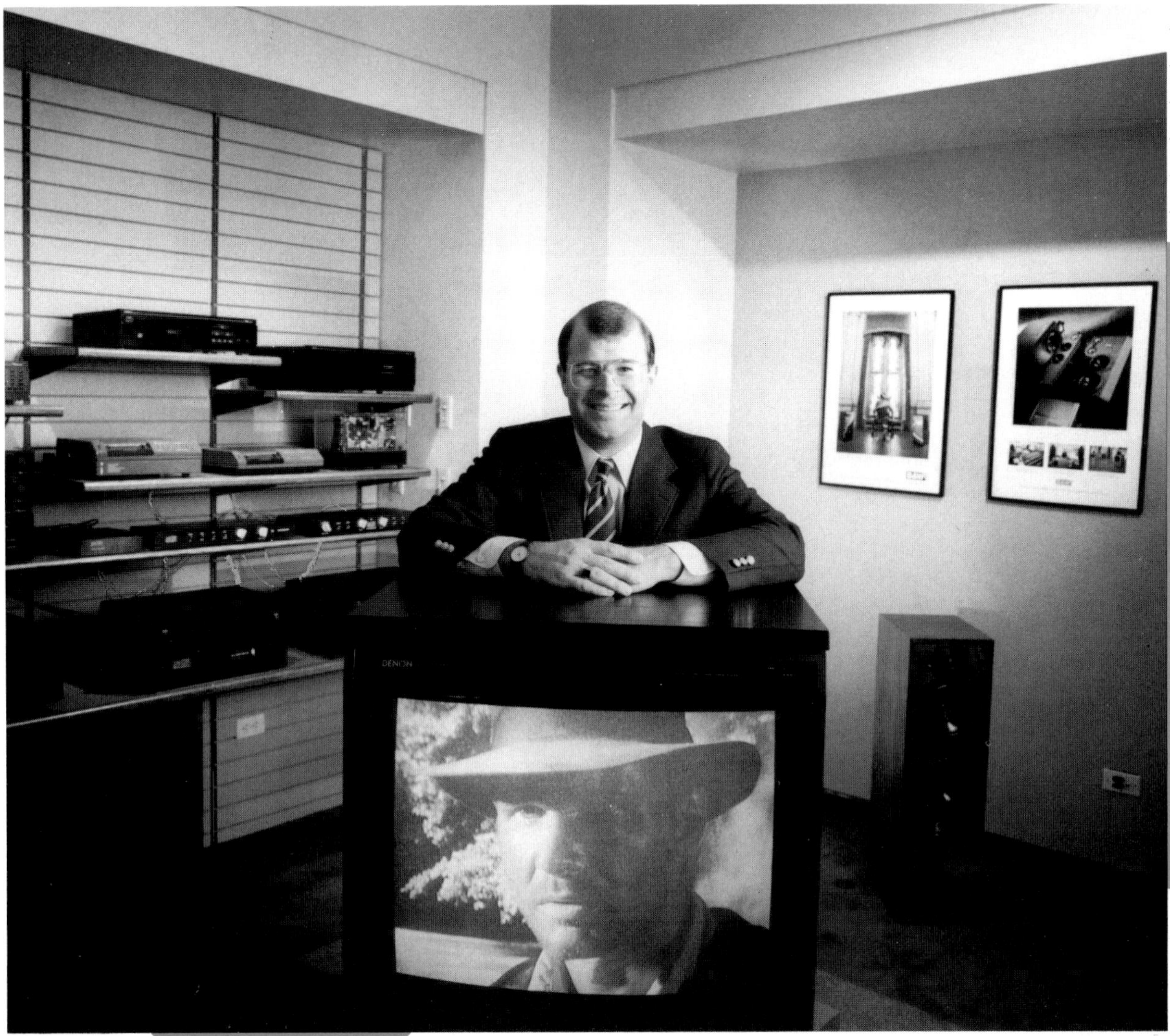

Audio and visual systems, installation and service.

Not so long ago, buying a fine stereo meant only three decisions: receiver, speakers, turntable. Then tape decks became commonplace. Now there are audio/video systems that integrate monitors and VCRs, a complete stereo, and entertainment technology's latest superstar, the compact disc player. Putting it all together — one piece or a room-full — requires more than fair prices and knowledgeable sales personnel. At Chelsea Audio Video, Ford Montgomery and Gary Taylor are guided by a simple philosophy never, ever, give customers reason to regret their patronage. That philosophy fused with quality, responsibility and service, makes the difference. You won't find 27 window-busting stereos blaring at once in Chelsea. Instead, the demonstration technique is honed to a high art, enabling the customer to experience the benefits of every product. And the selection covers every need; stereo equipment from $100 to many thousands; all manner of video products from VCRs to video surround-sound systems; car stereos, installed at Portland's largest facility; a complete service department; a custom home installation service that brings audio and video to every room; and the Bang & Olufsen stereo line, featuring audiophile quality and design worthy of permanent display at the New York Museum of Modern Art. Visa. MasterCard. Discover.

935 SW Washington Street
Portland 97205
226-3533

Monday-Thursday 10am-6pm
Friday 10am-7:30pm
Saturday 10am-6pm
Sunday noon-5pm

Beaverton Town Square
11693 SW Beaverton Hillsdale Highway
Beaverton 97005
641-3533

Monday-Friday 10am-9pm
Saturday 10am-6pm
Sunday noon-5pm

Car Stereo Store
1313 West Burnside
Portland 97209
226-0855

Monday-Thursday 9am-6pm
Friday 9am-7:30pm
Saturday 9am-6pm

Downtown

E23

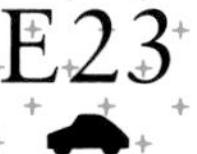

Beaverton

E2

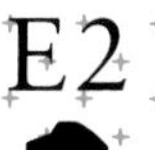

Downtown

E22

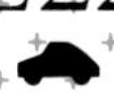

BOOKMERCHANTS BOOKSHOP, CAFÉ & ESPRESSO BAR

BOOKS

Book lover's best friend.

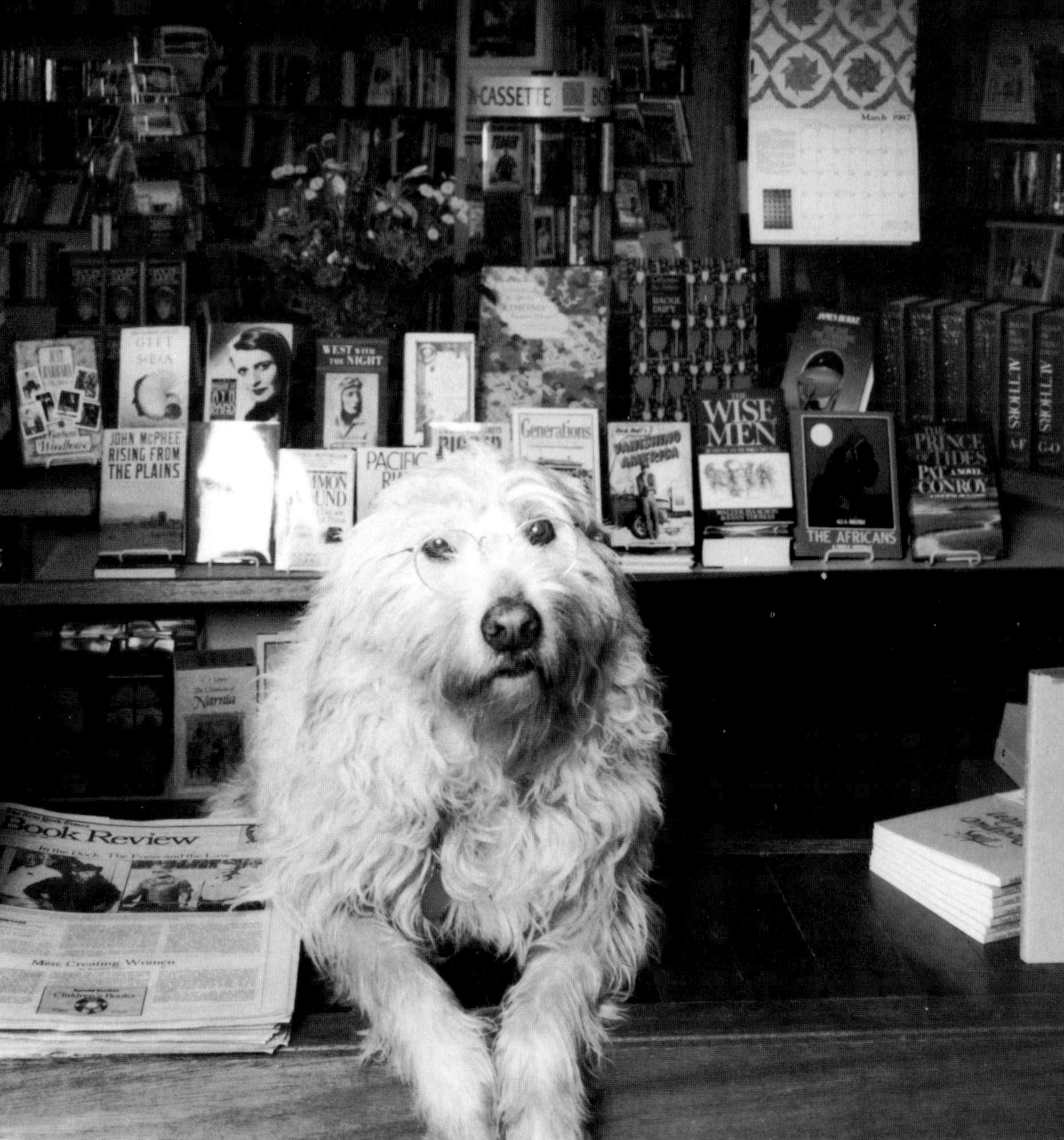

Yamhill Historic District
G25

Have you met Fingers, the Otterhound? Let her introduce you to Bookmerchants Bookshop, Café and Espresso Bar. Housed among old cast iron columns and pillasters, this bookshop features strong sections in travel, contemporary fiction, mysteries and children's literature. In addition, they have a wide variety of calendars and blank books. Bookmerchants is an independently owned full service bookstore with a broad selection of titles from best sellers to small press publications. In a relaxed, coffee house atmosphere you can browse through local and national newspapers or read periodicals from across the nation or around the world. Select one of their unusual cards and write a letter while sampling the daily special from their complete lunch menu or perhaps one of the baked goods made on the premises. As you step up to the Espresso and Wine Bar you may view work by Northwest artists. Choose from Oregon's finest wines, locally brewed beer and ale, or your choice of coffee and steamed milk drinks while you listen to a local author read from his or her work. No time today? They have food to go. The staff is knowledgeable and friendly, so if they don't have it they will order it for you. Visa. MasterCard.

818 SW First Street
Portland 97204
242-0087

Daily
10am-6pm
Call for evening hours

BOOK PORT

BOOKS

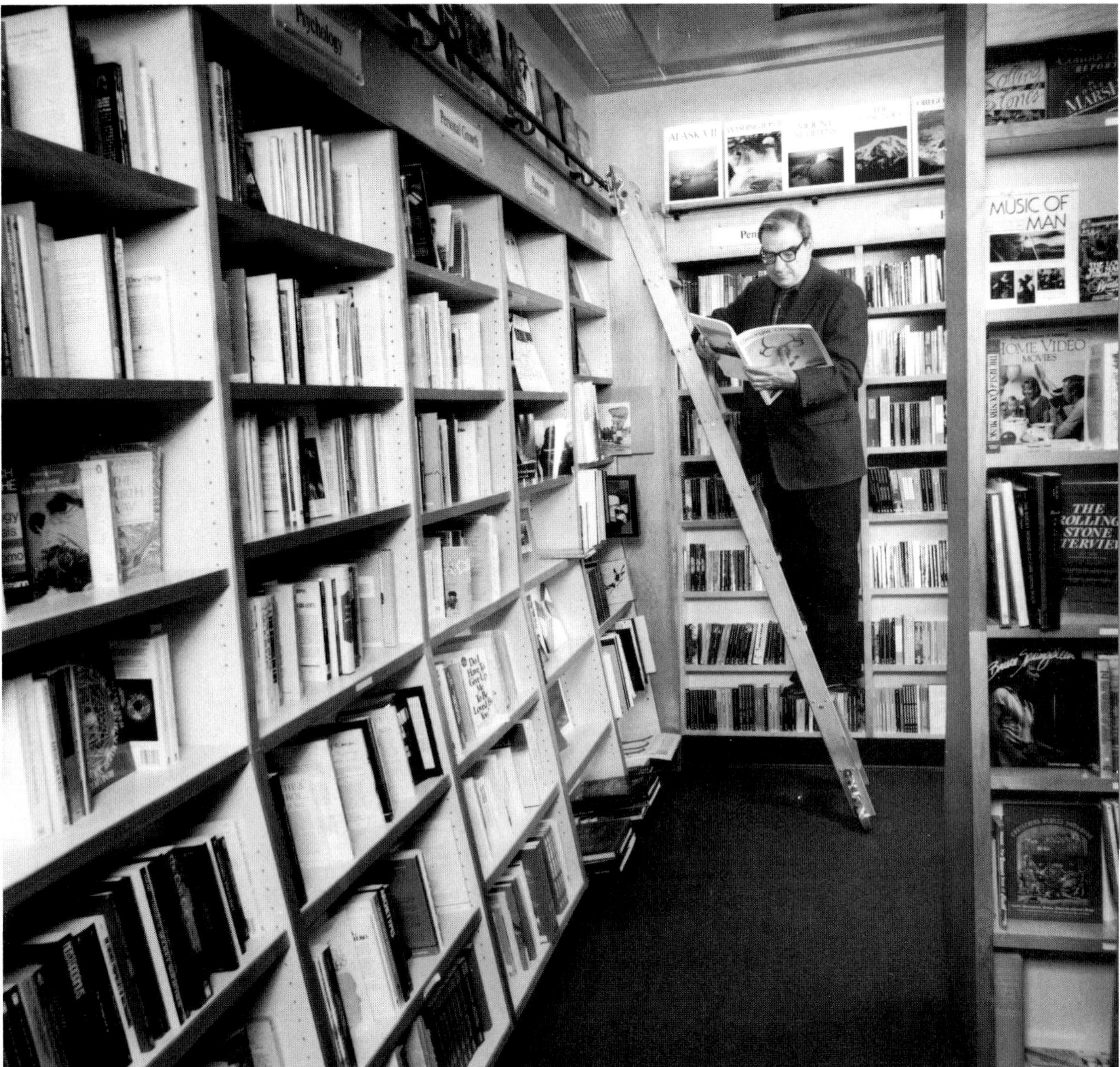

A friendly helpful bookstore overlooking the river.

In a recent 200-page report, a consultant to the Multnomah County Library suggested that the system could increase its appeal to users by creating a "popular library" in a bright corner of the main building. With books arranged by interest area on shelves and tables, the space would be "the most enticing and stimulating room in the building". A suitable example of such an attractive concept the consultant wrote, is Book Port at RiverPlace. By blending privacy, comfort and convenience, Book Port provides an atmosphere that makes browsing irresistible. To those attributes, owner Tom Dant has added a feature shared by only a tiny handful of West Coast book stores: A book rental service with a selection of hundreds of titles that include more than just best-sellers. There's also a Book Lovers Bonus Club that earns buyers one free book for each 10 purchased, select magazines, a special-order service, gift wrapping and shipping, downtown's biggest selection of religious reading materials, and, of course, a location in one of the city's most alluring developments. Book Port has it all. Visa. MasterCard. American Express. Diners Club.

0315 SW Montgomery
Suite #340
Portland 97201
228-2665

Summer:
Monday 10am-6pm
Tuesday-Thursday
10am-8pm
Friday-Saturday
10am-11pm
Sunday 10am-8pm

Winter:
Monday-Thursday
10am-6pm
Friday-Saturday
10am-10pm
Sunday 10am-6pm

RiverPlace
125

THE NOR'WESTER BOOKSHOP

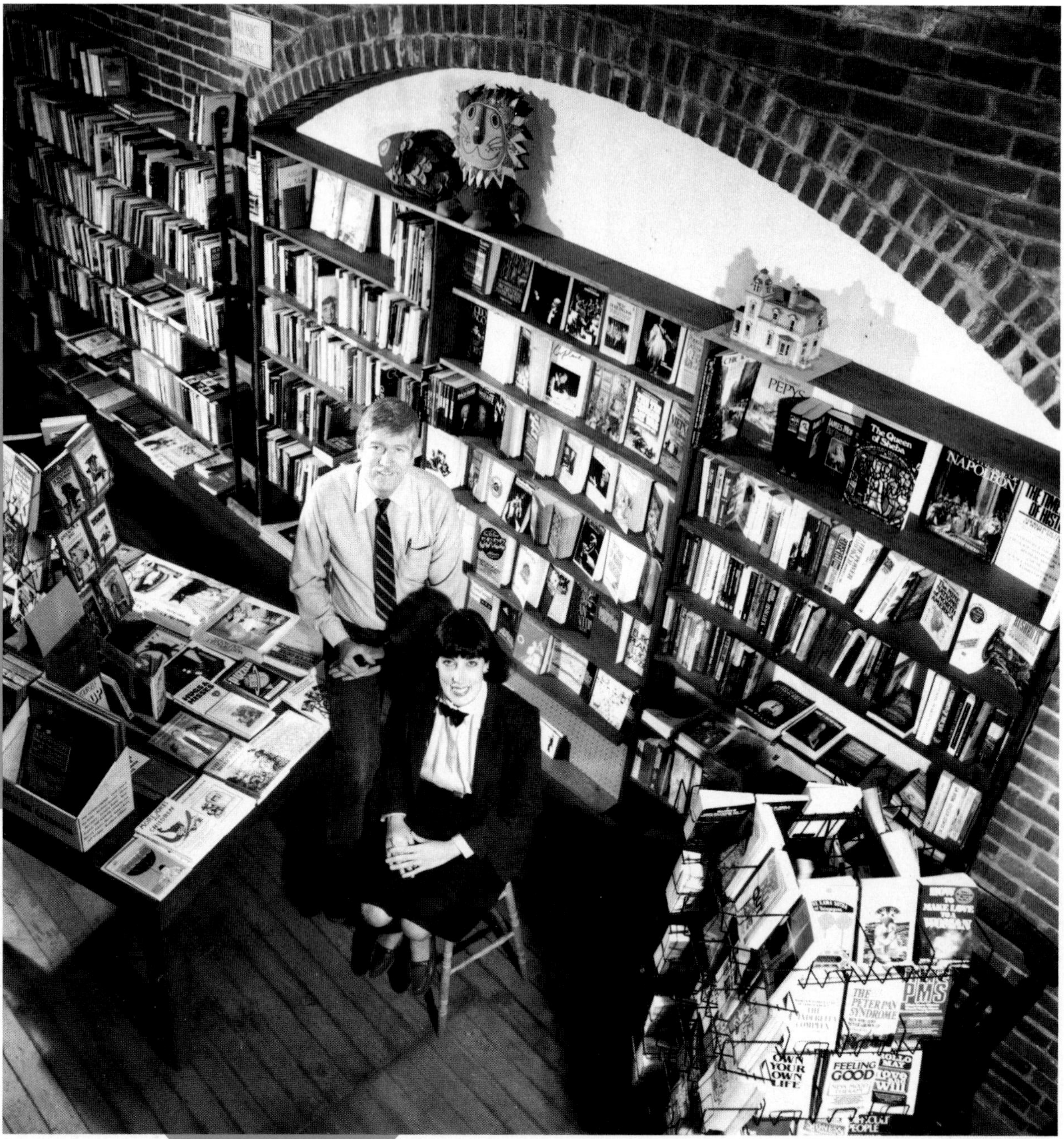

BOOKS

Unique books — knowledgeable service.

Skidmore Historic District

E25

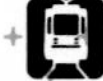

Phil Hubert wants you to enjoy his books. So when you visit his Nor'Wester Bookshop in New Market Village, don't be surprised by the personally selected classical music and the comfortable, relaxed ambience of the place. The atmosphere is delightfully different and so are the wares. Hubert, who selects all titles himself, prefers unusual, high quality books to those with purely commercial potential — another refreshing treat. One of the big categories at the Nor'Wester is design and architecture. "400 titles in architecture alone, and growing," Hubert says. The history and culture of the British Isles, Ireland and Japan are a specialty along with books on natural history, boats and boating, cooking, crafts, music and dance — and a strong selection of paperback mysteries. Look for Dover Scores and BBC Music Guides with the cassettes. There is also a wide selection of literature and poetry and more; including such items as paper dolls and model kits, a selection of fine and unusual cards, postcards and calendars, and the key works of Edward Gorey. If the title you're after isn't in stock, your special order will be handled quickly and efficiently. How can you lose? Comfort, good music and scads of good books. Visa. MasterCard.

New Market Village
58 SW Second Avenue
Portland 97204
228-2747

Daily
10am-6pm
And some evenings.

THE CATBIRD SEAT BOOKSTORE

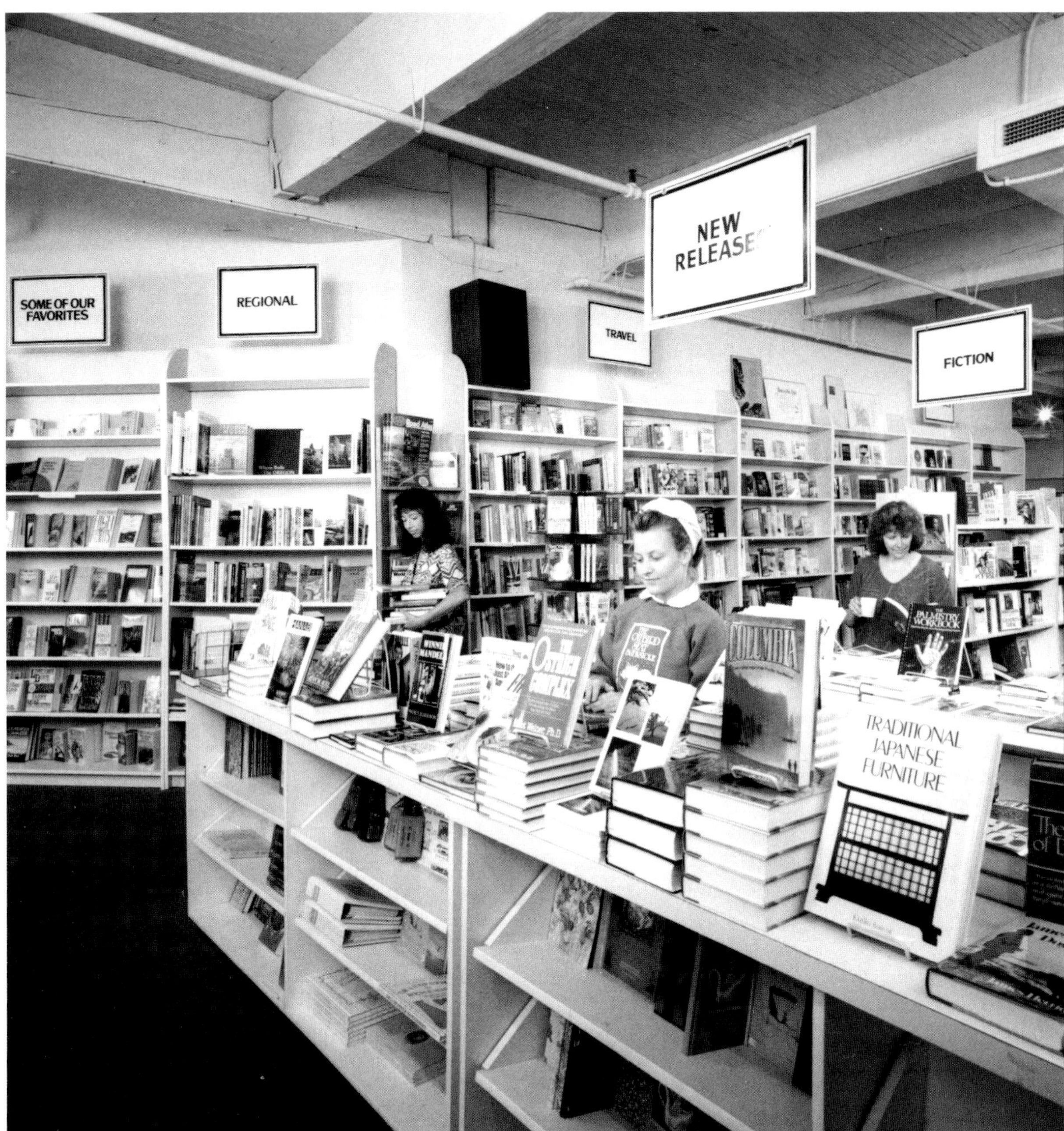

Personal, independent bookstore — customer service.

It's a book-lover's dream day — the skies are grey, the rain beats softly on the roof, the wind rattles the windowpanes. And that means just one thing. A trip to The Catbird Seat is definitely in order. Perhaps one of the most comprehensive bookstores in Oregon, The Catbird Seat offers a fascinating collection of carefully selected books. Psychology is a specialty — including a complete section of Jungian studies — as is health, women's studies, fashion, and cooking. English novelists and books from local small presses are well-represented; in fact, there's a complete selection from Prescott Street Press. Oregon and Northwest writers, many of whom have wandered through the aisles, are also featured. In addition, you'll find a broad range of fiction, mysteries, children's literature, art and photography, magazines and the leading bestsellers. Proprietor Deborah Robboy and her staff are avid readers themselves, so they can help you choose an especially good read. There's free coffee and tea and chairs in which to sit and read. Mail, phone, and special orders are always welcome as you are at The Catbird Seat Bookstore. Visa. MasterCard. American Express. Discover.

913 SW Broadway
Portland 97205
222-5817

Monday-Thursday
9:30am-9:30pm
Friday 9:30am-11pm
Saturday 10am-11pm
Sunday 10am-9:30pm

Downtown
F23

THE AUDIO ALTERNATIVE

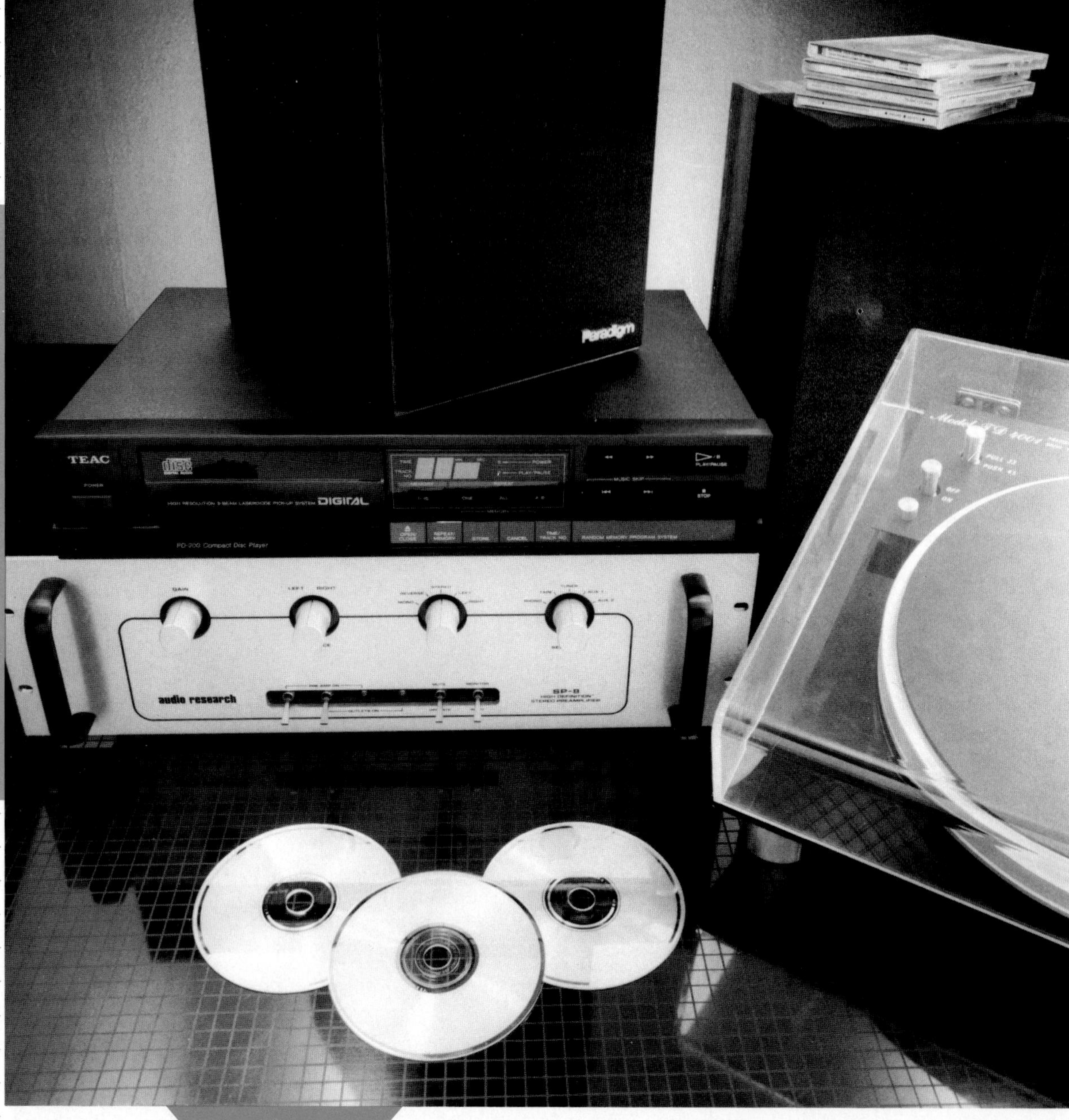

MUSIC

Your ears will appreciate the difference.

Southwest Portland

E3

The Audio Alternative is fanatically committed to the radical idea that making toast and listening to music have very little in common. In a business dominated by those who consider stereo equipment to be just another home appliance, owners Dave Herren and Mark Brannan remain staunchly unconvinced. To them, home audio shouldn't be judged by front panel conveniences or technological gimmickry, but by how transparently it reveals the spellbinding wonders of music. The aptness of its name is quickly evident to anyone who visits The Audio Alternative. The mood of personal service and real concern is clearly evident. Rather than walking among aisles of stacked boxes, one is encouraged to make decisions in listening rooms. Advice is given only after the real demands and desires of the listener are understood. The selection, from the modestly priced to the more esoteric, is obviously hand-picked for its musical quality. There is something to spell-bind everyone, whether one prefers rock rumbling through a stadium, Brahms sweeping across a concert hall, hot jazz blowing cool across a small club or a voice reaching for the next emotion. If one isn't a music lover when one enters, he will surely be one when he leaves. After a visit to the Audio Alternative, it will be hard to understand how anyone could ever have confused home audio with toasters in the first place. Visa. MasterCard.

West Slope
8680 SW Canyon Road
Portland 97225
297-1127

Tuesday-Saturday
11am-6pm
And by appointment.

MOE'S PIANOS

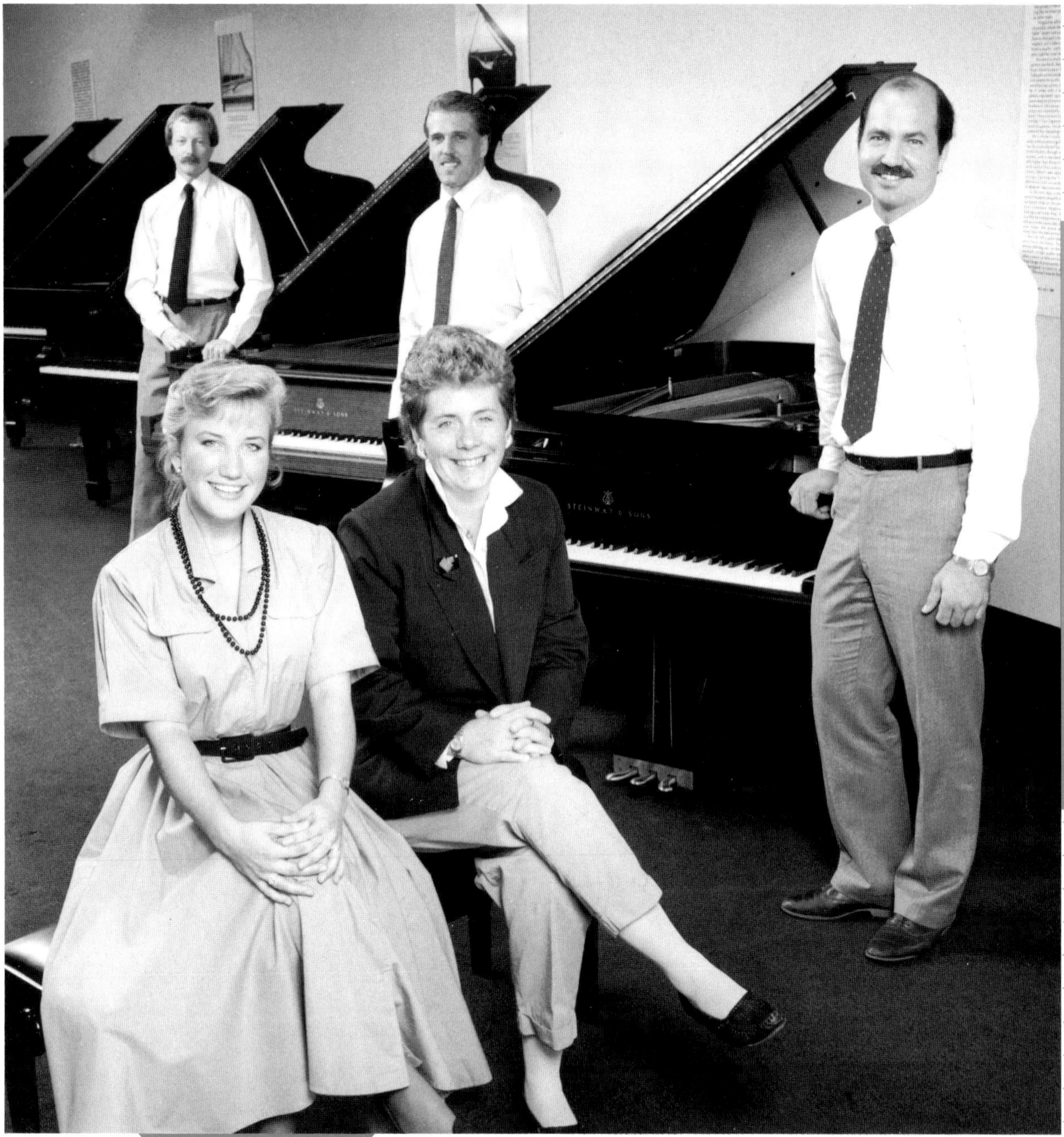

MUSIC

Most complete piano store in the Pacific Northwest.

Nowadays, when so much music is created on a computer and played with electronics, Moe's Pianos celebrates a time-honored instrument whose voice will endure for centuries. No addition to the home can be quite so appealing — to the eye or ear — as a piano. Alone before a concert audience, few instruments match the power, grace and delicacy of a piano. At a wedding or a party, the piano provides the right touch: a place to gather and celebrate the day's event in song. To all those ends, and many more, Moe's Pianos provides the technical expertise and uncompromising excellence that fine pianos and their owners deserve. In addition to a generous selection of fine grands and verticals from Young Chang, Bosendorfer and other respected names, Moe's now is Portland's exclusive dealer for the world-renowned Steinway & Sons instruments. Two fully equipped workshops offer reconditioned pianos for every taste and budget, backed by their own shop guarantees. In addition, Moe's has every imaginable service: moving, restoring, refinishing, tuning, storage, rentals, by the day, the month or more — supplies, appraisals and, as always, advice that only experts can give. Visa. MasterCard. Discover.

4500 SE Woodstock Boulevard
Portland 97206
775-2480

Monday-Thursday 10am-7pm
Friday 10am-9pm
Saturday 10am-6pm
Closed Sunday

Southeast Portland

F7

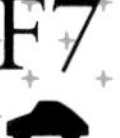

OREGON HISTORICAL SOCIETY

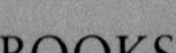

BOOKS

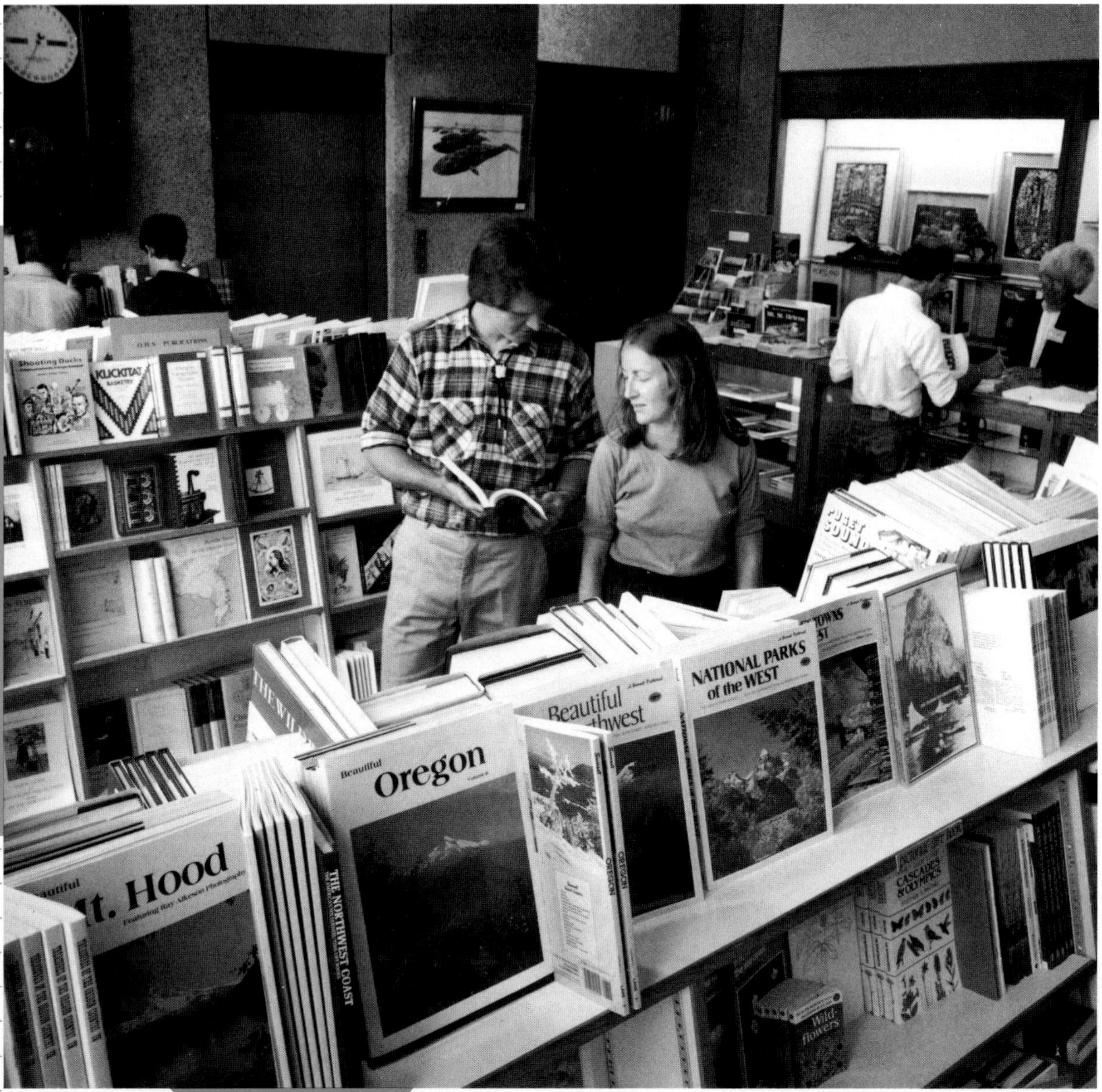

Collects, preserves, exhibits, and publishes Oregon history.

Downtown

G23

As the oldest statewide cultural institution in Oregon, the Oregon Historical Society has demonstrated leadership in the creative arts for 114 years. The Magna Carta: Liberty Under the Law exhibition of 1986, which was conceived and constructed by OHS staff and premiered in Portland before its nationwide tour, is an example of the internationally acclaimed exhibitions OHS has produced. Prize-winning books and precedent-making educational programs are other resources produced by OHS. The OHS regional research library with its collections of rare books, manuscripts, photographs, and films, attracts scholars from around the world. Founded in 1873 as an organization of enterprising pioneers, the Society today is an internationally recognized museum, publisher, and regional research and education center. Everyone benefits from its projects, as the library, exhibits and membership programs are open, free of charge to all. The Society's bookshop carries a full stock of publications — many available nowhere else — many ideally suited for gifts. The Oregon Historical Society Press has produced more than 150 books and maps covering regional history, biography and geography. The four-floor OHS Center ranks among the finest modern historical society homes in the nation and special events include lectures, tours, films and exhibition openings. With yearly membership starting at just $15, the Society enables everyone to play an important part in Oregon history. Visa. MasterCard.

MUSEUM
BOOKSHOP
LIBRARY & PRESS
1230 SW Park Avenue
Portland 97205
222-1741

Monday-Saturday
10am-4:45pm

PORTLAND STATE BOOKSTORE

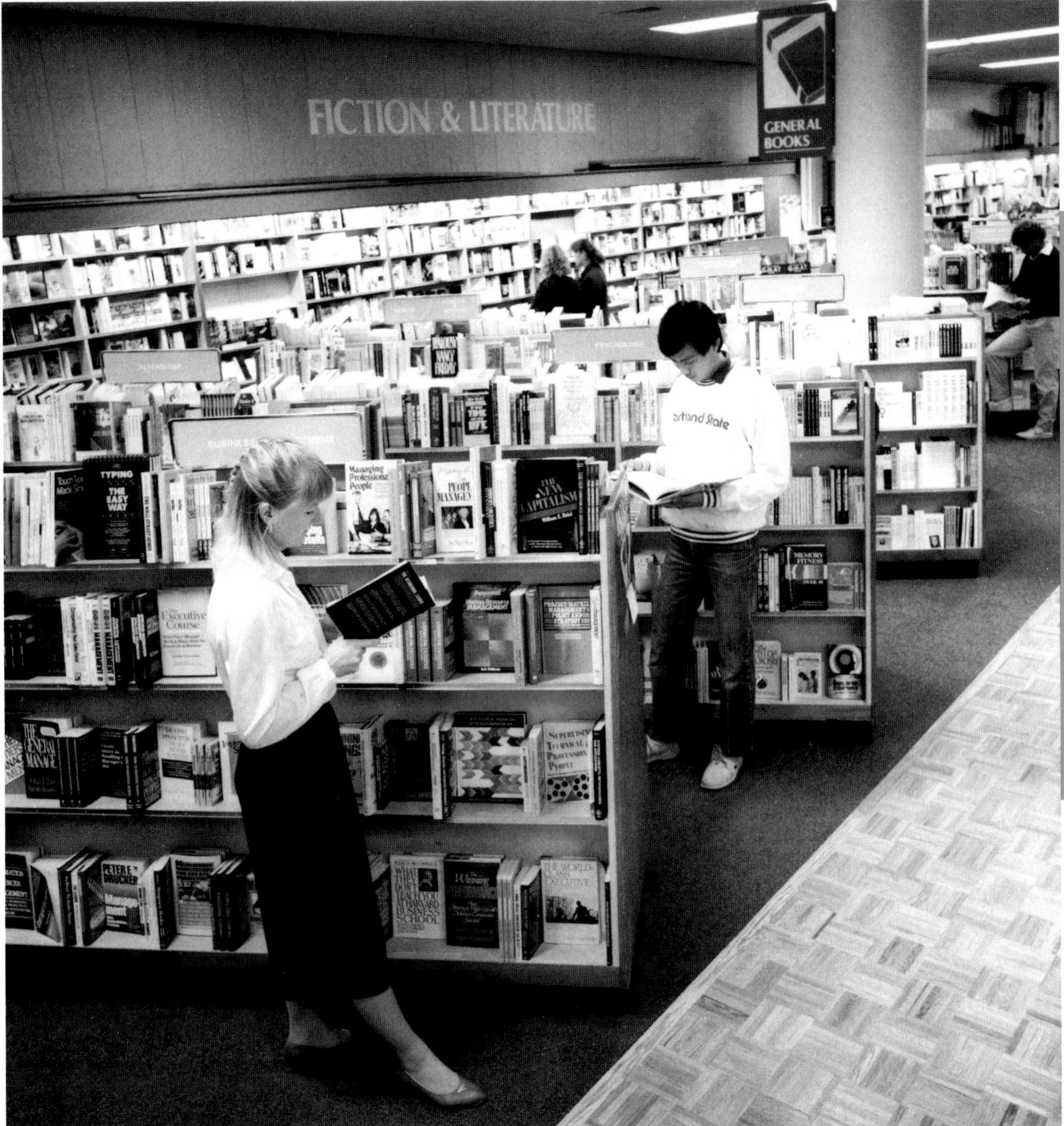

BOOKS

Books for all ages and interests.

Downtown
123

True book lovers glory in the vast selection of more than 20,000 general book titles — including the latest bestsellers — stocked at the Portland State Bookstore. Of course, university students get to ponder over 3,000 academic and technical books which also load the shelves. Alongside the volumes is a generous assortment of art supplies; Hewlett Packard calculators; greeting cards for every occasion; magazines; and sweats, shorts and shirts — many sporting the PSU insignia. And snacks and candies will nourish you after your exploration of the bookstore aisles. If, by chance, the book you seek is not on the premises, Portland State Bookstore will gladly make it available to you. Their special order service is thought to be one of the best in Portland. Casual browsers, along with members of the co- op — which is open to PSU faculty, staff, students and alumni — will find treasures by the thousands throughout the store. Visa. MasterCard.

531 SW Hall Street
Portland 97201
226-2631

Monday-Friday
8am-6pm
Saturday 9am-5pm

ANNIE BLOOM'S BOOKS FINE BOOKS AND WONDERFUL CARDS

BOOKS

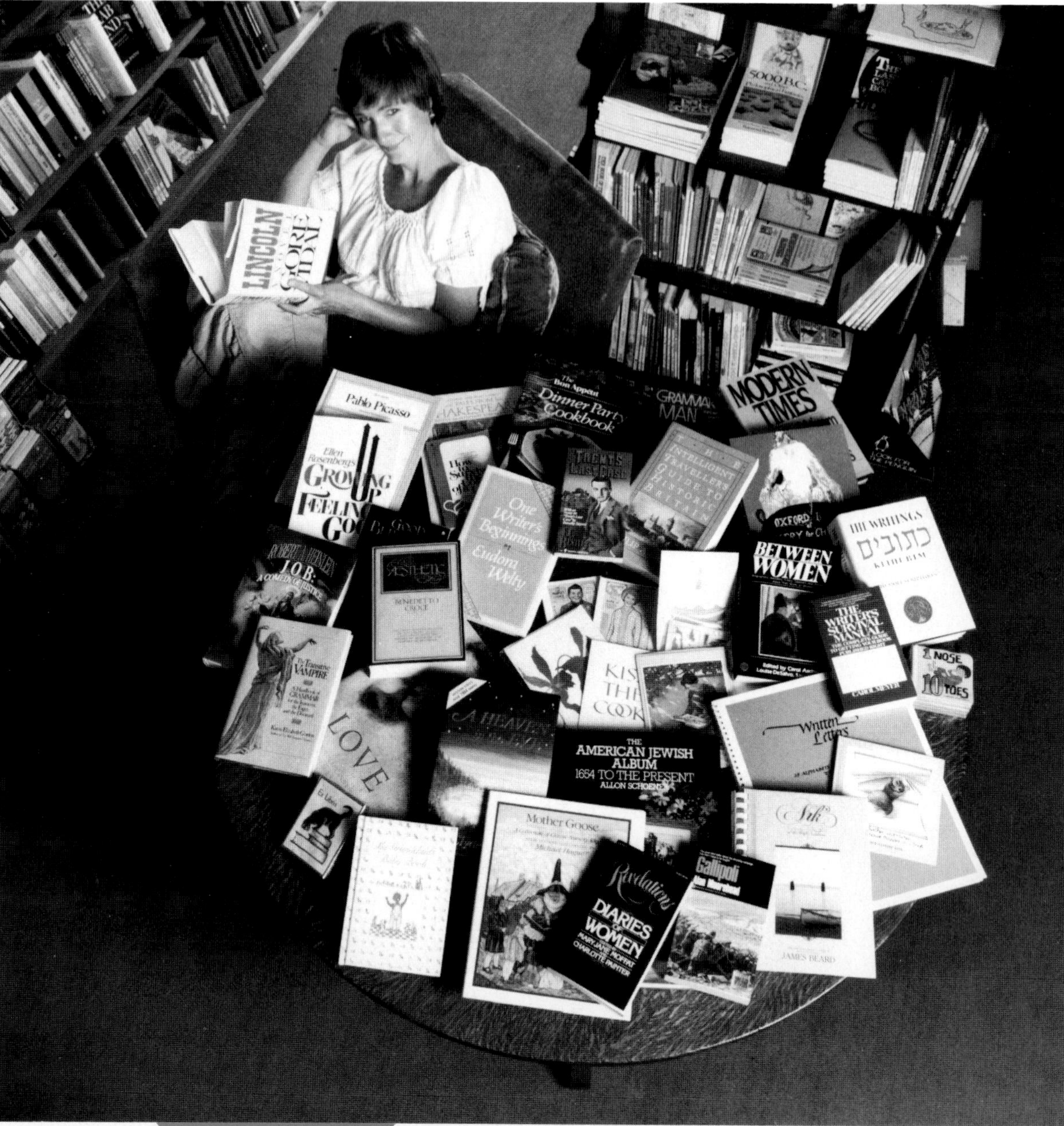

A book is like a garden, carried in the pocket.

Multnomah/ Hillsdale
F4

Northwest Portland
I17

Few places offer the sanctuary of a bookstore. In fact, the rainier the day, the better. If your enjoyment of reading demands something other than the commonplace, visit Annie Bloom's Books and be prepared to stay awhile. At Annie Bloom's the selection is top-notch, the service personalized, the gift- wrapping and ordering are all free. This is the place for fine literature, a scholarly reference section, plenty of cooking and poetry titles and a children's department with something for every visitor who's knee-high to a bookmark. The house specialty is Judaica, with a thorough and select collection of works on Jewish history. There are music cassettes for sale, the New York Times, cards for every occasion and even free calligraphy. Annie Bloom's recently opened second store in Northwest Portland is more of a good thing, featuring books and music on cassette, newspapers and magazines. In either location Annie Bloom's hallmark is always in abundant supply — the service of a warm and knowledgeable staff. Visa. MasterCard.

7834 SW Capitol Highway
Portland 97219
246-0053

Monday-Friday 9am-7pm
Saturday 9am-5pm
Sunday noon-4pm

406 NW 23rd Avenue
Portland 97210
221-4224

Monday-Friday 10am-7pm
Saturday 10am-6pm
Sunday noon-5pm

LOOKING GLASS BOOKSTORE

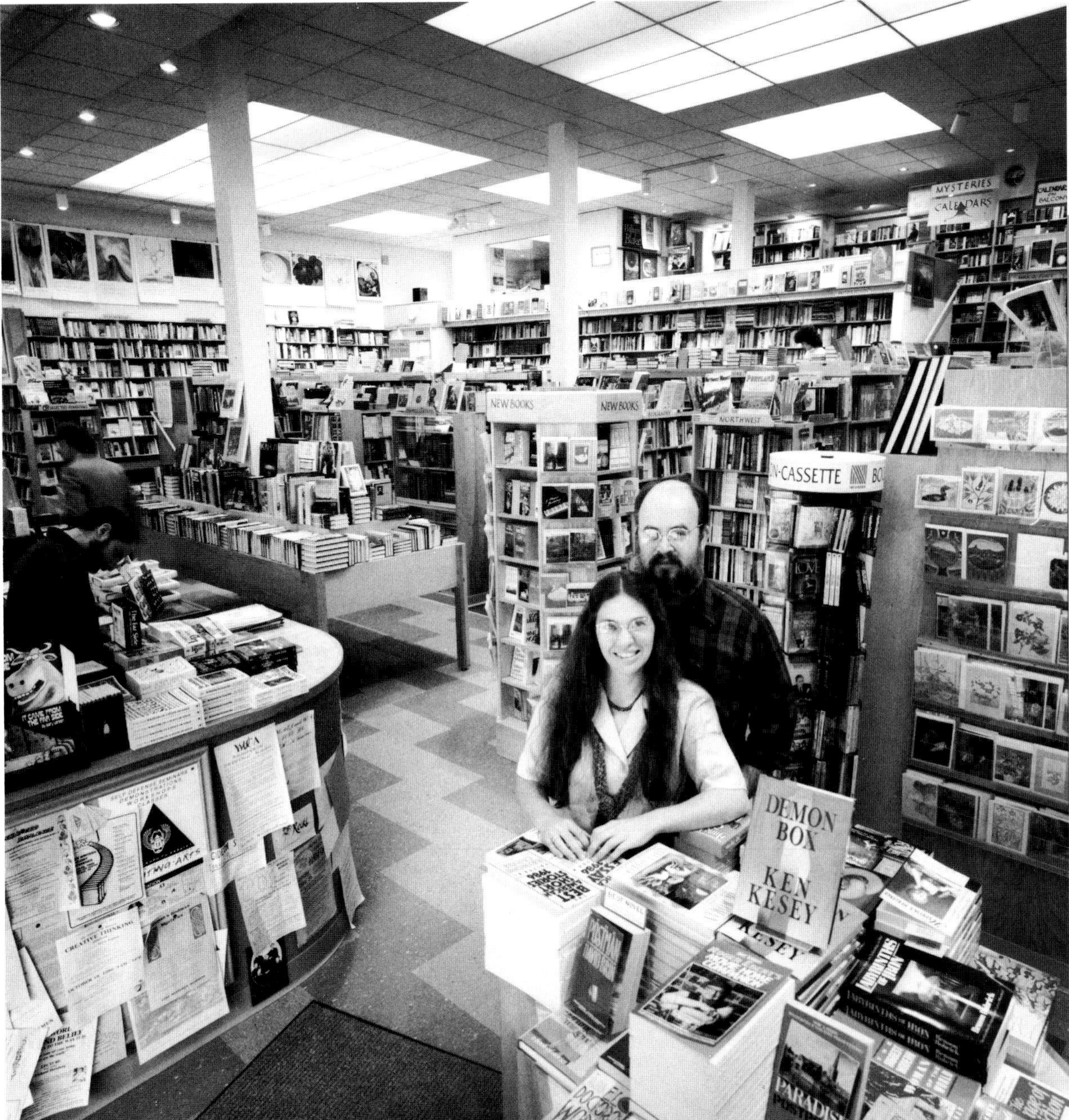

BOOKS

Downtown's oldest new book store.

Downtown

G24

With its skylights, blond woodwork, children's nook and three-tiered amphitheater of books, Looking Glass is perhaps Portland's most beautiful bookstore. Although the store has a full range of new books, it specializes in contemporary fiction, science fiction, psychology, health and religious thought, both Eastern and Western. It is the antithesis of the shopping mall book store: relaxing, contemplative music is always playing; art prints hang on the walls. There's a selection of literature in French and Spanish; a wide choice of hard-to-find magazines; a sale books balcony with a quality collection of hardback fiction and non-fiction at paperback prices. Employees willingly make special orders, provide a daily mailing service and handle gift wrapping. There's also a mailing list for Spring and Christmas catalogs and invitations to author autograph parties and readings. Among its counterparts, Looking Glass is probably best known for being on the forefront of thought, for weathering and flourishing amid downtown's changes, and for its steady, devoted and colorful mix of customers. It is an amusing, hospitable, sometimes invigorating, sometimes calming and always interesting place to spend a good bit of the day. Visa. MasterCard.

318 SW Taylor Street
Portland 97204
227-4760

Monday-Saturday
10am-6pm

OLD TOWN CAR TUNES

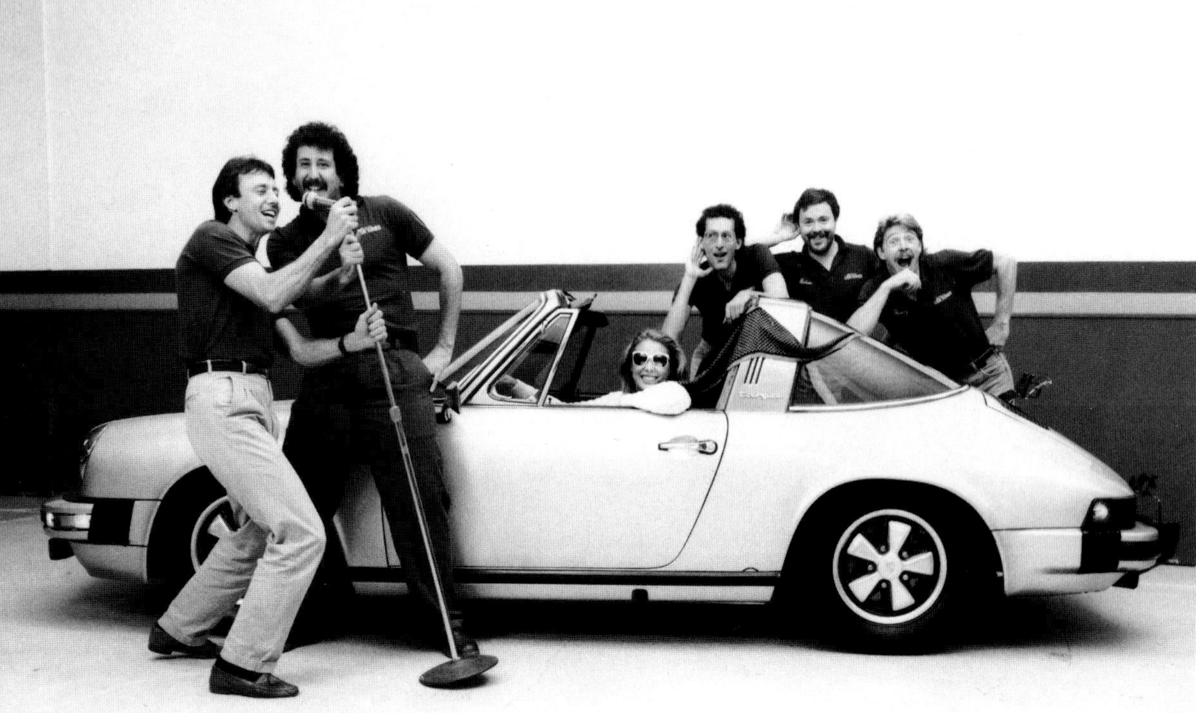

MUSIC

Mobile music systems for the discriminating buyer.

Old Town
D24

If your car's in need of a "tune-up", Don Stevenson and Dave Barr can guarantee you'll hear the difference after a visit to Old Town Car Tunes. Forget spark plugs, oil changes and valve adjustments: Don and Dave sell only the most important parts: electronic AM-FM/cassette receivers, compact digital disc systems, amplifiers and equalizers, and a broad range of speakers. By leaving the home systems to others, Old Town Car Tunes is an audio specialist that excels at being the best. Their expertise has become increasingly crucial as cars become more space-efficient; who wants to have a chainsaw-and-hammer installation in a $15,000 automobile? In addition to making every system look like it was built into the car at the factory, Old Town makes the whole process a convenient one. Its location is within walking distance of downtown's core, and customers can leave cars on the way to work and take advantage of a free shuttle service. Inside the shop, the recently remodeled showroom lends a hi-tech look and conveys the feeling of quality that is evident the second you turn on the sound. Other Old Town Car Tunes products complement the audio systems to help you keep your car (alarm equipment), keep your license (radar detectors) and keep in touch (cellular telephones). Visa. MasterCard. American Express. Discover.

34 NW Broadway &
Couch Street
Portland 97209
227-1668

Opening soon in Beaverton

Monday-Friday
7:30am-6pm
Saturday 10am-6pm

POWELL'S TRAVEL STORE

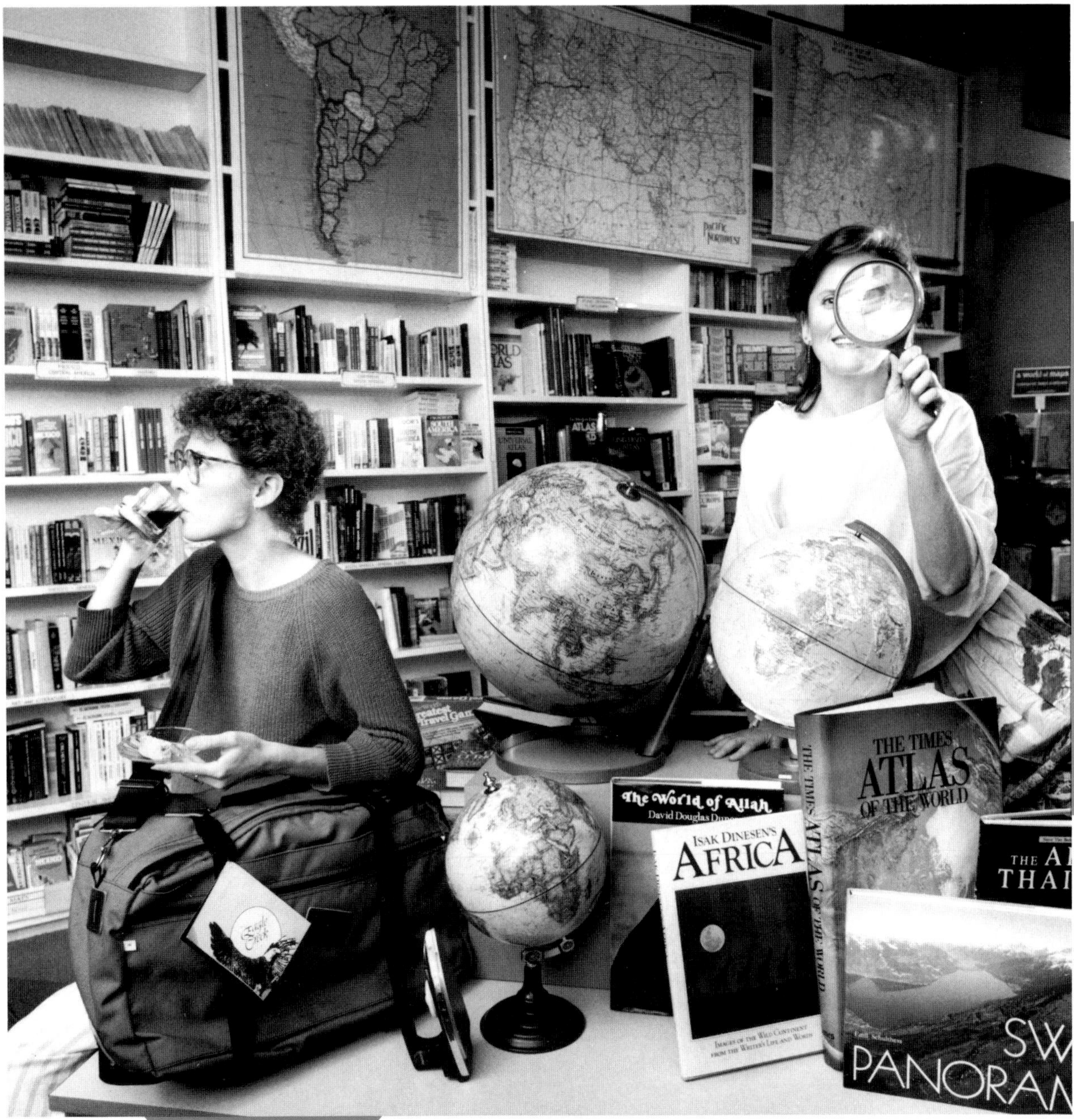

BOOKS

First stop for any trip: books, maps travel accessories.

Whether your destination is Dakar, Dusseldorf or Denver, the first required stop is as near as Pioneer Courthouse Square: Powell's Travel Store. With enough travel books, maps, hard-to- find travel accessories and well-engineered gadgets to fill a planeload of suitcases, Powell's Travel Store puts the world at your fingertips. The store boasts the largest selection of travel books and maps west of the Mississippi, with everything from a road map of Nepal to a street atlas of London to a natural history map of the Galapagos Islands. Once you've gotten there, indispensable Powell's Travel Store goodies will make your adventures even more enjoyable. For example, a butane-powered curling iron that works equally well in the Hilton or the Himalayas, an 8,000-word calculator/translator, or beach towel stakes good for gale-force winds. Travel irons, Eagle Creek's intelligently designed Overland Carryon luggage and dozens more items also await your perusal. Powell's Travel Store also offers its own brand of hospitality, in the form of an espresso bar that serves as the perfect spot to sip while comparing travel guides. Regularly scheduled travel slide presentations and language classes are but two other reasons that Arthur, "Europe on $25 a Day," Frommer remarked, "This store is a tremendous resource. Portland's lucky to have it." Visa. MasterCard.

Pioneer Courthouse Square
Portland 97204
228-1108

Monday-Saturday
9am-9pm
Sunday 11am-6pm

Downtown
F23

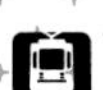

A WOMAN'S PLACE BOOKSTORE

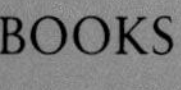

BOOKS

Feminist bookstore and resource center.

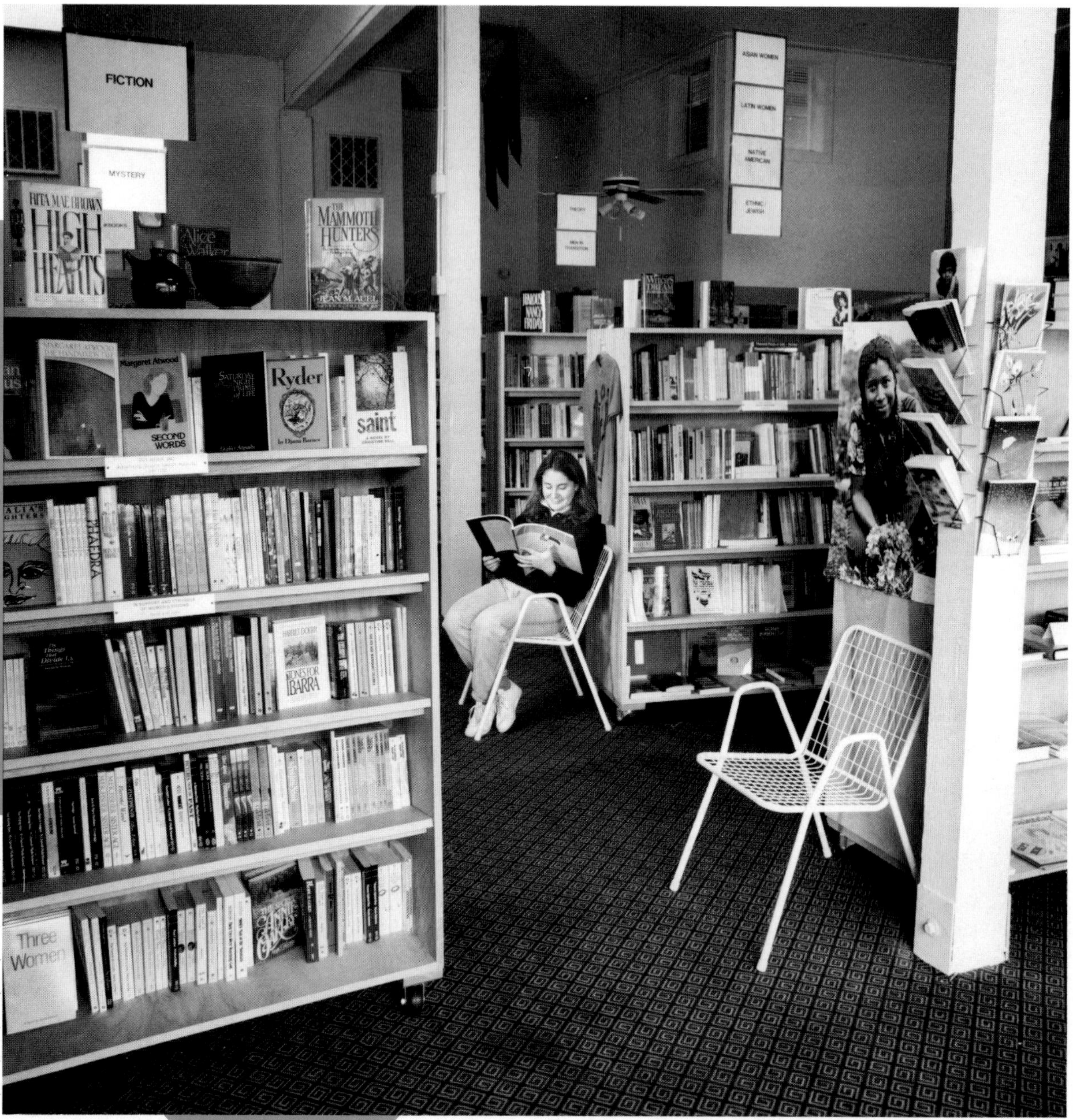

Northeast Portland

C6

In 1973, A Woman's Place Bookstore carried 50 titles and was operated as a non-profit corporation managed by a collective of women. Today, a volunteer board of directors oversees the operation; with a recent move to a new location, the space has tripled and the shelves display 6,500 titles. One thing has not changed — a reliance on volunteer help (only three persons are paid), and an abiding desire to provide a high-caliber resource center and outlet for feminist publications. Virtually everything here is by, for and about women, with book types and topics such as self-improvement, psychology, health, spirituality, women in business, gay men, incest survivors, domestic violence, and lesbians. Autobiographies and children's books with a feminist orientation are favorites here. T-shirts, custom clothing, jewelry, crystals, cards, art, stoneware, lotions and oils, records, cassettes and song books related to the feminist cause also are stocked. As a resource center, A Woman's Place provides referral services to women; a business card board; a ride, housing and events board; a free lending library with 1,000 contemporary feminist literature titles; and a women's events telephone recording that operates while the store is closed — 7 p.m. to 11 a.m. Every two months there's an art show featuring works by women in the community, further underscoring the atmosphere here: this is a place where a woman can feel at home. Visa. MasterCard.

1431 NE Broadway
Portland 97232
284-1110

Monday-Saturday
11am-7pm
Sunday noon-5pm

BEAVERTON BOOK COMPANY

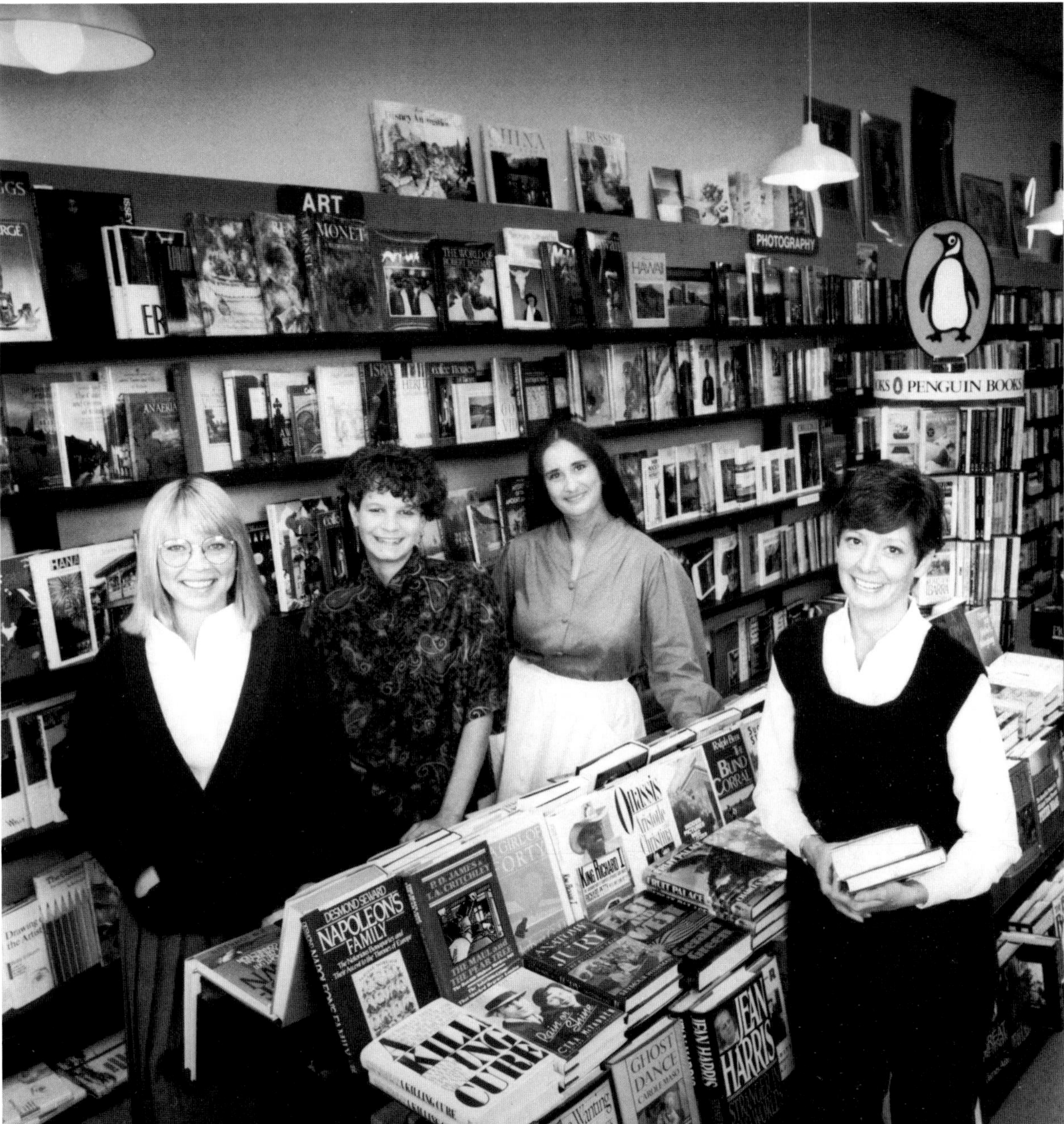

BOOKS

An extraordinary selection for the ardent reader.

Beaverton

E2

Proprietors John and Lee Ann Earlenbaugh's well-displayed written treasures are persuasive. Not only can you not judge a book by its cover, you can't judge a bookstore by its straightforward name. Books that slip from local best-seller lists can't be found in many stores. Yet here is a shop with both the room and inclination to display its surprisingly large variety of special titles.Particularly strong in food and children's literature, Beaverton Book Company showcases a potpourri of best-selling and high quality fiction. Charcoal shelving, gray carpeting, banners, colorful art prints, wood interiors, and a sky-lit interior enhance the browser's pleasures. The store's newspapers and magazines of international appeal are interspersed with well-displayed racks of greeting cards, and a broad selection of calendars. While browsing is encouraged, a literate, knowledgeable staff stands by, ready to assist you in your selections and gift wrap those special books. When Christmas decisions are pressing, the owners produce an annual, informative newsletter. Visa. MasterCard. American Express. Discover.

Beaverton Town Square
11773 SW Beaverton Hillsdale Highway
Beaverton 97005
644-7666

Monday-Friday 10am-9pm
Saturday 10am-6pm
Sunday noon-5pm

PORTLAND MUSIC CO.

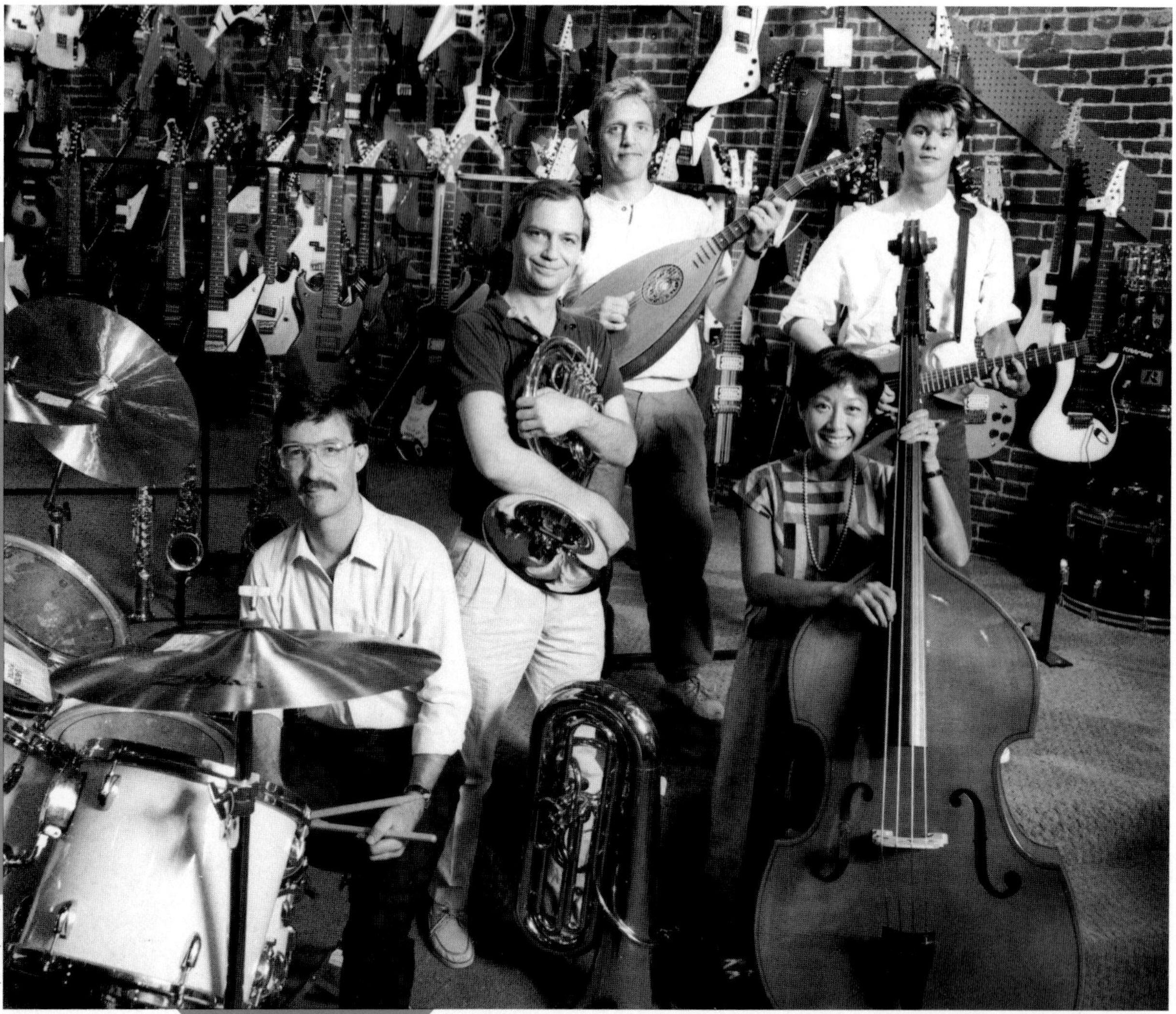

MUSIC

Leader of the band for 50 years.

Old Town
D25

Downtown
F25

Gresham
E13

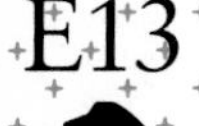

Beaverton
F3

Eric Clapton, Carlos Santana, Emmy Lou Harris, Jackson Brown, Kiss, Jeff Beck, Chuck Mangione, Earl Klugh, John Entwistle and local knowledgeable musicians all have something in common: they've done business with Portland Music Company. Legend has it that the store even sold Doc Severinsen his first trumpet. True or not, Portland Music doesn't need to toot its own horn — its inventory speaks for itself. State-of-the-art electronic keyboards and synthesizers, high quality new and used school instruments and a rent-to-own program; hundreds of electric and acoustic guitars, with rentals on student models; professional sound and home recording equipment that includes tape machines, signal processors and sale or rental of public-address equipment; sheet music and teaching materials; and a large drum and cymbal selection — it's all here. Complete instrument repair facilities also are at hand. In all, Portland Music offers thousands of instruments in a casual and comfortable atmosphere and has been serving the Northwest's musicians, for more than 50 years. Pay Portland Music Company a visit. Maybe, someday, they'll boast that they sold you a trumpet. Visa. MasterCard. Discover.

125 NW Fifth Avenue
Portland 97209
226-3719

Monday-Thursday
10am-6:30pm
Friday 10am-8pm
Saturday 10am-5pm

520 SW Third Avenue
Portland 97204
228-8437

Monday-Saturday
10am-6pm

576 NE Burnside
Gresham 97030
667-4663

Monday-Thursday
10am-6:30pm
Friday 10am-8pm
Saturday 10am-5pm

10075 SW Beaverton
Hillsdale Highway
Beaverton 97005
641-5505
Sheet Music 641-5691

Monday 10am-8pm
Tuesday-Thursday
10am-6:30pm
Friday 10am-8pm
Saturday 10am-5pm

LASKY'S VIDEO LIBRARY

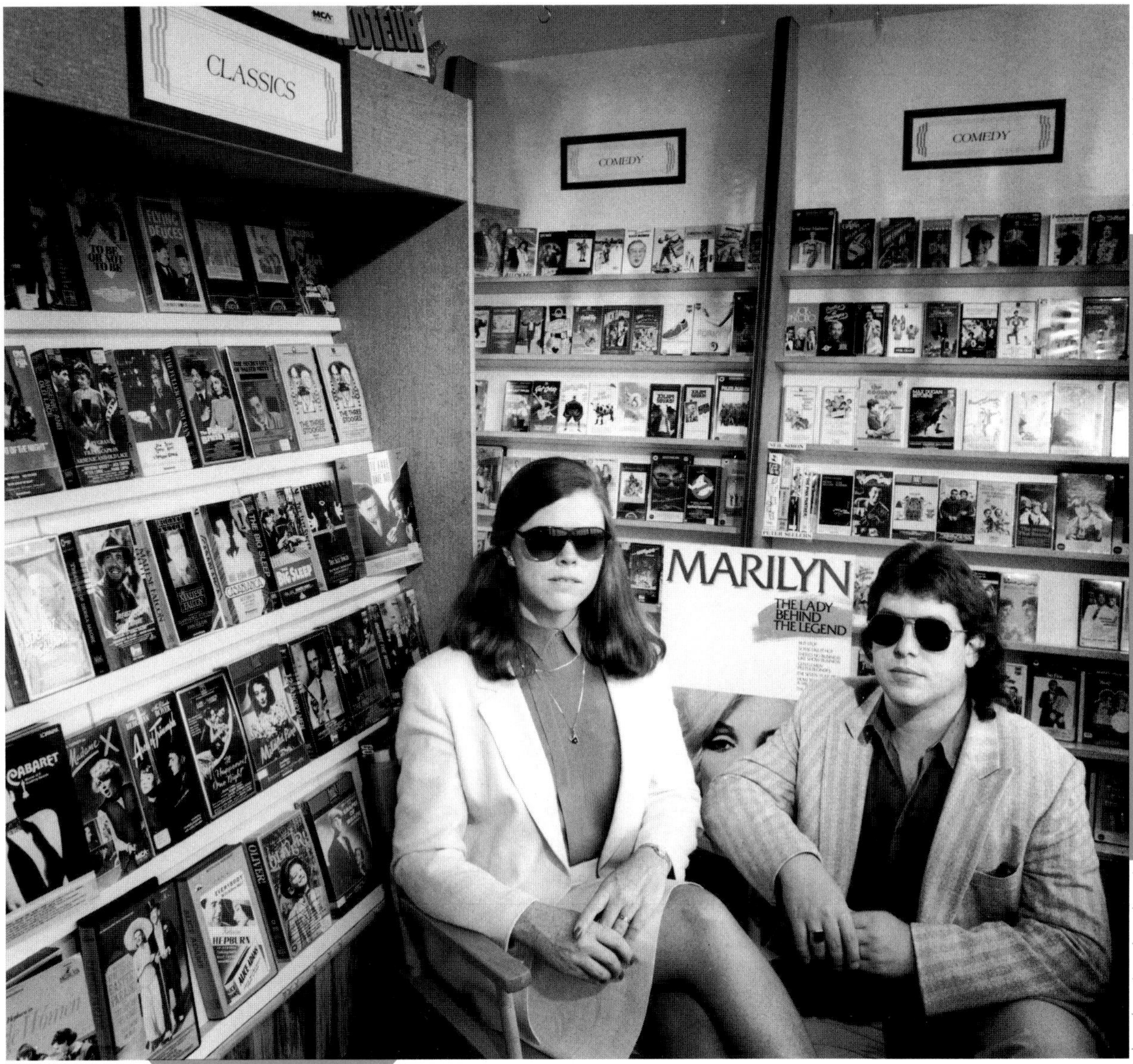

A real discovery for film lovers.

If most video stores leave you wanting, then Lasky's Video Library is for you. This inspiring collection of nearly 2,500 titles was amassed to quench a film buff's thirst for meaningful entertainment. In 1985, the store received an industry award as one of the country's top 12 video outlets; it also has been featured on "Best of Portland" lists compiled by both *Willamette Week* and *The Downtowner* magazines. The reason for this fame is as clear as a digital recording: Lasky's caters to customers whose tastes run to something more esoteric than "Rambo," and does it with finesse. A visit to Lasky's is like a tour of a motion picture vault. Andy and his wife, Katie, have collected a dazzling selection of VHS videotapes that includes foreign films, classics, ballet, opera, jazz, documentaries, cult films and many, many other hard-to-find items. The breadth of such a collection could be overwhelming, but the Laskys have categorized their inventory with libary-like logic. The comedy section, for example, has clearly marked subsections devoted to Woody Allen, Neil Simon, British comedy, Peter Sellers and so on, insuring that you'll spend more time watching your choices than looking for them. In addition to tape rentals, Lasky's has a tape sales section with an emphasis on special orders for affordable, collectible films; rental of VCRs and portable units with cameras; sales of equipment from every major line; and a video production unit for parties, reunions, weddings, sporting events, wills, bar mitzvahs and anything else that can be put on tape. Visa. MasterCard.

6345 SW Capitol Highway
Portland 97201
246-2157

Tuesday-Thursday
11am-9pm
Friday-Saturday
11am-10pm
Sunday — Summers
11am-9pm
Sunday — Winters
11am-7pm

Multnomah/ Hillsdale

F5

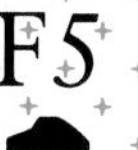

STILES FOR RELAXATION

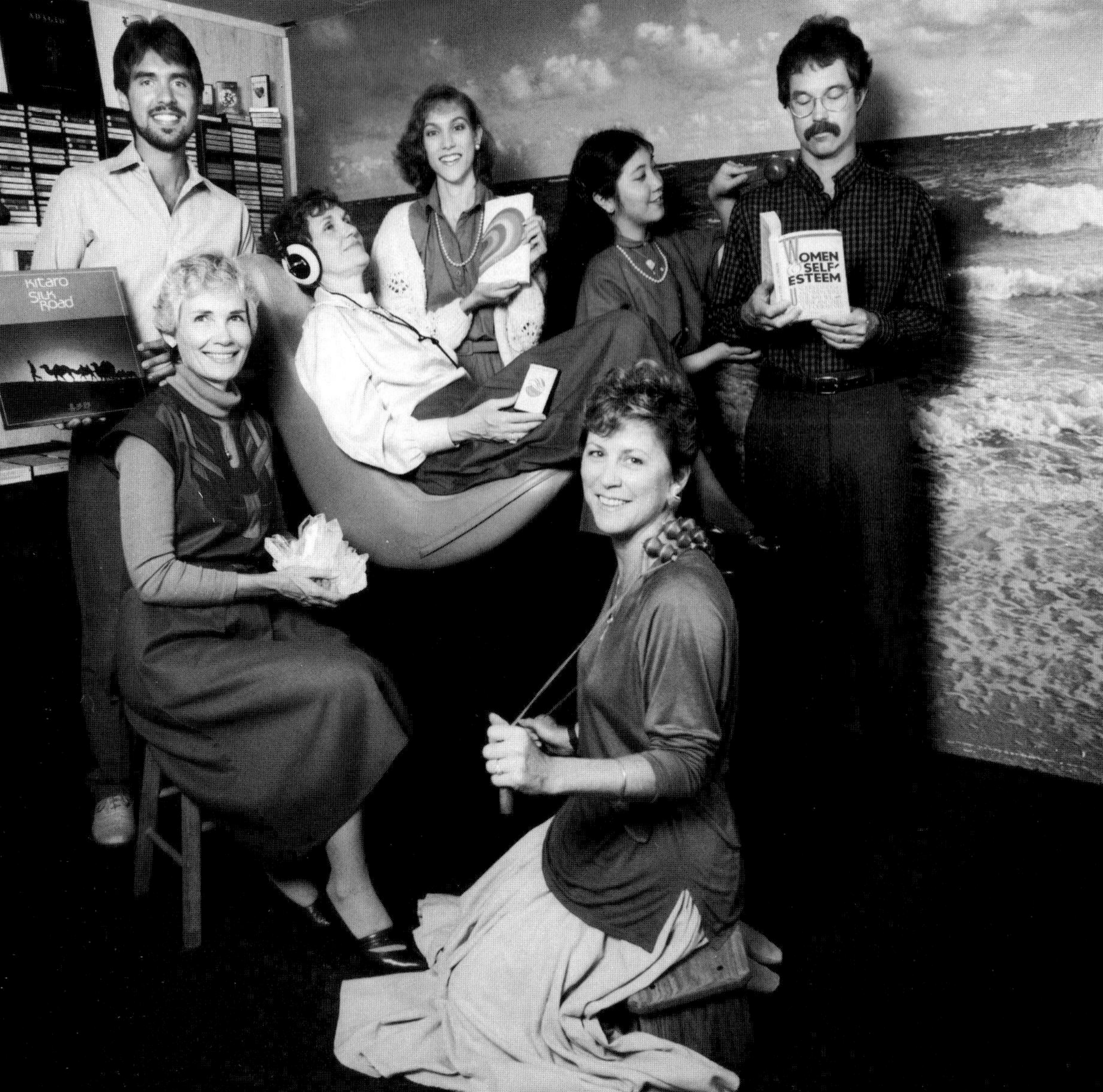

BOOKS AND MUSIC

Designed to increase your capacity for relaxation.

Northeast Portland

C7

During a recent visit, a Stiles for Relaxation customer spent more than an hour listening to relaxation tapes, sitting in the back-massage chair, browsing through books, looking at crystals and watching a video. Afterwards, she remarked, "This place is like a candy store for me!" Perhaps the same thought will cross your mind as you, like many customers, make a regular visit for a dose of the calming, peaceful atmosphere at Stiles for Relaxation. By turning their desire to help people into a source for specialized books, music, tapes, crystals, massage tools and furnishings, Marzenda and Oralee Stiles have created a most unique store. The shop is nothing less than an oasis for those who seek stress reduction, healing, self-improvement, emotional growth and spiritual awareness. Here, the customer is a guest. Concerned staff members devote their attention to your particular situation; the comfortable chairs allow you to relax while listening to any tapes before purchase. Through the use of guided imagery, self-hypnosis, affirmations, subliminal suggestions, music and nature sounds, a variety of recordings can help you make changes in health habits, weight, motivation, sports, sleep, self-esteem, study habits and stress level. There's also a bulletin board and business card resource file to keep you in touch with what's happening throughout Portland in the field of personal growth. Visit Stiles for Relaxation and learn how to improve the quality of your life. Visa. MasterCard.

4505 NE Tillamook Street
Portland 97213
281-6789

Monday-Wednesday 10am-6pm
Thursday 10am-8pm
Friday-Saturday 10am-6pm
Sunday noon-5pm

INCREDIBLES

One-of-a-kind shops and services so varied that no other category quite applies. Boutiques devoted to paper and cards, horse farms and Teddy bears, textiles, games and rentals for all occasions.

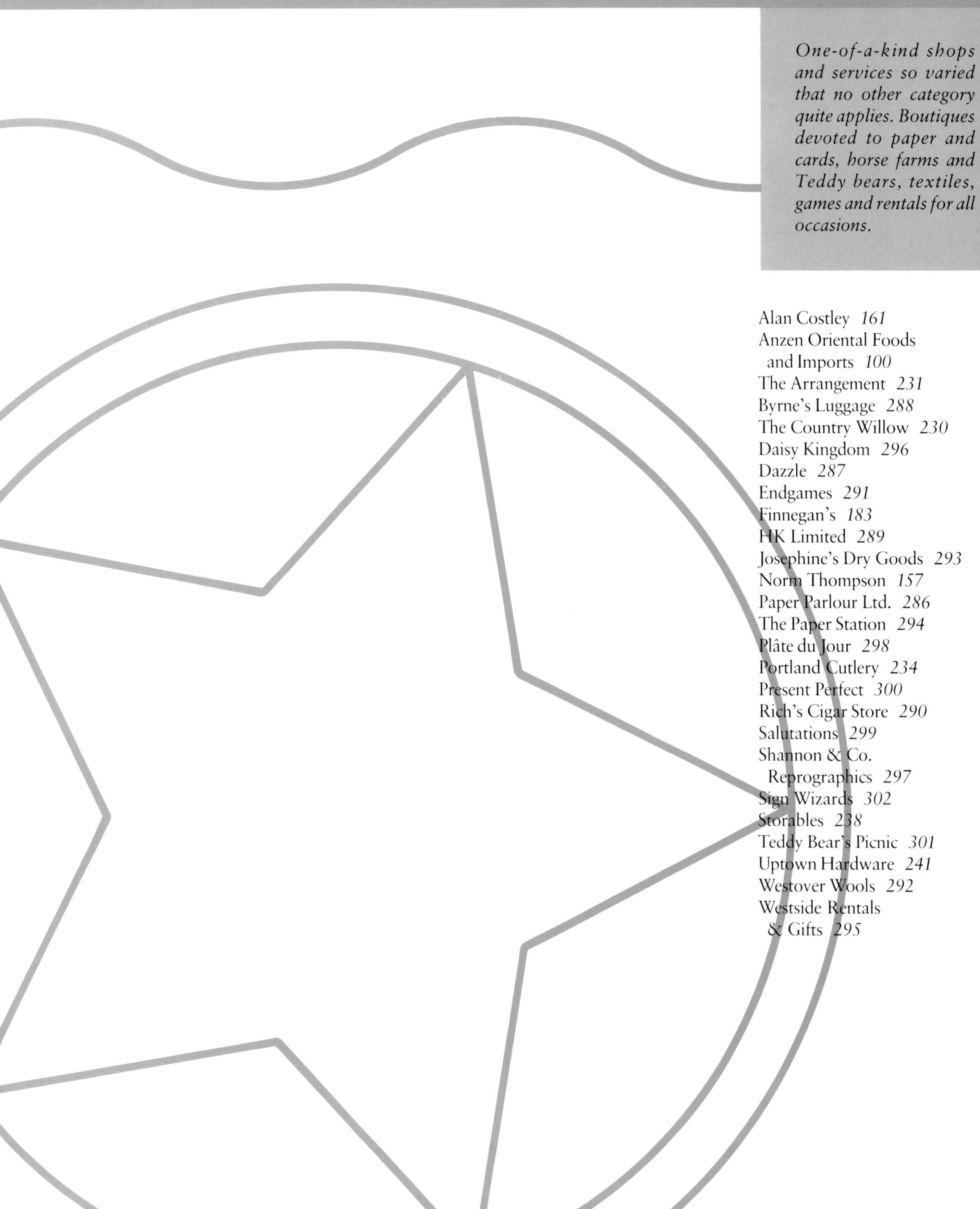

Alan Costley *161*
Anzen Oriental Foods and Imports *100*
The Arrangement *231*
Byrne's Luggage *288*
The Country Willow *230*
Daisy Kingdom *296*
Dazzle *287*
Endgames *291*
Finnegan's *183*
HK Limited *289*
Josephine's Dry Goods *293*
Norm Thompson *157*
Paper Parlour Ltd. *286*
The Paper Station *294*
Plâte du Jour *298*
Portland Cutlery *234*
Present Perfect *300*
Rich's Cigar Store *290*
Salutations *299*
Shannon & Co. Reprographics *297*
Sign Wizards *302*
Storables *238*
Teddy Bear's Picnic *301*
Uptown Hardware *241*
Westover Wools *292*
Westside Rentals & Gifts *295*

PAPER PARLOUR LTD.

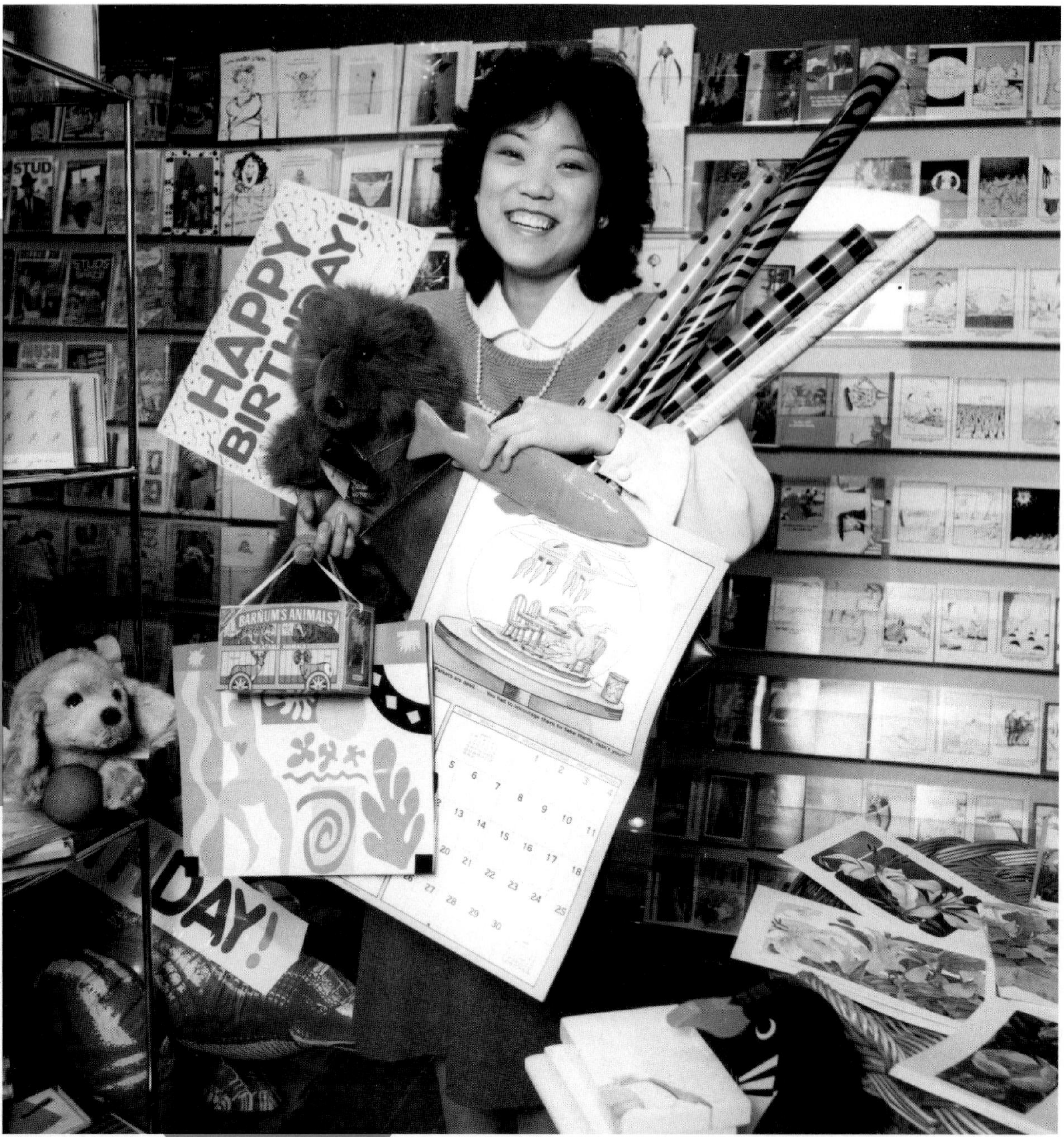

Celebrating the art of communication through writing.

Downtown

F23

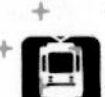

Paper Parlour Ltd. is a store that truly celebrates the art of communicating through writing. This fun, graphic, contemporary and sophisticated shop is filled to the brim with personalized stationery, birth announcements, wedding and party invitations, business cards, greeting cards and beautiful Italian and French social stationery. Stationery is available by the sheet, pound or box, and notepads for every reason abound. Paper Parlour Ltd. also offers fine pens from Italy, Germany and France as well as leather desk accessories and appointment diaries. With one of the largest selections of gift wrapping paraphenalia in the state, there is the opportunity of giving a package as attractive as the gift enclosed. The party goods department has napkins, plates, cups, balloons, banners, confetti, streamers and everything else needed for an instant celebration. Plus, there's a large selection of napkins that can be imprinted in short order — that's just two days! So stop by the Paper Parlour Ltd. — it's the write thing to do. Visa. MasterCard.

The Galleria
921 SW Morrison Street
Portland 97205
221-0700

Monday-Friday
10am-9pm
Saturday 10am-6pm
Sunday noon-5pm

DAZZLE

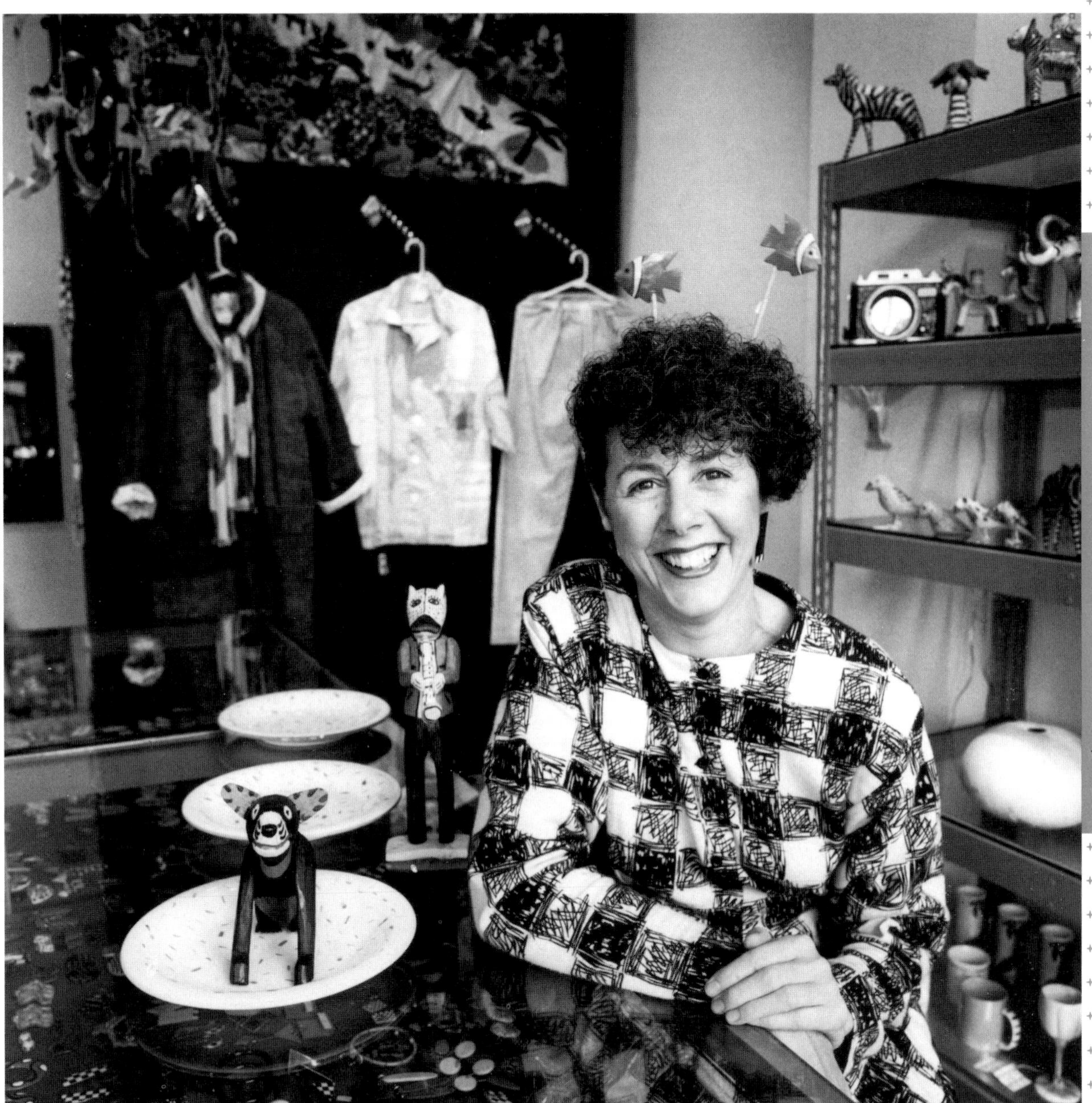

INCREDIBLES

Find the perfect gift in five seconds or less!

Hi, Barbie, Nancy here. I know you're brunching with Brad, but this is like important you know? I'm talking shopping! So I'm at Dazzle — you know, Dazzle — it's the same people who do the Sunbow Gallery. Like I heard I could find the perfect gift in five seconds or less here. Well, it's true — I'm dazzled! So I walk in and first I spot these great mobiles. Perfect, I go, but should I get the hearts or the dinosaurs? Next I check out the vases — should I get traditional crystal or go oriental with the Thai papier mâché bowls? I must be in a decorating mode because I fall all over this fabulous inflatable leopard-skin chair. Perfect again, I go, but how about a Party Animal? A Party Animal, Barbie — it's a blow-up dog, right? No fuss, no muss! So I'm patting the dog and I spot the earrings! Barbie, I'm talking earrings for days — Fernellas Jools, Joe Cool, Eve Kaplan! What? You're coming down as soon as your nails dry? What about Brad? Yeah, right, priorities — we'll do some serious trying on — the clothes are incredible. And Barbie, bring the Volvo wagon — we're going to need it! Sure, we can do lunch after — but it's your turn to do the check, dear! Visa. MasterCard. American Express.

709 Northwest 23rd & "Papa Haydn"
Portland 97210
224-1294

Monday-Friday
11am-6pm
Saturday 10am-6pm
Sunday 11am-4pm

Sunbow Gallery
206 SW Stark Street
Portland 97204
221-0258

Zany Gray
115 Stewart
Seattle 98101
(206) 448-8508

Northwest Portland
H17

Yamhill Historic District
F25

BYRNE'S LUGGAGE TRAVELWARE AND GIFTS

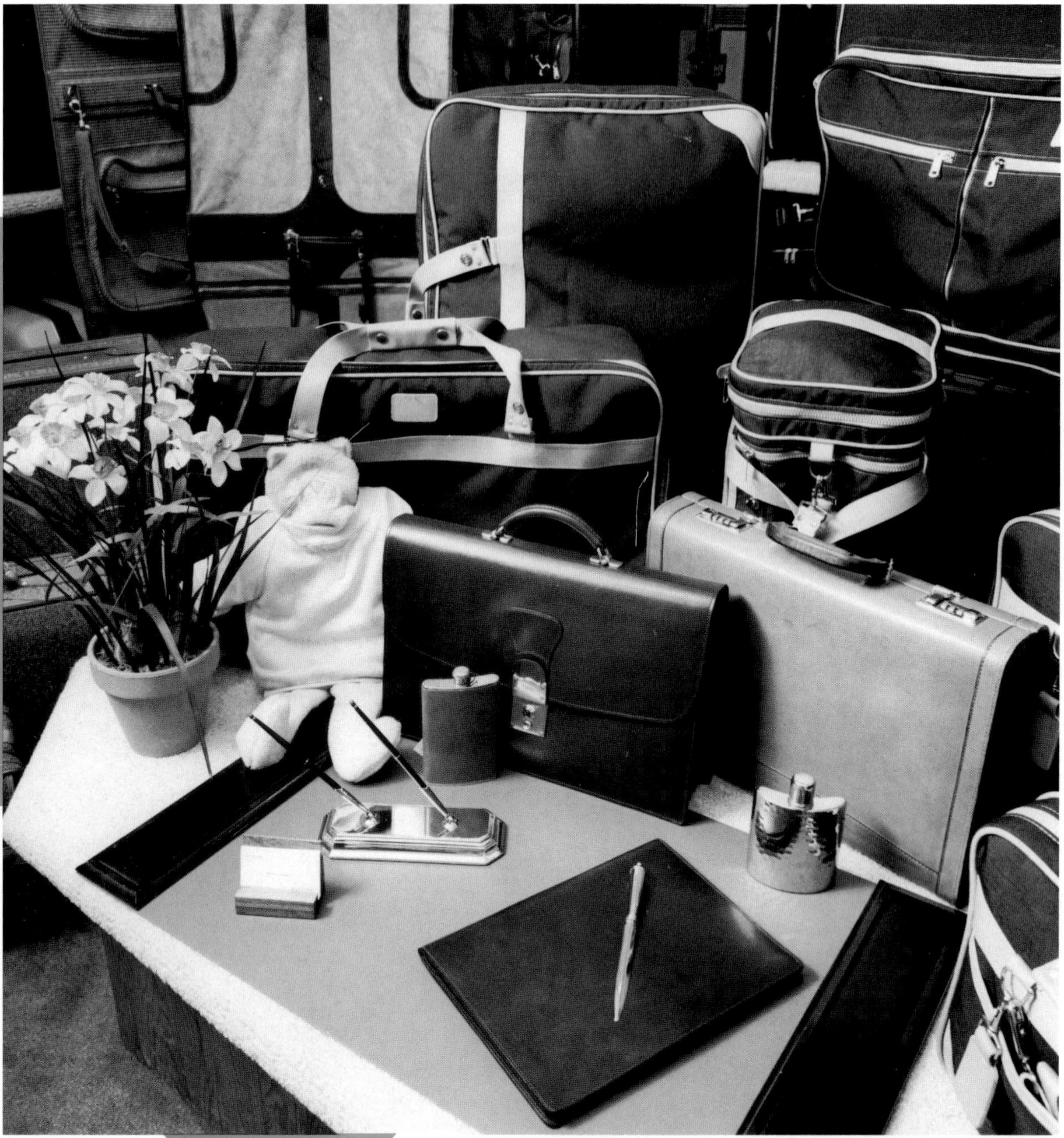

Go in style with luggage, travelware and gifts.

Downtown

F23

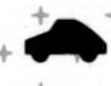

Blue highways. The Orient Express. Over the Pole. Across the Channel. Magic paths to faraway places — time to travel. Time for Byrne's Luggage to send you on the way in style. You'll find all necessities of travel under one roof at Byrne's Luggage, even if you're only traveling across town — fine quality attachés, briefcases, portfolios, travelware and small leather goods. Or say "bon voyage" to a friend with a unique executive or travel gift. Byrne's has a wide range of luggage brands to suit every purpose and mode of travel, business or pleasure. Brands include Fulton, Hartmann, Andiamo, Tumi, Renwick, Schlesinger and many others. Byrne's staff know that each traveler has special needs and will help tailor luggage selections to your travel plans. The wide variety of high quality pieces will ease the pain of parting with your old backpack and duffle bag. After a visit to Byrne's, you'll realize your luggage doesn't have to look like it's been around the world in the back of a pickup. Not anymore. Visa. MasterCard. American Express. Diners Club. Carte Blanche. Discover.

940 SW Morrison Street
Portland 97205
241-0969

Monday-Saturday
10am-6pm

HK LIMITED

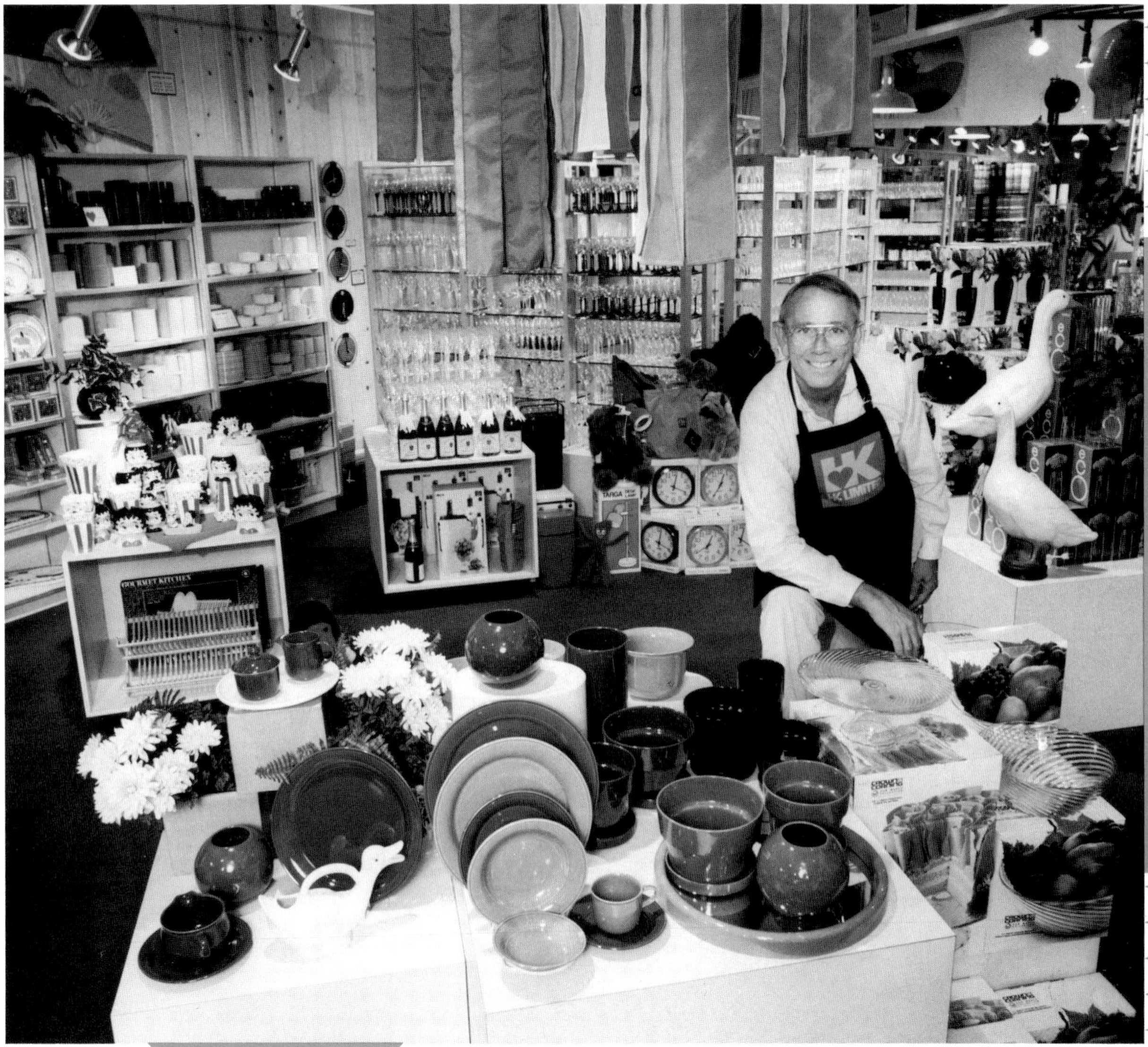

Come in with nothing in mind and leave with something you love.

Scattered about the Portland area are a collection of stores with inventories that are no less than mind-boggling. They are HK Limited, purveyors of thousands of items guaranteed to brighten your world. There's the bold and bizarre, charming and colorful, delicate and delightful, for everyone from age five to ninety-five. This is a home accessories and gift shop unmatched in Portland. The owners endeavor to select and introduce the newest in ideas and trends from domestic and international markets. They present merchandise in a contemporary setting, incorporating fantastic color and design into their displays. Upon entering HK Limited one is immediately attracted to the warm atmosphere and relaxed tone set by the sales staff, who allow you to browse and gather ideas at your leisure. You will find everything — except the food — for your table top, whether you dine in a castle or in a tent. Dinnerware — Health, Otagiri, Trend Pacific and others — flatware, glassware, mats and napkins are available. How about casual chairs and tables, lamps, baskets, clocks, cookware, candles, pillows, stoneware and ceramics? Or wall decor that runs the gamut from inexpensive paper prints to spectacular textiles. At no other establishment could HK's motto be more appropriate: "The store you come into with nothing in mind and leave with something you love." Visa. MasterCard.

Washington Square
Portland 97223
620-1217

Lloyd Center
Portland 97232
287-6911

Lancaster Mall
831 Lancaster Drive NE
Salem 97301
378-7040

Clackamas Town Center
Portland 97266
652-2273

Jantzen Beach Center
Portland 97217
289-2313

All locations
Monday-Friday
10am-9pm
Saturday 10am-6pm
Sunday noon-5pm

Progress-Washington Square

G3

Northeast Portland

D6

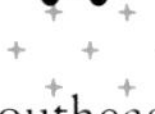

Southeast Portland

H9

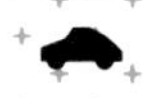

North Portland

A5

RICH'S CIGAR STORE

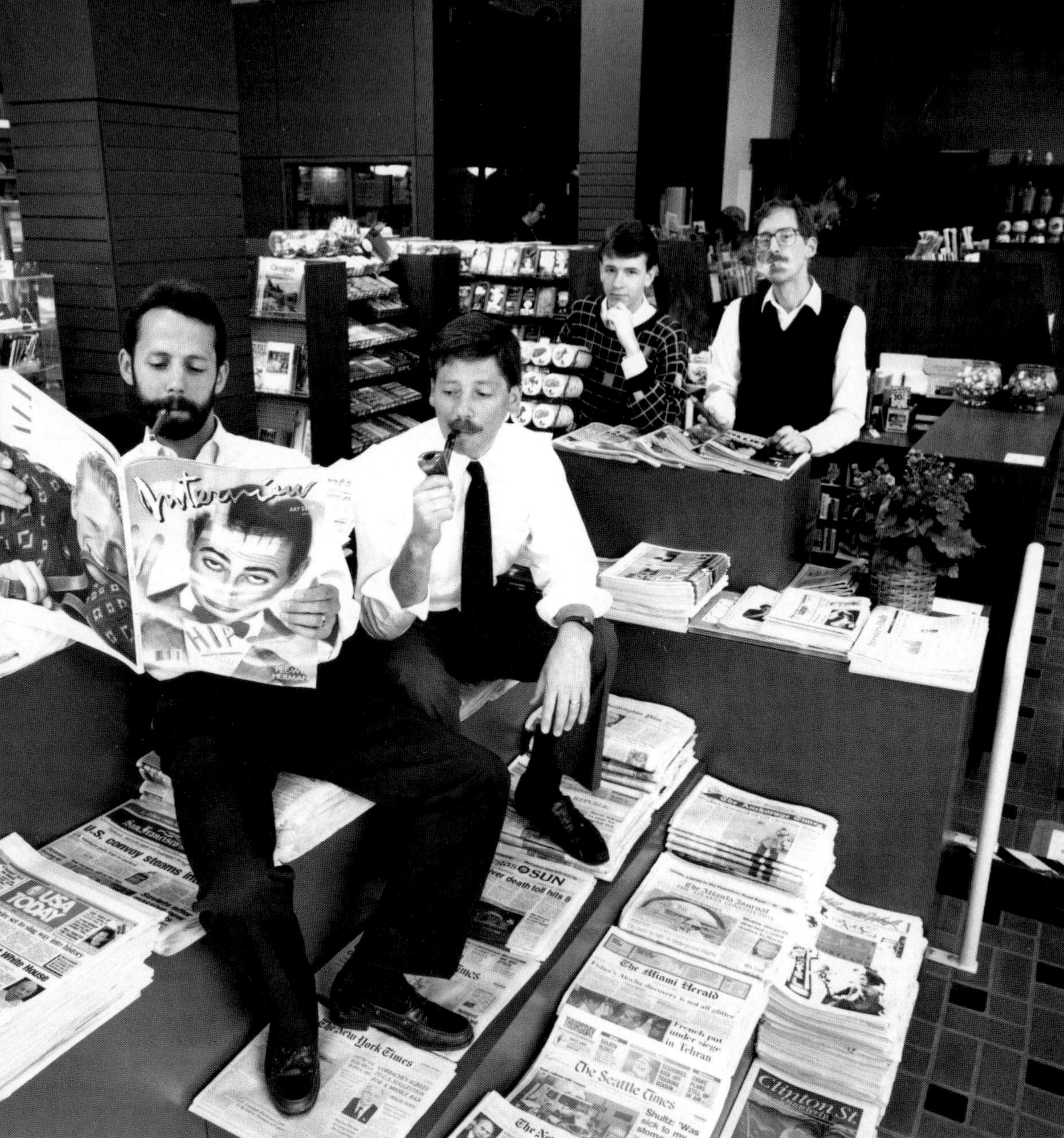

For the finest selection of tobacco and magazines.

Downtown
F23

A good five-cent cigar is a thing of the distant past, and so for the most part, are the fine little corner stores which sold them. One place in Portland that is still around, improving with age, is Rich's Cigar Store. It's been a movable city landmark since it was founded by Si S. Rich 92 years ago. Along the west wall of this always busy shop is a spread of smoking supplies — pipes in every price range, imported cigarettes, snuff, tobaccos and, of course, thousands of the world's finest hand-rolled cigars, the largest selection of cigars on the West Coast. Even for Portland's non-smokers, Rich's is a special place: it has an unbeatable stock of national and world-wide newspapers and magazines. You'll find every specialty journal you've ever heard of and some you likely haven't, and the Northwest's leading array of the latest European fashion magazines. Rich's takes great pride in its personal service and the staff work hard to meet all of your special needs and orders. In addition to excellent in- store service, Rich's offers mail order service for your convenience. Write or call for free catalogue. Visa. MasterCard.

801 SW Alder Street
Portland 97205
228-1700

Monday-Friday
7am-7pm
Saturday 8am-6pm
Sunday noon-5pm

ENDGAMES

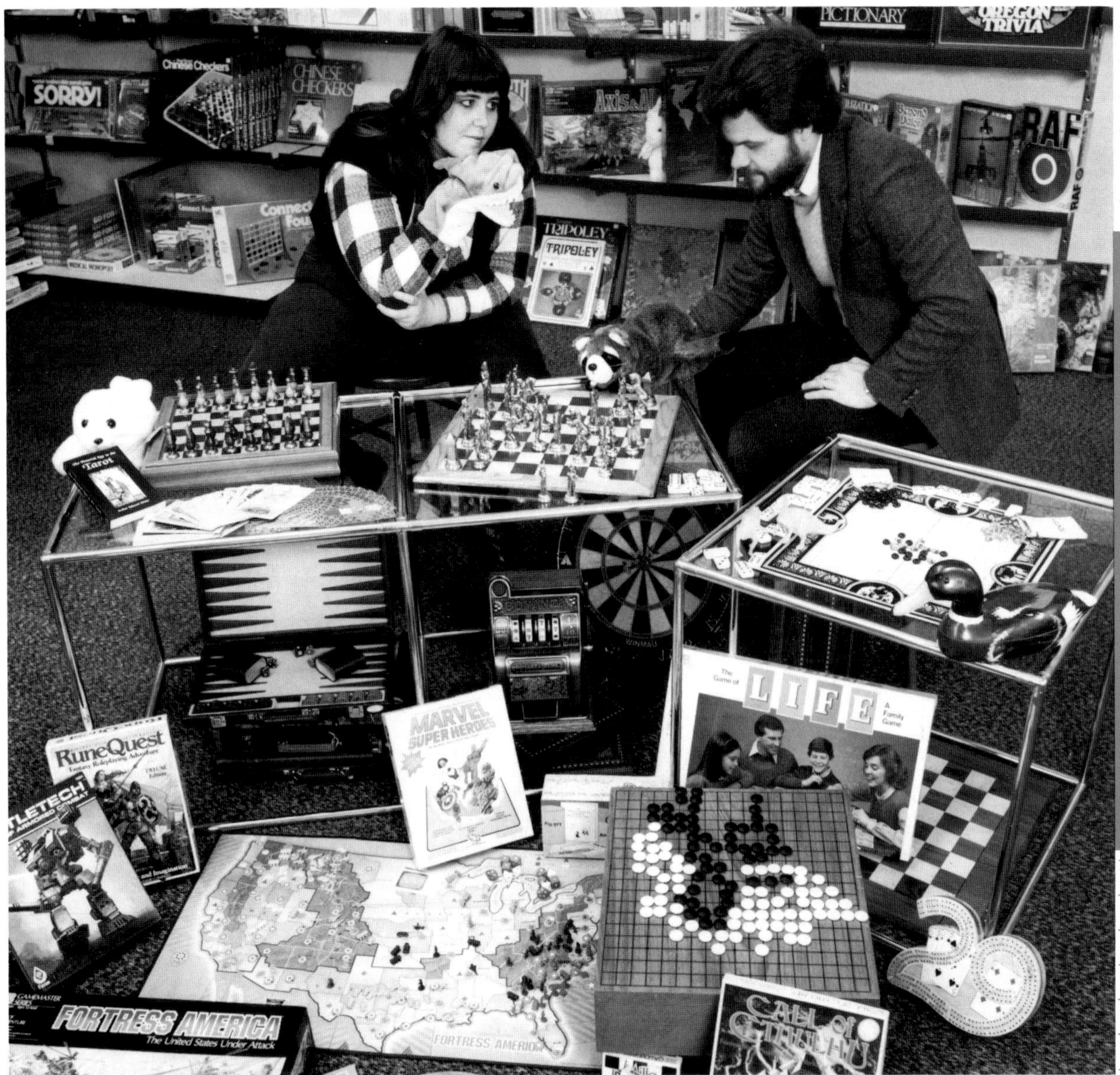

Deluxe games and puzzles.

Downtown
G24

Southeast Portland
H9

In chess, the endgame is the series of final moves. But when it comes to shopping for all manner of games and puzzles, a visit to Endgames should be the first move. Endgames is like winning at Scrabble, owning Boardwalk and Park Place and collecting the last pie wedge in Trivial Pursuit — a minor triumph at the very least. The stores display a comprehensive selection of board and table games, mostly for teenagers and adults; jigsaw puzzles and playing cards are featured in a wider selection than most outlets. Endgames got its start nearly a decade ago because owners Linda and Dennis Kilgore were frustrated by the lack of game variety in stores. They opened their first store in downtown Eugene and quickly did the same in Portland; now there are two in Portland. Among board games, you'll find all the old favorites like Monopoly and Clue, plus Pictionary, Scruples and all the other hot new entries. Traditional games are stocked in a wide variety of qualities and prices: cribbage boards, for example, range from \$2.50 to \$46.95. Endgames' employees are always willing to explain games to customers, and special orders, telephone and mail orders, shipping and gift-wrapping are all part of the package. Bonus question: who authored the play of the same name as the stores? Samuel Beckett. (Linda was a college English lit teacher.) Visa. MasterCard. American Express. Discover.

200 SW Salmon Street
Portland 97204
224-6917

Monday-Friday
10am-5:30pm
Saturday 10am-5pm

Clackamas Town Center
12092 Clackamas
Town Center
Portland 97266
652-1434

Monday-Friday
10am-9pm
Saturday 10am-6pm
Sunday 11am-6pm

WESTOVER WOOLS

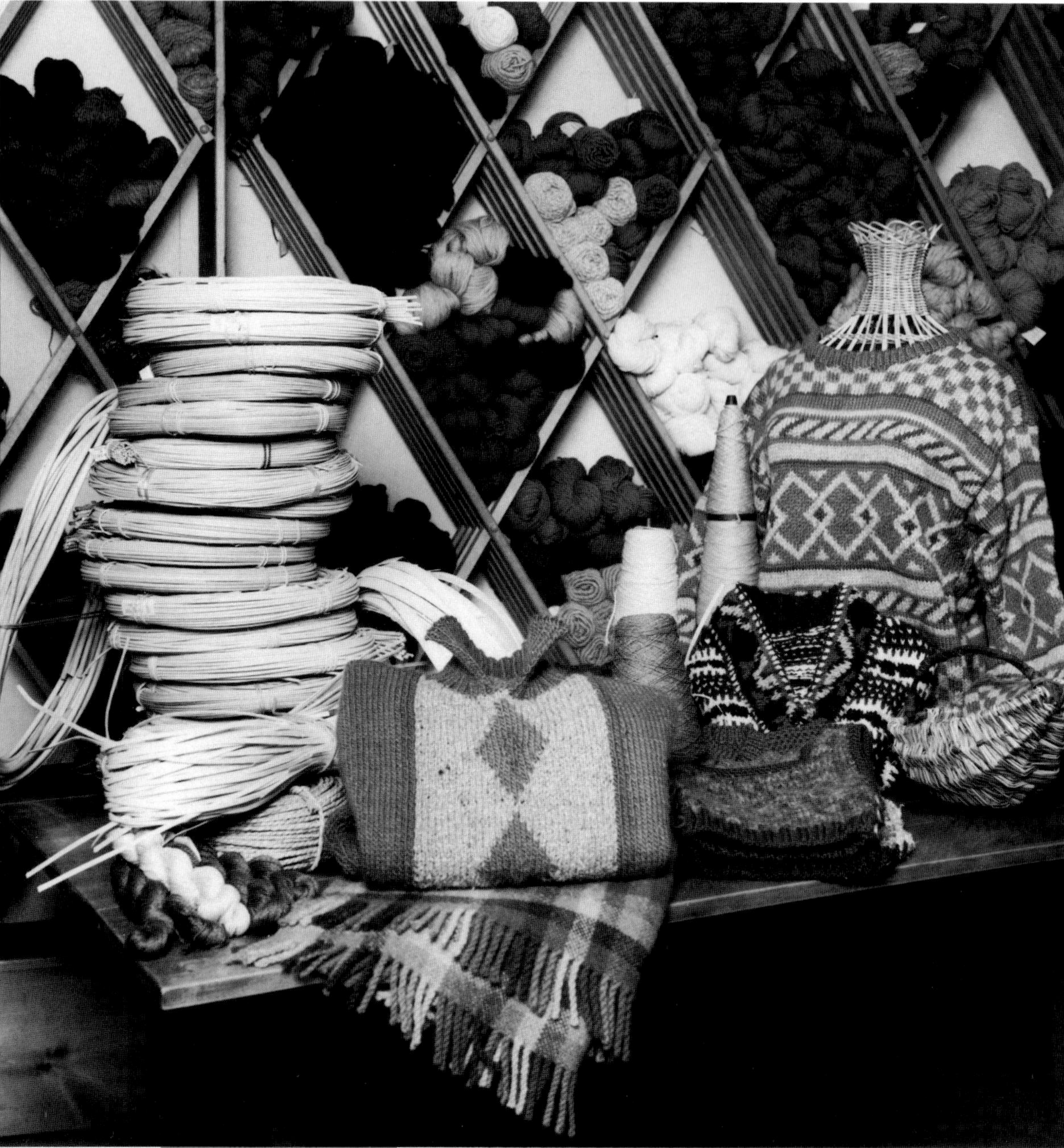

Weave some wool into your wardrobe.

Northwest Portland
F17

Why is it that just the thought of sitting inside on a cold, rainy day knitting a sweater gives us such a warm feeling? Maybe it's the feel of working with texturally pleasing yarns or the image of the completed project. Whether you're knitting a sweater or weaving a rug, Westover Wools has the best selection of textile supplies in the city. You can choose from a wide variety of natural fibers, including wools, silks, linens, alpacas and cotton as well as reed, raffias and sea grasses for your ventures into basketry. To put it all together you can bring your pattern or project to the shop, spread it out on a table, and discuss the details with any member of the knowledgeable staff. If you would rather not make it yourself, Westover has a handsome selection of handmade goods; and if you can't find what you're looking for they will gladly refer you to local artists. During school vacations and summer, childrens' classes offer an outlet for creativity through knitting, weaving, basketry, fabric painting and fabric dyeing. Similar classes are offered year-round for adults. In every case, expert help and friendliness are guaranteed. Visa. MasterCard.

2390 NW Thurman Street
Portland 97210
227-0134

Monday-Friday 10am-5:30pm
Saturday 10am-5pm
Classes available

JOSEPHINE'S DRY GOODS

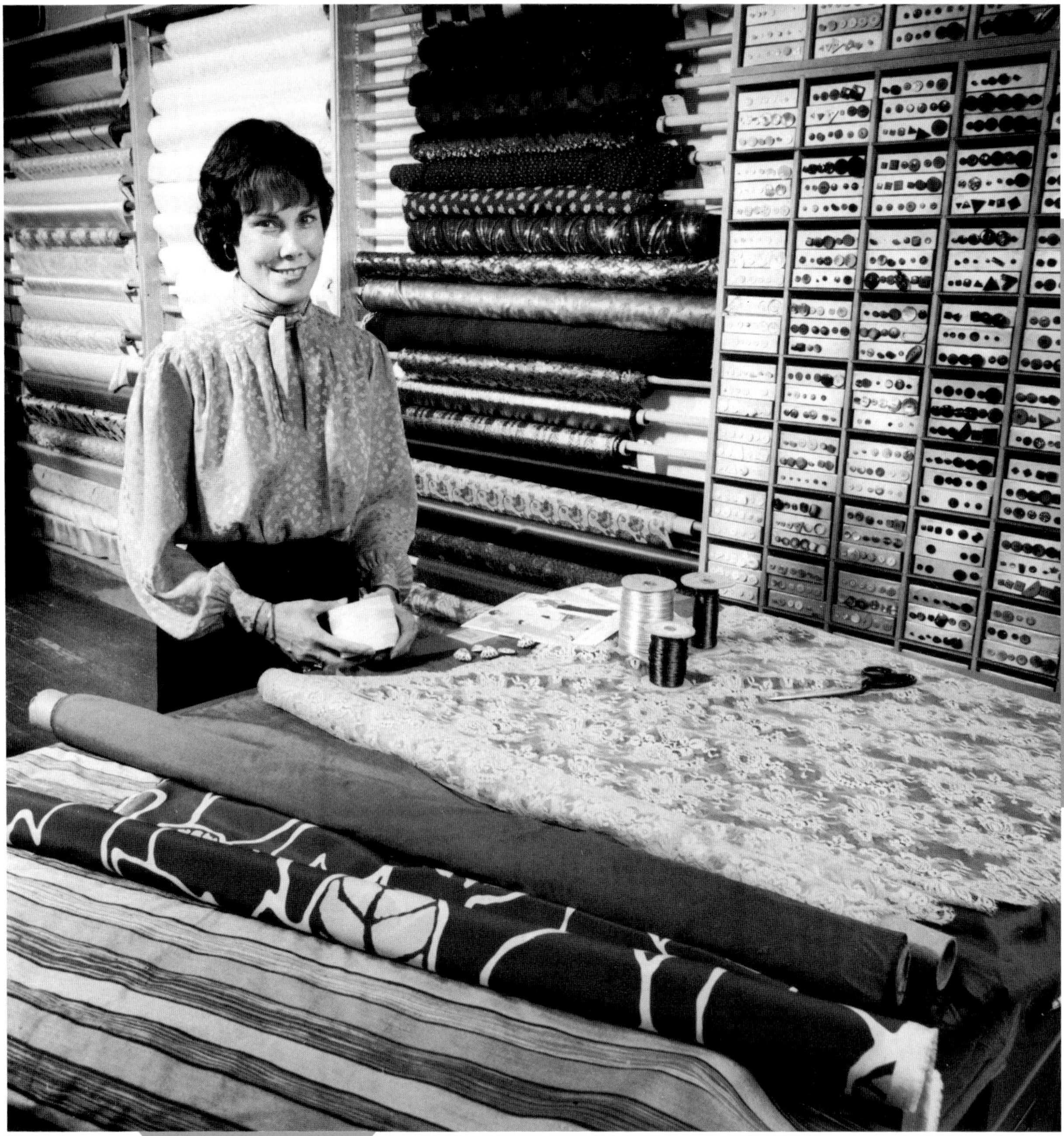

Beautiful fabrics for beautiful clothing.

Josephine's Dry Goods is a fabric lover's paradise, a world of natural fibers, luscious colors, sensuous textures. Here is a place to find sophisticated silks, cottons, woolens and linens. You'll recognize the names that mean prestige and quality worldwide: Liberty of London cotton and wool challis, Harris wool tweed, Moygashel linen and Viyella. Exquisite silk prints from Italy and France line the walls; fine Swiss and unusual Guatemalan cottons are a specialty. Owners Judith Head and Bonnie Harris opened Josephine's ten years ago in the Galleria in the heart of downtown Portland. Their idea was to specialize in natural fiber fabrics — a notion unheard of at that time. Every fabric is personally chosen. The sales people are ready to help with your sewing needs; they will coordinate fabrics for a Folkwear Ethnic pattern or choose the perfect button from Josephine's unique collection. If you need a seamstress, ask for suggestions. By popular demand Josephine's offers beginning sewing classes for teens during summer vacation. Josephine's Dry Goods is one of Portland's premier shops — a place to fulfill fantasies, to find beautiful fabrics for beautiful clothes. Visa. MasterCard.

The Galleria
921 SW Morrison Street
Portland 97205
224-4202

Monday-Friday
10am-9pm
Saturday 10am-6pm
Sunday noon-5pm

Downtown
F23

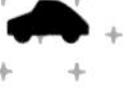

THE PAPER STATION

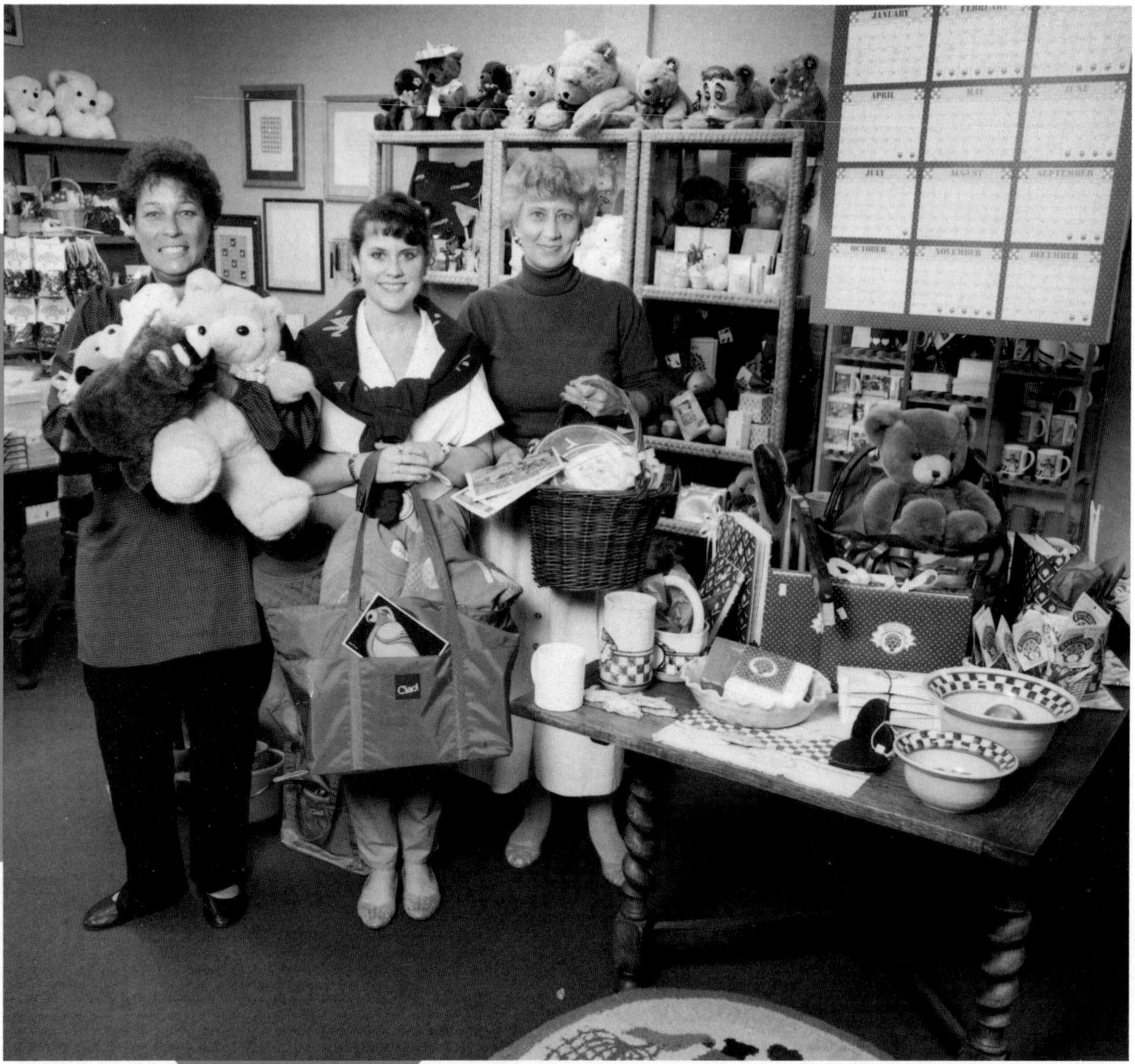

An uplifting gift and stationery store.

Lake Oswego/
Lake Grove

J7

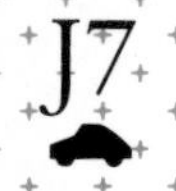

Progress-
Washington
Square

G3

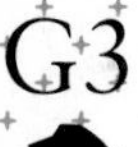

On the dreariest Portland day a visit to The Paper Station will lift your spirits. This cheerful gift and stationery shop is the perfect place to plan a party and to choose unique party goods, gifts and favors. Why not have messages written on helium-filled balloons of latex or mylar? There's no extra cost. Owners Bev and Gary Locker look all over the world to find gifts to please the child in all of us. They have filled this store with captivating treasures like stuffed animals, S.I. Ford sweatshirts, locally-made wreaths, beautifully designed stationery and photo albums, Crabtree and Evelyn soaps, as well as a full line of paper products. The Paper Station also offers a selection of Scarborough products for the home and baby gifts from Lucy Riggs and Beatrix Potter. Create a personalized gift by filling a straw or wire basket with your selections. The employees of The Paper Station will nestle your choices in tissue paper and, at no charge, giftwrap them with unique gift bags and boxes, ribbons and stickers. Select an up-beat message to accompany your gift from their carefully chosen cards. You'll find this family-oriented store has something to delight the heart of everyone, young or old. So come in out of the rain and enjoy. Visa. MasterCard. American Express.

Robinwood Center
19171 Willamette Drive
West Linn 97068
635-8486

Monday-Friday
10am-7pm
Saturday 10am-6pm
Sunday noon-5pm

Washington Square
9538 SW Washington
Square Road
Portland 97223
620-8426

Monday-Friday
10am-9pm
Saturday 10am-6pm
Sunday 11am-6pm

Sunriver Village Mall
Sunriver 97707
593-1982

Daily

WESTSIDE RENTALS & GIFTS

INCREDIBLES

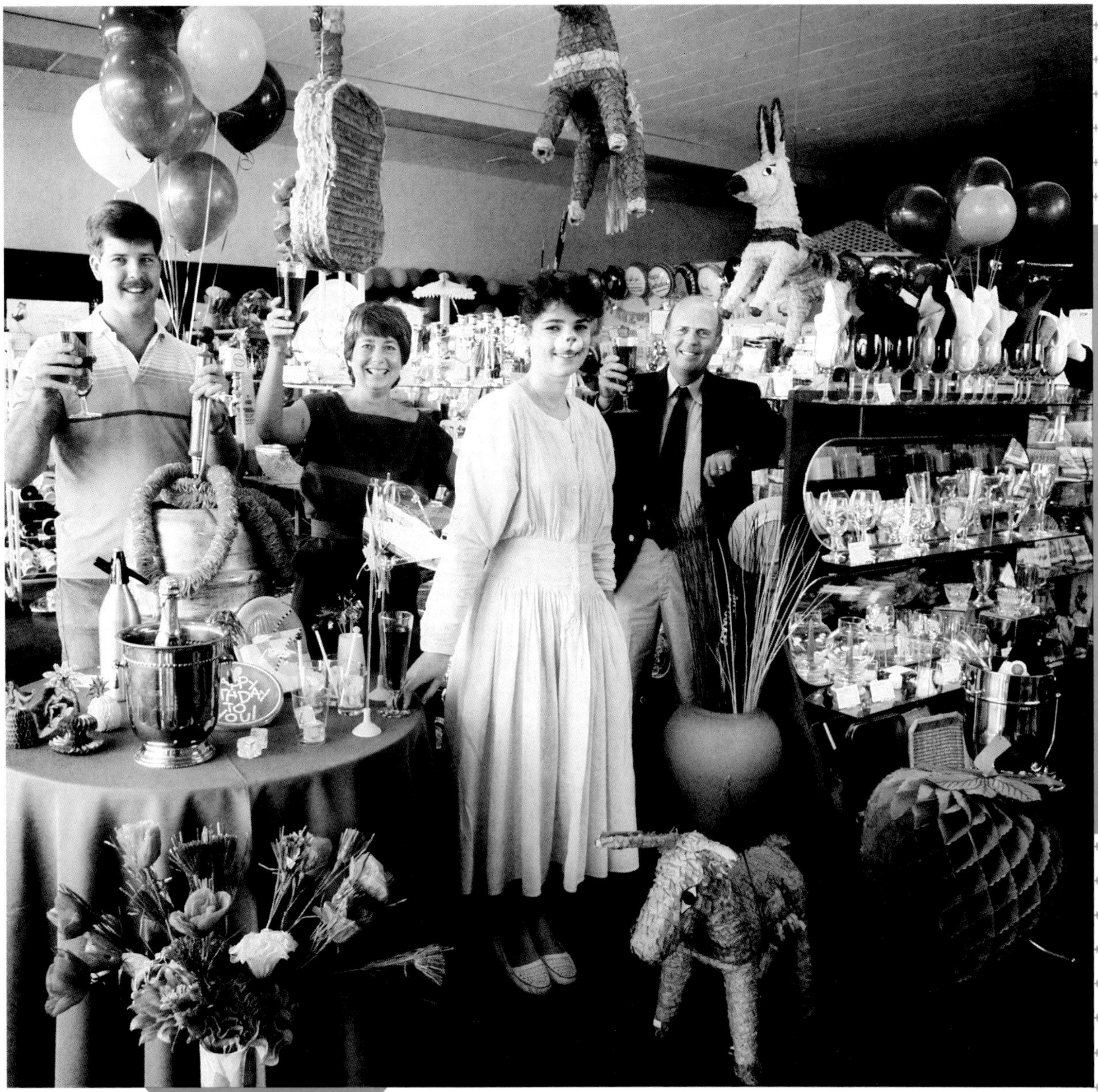

Catering to party animals.

When caterers such as Eat Your Heart Out, John's Meat Market, Jakes's, Food in Bloom and Northwest Sushi need party equipment, they turn to Westside Rentals & Gifts in Raleigh Hills. And so can you, whether it's for a soiree for a few friends or a shoot-the- budget wedding reception for five hundred. Westside owners Duane and Stephanie Selser are known for their attention to customer needs, a crucial ingredient in the orchestration of such major local undertakings as the OMSI auction, the PGA Golf Challenge and various Performing Arts Center events. That same attention awaits every customer who selects Westside's rental items, delivered day and night, weekdays and weekends. You'll find everything to make your affair a bright spot on anyone's social calendar: party rental items that include canopies, linen, china and silver; tables, chairs, easels and coat racks (of special interest to the corporate client); and candelabra, stemware and gazebos for weddings. The selection of smaller supplies is just as extensive: disposable items such as champagne glasses, napkins, plates and cups; paper streamers, bells and displays for decoration; and costumes and animal noses for an unforgettable Halloween blowout. The store is well appointed, without the warehouse appearance of some outlets, and the specialization in party and entertainment equipment means you won't have to step over lawnmowers and greasy automotive tools when you're trying to select goods for a dress-up lawn party. Visa. MasterCard.

Raleigh Hills
7308 SW Beaverton Hillsdale Highway
Portland 97225
297-8131

Monday-Saturday
9am-5:30pm

Southwest Portland

F3

DAISY KINGDOM

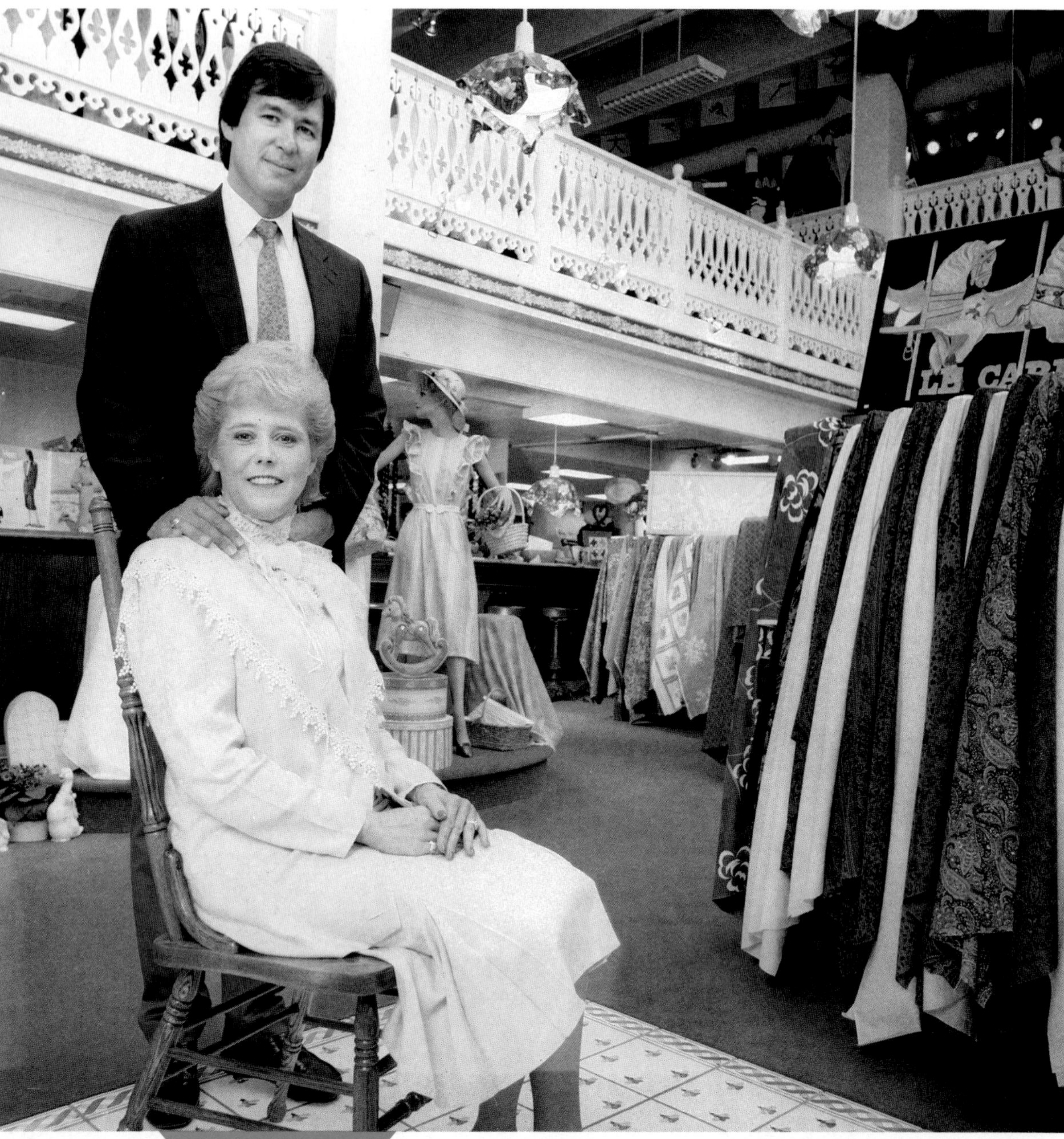

INCREDIBLES

Unique fabrics, glasses, gifts, craft supplies.

Northwest Portland
D24

It's easy to see why some people persist in thinking of Daisy Kingdom as a fabric showcase. The vivid patterns and fabrics, displayed against a delightful backdrop of nostalgia and antiques, take up an entire three-story building. In its way it's a tribute to what one woman with one-hundred-twenty-seven dollars worth of starting inventory and a talent for retailing fabrics can do. Sixteen years after Patricia Reed decided to unleash her own creative energies and "have fun," Daisy Kingdom has grown, like Topsy, in colorful new directions. Stenciling supplies, trims, notions, buttons, patterns, dress goods, calico, home decoration, sportswear and bridal fabrics can only suggest the overwhelming inventory. And Daisy Kingdom's nationally marketed line of skiwear patterns suggests something of the imaginative range of ideas to be found within. Interestingly, the fact that sewing skiwear was a little daunting to customers inspired an adult education program now offering over 45 different craft and specialty classes to several thousand customers a year. Such diversity and enthusiasm requires support, of course. The cheerful staff of talented specialists includes a graphic artist and designer, a pattern designer and technical writer, a color artist, and of course, teachers. Daisy Kingdom is a world of unique fabrics, including their own original design for nurseries and kitchen, related crafts, and education — a university of the sewing machine. Visa. MasterCard.

134 NW 8th Avenue
Portland 97209
222-9033

Monday-Saturday
10am-6pm
Sunday 1pm-5pm

SHANNON & CO. REPROGRAPHICS

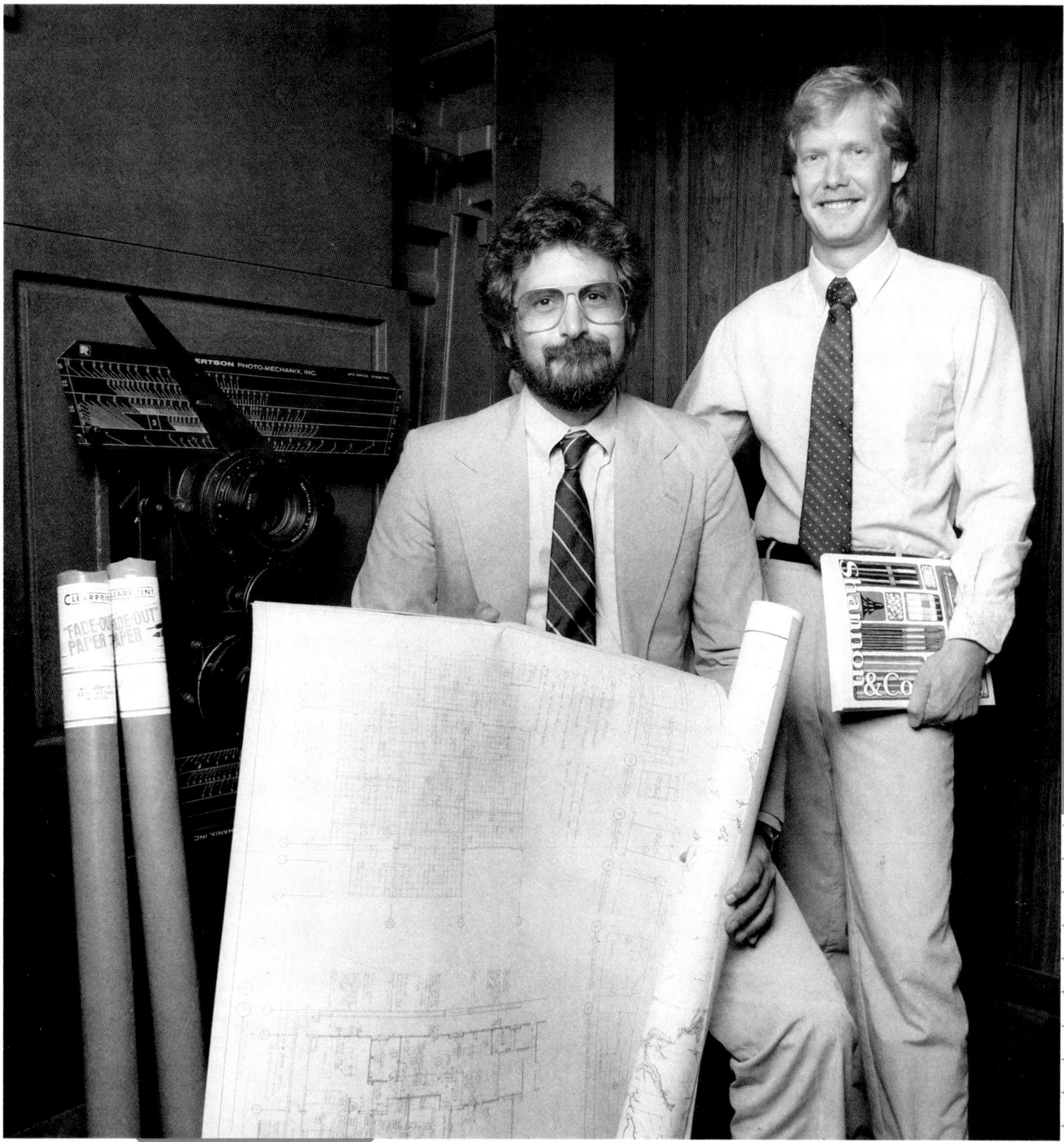

Reproduction — blueprints, PMT's, color and super stats, large Xerox.

Shannon & Co. offers Portland one of its largest Xerox copiers, capable of handling work 36 inches wide by length. People who need high-quality reproduction work on short notice have come to rely on the firm's three large process cameras for photographic enlargements up to 3 1/2 by 6 1/2 feet. There's also one-day service on photo work, a convenient location, while- you-wait small copying and free downtown pickup and delivery, with a five dollar minimum purchase. President Jeff Prideaux and his staff can produce blueprints up to 42 inches wide by any length, PMTs, negatives, Mylars, full-color stats, superstats to 42 by 80 inches, and film positives to 42 by 80 inches for silk screen masters. In short, the firm truly is a full-service shop for your reproduction needs. Shannon also does plastic lamination up to 24 inches wide by any length, and has recently begun carrying architectural, engineering and art supplies. Shannon & Co. Reprographics has served architects, engineers, graphic artists and the general public for more than 50 years — longer than any other Portland firm in the field. Its experience pays dividends to the customer. New or old, if your original can be photographed, drawn or designed, chances are Shannon & Co. can reproduce it. Visa. MasterCard.

1226 SW 12th Avenue
Portland 97205
222-1761

Monday-Friday
8:30am-5:30pm

Downtown
G22

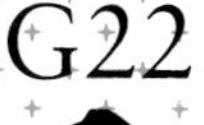

PLÂTE DU JOUR

Not just another pretty plate but... gleaming crystal and shining silver.

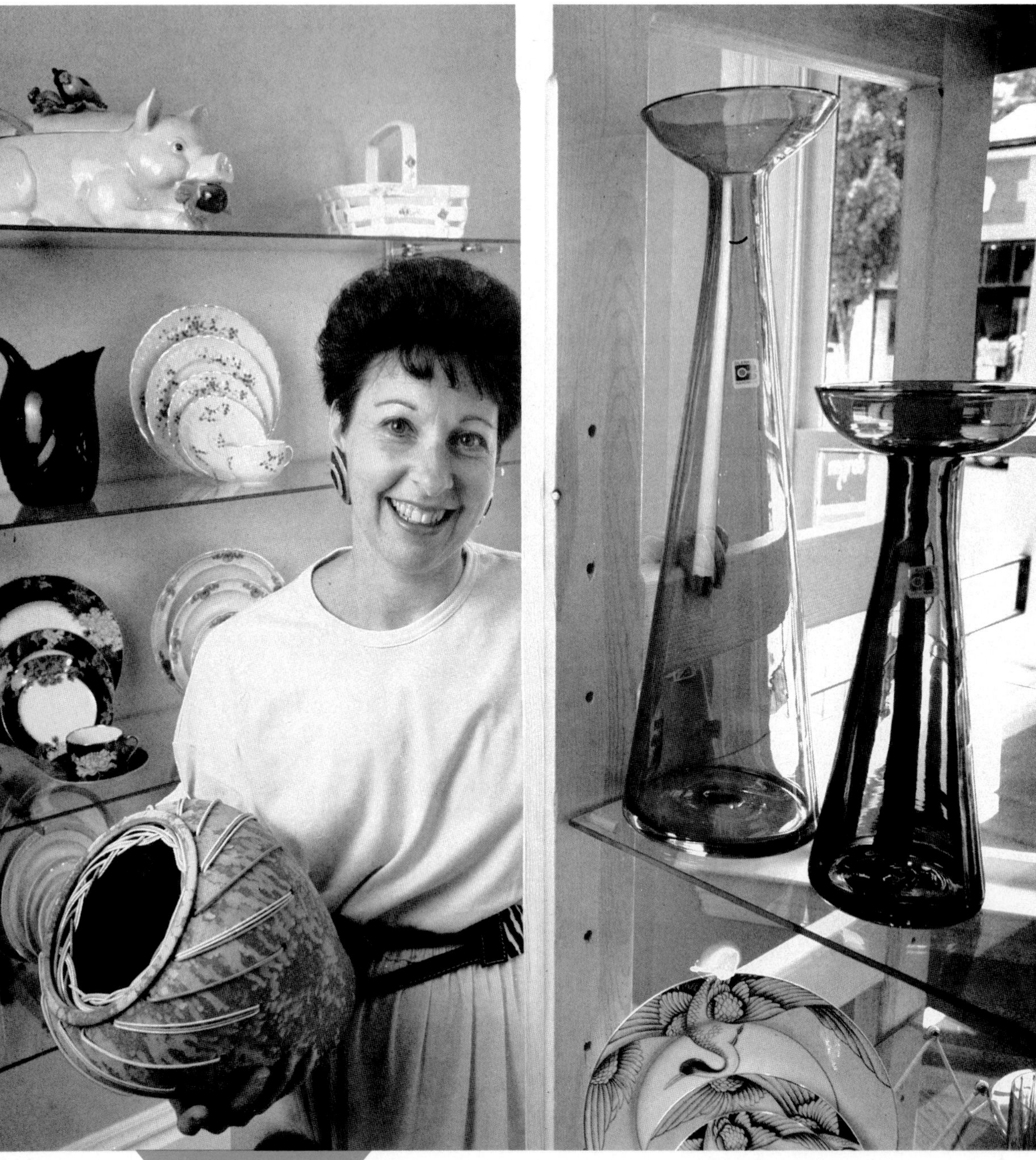

Northwest Portland

H17

Imagine a room decorated in the palest rose and gray with a delicate cream trim. Imagine this room filled with delightfully-set tables featuring lovely crystal and beautiful china patterns. Imagine the feeling you get from such a room—the feeling of comfortable surroundings and a friendly environment in which to choose gifts for close friends or special occasions. The ambiance of Plâte du Jour partially comes from a house built in 1910, the store Cookie Yoelin opened as an alternative to standard gift shops and department store china selections. Choose from the many traditional china, flatware and silver patterns available, or enjoy viewing a spectrum of newer and less conventional styles. Plâte du Jour features china by Fitz & Floyd, Sasaki, Limoge and others. Sasaki, Retroneau and Ricci flatware is displayed along with elegant crystal, and the store carries fine-quality imported linens found nowhere else in Portland. You can choose from inexpensive pieces to top-of-the-line tabletop accessories, from today's gifts to tomorrow's heirlooms. Cookie and her staff will be glad to work with you to design your bridal registry, or to choose the perfect gift for that hard-to-buy-for friend. When you're looking for something that's not just another pretty plate, visit Plâte du Jour. Visa. MasterCard. American Express.

728 NW 23rd Avenue
Portland 97210
248-0350

Tuesday-Saturday
10:30am-5:30pm
Sunday noon-4pm

SALUTATIONS

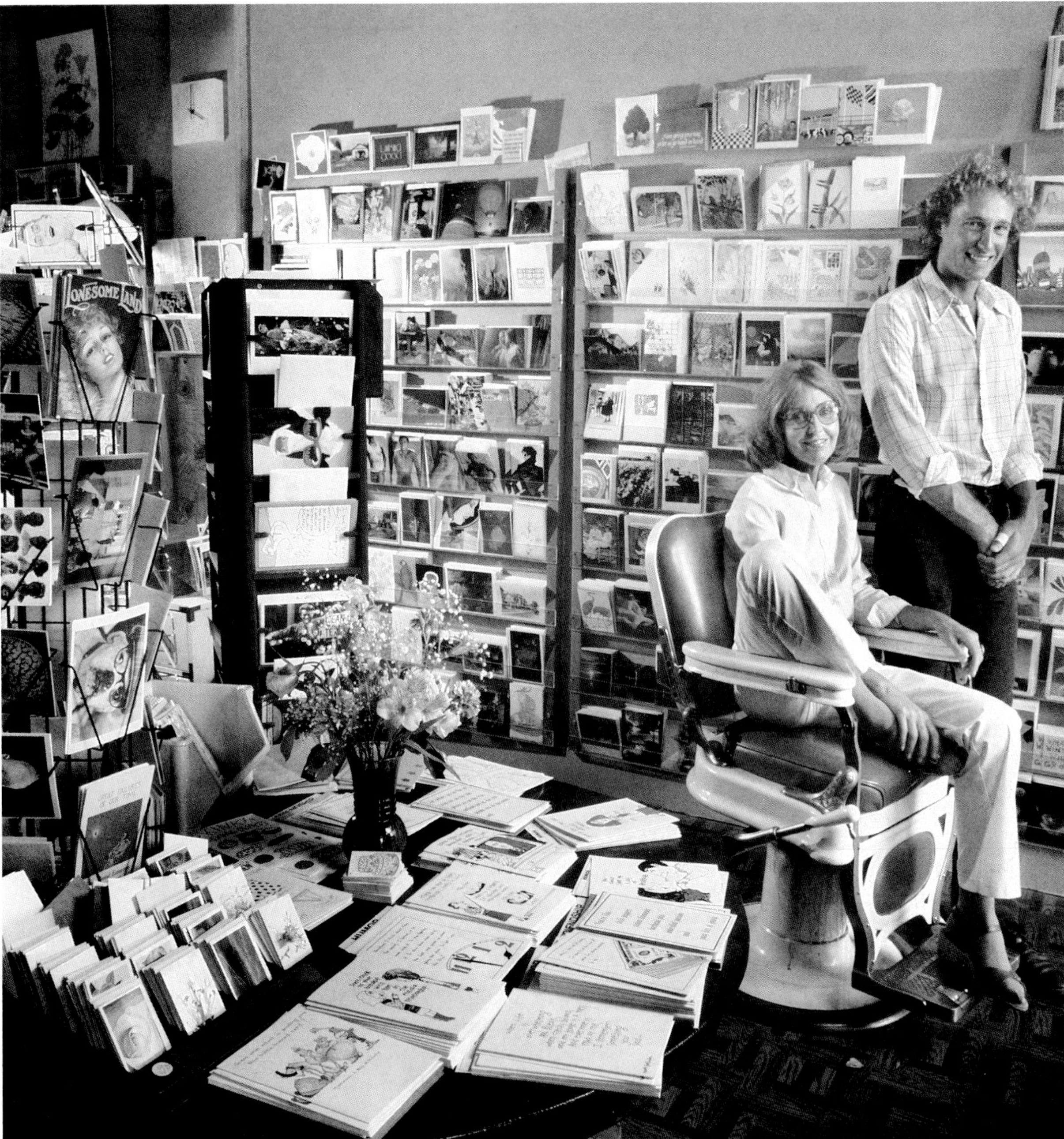

INCREDIBLES

City's largest selection of postcards.

As the pile of postcards, movie cards, photo art cards, handcrafted cards, humorous and audacious cards threatened to cascade over the counter, the customer just smiled with delight and exclaimed, "Here's five more — I can't stop!" Fifty-seven dollars and a whole lot of cards later she reluctantly left with a promise to return soon. At Salutations, finding the "perfect" card is an on-going challenge; there are so many unique and wonderful options. Hundreds — no thousands — of cards surround you, designed by all kinds of artists with every message imaginable, or with no message at all. There are inspirational cards by the Benedictine Sisters of Mt. Angel, strange humor cards by Hold the Mustard Productions, whimsical cards by Ken Brown, photo cards of movie stars, of sunsets, of boats, of bodies, and — only at Salutations — black and white postcard photos of Portland by store manager Brian Foulkes. Owner LouAnn Schreiber makes sure you'll never run out of choices. You'll find Salutations right around the corner from Le Panier in the Skidmore Historic District. You'll also want to return soon. Visa. MasterCard.

219 SW Ash Street
Portland 97204
224-8248

Monday-Friday
11am-6pm
Saturday 11am-5pm
April-December:
Sunday noon-5pm

Skidmore Historic District
E25

PRESENT PERFECT

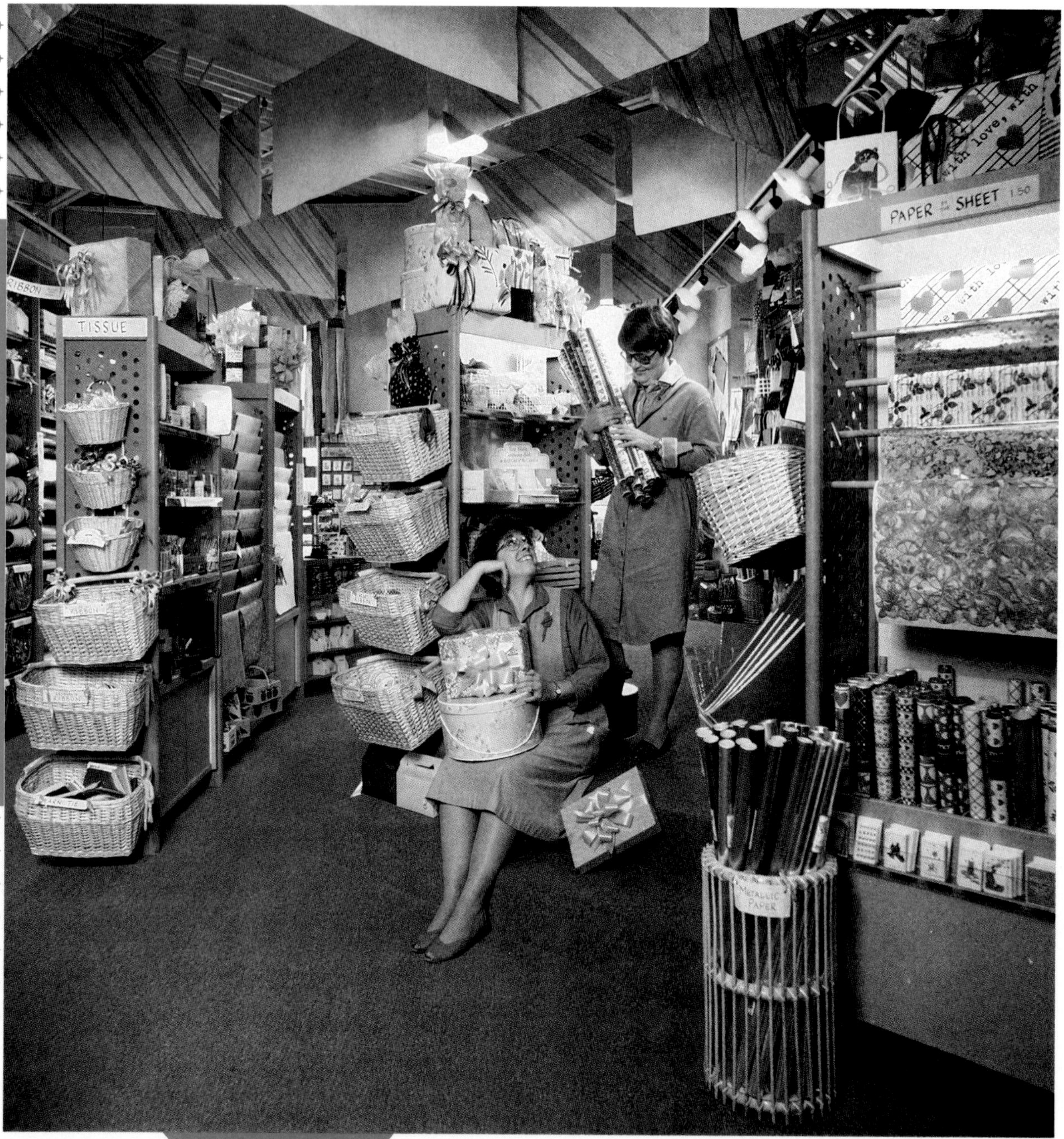

INCREDIBLES

Portland's most complete selection of gift wrap and accessories.

Yamhill Historic District

G25

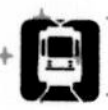

You won't find peach preserves on the shelves but "canning" presents is a specialty at Present Perfect, and cans are just one of many unique gift coverings. Rolls, reams and packages of colorful wrapping paper, finely textured rice paper, fancy fabric ribbons and bows, itty bitty bags, large shopping totes, boxes in all sizes, shapes, patterns and colors, tins, baskets, stickers, and rubber stamps abound at Present Perfect. Browsing under handpainted banners in a warm, inviting atmosphere is a continual delight, as each display is specially designed to provide new ideas for creating the package that everyone wants to open. Owners Jean Stephens and Fran Ranta have gathered together an incredible array of gift coverings and accessories, paper and writing tools, stationery, invitations and select hand-crafted gifts in one very special store that's definitely gift wrap "plus." And if you're all thumbs when it comes to ribbons and bows, Present Perfect will wrap — or can — your gift to be sure it's perfectly presented. Visa. MasterCard.

Yamhill Marketplace
110 SW Yamhill Street
Portland 97204
228-WRAP

Daily
10am-6pm

TEDDY BEARS PICNIC

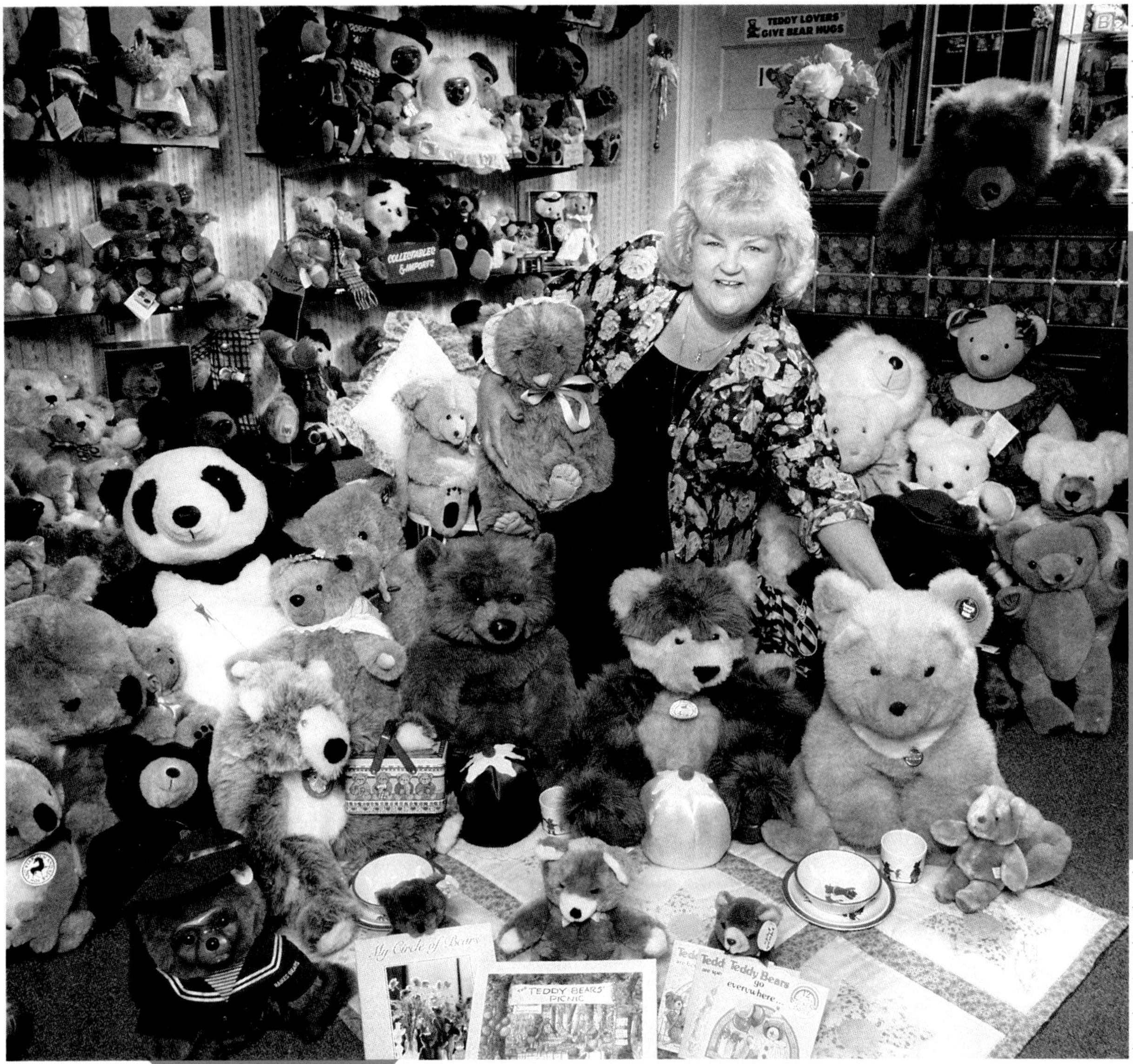

A picnic for bear lovers.

Teddy bears are a timeless treasure. While other toys may come and go, a child always remembers — and many adults still have — the teddy bear they grew up with! Today teddy bears are the fourth most collectible item in this country. Marilyn Weston, a bear collector herself, now serves as "Bearoness" of three Teddy Bear Picnic shops in the Portland area. Each is a fantasy world come true; the pink rosebud-covered wallpaper lends to the cozy feeling of a child's room and everywhere you look there are hundreds of bears to cuddle. The Glisan store is a bear-filled two story house, decorated with custom-made teddy-bear shutters. At Loehmann's Plaza and Jantzen Beach, the stores' logo is woven right into the carpeting. As for the inventory, well, if you're looking for anything that has a bear on it, you'll likely find it at Teddy Bears Picnic. There's a complete line of huggable, collectible hand-made and imported bears, and even a teddy bear tie for Dad. Naturally, the popular Gund line is represented, along with Steiff of West Germany, the Mercedes-Benz of bears. Northwest artists contribute the handmade bears, and there's a complete line of Lucy & Me Collectibles too! Visa. MasterCard.

House of Bears
2946 NE Glisan Street
Portland 97232
232-8221

Monday-Saturday
10am-5pm

Northeast Portland
D7

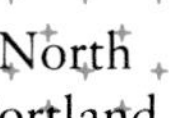

Jantzen Beach Center
1612 Jantzen Beach Center
Portland 97217
285-6664

Monday-Friday
10am-9pm
Saturday 10am-6pm
Sunday 11am-5pm

North Portland
G5

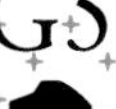

Cascade Plaza
8775 SW Cascade Avenue
Beaverton 97005
643-9255

Monday-Friday
10am-9pm
Saturday 10am-6pm
Sunday 11am-5pm

Beaverton
G2

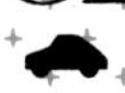

SIGN WIZARDS

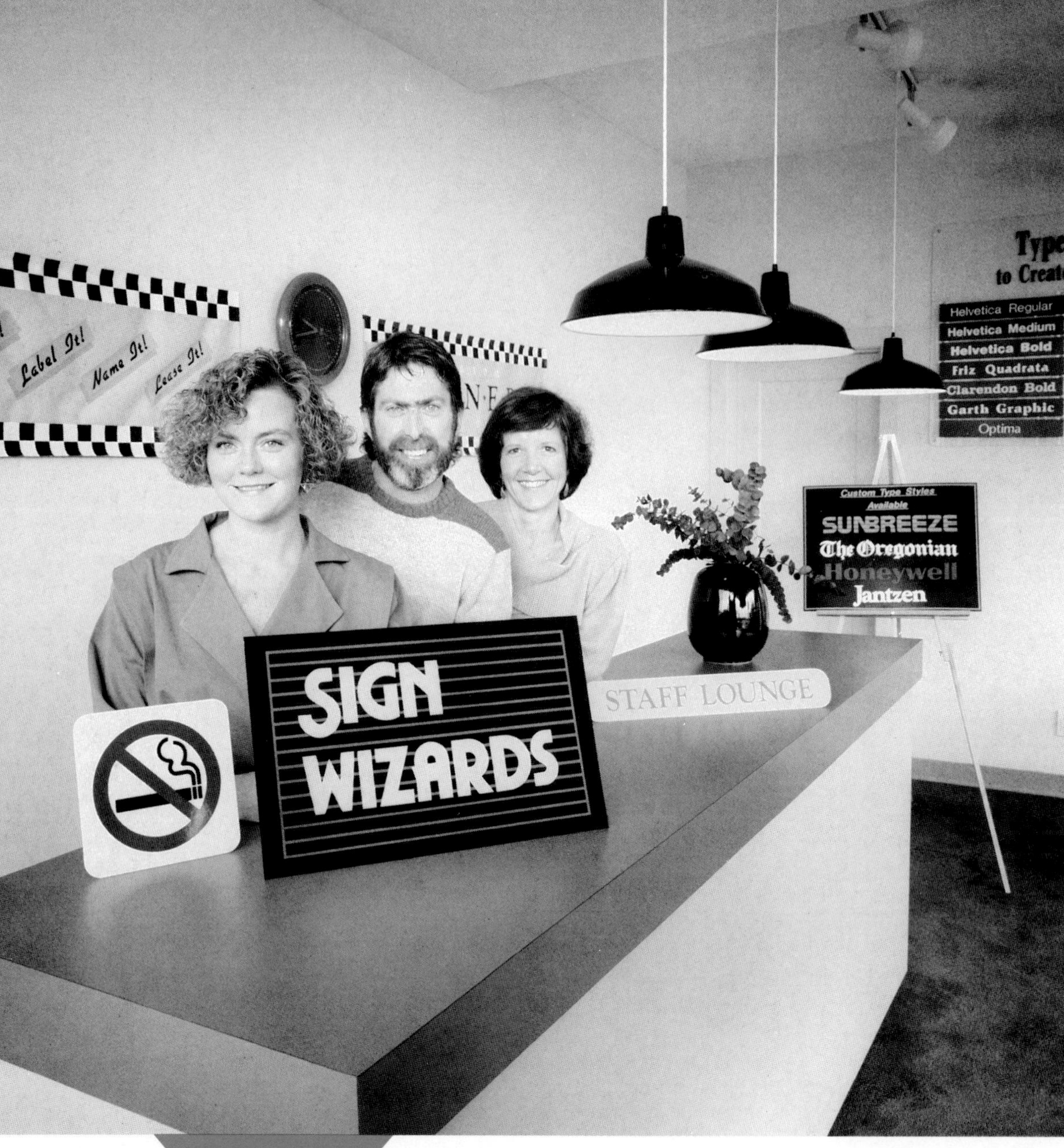

Quality custom signs and lettering.

Northeast Portland
C7

To create an effective visual message, you have to dabble in a little magic! Without a lot of hocus-pocus, Sign Wizards will create a variety of signs with the magic of graphics expertise and computerized state of the art technology. Introducing vinyl lettering and graphics as a new phase in sign making, Sign Wizards offers signs and banners suitable for interior and exterior display. Exciting trade show advertising, architectural signs, vehicle markings and boat names are all custom cut to fit your needs. The lettering generated is available in a single, pre-spaced line of type or a graphically complete visual message. A variety of typestyles is available and all may be varied by slanting, expanding or condensing them to impress your individuality upon any audience. They also offer the capabilities of logo reproduction. Choose the pressure sensitive vinyl from a splendid array of colors including a choice of metallic, reflective, pearlescent and translucent materials. Avoiding a lot of toil and trouble, skilled Sign Wizard employees will work with you to design a progressive visual image and offer step-by-step advice on installation, or they will install the signs for you. A twenty-four hour service is offered. When effective signage is limited only by your imagination, you begin to believe in magic. Visa. MasterCard.

2755 NE Broadway
Portland 97232
288-0037

Monday-Friday
8am-5:30pm
Saturday 10am-4pm

303

ENVIRONS

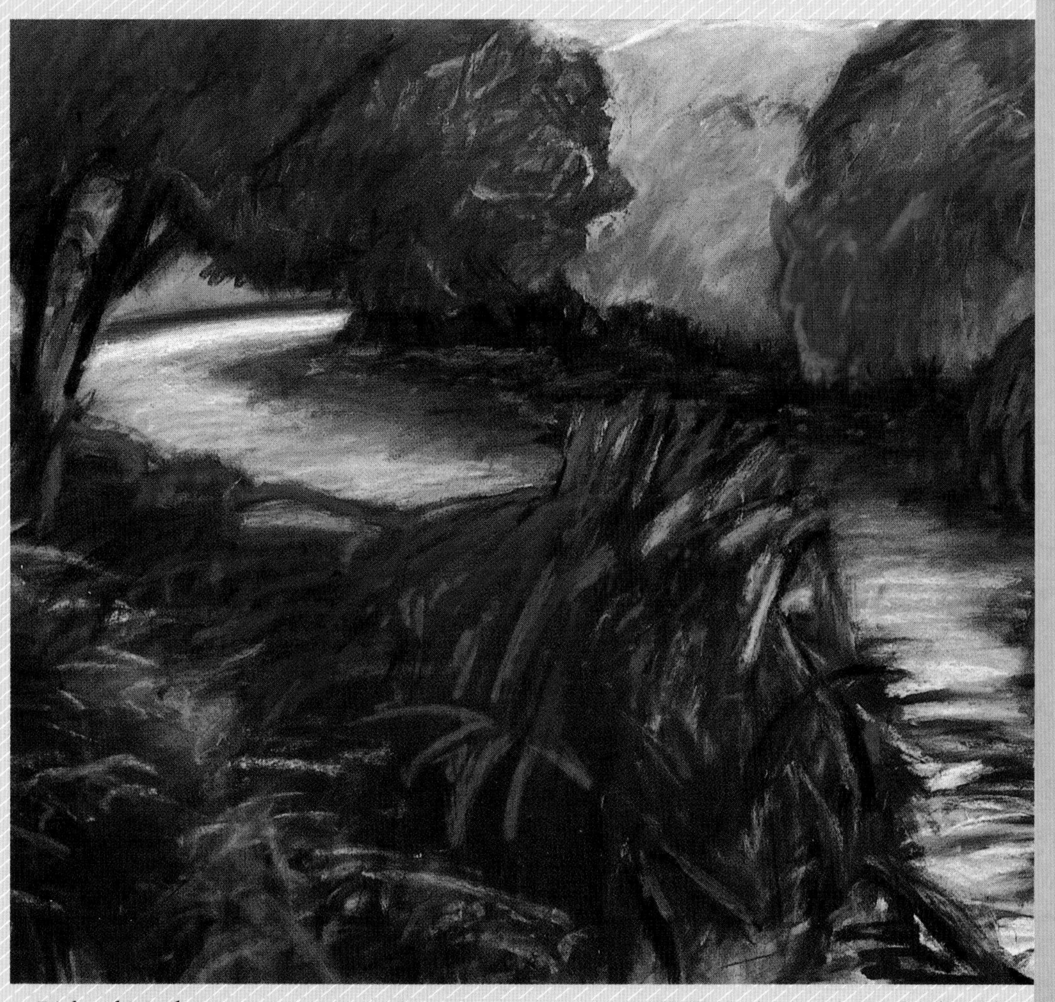

Richard Morhous *Derwent* ELIZABETH LEACH GALLERY

Portlanders, lucky people, are many times blessed. We insist, justifiably, that we inhabit a city of unsurpassed livability. Yet, we too need to escape. And when the time comes, our choices are not only abundant, they're close at hand. Without too much chauvinistic chest-pounding, it may reasonably be argued that no other major city within the continental U.S. offers such easy access to so many marvels of nature. Within an hour's drive of downtown Portland, one can ski the slopes of Mt. Hood, whale-watch along the Pacific Coast, windsurf in the Columbia Gorge, or tour a winery in Yamhill County. In short, what makes Portland so livable is not only the amenities within its boundaries, but the opportunities for escape that lie within easy driving distance.

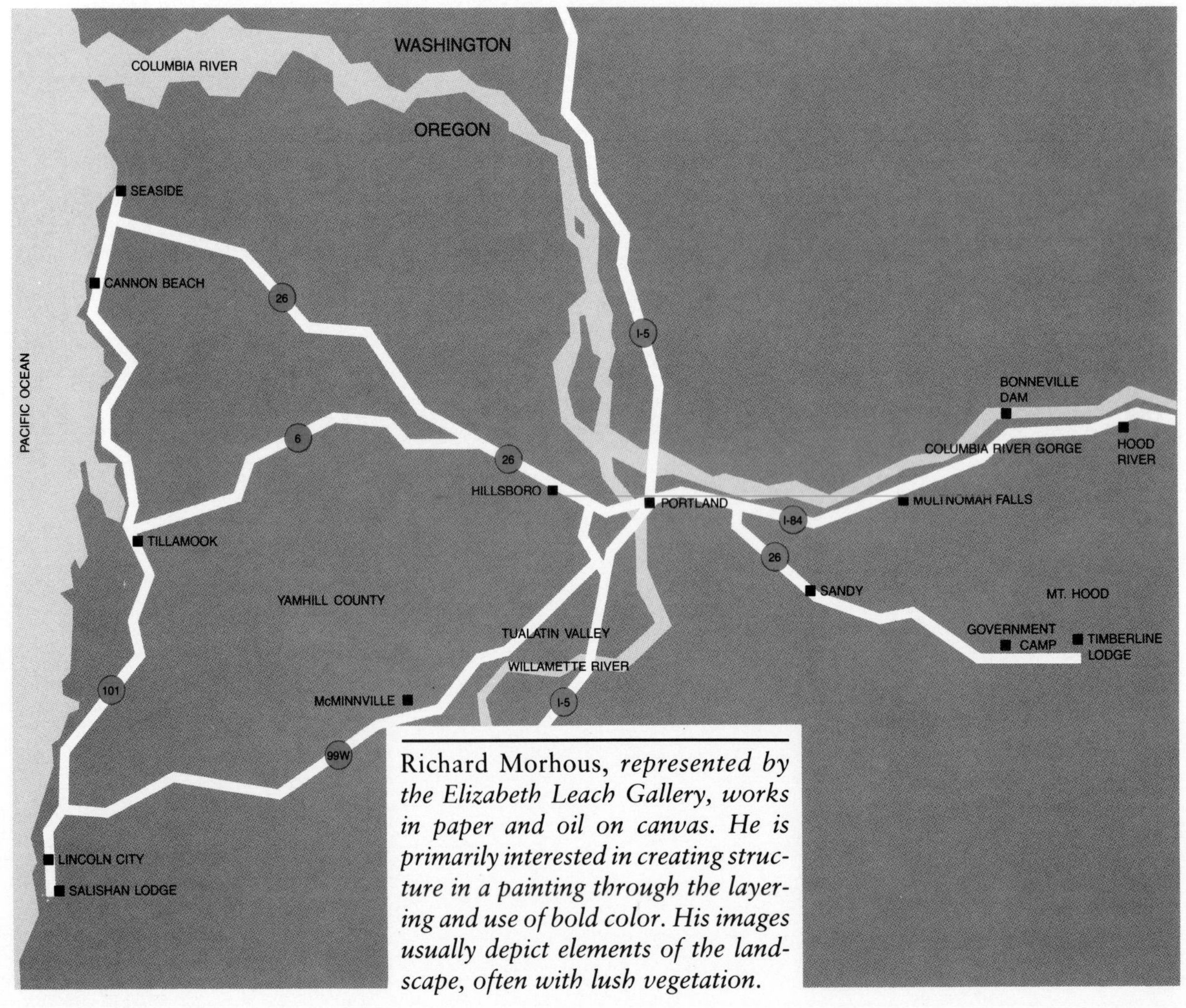

Richard Morhous, *represented by the Elizabeth Leach Gallery, works in paper and oil on canvas. He is primarily interested in creating structure in a painting through the layering and use of bold color. His images usually depict elements of the landscape, often with lush vegetation.*

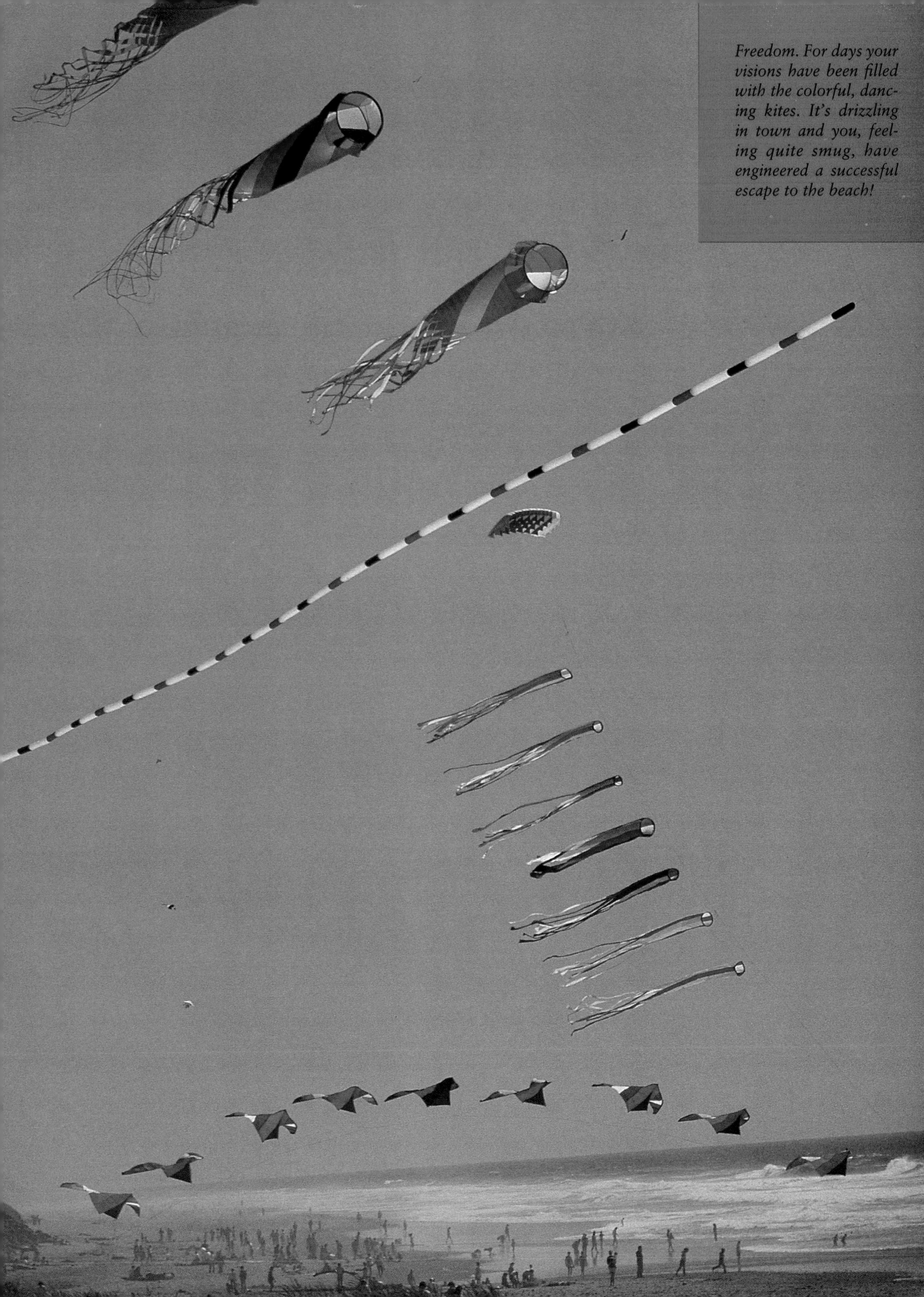

Freedom. For days your visions have been filled with the colorful, dancing kites. It's drizzling in town and you, feeling quite smug, have engineered a successful escape to the beach!

THE COAST

When a Portlander says, "Let's go to 'the Coast' for the weekend," the message is clear. The Coast can be defined simply as the Northwest portion of Oregon which borders the Pacific Ocean — from Seaside in the north to Lincoln City in the south. In other words, that part most easy to reach when you're fleeing Portland after work on Friday afternoon.

There are three routes available to the work-weary headed for a brief respite on the Coast. From north to south, they are Highway 26, which leads more or less directly to Seaside; Highway 6, which angles off Highway 26 some 25 miles outside of Portland and proceeds through the heart of the Coast Range to Tillamook; and the southernmost route, on Highway 99 W, which begins south of Portland and ends in Lincoln City. All three routes will bring you to the edge of the Pacific Ocean in 90 minutes or less.

Along this stretch of the Pacific Ocean, some 28 small towns, like Cannon Beach and Lincoln City, derive a large portion of their revenue from tourists. Others, like Wheeler and Netarts, are hardly large enough to notice when you pass by. Cabins, resorts, hotels and motels, restaurants and curio shops number in the hundreds — still the charm of the Oregon Coast is undisturbed. Although it is civilized, it is rustic and natural; not overdeveloped like much of the California Coast. You won't find Disneyland or Seaworld, L.A. or San Diego—just the ocean and a few amenities.

Speaking of amenities, I'd like to offer some suggestions. Starting at Seaside and traveling south, I'll point out a few of my favorite activities and establishments.

The Crab Broiler waits at the intersection of Highway 26 and Highway 101, "The Coast Highway." Owing to its prime location and decades of serving consistently good food, this restaurant is a favorite dining spot for Portlanders just arriving or about to leave the Seaside area. Although you'll enjoy any choice on the menu, the cracked crab and coleslaw plate, the barbecued crab and the onion rings are superlative!

If you need a little sustenance to see you through a day of beachcombing or hiking around Seaside, Harrison's Bakery is the place. This old-fashioned family bakery produces a staggering selection of homemade breads and tasty goodies which have nurtured visitors over the last seventy years. But don't overlook Seaside's essence: a stroll along the Boardwalk, the delicious taste of salt water taffy and Tom & Larry's homemade toffee.

Each February, Seaside is invaded by a motley throng of running fanatics, bent on finishing Oregon's most eccentric roadrace—the Trail's End Marathon. Started long before the running boom hit full stride, the Trail's End proves that a sizable number of Oregonians have a screw loose. How else to explain why anyone would willingly choose to face the daunting conditions prevalent on the Oregon Coast in February?

Twenty miles south of Seaside along Highway 101, Cannon Beach is Oregon's most tourist-oriented coastal community. Here the townsfolk boast an annual event every bit as popular as the Trail's End Marathon (and certainly more enjoyable): the Annual Cannon Beach Sand Sculpture Contest. The contest attracts delighted crowds and the level of creativity is always high. It's a perfect family outing.

Another attraction that has brought renown to Cannon Beach is the Coaster Theater. Established in 1966, when an old roller rink was refurbished, this intimate theater offers entertainment of many types.

The burgeoning Cannon Beach art community displays its works at the White Bird Gallery. One of the first in the U.S. to fully incorporate crafts with art — paintings, sculpture, prints, photographs, fibers, glass and ceramics—White Bird has become recognized at both the regional and national level.

After an afternoon browsing at the White Bird or before an evening of entertainment at the Coaster Theater, Ron Martin's Bistro is the perfect spot for a quiet little dinner for two. This restaurant is tucked away at the back of a courtyard and features Italian specialties and fresh seafood. When the following morning opens its eyes, several friendly eating spots will entice you quickly from the shower. If the mood is for light creative omelettes and other delights, try the Lazy Susan Cafe. Also keep in mind Osborne's, a wonderful homey old-fashioned grocery store and deli with wood plank floors, famous "two-star chili," and its great wine selection. Now, don't the skies look a little brighter?

Any discussion of Cannon Beach would be incomplete without a mention of both Haystack Rock and Ecola State Park. Haystack Rock, a 235-foot tall landmark is the third largest coastal monolith in the world — and has probably been photographed more often than any other feature along the Oregon Coast. Just before you leave Cannon Beach, a relaxing but exciting diversion awaits you at Ecola State Park. Wind your way to Indian Beach, take off your shoes, play in the surf, and watch kayakers and surfers battle the ocean's breakers.

Heading south again on Highway 101 past Neahkonie Mountain, we enter Tillamook, the heart of Oregon's dairy country. For local flavor, two cheese factories are worth a visit. Famous for Tillamook Cheese, the Tillamook County Creamery is the largest cheese processing plant in the world. But the highlight of any visit there is a stop at the dairy bar and tasting room where old-fashioned soft ice cream is available in two venerable flavors: chocolate and vanilla. The Blue Heron French Cheese Factory is smaller and newer, but a taste of their French-style breakfast cheese warrants a visit.

South of Tillamook, Highway 101 heads inland until it meets the Pacific, just north of Cascade Head, where the Sitka Center for Art and Ecology is located. Spend a quiet afternoon in this unique repository of art and educational information; the setting is majestic yet peaceful.

Our last stop is the Salishan Lodge in Gleneden Beach, just south of Lincoln City. As your mother used to say before serving dessert, we've saved the best for last. Indeed, there simply is no finer resort in the Northwest than Salishan. Designed to complement its spectacular setting, Salishan has nearly every possible amenity — a superb golf course, an indoor swimming pool with sauna and jacuzzi, tennis courts, a private beach, a pleasant bar and nature trails around the golf course where deer and jackrabbits roam. Amid this splendor sits a gourmet restaurant of national repute with a wine cellar unmatched north of San Francisco. Not content with near perfection, Salishan has added The Marketplace. This cluster of small specialty shops and art galleries offers unexpected delights, ranging from fresh seafood to children's toys.

Cannon Beach

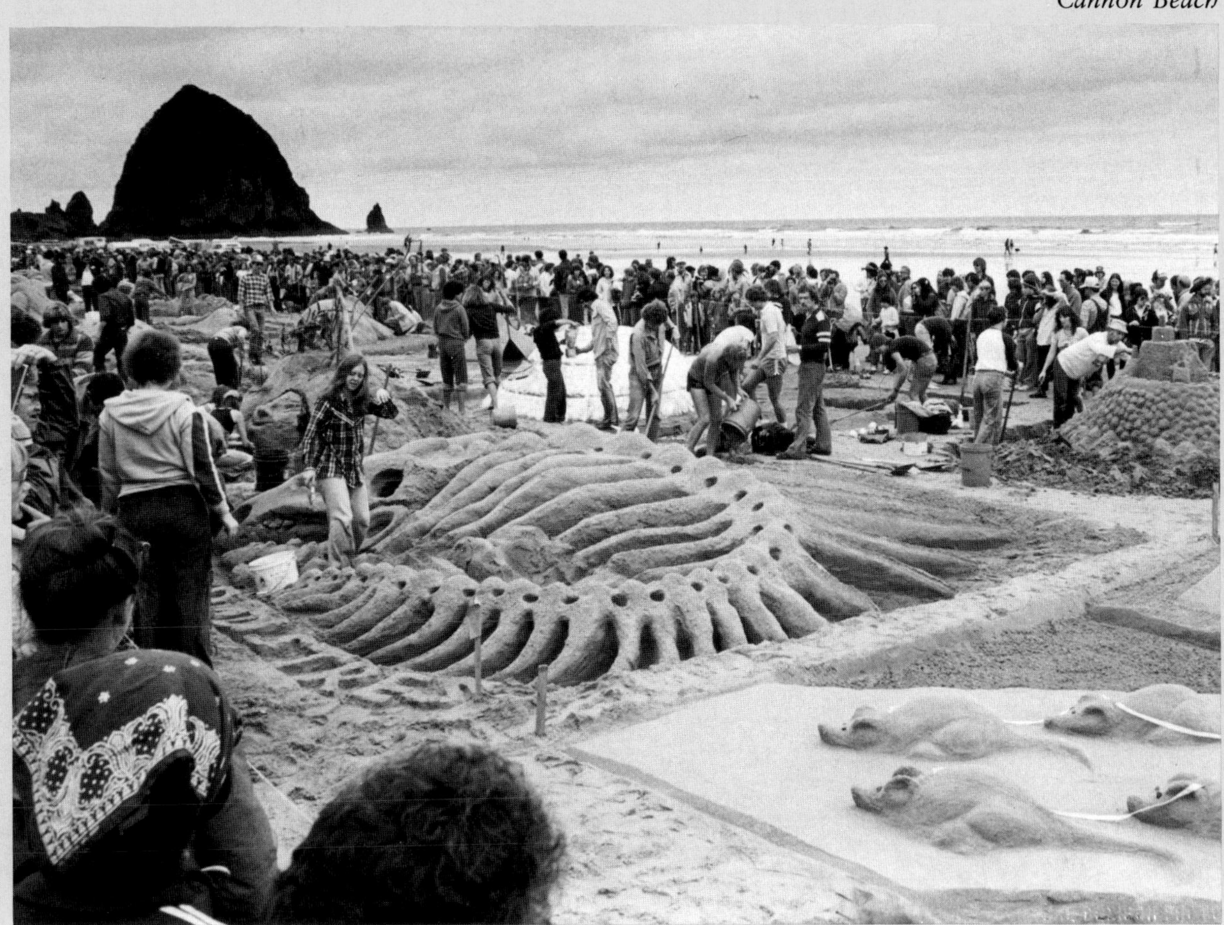

Hal Denison

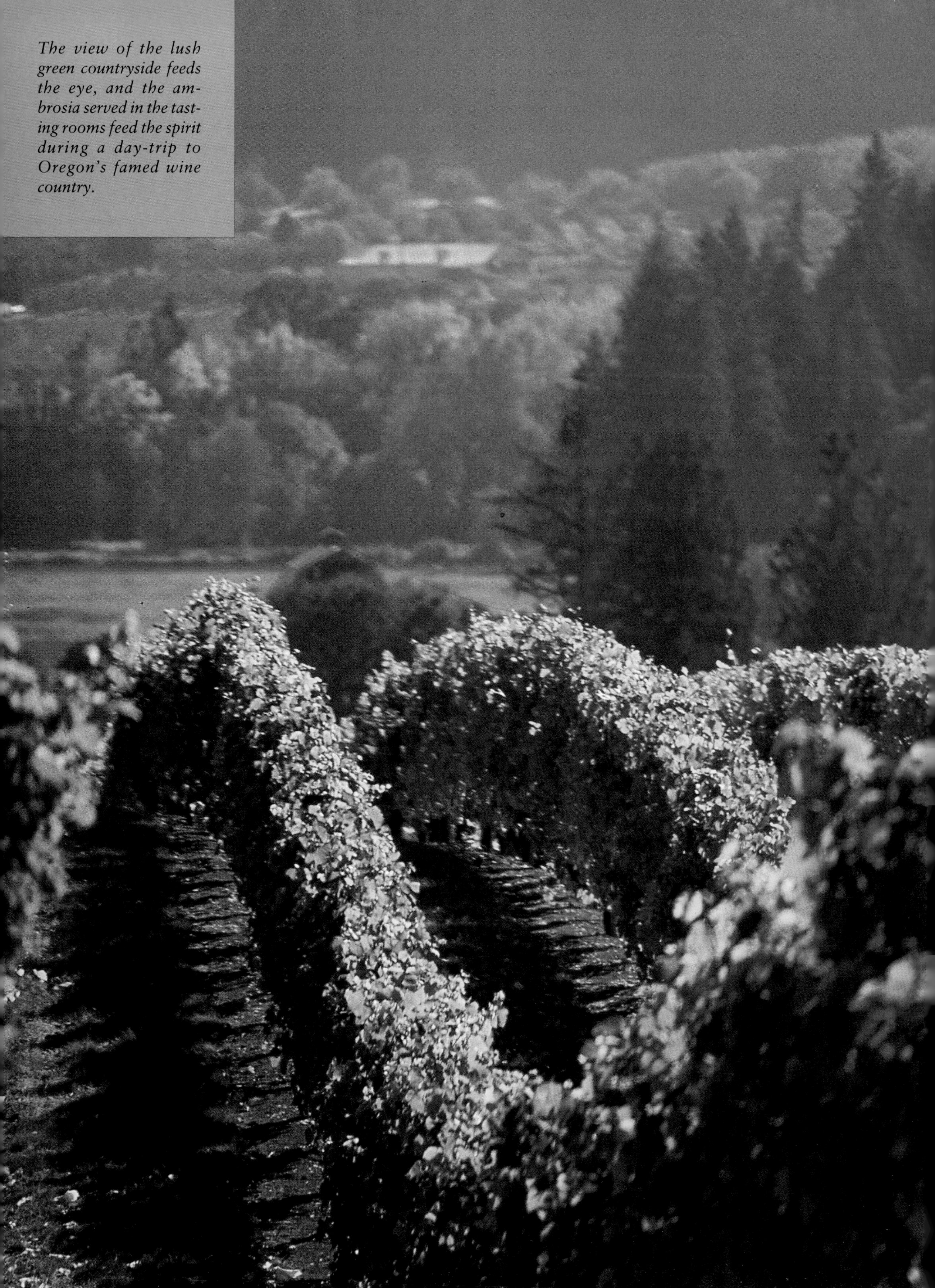

The view of the lush green countryside feeds the eye, and the ambrosia served in the tasting rooms feed the spirit during a day-trip to Oregon's famed wine country.

WINE COUNTRY

Certainly no recent development in Oregon has captured the natives' fancy as swiftly as the rise of the Northwest wine industry. Barely twelve years ago, the idea that the vineyards of this state would attract international attention was unheard of.

Today, over 50 wineries and vineyards are producing wines in Oregon, the vast majority clustered in Yamhill County and the Tualatin Valley of Washington County, though Polk and Marion Counties also boast many wineries. The opportunity for Portland's wine-lovers to visit these wineries during a leisurely day trip offers an experience few major cities share.

If you're contemplating a visit to the wine country, here's some basic advice. First, don't try to visit more than three wineries a day; you'll probably enjoy yourself more if you limit the itinerary to two. Second, although most wineries welcome visitors, not all do. Call ahead to find out when your favorite is open—both hours and days, and the best season to plan a visit.

The following wineries encourage visitors and offer the best experience for the wine tourist. And since part of the fun is planning a tour, explicit directions have not been provided. The wineries themselves will gladly give you that information or contact the Oregon Winegrowers' Association for a recent guidebook, P.O. Box 6590, Portland, Oregon 97228, 233-2377.

Tualatin Valley. Mulhausen Vineyard, Route 1, Box 99-C, Newberg 628-2417. Oak Knoll, Burkhalter Road, Hillsboro 648-8198. Ponzi Vineyard, Vandermost Road, Beaverton 628-1227. Shafer Vineyard Cellars, Star Route, Box 269, Forest Grove 357-6604. Tualatin Vineyard, Seavey Road, Forest Grove 357-5005.

Yamhill County. Chateau Benoit, Mineral Springs Road, Carlton 864-2991. Elk Cove Vineyards, Olson Road, Gaston 985-7760. Knudsen-Erath, Route 1, Box 368, Dundee 538-3318. Sokol Blosser Winery, Blanchard Lane, Dundee 864-2282. Amity Vineyards, 18150 Amity Vineyards Road S.E., Amity 835-2362. Arterberry Winery, 905 E. 10th Avenue, McMinnville 472-1587 or 244-0695. Hidden Springs Winery, 9360 SE Eola Hills Road, Amity 835-2782. Veritas Vineyard, 31190 NE Veritas Lane, Newberg 538-1470. Yamhill Valley Vineyards, Oldsville Road off Highway 18, McMinnville 843-3100.

While festivals and events take place throughout the year, two are worth special attention. The Yamhill County Wineries sponsor an Annual Wine Country Thanksgiving. On the Friday, Saturday, and Sunday following Thanksgiving, all of the wineries are open from 11am to 5pm. Special case discounts are offered, new wines are tasted and it is the only time the public is invited to visit Adelsheim Vineyards and the Eyrie Vineyards. The Washington County Winery Association sponsors an Annual Barrel Tasting Tour over the Fourth of July weekend. This is an opportunity to taste wine "before its time" straight from the barrel, meet the winemakers and discover why some wines are aged in wood. Admission to the wineries is free, light snacks and appetizers are available and mixed case discounts are given to buyers during the tour.

No discussion of touring Oregon's vineyards would be complete without noting some other discoveries. There are many fine restaurants, shops and villages to explore along the way. Here are two restaurants I recommend. Nick's Italian Cafe, 521 East Third Street, McMinnville 434-4471. All right. I'll say it up front. Nick's is the best Italian restaurant in Oregon — in the Northwest. Probably the best north of San Francisco. It's not just my opinion; every restaurant critic in the Portland area has paid homage to Nick's. And you won't find a friendlier establishment anywhere. Nick's serves dinners only, Tuesday through Saturday, at 6pm; Sundays at 5pm. The Brown Derby, 181 North Main Street, Banks 324-8121. At the Brown Derby, you'll find down home traditional American dishes, children's plates and a fine Sunday brunch—all of which are inexpensive. In this handsome, old-fashioned restaurant, a lace curtained window separates the lovely dining room from a loggers' bar. Take Grandma, Grandpa, Aunt Ivy and all the kids. It's that kind of place.

MT. HOOD & COLUMBIA GORGE

Nothing is so impressive to me as the sight of snowcapped Mt. Hood bathed in the last golden rays of daylight. Her "purple mountains' majesty" is a postcard image I never expected to see out my bedroom window.

When I first moved to Portland, I spent nearly every free weekend hiking and exploring the area around Mt. Hood. I quickly became aware of the highway loop that circles the mountain, the orchards of the Hood River Valley and the scenic splendor of the Columbia Gorge. It's one of my favorite stomping grounds.

Getting there. Although many backroads and some small highways will eventually lead you to Mt. Hood, Highway 26 is the avenue of choice. Between the outskirts of Gresham and the junction of Highways 26 and 35 is the small town of Sandy and a cluster of villages — Alder Creek, Brightwood, Welches, Wemme and Rhododendron. Rippling River in Welches is a gem of a small resort, handsomely designed, comfortably furnished and reasonably priced. The dining room is pleasing and the Sunday brunch worth a detour, not to mention eighteen holes of golf, cabins, and an upgraded lodge.

On the Mountain. Not only is the mountain lovely to look at and easy to reach but, once you arrive, there are great things to do. Ski downhill at Mt. Hood Meadows, Timberline Lodge or a number of other first-class ski areas. Timberline offers year-round skiing from its newest chairlift, the Palmer. For cross country enthusiasts, Hood River Meadows offers miles of wilderness uncluttered by downhillers. Snow Bunny Lodge and several other areas have sledding and tubing for the kids. When the snow has melted from all but the highest slopes, Mt. Hood becomes a hiker's and backpacker's dream. From Trillium Lake to Larch Mountain, there are miles of trails. In spring and early summer the mountain meadows come alive with brilliant colors as the mountain wildflowers — nonexistent in the village below — start to bloom.

How best to enjoy Mt. Hood? During the late fall or early spring, when the freezing level is well below 5,000 feet, spend a couple of days and at least one night at Timberline Lodge. Take off your watch, take a dip in the heated pool, enjoy a late breakfast, sip a warm brandy by the fireplace and just for awhile, forget the pressures of the outside world. In late spring, join a group of experienced climbers, such as the Mazamas, and scale the summit. You'll start at Timberline while it's still dark and, with a little luck, you'll reach the summit as the sun is rising. You don't need to be a triathlete to enjoy this experience; anyone in reasonable shape can successfully scale Mt. Hood. Once at the summit, you'll understand how the fabled holy men of Nepal find peace meditating on a mountaintop.

Multnomah Falls

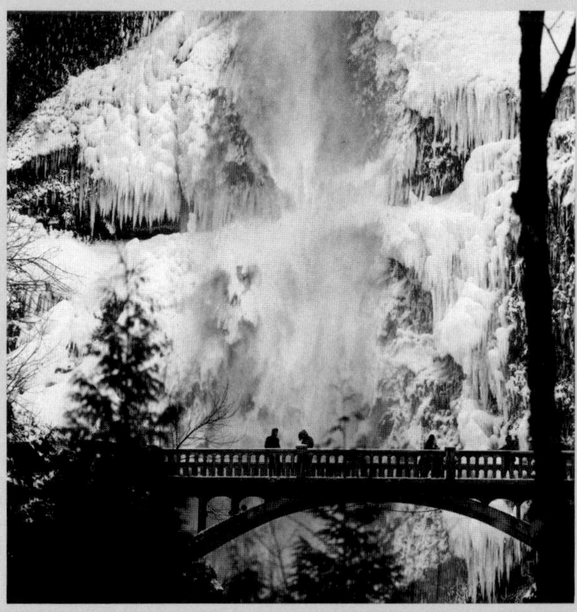

©1987 *Lawrence Hudetz*

Hood River Valley. On the far side of Mt. Hood lies Oregon's most scenic agricultural area: the Hood River Valley. Sloping down to the Columbia River, this picturesque area is famous for its harvest of apples and pears. In spring the fruit trees begin to color the orchards in shivers of pink and white, coming to a peak during April when the Annual Blossom Festival attracts thousands of visitors to the peaceful valley. Within the Valley, Hood River lies at the junction of Highway 35 and Interstate 84. For many years its location on the Columbia River guaranteed Hood River a position of commercial importance. Today it is gaining international recognition as a mecca for elite windsurfers. The nearly constant winds whipping down the Columbia Gorge create perfect conditions for enthusiasts of this sport.

After the Blossom Festival or a day of windsurfing, stop for a drink at the Hood River Inn. It's hard to leave this splendid location as you watch the sun set over the Columbia River. Hood River boasts one restaurant definitely worth a visit, The Stonehedge Inn, a turn-of-the-century house nestled in the trees overlooking Hood River. Dine on the porch and enjoy the view.

Heading home, the Columbia Gorge. Along the Columbia Gorge from Hood River to Portland, you can hike along scenic trails, gaze at imposing vistas and swiftly moving waterfalls and marvel at sights unique in the Continental United States. Turn off Interstate 84 just past Bonneville Dam where it meets the old Gorge Scenic Highway. From this point to just outside of Portland, make leisurely stops along the Sandy River and enjoy the beauty of Oregon. Here's a partial list of places I consider "must sees."

Multnomah Falls is one of the highest waterfalls in the United States. In the spring when the snowpack has melted in the mountains the falls are most powerful; but for unmatched beauty brave a trip when the mercury has dipped into the teens and the east wind rises out of the gorge. You'll be rewarded with an ice sculpture of shimmering textures and light that only nature can create. Further west is Latourell Falls, a lovely series of smaller falls connected by a well-maintained trail. This is nature at its simplest: not overwhelming or majestic—but rather, elegant and soothing — a perfect short hike for the kids. From the creations of nature, look next to a man-made wonder: The Columbia Gorge Hotel. Built in 1921 by Portland lumber baron Simon Benson as a haven at the end of the Scenic Highway, this imposing hotel has been restored to its former grandeur. It once again resembles a hotel in the fine European tradition. The views are magnificent, the public spaces grand, and the cuisine exceeds the standards one would expect. It's worth the price of an overnight stay or a stop for the Farm Breakfast. A scenic marvel like the Columbia River Gorge is best enjoyed from a particularly choice vantage point. Although many are available, Crown Point is easily accessible and affords a splendid view. Situated right in the middle of the highway, it's a good place to stop and walk around. Look east toward Idaho, west toward Portland, north to the wheatfields on the Washington side; watch the sun cast light and shadows across the mountain, fields and valley; then head back to Portland, refreshed. Welcome home!
Randal K. Shutt

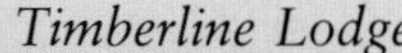

Timberline Lodge

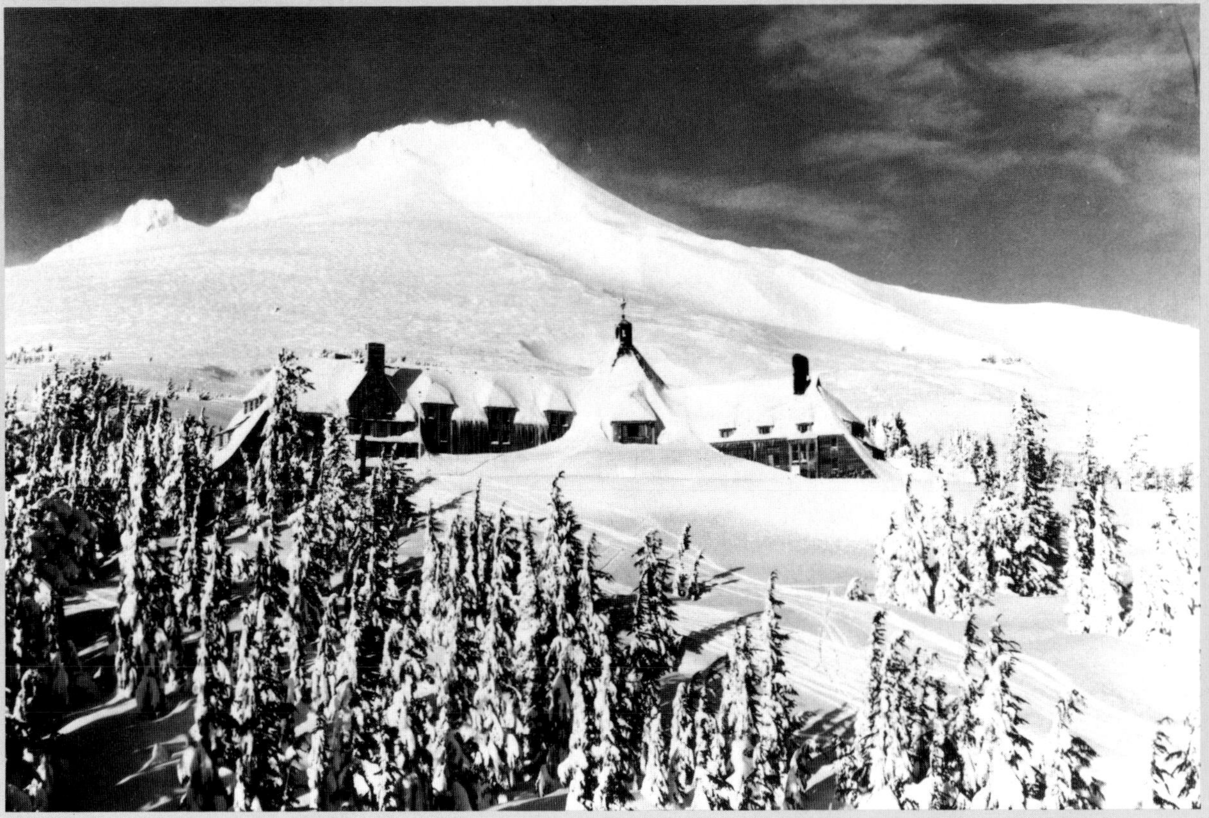

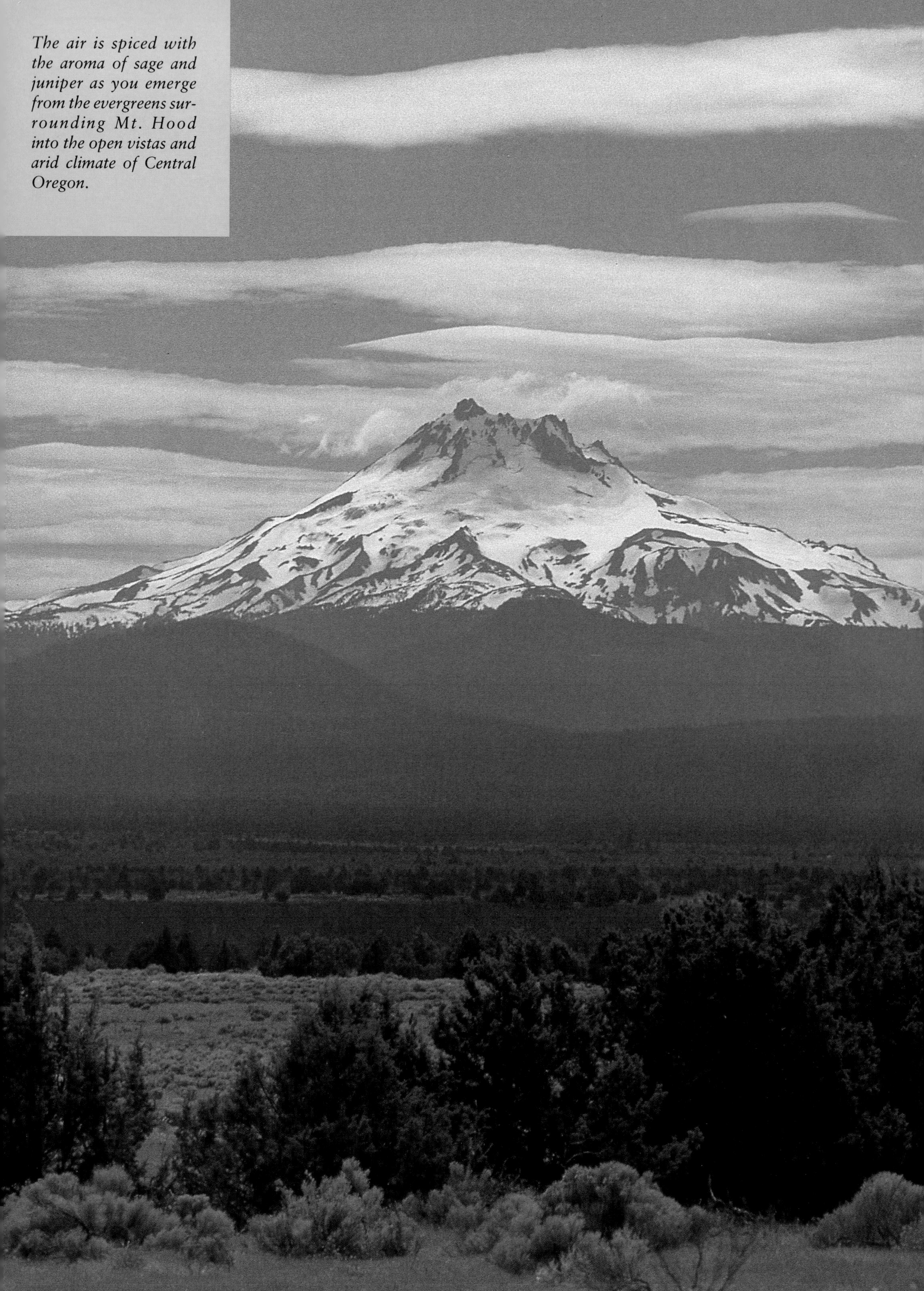

The air is spiced with the aroma of sage and juniper as you emerge from the evergreens surrounding Mt. Hood into the open vistas and arid climate of Central Oregon.

INSTANT INSPIRATIONS

It's a rare and clever person who knows without delay what is and where to get the perfect gift. Almost as rare are those who know immediate sources for all their own needs and luxuries. A Catalogue like this is such a splendid document to research the widest choice of Portland's selected best. Gifts or must-get-it, this is your best place to start.

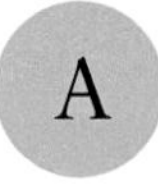

Antiques
American Primitives *227*
English *220*
European *220, 221*
Japanese *219*
Pine *220*
Architectural Supplies *260, 297*
Art
Appraisals *249, 250*
Art Search *250*
Brokerage *250*
Ceramics *246-248, 253, 257*
Children *191*
Collage *258*
Consultation *244, 246, 248, 249, 255*
Contemporary *244, 246, 247, 249, 250*
Crafts *72, 247, 252, 257*
Enamels *246*
Folk *151, 230, 246*
Glass Art *222, 247, 251, 256*
Installations *249*
International, Twentieth Century *250*
Japanese *219*
Metal Art *247*
Mobiles *251*
Pen and Ink *258*
Portraits *258*
Posters *254*
Prints *244, 245, 248, 254*
Rental *244*
Sculpture *244, 246, 248, 250, 251*
Supplies *259, 260, 275, 297*
Children *186*
Studio *258*
Watercolors *248, 254, 255, 258*
Weaving *247, 257*
West Coast *248, 251*
Attache
Renwick *288*
Schlesinger *161, 288*
Desa *288*
Stuart Kern *288*
Awnings *228*

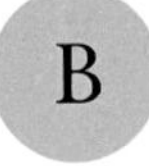

Baby Shower Registration *138, 188*
Balloons, helium *242, 294*
Baskets
Fruit *91*
Gift, custom *90, 91, 95, 96*
Straw *231, 242, 289*
Whitewash *254*
Banners, custom-made *302*
Bathroom Accessories *233*
Brass Faucets *241*
BBQ *228*
Weber *228*
Bears, teddy *301*
Bedding
Children *180, 188*
Cotton 100% *233*
Custom Designed *233, 239*
Designer Linen *233, 239*
Futon *100, 218*
Bicycles *199, 204*
Accessories *198, 199, 201, 204*
Children, tricycles *183*
European *204*
Italian *204*
Racing Club *204*
Touring *199*
Blankets
Monogrammed *233*
Boats
Mastercraft *206*
Boardgames *291*
Books
Academic *275*
Architecture *270*
Audio Tapes *264, 265, 258*
British Isles *270*
Cassettes, language *264, 268*
Children *182, 185, 264, 275-277, 281, 284*
Classical Music *270*
Cookbooks *94, 264, 270, 281*
Crafts *265*
Gardening *265*
Gift Books *265*
Gift Wrapping and Shipping *269*
Graphic Art *259*
Health *271, 277*
Imported, British *268*
Japan *270*
Judaica *276*
Language
French *277*
Spanish *277*
Foreign, children *187*
Large print *269*
Largest Selection *264*
Lending Library *269, 280*
Magazines *264, 265, 258, 269, 271, 276, 277*
Foreign *265, 281, 290*
Newspapers, International *268, 281, 290*
Children *190*
Northwest, Oregon *274*
Oriental *100*
Parenting *182, 187, 190*
Psychology *271, 277*
Relaxation *284*
Religion *269, 277*
Research, Northwest *274*
Self-development *284*
Science Fiction *277*
Teacher *182, 190*
Travel *268, 279*
Used *264*
Women's Studies *271, 280*
Brass *230*
Beds *239*
Faucets *241*
Business Cards *286*

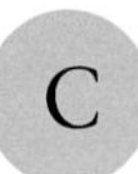

Cabinet Work, custom *214, 257*
Calenders *265, 268, 270, 281*
Calligraphy *276*
Candles *94, 230, 242*
Canoes *202*
Camping Equipment *198, 199*
Canopies, rental *295*
Camisoles, 100% cotton *144*
Car
Alarm System *267, 278*
Cassette Decks *267, 278*
Cellular Car Phones *278*
Compact Disc *278*
Installation *267, 268*
Stereo *267, 268*
Cards *183, 185, 268, 270, 276, 281, 286, 294, 299*
Carousel Horses *226*
Cash Registers, brass *226*
Catering — see Food
Cellulite Treatments *141*
Ceramics — see Pottery
Chairs, Queen Anne *221*
Chess *291*
Children
Arts and Crafts *191*
Basketry *292*
Books *182, 185, 264, 275-277, 281*
Clothing
Custom Design, Judy Johnson *178*
Florence Eiseman *178*
Hand-knit Sweaters *140, 181*
Infant Wear *138, 184, 188*
Mail Order *179*
Mako Originals *181*
Natural Fiber Clothing *162, 179, 181*
Osh Kosh *178*
Outerwear *184*
Patsy Aiken *178*
Sweatshirt, silk screen *181*
Swedish *179*
Concerts *187*
Dolls — see Dolls
Ear Piercing *189*
European Boutique *188*
Fabric Painting *292*
Furniture *180, 224, 232*
Gift Items *138, 180, 183, 188*
Gymnastics Lessons *192*
Hair Styling *189*
Knitting Lessons *292*
Multicultural Adventures *191*
Puppets *183*
Teddy Bears *184, 301*
Gund *301*
Lucy and Me *301*
Music Box *301*
Steiff *301*
Toys — see Toys
Weaving Lessons *292*
Christmas Tree Decorations *183*
Cigar
Imported *290*
Dunhill *290*
Cigarettes, Imported *290*
Curriculum Resources *182*
Clocks *220, 236, 289*
Estimate and Appraisals *236*
Grandfather *236*
Repair *236*
Trade-in *236*
Closet Accessories *238*
Clothing
Children — see Children
Men and Women
Alan Paine *153*
Arthur Freedberg *153*
Blanc Blu *158*
Byblos *154*
Cavaricci *158*
Corbin *153*
Farrell Reed *153*
Fitness *198, 201, 207*
Georgio Armani *154*
Handmade *257*
Harris tweed *157*
Hugo Boss *154*
Irish Country Hats *157*
M. Julian *158*
Martinique *158*
Natural Fiber *143, 162*
Norman Hilton *153*
Outdoor Wear *160, 198, 199, 203*

Patagonia *156, 160, 198, 199, 203*
Pendleton *156*
Perry Ellis *154*
Poco Lou *158*
Revolution *158*
Robert Talbot *153*
San Remo *154*
Sero *153*
Shirts
Custom-made *166*
Gittman *153*
Shoes — see Shoes
Suits
Hand Tailored *166*
Rental *155*
Tennis *206*
Ties, silk and woven *161*
Tuxedo
Rental *155*
Sale *155*
Wearable Art *256, 257*
Clothing, women
Adrienne Vittadini *149*
Anne Klein *139*
Balkan *143*
Belts *136, 139, 149*
Bogner *146*
British Khaki *137*
Briestle *139*
Byblos *142*
Calvin Klein *139*
Catcher *140*
C.P. Shades *137, 143*
Colour Me *143*
Contemporary, exotic *144, 151*
Custom-made *166*
Dennis Goldsmith *149*
Dresses
Evening and Professional *136, 139, 142, 145-147*
Eagle's Eye *140*
Ellen Tracy *147, 149*
E.S. Deans *136, 140*
Ethnic, tribal *151*
Fia *140*
Geiger of Austria *146, 198*
Georgio Armani *142*
Hosiery *136, 139, 145*
I.B. Diffusion *140*
IZEC *142*
Jeanne Pierre *140*
Joanie Char *146*
Joan Vass *136, 142*
J.G. Hook *147, 156*
Karen Kane *140*
Knitwear *136, 139, 140*
Levino *139*
Liz Claiborne *147*
Lingerie *139, 144, 145*
Luna *142*
Lyle & Scott *139*
Maternity *138*
Mondi *146*
Naf Naf *137*
Natural Fiber *143, 144, 145, 151, 162*
Nancy Heller *136*
Nicole Miller *136, 149*
Norma Kamali *142*
OK Sam *137*
One-of-a-Kind *137*
Outlander *140*
Pendleton *147, 156*
Petites *147*
Perry Ellis *149*
Richard & Co. *140*
Richard Warren *147*
Robes *144*
Scarves, handwoven *136, 140*
Shoes — see Shoes
Sportswear *136, 139, 142, 145, 149*
Sweaters *136, 139, 140, 145, 151*
Byford *154*
Cashmere *139*
Hand-knit *137, 140, 145, 157*
Susie Hayward *146*
Suzelle *139*
Trunk Shows *147*
Wardrobe Consultation, at home *145*
Comforters
Down *233, 239*
100% Cotton *233, 239*
Cooking — see Housewares
Copying — see Reproduction
Crafts *72, 247, 253, 256, 257, 296*
Glass *247, 251, 257*
Weaving *247, 292*
Crystal *287, 298*
Crystals *280, 284*

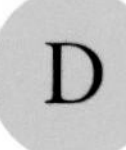

Decoys *230*
Delicatessans *90, 92, 95, 96, 99, 103*
Dinnerware *230, 232, 235, 289*
Dolls *184-186*
Clothing *185*
Houses *186*
Drafting Equipment *259, 260*
Delivery of Supplies *259*
Duvet Covers *233, 239*

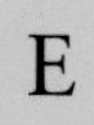

Ear Piercing, children *189*
Earrings
Eve Kaplan *287*
Fernellas Tools *287*
Joe Cool *287*
Electrolysis, waxing *150*
Engineering Supplies *260, 297*
Equestrian
Boarding *210*
Hunt-seat equitation *210*
Lessons *210*
Shows *210*

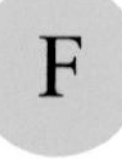

Fabric
Accessories *293, 296*
Dyes *292*
Natural Fiber *293*
Silk *293*
Silk Rainwear *293*
Wool *293, 296*
Facials *141*
Fireplace *228*
Fibre Arts *257, 292*
Film — see Video
Fishing, fly *198*
Flatware *289, 298*
Floorcoverings — also see Rugs
Carpet *215, 217, 223*
Flowers
Containers *242*
Dried *106, 231*
Fresh Cut *91, 95, 240, 242*
Seeds *240, 157*
Giverny Garden *157*
Silk *231, 242*
Food
Almond Torte *70*
Antipasto *44*
Apple Streudel, Viennese *105*
Autumn Meringue *70*
Bakery *94, 96, 98, 102, 103*
French *98*
Viennese *105*
Banana Leaves *100*
Bouillabaise *61*
Burgers *46, 47, 84, 85*
Burnt Creme *54, 69*
Caesar Salad *73, 77*
Cake *105*
Wedding, custom *105, 106*
Calamari *76*
Calamari Dijon *58*
Catalogue, mail order *94, 157*
Catering *59, 70, 77, 91, 92, 94-96*
Deli Trays *75, 91*
Japanese Cuisine *59*
Catfish *63*
Chang sa Chicken *65*
Cheese *89, 90, 91, 94-96, 101, 103*
Cheese Blintzes *75*
Chicken Matzo Ball Soup *75*
Chocolate *95-97, 104*
Swiss *104*
Cinnamon Rolls *75, 102, 105*
Clam Chowder *61*
Coffee espresso *56, 64, 69, 70, 73, 77, 79, 92, 94, 96, 97, 98*
Coffee, fresh bulk *91, 94, 95, 97, 104, 235*
Coffee Cakes, European *105*
Crab, Dungeness *54, 61*
Crab Cakes, Maryland Style *63*
Crab Legs and Scallops Beurre Blanc *54*
Crab Legs Toscana *45*
Cracked Crab w/Hunan Black Beans *65*
Crawfish *61*
Crepes, curried shrimp *64*
Deli *90-92, 95, 96, 99, 103*
Desserts, gourmet *106*
Fettuccine *101*
Feuillette *98*
Fish, fresh *90, 95*
Chemical free *103*
Smoked *157*
Flemish Hare *55*
Fruit Basket *91, 95, 298*
General Tso's Chicken *57*
Grains and Rice
Exotic *89, 103*
Grand Marnier Strawberries *45*
Hot and Sour Soup *57, 65*
Hushpuppies *63*
Kashmiri Birijani *66*
Kabobs, lamb *80*
Lamb Korma *66*
Lox, cream cheese and bagel *75*
Lobster *45*
Meat, fresh *90, 95*
Chemical free *103*
Milkshakes *73*
Muffins and Cookies, fresh *92, 96, 97, 102, 106*
Moussaka *76*
Mousse Pie, chocolate *106*
Mozzarella Di Bufala *89*
Olive Oils, extra virgin *89, 91, 95, 96, 103*
Onion Rings *47, 78*
Oriental *100*
Oyster, Cajun *54*
Oyster Rockefeller *61*
Pain Noel *98*
Pastries *75, 77, 79, 105*
Pasta, fresh *89, 96, 101*
Pasta, tomato, spinach, egg *53, 89, 101*
Pizza *62, 74, 78, 79, 82, 86, 96*
Gourmet *62, 82, 86, 96*
Pollo Dorado *81*
Poultry *90, 95, 103*
Chemical free *103*
Produce, organic *103*
Quail, stuffed with chutney *49*
Rabbit Paté *49*
Ravioli *101*
Ravioli Al Pesto *58*
Reuben Sandwich *75*
Roast Beef Hash *73*
Sake *59*

Salmon, Alder Smoked Chinook *54*
Salmon en Papilotte *70*
Salsa *73, 81, 83*
Sausage *99*
Scallop and Beef, with spicy sauce *57*
Scallopini Parmigiana Piccota *77*
Scones, fresh *92*
Shrimp Salad *87*
Snails Madrid *51*
Soft Shell Crab *63*
Southern Fried Chicken *63*
Spaghetti and Pasta, Neopolitan Style *74*
Spanish Coffee, flambé *60*
Spices, bulk *103, 235*
Tandori Murgh *66*
Tea, bulk *97, 103, 104, 235*
Torte Rustica *77*
Tortelini Della Cusa *71*
Tortelini, fresh *89, 101*
Tortillas, blue corn *81*
Triple Happiness Shrimp *65*
Truffle Cake *61, 86*
Turkey Corden Bleu *60*
Turkey Tettrozinni *60*
Veal, milk fed Provini *53*
Venison, New Zealand *55*
Vinegar, Imported *89, 90, 94-96*
Wild Boar, Australian *55*
Wine
Algerian, Tunisian, Moroccan *80*
Chinese *57*
French *46, 56, 90, 92, 95, 96*
Italian *44, 53, 58, 89, 90, 92, 95, 96*
Mexican and Spanish *81*
Footwear — see Shoes
Aerobic *201, 206*
Court *201, 206*
Golf *206, 207*
Fragrances *157, 164*
Custom Blending *164*
PH Fragrances Compatibility *164*
Rare *157*
Framing, custom *245, 248, 254, 255, 258*
Supplies *259, 260*
Furniture
Antique *219-221, 227*
Baker *215*
Contemporary *214, 215, 232, 257*
Country Pine *220, 221*
Custom *256, 257*
Drafting *259, 260*
Desk, children *180, 232*
Drexel Heritage *217*
Henredon *215*
Imported *214*
Japanese *219*
Leather *217, 232*
Mastercraft *215*
Mid Twentieth Century *227*
One-of-a-Kind *259*
Patio *216, 228*
Rattan & Wicker *216*
Tansu, Japanese *219*
Unfinished *224*
Victorian *227*
Futon *100, 218*

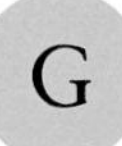

Games
Adults *291*
Children *183-186*
Special Orders *291*
Garden
Bedding Plants *91, 240*
Tools *240, 241*
Trees and Shrubs *240*
Gift Baskets — see Baskets
Gift Wrapping Supplies *286, 294, 300*
Glass
Art Glass *249, 251, 256*
Cloisonne *222*
Cut Glass *222*
Victorian *222*
Crystal *287, 298*
Glassware *289*
Disposable *295*
Golf
Footwear *206, 207*
Granite Tools *225*
Graphic Art Supplies *259, 260, 297*
Guitars *266, 282*
Gymnastics, children *192*

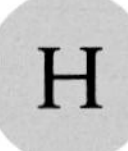

Hair
Children, styling, accessories *189*
Grooming Aids *150, 159, 165, 167, 168, 189, 234*
Styling *148, 150, 159, 165, 167, 189, 234*
Easycare *167*
Wig Sales and Service *148*
Halloween Supplies *183*
Costume *295*
Handbags *139, 161*
Hardware *241*
Hats
Dress *166*
Propellor *93*
Home Electronics — see Stereo and Video Equipment
Horse — see Equestrian
Boarding *210*
Shows *210*
Houseplants *240*
Housewares *94, 232, 235, 238, 289*
Asian cooking supplies *100*
Chantel *94, 232*
Cuisinart *94, 232, 235*
Le Cruiset *94, 232*
Master Chef *232*

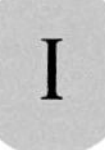

Inflatibles, animals *252, 287*
Instruction
Basketry *292*
Canoes and Kayaking *202*
Cooking *94, 95, 232*
Equestrian *210*
Fabric Painting *292*
Gymnastics, children *192*
Knitting *292*
Multicultural, children *191*
Sewing *296*
Weaving *292*
Interior Design Service *214, 215, 217, 257*
Invitations, personalized *286*

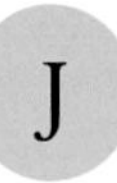

Jewelry *137, 143, 151, 170-174, 247, 248, 252-254, 256*
Appraisal *174*
Beadstringing *173*
Ceramic *253*
Custom Designed *170-174*
Diamonds *170-174*
European *164*
Gems *170-174, 256*
Gold *100, 170-174*
Handcrafted, contemporary *137, 143, 151*
Hand Engraved *174*
Logo and Trademarks *172*
Pearls *100*
Platinum *171*
Restyling and Updating *170-174*
Ruby Z *137*
Japanese, art and furniture *219*

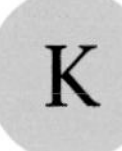

Kayaks
Folding *202*
Sea *202*
Whitewater *202*
Kimono's *100, 151, 218*
Kitchen Accessories — see Housewares
Knitting Accessories *292*
Knives
Gerber *234*
Henckel *232, 234*
Pocket *234*
Hunting *234*

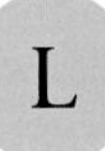

Lace *230, 239*
Leather
Accessories *161, 288*
Clothing *136*
Dooney and Bourke Belts *156*
Sofa *214, 232*
Lettering, custom *302*
Lighting *214, 216-218, 232, 237, 289*
Fabric Lampshades *237*
Halogen *232*
Import *214, 237*
Repair *237*
Luggage *161, 288*
Andiamo *288*
Frelton *288*
Hartman *288*
Members Only *288*
Schlesinger *161*
Tumi *288*

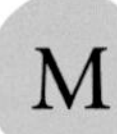

Magazines — see Books
Magic Wands
Glow in the Dark *287*
Make-up *141*
Massage *141, 150*
Massage Tools *284*
Maps *268, 279*
Marble Tiles *225*
Mobiles *251, 287*
Music Cassettes *284*
Compact Disc Players *267, 272*
Electronic Keyboards *282*
Drums and Cymbals *282*
Instruments *266, 282*
Instrument Repair *266, 282*
Organ *266, 273*
Piano *266, 273*
Sheet Music *266, 282*
Stereo Equipment *267, 272*
Museum, Oregon *274*
Educational Program *274*

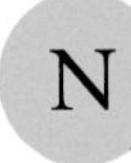

Nail Care *141, 148, 150, 168*
Newspapers — see Books

O

Oregon History *274*
Organs *266*
  Allens *266*
Oriental Gifts *100*
Outdoor Equipment *198, 199, 203*
  Hiking Boots, Danner *160*

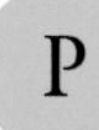

Party Goods *294, 295, 300*
  Rentals *295*
Pens
  Aurora *286*
  Lamy *161, 286*
  Mont Blanc *286*
Personal Care Products *150, 159, 165, 167, 168, 189, 234*
Pipe *290*
Piano
  Digital *266*
  Kawai *266*
  Reconditioned *266, 273*
  Service *266, 273*
  Steinway *273*

Quilting *296*

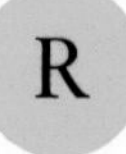

Rental, furniture and accessories
  Party *295*
  Seminars *295*
Reproduction Copying *297*
  Blueprings *297*
  PMT's *297*
  Super Stats *297*
Restaurants
  Afternoon Tea *50, 51, 77*
  Banquet Room *48, 50, 52, 57, 64, 80*
  Breakfast *50, 64, 71, 73, 75, 77, 78, 84*
  Burgers *46, 47, 84, 85*
  Cajun *62*
  Chinese *57, 65*
  Creole *63*
  Dance Floor *62*
  East Indian Cuisine *66*
  Eclectic Menu *51, 55, 62*
  Entertainment, live *50, 54, 56, 62, 63, 64, 78, 79, 85, 86*
  French Cuisine *46, 64*
  Game *49, 55*
  Games Room *78*
  Greek Cuisine *76*
  Home-style *74, 78*
  Italian
    Northern Cuisine *44, 53, 58*
    Southern Cuisine *74*
  Intercontinental *55, 72*
  Late Night *71, 78, 86, 87*
  Lebanese Cuisine *80*
  Mediterranean
    Specialties *52*
  Mesquite Broiler *52*
  Mexican Cuisine *81, 83*
  Outdoor *46, 50, 55, 58, 62, 64, 69, 70, 78, 80*
  Oyster Bar *71*
  Pakistani Cuisine *66*
  Pizza, take out *74, 82*
  Private Luncheon Club *48*
  Rock Lobster *45*
  Seafood Specialties *45, 49, 52, 54, 61, 62, 69*
  Scotch Selection *69*
  Steak and Onion *47*
  Sushi Bar *59*
  Tapas Bar *50, 51, 92*
  Tempura, Teriyaki Bar *59*
  Turn of the Century
    Restaurant *60*
  Twenty-four Hour
    Service *71*
  Vegetarian Menu *80*
  With a View
    City View *48, 72*
    Of the Water *48, 62*
Resource Center, women *280*
Ribbon, gift wrapping *300*
Riding Lessons, horse *200*
Ruanas *151*
Rubber Stamps *299, 300*
Rugs
  Antique *223*
  Appraisal *223*
  Contemporary *214, 215, 217*
  Dhurri *218, 223, 230, 255*
  Oriental *223*
  Persian *223*
  Repair *223*
  Used (Buy and Trade) *223*

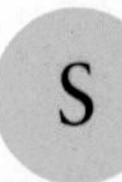

Scarves and Sashes *136, 162*
Scuba Diving, wet suit, dry suit *208*
Scent Bottles *164*
Screen Printing Supplies *259*
Scissors, professional *234*
Sewing — see Fabric
Shelving, wire *238*
Shoes, adult *154, 156, 157, 160, 161, 163*
  Fitness *160, 199, 201, 203, 206*
  Cole-Haan *153, 161*
  High Fashion *163*
  Italian *161*
  Kenneth Cole *161*
  Romika *156, 157*
Shopping Bags, hand-painted *252*
Signs, custom *302*
  Window and Store Display *302*
Sign, painter *302*
Silver
  Older Patterns *227*
Ski Equipment
  Cross-country *198, 199*
  Downhill *198, 203*
  Mastercraft, water *208*
Skin Care *141, 148, 150, 165*
Stained Glass *220*
Stationery Supplies *286, 294, 299, 300*
  Rubber Stamps *299, 300*
Stenciling Supplies *296*
Stereo Equipment
  Bang and Olufsen *267*
  Car *267, 278*
  Compact Disc *267, 272*
  Home *267, 272*
  Service *267, 272*
Stickers *300*
Storage Systems *238*
Stoves, wood *226, 228*
Stress Reduction *284*
Sundial, White Swan *241*
Sunglasses *203, 208*
  Vuarnet *203, 208*
Swimwear *202*

T

Tableware
  Ceramic *253*
  Contemporary *216, 232, 235, 289, 298*
  Fitz and Floyd *298*
  Heath *289*
  Otagiri *289*
Tennis
  Accessories *203, 206*
  Racquets *203, 206*
Telephone, cellular car *278*
Textile, dyes *259*
Ties *153, 154, 157, 161, 166*
Tobacco *290*
Tools, art *259, 260*
Toys
  Brio *178*
  Corolle *178*
  Developmental *186*
  European *185*
  Games *186*
  Infant *185*
  Newsletter *186, 190*
  Non-violent *186*
  Party Favors *186*
  Scientific *186*
  Stuffed Animals *183, 184-186, 301*
  Teddy Bears *301*
  Tricycles *183*
  Whimsical *287*
  Wind-up *183*
  Wooden *186*
Track Spikes *201*
Travel Accessories *161, 279, 288*
  Slide Presentations *279*

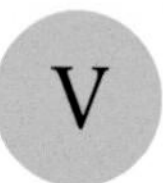

Vases *230-232, 287*
Video
  Equipment *267, 283*
  Equipment Rentals *283*
  Production *283*
  Service *267*
  Tapes *264, 283*
  Tape Rentals *283*

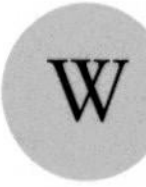

Watches
  Sport *198, 202, 203*
Wallpaper, children's *180*
Weather Instruments *234*
  Barometers *236*
Weaving
  Art *247*
  Supplies *292*
Wedding
  Cake *105, 106*
  Formal Wear *155*
  Invitations *286, 294*
  Rental Supplies *295*
Women's Studies *280*
Woodworking *256*
Wreath *231*

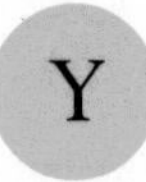

Yarns
  Imported *292*
  Natural Fiber *292*

PLACES TO GO

A

A Children's Place *187*
Abanté Fine Art Gallery *250*
Abou Karim *80*
Alan Costley *161*
Alder West *165*
Alexis Restaurant *76*
ANNUAL EVENTS *125*
Ann Sacks' Tileworks *225*
Annie Bloom's Books *276*
Anzen Oriental Foods and Imports *100*
Arlene Schnitzer Concert Hall *122*
The Arrangement *231*
ART AND CRAFT GALLERIES *243*
Art Media *259*
Attic Gallery *248*
Atwater's Restaurant & Lounge *48*
The Audio Alternative *272*
Augen Gallery *245*

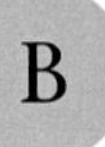

B

Bambini's Children's Boutique *188*
Beaverton Book Company *281*
Beyond Reason *257*
Bijou Cafe *73*
Bogart's Joint *85*
Bookport *269*
Bookmerchants *268*
BOOKS AND MUSIC *263*
Brasserie Montmartre *56*
Buffalo Gap Saloon and Eatery *78*
Byrne's Luggage *288*

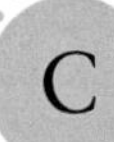

C

CAFÉS AND CASUAL RESTAURANTS *68*
Cafe Vivo *53*
Caro Amico *74*
Casa-U-Betcha *81*
Cast Iron and Cast Offs Antiques *226*
Catbird Seat Bookstore *271*
CATERING AND SPECIALTY FOODS *88*
Chelsea AudioVideo *267*
Chen's Dynasty *65*
CHILDREN *175*
Children's Country Store *180*
Children's Gym *192*
Children's Museum *191*
Child's Play *186*
Chris H. Foleen Goldsmith *174*
Ciclo Sport Shop *204*
City Kids *185*
Civic Auditorium *124*
Civic Stadium *121*
Claytrade *253*
Cloudtree & Sun and Main Street Grocery *94*
Coffee Bean *104*
Coffee Ritz *77*
The Coffee People *97*
Comella & Son & Daughter *91*
Contemporary Crafts Gallery *247*
Cool Temptations *93*
Couch Street Fish House *45*
The Country Willow *230*
Crane & Company *90*
Crêpe Faire Restaurant & Bistro *64*
Cromwell Formal Wear *155*

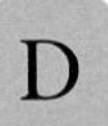

D

Daisy Kingdom *296*
DANCE *115*
Day Music Company *266*
Dazzle *287*
Delphina's *58*
DESTINATIONS *16*
Dimples *184*
DINING *43*
Dolores Winningstad Theater *123*

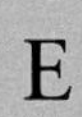

E

Early Childhood Bookhouse *182*
Ebb and Flow Kayak Center *202*
Echo Restaurant *49*
Edelweiss Sausage & Delicatessen *99*
Element 79 *171*
Elephants Delicatessen *96*
Elizabeth Leach Gallery *244*
Elizabeth Street *137*
Endgames *291*
ENTERTAINMENT *107*
ENVIRONS *303*
Equinox Fine Jewelry *173*
Executive Sweets, Desserts Etc. *106*
Expecting the Best *138*
Eye of Ra *151*

F

Faces Unlimited *141*
FASHION *133*
Fathertime Clocks *236*
FINAL TOUCHES *229*
Finnegan's *183*
Floral Trends Ltd. *242*
FOOD *41*
Foothill Broiler *84*
Francesca's Fragrances *164*

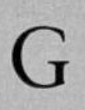

G

Gango Gallery *255*
Gary McKinstry Hair Design *159*
The Gazebo Gallery-Restaurant *72*
Gazelle Natural Fibre Clothing *162*
Genoa *44*
Goldmark Jewelers *170*
Great Harvest Bread Co. *102*

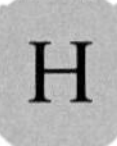

H

HK Limited *289*
Hall Street Bar & Grill *69*
Hanna Andersson *179*
Harbor Side Restaurant *62*
Harrington's Executive Clothiers *166*
The Heathman Hotel & Restaurant *50*
Hickox & Friends *167*
HOME *211*
Hot Lips Pizza *82*
Hot Cities *158*
House of Titles *265*
HOW TO USE THE BOOK *11*
Howell's Uptown Sports Center *203*
Huber's 60 Hunan Restaurant *57*

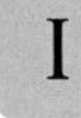

I

INCREDIBLES *285*
INDEX *313*
Intermediate Theater *123*
INTERIORS *213*
INTRODUCTION *10*

J

Jake's Famous Crawfish *61*
Jamison/Thomas Gallery *246*
Jazz de Opus *52*
Jean-Marie Fine Lingerie *144*
JEWELRY *169*
Josephine's Dry Goods *293*
Juleps *63*

K

Kasch's Garden Centers *240*
Kashmir *66*
KIDS AND TEENS *175*
Kid's Hair Parlour *189*
Kitchen Kaboodle *232*
The Kobos Company *235*
Koji Osakaya Fish House *59*

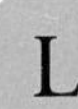

L

L'Auberge *46*
La Paloma *143*
Lasky's Video Library *283*
Lawrence Gallery *249*
Le Panier Very French Bakery *98*
Le Papillon *178*
Lloyd's Interiors *214*
Looking Glass Bookstore *277*
Ludeman's Fireplace & Patio Shop *228*

M

M. Willock *146*
Macheesmo Mouse *83*
Main Street Grocery *94*
Mako *181*
Malacca Rattan *216*
MAPS *19*
Mario's *154*
Mario's For Women *142*
Mastercraft of Oregon *208*
McCormick & Schmick's Seafood Restaurant *54*
Memorial Coliseum *120*
MEN AND WOMEN *152*
Mercantile *136*
Metro on Broadway *79*
Moe's Pianos *273*
More or Less Collectibles *222*
Mt. Park Pro Shop *206*
MUSIC *263*

N

Naomi's *237*
Napkin Folding Instructions *67*
Nature's Fresh Northwest *103*
NIGHTBEAT *117*
Nike Downtown *207*
Nofziger *163*
The Nor'Wester Bookshop *270*
Norm Thompson *157*
Northwest Futon Company *218*
Northwest Passage Boots & Clothing Company *160*

O

O'Connell Gallery *251*
Old Town Car Tunes *278*
Olde Favorites *227*
Opus Too/Jazz de Opus *52*
Oregon Mountain Community *198*
Oregon Historical Society *274*
Oriental Rug Gallery *223*

P

Pacific Crest Clothing Co. *156*
Papa Haydn *70*
Paper Parlour Ltd. *286*
The Paper Station *294*
Parchman Farm Restaurant and Bar *86*
Parker Furniture Design Center *215*
Pasta Cucina *101*
Pastaworks *89*
Paul Schatz Fine Furniture *217*
Paul*Bergen Catering and Charcuterie *92*
The Petite Woman's Shoppe *147*
Pettygrove House and Gardens *55*
Pharmacy Fountain *84*
Phidippides Fitness Center *201*
Piccolo Mondo *53*
Plâte du Jour *298*
PORTLAND: A PERFECT FIT *12*
Portland Antique Company *220*
Portland Center of the Performing Arts *122*
Portland Cutlery Company *234*
Portland Family Calendar *190*
Portland Music Co. *282*
Portland State Bookstore *275*
The Poster Gallery Etc. *254*
Powell's Books *264*
Powell's Travel Store *279*
Present Perfect *300*

R

The Real Mother Goose *256*
Recollections *221*
Rich's Cigar Store *290*
Richard Ltd. *153*
The Ringside *47*
Robert Eaton Jeweler-Designer *172*
Rose's Restaurant *75*
Rose's Viennese Bakery *105*

S

Salutations *299*
Scandia Down Shops *239*
SEATING PLANS *120*
Shannon & Co. *260*
Shannon & Co. Reprographics *297*
Shogun's Gallery *219*
SIGHTS *25*
Sign Wizards *302*
SPECIALTIES *261*
SPECTATOR SPORTS *195*
SPORTS AND RECREATION *193*
Stanton's Unfinished Furniture *224*
Stiles For Relaxation *284*
Storables *238*
Strohecker's *95*
Studio Artists *258*
Suite 360 *148*
Sunbow Gallery *252*
Sylvie, An Image Perfected For You *150*

T

13 Coins *71*
23rd Avenue Sweaters *140*
Tailwind Outfitters *199*
Teddy Bear's Picnic *301*
THEATER *112*
ThirtyOne Northwest *51*
The Towne Shop *139*
Trade Secrets *168*

U

Uptown Hardware *241*

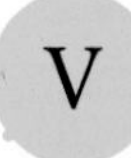

V

The Veritable Quandary *87*
Victoria's *149*
Virginia Jacobs *233*

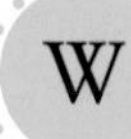

W

West End Ltd. *145*
Westover Wools *292*
Westside Rentals & Gifts *295*
A Woman's Place Bookstore *280*
WOMEN *135*
Woodmere Farm *210*

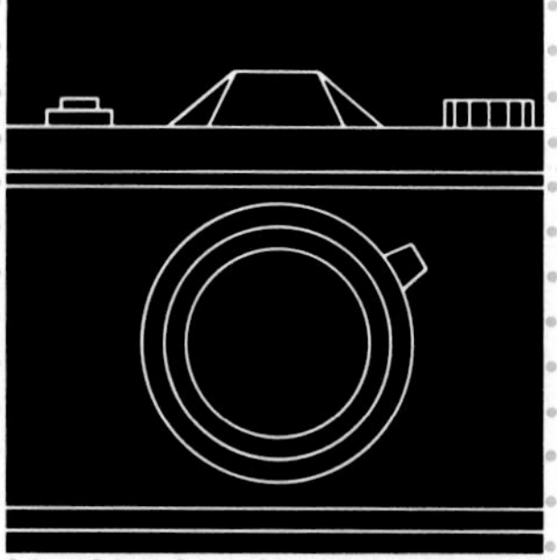

PHOTOGRAPHY CREDITS

Steven Bloch 45, 50, 56, 58, 62, 63, 64, 70, 71, 72, 75, 77, 78, 79, 82, 83, 89, 91, 92, 95, 98, 99, 100, 101, 103, 105, 136, 137, 141, 142, 144, 148, 149, 150, 154, 159, 161, 163, 165, 179, 181, 186, 198, 203, 224, 225, 238, 245, 246, 251, 252, 253, 254, 255, 260, 264, 267, 274, 279, 283, 287, 290, 298, 302

Ed Gowans 48, 54, 55, 57, 69, 81, 84, 93, 96, 97, 138, 139, 140, 145, 151, 158, 166, 168, 173, 201, 204, 207, 208, 215, 219, 223, 228, 230, 244, 248, 249, 250, 257, 259, 272, 273, 275, 288, 289, 293, 296, 301

Cathy Cheney 59, 65, 73, 90, 94, 102, 155, 164, 172, 184, 188, 189, 191, 210, 217, 232, 236, 237, 242, 258, 265, 268, 269, 278, 280, 281, 284, 286, 291, 292, 294, 297

Wayne Aldridge 46, 52, 53, 60, 74, 85, 86, 106, 146, 147, 153, 156, 157, 162, 170, 171, 199, 202, 214, 220, 222, 226, 227, 233, 239, 240, 241, 266, 271, 277, 282, 295

Ralph Perry 47, 49, 61, 66, 80, 87, 104, 160, 174, 182, 183, 216, 218, 221, 231, 234, 235, 247, 256, 270, 276, 299

Jerome Hart 44, 143, 167, 180, 185, 300

Harold Hutchinson 51

Kevin Haislip 76, 206

Bev Hawley 178

PHOTO GRAPHICS

C. Bruce Forster 2, 5, 12, 14, 34/35, 37, 39, 130, 209, 305, 308, 312

Kristin Finnegan 29, 126, 200, 205

Steven Bloch 15, 31, 32, 38

Dave Davidson 197

Molly Kohnstamm 27

Ronald Kirk, *a great fan of Portland, has been a driving force behind the formation of all four editions of* The First Portland Catalogue.™ *During his eight year involvement, he has managed to infuse the staff with his bizarre sense of humor.*

Ann Marra, *owner of Marra & Associates Graphic Design applies her design and artistic experience to special promotions, unusual communications problems, packaging and image revitalizations. For the last four years she has provided her expertise for the Catalogue design, content and organization of information. In 1987 she founded Earthlight Press Ltd. which, among other publishing projects, continues* The First City Catalogue™ *concept. She has taught at Pacific Northwest College of Art and played an advisory and consulting role to private and public organizations.*

Diana Masarie Leach *has a keen interest in the development and vitality of Portland which has led to her participation on several of the area's high visibility projects. From her position as General Manager's assistant at the Yamhill Marketplace — during the star-up through opening phases — Diana joined* The First Portland Catalogue™ *staff in 1984 to further promote many of the specialty retailers she had already become acquainted with.*

Catherine Windus *has been a public relations, marketing and special events specialist since 1977. She has directed the marketing and public relations for the Oregon Symphony, Oregon Art Institute and Portland Civic Theater and was the 1987 exhibit director of Portland Showcase, an annual economic development event. Her ongoing promotions business, "Interesting Projects Only" speaks for itself.*

Sharon Kolb, *publisher of Creative Scenic photographic books, has been a resident and lover of the Northwest for the past ten years. Besides publishing she has been involved in many freelance marketing projects. The love of shopping and her marketing skills have brought many exciting discoveries to the Catalogue this year.*

Joanne Forman, *a resident of Portland for ten years, has spent over fifteen years in politics, managing and coordinating political campaigns. In 1984 she began her own small business promoting international trade. She will continue to work with small business on international sales and promotion.*

Deanne Wong *brings to the Catalogue enthusiasm and creativity in her involvement in many aspects of production and research. For her, discovering the distinctive has always been a passion.*

Thomas H. Ryll, *a New Hampshire native, has lived for the past 21 years in Vancouver, Washington. His pen has now co-authored four editions of* The First Portland Catalogue™ *along with extensive reporting for the Vancouver "Columbian" on such diverse subjects as the eruption of Mt. St. Helens, transportation and municipal government.*

Steven Bloch *started his photographic career when he built a dark room at age twelve; he subsequently studied with Bernie Freemesser at the University of Oregon. His photographic career has taken him to twenty-six countries around the world; here at home he has been a free-lance photographer for the past eight years. He has made significant contributions to the last two Portland Catalogues. Away from work he serves as the President of the Pee Wee Herman Breakfast Club.*

Edward Gowans, *a native Oregonian, is best known for his gentle landscape photographs and intimate flower portraits. As a member of ASMP, he is equally comfortable shooting studio illustration assignments, or on location for corporate clients such as Soloflex, Speedo and The Nature Conservancy. Ed spends free time restoring his homestead on Bonny Slope, tending the kitchen orchard and honeybees. A year round vegetable gardener, he also grows bananas in the living room.*

Cathy Cheney, *a freelance photographer and resident of Portland for the past ten years, is a former* Willamette Week *staff photographer. Currently a corporate media photographer, she combines her career with raising the "world's most beautiful child" and riding and jumping horses.*

Ralph Perry, *a first-rate freelance photographer, has played a major role in the success of our Catalogues. The staff was very saddened to learn of his untimely death in the Spring of 1986. Ralph's contribution to Ensemble and the photographic world served as an inspiration to us all.*